PUBLISHED BY

Practical PowerShell Press
Naperville, IL 60565

Library of Congress Control Number: 2017934967
ISBN: 978-0-9987498-1-5

Paperback Edition - Printed and bound in the United States of America

First Printing

**Technical Reviewer**: Michel de Rooij and Jason Sherry
**Indexing:** Indexmatic2 by Indiscripts
**CopyEditor**: Deb Scoles

Cover: Damian Scoles * Lake O'Hara, Yoho National Park

The first time I heard about this thing called PowerShell it wasn't even called PowerShell. It was called Monad and I heard about it while being a student on the Exchange Ranger Program back in the days of Exchange 2003.

Back then Exchange was so hard to deploy and get right that there was an entire program set up to teach consultants (both inside Microsoft and from Partners) how to design, build and troubleshoot it.

I recall a Program Manager by the name of Vivek Sharma sitting at the front of the small room, with his feet up on the table talking about this thing he was working on called Monad, and telling us how it was going to change everything we did and we were all going to love it. I'm sure he used the word cool many, many times.

We, a group of experienced Exchange architects and engineers, all laughed and disagreed, and likely we asked if he was smoking something. He told us how, just like in Unix, when you do something right you get no response back from the command line – it's only when you make a mess of it does the interface tell you so. I'm sure again we laughed some more, and we told him it would never catch on. We are all GUI fans, we had all grown up using the 5.0 and 5.5 Admin tools, the Exchange Management Console, and we certainly didn't think a company like Microsoft would ever do something as radical as that. No GUI? Come on…

Well, he was right, of course. He was (and still is) a very smart guy and he knew then that it was only by building and using tool like that we'd stand any chance of building something like Exchange Online. (it should be noted for the sake of history that he was one of the key leading figures in the Friends and Family program which later built the foundation for Exchange Online and I think he ran the very first server from under his desk – so I think he knew more about the reasons why he was doing this than he let on at the time).

When you have ambitions of running a service with millions of mailboxes and hundreds of thousands of servers you can't use a GUI. The mouse clicking and scrolling alone would cause repetitive strain injuries throughout the ops team, no you must script or use a tool that allows you to operate on many objects sequentially. You must build a tool that allows an admin to perform large scale, broad ranging tasks, with accuracy, efficiency and repetition. And you need a cool name, because Monad is not going to get past the people in Marketing.

Fast forward a few years and now we have books such as this one explaining how to make the most of this powerful tool. While for some PowerShell is still challenging at first, there's no-one who uses it for some tasks and fails to see the advantages it offers. Certainly, you might argue that some tasks are quicker and easier in the GUI if you know where to look, but once you have multiple objects to manage, it's time for PowerShell. Once you get the hang of it, it's fast, powerful and easy to script. We manage Exchange Online using PowerShell, I'm pretty sure you can make it work for you too.

So whether you are still trying to figure out the basics, to grow your skills to make your day to day admin life easier, or are looking for some hard core scripting power to get tasks done with a single button push, you couldn't have found a better book to read.

Damian and Dave are two hardened grizzly pros (just look at the cover pics and tell me I'm wrong) who have spent years working with PowerShell and have picked up a ton of tricks along the way. In this book they'll show you the basics, how commands should be structured to avoid errors (my tip is when you get red text back… that's not usually a good sign), and how to take the output of one command and feed it into another. Once you have that down they'll show you a bunch of different tasks you can use PowerShell to accomplish, and automate or script, and then spend time showing you what to do when things go wrong or get PowerShell to help you find out when things went wrong.

All in all there's a lot of great information in here and you'll learn a lot by reading it and by trying it out.

When I eventually ran the Ranger Program for Exchange there was one thing I used to make sure to tell my instructors – don't just tell the class how something works and leave it at that – tell us how to use that knowledge to solve a problem, design a server, configure a connector or whatever it is. And more, you must tell the class how you personally use that knowledge to solve a problem or make a design decision or so on. If the class can see how you, the expert, tackle a problem they might face, they can try and model their behavior on you, they benefit from your experience and it's like having you there to help them.

Read the book, see how Damian and Dave take you from understanding how it works into putting it to use, and then you'll learn from their experience and become better at PowerShell for it.

Good luck and remember, red is bad, no response is good. What's up with that?


**Greg Taylor**
Principal Program Manager Exchange/O365
Microsoft Corporation

# AUTHORS

## DAMIAN SCOLES

Damian Scoles is an Office Servers and Services MVP (Exchange Specialization) based out of the Chicago area and started out managing Exchange 5.5 and Windows NT.  He has worked with Exchange Server since 1997 and has remained active in the Exchange community by contributing to TechNet forums, creating scripts for Exchange Admins on the TechNet wiki, writing detailed Exchange blog articles (https://justaucguy.wordpress.com/) and running an Exchange/Office 365 User Group in Chicago. As a first time author, Damian has poured his knowledge of Exchange and PowerShell into this book.  He hopes you will enjoy reading it as much as he did writing it.

## DAVE STORK

Dave Stork started his Exchange career with Exchange 2003 and that version got him hooked. He blogs (https://dirteam.com/dave) and tweets (https://twitter.com/dmstork) about Exchange and other relevant topcis for several years now and in time has expanded this community work with contributing to podcasts, speaking at several events and user group meetings in and outside his native Netherlands. And now he has tried to pour most of his knowledge and experience in this book, which he hopes will help IT pros properly manage Exchange 2016 with more ease and to ensure their end users achieve the best possible productivity.

## MICHEL DE ROOIJ

Michel de Rooij is a consultant and Office Servers and Services MVP from the Netherlands, and has been working in the IT industry for almost 20 years. Michel primary focus is Microsoft solutions involving Exchange Server, Office 365 or related technologies like PowerShell or Active Directory. Michel's background as a developer is a great asset when dealing with scripting challenges or development of supporting tools using PowerShell. Michel is also very active in the Exchange communities, like TechNet or the Dutch Network User Group NGN. He authors articles for his own Exchange blog www.eight-wone.com, but is also guest author for several other companies. Michel is also active on Twitter at @mderooij. Apart from speaking at events like IT/Dev Connections, he is also a contributor to The UC Architects podcast (http://theucarchitects.com).

## JASON SHERRY

Jason has been working as a Microsoft infrastructure expert for 21 years. He has worked with and focused on Exchange since the betas of 4.0 in 1995; with Office 365 and its predecessors since 2009. Jason has been a Microsoft MVP since 2006. He has also worked as an AD & Exchange product manager, consultant, and subject matter expert during this period. In his career, he has helped design, migrate and manage millions of users and systems, including some of the largest Microsoft environments in the world. Jason has built-out consulting practices, spoken at industry events, and written for websites and magazines. He current works as a Microsoft subject matter expert for Commvault. http://blog.jasonsherry.net | @JasonSherry

# Acknowledgments

## About this book

As PowerShell is a crucial tool in administrating servers and services, it's an important and valuable skill to possess. Unfortunately learning it by yourself can be a daunting task. That is why we decided to write this book, to help the average IT Pro/Administrator learn the fundamentals (and perhaps a little beyond that) of PowerShell. We believe that our practical approach will help the reader understand and learn these useful skills and help him or her to become proficient in Exchange PowerShell for all of their work and become more productive and a valuable employee almost immediately after reading this book.

Although this book is focused on Exchange Server 2016 in on-premises environments, quite a lot of the information can be reused for other versions of Exchange (such as 2013), Exchange Online and other products than Exchange, making the knowledge in this book even more valuable to have. So stop procrastinating, go read this book and go PowerShelling!

### Damian Scoles:

I would like to thank my wife and kids for their support and understanding while I worked on this book. The writing of this book took more effort and time than I anticipated.  However, as it is done now there is a profound sense of relief and realization that I can spend more time with them.  So thank you for that.

### Dave Stork:

I would like to thank my employer OGD ICT diensten for their support during the process of getting this book written and published. But especially would like to thank my wife, for her support and advice during the whole period I was working on this book. It's been tough at times, but you helped me through it. Thank you. And; it's finally done!

### From both authors:

We also like to acknowledge and thank other IT professionals/MVPs who have helped us is various ways with advice, feedback, etc. to achieve this end product. Those include: Tony Redmond, Paul Cunningham, Bhargav Shukla and many others. A special thanks goes to Jetze Mellema for his marathon reading of the book for a final review before publishing!

# Errata

In writing this book, we've put a lot of effort into making the information as accurate as possible.  Any errors that are reported will be recorded here:

*http://www.practicalpowershell.com/errata*

Expect this document to be updated if any issues are found.  If, for some reason, you want to report something that is not there go ahead and report it on that page.

Additional support can be found by emailing us at *input@practicalpowershell.com*.

# Table of Contents

# 3. Building Scripts



# 4. PowerShell Remoting



# 5. What's New

# 6. Server Configuration

## 7.  Server Management

## 9. Mail Flow - Compliance

# 10. IMAP and POP



# 11. Users

## Reporting



# 12. Non-User Objects



# 13. Mobile Devices

# 14. Migrations



# 15. Hybrid



# 16. Reporting

# 17. Troubleshooting



# 18. Miscellaneous

# Introduction

## Exchange Server 2016 and PowerShell

Beginning with Exchange Server 2007, Microsoft introduced PowerShell to enhance the Exchange Server product. PowerShell was a radical change at the time when Microsoft was known for its GUI interfaces.  Yes, Microsoft had some command line access to its OS's (think DOS).  By adding a command line interface, Microsoft had suddenly put the gauntlet down and announced to the world that it was serious about it products and providing an enhancement that would appeal to those who would look down on Microsoft because of the GUI based approach.

While Exchange Server 2007 ran what was then known as PowerShell 1.0, and while it was a good addition to existing Exchange Server management it was not perfect.  It was not as flexible as it is today and was sorely in need of enhancement.  With the introduction of Exchange Server 2010 and Exchange Server 2013, PowerShell advanced from 2.0 to 4.0.   Currently Exchange Server 2016 supports PowerShell version 4.0 and 5.0.   We won't cover the enhancements between versions, however suffice it to say that the product has changed drastically over the years since it was first introduced in 2007.

As PowerShell has advanced feature-wise, the commands that are exposed to Exchange Server have changed from 2007 to 2010 to 2013 to 2016.  This book is focused on Exchange Server 2016, however a lot of the cmdlets, one-liners and scripts will work on Exchange 2013, 2010 and even Exchange Online.  We will make references to changes that have occurred in case you have written scripts in previous versions and are unaware of changes that need to be made in those scripts.

## Why PowerShell and Not the Exchange Admin Center [a.k.a. the GUI]

There are many reasons to use PowerShell to manage and manipulate your Exchange Server 2016 environment. Some of the reasons are obvious while others may require some explanation.  Let's lay out why you should use and become familiar with when it comes to PowerShell for Exchange:

- PowerShell allows the use of standard Windows commands that you would run in the Command Prompt.
- PowerShell brings powerful commands to the table to enable you to work with a complex environment. These commands use a verb-noun based syntax.
- PowerShell allows for heavy automation.  While this would seem to be geared to larger environments, smaller shops can utilize scheduling for common tasks – reporting, maintenance, bulk maintenance, etc. – to reduce the time needed and human errors in managing their Exchange server(s).
- Some things just cannot be done in the GUI.  This is important. This is not advertised or spelled out by Microsoft.  There are many options or configurations that can ONLY be performed with PowerShell.  To make this clear, PowerShell is not limited in its management of Exchange as the GUI is.  So it is important to learn it when learning about Exchange Servers in general.
- PowerShell works with objects.  These objects can enable you to do powerful tasks in Exchange.
- PowerShell can get a task done in fewer lines than say VBScript. Some will find this to be an advantage as it can take less time to accomplish a task by writing it in PowerShell.
- PowerShell works with many technologies – XML, WMI, CIM, .NET, COM and Active Directory.  The last one is important as you will see later, we can tie scripts together between Active Directory queries and Exchange commands.

- PowerShell provides a powerful help and search function.  When working with PowerShell and a command is new to you, Get-Help is extremely useful as it can provide working examples of code.  Searching for commands is easy as well and if you know what you want to manipulate (e.g. mailboxes), just searching for commands with a keyword of 'mailbox' can help direct your Get-Help query to find the relevant command.

As we get further into the book, we will cover these important features and more.  One thing to remember about Exchange Server PowerShell is that it can be run local on an Exchange Server or remote (if PowerShell remoting is enabled).  This can ease manageability of your messaging environment.

** **Note** ** For this book, Exchange 2016 CU2 on Windows 2012 R2 is being used.  Future CUs could change the available cmdlets in PowerShell.

# Exchange Management Shell

Simply put, the Exchange Management Shell is the original Windows PowerShell with a module loaded specifically with Exchange Server oriented cmdlets.

**Cmdlet (definition)** – is a single PowerShell command like Get-Mailbox.  This is considered to be a cmdlet.

**Module (definition)** – is a collection of additional PowerShell commands that are grouped together for one purpose or function.  Example modules are Exchange Server, Active Directory and Windows Azure.  There are many, many more, but these examples are relevant to this book.

The Exchange Management shell is also visibly different from the Windows PowerShell interface that is installed on all Windows 2008+ servers.

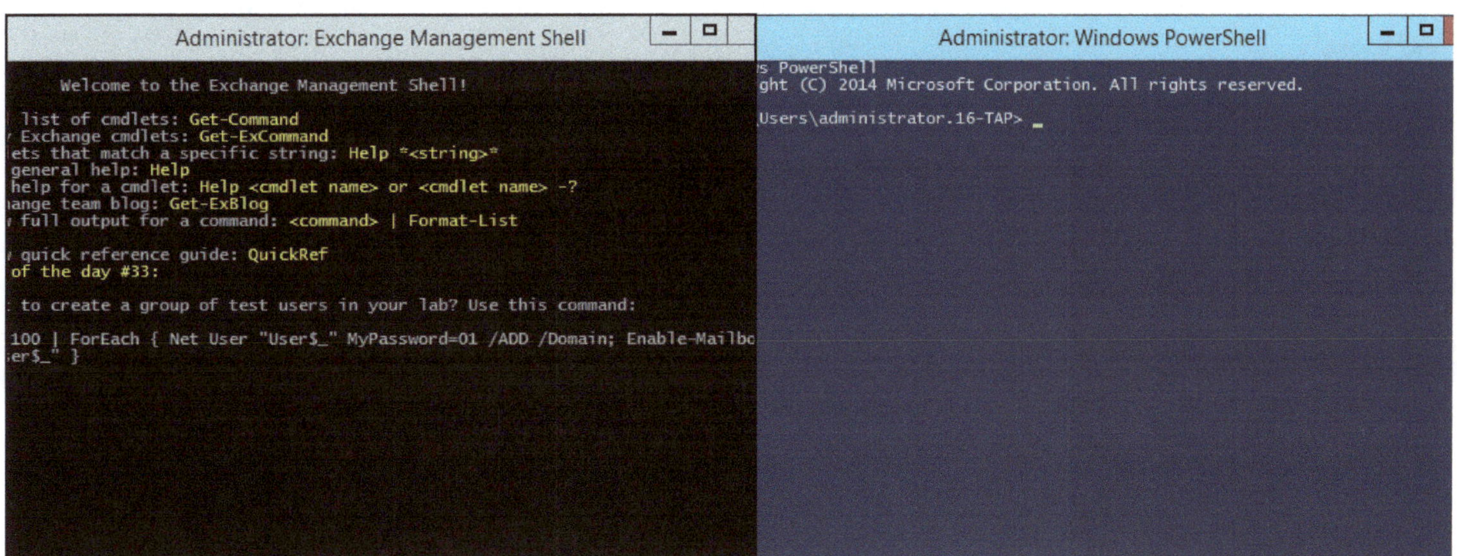


*(The above screenshots are from the same Windows 2012 R2 server.)*

On a server with Exchange Server 2016 installed, the shortcut for the Exchange Management shell can be found by click on the Windows Button, select the down arrow and the look for the Exchange Server 2016 shortcuts that have been placed there by the Exchange Server installation process.

Or, from the command line:

    C:\Windows\System32\WindowsPowerShell\v1.0\Powershell.exe -NoExit -Command ". 'C:\Program Files\Microsoft\Exchange Server\V15\bin\RemoteExchange.ps1'; Connect-ExchangeServer -Auto -ClientApplication:ManagementShell"

# Command Structure

PowerShell cmdlets come in two basic groupings - safe exploratory cmdlets (ones starting with 'GET' for example) and others that can configure or modify the Exchange configuration (not as safe and can be dangerous to a production Exchange messaging environment).

**Anatomy of a PowerShell Cmdlet:**

**Verb** - The action part of the cmdlet. Whether this is Get, Remove, List, Set or Add. These words are the first word of the Cmdlet and to the left of the dash of the cmdlet name.

**Noun** - The word or words to the right of the dash of the PowerShell cmdlet name. These words help describe what is being affected in Exchange Server 2016. Examples include - Database, ExchangeCertificate, AddressList and more.

**Parameter(s)** - These are the options which are selected and upon which the PowerShell cmdlet will act. To get an idea of what parameters are present for each cmdlet you will need to do run a Get-Help <cmdlet> -full. We will review that later in this chapter.

## Cmdlet Examples

### Get-ExchangeServer
Provides a list of Exchange Servers in the Exchange Organization.

### Set-ExchangeServer
Will change the configuration of the Exchange Server according to the parameters you chose.

When exploring PowerShell for Exchange for the first time, it is advisable to start with the Get cmdlets as these cmdlets will provide the beginner to PowerShell the following items:

- A view into Exchange and its configuration
- Practice with parameters, output, piping and more
- Non-destructive PowerShell practice
- A means to generating reports on Exchange

Get-cmdlets are benign in the sense that the current environment is not being changed or re-configured. This provides for safe learning or exploration not only for PowerShell but Exchange as well. It is highly recommended that you review some basic cmdlets like the following as a good starting point for your venture into Exchange PowerShell:

| | | |
|---|---|---|
| Get-ExchangeServer | Get-OutlookProvider | Get-AddressBookPolicy |
| Get-ExchangeCertificate | Get-OutlookAnywhere | Get-ClientAccessService |
| Get-Mailbox | Get-TransportService | Get-MailPublicFolder |
| Get-MailboxDatabase | Get-RetentionPolicy | Get-MobileDevice |

# Piping

Single cmdlets are the meat and potatoes of PowerShell. However you can combine the results gathered by one cmdlet and feed this to another cmdlet in PowerShell which then processes results from the previous cmdlet. This process is known as piping. By combing two cmdlets together like this we now have a very powerful tool to use to construct one-liners.

**One-liner (definition)** – In PowerShell a one-liner literally is either a single command that performs a function or it is comprised of a set of cmdlets that are paired together with a pipe symbol '|'.

For an example of piping we are passing information from Get-Mailbox to Get-MailboxStatistics to produce results in a single table. If we did not use the pipelining feature, you would have to perform the Get-MailboxStatistics for each mailbox instead of using the pipeline method, which will run this for all mailboxes in one cmdlet. The pipe allows us to do that in bulk, which saves time and produces a single table of results.

Get-Mailbox | Get-MailboxStatistics

Sample output:

```
DisplayName                    ItemCount StorageLimitStatus            LastLogonTime
-----------                    --------- ------------------            -------------
Administrator                  15                                      12/19/2014 3:39:49 PM
Backup                         6
Corporate User                 7
Corporate User2                12
Damian Scoles                  246359                                  1/28/2016 3:40:06 PM
Discovery Search Mailbox       1
John Smith                     10
Postmaster                     7                                       7/7/2013 8:18:25 PM
SCOM Agent                     3
SearchResults                  1
```

To see the advantage of this, if we needed to gather the same information using just Get-MailboxStatistics, we would need to run the command for each mailbox:

```
[PS] C:\>get-mailboxstatistics damian
Creating a new session for implicit remoting of "Get-MailboxStatistics" command...
DisplayName                    ItemCount       StorageLimitStatus
-----------                    ---------       ------------------
Damian Scoles                  252601

[PS] C:\>get-mailboxstatistics administrator
DisplayName                    ItemCount       StorageLimitStatus
-----------                    ---------       ------------------
Administrator                  15
```

As you can see, the pipeline method enables us to move past a simple single line. What this also allows us to do is save time and allow us to work more efficiently in our scripting.

An alternative to piping would require quite a bit more effort, and some techniques we have not covered yet. The code would involve basically gathering all the mailboxes and storing their identities in a variable and the reading through the variable and running Get-MailboxStatistics for each mailbox stored in that variable:

```
$Mailboxes = Get-Mailbox
Foreach ($Mailbox in $Mailboxes) {
    Get-MailboxStatistics $Mailbox.Alias
}
```

The results are the same, while the complexity has gone up substantially some combined cmdlets can save server resources in terms of CPU and memory usage.

For another example of pipeline, let's take a more advanced topic like Mailbox Database health in a mailbox cluster. In order to get a complete picture of database health in a cluster we need to find all the databases and then get a status of each copy on each node that has that copy. How do we do this? We pipe Get-MailboxDatabase to Get-MailboxDatabaseCopyStatus. These commands work in tandem to produce this:

```
[PS] C:\>get-mailboxdatabase |Get-MailboxDatabaseCopyStatus

Name                                Status      CopyQueueLength ReplayQueueLength ContentIndexState
----                                ------      --------------- ----------------- -----------------
DB01\EX01                           Mounted     0               0                 Healthy
Mailbox Database 0132631208\EX03    ServiceDown 0               0                 Unknown
```

Notice that we can see the status, as well as the ContentIndexStatus. Both of these are important in knowing the health of your mailbox databases.

## Caveats

Not all PowerShell cmdlets can be piped into all other PowerShell cmdlets. Most combinations are logical. So joining the Get-Mailbox and Get-MailboxDatabase PowerShell cmdlets won't produce any results because the identities from Get-Mailbox won't pass information that the Get-MailboxDatabase can use:

```
Get-Mailbox | Get-MailboxDatabase
```

While there were no errors, there were no results either. There are some cmdlets that will specify that they cannot be piped. These cmdlets do not include the issue of trying to pipe together cmdlets that are not supposed to work together. For example you would not run 'Get-Mailbox | Get-MailboxDatabaseCopyStatus'. This is because the identities that Get-Mailbox pulls are not valid mailbox database names needed by the Get-MailboxDatabaseC-opyStatus. If we were to instead use 'Get-MailboxDatabase | Get-MailboxDatabaseCopyStatus', then that would work fine and as expected.

# Protecting Yourself and What If

PowerShell is powerful. PowerShell can thus do some serious damage to Exchange and Active Directory. How can you protect your infrastructure from your missteps?

- Run Get cmdlets first to get a general familiarity of PowerShell in Exchange.
- Use the WhatIf switch when running cmdlets, this will show what would have occurred if a cmdlet was run.

An example of the WhatIf switch would be what would happen if you were to get all mailboxes in Exchange and remove the mailboxes:

Get-Mailbox | Remove-Mailbox -WhatIf

**What if**: Removing mailbox "16-01.local/Users/Administrator" will remove the Active Directory user object and mark the mailbox and the archive (if present) in the database for removal.
**What if**: Removing mailbox "16-01.local/Users/DiscoverySearchMailbox {D919BA05-46A6-415f-80AD-7E09334BB852}" will remove the Active Directory user object and mark the mailbox and the archive (if present) in the database for removal.

Notice the WhatIf statement in front of each result. If this command was run in production, all mailboxes would be deleted. However, because we ran the same command with the WhatIf switch only a simulation was run, no mailboxes were removed.

# Command Discovery Techniques

A certain amount of discovery involves knowing Exchange. With this knowledge, finding commands that are necessary to perform actions becomes easier. For example users in your environment that receive email have mailboxes. This may seem like a simple example, but it will help illustrate the idea of knowing Exchange will help with PowerShell cmdlets.

So, going back to mailboxes. We need to manipulate some information or create a report on mailboxes on your Exchange 2016 servers. If you don't know what commands that can be run, we rely on a specific cmdlet called 'Get-Command'. With this we can find cmdlets we need:

Get-Command *mailbox*

Running this will look for any PowerShell cmdlet that has the work mailbox in it. The wildcard '*' that is located in front and behind the word 'mailbox' just means that we are searching for any command that may or may not have additional letters before or after the word 'mailbox'. A small portion of the results are listed below:

```
[PS] C:\>get-command *mailbox*

CommandType        Name                              ModuleName
-----------        ----                              ----------
Function           _GetHubMailboxUMServers
Function           Add-MailboxDatabaseCopy           16-01-ex01.16-01.local
Function           Add-MailboxFolderPermission       16-01-ex01.16-01.local
Function           Add-MailboxPermission             16-01-ex01.16-01.local
Function           Connect-Mailbox                   16-01-ex01.16-01.local
Function           Disable-Mailbox                   16-01-ex01.16-01.local
Function           Disable-MailboxQuarantine         16-01-ex01.16-01.local
Function           Disable-RemoteMailbox             16-01-ex01.16-01.local
Function           Disable-UMMailbox                 16-01-ex01.16-01.local
Function           Enable-Mailbox                    16-01-ex01.16-01.local
Function           Enable-MailboxQuarantine          16-01-ex01.16-01.local
```

Now, let's say we actually need to look at the databases on the server:

```
Get-Command *database*
```

```
CommandType          Name                                         ModuleName
-----------          ----                                         ----------
Function             Add-DatabaseAvailabilityGroupServer          16-tap-ex02.16-tap.local
Function             Add-MailboxDatabaseCopy                      16-tap-ex02.16-tap.local
Function             Dismount-Database                            16-tap-ex02.16-tap.local
Function             Get-DatabaseAvailabilityGroup                16-tap-ex02.16-tap.local
Function             Get-DatabaseAvailabilityGroupConfiguration   16-tap-ex02.16-tap.local
Function             Get-DatabaseAvailabilityGroupNetwork         16-tap-ex02.16-tap.local
Function             Get-MailboxDatabase                          16-tap-ex02.16-tap.local
Function             Get-MailboxDatabaseCopyStatus                16-tap-ex02.16-tap.local
Function             Get-MailboxDatabaseRedundancy                16-tap-ex02.16-tap.local
Function             Get-PublicFolderDatabase                     16-tap-ex02.16-tap.local
Function             Mount-Database                               16-tap-ex02.16-tap.local
```

As you can see, the Get-Command is useful for finding cmdlets within PowerShell that you can use in Exchange.

# PowerShell Modules

When working with Exchange and because of its dependency on Active Directory we may need other cmdlets in order to perform certain actions. When working in the default Exchange Management Shell, PowerShell cmdlets for Active Directory are not pre-loaded. In order to load these cmdlets, a PowerShell module needs to be loaded. For Active Directory, the module is called 'ActiveDirectory':

```
Import-Module ActiveDirectory
```

After the PowerShell module has loaded, additional cmdlets are available.

# Getting Help!?!

Along with Get-Command, Get-Help will assist you in exploring PowerShell for Exchange Server 2016.

When faced with running a new cmdlet in PowerShell or just figuring out what other options are available for a PowerShell cmdlet, the Get-Help and Get-Command are extremely helpful. If you've used Linux or Unix they are like the man pages of old where a description of what the command can do, where it can be run, various examples of how the command can be used and more. When using the Get-Help and Get-Command, just like other PowerShell commands, there are switches that you can use to help enhance the basic cmdlet. For example, take this cmdlet:

```
Get-Help Get-ExchangeServer
```

The above command returns some information on the Get-Mailbox cmdlet:

```
NAME
    Get-ExchangeServer

SYNOPSIS
    This cmdlet is available only in on-premises Exchange Server 2016.

    Use the Get-ExchangeServer cmdlet to obtain the attributes of a specified server. If a server isn't specified, the
    cmdlet obtains the attributes of all the servers in the Exchange organization.

    When you run the Get-ExchangeServer cmdlet with no parameters, it returns the attributes of all the servers in the
    Exchange organization. To return specific server properties (including domain controller information) where the
    Get-ExchangeServer cmdlet has to contact servers directly or perform a complex or slow calculation, make sure you
    use the Status parameter.

    For information about the parameter sets in the Syntax section below, see Syntax.
```

```
SYNTAX
    Get-ExchangeServer [-Identity <ServerIdParameter>] [-DomainController <Fqdn>] [-Status <SwitchParameter>]
    [<CommonParameters>]

    Get-ExchangeServer -Domain <Fqdn> [-DomainController <Fqdn>] [-Status <SwitchParameter>] [<CommonParameters>]

DESCRIPTION
    To view all the Exchange server attributes that this cmdlet returns, you must pipe the command to the Format-List
    cmdlet.

    The ExchangeVersion attribute returned is the minimum version of Microsoft Exchange that you can use to manage the
    returned object. This attribute isn't the same as the version of Exchange displayed in the Exchange Administration
    Center when you select Server Configuration.

    You need to be assigned permissions before you can run this cmdlet. Although all parameters for this cmdlet are
    listed in this topic, you may not have access to some parameters if they're not included in the permissions
    assigned to you. To see what permissions you need, see the "Shell infrastructure permissions" section in the
    Exchange infrastructure and PowerShell permissions topic.

RELATED LINKS
    Online Version http://technet.microsoft.com/EN-US/library/96543903-10fa-46fe-9ea0-90570ca0ad2e(EXCHG.160).aspx

REMARKS
    To see the examples, type: "get-help Get-ExchangeServer -examples".
    For more information, type: "get-help Get-ExchangeServer -detailed".
    For technical information, type: "get-help Get-ExchangeServer -full".
    For online help, type: "get-help Get-ExchangeServer -online"
```

Notice the main sections: Name, Synopsis, Syntax, Description, Related Links and Remarks. The command we ran provided us with a nice summary of what this command can do and the Related Link section points you to the online documentation for this cmdlet. However, what is missing is the switches or options that are available for the cmdlet as well as some examples on how to use the cmdlet as well. To get these, run the following:

Get-Help Get-ExchangeServer -Full

The same first section appear: Name, Synopsis, Syntax and Description. However, a few addition sections appear now: Parameters, Inputs, Outputs and Examples:

```
PARAMETERS
    -Domain <Fqdn>
        The Domain parameter specifies the fully qualified domain name (FQDN) of the domain. If you use this
        parameter, you can't use the Identity parameter.

        Required?                    true
        Position?                    Named
        Default value
        Accept pipeline input?       False
        Accept wildcard characters?  false

    -DomainController <Fqdn>
        The DomainController parameter specifies the domain controller that's used by this cmdlet to read data from or
        write data to Active Directory. You identify the domain controller by its fully qualified domain name (FQDN).
        For example, dc01.contoso.com.

        The DomainController parameter isn't supported on Edge Transport servers. An Edge Transport server uses the
        local instance of Active Directory Lightweight Directory Services (AD LDS) to read and write data.

        Required?                    false
        Position?                    Named
        Default value
        Accept pipeline input?       False
        Accept wildcard characters?  false

    -Identity <ServerIdParameter>
        The Identity parameter specifies the identity of the server. If you use this parameter, you can't use the
        Domain parameter.

        Required?                    false
        Position?                    1
        Default value
        Accept pipeline input?       True
        Accept wildcard characters?  false

    -Status <SwitchParameter>
        The Status parameter specifies the status of the server.

        Required?                    false
        Position?                    Named
        Default value
        Accept pipeline input?       False
        Accept wildcard characters?  false

    <CommonParameters>
        This cmdlet supports the common parameters: Verbose, Debug,
        ErrorAction, ErrorVariable, WarningAction, WarningVariable,
        OutBuffer, PipelineVariable, and OutVariable. For more information, see
        about_CommonParameters (http://go.microsoft.com/fwlink/?LinkID=113216).

INPUTS

        To see the input types that this cmdlet accepts, see Cmdlet Input and Output Types
        (http://go.microsoft.com/fwlink/p/?linkId=616387). If the Input Type field for a cmdlet is blank, the cmdlet
        doesn't accept input data.
```

When you work with a command that you are unfamiliar with, it would be advisable to start with the -Full switch to get all information on the cmdlet as well as some examples on how to use the command. The major weakness of the help command as well as the Online help is that some commands are very complex and have so many options that they don't feel as complete as they might. This means that even after finding the right parameters, it may take some time to get the right results. If you find yourself in this situation, you can turn to your favorite Internet search engine to find the right syntax OR possibly get a close enough example that a bit of tweaking will make the cmdlet run the way you expect.

** **Note** ** Accessing the Online version of help required the use of the '-Online' switch. This allows PowerShell to access the Online version of help for the cmdlet.

# Idiosyncrasies

Let's end this chapter on a cautionary note. We covered commands like Get-Help and Get-Command. These will come in handy as you build your own scripts. After writing scripts for a while you may notice that not everything in Exchange PowerShell is perfect or logical. This is especially true when it comes to PowerShell cmdlet naming conventions. Let's take for example any cmdlet with the word 'database' in it. Here is the list of all the cmdlets:

```
Add-DatabaseAvailabilityGroupServer
Add-MailboxDatabaseCopy
Dismount-Database
Get-DatabaseAvailabilityGroup
Get-DatabaseAvailabilityGroupConfiguration
Get-DatabaseAvailabilityGroupNetwork
Get-MailboxDatabase
Get-MailboxDatabaseCopyStatus
Get-MailboxDatabaseRedundancy
Get-PublicFolderDatabase
Mount-Database
Move-ActiveMailboxDatabase
Move-DatabasePath
New-DatabaseAvailabilityGroup
New-DatabaseAvailabilityGroupConfiguration
New-DatabaseAvailabilityGroupNetwork
New-MailboxDatabase
Remove-DatabaseAvailabilityGroup
Remove-DatabaseAvailabilityGroupConfiguration
Remove-DatabaseAvailabilityGroupNetwork
Remove-DatabaseAvailabilityGroupServer
Remove-MailboxDatabase
Remove-MailboxDatabaseCopy
Restore-DatabaseAvailabilityGroup
Resume-MailboxDatabaseCopy
Set-DatabaseAvailabilityGroup
Set-DatabaseAvailabilityGroupConfiguration
Set-DatabaseAvailabilityGroupNetwork
Set-MailboxDatabase
Set-MailboxDatabaseCopy
Set-RDDatabaseConnectionString
Start-DatabaseAvailabilityGroup
Stop-DatabaseAvailabilityGroup
Suspend-MailboxDatabaseCopy
Update-DatabaseSchema
Update-MailboxDatabaseCopy
```

What you will notice is that some cmdlets have 'MailboxDatabase' and some have just 'Database'. This will throw you specifically if you need to say dismount and remount all mailbox databases on a particular servers. If you type in this:

```
Get-Database | Dismount-Database
```

You will generate an error since the 'Get-Database' cmdlet does not exist:

```
[PS] C:\>Get-Database | Dismount-Database
Get-Database : The term 'Get-Database' is not recognized as the name of a
cmdlet, function, script file, or operable program. Check the spelling of the
name, or if a path was included, verify that the path is correct and try again.
At line:1 char:1
+ Get-Database | Dismount-Database
+ ~~~~~~~~~~~~
    + CategoryInfo          : ObjectNotFound: (Get-Database:String) [], Comman
   dNotFoundException
    + FullyQualifiedErrorId : CommandNotFoundException
```

The correct syntax is:

Get-MailboxDatabase | Dismount-Database

Which will work successfully:

```
[PS] C:\>Get-MailboxDatabase | Dismount-Database

Confirm
Are you sure you want to perform this action?
Dismounting database "DB02". This may result in reduced availability for
mailboxes in the database.
[Y] Yes  [A] Yes to All  [N] No  [L] No to All  [?] Help (default is "Y"):
```

To remount all the databases, perform the opposite one-liner:

Get-MailboxDatabase | Mount-Database

As you can see this leaves a bit to be desired for consistency sake.  The best way to handle these situations is to do what we did above to get all cmdlets that have a similar word or function to them.  To get, for example, a list of cmdlets I can use to manipulate Mobile Devices, type in:

Get-Command *mobile*

Which will give us this for results:

```
[PS] C:\>Get-Command *mobile*

CommandType     Name
-----------     ----
Function        Clear-MobileDevice
Function        Get-MobileDevice
Function        Get-MobileDeviceMailboxPolicy
Function        Get-MobileDeviceStatistics
Function        New-MobileDeviceMailboxPolicy
Function        Remove-MobileDevice
Function        Remove-MobileDeviceMailboxPolicy
Function        Set-MobileDeviceMailboxPolicy
```

Notice in this case the consistency of cmdlets.  In the end, what matters is getting a familiarity with PowerShell cmdlets for Exchange Server 2016.  When searching for cmdlets, knowing Exchange and its various functions will help.  Search for words that you imagine you are looking for.  If the 'get-command' fails in your search, shorten your search string.  For example if you were to look for '*databases*' you may not find any cmdlets that are relevant.  Shorten your phrase to '*data*' or '*datab*' and results would appear.


# What's Next?

In this introduction we have just scratched the surface of what is available in PowerShell for Exchange Server 2016.  Let's go ahead and get in deep with PowerShell in Chapter 1.

# 1   PowerShell Basics



## Exchange Server 2016 PowerShell: Where to Begin

This book is not a beginner's guide to PowerShell and while we assume that you, the reader, know at least something about PowerShell, we will quickly cover some basic PowerShell topics. What is covered in this chapter is necessary in order to form our building blocks for the more advanced chapters later in this book. Those building blocks will provide practical knowledge for using PowerShell with Exchange Server 2016. Theory can be useful, but for production messaging environments, practical tips and tricks (and scripts!) are far more useful for working in your environment.

In the Introduction, we covered one-liners, cmdlets and getting help in the PowerShell interface. We are now going to turn our attention to building PowerShell parts that make up these elements in PowerShell. Remember that a PowerShell cmdlet consists of a verb and a noun. Remember that PowerShell cmdlets provide various parameters as we saw with the Get-Help in the Introduction to this book.

In the next few pages we will introduce you to some important concepts that are key to building your scripts for Exchange Server 2016. These concepts include variables, arrays, loops and more. Learning these will provide you with the building blocks for your scripts. There will be some basic topics which will introduce you to these elements. These topics will give you the tools to begin building scripts in future chapters of this book.

## Variables

When scripting, a variable is a place for storing data. A variable can store data for different lengths of time, but most importantly, the data stored in the variable can be retrieved or referenced by cmdlets later in a script for performing a task. The data stored in variables is of a certain type, such as strings, numerals, arrays and more. Variables are essential in PowerShell scripting, and it should become apparent how useful they are when working with Exchange Server.

### Example - Variables

| Variable | Variable Type |
| --- | --- |
| $Value = 1 | Numeric |
| $FirstName = "Damian" | String |

Variables are not restricted to static content or a single object or value, and they can store complex, nested structures as well. For example, if we use a variable to store information on all mailboxes:

$AllMailboxes = Get-Mailbox

The $AllMailboxes variable stores information on each mailbox as a single object and can contain as many objects as there are mailboxes in the Exchange environment. This content is unlikely to change as the script using that information will likely be stored for repeated use in a script.  However, a variable containing the current value of a property of a mailbox or server might change repeatedly in a script loop, replacing the variable content on each pass.  For example, while looping through an array (example on page 5), the mailbox name could be stored in a temporary variable (e.g. $name) and with each pass of in the loop, the contents of $name would change to the mailbox name in the current line of an array.  Thus, the contents of a variable is not necessarily static and can be changed during the processing of a script.

# Arrays

Arrays are used to store a collection of objects.  This collection of data is more complex than what would be stored in a normal variable (above).

### Example

$Values = 1,2,3,4,5
$Names = "Dave","Matt","John","Michael"

As you can see from the above example, the array contains a series of values which can be used by a script for queries or manipulation.

Even more complex than arrays are multi-dimensional arrays.  The $AllMailboxes variable example above is an example of this type of variable. This type is used to store more complex, structured information.

### Example of Arrays (Multi-dimensional)

If we were to store all the information about all the Exchange Servers in an array of arrays, there would be a 'list' of arrays.  Each line is essentially its own array of values.  Visually, this is how the data is stored in the array [the top line contains the column descriptions for the underlying values]:

Name, AdminDisplayVersion,ExchangeServerRoles
"EX03","Version 15.1 (Build 225.37)","Mailbox, ClientAccess"
"EX01","Version 15.1 (Build 225.37)","Mailbox, ClientAccess"
"EX02","Version 15.1 (Build 225.37)","Mailbox, ClientAccess"

# Hash Tables

Hash tables are similar in form and function to arrays, but with a twist.  To initialize a hash table, the command is similar to an array:

$Hash = @ { }

Notice the use of the '{' brackets and not '('.  Once initialized we can populate the data like so:

### Example

In the below data sample, the name of each server matched up with the location of the server.   As can be seen by the data set, the data is stored in pairs:

$Servers = @{Dallas = 'Exchange01'; Orlando = 'Exchange02' ; Chicago = 'Exchange03'}

To display the contents of the hash table, simply run '$Servers':

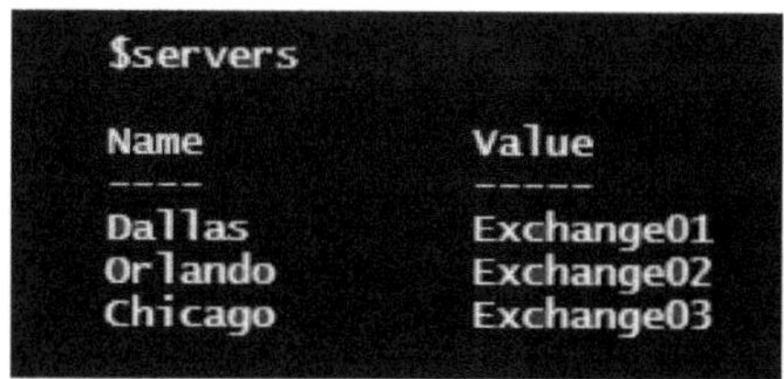


In most scenarios, an array is the way to go for data storage and manipulation.  However, hash tables provide for more complex data storage and indexing with its data pairs.

# CSV Files

CSV files are files used to store static data.  This data can be pre-created and then used by a script post creation or a CSV file can be generated by a script either as an end result or an intermediary step for a script to be used at a later point.  CSV files can be considered an alternative option to using arrays.  They can be used to contain data in a way similar to how an array would store data. One of the differences is that CSVs are files and arrays are stored in memory (RAM), which means that arrays only exist while a script is running and CSV files can be used to store information which should be kept, like for input or output purposes. They can also be looped through, like an array.  CSV files can be manually created in a program like Excel for total control or created by a running script with an Export-CSV cmdlet to export the data.

Arrays are preferable for storing data within a script because no file is created and left behind to cleanup at a later date.  The exception would be if I have an external program or process that generates a CSV file which contains lists of values that need to be imported or used for a process involving a PowerShell script.

The format of the CSV file looks something like this:

```
DisplayName,SamAccountName,PrimarySMTPAddress,MailboxServer,MailboxSizeMB
John Doe,JohnDoe,JohnDoe@practicalpowershell.com,Server01,1510
Damian Scoles,DamianScoles,DamianScoles@practicalpowershell.com,Server01,2400
Dave Stork,DaveStork,DaveStork@practicalpowershell.com,Server01,560
```

```
DisplayName,SamAccountName,PrimarySMTPAddress,MailboxServer,MailboxSizeMB
John Doe,JohnDoe,JohnDoe@practicalpowershell.com,Server01,1510
Damian Scoles,DamianScoles,DamianScoles@practicalpowershell.com,Server01,2400
Dave Stork,DaveStork,DaveStork@practicalpowershell.com,Server01,560
```

PowerShell scripts that use CSV files commonly read CSV files and store the contents in a variable to be used by the script.  Import-CSV is the command to perform this task.

### Example

$CSVFileData = Import-CSV "C:\temp\MailboxData.csv"

In the section on Loops, we will review what can be done with data stored in the variable, after it has been imported from a CSV file.

# Operators

Operators are used in PowerShell to compare two objects or values.  This can be particularly useful for when "If.. Then" or "Where-Object" is used.

Operators can include the following:

| | |
|---|---|
| -eq | Equal |
| -lt | Less Than |
| -gt | Greater Than |
| -ne | Not Equal |
| -ge | Greater Than or Equal |
| -le | Less Than or Equal |
| -like | Like<br><br>Good for single wildcards<br><br>e.g.   "*mailbox" |
| -Match | Matches criteria (non-case sensitive)<br><br>Also can use double wildcards<br><br>e.g.   "*mailbox*" |
| -Cmatch | Match criteria (case-sensitive)<br><br>e.g   "*Mailbox*" |
| -Contains | Exact match |

### Example

 $Mailbox = Get-Mailbox
If ($Mailbox -eq "Damian") {
    Set-Mailbox $Mailbox -ForwardingSMTPAddress DaveStork@PracticalPowershell.Com
}

The above example configures email forwarding for a mailbox that matches the name Damian and forwards all messages to the email address of ***DaveStork@PracticalPowershell.Com.***

Another example would be if there are mailboxes with small quotas (2GB) that need to be increased to 5GB:

```
If ($Quota -lt 2000000) {
    Set-Mailbox $Mailbox -IssueWarningQuota 5gb
}
```

Operators will work with strings and numbers types.  Less than and greater than operators will work against text:

```
If ("Mouse" -lt "Wolf) {
    Write-Host "The Wolf eats the Mouse!"
}
```

The output from this comparison would result in:

```
The Wolf eats the Mouse!
```

The operators, with strings, work off the numerical values of each letter in the words added together and compared.


# Loops

Loops can be used to process or generate a series of data, perhaps an array (or an array of arrays) of data stored in variables (like our $CSVFileData variable in the previous section).  A loop can also use a counter for a series of values as well.  Here are a few different ways to create loops in PowerShell:

## Types

```
Foreach { }
Do { } While ()
```


## Foreach

Foreach loops can be used to process each element of an array either stored in a variable or a CSV file.  The array can have a single or multiple elements.  The Foreach loop will stop when there are no more lines to read or process, although the more lines there are, the longer it will take to complete.

### Example

Let's take our $CSVFileData variable that has stored the data we pre-created in a CSV file.  The variable now contains three 'rows' of usable data.  We can use the data to manipulate mailboxes by changing parameters, creating a report to send to IT Admins or maybe to move mailboxes to different mailbox databases.

A simple example of a Foreach loop would look like this: (Complete code):

```
$CSVFileData = Import-CSV "C:\Data.csv"
Foreach ($Line in $CSVFileData) {
```

```
    $DisplayName = $Line.DisplayName
    $Size = $Line.MailboxSizeMB
    Write-host "The user $displayname has a mailbox that is $Size MB in size."
}
```

The output would look like this:

```
The user John Doe has a mailbox that is 1510 MB in size.
The user Damian Scoles has a mailbox that is 2400 MB in size.
The user Dave Stork has a mailbox that is 560 MB in size.
```

In this example, the loop created a simple visual representation of the data, but the representation was repeated in a standard manner using a loop and a write-host cmdlet.


## Do { } While ()

Do While and While loops allow a loop to continuously run until a condition has been met. The key difference between the two is that a While loop will evaluate a condition prior to any code executing (the code between the brackets of a While loop may not even run once) whereas a Do While loop will execute code first (guaranteeing at least one time execution of code) and then checking for a particular condition. Whether this conditional exit is an incremental counter, waiting for a query result or a certain key to be pressed, the Do While loop provides some interesting functionality that can be used in PowerShell and with your Exchange 2016 servers.

When looping code with a While loop, an example of conditional exit is the counter variable. Simply put, the counter variable keeps track of the number of times a loop has run. Each time the below loop runs, the counter value increases by 1 ($Counter++). When the $counter variable reaches 1,000, the script block will stop processing and PowerShell will move on to the next section of code.

Example – While Loop

** **Note** ** The $Counter++ near the end of the loop, which is shorthand for $Counter = $Counter +1.

Also notice that the 'While' statement is at the top of the loop unlike the Do...While loop that follows.

Example – Do While Loop

```
$Counter = 1
Do {
    Write-Host "This is pass # $counter for this loop."
    $Counter++
} While ($Counter -ne 1000)
```

In the above sample, we use a counter variable ($counter) which is incremented by 1's using $Counter++. On each pass the script writes a line to the screen (write-host "This is pass # $counter for this loop."). The resulting output from the code loops something like this:

```
This is pass # 4 for this loop.
This is pass # 5 for this loop.
This is pass # 6 for this loop.
This is pass # 7 for this loop.
This is pass # 8 for this loop.
This is pass # 994 for this loop.
This is pass # 995 for this loop.
This is pass # 996 for this loop.
```

Once the variable ($counter) gets to 1,000, the script will exit.

```
This is pass # 994 for this loop.
This is pass # 995 for this loop.
This is pass # 996 for this loop.
This is pass # 997 for this loop.
This is pass # 998 for this loop.
This is pass # 999 for this loop.
```

Notice that a result with 1,000 is not shown above and this is because the counter is increased after the write-host statement and the $counter variable is increased from 999 to 1,000 and exits. In order to show a result with 1,000 the $counter variable needs to be moved:

### Example

```
$Counter = 0
Do {
    $Counter++
    Write-Host "This is pass # $counter for this loop."
} While ($Counter -ne 1000)
```

## Export-CSV

Export-CSV – This cmdlet can create a CSV file to be used by another script or another section of code in the same script.

When exporting to a CSV file, make sure to use the –NoType option in order to remove the extraneous line that gets inserted into the exported CSV. This extra line can affect the use of the CSV file later. See below for an example of what happens when exporting a complete list of mailboxes to a CSV file:

**Export-CSV -NoType**

```
mailboxes.csv - Notepad
File  Edit  Format  View  Help
"PSComputerName","RunspaceId","PSShowComputerName","Database","MailboxProvisioningConstraint","
SendQuota","ProhibitSendReceiveQuota","RecoverableItemsQuota","RecoverableItemsWarningQuota","C
```

**Export-CSV**

```
mailboxes2.csv - Notepad
File  Edit  Format  View  Help
#TYPE Microsoft.Exchange.Data.Directory.Management.Mailbox
"PSComputerName","RunspaceId","PSShowComputerName","Database","MailboxProvisioningConstraint","
SendQuota","ProhibitSendReceiveQuota","RecoverableItemsQuota","RecoverableItemsWarningQuota","C
```

In order to use the CSV later in the script, the –NoType option should be used.

## How to Use these Cmdlets

These cmdlets are most useful for pulling in information from an external source or exporting the information for a later script or for reporting purposes.  When importing the contents of a CSV file, I will use a variable to store the contents to be pulled out later by a loop or some other method.

# Functions

Functions are blocks of code that can be called upon within the same script. This block of code becomes a reusable operation that can be called on multiple times in a script.  The function, since it is comprised of reusable code, helps to save time in coding by removing duplicate coding efforts as well as reducing the size of the script removing duplicate code. Which, depending on how much code is involved and how often it is called, can improve the performance and efficiency of a PowerShell script, as well as make it more maintainable.

### Example

```
# Check for Old Disclaimers
Function Check-OldDisclaimers {
    $RuleCheck = (Get-TransportRule).ApplyHtmlDisclaimerText
    $RuleCheck2 = Get-TransportRule | Where {$_.ApplyHtmlDisclaimerText -ne $Null}
    If ($RuleCheck -eq $Null) {
        Write-Host "There are no disclaimers in place now." -ForegroundColor Green
    } Else {
        Foreach ($Line in $RuleCheck2) {
        Write-Host "There is a transport rule in place called $line that is a disclaimer rule." -ForegroundColor
Yellow
        }
    }
} #End of the Check-OldDisclaimers function
Check-OldDisclaimers
```

The previous code sample checks for disclaimers configured in Exchange.  The last line of the script above calls the function (with the code contained within the '{' and '}' brackets) and the code in the brackets executes.  The PowerShell function by itself will not do anything unless it is called upon.

# PowerShell Tools

### PowerShell ISE

PowerShell ISE [*Integrated Scripting Environment*] is one of **THE** tools you should get familiar with when working with PowerShell.  The tool comes installed by default with Windows 2012, 2012 R2 and 2016.  If you are using an older version of Windows (2008R2 and before) ISE is not preinstalled and it will be necessary to download the installation and install it on the server.

The ISE has many useful features such as color coding of PowerShell cmdlet types as well as the indicators that are provided for loops (Foreach, If Else, etc.), to aid in checking matching brackets for example.   ISE's built-in spell checker make this tool very useful.  ISE is also PowerShell-aware which means you can quickly find the relevant cmdlet or recently defined variable after only typing a few characters.  If working with Exchange, the Exchange PowerShell Module needs to be available for ISE to use otherwise it won't be able to look up those cmdlets needed or used with Exchange Servers.

## PowerShell ISE Graphical Interface

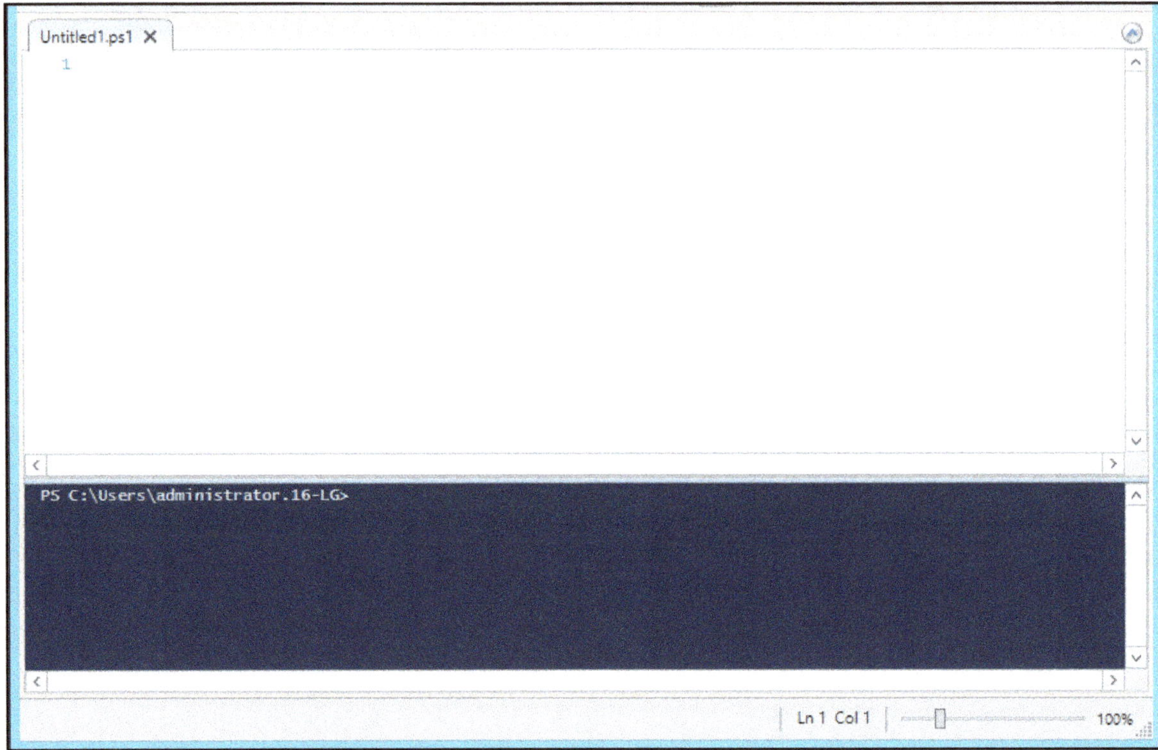

The ISE tool is a great way to help visualize a script (indentation, color, etc), while not necessary or required to assist the coder visually in writing PowerShell scripts. ISE can also be used to interactively debug scripts, stepping through the code as it is executed, allowing you to inspect variables for example.

Logical groupings are denoted by the '-' symbol on the left of the screen:

```
RC4Check.ps1  X
 1    $servers = get-exchangeserver
 2
 3    foreach ($server in $Servers) {
 4        # Set the initial value
 5        $name = $server.name
 6        $up = $true
 7        $success = $true
 8
 9        try {
10            $Registry = [Microsoft.Win32.RegistryKey]::OpenRemoteBaseKey("LocalMachine",$name)
11        } catch {
12            $up = $false
13        }
14
15        if ($up -eq $true) {
16
17            # Check the registry path - Cipher Stack
```

Different components of the PowerShell scripts are shown in different colors.  Comments are green, variables are red and cmdlets are color coded blue:

```
RC4Check.ps1  X

 1    $servers = get-exchangeserver ────────Cmdlet
 2                                          Comment
 3  ⊟foreach ($server in $Servers) {
 4       # Set the initial value
 5       $name = $server.name
 6       $up = $true          ────Variable
 7       $success = $true
 8
 9  ⊟    try {
10           $Registry = [Microsoft.Win32.RegistryKey]::Oper
11  ⊟    } catch {
12           $up = $false
13       }
14
15  ⊟    if ($up -eq $true) {
```

Loops can be verified by click at or near a bracket to see where the closing bracket is [paired brackets highlighted]:

```
66  ⊟    if ($success -ne $false) {
67           write-verbose "Test passed for server $name."
68  ⊟    } else {
69           write-verbose "Test failed for server $name."
70       }
```

If we click on the '-' sign on the left side, it will collapse A section of code is enclosed by a bracket pair:

```
66  ⊞    if ($success -ne $false) {...} else {
69           write-verbose "Test failed for server $name."
70       }
```

Some of the formatting is NOT done by the ISE tool.  Indentation is up to you to do.  I recommend the use of indenting each loop.  Following is an example of this.  This technique is used for readability and is not required for the code to run properly:

```
              $n = 0
            ⊟foreach ($line in $csv) {
One indent for →    if ($line -eq $true) {
each loop that →        if ($n -lt 10) {
is present.    →            write-host "We are at number $n"
                        }
                    }
                    $n++
            }
```

** **Note** ** Each indent is created by using the TAB key.

In the next example of indentation, without indentation, the script would be hard to read and understand where the different loops or groupings start / end:

```
2  ⊟    if( $tryWMI ) {
3           ## WMI depends on RPC. CIM depends on WinRM, but C]
4  ⊟        try {$Page_Managed = Get-WMIObject -computer $name
5  ⊟        } catch {Write-Verbose "$($TestID): Was not able t
6           $nulldata = $true
7           }
8       }
```

Now notice the red brackets highlight the bracketing to show the way cmdlets are grouped.

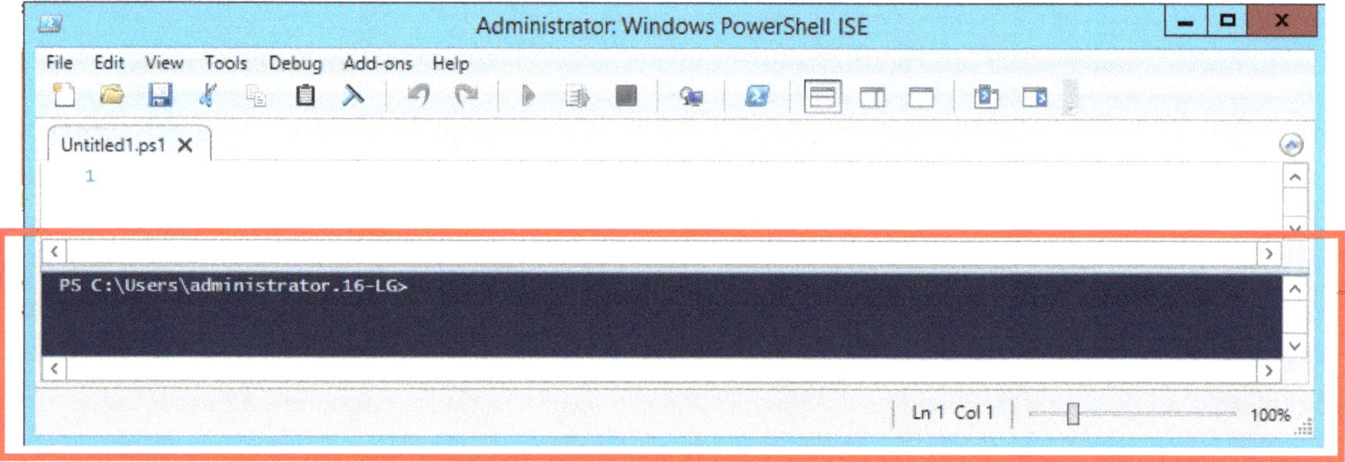



Indentation falls into the same category as comments. While not required to be used, they make the script much easier to use, understand and troubleshoot in case of problems or errors. Creating a script is one of many uses for the tool, as the ISE tool also allows for running the script. In the lower portion of the tool is a PowerShell interface used for script execution.



PowerShell modules can be imported in order to expand its capabilities. For Active Directory this module can be loaded with this one-liner.

**Active Directory**

```
import-module activedirectory
```

After the module is loaded, Active Directory cmdlets such as Get-AdUser and Get-ADDomain Controller can now be run.

** **Note** ** This module is loaded in the Exchange 2016 Management Shell by default.


## Alternatives to ISE

Notepad and Notepad++. Notepad is a very basic way to edit a PowerShell script. It is best used for quickly copying and pasting scripts or scripts that require very little work. Notepad++ is program similar to the PowerShell ISE in that it can handle multiple languages, however the ISE is much more versatile. AutoCompletion of PowerShell cmdlets and variable names are incredibly useful while coding longer scripts.

Visual Studio Code is also a via alternative to PowerShell ISE. The product is a noteworthy take on PowerShell script editing and is worth a look at here - https://4sysops.com/archives/visual-studio-code-vscode-as-powershell-script-editor/. Visually it has a more modern take on script editing:

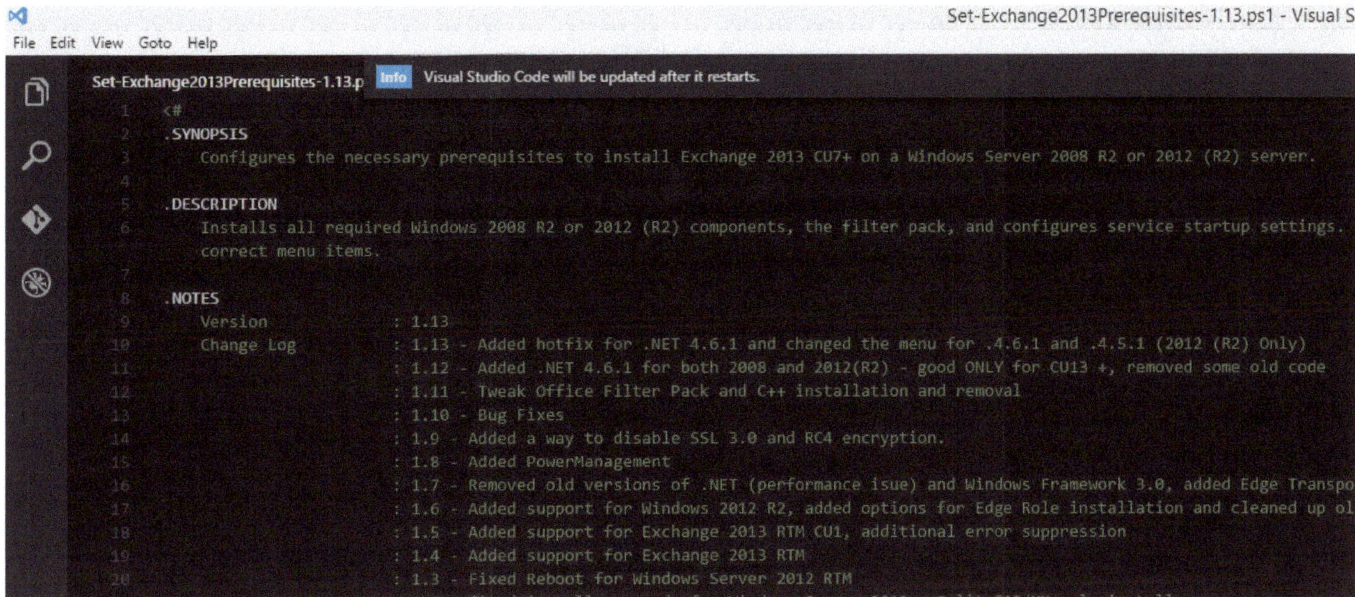

It has visual identifiers for comments, variables, text strings and has even more advanced features for identifying correct brackets keywords and more.

# ISE Plugins and Additional Tools

Plugins for ISE provide even more functionality for those coding in PowerShell.   Additional functionality and features can be added to PowerShell ISE with plugins created by third party authors.  Here are some sample plugins for the PowerShell ISE program:

**ISE Steroids -** http://www.powertheshell.com/isesteroids/

ISE Steroids makes coding within the ISE more interactive.  The plugin provides assistance with your coding, making sure that the correct syntax is used.  For example, the right use of quotes ' or " is shown below:

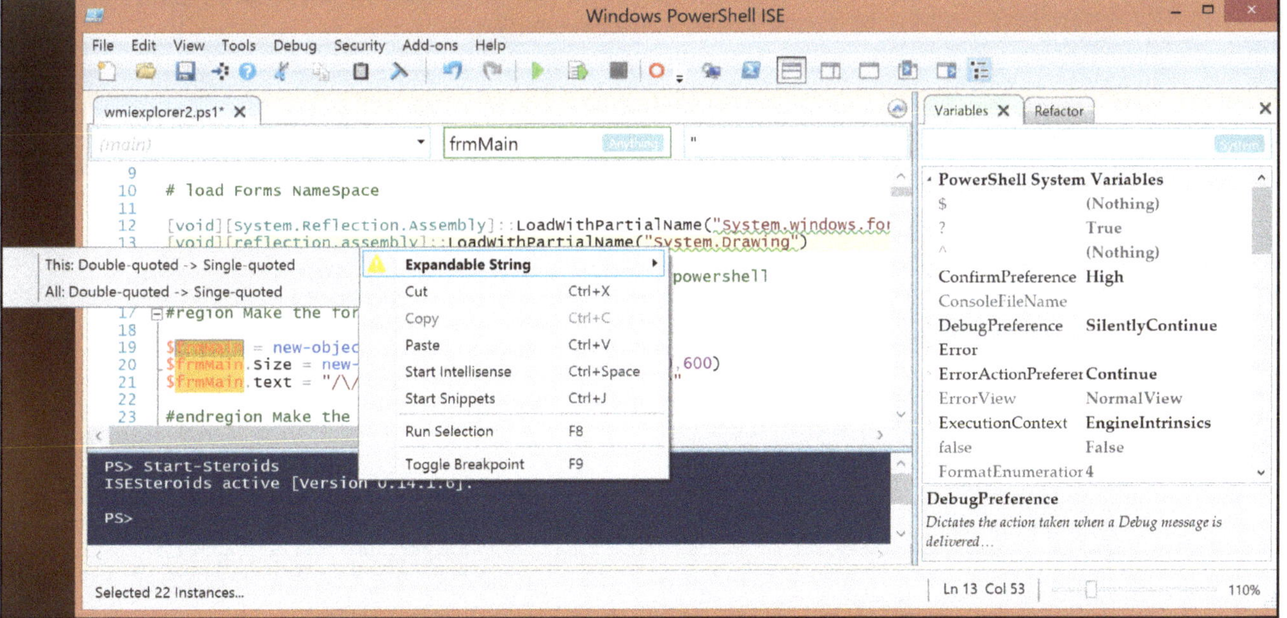

The plugin also provides help on PowerShell cmdlets:

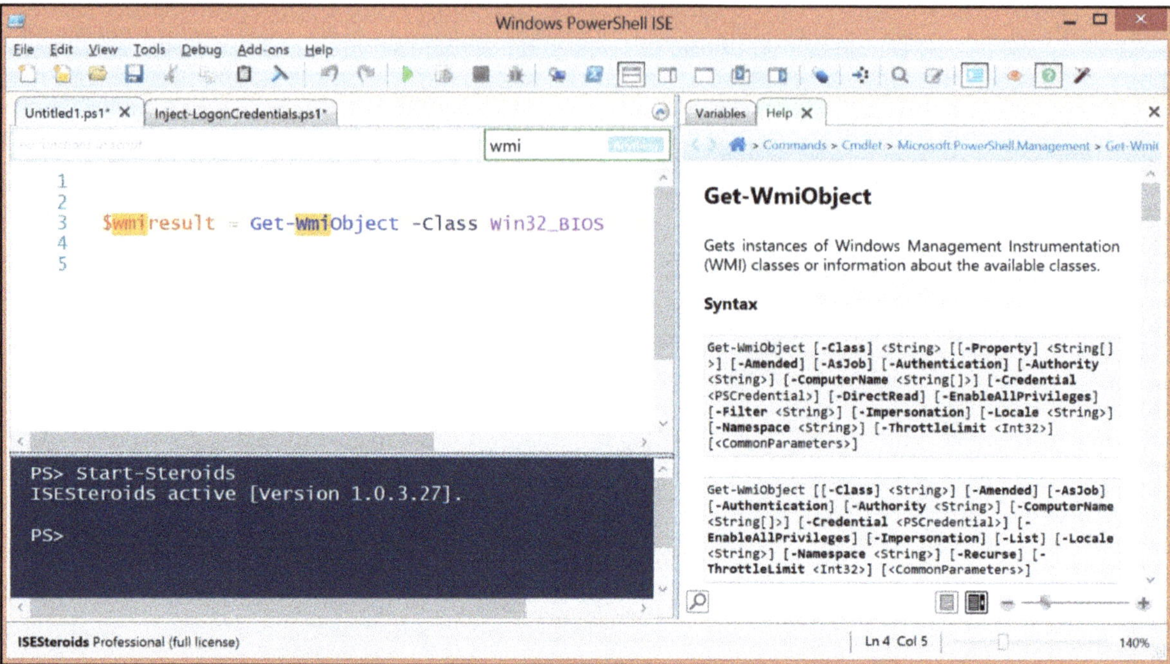

## PSharp Plugin for PowerShell

The PSharp ISE plugin, created by PowerShell MVP Doug Finke, was designed to make PowerShell ISE more powerful than it already is. The plugin allows for identifying variables, commands and functions with a single keystroke. Like any other, it is worth evaluating to see if it meets your needs.

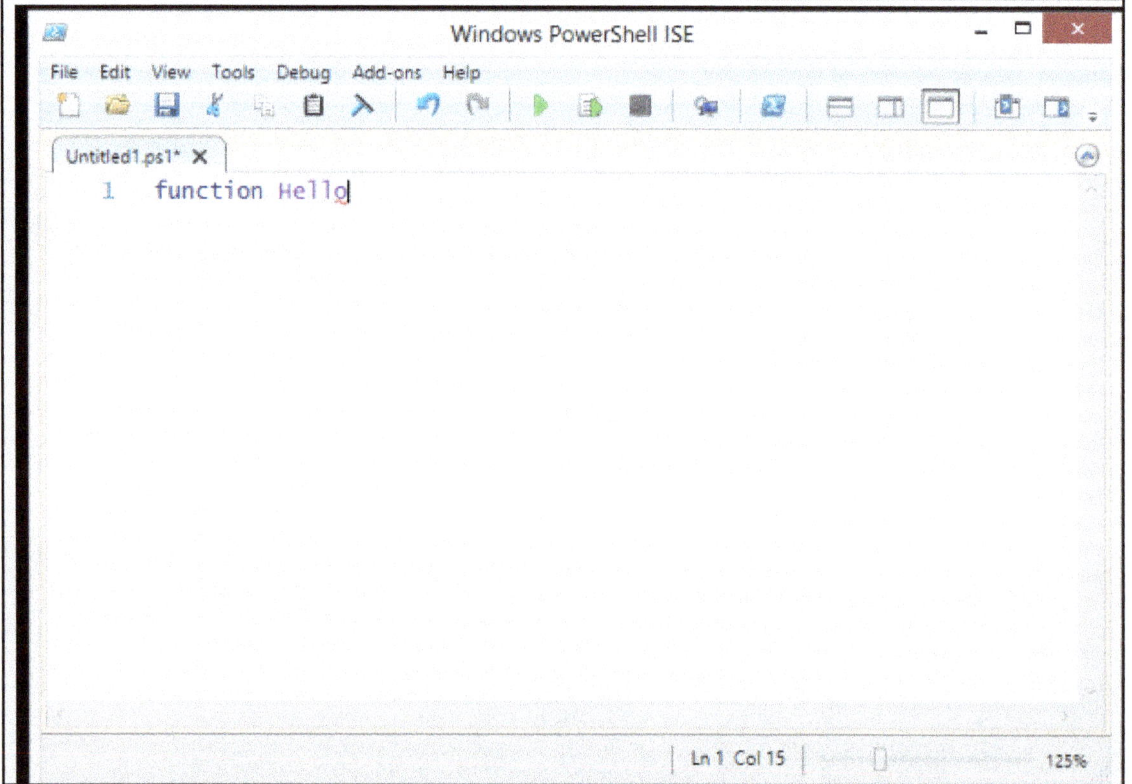

http://www.powershellmagazine.com/2013/08/18/psharp-makes-powershell-ise-better/

# 2 Beyond the Basics



## Formatting

A good working PowerShell script can be written quickly and without any formal formatting or standards. The script will probably function and perform the tasks it was coded for. However, a useful well-coded script should have more. A script should be easily read by another person, there should be a description of the script at the top and plenty of commenting in the script to provide information about its workings.

In this section, we will cover topics like capitalization, comments and bracketing. The use of these techniques will make your PowerShell scripts more usable and readily accessible to those who may use your scripts.

## Capitalization

We must note that even though capitalization can be used throughout our scripts, PowerShell is NOT case sensitive. One use case scenario for Capitalization is to help make PowerShell cmdlets and their arguments more readable:

**PowerShell Cmdlet Example:**

**No capitalization**
set-publicfoldermailboxmigrationrequest

**Each word is capitalized**
Set-PublicFolderMailboxMigrationRequest

Visually the second cmdlet example would make the scripts more readable. We can see the individual words in the cmdlet and possibly allow us to decipher what the cmdlet is used for. While the non-capitalized one seems flat, with the words seemingly running together.

Capitalization can vastly improve the readability of the script by providing visual clues for each new word in a variable where words are mashed together:

**Variable Example:**

**No capitalization**
$mailboxnames

**Each word is capitalized**
$MailboxNames

This capitalization is analogous to syllable emphasis in pronouncing words. The capital letters emphasize the important parts and give the read a visual cue as to what is being run. While this convention is not required by PowerShell as it is case-insensitive. Another example would be function names:

**Function Example:**

**No capitalization**
function pagefilesizecheckinitial {
}

**Each word is capitalized**
Function PagefileSizeCheckInitial {
}

In summary, while these changes will not increase the speed of your script, nor make the script run cleaner, it will make it easier for troubleshooting and understanding how a script is structured.


## Commenting

Comments. Do we really need these? Comments in PowerShell are not required, however they are extremely useful. If you have a team that shares scripts, then comments can be quiet beneficial to all. Not only can scripting logic be explained, or versioning be tracked, but each section of the script can be described and documented for yourself or others who will run the script.

**Exchange 2007 (Historical Note)**

If you write a script that needs to run on all versions of Exchange, even legacy versions, be aware that Exchange 2007, which uses PowerShell 1.0, does not like certain commenting syntax. The '#' is the only accepted way of making a block of comments. The '#' needs to be in front of each line that needs to be treated as a comment versus executable content.

```
#  **********************************************************
#  *       This section is for the Windows 2008 R2 SP1 OS   *
#  **********************************************************
```

## Exchange 2010 – 2016 (Modern PowerShell)

The more 'modern' versions of Exchange PowerShell have more options in formatting comments that are put into scripts. The below example shows the starting of a comment block with a '<#' and ending the same comment block with '>#'.

```
<#
.SYNOPSIS
        Configures the necessary prerequisites to install Exchang

.DESCRIPTION
      Installs all required Windows 2008 R2 or 2012 (R2) components

.EXAMPLE
        .\Set-Exchange2013Prerequisites-1-9.ps1

.INPUTS
        None. You cannot pipe objects to this script.
#>
```

Comments can also use the format of '#' in front of each line just like we have in Exchange 2007.   The example under Exchange 2007 (Historical Note) can also be used in Exchange 2016.  Comments can be single lines as well:

```
# Get-ADUser -Filter {SamAccountName -eq $UserID} | Set-ADUser …..
```

The example above is an instance where I wanted to comment out a line for troubleshooting other code around this one line. Another example is inline commenting, however that is not recommended as is makes reading more challenging:

```
Set-Mailbox –Identity UserA –PrimarySMTPAddress usera@contoso.com # Set Primary SMTP address
```

## Uses

What are the main drivers for comment utilization in scripts?

- Providing a detailed description of the purpose of the script as well as how to use the script
- Breaking the script into sections
- Providing a quick description of a section
- To block out a line of code for future use
- To block out a line of code that did not work

Take time to provide at least a very basic framework for other script users to get the gist of your script.  Adding comments will provide an additional benefit to your scripts. It allows you, the coder, to go back to an old script and quickly figure out what the script was for and allow for possible modification of one or more sections, as needed. Reusable code will also save time down the line when coding new scripts for new purposes.

With script writing, you might find it easier to comment as the script is built, if nothing else it provides a helpful reminder to yourself of which parts are performing certain functions in the script.  For example, while building a script for checking Pagefile settings, making sure to comment on what step you're on in the process: (the code below is a sample and not a complete script):

```
# Set the ideal PageFile size
$Page_Ideal = $RAMinMB + 10

# Retrieve the Minimum PageFile size
try {$Page_min = (Get-CIMInstance -ComputerName $name -ClassName win32_pagefilesetting -Property * -ErrorAction Stop).initialsize
}catch {$WMI=$true;write-host "The server $name is inaccessible by CIM, trying WMI." -foregroundcolor yellow}
if( $WMI ) {
    ## WMI depends on RPC. CIM depends on WinRM, but CIM failed, so we try WMI before we give up.
    try {$Page_min = (Get-WMIObject -Computer $name -Class win32_pagefilesetting -Property * -ErrorAction Stop).initialsize
    } catch {$up=$false;write-host " The server $name is inaccessible by WMI, this is not good." -foregroundcolor red}
}

# Retrieve the Maximum PageFile size
try {$Page_max = (Get-CIMInstance -ComputerName $name -ClassName win32_pagefilesetting -Property * -ErrorAction Stop).maximumsize
}catch {$WMI=$true;write-host "The server $name is inaccessible by CIM, trying WMI." -foregroundcolor yellow}
if( $WMI ) {
    ## WMI depends on RPC. CIM depends on WinRM, but CIM failed, so we try WMI before we give up.
    try {$Page_max = (Get-WMIObject -Computer $name -Class win32_pagefilesetting -Property * -ErrorAction Stop).maximumsize
    } catch {$up=$false;write-host " The server $name is inaccessible by WMI, this is not good." -foregroundcolor red}
}
```

Note the comments lines that are enclosed in red rectangles.  Each comment block describes a logical section of the script, almost like a script block.  I did this so I could describe each section of my script with a single concise line of text.

The symbol for commenting (#) can also be used to remove a line in the script from executing.  Using the '#' in front of a one-liner in a script would essentially turn the cmdlet into a comment and no longer be executable in PowerShell.  This technique is commonly used in order to duplicate a line of code, allowing for the original line to be saved while new versions of the line are concocted:

**Example – Troubleshooting Code**

**Original line (which fails and needs more options for output)**
Get-Mailbox DamianScoles | ft DisplayName, Server, Database

**Comment the line, duplicate and modify**
# Get-Mailbox DamianScoles | ft DisplayName, Server, Database
Get-Mailbox DamianScoles | ft DisplayName, ServerName, Database

Notice the original line above and the new corrected line below.  I did this because the first command failed to actually display the 'Server' where the mailbox was, because the parameter was incorrect and should have been 'Server Name'.

Another reason to comment out a line is PowerShell is to either remove old code or remove troubleshooting code.

**Example – Removing Old Code**
$Mailbox = Get-Mailbox $Name
Write-host "The current mailbox is $Mailbox."

**Becomes….**
$Mailbox = Get-Mailbox $Name
# Write-host "The current mailbox is $Mailbox."

Note on this, that after a script has tested out and verified as performing its function, these sorts of lines should be cleaned up to get rid of code no longer needed.

## Mind Your Brackets!

One of the more important aspects of writing loops and code sections in PowerShell is making sure your brackets are all correct and in the right place. Take a look at the code section below. Red arrows are drawn below to show which bracket goes with which set of code:

```
5 $files = get-childitem $location
7
8 # Loop for each file to get IP Addresses
9 foreach ($file in $files) {
10     $name = $file.name
11     $csv = import-csv $location"\"$name
12     foreach ($line in $csv) {
13         if ($line -like "#") { }
14         else {
15
16 # Get the Client IP
17         $info = $line.cip
18         if ($info -ne "cip") {
19             foreach ($value in $info) {
20                 if ($value -ne $null) {
21
22 # Client IP also contains the port number which we will remove here
23                 $ID = $value.Split([char]0x003A)
24                 $CIP = $ID[0]
25                 $cipresults += $cip
26             }
27         }
28         }
29     }
30     }
31 }
32
32 # Optional - Remove Duplicates
33 $location = (Get-POPSettings -server $server).logfilelocation
```

Why are brackets important? If each section of code is not closed properly, it could execute incorrectly or not execute at all. If you are using Windows PowerShell ISE, any issues with brackets should be obvious:

| Missing Bracket | All Brackets Present |
|---|---|
| ```foreach ($line in $var) {```<br>```    if ($line -eq "20") {```<br>```}``` | ```foreach ($line in $var) {```<br>```    if ($line -eq "20") {```<br>```    }```<br>```}``` |

As PowerShell ISE will show related brackets with grey marking the other bracket in a pair.

Notice the underlined bracket in the red rectangle in the left code sample as well as the missing '-' in the blue rectangle as well. These are two visual clues that the PowerShell ISE can provide for us while coding in PowerShell. These clues let us know that are brackets are not correct and that something is amiss. The only weakness with this visual clue is that sometimes the red squiggly does not mean that the exact same kind of bracket is missing:

### Example – Different Bracket Missing

```
foreach ($line in $csv) {

    if ($that -eq $that {

    }

}
```

The correct code block looks like this:

```
foreach ($line in $csv) {
    if ($that -eq $that) {
    }
}
```

Notice that the if () block on the top code block was missing the right bracket. Notice that the '{' bracket actually had the red squiggly under it, even though a ')' was missing. In the same vein, a missing quote can also cause a bracket to get a red squiggly placed under it:

```
write-host "B... Bl... Bla... Blah!"
foreach ($line in $csv) {
    write-host "
}
```

One missing quote causes all of this. Corrected:

```
write-host "B... Bl... Bla... Blah!"
foreach ($line in $csv) {
    write-host "That was the quote we needed."
}
```

No more issues.

# Command Output

The default results that are provided by PowerShell cmdlets are lackluster and in some cases not useful at all. The output needs to be tweaked. This section will cover ways to improve PowerShell cmdlet output, from filtering out unwanted results, to tweaking values stored in variables, to formatting tables and even adding a bit of color to PowerShell output.

## Cmdlet Output Formatting

Formatting. Boring. Do we really need to format our output? Who's going to care?

Any PowerShell script author should. By default the formatting for PowerShell leaves much to be desired. Property values on objects could be truncated, values you need may not be the defaults and more. Formatting will help you create better output, more usable output and allow you to get more out of Exchange 2016 via PowerShell.

How do we do this? Let's cover some of the basics. At the end of a PowerShell cmdlet we can add some more characters to change to format of the output. The characters are:

| Switch | Name | Purpose |
|---|---|---|
| \| FL | Format List | All object properties are displayed in a list format |
| \| FT | Format Table | Object properties displayed in a table format |
| \| FT -auto | Format Table + Auto | Object properties displayed in a table format extra spaces removed |
| \| FT -wrap | Format Table + Wrap | Object properties displayed in multi-line fashion |

Get-ExchangeServer cmdlet using FL which will display 'all' an objects properties in list format:

```
[PS] C:\>Get-ExchangeServer |fl


RunspaceId                  : a1194047-ac61-4a48-8932-ba9d558d0be0
Name                        : EX01
DataPath                    : C:\Program Files\Microsoft\Exchange Server\V15\Mailbox
Domain                      : EX0.local
Edition                     : StandardEvaluation
ExchangeLegacyDN            : /o=First Organization/ou=Exchange Administrative Group
                              (FYDIBOHF23SPDLT)/cn=Configuration/cn=Servers/cn=EX01
ExchangeLegacyServerRole    : 0
Fqdn                        : EX01.EX0.local
CustomerFeedbackEnabled     : True
```

Get-ExchangeServer cmdlet using FT which will  display a select number of attributes in a table format:

```
Creating a new session for implicit remoting of "Get-ExchangeServer" command...

Name       Site              ServerRole    Edition      AdminDisplayVersion
----       ----              ----------    -------      -------------------
EX01       EX0.local/Confi... Mailbox,...  Standard...  Version 15.0 (Bu...
EX02       EX0.local/Confi... Mailbox,...  Standard...  Version 15.0 (Bu...
```

Why would we want to use FT or FL?  FT allows us to create a usable table, mostly for reporting purposes.  It also allows us to copy and paste the information and share it outside of PowerShell.  FL will allow you to see all the properties on an object.  The list of attributes could then be used to create a better or more concise list of properties in table format:

```
[PS] C:\>get-mailboxdatabase db01 -status |fl *quota*


ProhibitSendReceiveQuota        : Unlimited
ProhibitSendQuota               : Unlimited
RecoverableItemsQuota           : 30 GB (32,212,254,720 bytes)
RecoverableItemsWarningQuota    : 20 GB (21,474,836,480 bytes)
CalendarLoggingQuota            : 6 GB (6,442,450,944 bytes)
QuotaNotificationSchedule       : {Sun.1:00 AM-Sun.1:15 AM, Mon.1:00 AM-Mon.1:15 AM
                                  AM-Wed.1:15 AM, Thu.1:00 AM-Thu.1:15 AM, Fri.1:00
                                  AM}
IssueWarningQuota               : Unlimited
```

Using the property list from the above FL we can now select relevant properties to put in a table format.  Also notice the use of an asterisk ('*') which is used as a wildcard character representing any number of characters on its side of the string. Let's pick Prohibit Send Quotas and the Issue Warning Quota.  We can now run this in a table format:

```
[PS] C:\>get-mailboxdatabase db01 -status |ft prohibitsend*,issuew*

ProhibitSendReceiveQuota        ProhibitSendQuota        IssueWarningQuota
------------------------        -----------------        -----------------
Unlimited                       Unlimited                Unlimited
```

What if we pick too many attributes and the values could become truncated as is evidenced above with the '...' displayed.

```
[PS] C:\>get-mailboxdatabase db01 -status |ft prohibitsend*,issuew*,*valid,name,objectcate* -auto

ProhibitSendReceiveQuota ProhibitSendQuota IssueWarningQuota IsValid Name ObjectCategory
------------------------ ----------------- ----------------- ------- ---- --------------
Unlimited                Unlimited         Unlimited         True    DB01 Domain.Com/Configuration/Schema/ms-Exc...
```

To fix this, first we need to widen the PowerShell Windows to a number greater that the normal 80.  You may need some trial and error on exact size numbers.  After that, we can run the same cmdlet with the | FT, but now followed by an '-auto' switch.  The '-auto' switch will take all of the results and create a 'neat table' that makes all property values fit on the screen.  The downside to the switch is that it will hold the results from being displayed as PowerShell is calculating how the properties will all fit on the screen properly.

```
[PS] C:\>get-mailboxdatabase db01 -status |ft prohibitsend*,issuew*,*valid,name,objectcate* -auto

ProhibitSendReceiveQuota ProhibitSendQuota IssueWarningQuota IsValid Name ObjectCategory
------------------------ ----------------- ----------------- ------- ---- --------------
Unlimited                Unlimited         Unlimited         True    DB01 Domain.Com /Configuration/Schema/ms-Exch-Private-MDB
```

This creates a readable output and displays the values properly in one table, auto adjusted (-auto) to condense the information displayed. FT and FL will become important tools for building reports or figuring out what properties to select from objects in Exchange.

## Filtering

In addition to formatting output with FL and FT we can also filter the output. Filtering with PowerShell involves selecting or limiting the reported set of properties on an object to a meaningful subset of properties of an object that can be used or manipulated. One use case for filtering is creating reports on items in Exchange like databases, mailboxes and servers. For example, the default output of 'get-mailbox' only displays the default properties name, alias, server name and ProhibitSendQuota. While these values are relevant to the object, it's hard to create a great report off this.

### Tweaking Our PowerShell Results

First we need to figure out what we want to filter or focus on. Do we want to find all mailboxes in a certain database, on a certain mail server or maybe create a list of mailboxes with a retention policy applied? Without a filter, the Get-Mailbox command will display all mailboxes on all Exchange Servers:

    Get-Mailbox

Results look like this:

```
[PS] C:\get-mailbox

Name                        Alias                   ServerName      ProhibitSendQuota
----                        -----                   ----------      -----------------
Administrator               Administrator           ex01            Unlimited
DiscoverySearchMailbox...   DiscoverySearchMa...    ex01            50 GB (53,687,091,200 bytes)
Damian Scoles               damian                  ex01            Unlimited
Bob Smith                   bob                     ex01            Unlimited
Test User                   TestUser2               ex01            Unlimited
ConferenceRoom Large        LargeConfRoom           ex01            Unlimited
```

In order to filter results based of a certain result, 'Where' can be used as a trigger for PowerShell cmdlets. Below are two examples.

Filter for all mailboxes whose 'database' property does not equal Database01 (notice the -ne operator):

    Get-mailbox | Where {$_.Database -ne 'Database01'}

```
Name                        Alias                   ServerName      ProhibitSendQuota
----                        -----                   ----------      -----------------
Administrator               Administrator           ex01            Unlimited
DiscoverySearchMailbox...   DiscoverySearchMa...    ex01            50 GB (53,687,091,200 bytes)
Damian Scoles               damian                  ex01            Unlimited
```

Filter for all mailboxes whose 'database' property equals Database02 (notice the -eq operator):

```
Name                        Alias                   ServerName      ProhibitSendQuota
----                        -----                   ----------      -----------------
Bob Smith                   bob                     ex01            Unlimited
Test User                   TestUser2               ex01            Unlimited
ConferenceRoom Large        LargeConfRoom           ex01            Unlimited
```

    Get-mailbox | Where {$_.Database -eq "Database02"}

The filters noticeably reduce the number of mailboxes that are reported by the PowerShell command. Contained inside the '{ }' is the criteria for the filter to work. The '$_.database' part allows us to specifically pick the database property on a mailbox. Then using an operator to decide the criteria to match a particular value in the property.

In the above example we are filtering the results to display only mailboxes that are in a database called 'Database01'. The below sample operators are all case insensitive.

### Sample operators:

| | |
|---|---|
| -eq | Equal To |
| -lt | Less Than |
| -gt | Greater Than |
| -ne | Not Equal To |

Filtering allows a search for common criteria on a bulk basis. This is useful for migrations to make sure no mailboxes are left on old legacy Exchange server, maybe find all mailboxes with a quota configured, etc.

## Splitting

### Scenario #1

Call it parsing, call it whatever. Sometimes the values stored in a CSV or variable have unwanted characters or need to be separated in order to be used for the rest of the script. Let's walk through a couple of scenarios that will better explain the usefulness of the technique.

In this book we have a script that will retrieve the IP addresses of clients that connect to Exchange 2010 servers using POP3 or IMAP4. The raw data is not ideal for creating a report. The value stored in CIP of the log file used by the POP3 or IMAP4 service looks something like this:

IP:port  --> 192.168.0.43:63475

If we want to display just the IP addresses of the clients, the information after the ':' is useless to us. In order to remove this information, we'll need to get the hex code for the ":" character. The hex code will allow us to specify which character to split the variable with. A good place to look for values is http://unicodelookup.com/:

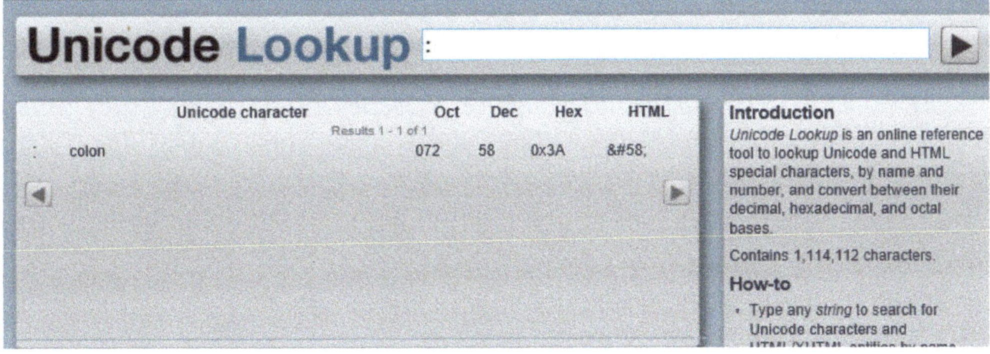


When looking for ":" we see that 0x3A is the code we will need in order to split up the value.

**In Action**

If we were able to work with the POP3 csv file and had a variable called $csv that contained the value of "192.168.0.43:63475" We can use the Split command in PowerShell to split this value.

```
$IP = $csv.Split([char]0x003A)
```

This transforms $csv into an array of 2 values, which is stored in $IP as 192.168.0.43,63475.  Once split we can chose one part of this variable and just use that information:

    $IP[0]

The above variable will give the first value in its array, which is '192.168.0.43'.  The port (63475) is stored as $IP[1].

**Scenario #2**

Using the same 'Split' cmdlet in PowerShell, let's explore another real scenario.  Translating Lotus Notes display names into aliases in Active Directory, this could be used in a migration to Exchange.  In this scenario we know

| Alias | First Name | Last Name |
|---|---|---|
| JohnSmith | John | Smith |
| MichaelLarraday | Michael | Larraday |

that Active Directory aliases are a combination of first and last names.

In some cases Lotus Notes uses the middle initials in their name.  We would have something like this:

    John M. Smith
    Michael G Larraday

Notice that John has a middle initial with a period and Michael does not.  We need to be able to account for both types of middle initials.  First, let's split the name up into its three parts:

    $Name = $SourceName.Split([Char]0x0020)
    (The 0x0020 character is a space)

The variable $name would look something like this for each name:

    $Name = John, M., Smith
    $Name = Michael, G, Larraday

Remember the data is stored like this:

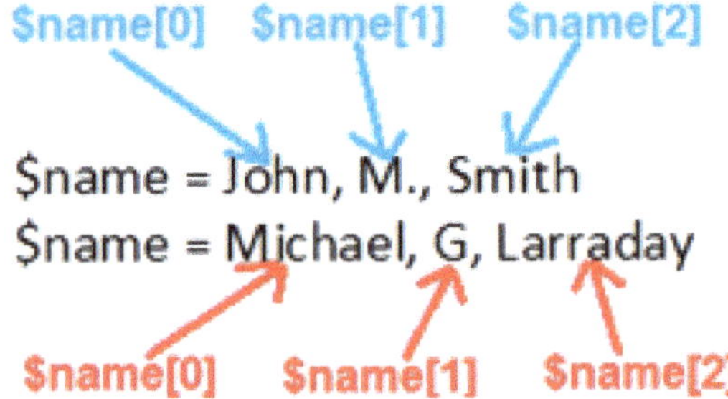


In order to get the alias, we need to add the last name to the first name and store it in the $alias variable.

    $Alias = $Name[0]+$Name[2]

This effectively ignores the middle initial which would be $name[1]:

    $Alias = JohnSmith
    $Alias = MichaelLarraday

## Possible Complication

Like a lot of technology used in production, nothing is ever that simple.  There is always some wrench thrown into the mix.  In the second scenario we assume that the user will have a middle name and we will have to ignore that to create the alias.  What if the user has no middle name listed in the source?  What would happen?

    Bob Delol

If we parsed it, we would get $Name[0] = "Bob" and $Name[1] = "Delol".  There would be no $Name[2].  Now we follow the same formula before:

    $Alias = $Name[0]+$Name[2]

Our results would be less than ideal:

    $Alias = "Bob"

To resolve this we would need some sort of logic to handle that:

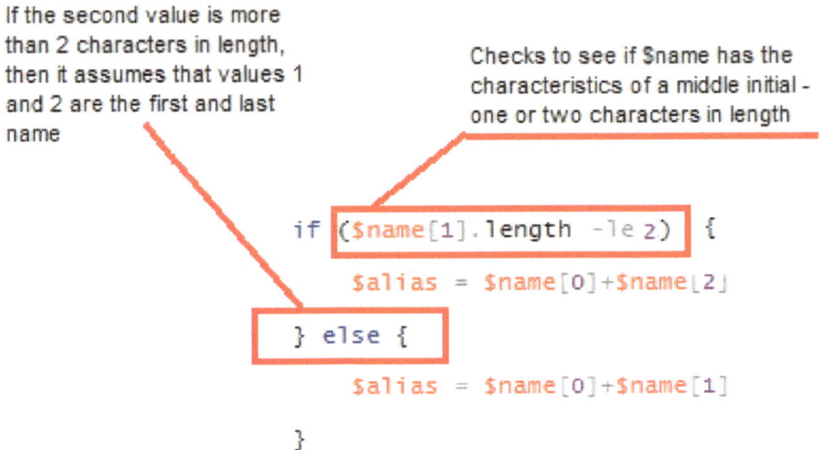

So Bob Smith would end up as "BobSmith".  The rest would have their middle initial ignore as well and put together.  The point of this exercise is that in real life scenarios, sometimes adjustments need to be made in order to get the results required.

# Scripting in Color

Why is color important in PowerShell?

Normally, while using PowerShell, we see Black and White or Blue and White.   PowerShell provides extra colors in its output for a more visual indication of the type of information presented on the console:

### Examples

- Report failures in red
- Reporting success in blue or white
- Warnings reporting in yellow
- Make different code sections
- Menus can be color coded

## Color Coding Examples

Reporting that a test failed: (This sample code verified that a certain hotfix is present on a server):

```
Write-Host "The server $name does not have the hotfix " -ForegroundColor White -NoNewLine;
Write-Host "$Hotfix" -ForegroundColor Red -NoNewLine
Write-Host " installed" -ForegroundColor White
```

```
16-lg-ex01 does not have the hotfix KB941345 installed
```

Notice the contrast of the red with the white in the results of the commands.  Also note that -NoNewLine was used as well to compress the result to one line in the output.  The '-NoNewLine' option allows for us to consolidate many lines of 'Write-Host' into one.  If we were to remove this switch from the above code and use this code sample:

```
Write-Host "The server $name does not have the hotfix " -ForegroundColor White
Write-Host "$hotfix" -ForegroundColor Red
Write-Host " installed at this time." -ForegroundColor White
```

The results would look vastly different:

```
The server 16-lg-ex01 does not have the hotfix
KB941345
 installed at this time.
```

Use care with –NoNewLine because too many lines can cause the formatting to look just as bad:

**Code Sample**

```
Foreach ($Name in $Names) {
    Write-Host "The server $name does not have the hotfix " -ForegroundColor White -NoNewLine
    Write-Host "$Hotfix" -ForegroundColor Red -NoNewLine
    Write-Host " installed at this time." -ForegroundColor White  -NoNewLine
}
```

Results:

```
[PS] C:\downloads>.\test.ps1
The server 16-lg-ex01 does not have the hotfix KB941345 installed at this time.The server 16-leg-ex02 does not have the
hotfix KB941345 installed at this time.The server 16-lg-ex03 does not have the hotfix KB941345 installed at this time.Th
e server 16-lg-ex04 does not have the hotfix KB941345 installed at this time.[PS] C:\downloads>
```

As you can see, too many can cause the output to be unusable and it even carries over to the PowerShell prompt being dragged into the mess. Another example is to create a colorful menu:

```
$a = {
    write-host "    *************************************************" -foregroundcolor cyan
    write-host "    **         This is a cool new menu !!     **" -foregroundcolor cyan
    write-host "    *************************************************" -foregroundcolor cyan
    write-host " "
    write-host "    Please select an option from the list below:" -foregroundcolor yellow
    write-host " "
    write-host "    1) Install Mailbox prerequisites - Part 1  [Includes 30 & 31]" -foregroundcolor white
    write-host "    2) Install Mailbox prerequisites - Part 2" -foregroundcolor white
    write-host "    3) Install Edge Transport Server prerequisites" -foregroundcolor white
    write-host " "
    write-host "    10) Launch Windows Update" -foregroundcolor red
    write-host "    11) Check Prerequisites for Mailbox role" -foregroundcolor red
    write-host "    12) Check Prerequisites for Edge role" -foregroundcolor red
    write-host " "
    write-host "    20) Install - One-Off - .NET 4.5.2 [MBX or Edge]" -foregroundcolor magenta
    write-host "    21) Install - One-Off - Windows Features [MBX]" -foregroundcolor magenta
    write-host "    22) Install - One Off - Unified Communications Managed API 4.0" -foregroundcolor magenta
    write-host " "
    write-host "    30) Set Power Plan to High Performance" -foregroundcolor green
    write-host "    31) Disable Power Management for NICs." -foregroundcolor green
    write-host "    32) Disable SSL 3.0 Support      ** NEW **" -foregroundcolor green
    write-host "    33) Disable RC4 Support      ** NEW **" -foregroundcolor green
    write-host " "
    write-host "    98) Restart the Server" -foregroundcolor white
    write-host "    99) Exit" -foregroundcolor white
    write-host " "
    write-host "    Select an option.. [1-99]?" -foregroundcolor yellow -nonewline
}
```

While the above code sample is a bit overboard, it illustrates the technique of coloring PowerShell output:

The key to making this work is the Invoke-Command used to display the $a variable as this colorful menu:

```
Invoke-Command -ScriptBlock $a
```

The ScriptBlock parameter specifies that code stored in the $a variable will execute, which is a colorful menu.

Lastly, an example of coloring would be HTML formatting. HTML color can be used, for example, in creating reports with cells of a particular mean. Red could be used to indicate an Error, yellow used to indicate a Warning and green to indicate Success. This would provide for a quick visual read of the data and allow for the recipient of the report to quickly determine what to concentrate efforts on or to troubleshoot as needed.

We could for example, check a server's patch level to see how close it is to a supportable version. Green could indicate the most recent, yellow could be for 1 to 2 CUs behind and Red could be for anything over 3 versions behind. HTML coding itself is a bit more complex, but it will covered later in the "**Chapter 16 - Reporting**".

The below code was created as sample testing code to use as a base for constructing an HTML report. The code checks the current version of Exchange Servers in an environment. If the version is current, then Green is used, Yellow means it is still supported, and its 1 or 2 CUs behind and if the server is 3 or more CUs behind, then Red is used to indicate that the server is out of the support range Microsoft has for Exchange.

**Sample Code**

```
$Current = "15.00.1178.004"
$CurrentMinus2 = "15.00.1130.007"
$Servers = Get-ExchangeServer

Foreach ($Server in $Servers) {
    $Test = $Null
    $ExchangeServer = $Server.Name
    $Script = { $Ver = Get-Command Exsetup |%{$_.FileVersionInfo} }

    Invoke-Command -ComputerName $ExchangeServer -ScriptBlock $Script

    If ($Ver -eq $Current) {
        Write-Host "The server $ExchangeServer is up to date [CU12]." -ForegroundColor Green
    }

    If (($Ver -lt $Current) -or ($Ver -gt $CurrentMinus2)) {
        Write-Host "The server $ExchangeServer is within two CUs of being up to date [CU10 or CU11]."
        -ForegroundColor Yellow
    }

    If ($Ver -lt $CurrentMinus2) {
        Write-Host "The server $ExchangeServer is out of date. This means it is running 3 or more CUs
        behind [CU9 or less]." -ForegroundColor Red
    }
}
```

By executing this against other servers we can test the logic without the added code for HTML. After validating the code, we can construct an HTML report that would fill in cells to correspond to the same colors listed above. A sample HTML report would look something like this:

| Exchange Build Check | |
| --- | --- |
| **Name** | **Version** |
| EX01 | 15.00.1130.007 |
| EX02 | 15.00.1178.004 |
| EX03 | 15.00.1130.007 |
| EX04 | 15.00.1104.005 |
| EX05 | 15.00.1104.005 |

# Miscellaneous Topics

In this section we'll cover a variety of topics that are important to PowerShell in general and Exchange PowerShell specifically.

# Quotes

Quotes are rather important when it comes to a PowerShell script. Missing quotes can throw off your script and cause it not to run. The wrong kind of quote can prevent a PowerShell script from functioning properly. The question is what quotes are good for what.

Quotes would seem to be an innocuous part of coding PowerShell. However, they are quite important. Microsoft has a set of rules to handle quotes and should be required reading for coding in PowerShell:

https://technet.microsoft.com/en-us/library/hh847740.aspx

**Single Quote ( ' )**

The single quote is the default quote to use for most, if not all quotes in PowerShell. The single quote is a literal interpretation of whatever exists between them. For example, if we take the code sample below, using a Write-Host command to display the contents of a quote, the information is who in a one to one fashion and all variables are ignored:

**Example Code**

```
$Score = 300
Write-Host 'My top score in bowling is $score.'
```

Results are:

```
My top score in bowling is $score.
```

As you can see, the variable was ignored with the single quote.

**Double Quote ( " )**

Double quotes will not allow a literal interpretation and will display values that are store in variables even when between the quotes.

**Example Code**

```
$Score = 300
Write-Host "My top score in bowling is $score."
```

Results are:

```
My top score in bowling is 300.
```

Notice the difference between the single and double quotes.

**Quotes within Quotes ( ' " " ' )**

There are two ways to handle a set of quotes within quotes and prove to be quite useful in a script. One use, shown in the example below, would be to display a book title in a sentence. Without this option, the title of the book would not be displayed in double quotes:

**Example 1**

```
Write-Host 'The title of this book is "Practical PowerShell: Exchange Server 2016".'
```

Results are:

```
The title of this book is "Practical PowerShell: Exchange Server 2016".
```

**Example 2**

```
Write-Host "The title of this book is ""Practical PowerShell: Exchange Server 2016""."
```

Results are the same as can be seen here:

```
The title of this book is "Practical PowerShell: Exchange Server 2016".
```

**Example 3**

```
Write-Host 'The title of this book is 'Practical PowerShell: Exchange Server 2016'.'
```

Results:

```
The title of this book is  Practical PowerShell: Exchange Server 2016.
```

Notice the complete lack of quotes in the resulting output. So if quotes are needed, the quotes need to be correctly ordered.

In summary, start with single quotes, unless a variable or a non-literal display of information is needed then use double quotes if needed. If a variable is in between quotes, use double quotes.

## Common Interface Model and Windows Management Interface

Where to start with this topic?  Whole books have been written about the topic… because there is so much to cover. When it comes to Exchange Server 2016, not all of these parts are of interest.  Think of Windows Management Interface (WMI) and Common Interface Model (CIM) as a database of hardware and software information for Windows servers. WMI is the Microsoft implementation of the CIM and WBEM standards.  Up until PowerShell 2.0 WMI was the only method in which to access server information.  Then with PowerShell version 3.0, Microsoft added CIM support as well, which can be used in addition to WMI.

WMI information is generated or accessible via providers.  Example providers are Active Directory, DFS, IIS, WIN32 and DNS as well as the server hardware.  Inside each of these providers are managed objects that can be queried for stored information.  PowerShell can query items via the WMI interface that store data about Windows OS Servers.  This data can include OS versions, RAM installed and more.

One of the notable differences for CIM and WMI is when querying servers or workstations that are inside or outside of a domain.  CIM works great when a computer is in the domain.  It relies on Windows Authentication and when making queries against non-domain machines, the queries made via CIM will fail.  WMI queries however will work as expected.  In an Exchange environment, CIM queries would fail against an Edge Transport server because the Exchange Server role can only be installed on a workstation machine, so being able to fail back to WMI from CIM would prove useful.

## Exchange Servers and CIM/WMI

For Exchange Server 2016, there are several components that can be utilized when it comes to CIM/WMI.  These components included reporting on the physical hardware (CPUS, cores, RAM and Pagefile) as well as software (Exchange configuration information and Operating System version).   For example, a report could be made to report on if all Exchange Servers in an environment are up to a certain standard – i.e. 4 cores and 24 GB of RAM. Adding to this report, the Pagefile configuration can be also be examined to make sure it matches Microsoft best practices of RAM + 10 MB to a max of 32 Gb + 10 MB.

### Example Code for Pagefile Analysis

The above code checks to see if (1) the Pagefile is managed, (2) the Pagefile minimum and (3) maximum size (4) as well as the current size.  Ideally Exchange Server 2016 would have a non-managed Pagefile of RAM + 10 MB with the same minimum and maximum.

```
$Page_Managed = Get-CIMInstance -computerName $name -ClassName Win32_ComputerSystem  -ErrorAction Stop| % {$_.AutomaticManagedPagefile}

$Page_min = (Get-CIMInstance -ComputerName $name -ClassName win32_pagefilesetting -Property * -ErrorAction Stop).initialsize

$Page_max = (Get-CIMInstance -ComputerName $name -ClassName win32_pagefilesetting -Property * -ErrorAction Stop).maximumsize

$Page_Current = (Get-CIMInstance -computername $name -classname Win32_PageFileUsage -ErrorAction Stop -property *).allocatedbasesize
```

> ** **Note** ** ErrorAction is specified in the one-liners above.  The ErrorAction specifies the action PowerShell should take in the case the one-liner generates an error message.

In a future chapter we will cover CIM and WMI more in-depth.

## Obfuscated Information

Is it possible that PowerShell would hide information when cmdlets are run querying for Exchange information? When running GET command, all available information is displayed, right? No. Not always. It depends on the command that is executed and if there is a switch to reveal more information.

**Special Switches**

The two switches that we need to cover are -Status and -IncludeReport. These two switches can reveal a bit more detail when it comes to certain commands and are available on a few cmdlets to retrieve additional information. Here are some examples:

### -Status

    Get-MailboxDatabase

This command reveals information about the mailbox databases on the server or servers that are running Exchange Server 2016. The above command produces a useful table like this:

```
Name                            Server        Recovery    ReplicationType
----                            ------        --------    ---------------
Mailbox Database 0794329553     16-LG-EX01    False       None
Mailbox Database 0128773553     16-LG-EX02    False       None
Mailbox Database 1790513196     16-LG-EX03    False       None
Mailbox Database 1654944653     16-LG-EX04    False       None
Mailbox Database 1051739237     16-LG-EX05    False       None
```

If we run the same command with Format-List like this….

    Get-MailboxDatabase | fl

…what we notice is that some values are not populated. This could mean that there really isn't anything stored and thus the property is truly empty. However, this is not the case for some of these properties. For a Mailbox Database, this is true for the 'Mounted' field:

```
MountAtStartup                                        : True
Mounted                                               :
Organization                                          : First Organization
```

Notice that this is blank. Why would this be blank? This would seem to be a rather important value. This is where the '-Status' switch comes into play:

    Get-MailboxDatabase -Status

Now we have an idea if the database is mounted or not:

```
MountAtStartup                                        : True
Mounted                                               : False
Organization                                          : First Organization
```

Now there are some PowerShell cmdlets where the '-Status' actually looks for the status of an object versus the switch revealing more information about something in Exchange.

Another example is:

    Get-ExchangeServer | fl

Without the -Status switch, there are many properties that are not populated:

- ErrorReportingEnabled
- CurrentDomainControllers
- CurrentGlobalCatalogs
- CurrentConfigDomainController

No '-Status'

```
ErrorReportingEnabled            :
StaticDomainControllers          : {}
StaticGlobalCatalogs             : {}
StaticConfigDomainController     :
StaticExcludedDomainControllers  : {}
MonitoringGroup                  :
CurrentDomainControllers         : {}
CurrentGlobalCatalogs            : {}
CurrentConfigDomainController    :
```

With '-Status'

```
ErrorReportingEnabled            : True
StaticDomainControllers          : {}
StaticGlobalCatalogs             : {}
StaticConfigDomainController     :
StaticExcludedDomainControllers  : {}
MonitoringGroup                  :
CurrentDomainControllers         : {16-LG-DC03.16-lg.local, 16-LG-DC04.16-lg.local, 16-LG-DC01.16-lg.local,
                                   16-LG-DC02.16-lg.local}
CurrentGlobalCatalogs            : {16-LG-DC03.16-lg.local, 16-LG-DC04.16-lg.local, 16-LG-DC01.16-lg.local,
                                   16-LG-DC02.16-lg.local}
CurrentConfigDomainController    : 16-LG-DC03.16-lg.local
```

To see which one of the commands have an option for '-status' and found that there are quite a few that do. If we were to explore each one by simply typing the cmdlet name followed by the '-Status' parameter we can see which cmdlets use the -status to reveal more information and which use the switch for filtering the results of the cmdlet.

## '-Status' Used for Filtering

Get-MailboxRestoreRequest -Status

```
[PS] C:\>Get-mailboxrestorerequest -status
Get-MailboxRestoreRequest : Missing an argument for parameter 'Status'. Specify a parameter of type 'System.Obje
and try again.
At line:1 char:27
+ Get-mailboxrestorerequest -status
+                           ~~~~~~~
    + CategoryInfo          : InvalidArgument: (:) [Get-MailboxRestoreRequest], ParameterBindingException
    + FullyQualifiedErrorId : MissingArgument,Get-MailboxRestoreRequest
```

Notice the red error message, this means that a word or 'argument' is missing after the '-Status' parameter. The same results can be seen for these cmdlets:

- Get-MessageTrackingReport -Status
- Get-MigrationBatch -Status
- Get-MigrationUser -Status
- Get-PublicFolderMailboxMigrationRequest -Status
- Get-PublicFolderMigrationRequest -Status
- Get-PublicFolderMoveRequest -Status
- New-UMAutoAttendant
- New-UMIPGateway
- Set-UMIPGateway
- Set-UMService

## -IncludeReport

The '-IncludeReport' switch could be considered a verbose switch for certain PowerShell cmdlets. The most commonly used cmdlets with the -IncludeReport switch are move request commands because they pertain to migration reports generated by Exchange. Examples of this are Get-MigrationBatch, Get-MoveRequestStatistics, and Get-PublicFolderMigrationRequestStatistics.

To see what the -IncludeReport switch brings to the table, the Get-MigrationBatch is a good example. Make sure to use the Format-List option to provide the full extent of the command. Without the -IncludeReport switch, displayed would be the base set of information on the migration that is being reported by the Get-MigrationBatch:

```
[PS] C:\>Get-MigrationBatch |fl

RunspaceId              : 5963e5f0-bd3a-4c5c-a8b2-bec8a3b4c3d1
Identity                : test
Status                  : Syncing
State                   :
Flags                   :
SubmittedByUser         : Administrator@16-lg.local
OwnerId                 : 16-lg.local/Users/Administrator
OwnerExchangeObjectId   : 5c24c780-bee6-4e29-b746-2483d2e0a816
NotificationEmails      : {Administrator@16-lg.local}
ExcludedFolders         : {}
MigrationType           : ExchangeLocalMove
BatchDirection          : Local
Locale                  : en-US
Reports                 : {}
IsProvisioning          : False
BatchFlags              : UseAdvancedValidation, AutoComplete
WorkflowControlFlags    : None
Workflow                :
WorkflowTemplate        :
Report                  :
StartAfter              :
```

Notice that two fields, one field called 'Report' and another called 'Reports' that are empty. If we run this one-liner:

    Get-MigrationBatch -IncludeReport | fl

The Report/Reports fields will be populated and include information like this:

```
Reports     : {When migration report was created:3/8/2016 2:45:56 PM; Migration report URL:https://16-lg
              -ex01.16-lg.local/ecp/Migration/DownloadReport.aspx?HandlerClass=MigrationReportHandler&Na
              me=MigrationStatistics.csv&OrganizationContext=ForestWideOrganization&realm=ForestWideOrga
              nization&exsvurl=1&Identity=RgAAAACPvJ3akmrgRqYwUH1BmjU1BwDPfG4BT0uzRIcnIIZydZ8bAAAAAAEaAA
              DPfG4BT0uzRIcnIIZydZ8bAAAAAA0hAAAJ; Error report URL:}

Report      : 3/8/2016 8:30:52 AM [16-LG-EX01] '16-lg.local/Users/Administrator' created the
              'ExchangeLocalMove' batch.
              3/8/2016 8:30:52 AM [16-LG-EX01] Batch will automatically start per user request.
              3/8/2016 8:31:14 AM [16-LG-EX01] migration user 'Administrator@16-lg.local' created.
              3/8/2016 8:45:24 AM [16-LG-EX01] The migration batch is now complete.
```

While that information is good for migrations, we can reveal even more information when applying this switch to Get-MoveRequestStatistics:

```
Report   : 3/8/2016 8:35:22 AM [16-LG-EX01] '' created move request.
           3/8/2016 8:35:22 AM [16-LG-EX01] '' allowed a large amount of data loss when
           moving the mailbox (100 bad items, 0 large items).
           3/8/2016 8:39:38 AM [16-LG-EX03] The Microsoft Exchange Mailbox Replication
           service '16-LG-EX03.16-lg.local' (15.1.225.37 caps:7FFF) is examining the
           request.
           3/8/2016 8:39:43 AM [16-LG-EX03] Connected to target mailbox
           'a2595af5-babd-4608-bd27-ddf152f81a57 (Primary)', database 'Mailbox Database
           1790513196', Mailbox server '16-LG-EX03.16-lg.local' Version 15.1 (Build
           225.0).
           3/8/2016 8:39:46 AM [16-LG-EX03] Connected to source mailbox
           'a2595af5-babd-4608-bd27-ddf152f81a57 (Primary)', database 'Mailbox Database
           0794329553', Mailbox server '16-LG-EX01.16-lg.local' Version 15.1 (Build
           225.0), proxy server '16-LG-EX01.16-lg.local' 15.1.225.37
           caps:01FFBF7FFFFFCB07FFFF.
           3/8/2016 8:39:49 AM [16-LG-EX03] Request processing started.
           3/8/2016 8:39:49 AM [16-LG-EX03] Source mailbox information:
           Regular Items: 3, 12.27 KB (12,563 bytes)
           Regular Deleted Items: 0, 0 B (0 bytes)
           FAI Items: 6, 7.035 KB (7,204 bytes)
           FAI Deleted Items: 0, 0 B (0 bytes)
           3/8/2016 8:39:49 AM [16-LG-EX03] Cleared sync state for request
           a2595af5-babd-4608-bd27-ddf152f81a57 due to 'CleanupOrphanedMailbox'.
```

As you can see, for this cmdlet, -IncludeReport is like Verbose for mailbox move requests.

## Code Signing

**What is it?**

When a PowerShell script is signed, the code block only validates if a script has not been modified by anyone other than the original author.  Code signing does not validate that the script is functional or certified.  The intention of code signing is solely to make sure that the code written by the author is not modified by another scripter and passed along as the authors work.

**Why Use It?**

By default, PowerShell execution is restricted to Remote Signed scripts:

**Remote Signed:** Requires that all scripts and configuration files downloaded from the Internet be signed by a trusted publisher.

When a script is not digitally signed, the script will not run.  If a script is signed, but cannot be validated, it cannot be run.  Verification at this level is just one level of protection against running rogue PowerShell scripts.  However, it should not be the only level of protection.  Ideally, a Dev or QA environment should be used for PowerShell script testing to validate both the code signing and functionality of the script.

**How to Use It**

There are a few configuration options to use when configuring digital signing options in Windows PowerShell. The PowerShell cmdlet used to configure this is Set-ExecutionPolicy.

- **Restricted:** Does not load configuration files or run scripts. "Restricted" is the default execution policy.
- **AllSigned:** Requires that all scripts and configuration files be signed by a trusted publisher, including scripts that you write on the local computer.
- **RemoteSigned:** Requires that all scripts and configuration files downloaded from the Internet be signed by a trusted publisher.
- **Unrestricted**: Loads all configuration files and runs all scripts. If you run an unsigned script that was downloaded from the Internet, you are prompted for permission before it runs.
- **Bypass:** Nothing is blocked and there are no warnings or prompts.
- **Undefined:** Removes the currently assigned execution policy from the current scope. This parameter will not remove an execution policy that is set in a Group Policy scope.

In order to run a script that has not been digitally signed, you must set the Execution Policy for PowerShell scripts to Unrestricted:

```
Set-ExecutionPolicy –ExecutionPolicy Unrestricted
```

When installing a new Cumulative Update for Exchange, Microsoft recommends that command be run to prevent any issues with the installation - https://blogs.technet.microsoft.com/exchange/2015/09/15/released-september-2015-quarterly-exchange-updates/.

In some organizations, PowerShell is restricted and locked down to prevent unauthorized scripts from running. The Execution Policy for PowerShell would be set to 'Restricted' in this case. If an unsigned script with this execution policy set, you will receive an error like so:

```
PS C:\> .\prereq1.ps1
.\prereq1.4.ps1 : File C:\prereq1.ps1 cannot be loaded because running scripts is disabled on this system.
For more information, see about_Execution_Policies at http://go.microsoft.com/fwlink/?LinkID=135170.
At line:1 char:1
+ .\prereq1.4.ps1
+ ~~~~~~~~~~~~~~~
    + CategoryInfo          : SecurityError: (:) [], PSSecurityException
    + FullyQualifiedErrorId : UnauthorizedAccess
PS C:\>
```

The policy for PowerShell execution restrictions can be implemented with a GPO in the following GPO location:

Computer Configuration -- Policies -- Administrative Templates: Policy Definitions (ADMX) -- Windows Components -- Windows PowerShell

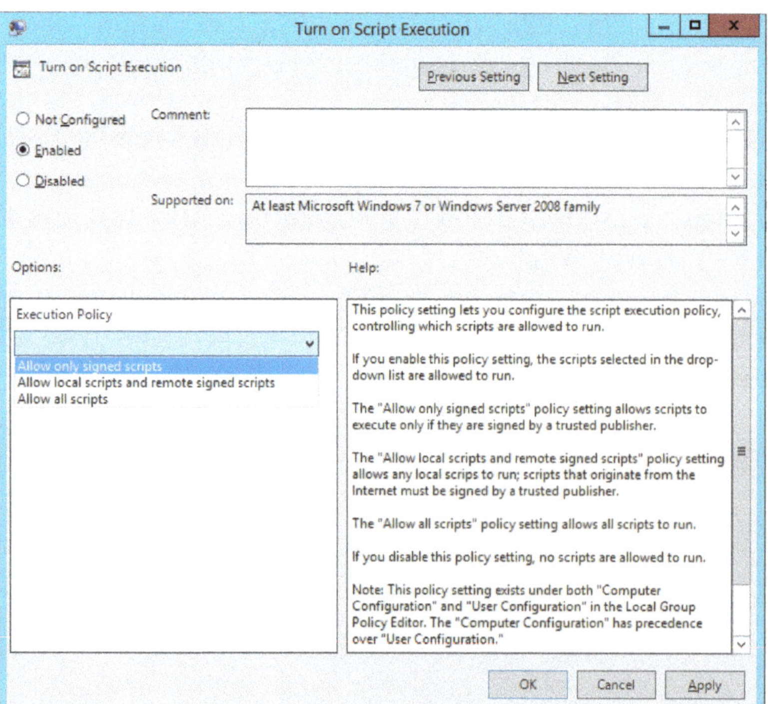

By default, this setting is not configured for the GPO:

To restrict PowerShell code execution in the GPO, the setting needs to be enabled and a setting chosen:

**Signing Your Code**

So how do you sign your scripts and what are the requirements?

Requirements – your script and a certificate to sign it with.

To sign it, the Set-AuthenticodeSignature cmdlet needs to be used.  First acquire a signing certificate either from a third party or internally.  Then bring up a PowerShell session in order to sign the script.  One method, which was spelled out by the Scripting Guy! From Microsoft is to store the certificate in a variable and then run the Set-AuthenticodeSignature cmdlet to sign the script:

```
$Cert=(dir cert:currentuser\my\ -CodeSigningCert)
Set-AuthenticodeSignature .\MyScript.ps1 $Cert –TimeStampServer “http://timestamp.globalsign.com/
scripts/timstamp.dll”
```

Using the TimeStampServer option is recommended:

```
-TimestampServer <String>
    Uses the specified time stamp server to add a time stamp to the signature. Type the URL of the time stamp server as a string.

    The time stamp represents the exact time that the certificate was added to the file. A time stamp prevents the script from failing
    if the certificate expires because users and programs can verify that the certificate was valid at the time of signing.
```

What is added to the script once it is signed?

When a script is signed, a code block is added to the end of a PowerShell script.

```
AntispamCommon.ps1 - Notepad
File  Edit  Format  View  Help

filter topN
{
  param (
    $top = 10)

  if ($script:count -lt $top)
  {
    write-output ($_)
    $script:count = $script:count + 1
  }
}

# SIG # Begin signature block
# MIIavQYJKoZIhvcNAQcCoIIarjCCGqoCAQExCzAJBgUrDgMCGgUAMGkGCisGAQQB
# gjCCAQSgwzBZMDQGCisGAQQBgjCCAR4wJgIDAQAABBAfzDtgwUsITrckOsYpfVNR
# AgEAAgEAAgEAAgEAAgEAMCEwCQYFKw4DAhoFAAQUKOzFl7KMitsRe2naqD/c+ump
# KAmgghwCMIIEwzCCA6ugAwIBAgITMwAAAG9lLVhtBxFGKAAAAAAAbzANBgkqhkiG
# 9w0BAQUFADB3MQswCQYDVQQGEwJVUZETMBEGA1UECBMKV2FzaGluZ3RvbjEQMA4G
# A1UEBxMHUmVkbW9uZDEeMBwGA1UEChMVTWljcm9zb2Z0IENvcnBvcmF0aW9uMSEw
# HwYDVQQDExhNawNvb3NvZnnQqvGltZS1TdGFtcCBQQ0EwHhcNMTUwMZIwMTczMjAy


# BgNVBAoTFU1pY3Jvc29mdCBDb3Jwb3JhdGlvbjEhMB8GA1UEAxMYTWljcm9zb2Z0
# IFRpbwUtU3RhbXAgUENBAhMzAAAAb2UtWG0HEUYoAAAAAABvMAkGBSsOAwIaBQCg
# XTAYBgkqhkiG9w0BCQMxCwYJKoZIhvcNAQcBMBwGCSqGSIb3DQEJBTEPFw0xNTA3
# MTAwMDIzMTRaMCMGCSqGSIb3DQEJBDEWBBSO+72hib43aVD/cYMaY9DgkEixWjAN
# BgkqhkiG9w0BAQUFAASCAQCneZqiN1u0lBo1S419v5kkIU0l5XBCt3jkQashnmTs
# xBFuShkfl60kqlQqzNP5k94rPX2hKFP9c7NVWB/1rXp+g4ExvCH0FhgK8/S8C5NI
# CE4Q1fgVlo4BstrUAcyvdfPerHrxeTVRfZEh1B3SCZixObTYirwJ76kzLI7P5HkZ
# 63peq8yZE+hd3c2FEYMuknrYFezosmvlnDKi8XFdwf/xlX3cbLEkviNXzItprsP1
# Z5DIJONQRkCqckzxT0nhIKJ8vQQqsLPbCCzdRDZcQ8UZFANUnXFuGGWPQpn3bqj2
# beNm5c1+6i1kXws6AJ591RmwtlikLFLtlnD2P6KjpbkI
# SIG # End signature block
```

Notice that the code signature is commented out to prevent any execution issues within the script.

For internal only scripts, a self-signed certificate can be sufficient.  If the script is going to be used outside of your environment, a third party certificate must be used.  The key is to use the correct kind of certificate – Class III or code-signing certificate – to generate the signature block.

# 3    **Building Scripts**

**In This Chapter**

- How To Begin
- Script Build Summary
- PowerShell and Change

In the previous two chapters quite a few topics concerning PowerShell were covered, with some Exchange Server topics sprinkled into the mix. Now that some basic options have been covered let's see how these can be used in a PowerShell script and begin building your own scripts. This chapter will cover what to start with, how to add to the script, how to enhance the script, perform detailed testing and finally how to transition and use this in production with your Exchange Servers. The end result will be a working script for Exchange Server 2016.

## How to Begin

When script building, having a clear goal of what is to be accomplished is advisable. In the past programmers used various methods to build scripts. The key to our method is that we need a beginning and we need an end. This method requires a seed or first cmdlet to start with and from that we need to aim for the end goal, what could be called the purpose of the script. Let's start with a real life example.

To build a complete script, to keep the process ordered and to complete the task at hand there are a series of steps that can provide a useful guide to the process. Provided below is a series of suggested steps for creating a Power-Shell script.

- Seed to start the script - usually a core concept with a corresponding PowerShell cmdlet
- Look for samples on the Internet to save time – code blocks, one-liners, routines and usage
- Loops if needed to perform iterations (Foreach, arrays, etc.) or objects in Exchange
- Define arrays if needed for the loops or other parts of the scripts
- Functions if a process is repeatable or needs to be called on from multiple parts of a script
- Export the results
- Build in some error checking or fail safes
- Commenting - top of the script - detailed description
- Commenting - document the script

> **TIP**
>
> On the first run of any new script, either the script needs to be run in a lab environment or all PowerShell cmdlets that make changes should be commented to prevent their execution. Alternatively, you can leverage the WhatIf switch to see what the cmdlet would do. However, trailing code can react as if the cmdlet failed, as the cmdlet did not actually run.

## Sample Scenario

This book is built on practical ways to use PowerShell and building a script in a practical manner is the goal of this sample scenario.

You are the Exchange engineer that is in charge of all the Exchange 2013 Servers at a large company. Your boss has just given the green-light to build-out new Exchange Server 2016 production and lab environments. He wants you to begin with the lab environment, which will be a replica of production with twelve new Exchange 2016 servers that will need to be built. In addition to that, there was an additional requirement to install two Edge Transport servers in the lab and production environments. In the end, twenty-eight new Windows 2012 R2 servers that will be running Exchange Server 2016 need to be built. Each of these servers needs to be prepared for installing Exchange. You review the list of requirements for Exchange Server 2016 and decide that a script to install these requirements will save time.

### Coding the Script

First a list of the requirements needed for Exchange Server 2016 is needed and these requirements can be found in TechNet:

https://technet.microsoft.com/en-us/library/bb691354(v=exchg.160).aspx

- .Net 4.6.1 (or 4.5.2)
- Microsoft Unified Communications Managed API 4.0, Core Runtime 64-bit
- Windows features:

| | | |
|---|---|---|
| AS-HTTP-Activation | Web-Digest-Auth | Web-Net-Ext45 |
| Desktop-Experience | Web-Dir-Browsing | Web-Request-Monitor |
| NET-Framework-45-Features | Web-Dyn-Compression | Web-Server |
| RPC-over-HTTP-proxy | Web-Http-Errors | Web-Stat-Compression |
| RSAT-Clustering | Web-Http-Logging | Web-Static-Content |
| RSAT-Clustering-CmdInterface | Web-Http-Redirect | Web-Windows-Auth |
| RSAT-Clustering-Mgmt | Web-Http-Tracing | Web-WMI |
| RSAT-Clustering-PowerShell | Web-ISAPI-Ext | Windows-Identity-Foundation |
| Web-Mgmt-Console | Web-ISAPI-Filter | RSAT-ADDS |
| WAS-Process-Model | Web-Lgcy-Mgmt-Console | |
| Web-Asp-Net45 | Web-Metabase | |
| Web-Basic-Auth | Web-Mgmt-Console | |
| Web-Client-Auth | Web-Mgmt-Service | |

To begin the script, we'll start with the .Net requirements, then work out the UCM and Windows features to round out the script coding.

## .Net Requirement Installation

Exchange Server 2016 requires a version of .Net of version 4.5.1 or greater. In the Cumulative Update for Exchange Server 2016 that was released when this book was published (CU2), .Net 4.6.1 support was introduced. Thus, on a Windows 2012 R2 server where Exchange Server 2016 will be installed, the current .Net version should be verified to make sure that the correct .Net version is installed for Exchange.

Some logistical processes that will need to be worked out are:

- Where is the version of .Net installed on a server stored?
- What criteria can a script review to verify if this has been installed?
- If the version of .Net is too low, can the script download the latest version, install that version and then verify that the installation was successful?

*What version is installed on the server?*

How can this be checked? Use your favorite search engine to find this information (Bing, Google, Yahoo):

**Search terms** - ".Net 4.6.1 version number"

** Why these terms? Started with the primary search term of '. NET 4.6.1' and followed it with 'descriptors' like version numbers.

Notice the results from the search engine, the first being a MSDN link, what would be considered a trusted source as it is from Microsoft on their own product:

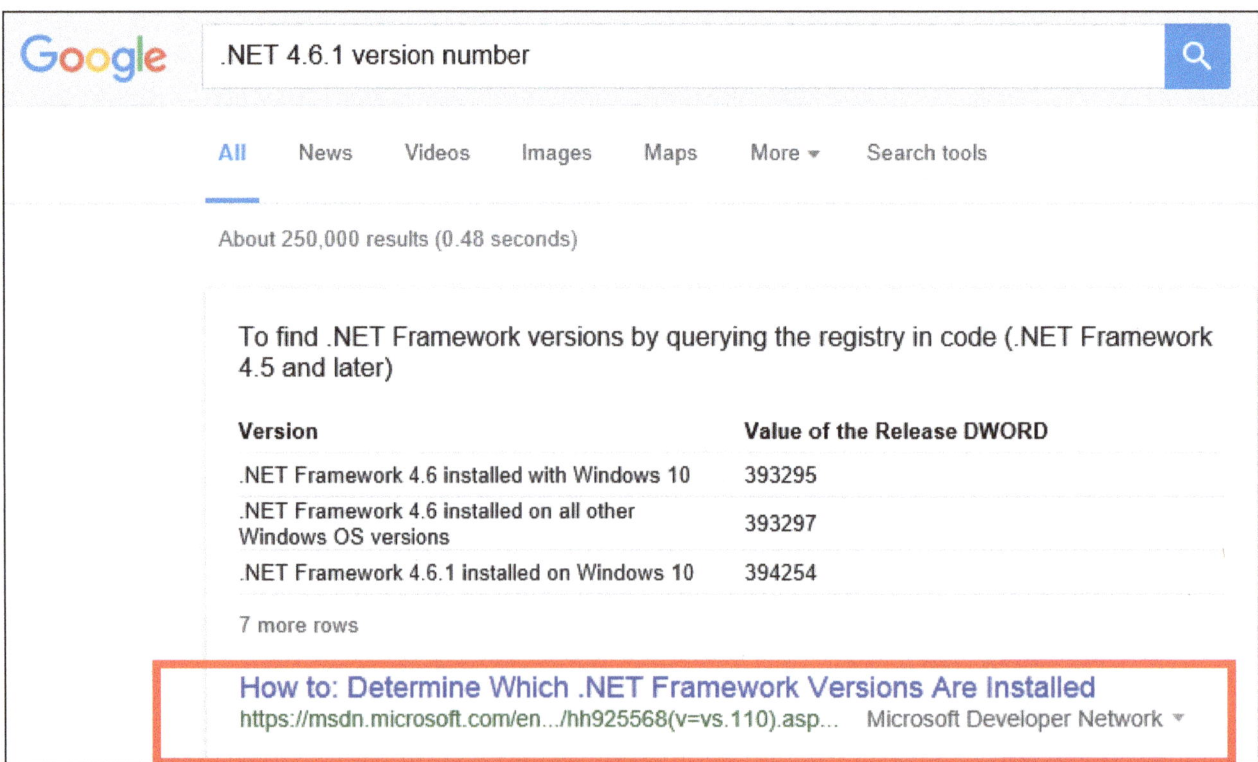


| Version | Value of the Release DWORD |
| --- | --- |
| .NET Framework 4.6 installed with Windows 10 | 393295 |
| .NET Framework 4.6 installed on all other Windows OS versions | 393297 |
| .NET Framework 4.6.1 installed on Windows 10 | 394254 |



The link provided - https://msdn.microsoft.com/en-us/library/hh925568(v=vs.110).aspx - leads to a page that provides version numbers for each version of .Net. Scrolling down, there is a table of .Net version numbers:

| Value of the Release DWORD | Version |
| --- | --- |
| 378389 | .NET Framework 4.5 |
| 378675 | .NET Framework 4.5.1 installed with Windows 8.1 or Windows Server 2012 R2 |
| 378758 | .NET Framework 4.5.1 installed on Windows 8, Windows 7 SP1, or Windows Vista SP2 |
| 379893 | .NET Framework 4.5.2 |
| On Windows 10 systems: 393295<br><br>On all other OS versions: 393297 | .NET Framework 4.6 |
| On Windows 10 November Update systems: 394254<br><br>On all other OS versions: 394271 | .NET Framework 4.6.1 |
| On Windows 10 Insider Preview Build 14295: 394747<br><br>On all other OS versions: 394748 | .NET Framework 4.6.2 Preview |

For .Net Framework 4.6.1, the version number is '394271'. Where is this value stored? On the same page there is also a clue left about where to find this stored value.

> **To find .NET Framework versions by querying the registry in code (.NET Framework 4.5 and later)**
>
> 1. The existence of the **Release** DWORD indicates that the .NET Framework 4.5 or later has been installed on a computer. The value of the keyword indicates the installed version. To check this keyword, use the OpenBaseKey and OpenSubKey methods of the Microsoft.Win32.RegistryKey class to access the Software\Microsoft\NET Framework Setup\NDP\v4\Full subkey under HKEY_LOCAL_MACHINE in the Windows registry.

This same web page also provides some coding on how to find the values, but only in VB or C#. No PowerShell is listed. If we want to use PowerShell, we will have to create our own coding. How can PowerShell query for that value?

The first web search provided the location and a list of possible values for the .Net release, which is stored in the Registry. We need a way to query the registry with PowerShell. Back to your favorite search engine:

**Search terms** – 'find registry values using PowerShell'

For this search a complete phrase was used but key words could work as well. The search provided these results:

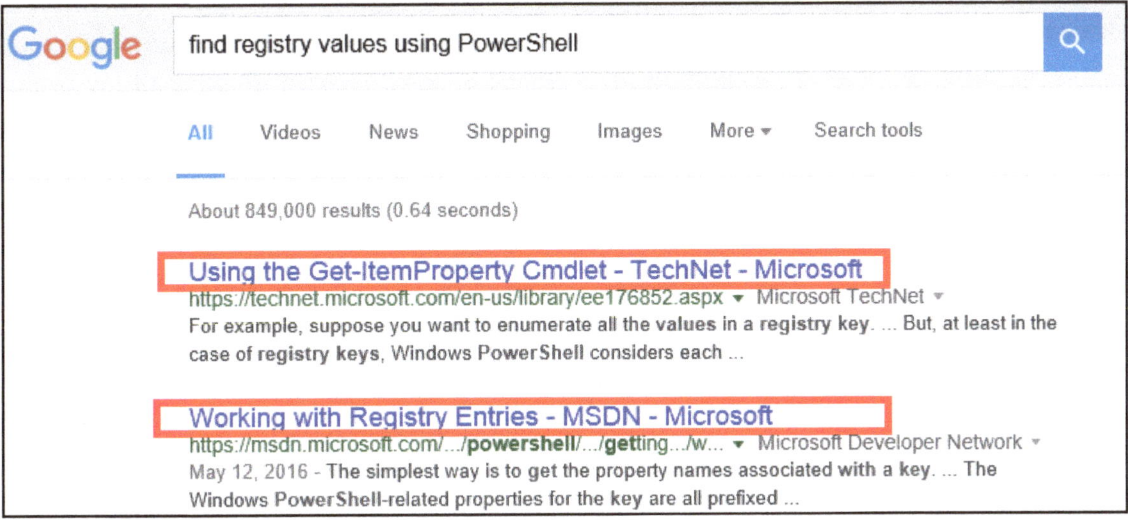

The top two links look appropriate for querying the registry and the first link does provide the correct cmdlet we need. To find a registry entry with PowerShell, the Get-ItemProperty cmdlet is the way to go:

**Example:**
Get-Help Get-ItemProperty -Examples

```
------------------------- EXAMPLE 3 -------------------------

PS C:\>Get-ItemProperty -Path HKLM:\SOFTWARE\Microsoft\Windows\CurrentVersion
```

**** Note **** Use a search engine if the Get-Help doesn't clarify the option needed

We know the registry key where the value is stored - SOFTWARE\Microsoft\NET Framework Setup\NDP\v4\Full and we know that the value is a DWORD called 'RELEASE'. First, following the example above a query of the registry path would look like this:

Get-ItemProperty -Path 'HKLM:\SOFTWARE\Microsoft\NET Framework Setup\NDP\v4\Full'

Running that PowerShell one-liner on any server will display something similar to this:

```
Release       : 378389
PSPath        : Microsoft.PowerShell.Core\Registry::HKEY_LOCAL_MACHINE\SOFTWARE\Microsoft\NET Framework
                Setup\NDP\v4\Full
PSParentPath  : Microsoft.PowerShell.Core\Registry::HKEY_LOCAL_MACHINE\SOFTWARE\Microsoft\NET Framework Setup\NDP\v4
PSChildName   : Full
PSDrive       : HKLM
PSProvider    : Microsoft.PowerShell.Core\Registry
```

To filter the results to get just the version number requires isolating the 'Release' property in the above results, to do so, we wrap the one-liner with a pair of brackets '(' and ')' then specify the property we want the value of with a '.Release' on the outside of the brackets. This specifically selects the Release value that is stored in the results:

(Get-ItemProperty -Path "HKLM:\SOFTWARE\Microsoft\NET Framework Setup\NDP\v4\Full").Release

This provides this result:

```
PS C:\> (Get-ItemProperty -Path "HKLM:\SOFTWARE\Microsoft\NET Framework Setup\NDP\v4\Full" -Name "Release").release
379893
```

With this information, a .Net release version of 379893, we now know that the server has .Net 4.5.2. If we want the latest version, which is recommended with CU2, then version 4.6.1 is needed. With multiple servers to install this update from, there are two options, we can either put it on a network share or download / copy it locally to the server. In either case a download link for the .Net executable will be needed in order for the file to be downloaded from Microsoft. The easiest way to do this is to manually download the file once and get the path from the downloaded file. Make sure to get the offline installer as well as this provides a complete install file with no need for further downloads or prompts.

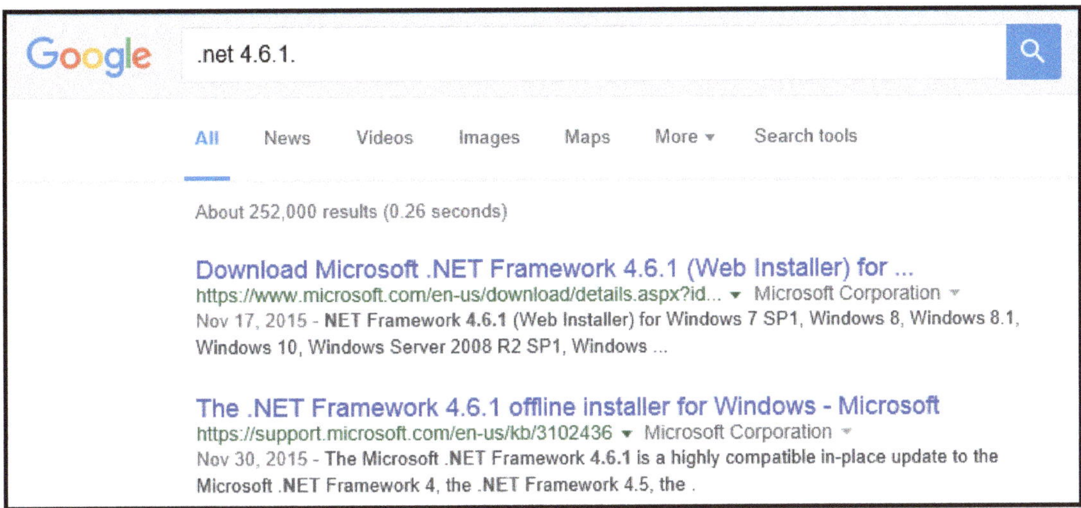

To get the download path, in a browser use View Downloads and right click on the download:

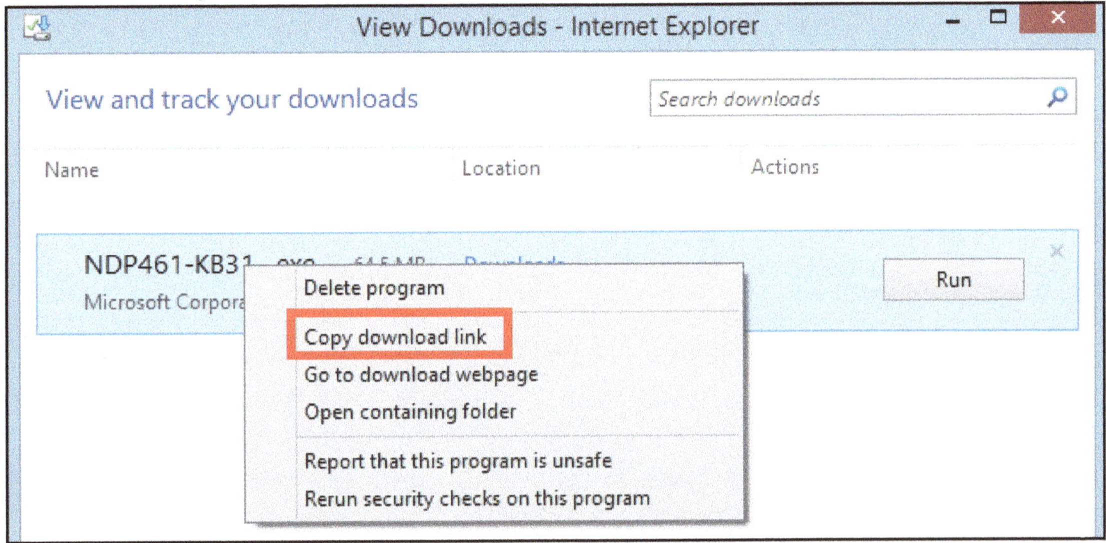

Copy the link and save it for later. For the .Net 4.6.1 installer, this is the download link:

https://download.microsoft.com/download/E/4/1/E4173890-A24A-4936-9FC9-AF930FE3FA40/NDP461-KB3102436-x86-x64-AllOS-ENU.exe

The file download needs to be stored locally and thus a variable will be used to store the download path for the .Net 4.6.1 offline installer executable. The variable used, $TargetFolder, is meant to be descriptive and easy to understand. Which would make troubleshooting easier if there is an issue.

```
$DownloadFolder = "c:\install"
```

The download link will also be stored in a variable to call on later:

```
$File = "https://download.microsoft.com/download/E/4/1/E4173890-A24A-4936-9FC9-AF930FE3FA40/NDP461-KB3102436-x86-x64-AllOS-ENU.exe"
```

To sort off the file name from the download link, the below line will split the file name up logically by the "/" character and choose the very last item in the array variable:

```
$DownloadFile = $File.Split([char]0x02F)
$DownloadedFile = $DownloadFile[-1]
```

The breakdown would look like this:



To execute the download process, a cmdlet needs to be found within PowerShell to handle this process. Using a search engine and the terms "PowerShell download files" we can find a well written blog article that provides a clue to some cmdlets:

https://blog.jourdant.me/post/3-ways-to-download-files-with-powershell

The one that we will use for this script will be "Start-Bits Transfer". Looking at examples from Get-Help Start-BitsTransfer, the PowerShell cmdlet that can be used to download the file would be constructed to look like this:

```
Start-BitsTransfer -Source "$DownloadFile" -Destination "$DownloadFolder\$DownloadedFile"
```

Alternatively, you can use a Join-Path cmdlet for the destination like so:

```
$Destination = join-path -path $DownloadFolder -ChildPath $DownloadedFile
Start-BitsTransfer -Source "$DownloadFile " -Destination $Destination
```

Taking all of the above single line cmdlets, a cohesive script to download the .Net installation files can be constructed as such:

```
$DownloadFolder = "c:\install"
$File = "https://download.microsoft.com/download/E/4/1/E4173890-A24A-4936-9FC9-AF930FE3FA40/
NDP461-KB3102436-x86-x64-AllOS-ENU.exe"
$DownloadFile = $DownloadFile.Split([char]0x02F)
$DownloadedFile = $DownloadFile[-1]
Start-BitsTransfer -Source "$File" -Destination "$DownloadFolder\$DownloadedFile"
```

Once the code block is validated, it can be reused for the next download - Unified Communications Managed API 4.0 or even future scripts that need to download files. With the .Net 4.6.1 executable in an installation directory, these files now need to be installed. For installing files via PowerShell, the Start-Process is a cmdlet that can be used. This cmdlet was found using a Search Engine query:

**Search terms:**   'PowerShell run executable file'

One of the results is a TechNet article:

PowerShell: Running Executables - TechNet Articles - United States ...
social.technet.microsoft.com › Wiki › TechNet Articles
Feb 22, 2012 - There are several different methods for running executables as well as ... If for
example you invoke-item with a PDF file, it opens it in whatever ...
You've visited this page 2 times. Last visit: 7/17/16

The article provides many options for running executable files in PowerShell. Number seven is Start Process. This command will allow the execution on the current server. First the file name gets stored as a variable and then use the variable in the Start-Process command. The use of a variable allows the use of switches available for executables. For .Net, the syntax below stores the file and options in a variable:

```
Start-Process '.\NDP461-KB3102436-x86-x64-AllOS-ENU.exe' -ArgumentList '/quiet','/norestart' –Wait
```

In the above variable, not only is the executable name stored, so are the '/quiet', '/norestart' and /l' options which allow for the installation to occur quietly, without requiring a reboot and log to a file for later review.

One caveat for the .Net installation is that the server should be rebooted after the .Net is installed or upgraded. A visual reminder could be coded into the script to remind the person running the script that a reboot is needed, but this is an optional portion of the script that would depend on the intention of the script. If this is written for one's own environment, the reminder might not be needed. However if the script is being shared, this may need to be coded:

```
Write-Host "A REBOOT is required after the .Net installation." –ForegroundColor Red
```

## Unified Communications Managed API 4.0 Requirement Installation

The great part about PowerShell code is that once a set of code is written, there is the potential of code being re-used for similar requirements. To that end, we have completed the .Net installation and now we need to install the Unified Communications Managed API 4.0. Following the same process that was used for .Net 4.6.1 download, we need to get the URL for the file. Going back to the Exchange Server 2016 requirements page:

https://technet.microsoft.com/en-us/library/bb691354(v=exchg.160).aspx

There is a link for the UCM download page:

https://www.microsoft.com/en-us/download/details.aspx?id=34992

Then right click the download and 'Copy Download link" to get the URL to use in our script. Using the download function we now need to add a single line of code to download this file:

http://download.microsoft.com/download/2/C/4/2C47A5C1-A1F3-4843-B9FE-84C0032C61EC/UcmaRuntimeSetup.exe

We adjust the code from the .Net download and come up with this download code:

```
$DownloadFolder = "c:\install"
$File = "http://download.microsoft.com/download/2/C/4/2C47A5C1-A1F3-4843-B9FE-84C0032C61EC/UcmaRuntimeSetup.exe"
$DownloadFile = $DownloadFile.Split([char]0x02F)
$DownloadedFile = $DownloadFile[-1]
Start-BitsTransfer -Source "$File" -Destination "$DownloadFolder\$DownloadedFile"
```

And run the installation:

```
Start-Process ".\$DownloadedFile" -ArgumentList '/quiet','/norestart' –Wait
```

## Windows Feature Requirement Installation

Perhaps the easiest part to install are the Windows features that are required for Exchange 2016. This is simply because Microsoft provides the necessary code in order to install these features:

```
Install-WindowsFeature RSAT-ADDS
Install-WindowsFeature AS-HTTP-Activation, Desktop-Experience, NET-Framework-45-Features, RPC-over-HTTP-proxy, RSAT-Clustering, RSAT-Clustering-CmdInterface, RSAT-Clustering-Mgmt, RSAT-
```

Clustering-PowerShell, Web-Mgmt-Console, WAS-Process-Model, Web-Asp-Net45, Web-Basic-Auth, Web-Client-Auth, Web-Digest-Auth, Web-Dir-Browsing, Web-Dyn-Compression, Web-Http-Errors, Web-Http-Logging, Web-Http-Redirect, Web-Http-Tracing, Web-ISAPI-Ext, Web-ISAPI-Filter, Web-Lgcy-Mgmt-Console, Web-Metabase, Web-Mgmt-Console, Web-Mgmt-Service, Web-Net-Ext45, Web-Request-Monitor, Web-Server, Web-Stat-Compression, Web-Static-Content, Web-Windows-Auth, Web-WMI, Windows-Identity-Foundation

## Completing the Code Section

One complication with the requirements for Exchange Server 2016 is that reboots are required in between some of the installations. This is simply due to the fact that the server may not see the changes made until the OS has restarted and reloaded certain services, files, etc. The ideal feature install order is:

- Install .Net and Windows features
- Reboot server
- Install UCM
- Reboot server
- Install Exchange Server 2016 as required

For the reboot don't forget the PowerShell code reminder might be required, like this:

```
Write-Host "`t`t`t`t`t`t`t`t`t`t" -BackgroundColor Red -ForegroundColor Black
Write-Host "A reboot is required!  Please Use Option 98!" -ForegroundColor Red
Write-Host "`t`t`t`t`t`t`t`t`t`t" -BackgroundColor Red -ForegroundColor Black
```

Which will display this message:



The `t in the code in the above represents a TAB character in PowerShell. It is used above to show a red line as it is combined with the *foregroundcolor red* parameter.

Improving the script further would be to add comment lines before each section so that the section's function is clearer. On a brand new server, the script will now install UCM, .Net and the Windows Features needed to install Exchange 2016. However, the script does not take into account a few issues that may occur.

- What if the script is run on the wrong Operating System – That should be verified
- .Net 4.6.1 requires a certain hotfix to be installed – That should be verified
- There is a need for multiple reboot – That needs to be accounted for
- Commenting in the script is very light – need a comment block at the top
- The feedback from the script is very limited – this should be enhanced

These improvements will make a better script that will run consistently and accurately install all prerequisites. Let's tackle each issue and then create a final working version of the script for use on the future Exchange 2016 servers.

## Operating System Check

Exchange Server 2016 is currently supported on Windows Server 2012, Windows Server 2012 R2 and Windows Server 2016 as of Exchange 2016 CU3. Checking Microsoft's documentation on the version numbers for Operating Systems, we can check against this with PowerShell:

https://msdn.microsoft.com/en-us/library/windows/desktop/ms724832(v=vs.85).aspx

| Operating System | Version Number |
| --- | --- |
| Windows Server 2016 | 10 |
| Windows Server 2012 R2 | 6.3 |
| Windows Server 2012 | 6.2 |
| Windows Server 2008 R2 | 6.1 |

The script, will need to verify that the Operating System is either '6.2' or '6.3' as this corresponds to Windows Server 2012 or 2012 R2. How can we verify this? Using a search engine with these terms:

**Search Terms**    PowerShell Operating System Version

For this search just choose a reliable looking source (in this case TechNet blog):

**Resulting link**
https://blogs.technet.microsoft.com/heyscriptingguy/2014/04/25/use-powershell-to-find-operating-system-version/

From that page we can determine that the simplified command for finding the Operating System version uses CIM:

(Get-CimInstance Win32_OperatingSystem).Version

On Windows Server 2012 R2, the version should come back with 6.3.xxxx and with Windows 2012, the result should match the above table and show 6.2.xxxx. Now that we have the command to get the version, we need some way to have PowerShell validate the OS for 2012 and 2012 R2. For these situations, an If…Else block usually works best. We can even use it to exit the script entirely if the OS is not correct. Let's build a check for each version:

**Windows Server 2012**
If ((Get-WMIObject Win32_OperatingSystem).Version -NotMatch '6.2')

**Windows Server 2012 R2**
If ((Get-WMIObject Win32_OperatingSystem).Version -NotMatch '6.3')

**Windows Server 2016**
If ((Get-WMIObject Win32_OperatingSystem).Version -NotMatch '10')

** **Note** ** The order of checking OS does not matter as long as all are checked.

The '-nomatch' operator, is in use because the script will exit if the Operating System is not 6.2, 6.3 or 10. This is a desired result because no other operating systems will work with Exchange Server 2016. The complete code block would resemble this.

**Option 1**

If ((Get-WMIObject Win32_OperatingSystem).Version -NotMatch '6.2') –and ((Get-WMIObject Win32_OperatingSystem).Version -NotMatch '6.3')) {
    Write-Host "This server is not Windows Server 2012 or 2012 R2. Exiting." -ForegroundColor Red
    Exit

```
}
```
**Option 2**

Check for the OS version first and store in a variable.  This will help shorten the code:

```
$OSVersion = (Get-WMIObject Win32_OperatingSystem).Version
If (($OSVersion -NotMatch '6.2') -and ($OSVersion -NotMatch '6.3') -and ($OSVersion -NotMatch '10')) {
    Write-Host "This server is not Windows Server 2012, 2012 R2 or Windows 2016. Exiting."
    -ForegroundColor Red
Exit
}
```

If the above code block is run on a Windows 2012 or 2012 R2 server, no feedback will be returned and the script will continue without exiting.  However, on a server with 2008 R2 and lower or Windows Server 2016 the script will exit with an error message about the wrong version.

Notice that the lines are indented.  PowerShell does not require indents and they are of used for the scripter to recognize what code blocks or sections go together, what code is nested, i.e. in loops. Also, use consistent indentation – ISE allows for easy indentation of pieces of code by selecting the code and pressing tab or alt-tab (refer to 'Mind The Brackets' section in Chapter 2).

```
Source          Description       HotFixID        InstalledBy             InstalledOn
------          -----------       --------        -----------             -----------
16-02-EX01      Update            KB2919355       16-02\administrator     7/2/2016 12:00:00 AM
```

## .Net 4.6.1 Hotfix Prerequisite Verification

.Net 4.6.1 has one required hotfix that will need to be installed before .Net is installed.  This requirement was determined by installing .Net on a brand new Windows 2012 R2 server and received an error that KB2919355 is needed to install .Net 4.6.1 and is referenced on MSDN here - https://msdn.microsoft.com/en-us/library/hh925569(v=vs.110).aspx. In order to validate the installation, we need to determine the proper way to check for a particular hotfix. 'Get-Command *hotfix*' which returns on value of 'Get-HotFix'. The hotfix is KB2919355 is what needs to be verified.  One thing to note is that not all hotfixes will be reported this way.  Specifically with .Net, the hotfixes have to be queried by reviewing the registry.  The command 'Get-HotFix' displays a list of ALL hotfixes installed on the server.  The results need to be filtered to KB2919355 only.  Let's try one of our filters from Chapter 2 - '| Where' – which will be very useful here:

```
Get-Hotfix | Where {$_.HotfixID -eq "kb2919355"}
```

If the command returns a result, the PowerShell window will display this:

If the hotfix is missing, no results are returned.  How can we use this knowledge to create a proper check on a server?  Using a variable.  We will use the $hotfix variable to store our results.

```
$Hotfix = Get-Hotfix | Where {$_.HotfixID -eq "kb2919355"}
```

We can use an If..Else block again for a checking values.  If..Then allows for a choice between two actions (1) if the hotfix can be found and (2) if the hotfix is missing.  The If..Else would look like this:

```
$Hotfix = Get-Hotfix | Where {$_.HotfixID -eq "kb2919355"}
If ($Hotfix -eq $Null) {
    Write-Host "Hotfix kb2919355 is missing." -Foregroundcolor Red
} Else {
    Write-Host "Hotfix kb2919355 is installed." -Foregroundcolor Green
}
```

With the above code block, if the hotfix is missing, the $Hotfix variable will be empty as there are no results and PowerShell will display a warning message in red, but if the hotfix is present a different message will be displayed in green.  Now to properly integrate this into our script, we can either (1) insert the .Net installation code into the section with the 'green' (hotfix was found) or (2) create a function for the .Net install code and then call the function from this same section.

Option two is usually preferable because it allows PowerShell to potentially call on the same code, the .Net install, in another instance:

Notice that the .NET 4.6.1 install is now enclosed by the start of the function at the top and closed off at the bottom to end the function

```
Function DotNET461Install    {
        $DownloadFolder = "c:\install"
        $File = "https://download.microsoft.com/download/E/4/1/E4173890-A24A-4936-9FC9-AF930FE3F
        $DownloadFile = $DownloadFile.Split([char]0x02F)
        $DownloadedFile = $DownloadFile[-1]
        Start-BitsTransfer -Source "$File" -Destination "$DownloadFolder\$DownloadedFile"
        Start-Process ".\$DownloadedFile" -ArgumentList '/quiet','/norestart' -Wait
} # End of DotNET461Install function
```

** **Note** ** The ISE allows for collapsing functions and bracket pairs to make it easier to navigate a script and see other sections of code easier.

With the .Net 4.6.1 installation process turned into a function, this can be placed in the If…Else block of code.  To call a function, we just need to use the name of the function – 'DotNet461Install'.  Remember the function name needs to be unique and cannot conflict with any existing PowerShell cmdlets or other functions.

```
$Hotfix = Get-Hotfix | Where {$_.HotfixID -eq "kb2919355"}
If ($Hotfix -eq $Null) {
    Write-Host "Hotfix kb2919355 is missing." -Foregroundcolor Red
} else {
    DotNet461Install
}
```

Notice that the script checks to see if the $Hotfix variable has a value of $null.  The $null value means that the variable is empty.  So if the Get-Hotfix cmdlet did not return any results, the $Hotfix variable will be empty and equal to $Null.

The script now needs a section of code to handle the download and installation of the hotfix from KB2919355.  This code section should also be coded in the form of a function.  Remember to get the download link after trying to download the file from the Internet.  First and last lines define the function's beginning and end.  In between these lines are the same code block that has been used for .Net and UCM, can be modified for KB2919355.

```
Function Install-KB2919355 {
   # KB2919355 Section
   $DownloadFolder = "c:\install"

   $SourceFile = https://download.microsoft.com/download/2/5/6/256CCCFB-5341-4A8D-A277-
   8A81B21A1E35/Windows8.1-KB2919355-x64.msu"
   $DownloadFile = $DownloadFile.Split([char]0x02F)
   $DownloadedFile = $DownloadFile[-1]
   Start-BitsTransfer -Source "$File" -Destination "$DownloadFolder\$DownloadedFile"
   Start-Process ".\$DownloadedFile" -ArgumentList '/quiet','/norestart' –Wait
} # End Install-KB2919355
```

Notice that there are no options selected for what is stored in $expression. The reason for this is that the hotfix for KB2919355 is very much an interactive install. Using the /quiet /norestart switches do not work with this installation. This hotfix also requires a reboot.

With the above code, we can now insert the function name into the check for .Net:

```
$Hotfix = Get-Hotfix | Where {$_.HotfixID -eq "kb2919355"}
If ($Hotfix -eq $Null) {
   Install-KB2919355
} Else {
   DotNet461Install
}
```

First the script checks for the hotfix, if the hotfix is not installed, the $Hotfix variable is blank. When the value is checked, PowerShell determines that $Hotfix is $Null and thus runs the Install-KB2919355 function. If the hotfix is found, then .Net 4.6.1 is installed using the DotNetInstall function.

**Multiple Reboots**

The requirements for Exchange 2016 require reboots of the server after they are installed. The act of rebooting a computer from PowerShell requires another PowerShell cmdlet. Let's try to find a relevant command. First let's try to look for any PowerShell cmdlet with 'start' in it:

```
Get-Command *start*
```

The results provided by this command is a list of about 25+ cmdlets, but there is one of use:

```
Cmdlet              Import-StartLayout
Cmdlet              Restart-Computer
Cmdlet              Restart-Service
Cmdlet              Start-BitsTransfer
Cmdlet              Start-DscConfiguration
```

To get code samples using Get-Help and the '-examples' switch for the Restart-Computer cmdlet provide examples of how to use the cmdlet to reboot the computer:

```
Get-Help Restart-Computer -Examples
```

Reading through the examples, the one that will be effective is Example 5. Shortening up one of the examples, we can use this:

```
Restart-Computer -ComputerName LocalHost -Force
```

or

```
Restart-Computer LocalHost -Force
```

This cmdlet satisfies another requirement for the script.

## Additional Commentary

When coding in PowerShell, comments should be provided in order to document script features and possibly explain what a code section does. A comment block at the top can also be used to help define a script and provide vital information about the script to those who may run it while the original coder is not around to explain the script. Let's start with a code section devoid of comments and add commentary on the purpose of the code block. Then we will create a special code block for the top of the script.

**No Description:**
```
Function DotNet461Install  {
    $DownloadFolder = "c:\install"
    $File = "https://download.microsoft.com/download/E/4/1/E4173890-A24A-4936-9FC9-AF930FE3FA40/
        NDP461-KB3102436-x86-x64-AllOS-ENU.exe"
    $DownloadFile = $DownloadFile.Split([char]0x02F)
    $DownloadedFile = $DownloadFile[-1]
    Start-BitsTransfer -Source "$File" -Destination "$DownloadFolder\$DownloadedFile"
    Start-Process ".\$DownloadedFile" -ArgumentList '/quiet','/norestart' –Wait
} # End of DotNet461Install Function
```

**Descriptive Commenting Between Code Lines:**
```
Function DotNet461Install  {
    # Set the download folder for the .Net executable
    $DownloadFolder = "c:\install"

    # Set the file location to be downloaded
    $File = "https://download.microsoft.com/download/E/4/1/E4173890-A24A-4936-9FC9-AF930FE3FA40/
        NDP461-KB3102436-x86-x64-AllOS-ENU.exe"

    # Split the file name up to remove the '/' character
    $DownloadFile = $DownloadFile.Split([char]0x02F)
    $DownloadedFile = $DownloadFile[-1]

    # Download the file
    Start-BitsTransfer -Source "$File" -Destination "$DownloadFolder\$DownloadedFile"

    # Install .Net 4.6.1 with the local file
    Start-Process ".\$DownloadedFile" -ArgumentList '/quiet','/norestart' –Wait

} # End of DotNet461Install function
```

Without the comments the code seems to bleed together and really only makes sense to someone with previous PowerShell experience.  With commenting we can provide a quick explanation of each line or at least each pair of lines that perform a certain function.  This helps quickly orient an individual to the layout and function of the script code lines.


## Top Code Block

```
<#
.SYNOPSIS
    Install Exchange Server 2016 Prerequisites

.DESCRIPTION
    Install Exchange Server 2016 Prerequisites using PowerShell

.NOTES
    Version             : 1.0
    Change Log          : 1.0 - First iteration
    Rights Required     : Local admin on server
    Exchange Version    : 2016
    Author              : Just A UC Guy [Damian Scoles]
    Blog                : http://justaucguy.wordpress.com
    Disclaimer          : No support provided by Microsoft

.EXAMPLE
    .\Configure-ExchangePrereq-1.1.ps1
#>
```

Sections contained in this information comment block at the top of the script:

- Synopsis – Short description of the script
- Description – Longer, more informative description
- Notes – Quick facts on the script – version, change log, author, and more
- Example – How to run the script

For further reading on what tags can be used in a script header, check out 'about_comment_based_help' which can be found on TechNet:

https://technet.microsoft.com/en-us/library/hh847834.aspx


### Putting it all together

Coding for hotfix the check, comments, operating system check and more are complete, putting all the pieces together in one cohesive script is the last step.  However there is one more hurdle to cover.  The script could require multiple reboots, from the KB2919355 install, to the .Net install to the Windows features and finally to the UCM 4.0 install.  .Net and the Windows features can be grouped and then the UCM install can be done after the server reboots.  The easiest way to handle this is with a flowchart for coding the updates as writing down a script flow makes the building of the script easier:

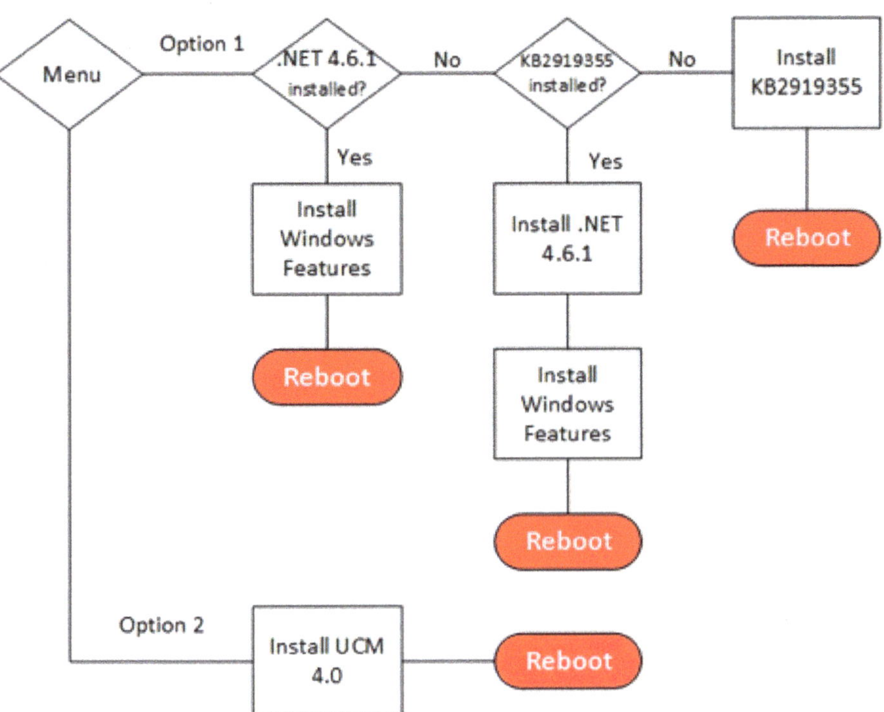


To handle multiple options and install path options, a menu can be used, powered by PowerShell. Potentially the script could be run three times with reboots after each install. The reason for this is to separate out sections of code depending on what needs to be installed. Option one could potentially require one or two reboots. To handle this, build a block of code to display a menu of options. In order to create a proper working menu, two sections of code will need to be used – one will be the menu, the other will be how PowerShell interprets the input from the menu (i.e. read-host):

**Sample Menu**

```
$menu = {

    write-host "*********************************************"
    write-host "Exchange Server 2016 PreRequisite Installation"
    write-host "*********************************************"
    write-host " "
    write-host "Please select an option from the list below:"
    write-host " "
    write-host "   1) Prerequisites Part 1 - .Net and Windows Features"
    write-host "   2) Prerequisites Part 2 - UCMA 4.0"
    write-host " "
    write-host "   98) Restart the Server"
    write-host "   99) Exit"
    write-host " "
    write-host "Select an option.. [1-99]?"

}
```

The second section of code interprets the keyboard input after the menu is displayed:

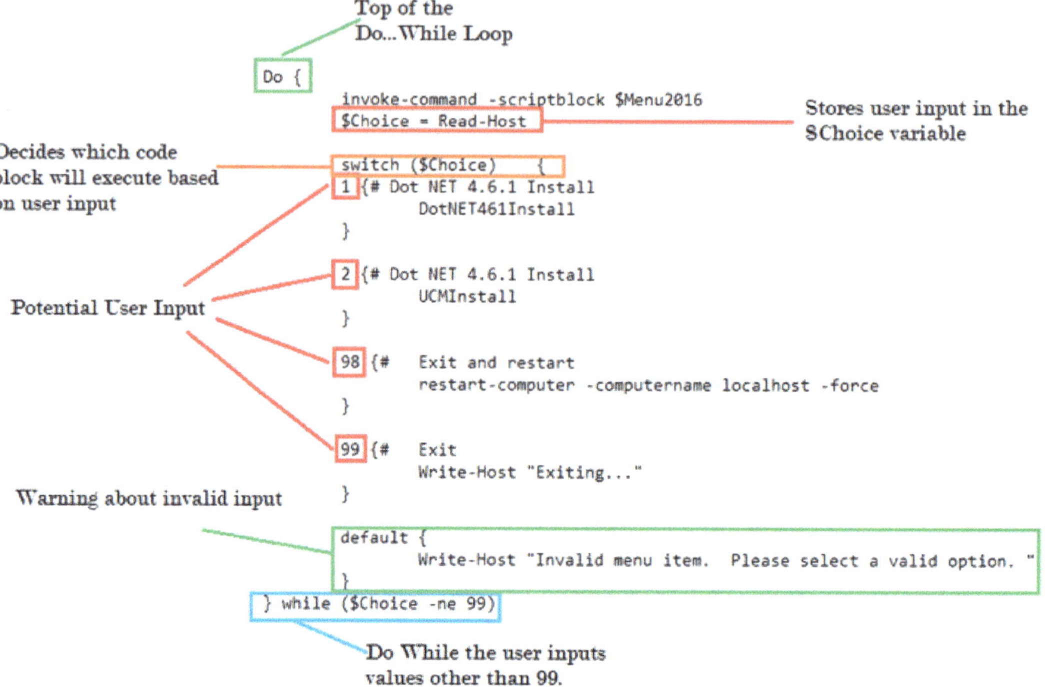


A Do..While loop was chosen because then the menu can be redrawn after each execution of an available option (1 or 2 in this case).  Also note that Option 1 and 2 will display a Reboot message when completed.  Option 98 is available for an immediate reboot and Option 99 is just for exiting the script.  When the script is first run, the menu will display like so:

```
********************************************************
Exchange Server 2016 PreRequisite Installation
********************************************************

Please select an option from the list below:

    1) Prerequisites Part 1 - .NET and Windows Features
    2) Prerequisites Part 2 - UCM 4.0

    98) Restart the Server
    99) Exit

Select an option.. [1-99]?:
```

Next step is to put all the code sections together.  Remember to follow the flowchart above, include the new menu as well as the previous sections with code for .Net, the hotfix and UCM 4.0 installations.

The entire script is available on Microsoft's TechNet Gallery:

https://gallery.technet.microsoft.com/Install-Exchange-2016-48983e13

** **Note** ** This script was written based off a script that Pat Richards, Skype MVP, had co-written for Exchange 2010.  This script has been modified over the years replacing code with the newer requirements and rewriting of certain functions and other code sections.  The original script and code can be found here:

https://www.ucunleashed.com/152

## Explanation

Taking time to read through the above script, 95% of the code is from the previous pages. The major difference is that there is now a flow, some checks for .Net and some additional commenting. The general flow of the script is as follows:

- Comment Block
- Variable Definitions
- Operating System Check
- Menu
- Functions
- Do..While Script for User Input

While the script is organized in this manner, there is nothing to prevent the code from being a bit more disorganized. About the only requirement is for the menu to be before the Do..While because the Do..While makes a call to the $Menu variable as well as the '# Variables' section needs to be defined first because it is used in the script a few times.

### Last Note the Requirements Script

While the script will cover all the requirements, other options can be added that will further prepare the Exchange Server for a production environment. Here are some other options that could be configured:

- Server Power Management - https://support.microsoft.com/en-us/kb/2207548
- NIC Power Management - https://blogs.technet.microsoft.com/exchange/2013/10/22/do-you-have-a-sleepy-nic/
- Disable SSL 3.0 - https://blogs.technet.microsoft.com/exchange/2015/07/27/exchange-tls-ssl-best-practices/
- Transcript - https://technet.microsoft.com/en-us/magazine/ff687007.aspx

While none of these are required, they are good options to code for in the requirements script.

# Script Build Summary

The previous page demonstrates that there are quite a few moving pieces that can occur in script building. From a core of one liners to using variables, functions and decision points to enhance our experience. More of the Power-Shell scripting building process will be covered in the remaining chapters. Troubleshooting steps are not covered yet, but these steps will be covered in Chapter 17 for troubleshooting assistance.

In this chapter, we covered building a script from scratch and utilized the following techniques to construct it:

- Get-Help
- Search Engine
- Borrowing code
- Functions
- If..Else

- Do..While
- Menu
- Commenting

In the chapters following this one, the above methods and below methods will be used in building more scripts:

- Execute successfully against one server, mailbox, etc.
- Set arrays
- Use Foreach
- Use Try {} Catch {}
- CIM queries need backup WMI queries

As can be seen from the above lists there are quite a few steps involved in building a script. At the end of the build process, precautions should be taken, WhatIf should be utilized and if possible a QA/Dev environment should be used as well. This will minimize any accidents or RGE's (Resume Generating Events).


# PowerShell and Change

Before ending this chapter on the basics of building a script, a thought should be given to the longevity of your script…. PowerShell cmdlets change with features added, remove, deprecated and more….

Change is a constant at Microsoft. By the time you read this Microsoft has changed the way Exchange 2016 handles the initial server connection when the shell is fired up. This is described as 'Mailbox Anchoring'. This is described in more detail on their EHLO blog here - https://blogs.technet.microsoft.com/exchange/2015/12/15/exchange-management-shell-and-mailbox-anchoring/ in Chapter 4. Office 365 changes every month, week and day. PowerShell change is less often, but the results are no different. New editions are made, old commands deprecated and eventually removed.

## Why does this matter?

As scripts are built, effort may be required to make sure the cmdlets being used are not being deprecated. Cmdlets that are being deprecated can be found in a few ways. Simply run a cmdlet in PowerShell and if the cmdlet is being deprecated a message in yellow will reveal itself. There are cmdlets still in Exchange 2016 that were listed as 'deprecated' in Exchange 2010 and 2013, so deprecated cmdlets may not always go away.

Examples of a deprecated cmdlets are the 'Get-TransportServer' and 'Get-TransportService'. The Get-Transport-Services does not exist in Exchange 2010. This cmdlet was added to Exchange 2013. Within the timeline of the CU releases the Get-TransportServer cmdlet started to report that the cmdlet was deprecated and that it would be removed in a future release. Get-TransportService is the replacement for Get-TransportServer:

```
[PS] C:\>Get-TransportServer
WARNING:  The Get-TransportServer cmdlet will be removed in a future version of Exchange.
Use the Get-TransportService cmdlet instead. If you have any scripts that use the Get-TransportServer
cmdlet, update them to use the Get-TransportService cmdlet.  For more information, see
http://go.microsoft.com/fwlink/p/?LinkId=254711.
```

For the moment, Exchange Server 2016 still has this cmdlet, with the same warning. The help file of the Get-TransportServer cmdlet still reports the same statement:

```
TransportServer cmdlet will be removed in a future version of Exchange. You should use the Get-TransportService cmd
```

How do we find out if the cmdlets will be deprecated?  One way is to try each cmdlet at a time to see if the yellow text seen above is displayed for a particular cmdlet.  Another way is to search the Help for each PowerShell cmdlet. Examining each cmdlet's Get-Help will reveal which cmdlets are being deprecated:

```
For information about the parameter sets in the Syntax section below, see Syntax.

The Clear-ActiveSyncDevice cmdlet will be removed in a future version of Exchange. Use the Clear-Mobile
cmdlet instead. If you have any scripts that use the Clear-ActiveSyncDevice cmdlet, update them to use
Clear-MobileDevice cmdlet.
```

## Script to Discover Deprecated Cmdlets

```
$Name = "16-lg-ex01.16-lg.local"
$Commands = (Get-Command | Where {$_.ModuleName -eq $Name}).Name
Foreach ($Line in $Commands) {
    Get-Help $Line -Full > c:\downloads\command.txt
    $Search = Select-String -Path c:\downloads\command.txt -pattern "cmdlet will be removed in a future
    version of"
    $Search2 = Select-String -Path c:\downloads\command.txt -pattern "cmdlet has been deprecated"
    If ($Search -ne $Null) {
        Write-Host "$line is going to be deprecated!" -ForegroundColor Yellow
    }
    If ($Search2 -ne $Null) {
        Write-Host "$Line is going to be deprecated!" -ForegroundColor Yellow
    }
    Remove-Item c:\downloads\command.txt
}
```

The code block above will run through each PowerShell cmdlet from the PowerShell module "16-lg-ex01.16-lg. local" (a PowerShell snap-in or remote session providing PowerShell cmdlets), and store the Get-Help results in a variable.  The variable will then be checked for two key phrases "cmdlet will be removed in a future version of" or "cmdlet has been deprecated".

(Below is an example of an old deprecated cmdlet that is still present in Exchange Server 2016)

```
NAME
    Enable-AntispamUpdates

SYNOPSIS
    The Enable-AntispamUpdates cmdlet has been deprecated in Microsoft Exchange Server 2010 Service Pack 1.
```

(Also found is a cmdlet that is deprecated and 'removed' but no longer in use)

```
NAME
    Get-LogonStatistics

DESCRIPTION
    This cmdlet has been deprecated and is no longer used.
```

Another option is to export the cmdlets of the reference release with:

```
Get-Command –Module A | Export-CliXml CmdletsA.xml
```

Do the same for the new release:

```
Get-Command –Module B | Export-CliXml CmdletsB.xml
```

Then compare the two result sets by checking the Name property (which corresponds to cmdlet names):

```
$CmdA= Import-CliXml .\CmdletsA.xml
$CmdB= Import-CliXml .\CmdletsB.xml
Compare-Object -ReferenceObject $CmdA -DifferenceObject $CmdB -Property Name
```

4 PowerShell Remoting

# 4 PowerShell Remoting

**In This Chapter**

- A Brief History
- Remote PowerShell - HTTP
- Remote PowerShell - HTTPS
- Invoke-Command
- Mailbox Anchoring

# A Brief History

Remote PowerShell has not always worked the same for all versions of Exchange. In fact, Exchange Server 2007 by default does not have the ability to handle remote PowerShell. The reason is that PowerShell 1.0 was not designed for these connections. Exchange Server 2010, with its PowerShell 2.0 requirement, was the first Exchange server version to allow for remote PowerShell. Microsoft retroactively added the ability of remote PowerShell with Exchange 2007 Service Pack 2 with PowerShell 2.0 installed. All later generations of Exchange Server allow for Remote PowerShell through PowerShell 3 and up. By default the Exchange Management Shell on Exchange 2016 opens a remote connection to Exchange even though the shortcut is opened on the server it connects to.

When managing a large Exchange Server environment, the capability to run PowerShell cmdlets on remote servers as if these are being run local to the server is a useful feature. The remote sessions can be initiated from any computer that has PowerShell installed. The remote session should be initiated from a management PC that is used for managing servers. This is done to limit the insecure connections that could be made to an Exchange Server by locking down external access to the server via GPO or firewall rules on the server. Remote management also allows an administrator to manage servers without locally logging in.

This chapter will cover how to remotely connect to Exchange servers with PowerShell connections over the HTTP and HTTPS protocols.

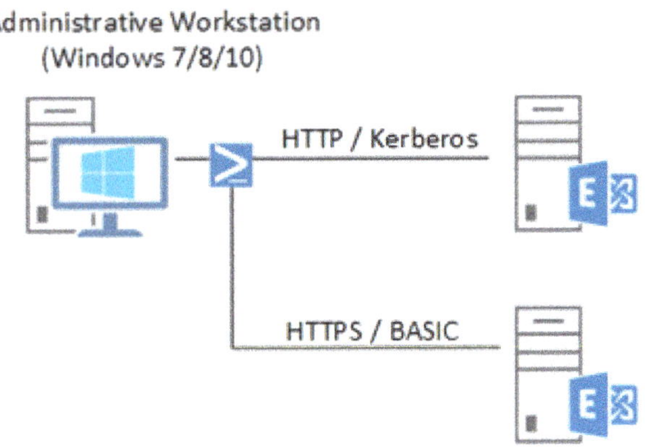

# Remote PowerShell – HTTP

A remote PowerShell sessions allows an administrator to run PowerShell cmdlets, one-liners, scripts and more as if he or she were logged on the remote server itself.   When connecting to a server that has PowerShell remoting enabled the default connection method is HTTP and not HTTPS.  This is the default configuration as HTTPS is not initially enabled.  For those who manage an Office 365 tenant with PowerShell, the connections to the cloud, made via PowerShell would be accomplished with three PowerShell cmdlets:

### Example – Office 365

```
$LiveCred = Get-Credential
$Session = New-PSSession -Name ExchangeOnline -ConfigurationName Microsoft.Exchange
-ConnectionUri https://ps.outlook.com/powershell/ -Credential $LiveCred -Authentication Basic –
AllowRedirection
Import-PSSession $Session
```

** **Note** ** The ConnectionUri is HTTPS and that the Authentication method is Basic.

The first line stores the administrative credentials (Office 365 Global Administrator) in the $LiveCred variable.  On the second line, the credentials are used to create a new session over HTTPS and basic authentication.  The last line initiates the session, imports all available cmdlets through the remote session, and you are connected to Office 365 tenant.  For Exchange Server 2016, the cmdlets are very similar.  Line one can use a different variable name (perhaps $cred) for gathering the login information for an account that is a member of the Organization Management group which has full permission in Exchange.  The next line would have to be modified (if the servers have not been changed from the defaults) to use HTTP and Kerberos for authentication.  The last line would remain the same because that is the method used for remote PowerShell connections:

### Example – Exchange Server 2016

```
$Cred = Get-Credential
$Session = New-PSSession -ConfigurationName Microsoft.Exchange -ConnectionUri http://<exchange
server FQDN>/PowerShell/ -Credential $Cred -Authentication Kerberos
Import-PSSession $Session
```

When the above lines are run, a pop-up box for credentials is displayed and needs to be entered:

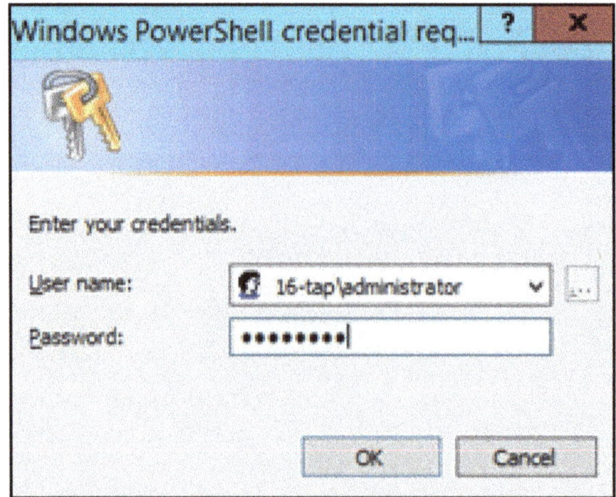

Then, the $Session variable stores the connection information.  No feedback is given in PowerShell unless there is an error.  By running the last line, the PowerShell connection is made, and when successful, a list of available cmdlets is eventually displayed:

```
[PS] C:\>Import-PSSession $Session
WARNING: Proxy creation has been skipped for the following command: 'Add-ADPermission, Add-AvailabilityAddressSp
Add-ContentFilterPhrase, Add-DatabaseAvailabilityGroupServer, Add-DistributionGroupMember, Add-FederatedDomain,
Add-GlobalMonitoringOverride, Add-IPAllowListEntry, Add-IPAllowListProvider, Add-IPBlockListEntry,
Add-IPBlockListProvider, Add-MailboxDatabaseCopy, Add-MailboxFolderPermission, Add-MailboxLocation,
Add-MailboxPermission, Add-ManagementRoleEntry, Add-PublicFolderClientPermission, Add-ResubmitRequest,
Add-RoleGroupMember, Add-ServerMonitoringOverride, Clear-ActiveSyncDevice, Clear-MobileDevice,
Clear-TextMessagingAccount, Compare-TextMessagingVerificationCode, Complete-MigrationBatch, Connect-Mailbox,
Disable-AddressListPaging, Disable-App, Disable-CmdletExtensionAgent, Disable-DistributionGroup, Disable-InboxRu
Disable-JournalRule, Disable-Mailbox, Disable-MailboxQuarantine, Disable-MailContact, Disable-MailPublicFolder,
Disable-MailUser, Disable-MalwareFilterRule, Disable-OutlookProtectionRule, Disable-PushNotificationProxy,
Disable-RemoteMailbox, Disable-ServiceEmailChannel, Disable-TransportAgent, Disable-TransportRule
```

With a successful connection to the remote server, initiated from a workstation that can now execute cmdlets as if directly logged onto that server.

One issue here is that the connection was initiated over HTTP and not HTTPS.  Although Kerberos authentication was used, some companies require all connections secured by SSL to the remote server per their security policies.  Some consideration should be given to this as any PowerShell connection to Office 365, Microsoft's own bread and butter, is made with SSL only.  HTTP is not allowed for connections to manage your tenant via PowerShell.

# Remote PowerShell – HTTPS

In order to provide a SSL connection to PowerShell on a remote Exchange Server some configuration is necessary.  Where do we start in order to configure SSL for PowerShell?  What if the PowerShell Virtual Directory was forced to require SSL?  Would that solve the issue?   First we need to get the name of the PowerShell Virtual Directory:

    Get-PowerShellVirtualDirectory –Server 16-Tap-Ex01

```
Name                                                                    Server
----                                                                    ------
PowerShell (Default Web Site)                                           16-TAP-EX01
```

    Set-PowerShellVirtualDirectory "16-tap-ex01\PowerShell (Default Web Site)" -RequireSSL $True

This setting kills local PowerShell access:

```
VERBOSE: Connecting to 16-TAP-EX01.16-TAP.Local.
New-PSSession : [16-tap-ex01.16-tap.local] Connecting to remote server 16-tap-ex01.16-tap.local failed with the
following error message : The WinRM client received an HTTP status code of 403 from the remote WS-Management se
For more information, see the about_Remote_Troubleshooting Help topic.
At line:1 char:1
+ New-PSSession -ConnectionURI "$connectionUri" -ConfigurationName Microsoft.Excha ...
+
    + CategoryInfo          : OpenError: (System.Manageme....RemoteRunspace:RemoteRunspace) [New-PSSession], PS
   gTransportException
    + FullyQualifiedErrorId : -2144108273,PSSessionOpenFailed
VERBOSE: Connecting to 16-TAP-EX01.16-TAP.Local.
New-PSSession : [16-tap-ex01.16-tap.local] Connecting to remote server 16-tap-ex01.16-tap.local failed with the
following error message : The WinRM client received an HTTP status code of 403 from the remote WS-Management se
For more information, see the about_Remote_Troubleshooting Help topic.
At line:1 char:1
+ New-PSSession -ConnectionURI "$connectionUri" -ConfigurationName Microsoft.Excha ...
+
    + CategoryInfo          : OpenError: (System.Manageme....RemoteRunspace:RemoteRunspace) [New-PSSession], PS
   gTransportException
    + FullyQualifiedErrorId : -2144108273,PSSessionOpenFailed
```

Now that PowerShell is unavailable, how do we modify the PowerShell virtual directory? With the IIS Manager.  Reviewing the settings on the PowerShell virtual directory we see that 'Require SSL' is checked:

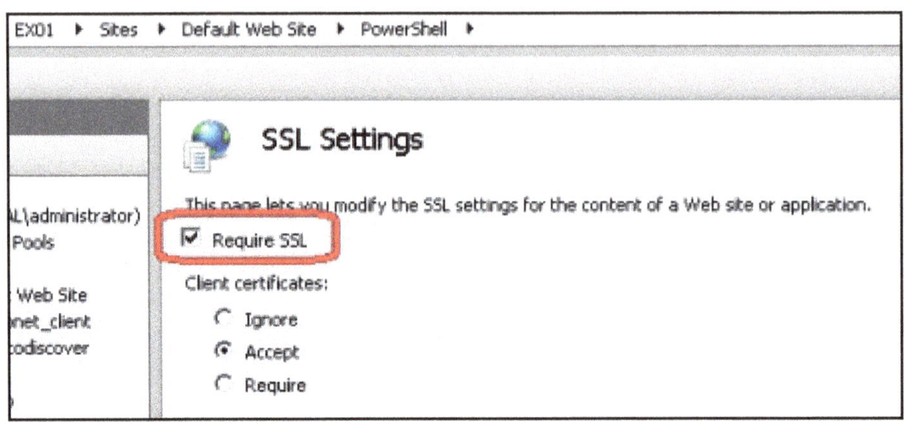

Simply uncheck the box and click apply.

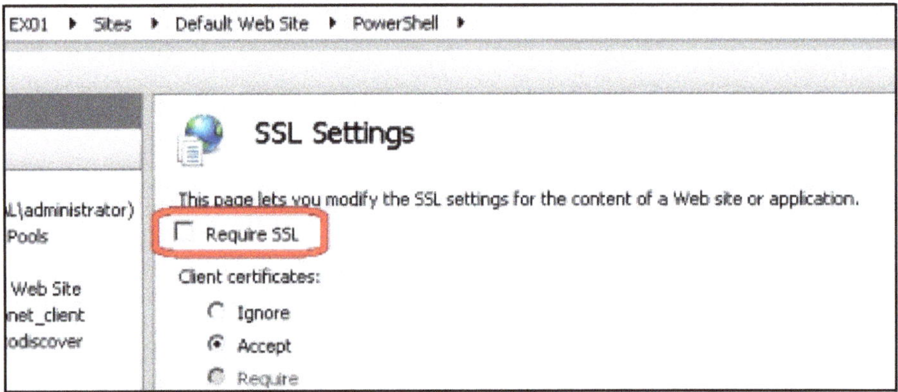

Then PowerShell works again:

```
VERBOSE: Connecting to 16-TAP-EX01.16-TAP.Local.
VERBOSE: Connected to 16-TAP-EX01.16-TAP.Local.
```

Knowing that requiring SSL on the PowerShell virtual directory will cause PowerShell to fail on the local server means that a different approach to these connections needs to be reviewed. TechNet refers to remote connections with the HTTP protocol and does not define how to connect via HTTPS. The default authentication method is Kerberos.

First, verify that PowerShell remoting over HTTP is allowed on the Exchange 2016 server:

    Enter-PSSession -ComputerName LocalHost

If an error occurs, then PowerShell remoting can be enabled with this command:

    Enable-PSRemoting

This one-liner will display information about the changes to the WinRM configuration. Choose 'A' for the answer to the two questions:

```
[PS] C:\>enable-psremoting

WinRM Quick Configuration
Running command "Set-WSManQuickConfig" to enable remote management of this computer by using the Windows Remote Management (WinRM)
service.
 This includes:
    1. Starting or restarting (if already started) the WinRM service
    2. Setting the WinRM service startup type to Automatic
    3. Creating a listener to accept requests on any IP address
    4. Enabling Windows Firewall inbound rule exceptions for WS-Management traffic (for http only).

Do you want to continue?
[Y] Yes  [A] Yes to All  [N] No  [L] No to All  [S] Suspend  [?] Help (default is "Y"): a
Confirm
Are you sure you want to perform this action?
Performing operation "Set-PSSessionConfiguration" on Target "Name: microsoft.powershell SDDL:
O:NSG:BAD:P(A;;GA;;;BA)S:P(AU;FA;GA;;;WD)(AU;SA;GXGW;;;WD). This will allow selected users to remotely run Windows PowerShell commands on
this computer".
[Y] Yes  [A] Yes to All  [N] No  [L] No to All  [S] Suspend  [?] Help (default is "Y"): a
```

Now that PowerShell remoting is enabled, verify the user account has access:

Get-User <Alias> | ft DisplayName,*power*

If the result is 'True', then the user has permission to connect remotely via PowerShell.

Back to the SSL connection.  We can review what happens by default:

New-PSSession -ConfigurationName Microsoft.Exchange -ConnectionUri http://<exchange server FQDN>/PowerShell/ -Credential (Get-Credential) -Authentication Kerberos

** Note ** Using Basic for the Authentication method will cause the connection to fail.  Either have no Authentication defined or choose something like Kerberos in our example.

The one-liner will prompt for credentials and allow a connection with the correct credentials. If, however, the ConnectionURI contains HTTPS and not HTTP, so the connection will fail:

New-PSSession -ConfigurationName Microsoft.Exchange -ConnectionUri https://<exchange server FQDN>/PowerShell/ -Credential (Get-credential) -Authentication Basic

```
cmdlet Get-Credential at command pipeline position 1
Supply values for the following parameters:
Credential
New-PSSession : [16-tap-ex01.16-tap.local] Connecting to remote server 16-tap-ex01.16-tap.local failed with the
following error message : WinRM cannot process the request. The following error with errorcode 0x80090311 occurred
while using Kerberos authentication: There are currently no logon servers available to service the logon request.
 Possible causes are:
   -The user name or password specified are invalid.
   -Kerberos is used when no authentication method and no user name are specified.
   -Kerberos accepts domain user names, but not local user names.
   -The Service Principal Name (SPN) for the remote computer name and port does not exist.
   -The client and remote computers are in different domains and there is no trust between the two domains.
 After checking for the above issues, try the following:
   -Check the Event Viewer for events related to authentication.
   -Change the authentication method; add the destination computer to the WinRM TrustedHosts configuration setting or
use HTTPS transport.
 Note that computers in the TrustedHosts list might not be authenticated.
   -For more information about WinRM configuration, run the following command: winrm help config. For more
information, see the about_Remote_Troubleshooting Help topic.
At line:1 char:1
+ New-PSSession -ConfigurationName Microsoft.Exchange -ConnectionUri https://16-ta ...
    + CategoryInfo          : OpenError: (System.Manageme...RemoteRunspace:RemoteRunspace) [New-PSSession], PSRemotin
```

What is the fix? IIS Authentication. The PowerShell virtual directory has no authentication settings configured. The one-liner above is set for Basic Authentication which is not allowed by default on the PowerShell virtual directory.  These settings can be verified running:

Get-PowerShellVirtualDirectory -Server <Exchange Server> | fl *auth*

```
CertificateAuthentication         : True
InternalAuthenticationMethods : {}
ExternalAuthenticationMethods : {}
LiveIdNegotiateAuthentication : False
WSSecurityAuthentication          : False
LiveIdBasicAuthentication         : False
BasicAuthentication               : False
DigestAuthentication              : False
WindowsAuthentication             : False
OAuthAuthentication               : False
AdfsAuthentication                : False
```

Notice that no authentication is configured by default. Using PowerShell to enable Basic Authentication will allow the use of a SSL connection to remotely connect via PowerShell:

> Get-PowerShellVirtualDirectory -Server <exchange server> | Set-PowerShellVirtualDirectory
> -BasicAuthentication $True

```
[PS] C:\>Get-PowerShellVirtualDirectory -server ex01 !fl *auth*


CertificateAuthentication         : True
InternalAuthenticationMethods : {Basic}
ExternalAuthenticationMethods : {Basic}
LiveIdNegotiateAuthentication : False
WSSecurityAuthentication          : False
LiveIdBasicAuthentication         : False
BasicAuthentication               : True
DigestAuthentication              : False
WindowsAuthentication             : False
OAuthAuthentication               : False
AdfsAuthentication                : False
```

Now that PowerShell Remoting is verified as enabled, that the user account has access and that Basic Authentication is enabled, setting up an HTTPS connection should now be successful:

```
[PS] C:\>New-PSSession -ConfigurationName Microsoft.Exchange -ConnectionUri https://16-tap-ex01.16-tap.local/Po
werShell/ -Credential $cred -authentication basic

 Id Name              ComputerName      State     ConfigurationName       Availability
 -- ----              ------------      -----     -----------------       ------------
 14 Session14         16-tap-ex01....   Opened    Microsoft.Exchange         Available
```

In summary, to enable a PowerShell connection over HTTPS, the following is required:

- PowerShell remoting is enabled
- User has access to a remote PowerShell session
- PowerShell Virtual Directory has Basic Authentication turned on


# Invoke-Command

Another option for connecting to an Exchange Server remotely using native PowerShell cmdlets is 'Invoke-Command'. Invoke-command will allow running a single cmdlet or an entire block of code on a remote server called by the cmdlet. Let's review the Invoke-Command with Get-Help to see what can be done with this cmdlet:

```
-------------------------- EXAMPLE 1 --------------------------

PS C:\>Invoke-Command -FilePath c:\scripts\test.ps1 -ComputerName Server01

This command runs the Test.ps1 script on the Server01 computer.
```

Or:

```
------------------------------ EXAMPLE 2 ------------------------------
PS C:\>Invoke-Command -ComputerName server01 -Credential domain01\user01 -ScriptBlock {Get-Culture}

This command runs a Get-Culture command on the Server01 remote computer.
```

** **Note** ** *Invoke-Command uses WinRM to work properly. If this is disabled on the remote server, this method will fail.*

Why use the Invoke-Command? Invoke-Command will increase the speed of scripts that need to query information on remote Exchange Servers. This is especially true if slow WAN links are between the PowerShell source workstation and the remote Exchange Server being queried. Here is a traffic sample of a remote script query without Invoke-Command.

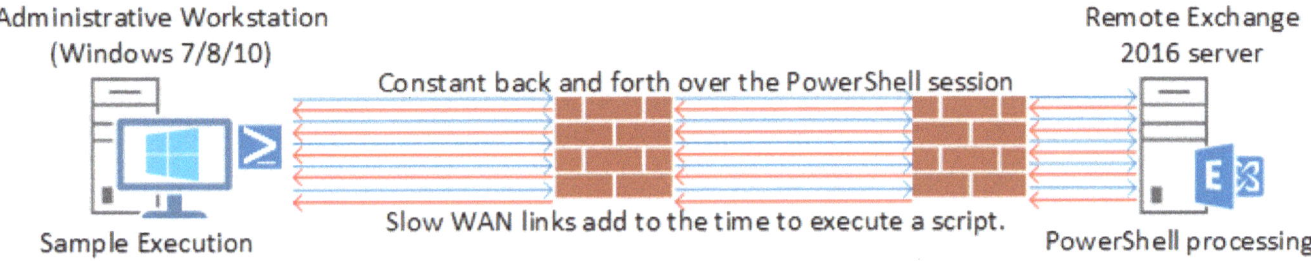



Notice the number of times the traffic passes over the WAN links. This could substantially slow down a script that queries remote servers (for example: Event Log reporting). The problem is that variables are being populated and the data is being sent back to the place where the PowerShell script it kicked off. In order to combat this, Invoke-Command can be used instead.

With Invoke-Command, the traffic crosses the WAN links just twice. Once out to initialize and run the code, and once back with the results. As can be seen by the diagram below, this would significantly speed things up and provide a better use of WAN bandwidth as well, as processing occurs at the local level:

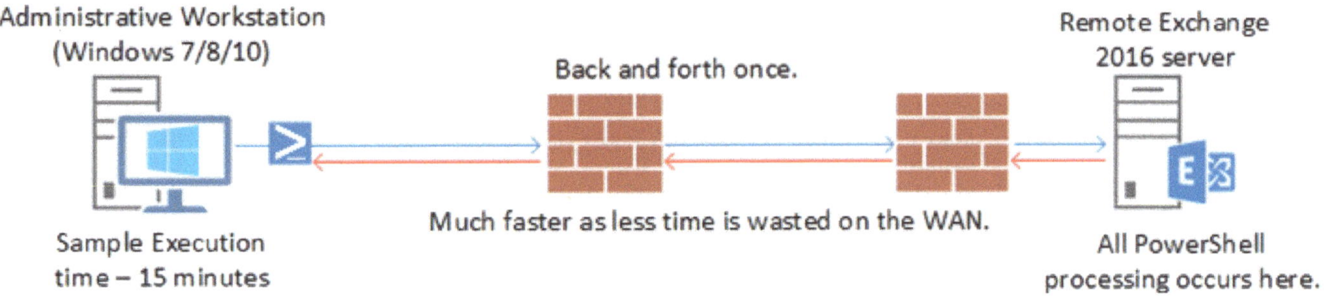



Inferred in the above diagram is that Invoke-Command can provide an advantage in situations where servers are accessible over the WAN. The Invoke-Command is great for WAN links or slow local links. For the example below we will explore the use of Invoke-Command in a real world scenario where Event Logs need to be examined for warning and critical events:

## Example

In this example there is a need to pull critical and warning events from the Application log for all Exchange Servers that exist. The first block of code will be used to get all Exchange Servers in AD. The script can be run on any server as the query used is an Active Directory query with no reliance on Exchange Server. The query looks for servers that are a member of the 'Exchange Install Domain Servers' group:

```
# Get list of all Exchange Servers
$Servers = Get-ADComputer -Filter *

Foreach ($Server in $Servers) {
   $MemberOf = (Get-ADComputer $Server | Get-ADObject -Properties MemberOf).MemberOf
   If ($MemberOf -Match "Exchange Install Domain Servers") {
      $Name = [string]$Server.Name
      $ExchangeServers += ,@($Name)
   }
}
```

Next, the Invoke-Command is used in a loop to execute large code section to run on the remote server as if the administrator were logged directly into the server. The Invoke-Command uses the 'ComputerName' parameter to specify which server to execute the script block on, the 'ScriptBlock' parameter specified the code to run, in this case it is stored in a variable. Storing code in a variable is typical for this type of script. Lastly, the 'ArgumentList' passes the server name to be used in the Script Block defined below.

```
Foreach ($Server in $ExchangeServers) {
   Invoke-Command -ComputerName $Server -ScriptBlock $Script -ArgumentList $Computer
}
```

Lastly, for the code section that queries the Application log for Critical events, we will examine chunks of code as to explain what the process and cmdlets that were used in order to accomplish this task.

First, $Script is used to store the entire code block to be executed by Invoke-Command:

```
$Script = {
```

We didn't close the brackets as we are now entering code in the script block. First, the server name is stored in $server variable which was passed from Invoke-Command (see above). For this, we grab the first parameter – or argument, hence args - passed. Args is a built-in array variable which contains parameters passed.

```
$Server = $Args[0]
```

Then, an appropriate description of what is occurring is displayed with this series of Write-Host cmdlet.

```
Write-Host " "
Write-Host "Analyzing event logs for server $server" -ForegroundColor White
Write-Host " "
Write-Host "PROCESSING" -ForegroundColor Yellow
Write-Host " "
```

This would look like this:



Next, define a few variables, one nullifying variable to clear out old data so the variables can be reused within each loop.

The $Log variable is populated with the Application variable as this is the log to be analyzed:

```
# Get a list of Critical Events
# Application Log
$Info = $Null
$App = $Null
$Log = "Application"
```

Next a new cmdlet 'Get-WinEvent' is being used to verify that the log can be queried. The switches used are –ListLog which is to define which log is to be analyzed and –ComputerName just specifies the server to be analyzed. This one line just checks to make sure the application log can be queried:

```
$LogCheck = Get-WinEvent -ListLog $Log -ComputerName $Server -ErrorAction SilentlyContinue
```

Next, if $LogCheck is not empty, PowerShell will begin to examine the event log for warning and critical events:

```
If ($LogCheck -ne $Null) {
```

A quick one line description is provided letting the administrator know that the App log for what server is being analyzed:

```
Write-Host "Application Log Analysis" -ForegroundColor Cyan
```

In the next section the $events variable is used to store events found by a filter applied to the application log. This section uses the 'get-eventlog' cmdlet to get events from the server. Then a 'where' filtering technique is used to find the events that are critical or warning level events. At the end of the line are Sort-Object and Group-Object cmdlets, which will help sort and group these events for better viewing:

```
$Events = Get-EventLog -ComputerName $Server -LogName $Log | Where {($_.EntryType -eq "Error")
-or ($_.EntryType -eq "Warning") -or ($_.EntryType -eq "Critical")} | Sort-Object EventID | Group-
Object EventID
```

Next, an If..Else section is used to check if any critical or warning events were stored in the $events variable. If $events is empty, the script moves on, and if there are any values stored in $events, the script will work within the If..Then section:

```
If ($Events -ne $Null) {
```

This section manipulates all events found in the $Events variable.

```
$App = Foreach ($Line2 in $Events) {
$Event = $Line2.Name
```

A PowerShell object is created for each event type found. The key parts of the PowerShell object are that $info2 calculates information about a particular event time – last date occurred, how many times this event occurred, the name of the event and the eventID.

In the below example, we will use a custom PowerShell object to store event data. A PowerShell object is essentially a collection of properties that can be gathered from different sources. It is vastly more powerful than using just a variable or array to construct due to its nature. The object created below has four fields – LastOccurred, Count, Name and Event. LastOccurred and Count are populated by $line2, Name by $Info2 and Event by $Event. This makes for an easy way to assemble data into a table format ready for output:

```
$Info2 = Get-WinEvent -ComputerName $Server -FilterHashTable @{LogName=$Log;ID=$Event}
-MaxEvents 1 -Erroraction SilentlyContinue

New-Object PSObject -Property @{
LastOccured = ($Info2.TimeCreated).DateTime
Count = $Line2.Count
Name = $Info2.ProviderName
Event = $Event

} Else {
        Write-Host "No events were found." –ForegroundColor Yellow
}
```

After all the events are gathered, a $App variable is called in order to display the end results that were gathered.

```
$App
```

If events are found, each server is processed and the results look like this:

From the first server:

```
Analyzing event logs for server 16-TAP-EX01

PROCESSING

Application Log Analysis

Name            : MSExchange RBAC
Event           : 74
LastOccured     : Monday, September 5, 2016 6:17:54 PM
Count           : 4
PSComputerName  : 16-TAP-EX01
RunspaceId      : 01278e2e-d658-4c58-a4ba-dc3f98cacab6

Name            : MSExchange Common
Event           : 106
LastOccured     : Monday, September 5, 2016 5:07:35 PM
Count           : 219
PSComputerName  : 16-TAP-EX01
RunspaceId      : 01278e2e-d658-4c58-a4ba-dc3f98cacab6

Name            : MSExchange Front End HTTP Proxy
Event           : 1003
LastOccured     : Monday, September 5, 2016 3:56:11 PM
```

… to the last server:

```
Name            : MSExchange UnifiedPolicyFileSync
Event           : 14005
LastOccured     : Monday, September 5, 2016 6:31:37 PM
Count           : 5
PSComputerName  : 16-TAP-EX01
RunspaceId      : 01278e2e-d658-4c58-a4ba-dc3f98cacab6


Analyzing event logs for server 16-TAP-EX02

PROCESSING

Application Log Analysis
Name            : MSExchange RBAC
Event           : 74
LastOccured     : Monday, September 5, 2016 3:42:04 PM
Count           : 2
PSComputerName  : 16-TAP-EX02
RunspaceId      : a9cb1823-7613-4196-a6fd-e6115ce452eb

Name            : VMware Tools
Event           : 1000
LastOccured     : Monday, September 5, 2016 5:07:44 PM
```

The above information could be populated into an HTML file after each servers finds all of these events. See *Chapter 16: Reporting* for more information on how to do so.

# **5**     What's New

---

**In This Chapter**

- Requirements
- Coexistence
- New Features
- De-Emphasized Features
- Frequency Asked Questions (FAQ)

---

# Introduction

With every major release of Exchange Server, the requirements and feature set gets an update. Requirements like CPU, memory and storage are changed in order to solve current and future challenges. New features are added to enable new ways of working, for the user and/or the administrator.

Such is the same with Exchange Server 2016. Since the release of previous versions, the way people work has changed. Despite all predictions that mail is going away (and some organizations have discarded the use of mail in favor of IM or Enterprise Social solutions), it's still considered business critical by most. However, it is important to address and support new ways people work.

One of the big drivers for Microsoft is obviously Office 365 or Exchange Online, cloud based solutions that use Exchange Server. Or should we say that whatever is present in Exchange Server 2016 is dependent on what is implemented in the cloud? It's no secret that Office 365 is the platform that will receive new capabilities first and some of it will trickle down to the on-premises build. Keep this in mind when browsing through the new list of features.

The features listed here are new in comparison with Exchange Server 2013, so if you are running an older version you might miss features that were introduced in 2013. Some features might be discussed more extensively in other chapters.

# Requirements

### Install OS

You will be able to install Exchange Server 2016 on the following Operating Systems:

- Windows Server 2012 R2
- Windows Server 2016 - Requires Exchange 2016 CU3 or greater

## Active Directory

The Active Directory forest in which you want to install Exchange Server 2016 will be at the following levels:

- Windows Server 2008 Forest/Domain Functional Level (FFL/DFL)
- Windows Server 2008 Domain Controllers

  ** **Note** ** If Windows 2016 Domain Controllers is installed, then the Forest Functional Level will need to be Windows 2008 R2 Functional Level.

This is a change compared to previous versions, from 2000 up until 2013 an FFL/DFL at Windows Server 2003 was supported. Please note that even if you have no longer have Windows Server 2003 domain controllers, both the FFL and DFL still might be on that level. Check this during your planning stage to prevent unexpected delays.

# Coexistence

Coexistence with previous versions of Exchange (in the same Active Directory Forest) is important for migration scenarios. You can install Exchange Server 2016 in combination with the following (already existing installations) versions at minimum:

- Exchange Server 2010 SP3 UR11
- Exchange Server 2013 CU10

Note that the specific Service Pack (SP), Update Rollup (UR) and Cumulative Update (CU) are subject to change. So verify these requirements here - https://technet.microsoft.com/en-us/library/aa996719(v=exchg.160).aspx

Exchange Server 2007 is not supported in a coexistence scenario. This is not unexpected, as previously Microsoft supported two previous versions for coexistence. This means that if you still have Exchange Server 2007, you will have to migrate to 2010 or preferably 2013 first and then introduce Exchange Server 2016. It's a hassle, but keep in mind that Exchange Server 2007 is out of mainstream support since April 10, 2012. This is the price organizations have to pay for not keeping up-to-date.

## Desktop Clients

Most organizations use Outlook, even if the web interface from Outlook Web App is getting more and more usable for day to day operations with each version of Exchange. The following versions are supported with Exchange Server 2016:

- Outlook 2010 SP2 (with KB2956191 and KB2965295) or later
- Outlook 2013 SP1 (with KB3020812) or later
- Outlook 2016

Note that the specific update KB's are subject to change, so be sure to check whether these requirements are still valid when you deploy Exchange Server 2016. However, also note that these are minimum requirements in order to work with Exchange Server 2016. It is probably best to keep each version fully updated.

At the time of writing support of Outlook for MacOS has been added to Exchange 2016. However, as it uses Exchange Web Services (EWS).

# New Features

## Single Role

Exchange Server 2007 introduced us to the concept of multiple roles; Client Access (CAS or CA) for client connectivity and OWA, Hub Transport (HT or HUB) for SMTP mail receiving, sending and processing, Mailbox (MBX) for database and database high availability, Unified Messaging for voice mail and Auto attendant features and the Edge Transport server for SMTP mail receiving, sending and cleaning within the perimeter network. Edge Transport servers can be non-domain joined or part of a DMZ only domain, separate from production.

We already saw a change in Exchange Server 2013 where there were only three roles left: Client Access role for client connectivity and proxying, Mailbox role for the actual business logic (i.e. rendering OWA etc.) as well as database storage and high availability. The Edge Transport server role returned after Service Pack 1.

Separate roles were created to enhance security or to balance the load of different tasks onto different separate servers. However, Exchange has been made safer and developments in CPU infrastructure has limited the need for separate roles. This is why the Exchange Product Team's recommendation is to deploy multi-role servers since Exchange Server 2010 and resulted in the convergence of all roles within Exchange Server 2016.

Now they have taken this step even further by only making one role install possible (with the exception of the Edge Transport role, which should be placed in the perimeter network, separate from your internal network).

The role consolidation forces you to implement the multi-role deployment recommendation which was also presented in the Preferred Architecture of Exchange Server 2013 and the revision for Exchange Server 2016.

## Modern Attachments

With the growing use of Office 365 users might have their files stored on OneDrive for Business. This creates certain advantages; files are available online and can be synced offline to a myriad of devices.

Within OWA (Webmail) users can now read attachments inline in OWA, which was possible in Exchange 2010 and 2013 with the latter having a more native look when an Office Web App server was used in conjunction. This was a welcome addition for OWA users, especially those who didn't have a full-fledged Office suite installed on their device. However, OWA Attachment preview was read-only. If you wanted to edit the document, you had to download the file and edit it offline with your Office suite.

But with OWA 2016, users can immediately reply and edit the office document before sending it. No more downloading and editing the file offline. No need for an Office suite installed on your device. For this purpose, a copy of the document is created in the Drafts folder, from where it can be edited. Furthermore, attachments can be added from your device or directly from your OneDrive either as a full attachment or a link with view or edit permissions to those recipients. Permissions on the file are set automatically. This works from OWA but also from Outlook (2016).

This allows the user to collaborate more easily and keep the mailbox leaner by leveraging OneDrive (basically SharePoint) storage, and not Mailbox Storage. You will require an Outlook Online Server 2016 (OOS) for viewing and editing attachments in OWA. For adding links to files, instead of adding the file to a mail you require either

OneDrive for Business or SharePoint Server 2016 on-premises.

## REST API

Consumers of Exchange have had Exchange Web Services (EWS) since Exchange Server 2007, and this was the first Exchange focused API available. Outlook uses it for looking up Free/Busy information, Mail Tips etc.. Outlook for Mac uses EWS for all its communication as it doesn't use Outlook Anywhere.

While EWS suits its purpose, it is a proprietary protocol and not based on an open standard. So it is interesting to see the introduction of the Representational State Transfer (REST) API in Exchange Server 2016. It is an open standard and uses:

- **JSON (JavaScript Object Notification)** – Is a method for storing information logically and in a human readable format.
- **OAUTH 2.0 (Open Authorization)** – Used for authentication for end users connecting to Exchange.  It is a more secure method than Basic Authentication and requires a third party provider.
- **ODATA 4.0 (Open Data Protocol)** – Use for Exchange data manipulation and querying.

REST API consists of several elements: The Mail API you can read, compose, send messages and manage folders and attachments, and the Calendar API and Contacts API provide access to calendar and contacts data. You can limit access with granular scoped permissions, and it can be used in conjunction with EWS.

Yes, EWS is still present and supported despite the fact REST API was introduced in Exchange Server 2016.  REST is also available in Office 365 (not only for Exchange Online). CU3 makes it an option on Exchange Server 2016.

## No MAPI/CDO Support

As announced during the Microsoft Exchange Conference (MEC) in 2012, and other following events, the MAPI/CDO protocol was deprecated in Exchange Server 2013 meaning it would no longer be developed and would not become available in following versions of Exchange Server. And indeed, there is no MAPI/CDO support in Exchange Server 2016.

Be sure to check your applications whether they use MAPI/CDO and investigate other solutions when planning for Exchange Server 2016. Those solutions should use EWS or the aforementioned REST API.

## Lagged Copy Enhancements

This feature has been introduced in Exchange 2013 but was further enhanced in Exchange 2016 RTM and CU1. When the Replay Lag Manager is enabled (per 2016 CU1 this is now the default setting), lagged database copies will replay logs automatically in the following scenarios:

- Low disk space (~10GB)
- Corruption in lagged copy
- Less than three healthy database copies for more than 24 hours

With CU1 it takes the health of the server into account, specifically the read IO latency of the disk. If the latency is above 25ms the log replay will be delayed, unless there is a low disk space trigger. This prevents user experience performance issues when a replay event has to be initiated.

## Preferred Architecture 2016

The Preferred Architecture has been updated with Exchange Server 2016 in mind. It is a framework made by the Exchange Product Team to educate how they feel Exchange Server 2016 should be deployed when possible. You could consider it a best practice description and should always be referenced if you design your Exchange Server 2016 environment. Every deviation should be clearly explained and documented. Preferred Architecture is defined here - https://blogs.technet.microsoft.com/exchange/2015/10/12/the-exchange-2016-preferred-architecture/

## MAPI/HTTP is Now Default

Introduced in Exchange Server 2013, the MAPI/HTTP protocol is the successor to the RPC/HTTP protocol, which was introduced in Exchange Server 2003. Yes, more than ten years ago! In this time end users habits have changed as have clients connecting to Exchange.  A newer, standards based protocol was thus created with the thought being to improve client experience and make it more efficient at the same time.

This protocol was designed with the Internet in mind and should provide more reliable connections, even when connected from mobile Internet connections. It also provides new capabilities such as Multi Factor Authentication (MFA). It requires a supported Outlook version (Outlook 2010 (KB2899591),  2013 SP1 and 2016).

In Exchange Server 2013 it had to be enabled specifically, unfortunately not with granularity: it was active for all users. It will now be enabled by default in Exchange Server 2016 and has a per-user settings control (to accommodate users that don't have a supported client, for instance). If you enable such a user, it will be discovered by Auto-Discover and after a client restart (no user notification is given as it is not that interesting for the average user), Outlook will start using with the new protocol. You can verify this, by checking the Outlook connections window for HTTP connections, as Outlook Anywhere connections will display RPC/http instead.

| Server name | Status | Protocol | Authr |
|---|---|---|---|
| https://outlook.office365.c... | Established | HTTP | Clear |
| https://outlook.office365.c... | Established | HTTP | Bear. |
| https://outlook.office365.c | Established | HTTP | Clear |

## Search Improvements

Search has now improved performance. The search results should also be more accurate and complete as it uses fuzzy logic and search refiners. The results are now consistent between Outlook and OWA, because Outlook (as of Outlook 2016) will no longer search in its own cached OST file, but delegate the search query to Exchange.

A notable improvement, known as "read from passive", was introduced with CU3 and now reduces network traffic for DAGs.  The reduction is due to the fact that Exchange 2016 now pulls search data from a local copy and the various copies do not need to coordinate index updates.  These changes are reflected in the Exchange Server Role Requirements Calculator.

## Extensibility

Exchange 2013 already introduced Outlook/OWA Apps, now they are even more functional and rebranded as Outlook Add-Ins. Outlook Apps controls were only available right above the message pane, but the Outlook Add-Ins have multiple possible integration points: the Ribbon, Command Bar, Context Menu, Body Text and Task Pane.

There are already add-ins from DocuSign, SalesForce, Wunderlist and Uber for example.

## Inbox Enhancements

In the Outlook interface there are several improvements as well, for example there is now an inline URL preview for messages, as well as an inline video player, which would reduce the need leaving Outlook and starting a browser or video player.

The recipient selection and people search is now more intelligent. And there is a "Tell me what you want to do" box in Outlook, which is a similar to Cortona in Windows Phone and Windows 10.

## Simplified Coexistence with Exchange 2013

When transitioning to Exchange Server 2016, there is no need to create a separate namespace (like legacy.contoso.com) which handles client traffic for mailboxes on the legacy server. There is also no need to switch the general client access URLs to the highest version of Exchange which then redirects (i.e. legacy.contoso.com) or proxy's connections to the server that contains the user mailbox.

You can now add Exchange 2016 servers to the same namespace via your load balancers. Whether a client connection first connects to 2013 or 2016, data is proxied to the correct server that holds your database. Yes, this is even true for mixed 2013 and 2016 Exchange servers. In this way there is no client access switchover as there used to be with 2007 or 2010 to 2013 transitions. This enables very simple transitions. Simply put: add 2016 servers to your load balancing services, move the data, remove 2013 servers from your load balancers, and you're done.

## Faster Recovery

Failover times have now been improved to about 18 seconds, almost a 50% reduction compared to Exchange 2013, and a welcome improvement for high demanding environments.

And of course the previously mentioned Replay Lag Manager that is now enabled per default, which will play down lagged database transaction logs when there aren't sufficient available copies insuring the required high availability you designed for while you sleep and not causing a rush on Monday morning to get that availability up to specs.

But that's not the only automatic process, there is automated database repair of corruptions due to divergence detections. Loose truncation doesn't cause database dismounts and the supported ReFS file system decreases chances of file system corruption, which could trigger database reseeds or rebuilds.

## Simpler Deployments

Now there is only one role to implement in your internal network: all roles are consolidated in a single role, the Mailbox server. There is no option anymore allowing for split-role installations. The only exception is the Edge Transport server, which is a role specifically designed to be deployed in perimeter networks as an SMTP gateway, and is not required for Exchange to function properly.

## Hybrid Enhancements

A Hybrid Exchange environment is one that has on-premises Exchange servers as well as Exchange Online mailboxes. Organizations requiring hybrid Exchange environments, can now use the Microsoft Office 365 Hybrid Configuration Wizard. This is an online wizard and is no longer tied to the on-premises installation of Exchange. This enables the product team to monitor experiences, collect statistics and respond and implement changes more quickly in the wizard. This ensures a lot smoother creation of your hybrid Exchange environment.

## Security and Compliance

The Data Loss Prevention (DLP) was added with new information types, Office applications other than Outlook have support for PolicyTips (2016) and DLP has been introduced into SharePoint making more data than just your email safer.

eDiscovery and Auditing have been improved in reliability and speed and for those using Public Folders, they can now put them on Hold just like mailboxes.

## Outlook on the Web

Previously called Outlook Web App (and before that Outlook Web Access). Improvements include:

Platform specific experiences (iOS/Android), Performance improvements, new Option screen, improved Search including suggestions, Contact linking, Undo feature, Pinning or flagging messages and new themes (Our favorite Super Sparkle Happy is still in there!).

# De-Emphasized Features

As with every new version of Exchange, some features may be "de-emphasized", which means that they are currently still present but might be removed in upcoming versions of Exchange. These announcements are to guide organizations with long term planning and investments.

## Third Party Replication API

Normally a Database Availability Group (DAG) will be replicated by Exchange services. However, there are storage solutions that, next to their own replication to other devices or locations, can leverage DAG replication. Now, this was never implemented on a large scale as the preference is to keep it simple and use native DAG replication. This de-emphasis supports this practice.

## RPC over HTTP

Introduced with Exchange 2003 in order to provide Outlook access outside the corporate network via HTTP(s) connections. Normal communications between Exchange and Outlook where based on the MAPI RPC protocol, which can't be routed over the Internet, has a dynamic port range and is very susceptible to high latency connections. By wrapping this protocol within HTTP packets, most issues were resolved. However, times have changed and over time other specific requirements and features are needed, made possible by MAPI over HTTP introduced in Exchange Server 2013.  See Chapter 6 for more information on this.

## Failover Cluster Administrative Access Point for DAGs

Since Exchange 2010 up until Exchange 2013 (on Windows Server 2012) it was required to create a Cluster Node Object (CNO) in Active Directory and provide a valid IP address, as a result from Windows Server Failover Clustering requirements. However, due to improvements this is no longer required for Failover Clustering as of Windows Server 2012 R2.

As it served no purpose and only increased complexity you are probably better off. The use of an IP Less DAG reduces complexity with one less point of failure.  Do check third party applications that sometimes, despite advisories from Microsoft, require this administrative access point such as backup solutions.

# Frequently Asked Questions (FAQ)

**Why the change in Forest and Domain Functional level? Will that give me more features?**

No, the fact that Windows Server 2008 Forest and Domain Functional Level (respectively FFL/DFL) is mainly because Windows Server 2003 (the previously "golden" version, supported by each Exchange version from 2000 up to 2013) will be out of mainstream support when Exchange Server 2016 is expected to be released. Why allow a FFL/DFL of a Windows Server version that is no longer supported and tested in combination with new products? In the future, 2008 R2 FFL/DFL will become the new standard and organizations should plan to be there if they are deploying Exchange 2016.

**Why only one role? We always deployed each role separately as it is safer/faster/stronger/better.**

Previous limiting factors like CPU power and memory prices required the splitting of functionality in order to get the required performance. This was during the Exchange 2003/2007 era, but even then things changed rapidly with multi-core processors and cheaper memory. So, there is no longer a clear benefit in splitting roles, the downside is of course a more complex Exchange environment when every role is on a separate server. So, somewhere during the lifetime of Exchange 2010 the recommendation changed from separate roles to multi-role Exchange deployments. The deployment setup has now fully adopted that recommendation, and offers only deploying (Edge excluded) multi-role servers.

**Wait, didn't Exchange 2016 require less IOPS than Exchange 2013?**

Unfortunately, no. Before the release of Exchange 2016, there were perhaps some mentions about even less IOPS but those statements where subject to change and they did. Exchange 2016 has the same IOPS profile as Exchange 2013 under the same circumstances.

Having said this, some new features have or will affect the IOPS requirement somewhat. For instance, building the Content Index from a passive database copy instead of copying the Index from another server with the active copy will change the IOPS behavior somewhat in specific circumstances.

<table><tr><td>6</td><td># Server Configuration</td></tr></table>

## In This Chapter

- Base Installation Requirements
- Configuring the Pagefile
- Event Log Configuration
- Certificates
- Exchange Virtual Directories
- Client Access – OWA, Outlook Anywhere and MAPI over HTTP
- Databases
- Database Availability Group
- Address Lists
- Accepted Domains
- Putting It All Together

As important as the rest of the book is, nothing is more important than the installation and configuration of your new Exchange 2016 servers.  Whether these servers are part of an upgrade from Exchange 2010 and/or 2013 or these are a brand new install (Greenfield), this stage is important and PowerShell can and should be used to handle the initial configuration.

Plenty of PowerShell scripts have been written to handle the installation and prep work needed before Exchange 2016 can be installed on your servers.  We will cover the basics in this chapter as these scripts tend to get complicated fast and exploring these in their entirety would take more space then we have available in this book.

Additionally PowerShell can be used to configure some server options like the Server's Pagefile and Event Logs.  These can be performed before or after Exchange is installed.  The Event Log can be configured in terms of size and when events are overwritten.  The Pagefile needs to be configured as the amount of RAM+10MB using PowerShell on all Exchange 2016 servers.

Client access to Exchange servers can also be configured with PowerShell.  This includes configuring URLs needed for client connections, as well as OWA and Outlook access options. Planning out what names are to be used should be done prior to allowing client devices to connect to the mailboxes hosted or front-ended by Exchange 2016.

Securing Exchange via certificates can also be done with PowerShell.  From requesting, importing and exporting certificates to enabling, disabling and removing certificates, PowerShell cmdlets exist for all of these tasks.  These will need to be performed prior to users connecting to Exchange 2016.

Databases can also be created, deleted and configured using PowerShell.  In this chapter we will cover some of the ways that this can be done with PowerShell with practical tips for everyday usage.

# Base Installation Requirements

Microsoft posts the requirements for each version of Exchange Server on TechNet. Usually these requirements are different depending on the Operating System or Exchange role to be installed. Exchange 2016 is no different. Let's review the requirements and build PowerShell cmdlets around these to make installation a breeze.

**Exchange 2016 CU2, Mailbox Role, Windows 2012 (R2)**

First, Exchange requires numerous Windows features in order to be installed:

- **Windows Features**

| | | |
|---|---|---|
| AS-HTTP-Activation | Web-Client-Auth | Web-Mgmt-Console |
| Desktop-Experience | Web-Digest-Auth | Web-Mgmt-Service |
| NET-Framework-45-Features | Web-Dir-Browsing | Web-Net-Ext45 |
| RPC-over-HTTP-proxy | Web-Dyn-Compression | Web-Request-Monitor |
| RSAT-Clustering | Web-Http-Errors | Web-Server |
| RSAT-Clustering-CmdInterface | Web-Http-Logging | Web-Stat-Compression |
| RSAT-Clustering-Mgmt | Web-Http-Redirect | Web-Static-Content |
| RSAT-Clustering-PowerShell | Web-Http-Tracing | Web-Windows-Auth |
| Web-Mgmt-Console | Web-ISAPI-Ext | Web-WMI |
| WAS-Process-Model | Web-ISAPI-Filter | Windows-Identity-Foundation |
| Web-Asp-Net45 | Web-Lgcy-Mgmt-Console | RSAT-ADDS |
| Web-Basic-Auth | Web-Metabase | |

- **.Net 4.5.2**
- **Microsoft Unified Communications Managed API 4.0, Core Runtime 64-bit**

These are the minimum requirements. The moving target in this group is .Net. With the release of CU2 and greater, .Net 4.6.1 is now supported and can be installed. Since this section deals with base listed requirements, we'll stick with .Net 4.5.2 for PowerShell scripting.

***SEE CHAPTER 3 FOR INSTALLATION OF THESE PREREQUISITES***

# Configuring the Pagefile

When it comes to initial server configuration, the Pagefile can be an important, but often overlooked item to configure for a Windows server. This is because, by default, the Pagefile is configured automatically. With servers configured with 16, 32, 64 and even 96 GB of RAM, one would think that the Pagefile would no longer be needed. However, Microsoft has recommended the Pagefile be configured specifically to be RAM + 10 MB to a maximum of 32 GB + 10 MB of RAM. In order to configure this, there are two options, either done from the GUI (Server Manager) or with PowerShell and WMI. With the focus of the book on PowerShell, we'll configure the Pagefile to match best practices with PowerShell. This means removing the automatically size Pagefile and replacing it with a Pagefile that has the same Initial and Maximum size.

Information about a server's Pagefile can be found using either CIM or WMI. PowerShell can leverage these two methodologies to discover information about the configuration of a Windows Operating System. Currently, CIM is the preferred method for querying information.  WMI should only be used if CIM queries fail.  When building a script, it would be perfectly acceptable to use just CIM to gather Operating System configuration items.  However, using WMI as a failback would be preferred, if only to give the script some redundancy in case of failure.  Also, some servers will not allow CIM to connect – this can happen with Edge Transport Servers which are not in the domain.

The Windows Pagefile configuration, as far as Exchange cares, has four components that need to be configured.

- **Automatically Managed** – By default the Pagefile is System Managed and this is not an Exchange Server best practice
- **Location** – By default this is on the C drive, depending on your available disk space, it may be preferable to move the Pagefile to a separate disk and not on the same drive as the Operating System
- **Initial Size** – By default, this is not configured as the server will be managing it
- **Maximum Size** – Same as the Initial Size

## Starting Point

First we need a baseline to discover this information we want to change, how can we find out what the initial configuration is?  CIM.  The Get-CimInstance cmdlet will provide that information.  In Chapter 2 we discussed some ways to work with the Pagefile using CIM to do so.

```
Get-CimInstance -Query "Select * from Win32_ComputerSystem"
```

```
Name         PrimaryOwnerName    Domain        TotalPhysicalMemory    Model                    Manufacturer
----         ----------------    ------        -------------------    -----                    ------------
16RTM-EX01   Windows User        WIN16.LOCAL   17179332608            VMware Virtual Platform   VMware, Inc.
```

## Complete Script Block

```
Function ConfigurePagefile {
$Stop = $False

# Remove Existing Pagefile
Try {
    Set-CimInstance -Query "Select * From Win32_ComputerSystem" -Property @{
    AutomaticManagedPagefile = "False" }
} Catch {
    Write-Host "Cannot remove the existing pagefile." -ForegroundColor Red
    $Stop = $True
}
# Get RAM and Set ideal PagefileSize

Try {
    $RamInMB = (Get-CIMInstance -ComputerName $Name -ClassName Win32_PhysicalMemory
    -ErrorAction Stop | Measure-Object -Property Capacity -Sum).Sum/1GB
} Catch {
    Write-Host "Cannot acquire the amount of RAM in the server." -ForegroundColor Red
    $Stop = $True
```

```
}
$ExchangeRAM = $RAMinMB + 10

If ($Stop -ne $True) {
   # Configure Pagefile
   Try {
      Set-CimInstance    -Query   "Select   *   From   Win32_PagefileSetting"   -Property   @
      {InitialSize=$ExchangeRAM;MaximumSize=$ExchangeRAM}
   } Catch {
      Write-Host "Cannot configure the Pagefile correctly." -ForegroundColor Red
   }
   $Pagefile   =   Get-CimInstance   Win32_PagefileSetting   -Property   *   |   Select-Object
   Name,initialSize,Maximumsize
   $Name = $Pagefile.Name
   $Max = $Pagefile.MaximumSize
   $Min = $Pagefile.InitialSize
   Write-Host "
   Write-Host "The page file of $name is now configured for an initial size of " -ForegroundColor White
   -NoNewline
   Write-Host "$Min " -ForegroundColor Green -NoNewline
   Write-Host "and a maximum size of " -ForegroundColor White -NoNewline
   Write-Host "$Max." -ForegroundColor Green
   Write-Host " "
   } Else {
      Write-Host "The Pagefile cannot be configured at this time." -ForegroundColor Red
   }
}

# Call the Pagefile Function
ConfigurePagefile
```

One caveat we have not covered is when a server has greater than 32 GB of RAM. For this scenario Microsoft has deemed it a best practice not to set the Pagefile to a size greater than 32 GB + 10 MB. Converting 32 GB into MB provides a nuMBer of 32768. Adding 10 MB to 32768 provides us with the maximum Pagefile size of 32778 MB. In order to accommodate this in the script, we will adjust this line here:

```
$ExchangeRAM = $RAMinMB + 10
```

To include a check for the size of the $ExchangeRAM and if it is above the maximum value of 32778, then the variable will be set to 32778.

```
# Set maximum pagefile size to 32 GB + 10 MB
If ($ExchangeRAM -gt 32778) {$ExchangeRAM = 32778}
```

Now that the script above can handle one server, we can modify the code to make it more useful and allow the configuration of multiple servers.

## Multiple Servers

With the above script, the local server will have its Pagefile configured. What if the same process needed to be run on a dozen servers? Is there an easy way to do this? Let's do some testing to see if this is the way to change multiple servers.

First, we need a list of servers:

```
$Servers = Get-ExchangeServer
```

Then a Foreach loop needs to be constructed around the code block:

```
Foreach ($Server in $Servers) {
   <Code Block>
}
```

Next, each of the cmdlets needs to query the specific server name in order to make this work. The caveat to this is that if these CIM queries fail, a failback to WMI will be needed. Refer to Chapter 18 for more on CIM and WMI, but for this case, the Edge Transport will not allow CIM connections, but WMI only, hence the failback in case CIM queries fail on an Exchange Server. Edge Transport servers will require a WMI install.

Add specific server to each CIM cmdlet:

**Initial cmdlets:**
```
Set-CimInstance -Query "Select * From Win32_ComputerSystem" -Property @
{AutomaticManagedPagefile="False"}
(Get-CIMInstance -ClassName Win32_PhysicalMemory -ErrorAction Stop | Measure-Object -Property
Capacity -Sum).Sum/$GB
Set-CimInstance -Query "Select * From Win32_PagefileSetting" -Property @
{InitialSize=$ExchangeRAM;MaximumSize=$ExchangeRAM}
$Pagefile = Get-CimInstance Win32_PagefileSetting -Property * | Select-Object
Name,InitialSize,MaximumSize
```

**Modified cmdlets:**
```
Set-CimInstance –ComputerName $Server -Query "Select * From Win32_ComputerSystem" -Property
@{AutomaticManagedPagefile="False"}
(Get-CIMInstance –ComputerName $Server -Classname Win32_PhysicalMemory -ErrorAction Stop |
Measure-Object -Property Capacity -Sum).Sum/$GB
Set-CimInstance –ComputerName $Server -Query "Select * From Win32_PagefileSetting" -Property @
{InitialSize=$ExchangeRAM;MaximumSize=$ExchangeRAM}
$Pagefile = Get-CimInstance –ComputerName $Server Win32_PagefileSetting -Property * | Select-
Object Name,InitialSize, MaximumSize
```

**WMI Failback**

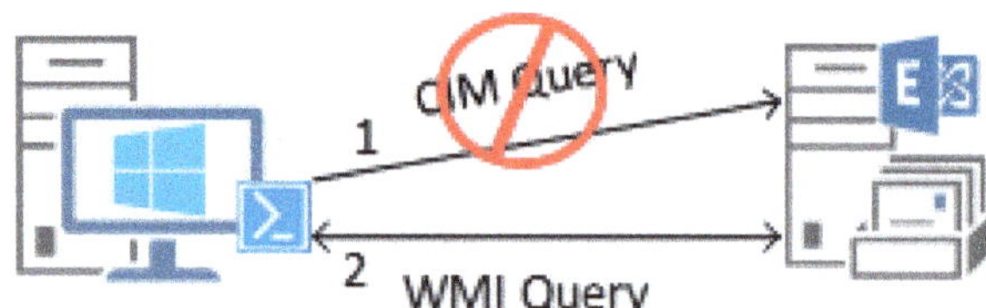

As stated above, CIM queries can and will fail on Edge Transport servers and thus need a WMI failback to be able to query and make changes on the servers.  Let's take one of the CIM queries and modify it to handle a failure and check WMI as a failback:

## Initial CIM Query

For this code section, we will wrap our original code with a 'Try..Catch' block for error handling.  In the 'Try { }' lines, the original CIM query is executed.  If an error occurs in the query, the Erroraction switch stops the query and then PowerShell executes the 'Catch { }' code block.  In this section the $WMIQuery variable is set to $true:

```
Try {
    Set-CimInstance -Query "Select * From Win32_ComputerSystem" -Property @{AutomaticMan-
    agedPagefile="False"} –ErrorAction STOP
} Catch {
    Write-Host "Cannot remove the existing pagefile." -ForegroundColor Red
    $WMIQuery = $True
}
```

### Fail WMI from CMI Queries

If the $WMIQuery is set to $true the WMI code section is executed.  Just like the CIM Query section above, the WMI query code block will remove the Pagefile via WMI.  If the action fails, then the Catch section notes the error:

```
If ($WMIQuery) {
    Try {
        $CurrentPagefile = Get-WmiObject -ComputerName $Server -Class Win32_PagefileSetting -Er-
        rorAction STOP
        $Name = $CurrentPagefile.Name
        $CurrentPagefile.Delete()
    } Catch {
        Write-Host "The server $server cannot be reached via CIM or WMI." -ForegroundColor Red
    }
}
```

Now that we have code for the coMBination of CIM and WMI queries, we can code for running the queries against multiple servers.

## Multiple Servers

In order to scale the script, we'll need the names of each Exchange Server.  The last five lines will call a function, passing just the server name, and run the entire set of cmdlets from before.  All WMI and CIM queries were modified to handle remote servers and not just work on the local server:

```
Function ConfigurePagefile {
    Param ($Server)
    $Stop = $False
    $WMIQuery = $False
    $Name = $Null
```

```powershell
# Remove Existing PageFile with CIM
Try {
    Set-CimInstance -ComputerName $Server -Query "Select * From Win32_ComputerSystem"
    -Property @{AutomaticManagedPagefile="False"} –Erroraction STOP
} Catch {
    Write-Host "Cannot remove the existing pagefile." -ForegroundColor Red
    $WMIQuery = $True
}

# Remove Pagefile with WMI if CIM fails
If ($WMIQuery) {
    Try {
        $CurrentPagefile = Get-WmiObject -ComputerName $Server -Class Win32_PagefileSetting –
        Erroraction STOP
        $Name = $CurrentPagefile.Name
        $CurrentPagefile.Delete()
    } Catch {
        Write-Host "The server $server cannot be reached via CIM or WMI." -ForegroundColor Red
        $Stop = $True
    }
}
# Reset WMIQuery
$WMIQuery = $False
# Get RAM and set ideal PagefileSize - CIM method
Try {
    $RamInMB = (Get-CIMInstance -ComputerName $Server -ClassName Win32_PhysicalMemory
    -ErrorAction Stop | Measure-Object -Property Capacity -Sum).Sum/1GB
    $ExchangeRAM = $RAMinMB + 10
} Catch {
    $WMIQuery = $True
}
# Get RAM and set ideal PagefileSize - WMI Method
If ($WMIQuery) {
    Try {
        $RamInMB = (Get-WmiObject -ComputerName $Server -ClassName Win32_PhysicalMemory
        -ErrorAction Stop | Measure-Object -Property Capacity -Sum).Sum/1GB
        $ExchangeRAM = $RAMinMB + 10
        # Set maximum pagefile size to 32 GB + 10 MB
        if ($ExchangeRAM -gt 32778) {$ExchangeRAM = 32778}
    } Catch {
    Write-Host "Cannot acquire the amount of RAM in the server with CIM or WMI queries."
    -ForegroundColor Red
    $Stop = $True
    }
}
# Reset WMIQuery
```

```
      $WMIQuery = $False
      If ($Stop -ne $True) {
        # Configure Pagefile
        Try {
          Set-CimInstance  -Computername  $Server  -Query  "Select  *  from  Win32_PagefileSetting"
          -Property @{InitialSize=$ExchangeRAM;MaximumSize=$ExchangeRAM}
        } catch {
          write-host "Cannot configure the Pagefile correctly." -ForegroundColor Red
          $WMIQuery = $True
        }
        If ($WMIQuery) {
          Try {
            Set-WMIInstance -ComputerName $Server -Class Win32_PagefileSetting -Arguments @{Name
            ="$Name";InitialSize=$ExchangeRAM;MaximumSize=$ExchangeRAM}
          } catch {
            Write-Host "Cannot configure the Pagefile correctly." -ForegroundColor Red
            $Stop = $True
          }
        }
        If ($Stop -ne $True) {
          $Pagefile = Get-CimInstance -ComputerName $Server Win32_PagefileSetting -Property * | Select-
          Object Name,InitialSize,MaximumSize
          $Name = $Pagefile.Name
          $Max = $Pagefile.MaximumSize
          $Min = $Pagefile.InitialSize
          Write-Host " "
          Write-Host "On the server $server The Pagefile of $name is now configured for an initial size of "
          -ForegroundColor White -NoNewline
          Write-Host "$Min " -ForegroundColor Green -NoNewline
          Write-Host "and a maximum size of " -ForegroundColor White -NoNewline
          Write-Host "$Max." -ForegroundColor Green
          Write-Host " "
        } Else {
          Write-Host "The Pagefile cannot be configured at this time." -ForegroundColor Red
        }
      } Else {
        Write-Host "The Pagefile cannot be configured at this time." -ForegroundColor Red
      }
    }
    $Servers = Get-ExchangeServer
    Foreach ($Server in $Servers) {
      ConfigurePagefile $Server
    }
}
```

# Event Log Configuration

Event Logs are an important tool in troubleshooting Exchange Servers. The problem is that the default settings on Windows Servers may not fit your organization's needs. In this section we'll explore how changes can be made and what best practices (if any) should be followed for configuring your server Event Logs. Every Windows administrator should be familiar with common Event Logs on Windows servers:

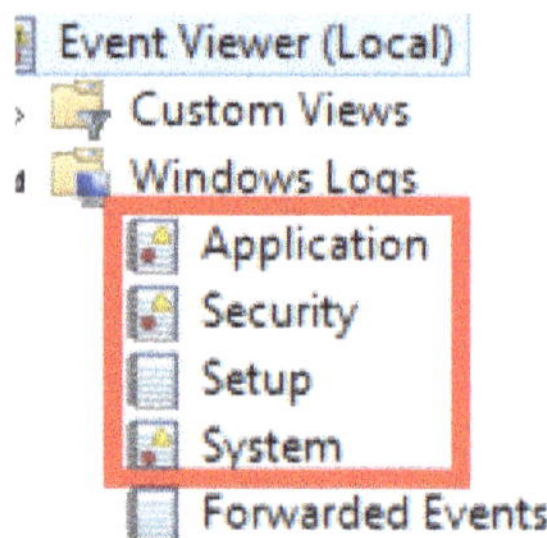

In particular, we are interested in the Application and System logs as that is where the majority of Exchange related events will be logged on your Exchange Servers. Now, we need to figure out how to manage these logs via PowerShell. In addition to these generic server Event Logs, there are also a few that are Exchange Server specific - Crimson channel Event Logs – stores application or component specific events:

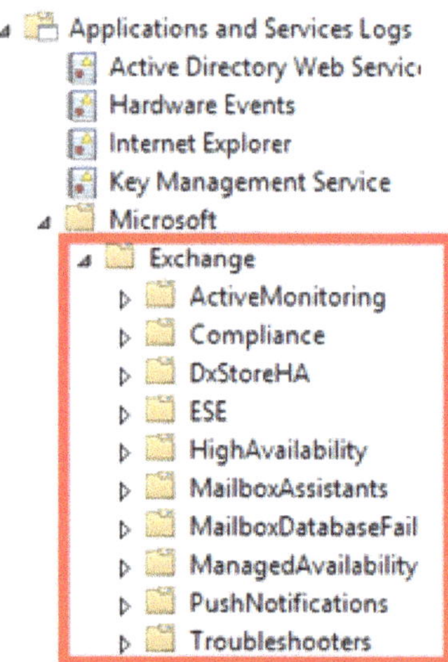

In any case, these Event Logs may need some settings adjusted so that if a troubleshooting issue arises, there will be enough information logged to assist in the effort.

What cmdlets are available for us to do so?

```
Get-Command *EventLog*
```

This provides us with a working list of PowerShell cmdlets for managing server Events Logs:

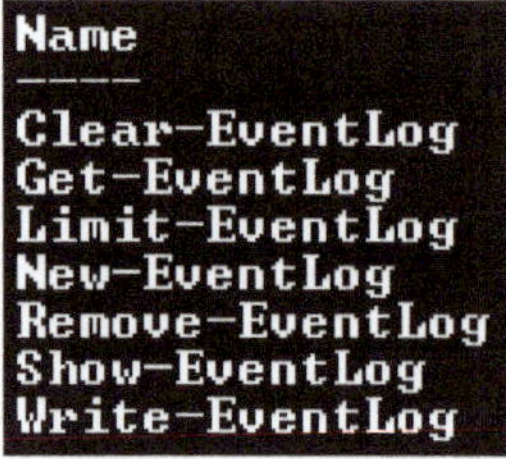

Using one of the above Powershell cmdlets, the Get-EventLog cmdlet, we are able to get some basic information on all the Event Logs.  However, a special switch is needed in order to do this (-List) which will provide a list of all logs and sizes. With -list this table is provided for us:

```
[PS] C:\>get-eventlog -list

 Max(K) Retain OverflowAction            Entries Log
 ------ ------ --------------            ------- ---
    512      7 OverwriteOlder                  0 Active Directory Web Services
 20,480      0 OverwriteAsNeeded          50,459 Application
 20,480      0 OverwriteAsNeeded               0 HardwareEvents
    512      7 OverwriteOlder                  0 Internet Explorer
 20,480      0 OverwriteAsNeeded               0 Key Management Service
153,600      7 OverwriteOlder              3,128 MSExchange Management
 20,480      0 OverwriteAsNeeded          33,363 Security
 20,480      0 OverwriteAsNeeded          47,649 System
 15,360      0 OverwriteAsNeeded           9,845 Windows PowerShell
```

Notice the first three columns provide the configuration information for each of the logs files.  Before these settings are adjusted we need to take a few things into consideration:

**OverwriteOlder [OverFlowAction]** - This setting allows the events to be overwritten ONLY if the events are older than 'X' amount of days.  This setting is typically seven days (as seen above). If the maximum log size is too small and the the server hits the cap, no new logs are written which can cause issues on the affected server.

**OverwriteAsNeeded [OverFlowAction]** - This setting allows all events to be overwritten.

**Max(K)** – Configuring this puts a cap on how large the .EVT files can grow to.  When configuring the maximum size we'll keep the max size lower than 300M.  Keep in mind that setting this too small could cause issues with the OverwriteOlder setting.  The minimum recommended size on common Event Logs on an Exchange Server is 40 MB.

**Example**

In this example the IT manager has asked you to create a standard Event Log size and retention period for various log types on the Exchange Servers.  The manager suggests seven days and 100 MB.  After doing some research and reviewing other servers, you decide that 100 MB would provide sufficient protection against the log files being overwritten too soon.  For this standard all Exchange Servers need to be configured the same and because there are 16 servers configured in a single DAG that need to be configured, a script is needed. The logs to be configured will be the Server and Application logs.

First, let's create the base cmdlets needed for this to work locally.  Then use these one-liners to build a loop to handle all Exchange Servers. Reviewing the list of EventLog PowerShell cmdlets, there appears to be no 'Set-EventLog' cmdlet.  What about the cmdlet that sticks out? 'Limit-EventLog' cmdlet.  To see what the cmdlet can do, simply run this:

Get-Help Limit-EventLog –Examples

This reveals a few ways to configure the log files:

```
-------------------------------- EXAMPLE 1 --------------------------------
PS C:\>limit-eventLog -logname "Windows PowerShell" -MaximumSize 20KB
```

```
-------------------------------- EXAMPLE 2 --------------------------------
PS C:\>limit-eventlog -logname Security -comp Server01, Server02 -retentionDays 7
```

Our resulting one-liner looks like this:

```
Limit-EventLog –LogName Application –RetentionDays 7 –MaximumSize 100MB –OverFlowAction
OverWriteAsNeeded
```

Now that the local server can be configured with this line, a loop needs to be created to enable the configuration of the remaining 15 servers.

```
$Servers = (Get-ExchangeServer).Name
$Logs = "Application", "Server"
Foreach ($Server in $Servers) {
   Foreach ($Log in $Logs) {
      Limit-EventLog  –ComputerName  $Server  –LogName  $Log  –RetentionDays  7  –MaximumSize
      100MB –OverFlowAction OverWriteAsNeeded
   }
}
```

In the above script, the Exchange Server names are stored in the $Servers variable. The logs to be modified are stored in the $Logs variable. In order to modify each Event Log for each server, a dual 'ForEach' loop must be used. The outer loop cycles through each server while the inner loop circles through each Event Log in the $Logs variable. This way each server's Application Log and Server Log are configured for 100 MB, seven days retention and overwrite as needed.

We can verify these settings with another loop or add a single line added to the above script. The ideal place for this code would be when the configuration for the current server's Event Log in the loop has been completed and the loop is about to go to the next Event Log. This way the verification can take place after the log has been configured:

**Simple:**

```
Get-EventLog -ComputerName $Server -List | Where {$_.Log -eq $Log}
```

```
Max(K)  Retain  OverflowAction            Entries  Log
------  ------  --------------            -------  ---
102,400      0  OverwriteAsNeeded          51,537  Application
102,400      0  OverwriteAsNeeded          10,922  System
102,400      0  OverwriteAsNeeded          33,087  Application
102,400      0  OverwriteAsNeeded           6,189  System
102,400      0  OverwriteAsNeeded          37,683  Application
102,400      0  OverwriteAsNeeded           4,888  System
```

**Complex**

```
Get-EventLog  -ComputerName  $Server  -List  |  Where  {$_.Log  -eq  $Log}  |  ft  @
{Label="Server";Expression={$Server}},MaximumKiloBytes,OverflowAction,Log
```

```
Server        MaximumKilobytes      OverflowAction Log
------        ----------------      -------------- ---
16RTM-EX01              102400 OverwriteAsNeeded Application
Server        MaximumKilobytes      OverflowAction Log
------        ----------------      -------------- ---
16RTM-EX01              102400 OverwriteAsNeeded System   |
Server        MaximumKilobytes      OverflowAction Log
------        ----------------      -------------- ---
16RTM-EX02              102400 OverwriteAsNeeded Application
Server        MaximumKilobytes      OverflowAction Log
------        ----------------      -------------- ---
16RTM-EX02              102400 OverwriteAsNeeded System
Server        MaximumKilobytes      OverflowAction Log
------        ----------------      -------------- ---
16RTM-EX03              102400 OverwriteAsNeeded Application
Server        MaximumKilobytes      OverflowAction Log
------        ----------------      -------------- ---
16RTM-EX03              102400 OverwriteAsNeeded System
```

In the end, simple was chosen for its clean look and readability. Here is the final script:

```
$Servers = Get-ExchangeServer
$Logs = "Application","Server"
Foreach ($Server in $Servers) {
    Foreach ($Log in $Logs) {
        Limit-EventLog –ComputerName $Server –LogName $Log –RetentionDays 7 –MaximumSize
        100MB –OverFlowAction OverWriteAsNeeded
        Get-EventLog -ComputerName $Server -List | Where {$_.Log -eq $Log}
    }
}
```

The above script now provides a simple mechanism for configuring Windows Event Logs.


# Certificates

One of the next configuration items on a server is to either import an existing certificate or to create a new certificate request and import the certificate from that. A certificate can be used by Exchange to secure OWA, Outlook Anywhere, PowerShell, Activesync, AutoDiscover and SMTP connections. A SSL certificate is a core component to securing Exchange Server communications for production. In this section we will cover the following topics:

- Create a request
- How to import a certificate
- How to export a certificate
- How to enable a certificate
- How to disable a certificate
- How to assign the certificate to Exchange services
- How to report on active/inactive certificate

## Certificate PowerShell Cmdlets

Before diving into the certificates themselves, let's explore what cmdlets are available for the management of Exchange certificates:

```
Get-Command *ExchangeCertificate*
```

Or

```
Get-Command –Noun ExchangeCertificate
```

```
Name
----
Enable-ExchangeCertificate
Export-ExchangeCertificate
Get-ExchangeCertificate
Import-ExchangeCertificate
New-ExchangeCertificate
Remove-ExchangeCertificate
```

These cmdlets mimic the list of options discussed just prior.  Now, on to working with Certificates:

## Create a Request (New-CertificateRequest)

Creating a new request for a certificate requires some forethought before running PowerShell cmdlets to create a request for a new SSL certificate.  First, what names will be used on the certificate?  Will the certificate contain the bare minimum of two FQDNs for Exchange [AutoDiscover and the FQDN for all services]? Will the certificate require different names for internal and external services? Will it be a wildcard certificate? Or will each service name (OWA, ActiveSync, etc.) be spelled out as a separate name in the certificate?

To get a new certificate issued for an Exchange server, we can use the New-CertificateRequest to generate a request for a third party certificate. Using a self-signed certificate is not recommended for securing Exchange services. First, if we don't know how to use the cmdlet, using Get-Help for the cmdlet and adding the '-Examples' switch should be used, providing us with one relevant example:

```
Get-Help New-ExchangeCertificate –Examples
```

```
--------------------------- Example 1 ---------------------------
New-ExchangeCertificate -GenerateRequest -RequestFile "C:\Cert Requests\woodgrovebank.req"
-SubjectName "c=US,o=Woodgrove Bank,cn=mail.woodgrovebank.com" -DomainName
autodiscover.woodgrovebank.com,mail.fabrikam.com,autodiscover.fabrikam.com
```

For this example, the certificate needs to be stored on the C: drive of the server and have the following names on it:

- Autodiscover.BigCorp.com
- Mail.BigCorp.Com

Using the example as our model for the cmdlet, we should come up with this certificate request:

```
New-ExchangeCertificate -GenerateRequest -RequestFile "C:\Cert\Exchange-Mail.BigCorp.Com.req"
-DomainName Autodiscover.BigCorp.Com,Mail.BigCorp.Com
```

If the certificate request is successful, generate a text file that can be used with a third party to generate a certificate for Exchange:

```
-----BEGIN NEW CERTIFICATE REQUEST-----
MIID5zCCAs8CAQAwIzEhMBBGA1UEAwwYQXU0b2Rpc2NvdmUyLkJpZ0NvcnAuQ29t
MIIBIjANBgkqhkiG9w0BAQEFAAOCAQ8AMIIBCgKCAQEA1qEIAs8TycyU13Gio2K1
4eccXFcoSdPnmzdyqydnWcddQOSUdP7E0kGUg6INHTy7dizEgqdhMJkrQ9vR4mo+
4xHtL4h9wW0b48jvTU0DhM1ySB7CF9mw4/gvBAdgssJll4esDwhUvGny1Okfg1W5
uV3HmHingUBc7Wj0AfpIHJkiKFumzIQXw8tbYaEw1UC0yimQnn3zoUaLePNxISsp
xUUETJ9K7s1YOCk28n2NAJMvE/Iw0sdRw6FQdNa0IUE5aS0RijgT8tWwyJxcW1ic
z58rRUj6tcFCAJzyoYYWncE0+Itvx0Zz1P1EAEslzeYUBscbMXsP0IjdIGkqU/QP
BQIDAQABoIIBfTAaBgorBgEEAYI3DQIDMQwWCjYuMi45MjAwLjIwZQYJKwYBBAGC
NxUUMVgwUgIBBQwYMTYtUEFQLUVYMDEuMTYtUEFQLkxvY2FsDBMxNi1UQUBcMTYt
UEFQLUVYMDEkDCJNaWNyb3NvZnQuRXhjaGFuZ2UuU2UydmljZUhvc3QuZXhlMHIG
CisGAQQBgjcNAgIxZDBiAgEBHloATQBpAGMAcgBvAHMAbwBmAHQAIABSAFMAQQAg
AFMAQvBoAGEAbgBuAGUAbAAgAEMAcgB5AHAAdABvAGcAcgBhAHAAaABpAGMAIABQ
AHIAbwB2AGkAZABlAHIDAQAwgYMGCSqGSIb3DQEJDjF2MHQwDgYDUR0PAQH/BAQD
AgWgMDUGA1UdEQQuMCyCGEF1dG9kaXNjb3Z1ci5CaWdDb3JwLkNvbYIQTWFpbC5C
aWdDb3JwLkNvbTAMBgNUHRMBAf8EAjAAMB0GA1UdDgQWBBTqqqU1XnpCU7FKMH0k
/p1zYisq/zANBgkqhkiG9w0BAQUFAAOCAQEAjp9uQ6ZYEYxazSem+S3bMovy/5nF
cLKxtRZ1UvquvhyegtUIEY47XvycpTLkM49sP4KK1AeIL8+vIu92PjWr6YizZy84
EJmiE7AiWIo+ov0zyTTbY/BroNY4l+IrD4yH7BsQ0UqWd47saR53IM1W6EI1yejX
IekOcR2/7YrQNQ/CZ4YrMKWDdGq32CPuIdJjSsRI9RbPFqk6yxgnZZwcGfIR/DUs
hUjvxm+y6I/UXfuCHxA0TvJ13UzkrLqsGa3X4ccLORj983iIaHMFoRgnzEd+qUKj
3IG0qHM5QKNqET7gYW7CNdod3eYyIK956w1qHPp9p+zIidzL497bTz0ebg==
-----END NEW CERTIFICATE REQUEST-----
```

## Import Request (Import-ExchangeCertificate)

After the request has been created and the Certificate Authority you are using provides the certificate for you to import, importing the certificate is the next step. Exchange can import .cer, .crt, .der, .p12, or .pfx based certificates using the Import-ExchangeCertificate cmdlet.

The correct syntax for the command is the following:

```
Import-ExchangeCertificate -FileData ([Byte[]](Get-Content -Path "$Certificate" -Encoding Byte
-ReadCount 0))
```

> **Certificate Authority**
>
> Microsoft prefers that a third party Certificate Authority be used for the simple fact that all devices will be able to verify a certificate issued by a third party, whereas an internally generated certificate may only validate while the device is connected internally.

Which will give this as a result:

```
Thumbprint                                Services    Subject
----------                                --------    -------
A57A99759DA531A7AB85B5E953001979F8B0C398  IP.WS..     CN=16-TAP-EX01
```

If you do not know the name of the certificate file, a script can be written to read on one or more file types to handle that scenario:

```
$Certificates = Get-ChildItem c:\downloads\*.p7b
ForEach ($Certificate in $Certificates) {
    Write-Host "This script will now import $Certificate."
    Import-ExchangeCertificate -FileData ([Byte[]](Get-Content -Path $Certificate -Encoding Byte
    -ReadCount 0))
}
```

When run, the script will fine the correct file in the downloads directory and import it into Exchange:

```
This script will now import C:\Downloads\ex02.p7b.

Thumbprint                                          Services    Subject
----------                                          --------    -------
A57A99759DA531A7AB85B5E953001979F8B0C398            IP.WS..     CN=16-TAP-EX01
```

## Export Certificate (Export-ExchangeCertificate)

PowerShell also allows for exporting a certificate in Exchange 2016. Exporting the certificate provides for the ability to backup the existing installed certificate. Exporting the certificate also allows for a PFX version of the certificate to be created and then imported into another Exchange 2016 server via PowerShell or the EAC. An old certificate may also be exported and then removed from the server as way to clean up old certificates from Exchange. So how do we export a certificate?

Get-Help Export-ExchangeCertificate –Examples

```
------------------------------ Example 1 ------------------------------
Export-ExchangeCertificate -Thumbprint
5113ae0233a72fccb75b1d0198628675333d010e -FileName "C:\Data\HT cert.pfx"
-BinaryEncoded -Password (ConvertTo-SecureString -String 'P@ssw0rd1'
-AsPlainText -Force)
```

```
------------------------------ Example 2 ------------------------------
Export-ExchangeCertificate -Thumbprint
72570529B260E556349F3403F5CF5819D19B3B58 -Server Mailbox01 -FileName
"\\FileServer01\Data\Fabrikam.req"
```

For the example of exporting to a PFX, Example 1 above is exactly what we need. In this example we will export a non self-signed certificate. To export a certificate, to the PFX format, with a password of '3xch@ng31sb35t'. First we need the thuMBprint of the certificate to export. The search criteria is that the certificate cannot be a self-signed one as that one will not be assigned to any services like a third party certificate would be. Find all Exchange certificates:

Get-ExchangeCertificate

```
Thumbprint                                          Services    Subject
----------                                          --------    -------
82CBB184A50CB7B89209D04D3280C04146BE7268            IP.WS..     CN=16TAP.COM
549C4182CB7073B184A50CB7BE9FC39FEC726778            ....S..     CN=Microsoft Exchange Server Auth Certif
A57A99759DA531A7AB85B5E953001979F8B0C398            IP.WS..     CN=16-TAP-EX01
B892095CAD99E0855D04D328E9750C04146BE448            .......     CN=WMSvc-16-TAP-EX01
```

Filtered search:

Get-ExchangeCertificate | Where {$_.IsSelfSigned -ne $True}

Or

Get-ExchangeCertificate | Where {-Not $_.IsSelfSigned }

```
Thumbprint                                          Services    Subject
----------                                          --------    -------
82CBB184A50CB7B89209D04D3280C04146BE7268            IP.WS..     CN=16TAP.COM
```

This provides the thuMBprint needed for the next step which is the export cmdlet. Note the 'string' is the password secret:

Export-ExchangeCertificate -ThuMBprint 82CBB184A50CB7B89209D04D3280C04146BE7268 -FileName "c:\cert.pfx" -BinaryEncoded -Password (ConvertTo-SecureString -String 'c3rt123' -AsPlainText -Force)

Once exported, the PFX file can be stored safely or imported into another server.

## Enabling Certificates and Assigning Exchange Services

Exchange services are typically assigned to a certificate when it is enabled for Exchange usage with the Enable-ExchangeServices cmdlet. In some cases, additional Exchange services are added after a certificate is installed, for example - POP3 or IMAP4. This would require the assignment of the certificate to these newly enabled services (if a secure connection is needed). This would be accomplished in the same manner as the original Enable-ExchangeCertificate cmdlet. For example, if we have the ThuMBprint of the certificate (82CBB184A50CB7B89209D-04D3280C04146BE7268 from the above example), the additional services can be assigned as follows:

```
Enable-ExchangeCertificate -ThuMBprint 5113ae0233a72fccb75b1d0198628675333d010e -Services POP,IMAP
```

** **Note** ** *What is perhaps the hardest part of changing the assignment of some services is removing excess Exchange services assigned to a certificate. For example we have a scenario for removing services that are assigned to a certificate, the 'none' option for services would seem the appropriate answer. However, this option does not actually do anything. If this option is used for an Enable-ExchangeCertificate cmdlet, no service changes occur. All previously assigned services will remain. Microsoft's help for this states that "The values that you specify with this parameter are additive" and that "you can't remove the existing services." Which explains the results.*

If services need to be removed from a particular certificate, either change can be made in the EAC:

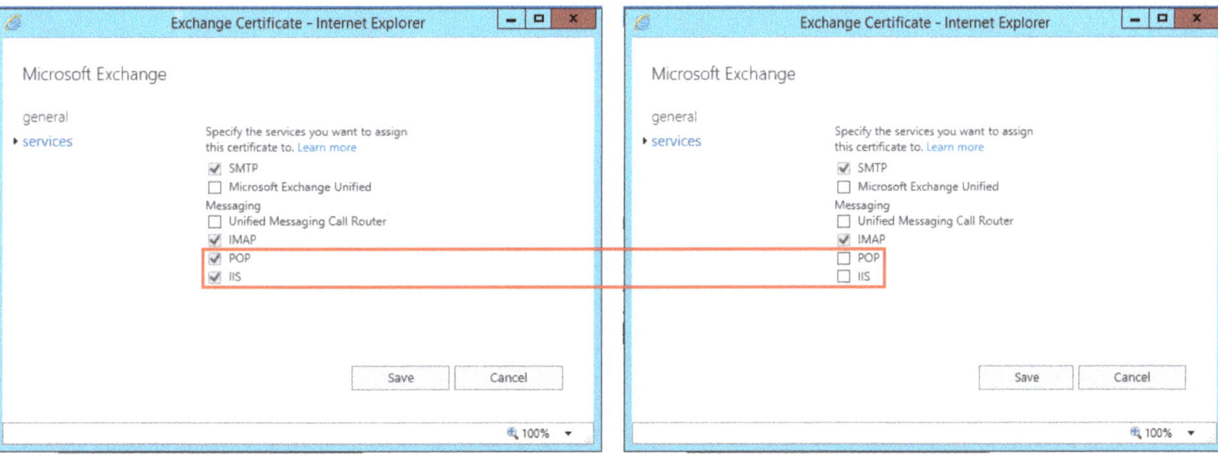


It's either that or use PowerShell to make sure a certificate is exported, removed, reimported and enabled for the correct services.

## Removing Certificate (Remove-ExchangeCertificate)

If a certificate needs to be removed, for example in the last example, or maybe removed for cleanup, the Remove-ExchangeCertificate can be used. CoMBining this cmdlet with the Get-ExchangeCertificate enabled for a quick removal of the certificate:

```
Remove-ExchangeCertificate -ThuMBprint 1AB65D6DFA6B2F6555B6977BF49DFC205BC88CC8

Confirm
Are you sure you want to perform this action?
Remove certificate with thumbprint 1AB65D6DFA6B2F6555B6977BF49DFC205BC88CC8 from the computer's certificate store?
[Y] Yes  [A] Yes to All  [N] No  [L] No to All  [?] Help (default is "Y"): a
```

### Server Certificate Report (Get-ExchangeCertificate)

As a maintenance task, PowerShell can be used to check for certificates installed on an Exchange server to see if the need to be cleaned up as names change and needed change.  For example, in the transition from certificates containing names not needed (Exchange 2010 CAS arrays) or internal names (domain.local).  Those old certificates tend to remain behind for a lot of Exchange installations.  Generating a report to determine if there are any old certificates, self-signed certificates and more could be generated:

```
Get-ExchangeCertificate | ft Subject, ThuMBprint, Services, Status, NotBefore, NotAfter, *Domains
-Auto
```

```
Subject                                         Thumbprint                                       Services        Status NotBefore               NotAfter
CN=Autodiscover.BigCorp.Com                     1AB65D6DFA6B2F6555B6977BF49DFC205BC88CC8             None PendingRequest 10/22/2016 6:22:59 PM 10/22/2017 6:42
CN=Microsoft Exchange Server Auth Certificate   549C4182CB7073B184A50CB7BE9FC39FEC726778             SMTP          Valid 7/6/2016 10:07:58 PM  6/10/2021 10:07
CN=16-TAP-EX01                                  A57A99759DA531A7AB85B5E953001979F8B0C398 IMAP, POP, IIS, SMTP          Valid 7/6/2016 10:02:57 PM  7/6/2021 10:02:
CN=WMSvc-16-TAP-EX01                            B892095CAD99E0855D04D328E9750C04146BE448             None          Valid 7/5/2016 5:51:02 PM   7/3/2026 5:51:0
```

The one-liner also can reveal pending requests that may or may not need to be completed.

# Exchange Virtual Directories

Exchange uses quite a few URLs in order for it to function correctly.  These URLs cover the following services:

- Outlook Web Access (OWA)
- Offline Address Book (OAB)
- MAPI over HTTP (MAPI)
- AutoDiscover
- Outlook Anywhere (OA)
- Web Services (EWS)
- Exchange Control Panel (and Exchange Administration Center) (ECP)
- ActiveSync (EAS)

In the previous section the names and options were discussed and in this section we'll configure those URLs as per the previous example.

### PowerShell Cmdlets for Virtual Directories

```
Get-Command *VirtualD*
```

Which provides a list of 54 cmdlets.  For the sake of this section, we only need the set-*virtualdirectory cmdlets:

```
Set-ActiveSyncVirtualDirectory            Set-OabVirtualDirectory
Set-AutodiscoverVirtualDirectory          Set-OutlookServiceVirtualDirectory
Set-ComplianceServiceVirtualDirectory     Set-OwaVirtualDirectory
Set-EcpVirtualDirectory                   Set-PowerShellVirtualDirectory
Set-LogExportVirtualDirectory             Set-RestVirtualDirectory
Set-MailboxDeliveryVirtualDirectory       Set-WebServicesVirtualDirectory
Set-MapiVirtualDirectory
```

## Brief Description of Exchange Virtual Directories

**ActiveSync Virtual Directory** – Aptly named, this virtual directory controls the connections made to Exchange 2016 for SmartPhone devices using the Active Sync Protocol.

**Exchange Control Panel (ECP) Virtual Directory** – This virtual directory is used for two items in Exchange (1) for OWA users it is their Options page where options within OWA can be configured (2) for administrators, this URL is used to load the Exchange Admin Center (EAC) for managing Exchange in a non PowerShell fashion.

**MAPI Virtual Directory** – Outlook uses this virtual directory if the Exchange organization is configured to use MAPI and the end users account is configured to use the protocol to connect to Exchange. MAPI over HTTP is the modern replacement for RPC over HTTP and Outlook Anywhere.

**Offline Address Book (OAB) Virtual Directory** – Where the Offline Address Book is published in IIS. Outlook uses web services to access the GAL using this URL. Older versions of Exchange used Public Folders up until this was devised and the web publishing method is now the only option for accessing the Offline Address Book.

**Outlook Web App (OWA)Virtual Directory** – Self explanatory, the OWA virtual directory allows access to a users mailbox from a browser.

**Web Services Virtual Directory** – The web services virtual directory is responsible for some hidden features of Exchange and it also needs to be configured for proper client operation. The Web Services directory (a.k.a. EWS) is used to provide a large swath of client services – Availability, Conversations, Delegation, Sharing, Inbox Rules, Mail Tips and more. Configuring this incorrectly will adversely affect end users by providing a terrible client experience.

## Configuring the Virtual Directories

The first settings that are changed on the virtual directories are the Internal and External URL that the clients will be connecting on. It is common to use the same base FQDN on all virtual directories for both Internal and External naming. However, this may not always be the case as a configuration will vary based on how many servers, locations affected and company access policies.

First, let's review the default configuration for these virtual directories. Below is a sample from the OWA and OAB directory, note the server name is listed in the description:

```
Name                                   InternalUrl                         ExternalUrl
----                                   -----------                         -----------
owa (Default Web Site)                 https://ex01.domain.com/owa
owa (Default Web Site)                 https://ex01.domain.com/owa

Name                                   InternalUrl                         ExternalUrl
----                                   -----------                         -----------
OAB (Default Web Site)                 https://ex01.domain.com/OAB
OAB (Default Web Site)                 https://ex01.domain.com/OAB
```

Next, we can build a script to adjust the virtual directories on the current server. This same script could then be copied to each server (maybe run from a central location) and used to configure all Exchange 2016 servers with one code set:

```
$FQDN = "Mail.BigCorp.Com"
$Server = $Env:ComputerName


Set-ActiveSyncVirtualDirectory -Identity "$Server\Microsoft-Server-ActiveSync (Default Web Site)"
-InternalURL https://$FQDN/Microsoft-Server-ActiveSync -externalurl https://$ FQDN /Microsoft-Server-
ActiveSync -Confirm:$False


Set-EcpVirtualDirectory -Identity "$Server\ecp (Default Web Site)" -InternalURL https://$FQDN/ecp
-Externalurl https://$FQDN/ecp -Confirm:$False


Set-MAPIVirtualDirectory -Identity "$Server\MAPI (Default Web Site)" -Internalurl https://$FQDN/MAPI
-Externalurl https://$FQDN/MAPI -Confirm:$False


Set-OabVirtualDirectory -Identity "$Server\OAB (Default Web Site)" -InternalURL https://$FQDN/oab
-Externalurl https://$FQDN/oab


Set-OWAVirtualDirectory -Identity "$Server\owa (Default Web Site)" -InternalURL https://$FQDN/owa
-Externalurl https://$FQDN/owa -Confirm:$False


Set-WebServicesVirtualDirectory -Identity "$Server\EWS (Default Web Site)" -InternalURL https://$FQDN/
ews/exchange.asmx -Externalurl https://$FQDN/ews/exchange.asmx -Confirm:$False
```

One URL that is not configured in the above script also needs to be completed. This is the URL for the AutoDiscover service. For that, the Set-ClientAccessService cmdlet must be used. And the parameter for AutoDiscover is 'AutoDiscoverServiceInternalUri'. Do not use the Set-AutoDiscoverVirtualDirectory.

```
Set-ClientAccessService –AutoDiscoverServiceInternalUri https://$FQDN/autodiscover/autodiscover.
xml
```

While running this script would be useful for a single server, or a couple of servers, what if there is a 16 node DAG in your corporate office and all 16 servers need the same settings, can a loop be leveraged for this as well? Of course:

```
$Servers = (Get-ExchangeServer).Name
$FQDN = "Mail.BigCorp.Com"
Foreach ($Server in $Servers) {
    Set-ActiveSyncVirtualDirectory -Identity "$Server\Microsoft-Server-ActiveSync (Default Web Site)"
    -InternalURL https://$FQDN/Microsoft-Server-ActiveSync -ExternalUrl https://$ FQDN /Microsoft-
    Server-ActiveSync -Confirm:$False
    Set-EcpVirtualDirectory -Identity "$Server\ecp (Default Web Site)" -InternalUrl https://$FQDN/ecp
    -ExternalUrl https://$FQDN/ecp -Confirm:$False
    Set-MAPIVirtualDirectory -Identity "$Server\MAPI (Default Web Site)" -InternalUrl https://$FQDN/
    MAPI -Externalurl https://$FQDN/MAPI -Confirm:$False
    Set-OabVirtualDirectory -Identity "$server\OAB (Default Web Site)" -InternalUrl https://$FQDN/oab
    -ExternalUrl https://$FQDN/oab
    Set-OWAVirtualDirectory -Identity "$Server\OWA (Default Web Site)" -InternalURL https://$FQDN/
    owa -Externalurl https://$FQDN/owa -Confirm:$False
    Set-WebServicesVirtualDirectory -Identity "$Server\EWS (Default Web Site)" -InternalUrl
    https://$FQDN/ews/exchange.asmx -ExternalUrl https://$FQDN/ews/exchange.asmx -Confirm:$False
}
```

From the script above we see that the URLs are all now uniform. However, what if the environment is more complex? Consider a medium side corporation that has five main datacenters with a DAG configured at each site for redundancy. Each of these DAGs has its own naming convention for its URLs. One way to handle this scenario is to filter the Exchange servers by site and apply site specific URLs.

First, we can store the site names in a variable to reference later. The names do not have to be the entire site name:

```
$Sites = "Corporate","Location02","Location03","Location04","Location05"
```

Then we begin the loop like the last example:

```
Foreach ($Site in $Sites) {
```

After that we need to get a list of Exchange servers in that site, which is a value we can filter by:

```
$Servers = Get-ExchangeServer | Where {$_.Site -Like "*$site*"}
```

Then, using the site name, we assign the FQDN to the $FQDN variable based on the site name. We need one line per site for this:

```
Switch($Site) {
   'Corporate' { $FQDN = 'mail.bigcorp.com'  }
   'Location02' { $FQDN = 'chicago.bigcorp.com'}
   'Location03' { $FQDN = 'newyork.bigcorp.com'}
   'Location04' { $FQDN = 'orlando.bigcorp.com'}
   'Location05' { $FQDN = 'dallas.bigcorp.com' }
}
```

Now that the FQDN is defined, the virtual directories can be configured just like the last script. Now the final script looks like this:

```
$Sites = "Corporate","Location02","Location03","Location04","Location05"
Foreach ($Site in $Sites) {
   $Servers = Get-ExchangeServer | Where {$_.Site -Like "*$site*"}
   Switch($Site) {
      'Corporate' { $FQDN = 'mail.bigcorp.com'  }
      'Location02' { $FQDN = 'chicago.bigcorp.com'}
      'Location03' { $FQDN = 'newyork.bigcorp.com'}
      'Location04' { $FQDN = 'orlando.bigcorp.com'}
      'Location05' { $FQDN = 'dallas.bigcorp.com' }
   }
   Set-ActiveSyncVirtualDirectory -Identity "$server\Microsoft-Server-ActiveSync (Default Web Site)"
   -InternalUrl https://$FQDN/Microsoft-Server-ActiveSync -ExternalUrl https://$ FQDN /Microsoft-
   Server-ActiveSync -Confirm:$False
   Set-EcpVirtualDirectory -Identity "$server\ecp (Default Web Site)" -InternalUrl https://$FQDN/ecp
   -externalUrl https://$FQDN/ecp -Confirm:$False
   Set-MAPIVirtualDirectory -Identity "$server\MAPI (Default Web Site)" -InternalUrl https://$FQDN/
   MAPI -ExternalUrl https://$FQDN/MAPI -Confirm:$False
   Set-OabVirtualDirectory -Identity "$server\OAB (Default Web Site)" -InternalUrl https://$FQDN/oab
   -ExternalUrl https://$FQDN/oab
```

```
    Set-OWAVirtualDirectory -Identity "$server\owa (Default Web Site)" -InternalUrl https://$FQDN/owa
    -ExternalUrl https://$FQDN/owa -Confirm:$False
    Set-WebServicesVirtualDirectory -Identity "$Server\EWS (Default Web Site)" -InternalURrl
    https://$FQDN/ews/exchange.asmx -ExternalUrl https://$FQDN/ews/exchange.asmx -Confirm:$False
}
```

Once completed, servers in each site will have their site related URLs configured.


# Client Access – OWA, Outlook Anywhere and MAPI over HTTP

End user access is key to a functional messaging system. This goes for Exchange servers as well. Access for clients comes in the form of OWA, EWS, Outlook and ActiveSync. For this chapter we will cover OWA, Outlook Anywhere and MAPI over HTTP. These items need to be configured before clients begin to connect to the Exchange 2016 servers.

### Outlook Web Access (OWA)

Of the protocols to configure for user access OWA is the easiest to configure. Configuring OWA consists of a name for the URL, a SSL certificate to secure communications between the browser and Exchange:

```
Get-command *owa*
```

```
Name
----
Get-OwaMailboxPolicy
Get-OwaVirtualDirectory
New-OwaMailboxPolicy
New-OwaVirtualDirectory
Remove-OwaMailboxPolicy
Remove-OwaVirtualDirectory
Set-OwaMailboxPolicy
Set-OwaVirtualDirectory
```

Previously we covered how to set the URL for the OWA directory. The OWA directory has quite a few options that can be configured, care needs to be taken as to which options are set because not all options will work for an on-premises Exchange 2016 server or parameters have been deprecated. For example:

```
    -DefaultClientLanguage <Int32> - This parameter has been deprecated and is no longer used.
    -OAuthAuthentication <$True | $False> - This parameter is reserved for internal Microsoft use.
```

Upon configuring a new server the typical setting changes on the OWA virtual directory are URL values (Internal and External), LogonFormat (Domain or user name only), AllowOfflineOn (For OWA Offline mode) and any Authentication changes (default is basic and FBA). Further customizations can be made in the form of changing parameters relating to what is displayed in OWA - Tasks, Themes, UM Integration and photos for example. Using the below one-liner we can set OWA to change the login from to just the user name instead of domain\username, turned off OWA Offline Mode and set the Authentication to just Basic.

```
    Set-OWAVirtualDirectory "EX01\OWA (Default Web Site)" –LogonFormat UserName –DefaultDomain
    Domain.Com –AllowOfflineOn NoComputers –Authentication Basic
```

** **Note** ** if the Authentication is changed, make sure to set the ECP Virtual Directory to the same authentication method as this controls the Options Page an end user would open to change OWA settings.

If these changes are required of multiple servers, we can again use a Foreach loop to craft a quick script like so:

```
$ExchangeServers = (Get-ExchangeServer).Name
Foreach ($Server in $ExchangeServers) {
    Set-OWAVirtualDirectory "$server\OWA (Default Web Site)" –LogonFormat UserName –
    DefaultDomain Domain.Com –AllowOfflineOn NoComputers –Authentication Basic
}
```

## Outlook Anywhere

Outlook Anywhere is a hold over from Exchange 2010 and Exchange 2013.  Outlook Anywhere provides for a secure SSL connection between Outlook and Exchange 2016.  Using Outlook Anywhere has simplified the setup and connection of Outlook with Exchange Server.  First, we can start with the PowerShell command available for Outlook Anywhere:

```
Get-Command *Any*
```

As you can see there are not a lot of cmdlets used to manage this.  So let's start with Get-OutlookAnywhere to see what settings are in place by default:

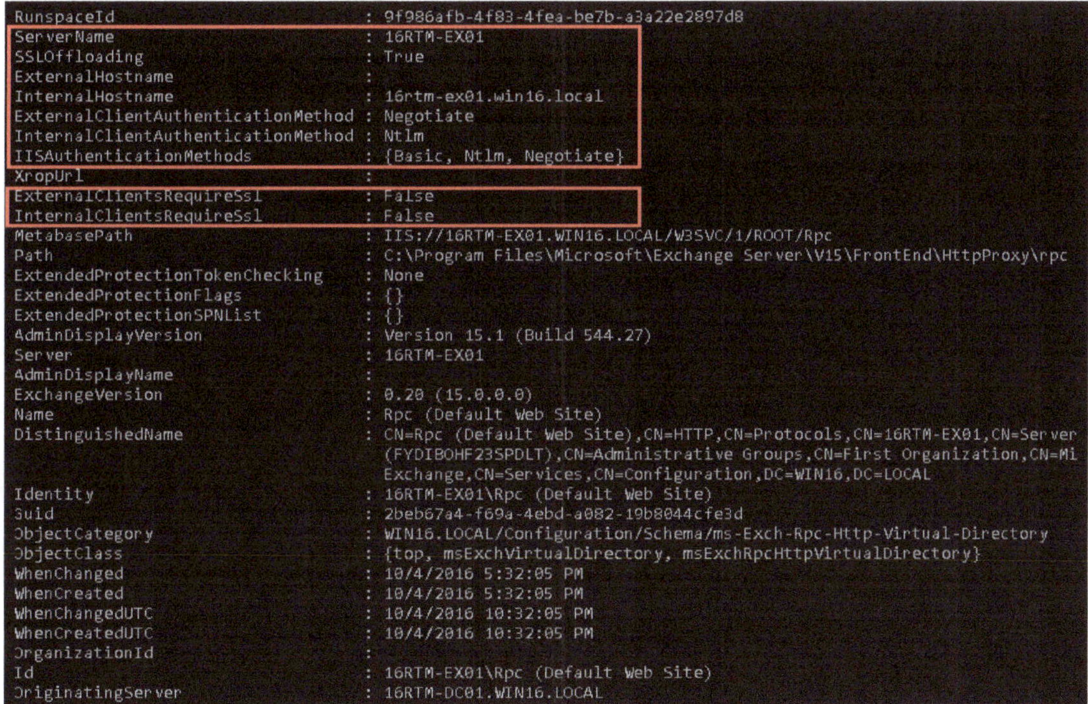


The settings enclosed in red rectangles are ones the will be customized to match your environment (shown below):

- SSLOffloading – used in conjunction with a loadbalancer that would handle SSL encoding and decoding
- ExternalHostname - External hostname for Outlook Anywhere
- InternalHostname - External hostname for Outlook Anywhere
- ExternalClientAuthenticationMethod – Authentication method for connecting to the external hostname
- InternalClientAuthenticationMethod– Authentication method for connecting to the internal hostname
- IISAuthenticationMethods – Authentication methods defined in IIS for the RPC Virtual Directory

- ExternalClientsRequireSsl – Require the use of SSL
- InternalClientsRequireSsl – Require the use of SSL

Now using the Set-OutlookAnywhere cmdlet, we can configure these settings:

```
Set-OutlookAnywhere –Server EX01 -SSLOffloading $False -ExternalHostname mail.domain.com
-InternalHostname mail.domain.com -ExternalClientsRequireSsl $True -InternalClientsRequireSsl $True
-ExternalClientAuthenticationMethod NTLM -InternalClientAuthenticationMethod NTLM
```

The above one-liner is good for a greenfield environment where no other versions of Exchange are involved, however, if Exchange 2013 or 2013 exist in the Exchange Organization, other steps may need to be taken, specifically with URLs and authentication methods.  The reason is that traffic will eventually be passed from Exchange 2016 to Exchange 2010 as client access features are transferred to Exchange 2016:

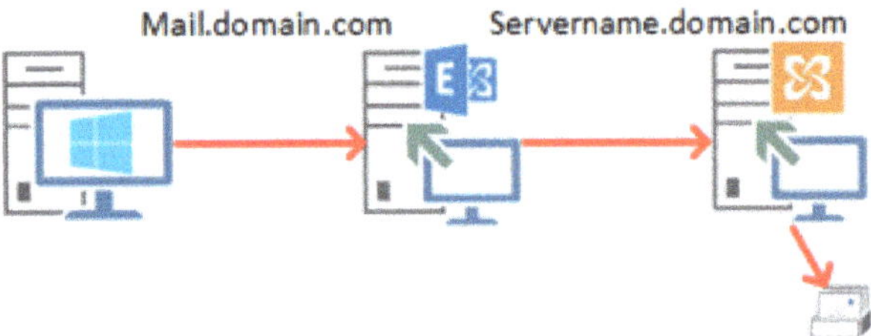


The major change in this architecture is that you no longer need to specify or create a legacy name space for the Exchange 2010 servers as Exchange 2016 will proxy requests back to Exchange 2010 based on the host name.  The communication is secured by the self-signed certificates.

If there are legacy servers, more than likely the Authentications methods will need to be changed to match and pass traffic back to the Exchange 2010 servers.  This will enable a smooth transition from 2010 to 2016 servers.


## MAPI over HTTP

MAPI over HTTP is the successor to Outlook Anywhere because Outlook Anywhere utilizes RPC communications in order to function.  RPC is a rather older protocol and inefficient as well.  Microsoft has decided to use standard HTTP(s) commands in order for Outlook to connect to Exchange 2016. While this has resulted in slightly higher traffic volumes between clients, it has also enabled the clients to communicate more efficiently and with a recognized standard (HTTP).

Let's explore what PowerShell cmdlets are available for MAPI over HTTP:

```
Get-Command *MAPI*
```

With MAPI, we are given over double the cmdlets to work with. Interestingly there are cmdlets for testing MAPI (Test-MAPIConnectivity) and removing MAPI (Remove-MAPIVirtualDirectory). As can be seen from just the names of the cmdlets, it is apparent that MAPI can be configured in a similar manner to OWA and ActiveSync as they are all Virtual Directories on Exchange 2016.

We can use 'Get-MapiVirtualDirectory' to get a sense of what can be configured for MAPI in Exchange:

```
RunspaceId                       : 781f39b3-38ff-4bbb-8221-73bd44ab14c6
IISAuthenticationMethods         : {Ntlm, OAuth, Negotiate}
MetabasePath                     : IIS://16-TAP-EX01.16-TAP.Local/W3SVC/1/ROOT/mapi
Path                             : C:\Program Files\Microsoft\Exchange Server\V15\FrontEnd\HttpProxy\mapi
ExtendedProtectionTokenChecking  : None
ExtendedProtectionFlags          : {}
ExtendedProtectionSPNList        : {}
AdminDisplayVersion              : Version 15.1 (Build 466.34)
Server                           : 16-TAP-EX01
InternalUrl                      : https://16-tap-ex01.16-tap.local/mapi
InternalAuthenticationMethods    : {Ntlm, OAuth, Negotiate}
ExternalUrl                      :
ExternalAuthenticationMethods    : {Ntlm, OAuth, Negotiate}
AdminDisplayName                 :
ExchangeVersion                  : 0.10 (14.0.100.0)
Name                             : mapi (Default Web Site)
DistinguishedName                : CN=mapi (Default Web Site),CN=HTTP,CN=Protocols,CN=16-TAP-EX01,CN=Serv
                                   Groups,CN=TAP,CN=Microsoft Exchange,CN=Services,CN=Configuration,DC=16-
Identity                         : 16-TAP-EX01\mapi (Default Web Site)
Guid                             : 6e579b30-eba1-4408-8b22-d28107f7d23f
ObjectCategory                   : 16-TAP.Local/Configuration/Schema/ms-Exch-Mapi-Virtual-Directory
ObjectClass                      : {top, msExchVirtualDirectory, msExchMapiVirtualDirectory}
WhenChanged                      : 7/6/2016 10:50:11 PM
WhenCreated                      : 7/6/2016 10:50:11 PM
WhenChangedUTC                   : 7/7/2016 3:50:11 AM
WhenCreatedUTC                   : 7/7/2016 3:50:11 AM
OrganizationId                   :
Id                               : 16-TAP-EX01\mapi (Default Web Site)
OriginatingServer                : 16-TAP-DC01.16-TAP.Local
IsValid                          : True
ObjectState                      : Changed
```

Similar to other virtual directories in Exchange 2016, the internal and external URLs as well as the internal and external authentications can be configured.

```
Set-MapiVirtualDirectory –Identity "16-TAP-EX01\MAPI (Default Web Site)" -ExternalUrl mail.
domain.com -InternalUrl mail.domain.com –ExternalAuthenticationMethods NTLM, OAuth –
InternalAuthenticationMethods NTLM, OAuth
```

Just like other URLs, the cmdlet can be placed in a loop and be applied to all servers.

MAPI is enabled by default in Exchange 2016. This setting can be verified with PowerShell:

```
Get-OrganizationConfig | ft *mapi*
```

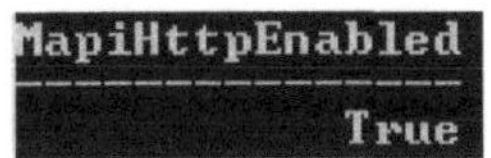



This can be disabled, but Microsoft has made it clear that MAPI over HTTP is the replacement for Outlook Anywhere.


# Databases

As part of the initial configuration of Exchange 2016 servers, additional databases will probably be needed before users are created on or migrated to the new servers. In order to facilitate this, there is a set of PowerShell cmdlets for database management. What are these cmdlets?

```
Get-Command *database*
```

Which provides us this list of cmdlets:

**NOTE** Two quirks in these cmdlets: Dismount-Database and Mount-Database instead of following the pattern of the other cmdlets with 'MailboxDatabase'.

## New Databases

Creating new databases can be done when the server is initially configured for user access or on an existing server that may need more databases due to higher usage or user counts. To create a database, we need the minimum information:

- Database Name
- Database File Location (EdbFilePath)
- Server Name

While those are the minimum requirements, the following should also be configured:

- Log Files Location (LogFolderPath)

Sample cmdlet with the above parameters:

```
New-MailboxDatabase –Name "DB01" –EdbFilePath "E:\Databases\DB01\DB01.edb" -LogFolderPath "F:\Logs\DB01" –Server Server01
```

The one-line above creates a new database called 'DB01' with the database file (.edb) located at E:\Databases\DB01\DB01.edb and the logs for the database stored in this directory - F:\Logs\DB01. There are other options that are useful when creating a new database:

- IsExcludedFromInitialProvisioning
- IsExcludedFromProvisioning
- IsSuspendedFromProvisioning

These parameters control how the database is to be used when a new mailbox is created. This is important because if a database resides on a disk that is becoming full, then you may not want new mailboxes placed in this database. Once a new database is created, remeMBer to restart the Information store service. The reason for this is that there was an architecture change that allows Exchange 2016 to optimize resources based on databases on a server:

```
Get-Service "Microsoft Exchange Information Store" | Restart-Service
```

## Removing Databases

Removing a database from Exchange can be done after all mailboxes have been removed from the database or if the database is simply not needed any more (all users are inactive). To remove a database we just need the name of the database:

```
Remove-MailboxDatabase –Identity "OldDatabase"
```

Make sure no user archive, arbitration, auditlog or system mailboxes are on that database. To check for mailboxes run these PowerShell one-liners:

```
Get-Mailbox -Database "<database name>"
Get-Mailbox -Database "<database name>" -Arbitration
Get-Mailbox -Database "<database name>" - Archive
Get-Mailbox -Database "<database name>" -Monitoring
Get-Mailbox -Database "<database name>" -Auditlog
```

Then once all mailboxes are moved, the database can be removed from the server.

** **Note** ** If the database is part of a DAG, all copies need to be removed first.

## Moving Databases

One use case for moving a database is to rename and relocate the default first database on an Exchange 2016 server. There are a couple of ways to handle the default database:

**(1) Rename, move database location and move log location.**

By making changes to the default database, this eliminates the need to move all system mailboxes, like the ones found above and should be done prior to any mailboxes are placed on the database. The reason is that during the move processes, the database is dismounted.

## Example

In this scenario, Exchange is installed on the C: Drive in the default directory. Thus the default database is located in this directory as well:

```
C:\Program Files\Microsoft\Exchange Server\V15\Mailbox\<default database>
```

The Exchange Server has two other drives, an E drive with 2 TB allocated for mailbox databases and an F drive with 500 GB allocated for Exchange database logs. To move the location of the database edb and logs files while also renaming the database, the following PowerShell cmdlets should be used:

```
Move-DatabasePath, Get-MailboxDatabase and Set-MailboxDatabase
```

First, moving log and database files use the first cmdlet to do so:

```
Move-DatabasePath –identity <default database>  –edbfilepath e:\databases\db01\database01.edb
–LogFolderPath "F:\logs\DB01"
```

This one-liner will prompt asking if you are sure this change is what you want:

```
Confirm
To perform the move operation, database"Mailbox Database 0576450030" must be temporarily dismounted,
which will make it inaccessible to all users. Do you want to continue?
[Y] Yes  [A] Yes to All  [N] No  [L] No to All  [?] Help (default is "Y"): y
```

After the database is moved, it can be renamed as well:

```
Get-MailboxDatabase –Identity <default database> | Set-MailboxDatabase –Name "DB01"
```

Now the default database has been renamed and placed at another location and ready for mailbox usage.

## (2) Moving System Mailboxes

The first database on an Exchange Server also contains system mailboxes that are used for internal processes. Note that using just the Get-Mailbox only reveals the Discovery Search Mailbox:

```
Name
----
Administrator
DiscoverySearchMailbox {D919BA05-46A6-415f-80AD-7E09334BB852}
```

However, there are other hidden mailboxes. Checking the help for the Get-Mailbox cmdlet:

    Get-Help Get-Mailbox –Full

We see that there is a couple of other switches that can show hidden system mailboxes. System mailboxes are used to perform many underlying functions for Exchange. These functions include eDiscovery Searches, Federation moderation with Office 365, mailbox move arbitration, moderation message holding (until approved) and Admin Audit logging.

- Arbitration – System Mailboxes
- Archive – would not be present on the default database when created
- Audit Log
- Monitoring – Healthcheck mailboxes

### Arbitration Mailboxes

    Get-Mailbox -Database <default database>  -Arbitration | ft Name, Alias -Auto

```
Name                                                 Alias
----                                                 -----
SystemMailbox{1f05a927-b837-44d3-98f1-4da7c4dfb39d}  SystemMailbox{1f05a927-b837-44d3-98f1-4da7c4dfb39d}
SystemMailbox{bb558c35-97f1-4cb9-8ff7-d53741dc928c}  SystemMailbox{bb558c35-97f1-4cb9-8ff7-d53741dc928c}
SystemMailbox{e0dc1c29-89c3-4034-b678-e6c29d823ed9}  SystemMailbox{e0dc1c29-89c3-4034-b678-e6c29d823ed9}
Migration.8f3e7716-2011-43e4-96b1-aba62d229136       Migration.8f3e7716-2011-43e4-96b1-aba62d229136
FederatedEmail.4c1f4d8b-8179-4148-93bf-00a95fa1e042  FederatedEmail.4c1f4d8b-8179-4148-93bf-00a95fa1e042
```

### Monitoring Mailboxes

    Get-Mailbox -Database <default database> -Monitoring | ft Name, Alias -Auto

```
Name                                             Alias
----                                             -----
HealthMailbox58d467eb6ad04993a08b5ebdfcd9c73f    HealthMailbox58d467eb6ad04993a08b5ebdfcd9c73f
HealthMailbox5d415ab7450045518cea8ce583d3d9a3    HealthMailbox5d415ab7450045518cea8ce583d3d9a3
HealthMailboxdfe6cbca500d4a14a9158ea396c53464    HealthMailboxdfe6cbca500d4a14a9158ea396c53464
HealthMailbox0c2bc0908e6048dba7b696844ea90831    HealthMailbox0c2bc0908e6048dba7b696844ea90831
HealthMailbox49e3b71f711c476c9a0a25f8c9b35d28    HealthMailbox49e3b71f711c476c9a0a25f8c9b35d28
HealthMailbox04a4183edd1146d38efa2bc5f8e80df7    HealthMailbox04a4183edd1146d38efa2bc5f8e80df7
HealthMailbox5296ccf13a804c499300ecb652ce40c8    HealthMailbox5296ccf13a804c499300ecb652ce40c8
HealthMailbox7e1a6c8115674c51ac0e62791da91538    HealthMailbox7e1a6c8115674c51ac0e62791da91538
HealthMailbox33e3882356f540d29aa849381d044c7c    HealthMailbox33e3882356f540d29aa849381d044c7c
HealthMailbox143cfeab318c489f9ec7fa107b59f512    HealthMailbox143cfeab318c489f9ec7fa107b59f512
HealthMailboxa07048b621b34c9dbf007d99dad598ad    HealthMailboxa07048b621b34c9dbf007d99dad598ad
HealthMailboxa645272c108e4295837dfcce17a7fcd8    HealthMailboxa645272c108e4295837dfcce17a7fcd8
HealthMailbox4b53dad7dc3a4ab48017218af16ae03a    HealthMailbox4b53dad7dc3a4ab48017218af16ae03a
HealthMailbox7f8f74049bc74022828e773c7c5fb63a    HealthMailbox7f8f74049bc74022828e773c7c5fb63a
HealthMailboxb5817f2cb8984685b06502dd7e66cd07    HealthMailboxb5817f2cb8984685b06502dd7e66cd07
HealthMailboxaeaa2b25830b436688533f5bb2aea06e    HealthMailboxaeaa2b25830b436688533f5bb2aea06e
HealthMailbox3d927c9183454a55ad5db24587affe9d    HealthMailbox3d927c9183454a55ad5db24587affe9d
```

**AuditLog Mailboxes**

Get-Mailbox -Database <default database> -AuditLog | ft Name, Alias -Auto

```
Name                                                  Alias

SystemMailbox{8cc370d3-822a-4ab8-a926-bb94bd0641a9}   SystemMailbox{8cc370d3-822a-4ab8-a926-bb94bd0641a9}
```

In order to delete the default database, these mailboxes would then need to be moved with the 'New-MoveRequest' cmdlet like so:

```
Get-Mailbox -Database db02 -Arbitration | New-MoveRequest -TargetDatabase db01
Get-Mailbox -Database db02 -Monitoring | New-MoveRequest -TargetDatabase db01
Get-Mailbox -Database db02 -AuditLog | New-MoveRequest -TargetDatabase db01
```

Once all the jobs are complete, then the database can be removed and the Move Requests removed.

```
Remove-MailboxDatabase –Identity <default database>
Get-MoveRequest | Remove-MoveRequest
```

**Example**

In the first example, the default database is moved to a new location and renamed. What if all 16 servers in a DAG needed the same treatment? Using the technique we have shown earlier, we will construct a Foreach loop around the existing cmdlets and adding a parameter for the server where the database is located:

```
$Servers = (Get-ExchangeServer).Name
Foreach ($Server in $Servers) {
    $Database = Get-MailboxDatabase –Server $Server
    Get-MailboxDatabase $Database | Set-MailboxDatabase –Name "$Server-DB01"
    Move-DatabasePath –Identity $Server –EdbFilePath e:\databases\$server-db01\$server-db0101.edb –LogFolderPath "F:\logs\$server-DB01"
}
```

Before and after the script was run:

```
[PS] C:\>get-mailboxdatabase

Name                             Server      Recovery       ReplicationType
----                             ------      --------       ---------------
Mailbox Database 0850444486      EX01        False          None
Mailbox Database 1615679643      EX02        False          None
Mailbox Database 0117931694      EX03        False          None


[PS] C:\>get-mailboxdatabase

Name                             Server      Recovery       ReplicationType
----                             ------      --------       ---------------
EX01-DB01                        EX01        False          None
EX02-DB01                        EX02        False          None
EX03-DB01                        EX03        False          None
```

Notice that just the name changed and the server name is incorporated into the database name now.

One caveat is that this assumes no other databases exist except the default databases exist, otherwise this will fail or cause havoc with the naming conventions. The script could be further enhanced with a filter based on the name of the database.

PowerShell code line before the change:

    $Database = Get-MailboxDatabase –Server $Server

Line modified to look for a specific name pattern:

    $Database = Get-MailboxDatabase –Server $Server | Where {$_.Name –Like 'Mailbox Database *'}

The pattern of 'Mailbox Database *' was chosen since all default databases follow this pattern.  The wildcard of '*' is used to cover the random nuMBers portion.


# Database Availability Group

A Database Availability Group (DAG) is the high availability feature for mailbox servers and databases.  A DAG is a type of clustering for Exchange 2016.  The feature was first introduced in Exchange 2010 as a much better form of high availability. This form of cluster is scalable up to 16 nodes and not all nodes need to have a copy of all databases.  Each node consists of a single Exchange 2016 server configured with Windows failover.

Creating a DAG requires a few steps:

- Install Exchange 2016 on two or more nodes (up to 16)
- Create mailbox databases
- Create the DAG in Exchange
- Create mailbox database copies

Now let's take a look at how we can manage DAG's with PowerShell.

**PowerShell**

There are quite a few PowerShell cmdlets for Database Availability Groups:

    Get-Command *databaseav*

```
Name
----
Add-DatabaseAvailabilityGroupServer
Get-DatabaseAvailabilityGroup
Get-DatabaseAvailabilityGroupConfiguration
Get-DatabaseAvailabilityGroupNetwork
New-DatabaseAvailabilityGroup
New-DatabaseAvailabilityGroupConfiguration
New-DatabaseAvailabilityGroupNetwork
Remove-DatabaseAvailabilityGroup
Remove-DatabaseAvailabilityGroupConfiguration
Remove-DatabaseAvailabilityGroupNetwork
Remove-DatabaseAvailabilityGroupServer
Restore-DatabaseAvailabilityGroup
Set-DatabaseAvailabilityGroup
Set-DatabaseAvailabilityGroupConfiguration
Set-DatabaseAvailabilityGroupNetwork
Start-DatabaseAvailabilityGroup
Stop-DatabaseAvailabilityGroup
```

## Creating a DAG

Creating a new Database Availability Group will require a few items to be successful in PowerShell:

- Name
- File Witness Server Name
- File Witness Server Directory Path
- IP Address (or not with IP Less DAGs)

A sample command that could be used to create a DAG is shown below:

```
New-DatabaseAvailabilityGroup -Name DAG01 -WitnessServer 16RTM-FS01 -WitnessDirectory C:\FSW
-DatabaseAvailabilityGroupIpAddresses 192.168.0.233
```

A DAG can be created without an IP (e.g. Administrative Access Point) using this one-line below:

```
New-DatabaseAvailabilityGroup -Name DAG01 -WitnessServer 16RTM-FS01 -WitnessDirectory C:\FSW
-DatabaseAvailabilityGroupIpAddresses ([System.Net.IPAddress]::None)
```

Once the DAG has been created successfully, we need to add some servers to the mix. Adding a node to the DAG will install the Windows Failover Service. To add these we can use the following cmdlet:

```
Add-DatabaseAvailabilityGroupServer
```

## Potential FSW Creation Issues

When creating a Database Availability Group, the creation of a File Share Witness is important. However, things can fail in the initial creation of the File Share Witness. This will not prevent the DAG from being created or servers from being added. However, a defective FSW share will prevent the cluster from working. If there is an issue populating the File Share Witness, the using the 'Set-DatabaseAvailabilityGroup' will need to be run to determine the error message:

```
Set-DatabaseAvailabilityGroup -Identity DAG01
```

Common errors that are found are permissions set on the fileshare are incorrect or that the fileshare could not be reached. The first requires a review of Microsoft's share requirements, match the permissions set on the share:

- Server with file share – Administrator Group – Add Exchange Trusted System
- File Share permissions – Exchange Trusted Subsystem has full control

Other items to check for the File Witness Server:

- Firewall
- DNS
- Domain MeMBership

To verify whether or not a FSW it being correctly used, the following one-liner provides information on the witness file share:

```
Get-DatabaseAvailabilityGroup -Identity dag01 -Status | fl *witness*
```

The desired result will look like this:

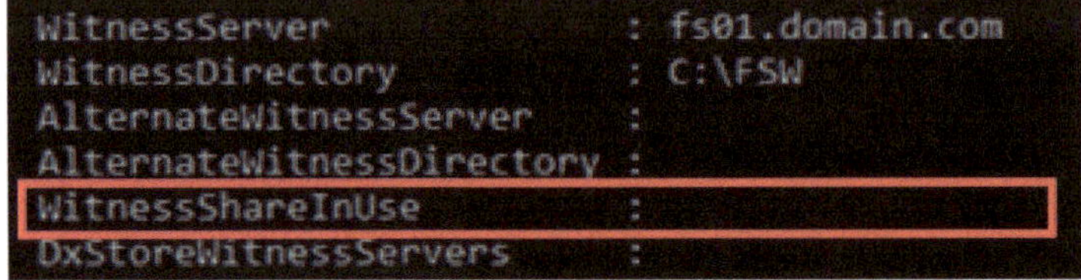

Bad results will look like this:

Or:

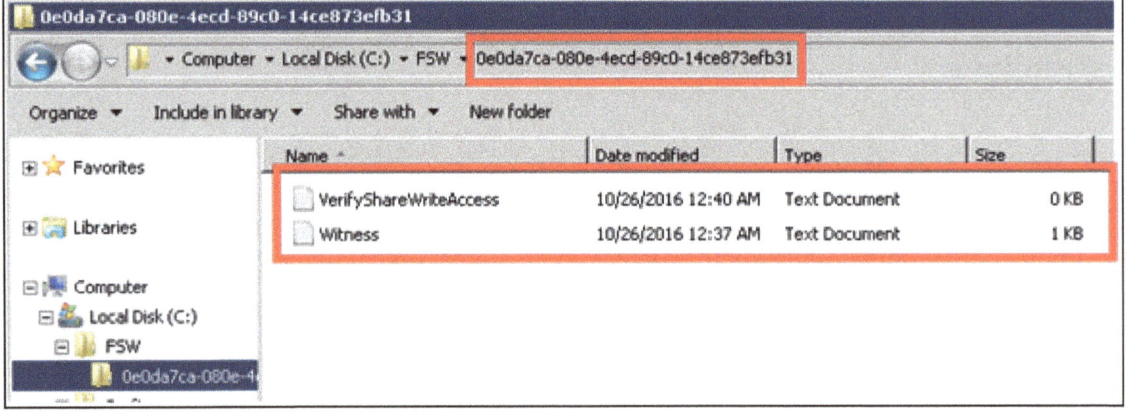

Once the File Share Witness is correctly configured, re-running the 'Set-DatabaseAvailabilityGroup -Identity <DAG Name>' which should reset the DAG and the DAG meMBers should have access and write to the file share. A sample FSW file directory is shown below:

## Removing a DAG

DAGs sometimes need to be removed from an Exchange environment. This could occur when a location is closed in a business or if DAG with a newer version of Exchange is being installed and the older one is no longer needed.

PowerShell will allow for removing the Database Availability Group. However, before a DAG can be removed, other items need to be removed first – mailboxes, databases, database copies and database servers.

## Example

To remove one node from a DAG, first we need to remove any database copies that exist on other nodes. In this sample environment, there are three Exchange servers in a DAG and each server has a database each of which has a copy on another server. The server names are EX01, EX02 and EX03. To remove a copy, the 'Remove-MailboxDatabaseCopy' cmdlet can be used in PowerShell to handle its removal.

First a list of copies for each database is needed:

Get-MailboxDatabase -Server EX01 | Get-MailboxDatabaseCopyStatus

```
ame                          Status
--                           ------
01-DB01\EX01                 Mounted
01-DB01\EX02                 Healthy
```

Once we have the names, we can remove one copy:

Remove-MailboxDatabaseCopy EX01-DB01\EX02

```
Confirm
Are you sure you want to perform this action?
Removing database copy for database "EX01-DB01" on server "EX02".
[Y] Yes  [A] Yes to All  [N] No  [L] No to All  [?] Help (default is "Y"): y
WARNING: The copy of mailbox database "EX01-DB01" on server "EX02" has been removed. If necessary, manuall
"C:\Program Files\Microsoft\Exchange Server\V15\Mailbox\Mailbox Database 0850444486" and "C:\Program File
0850444486\Mailbox Database 0850444486.edb" on that server.
```

This step should be repeated for all databases that contain additional copies in the DAG.

After all copies have been removed the next step is to remove each server from the DAG:

Remove-DatabaseAvailabilityGroupServer EX01

```
Confirm
Are you sure you want to perform this action?
Removing Mailbox server "EX01" from database availability group "DAG01".
[Y] Yes  [A] Yes to All  [N] No  [L] No to All  [?] Help (default is "Y"): y
```

Repeat this for each server in the DAG. Then, once all servers have been removed, the DAG can be removed from Exchange as well.

Remove-DatabaseAvailabilityGroup -Identity DAG01

```
Confirm
Are you sure you want to perform this action?
Removing database availability group "DAG01".
[Y] Yes  [A] Yes to All  [N] No  [L] No to All  [?] Help (default is "Y"): y
```

Now the Exchange servers are back to their original stand alone versions and not part of a highly available cluster.

# Address Lists

Address Lists are grouping of objects (mailboxes, groups, Rooms, etc.) that allows for the quick lookup of a certain type of recipient. The default groups in Exchange are All Contacts, All Distribution Lists, All Rooms, All Users and Public Folders. Each of these lists are constructed from a Recipient Filter. These addresses lists are entirely dynamic and change as objects are added and removed. These filters look something like this:

**All Contacts**
((Alias -ne $Null) -And (((ObjectCategory -Like 'Person') -And (ObjectClass -eq 'Contact'))))

**All Groups**
((Alias -ne $Null) -And (ObjectCategory -Like 'Group'))

Custom Address Lists are created in order to organize a group of users into a list based on a single criteria like office, country or maybe job title / function. Address Lists appear as a subset of the GAL for Outlook like this:

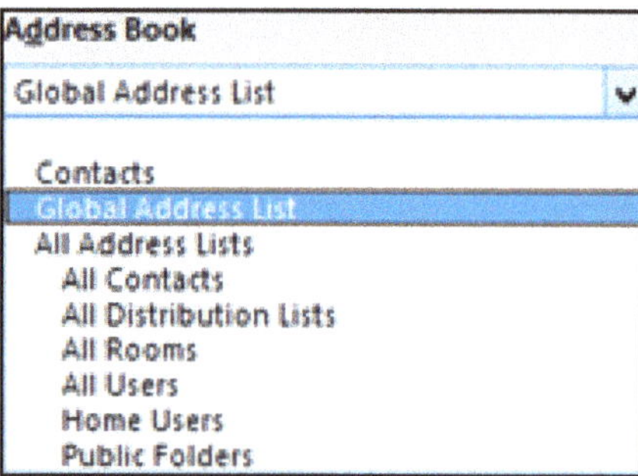


**PowerShell**

To manage the Address Lists, we need some PowerShell cmdlets:

```
Get-Command *addressl*
```

This provides a list of all cmdlets that deal with Address Lists:

```
Name
Get-AddressList
Get-GlobalAddressList
Move-AddressList
New-AddressList
New-GlobalAddressList
Remove-AddressList
Remove-GlobalAddressList
Set-AddressList
Set-GlobalAddressList
Update-AddressList
Update-GlobalAddressList
```

Using the Get-AddressList cmdlet, we should see the same Address lists that were displayed in Outlook:

```
Name                      DisplayName
All Contacts              All Contacts
All Distribution Lists    All Distribution Lists
All Rooms                 All Rooms
All Users                 All Users
Public Folders            Public Folders
```

The above lists are the default for Exchange installations. However, what if we wanted to add additional lists that were for a particular country, say Italy or Canada? How could a list be built to handle this? First, we would need to construct the appropriate RecipientFilter so that Exchange can look them up and insert them into the address list.

First, some examples from the cmdlet Help:

```
------------------------- Example 1 -------------------------
New-AddressList -Name MyAddressList -RecipientFilter {((RecipientType -eq 'MailboxUser') -and ((StateOrProvince
-eq 'Washington') -or (StateOrProvince -eq 'Oregon'))))
```

```
------------------------- Example 3 -------------------------
New-AddressList -Name "AL_AgencyB" -RecipientFilter {((RecipientType -eq 'MailboxUser') -and (CustomAttribute15
-like *AgencyB*)))
```

Now, one thing to remeMBer is that these recipient filters are constructed using an OPATH filter. A list of filterable properties can be found from Microsoft at this link - https://technet.microsoft.com/en-us/library/bb738157(v=-exchg.150).aspx

### Example – Custom Address List

For this example, an address needs to be created on a per country basis. The company that wants these lists has large groups of users in the United States, Poland, Sweden and India. Reviewing the list of criteria that is filterable for a recipient filter, we see that there are quite a few, but which ones will work? As it turns out, several will work just fine:

Co, Country and Country Code  The country of 'Unites States' populates these properties:

| Co | Country | CountryCode |
|---|---|---|
| United States | US | 840 |

What about the other countries on our list?

| | | |
|---|---|---|
| Poland | PL | 616 |
| Sweden | SE | 752 |
| India | IN | 356 |

> **TIP**
>
> Populating the 'Co' value (Country/Region on a user account) will also populate the corresponding value on the 'CountryCode' value.

Now that we have a list of codes, we can now build a simple OPATH query to look for only users with this information. We'll use the 'CountryCode' to build the Address List off of.

```
New-AddressList -Name "US Mailboxes" -RecipientFilter {((RecipientType -eq "UserMailbox") -And (CountryCode -eq "840"))}
```

For the Recipient Type, verify that the value is correct as the Example for the cmdlet is incorrect ('MailboxUser') and if a mailbox is checked for the correct Recipient type, we see that "UserMailbox" is the correct value to use. For the rest of the countries:

```
New-AddressList -Name "Poland Mailboxes" -RecipientFilter {((RecipientType -eq "UserMailbox") -and (CountryCode -eq "616"))}
New-AddressList -Name "Sweden Mailboxes" -RecipientFilter {((RecipientType -eq "UserMailbox") -and (CountryCode -eq "752"))}
New-AddressList -Name "India Mailboxes" -RecipientFilter {((RecipientType -eq "UserMailbox") -and (CountryCode -eq "356"))}
```

# Accepted Domains

Accepted domains are the SMTP domains that an Exchange server will accept email for. By default the only domain defined is the name of the Active Directory domain. For example, if the Active Directory domain is Corp. com, any mailbox created before custom or vanity domains are configured will get an email address:

**PowerShell**

    Get-Command *accepted*

```
Get-AcceptedDomain
New-AcceptedDomain
Remove-AcceptedDomain
Set-AcceptedDomain
```

Adding an accepted domain for routing email through Exchange is easy with the New-AcceptedDomain cmdlet. We just need the domain name and if it's authoritative:

    New-AcceptedDomain -DomainName BigBox.Com -DomainType Authoritative -Name BigBox

Notice that the domain is not set to the default, which would be needed to change the default domain from the current default to the correct external domain:

    Set-AcceptedDomain -Identity BigBox -MakeDefault $True

Other Domain types are 'ExternalRelay' and 'InternalRelay'. The ExternalRelay one allows emails to exit Exchange an be delivered to an Internet destination. While the InternalRelay type allows for only local relay, possibly to another internal mail server.

The Remove-AcceptedDomain cmdlet is useful for cleaning up old domains that may not be needed anymore or if, for example the migration is to Office365 and the domain is not yours and you do not control DNS.

    Remove-AcceptedDomain BigBox

```
Confirm
Are you sure you want to perform this action?
Removing Accepted Domain "BigBox".
[Y] Yes  [A] Yes to All  [N] No  [L] No to All  [?] Help (default is "Y"): a
```

# Putting It All Together

In this chapter we covered information relating to the setting up of a new server. Each piece had its own section, explanation and PowerShell scripting. Now what if we wanted to take all of the pieces above to create a script that would allow for the duplication of all settings. Doing so would save time in configuring a set of new servers and would ensure that the configuration was correct among all servers.

**Scenario**

You have been tasked with creating a 16 node DAG in the central datacenter for BigBox.Com network. All the nodes needs to be standardized in their configuration. A load balancer will be placed on front of all nodes to handle traffic routing to the 16 nodes in the DAG. Each server has 32 GB of RAM. The company's Windows Server team has installed Windows 2012 R2 and the latest approved patches on the server and have given you full control of the servers to install Exchange 2016.  After installing Exchange 2016 in the default configuration, you now need to configure all the servers in a standard fashion.

## Script Example

For this example, we will use code samples from above to create a cohesive configuration for all Exchange 2016 servers in the DAG.  Comments will be used in order to guide you as to what the script is doing for each code section:

```powershell
### Set variables for later use
$ExchangeServers = (Get-ExchangeServer).Name
$Logs = "Application","Server"
$FQDN = "mail.domain.com"


### Begin Foreach loop to configure each server
Foreach ($Server in $ExchangeServers) {
   ### Configure Pagefile ###
   $Stop = $False
   # Remove Existing Pagefile
   Try {
      Set-CimInstance -Query "Select * From Win32_ComputerSystem" -Property @
      {AutomaticManagedPagefile="False"}
   } Catch {
      $Stop = $True
   }
   Try {
      $RamInMB = (Get-CIMInstance -ComputerName $Name -ClassName Win32_PhysicalMemory
      -ErrorAction Stop | Measure-Object -Property Capacity -Sum).Sum/1GB
   } Catch {
      $Stop = $True
   }

   $ExchangeRAM = $RAMinMB + 10

   If ($Stop -ne $True) {
      Try {
         Set-CimInstance -Query "Select * From Win32_PagefileSetting" -Property @
         {InitialSize=$ExchangeRAM;MaximumSize=$ExchangeRAM}
      } Catch {
         Write-Host "Cannot configure the Pagefile correctly." -ForegroundColor Red}
         $Pagefile = Get-CimInstance Win32_PagefileSetting -Property * | Select-Object
         Name,InitialSize,MaximumSize
         $Name = $Pagefile.Name
         $Max = $Pagefile.MaximumSize
         $Min = $Pagefile.InitialSize
      }
   }
```

```
### Configure Event Logs ###
# Configure each event log (from $Logs) with the same settings
Foreach ($Log in $Logs) {
    Limit-EventLog  –ComputerName  $Server  –LogName  $Log  –RetentionDays  7  –MaximumSize
    100MB –OverFlowAction OverWriteAsNeeded
}

### Import certificate for all servers (IISRESET included) ###
Import-ExchangeCertificate -Server $Server -FileName"\\DC01\Cert\Exchange2016.pfx" -Password
(ConvertTo-SecureString -String '3xch@ng31sb35t' -AsPlainText -Force)

# URL Information ###
Set-ActiveSyncVirtualDirectory -Identity "$Server\Microsoft-Server-ActiveSync (Default Web Site)"
-InternalUrl https://$FQDN/Microsoft-Server-ActiveSync -ExternalUrl https://$FQDN/Microsoft-
Server-ActiveSync -Confirm:$False

Set-EcpVirtualDirectory -Identity "$Server\ecp (Default Web Site)" -InternalURL https://$FQDN/ecp
-externalurl https://$FQDN/ecp -Confirm:$False

Set-MAPIVirtualDirectory -Identity "$Server\MAPI (Default Web Site)" -InternalURL https://$FQDN/
MAPI -ExternalURL https://$FQDN/MAPI -Confirm:$False

Set-OabVirtualDirectory -Identity "$Server\OAB (Default Web Site)" -InternalUrl https://$FQDN/oab
-ExternalUrl https://$FQDN/oab

Set-OWAVirtualDirectory -Identity "$Server\owa (Default Web Site)" -InternalUrl https://$FQDN/owa
-ExternalUrl https://$FQDN/owa -Confirm:$False

Set-WebServicesVirtualDirectory -Identity "$Server\EWS (Default Web Site)" -InternalUrl https://$FQDN/ews/
exchange.asmx -ExternalURL https://$FQDN/ews/exchange.asmx -Confirm:$False

# Configure Outlook Anywhere ###
Set-OutlookAnywhere –Server $Server -SSLOffloading $False -ExternalHostName mail.domain.com
-InternalHostName  mail.domain.com  -ExternalClientsRequireSsl  $True  -InternalClientsRequireSsl
$True -ExternalClientAuthenticationMethod NTLM -InternalClientAuthenticationMethod NTLM
}
```

With this one PowerShell script we have a standard configuration for all existing servers and it can be modified for a single new server as well:

**Old line**

```
$ExchangeServers = (Get-ExchangeServer).Name
```

**New Line**

```
$ExchangeServers = 'NewExchange01"
```

# 7    Server Management

**In This Chapter**

- Patch Management
- Starting and Stopping Services
- Database Management
- Verifying Backups
- Circular Logging
- Monitoring Disk Space
- Command Logging
- Offline Address Book

Installing your first Exchange 2016 server is just the beginning of your adventures when it comes to supporting Microsoft's latest and greatest messaging platform.  Once the server is patched, next comes users asking for features and connections and the like.  Then it's your boss with his requirements and his boss' business requirements.  All of this leads to one place.  Management.

Now you have your shiny new Exchange 2016 server.  It's configured.  Users are connecting.  Your boss is getting his or her reports.  All of the old legacy servers are gone.  Now you can work on managing Exchange 2016.  Tasks such as backups, database management, patching, tweaking and patching are key as are troubleshooting and fixing issues that occur with daily usage by your end users.

This chapter will cover maintenance of Exchange 2016 using PowerShell.  Tips and script provided will be practical and real world vetted.  We will cover things like database management, services, back-ups and Offline Address Books.

# Patch Management

Keeping your Exchange 2016 servers up to date is an important task that should be performed on a regular basis, as not patching could leave your server vulnerable or without a properly working feature.  Keeping up to date is even more important if your Exchange 2016 servers are running in a Hybrid environment as Microsoft requires that your servers remain within N-1, with N being the most current version.  With the current release cycle for Exchange Server, with the CU releases being every three months or so, your servers need to be updated every three to six months depending on your current version of Exchange when running in a hybrid Exchange 2016 server.

Updating servers should be a planned event, some Cumulative Updates have Active Directory updates, in case there are any issues with the newest Exchange Update Rollup.  There is no uninstall option either for Cumulative Updates for Exchange 2016.  Planning should include:

- **Proper Change Management** – one to two weeks before patch is applied
- **Proper Backups** – full backups with your backup software's Exchange agent
- **Support plan** – phone tree if needed

Other factors to take into consideration are what servers are to be patched first?  A first target for patching should be a lightly used server or a server in the DR site.  If the choice is between Edge and Mailbox, Mailbox servers should be updated first because if a mailbox server is down, the Edge Transport server can queue the email until it can be delivered.  If an Edge server will be down for a long time, the email could timeout and generate an NDR (for external emails).

When choosing a server to update, you must consider the architecture of the environment. Below is a sample decision check on which server to patch first:

- **Disaster Recovery Site** – Ideal to patch a server from here first
- **Secondary (or passive node)** – Passive is good as it will have less users, possibly limiting High Availability
- **Single Server** – No choice, only that node

Once the update has been tested, it would be advisable to patch Mailbox servers first, then Edge Transport servers.

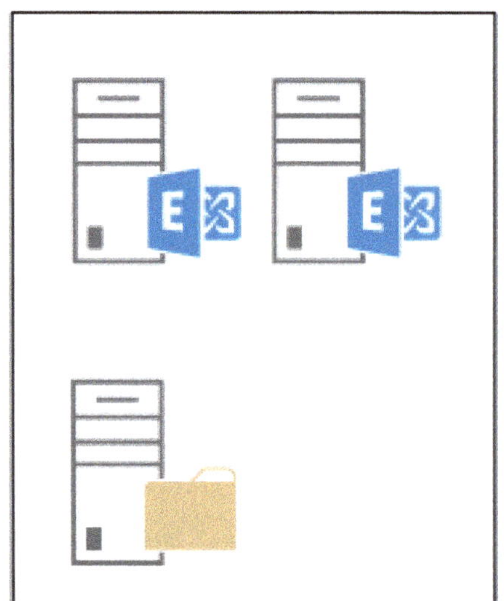

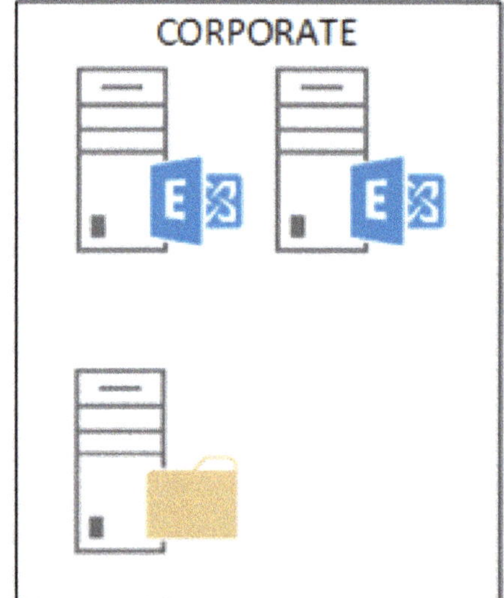


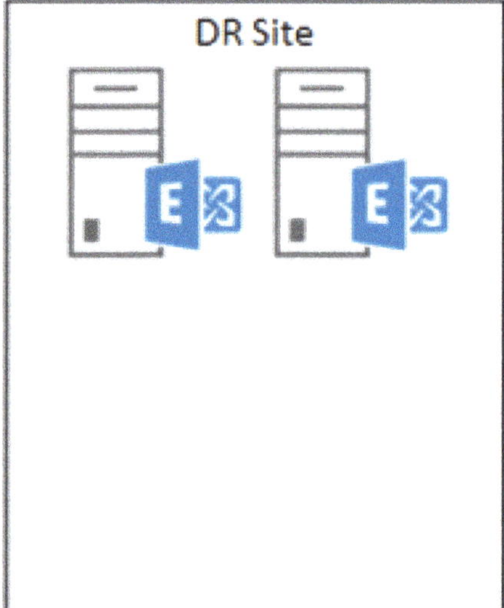


**Figure 1** - Single Site/Multiple Servers        **Figure 2** - Multiple Servers and Sites

For Figure 1, one server would be picked to test the updates on in order to validate the update is successful, while in Figure 2, one server from DR should be chosen first.  If the update is successful, then the other DR server would be next, followed by the two in the Corporate office.  Upgrade one, reboot, validate operation and then update the last server.

Using Microsoft's guidance for putting Exchange into maintenance mode, the script was built and enhanced.  The script is to be used in a multi Exchange server environment.

## Microsoft's Guidance on Exchange Server Patching:

https://blogs.technet.microsoft.com/nawar/2014/03/30/exchange-2013-maintenance-mode

# Start Maintenance

First, we will save the current server's FQDN in a variable called $CurrentServer, along with the domain (for constructing a FQDN:

```
# Current Server
$Domain = $Env:UserDNSDomain
$CurrentServer= $Env:ComputerName+"."+$Domain
```

Then a target server which will take over some functionality needs to be defined. In this script block, PowerShell will look for the first server to not match the current server's name. This server name is stored in a variable and the loop is exited with the 'Break' cmdlet. The Break prematurely exits the loop as we don't want PowerShell to loop through all servers that are not the current server:

```
#Remote Server

$Target = (Get-ExchangeServer).Name

Foreach ($Line in $Target) {
   if ($Line -ne $CurrentServer) {
      $TargetFQDN = $Line+"."+$Domain
      Break # Exit this loop with first non-match
   }
}
```

In the below section, each step is taken to put the server in maintenance mode. First the Hub Transport component is set to draining which will drain the SMTP queues so no messages are stuck during maintenance mode. The second component 'ServerWideOffline' managed all server components and sets them all to inactive in one one-liner:

```
# Script Body

Set-ServerComponentState $CurrentServer -Component HubTransport -State Draining -Requester
Maintenance
Set-ServerComponentState $CurrentServer -Component ServerWideOffline -State Inactive -Requester
Maintenance
```

## Reference

https://blogs.technet.microsoft.com/exchange/2013/09/26/server-component-states-in-exchange-2013

Then SMTP messages bound for the server to be patched are redirected at a different server:

```
Redirect-Message -Server $CurrentServer -Target $TargetFQDN -Confirm:$False
```

Next, services are restarted in order to make these changes effective:

```
Restart-Service MSExchangeTransport
Restart-Service MSExchangeFrontEndTransport
```

Suspending DAG operations – if the servers are not in a DAG, either remove the lines or comment them out with '#' in the front.

```
Suspend-ClusterNode $CurrentServer
Set-MailboxServer $CurrentServer -DatabaseCopyActivationDisabledAndMoveNow $True
Get-MailboxServer $CurrentServer | Select DatabaseCopyAutoActivationPolicy
Set-MailboxServer $CurrentServer -DatabaseCopyAutoActivationPolicy Blocked
```

Lastly, the components we put offline earlier are brought out of maintenance mode:

```
Set-ServerComponentState $CurrentServer -Component ServerWideOffline -State Inactive -Requester Maintenance
Get-ServerComponentState $CurrentServer | ft Component,State –AutoSize
```

When all is done a visual indicator is provided:

```
Write-Host "The server $CurrentServer is ready to update." -ForegroundColor Yellow
```

A sample run-through of setting maintenance mode up so that patches and updates can be applied:

```
WARNING: Waiting for service 'Microsoft Exchange Transport (MSExchangeTransport)' to start...
WARNING: Waiting for service 'Microsoft Exchange Frontend Transport (MSExchangeFrontEndTransport)' to start...

Name                    ID    State
----                    --    -----
16-TAP-EX01             2     Paused

DatabaseCopyAutoActivationPolicy : Unrestricted


Component                     State
---------                     -----
ServerWideOffline             Inactive
HubTransport                  Inactive
FrontendTransport             Inactive
Monitoring                    Active
RecoveryActionsEnabled        Active
AutoDiscoverProxy             Inactive
ActiveSyncProxy               Inactive
EcpProxy                      Inactive
EwsProxy                      Inactive
ImapProxy                     Inactive
OabProxy                      Inactive
OwaProxy                      Inactive
PopProxy                      Inactive
PushNotificationsProxy        Inactive
RpsProxy                      Inactive
RwsProxy                      Inactive
RpcProxy                      Inactive
UMCallRouter                  Inactive
XropProxy                     Inactive
HttpProxyAvailabilityGroup    Inactive
ForwardSyncDaemon             Inactive
ProvisioningRps               Inactive
MapiProxy                     Inactive
EdgeTransport                 Inactive
HighAvailability              Inactive
SharedCache                   Inactive
MailboxDeliveryProxy          Inactive
RoutingUpdates                Inactive
RestProxy                     Inactive
DefaultProxy                  Inactive
```

## Stop Maintenance Mode

Once the patches and Cumulative Updates have been applied, you may need to reboot the Exchange server. Then, when the reboot cycle completes, there are further steps that must be taken to reverse the maintenance mode the Exchange Server is placed in. Here is a sample script to handle this functionality:

First, the current server's FQDN needs to be saved in a variable called $CurrentServer (just like the script that was used to put the server in maintenance mode):

```
# Current Server
$Domain = $Env:UserDNSDomain
$CurrentServer= $Env:ComputerName+"."+$Domain
```

Then server components are brought out of maintenance mode:

```
# DAG or Not
Set-ServerComponentState $CurrentServer -Component ServerWideOffline -State Active -Requester
Maintenance
```

A DAG only section which resets some settings for servers who are DAG members and it does not apply to single servers or server not in a DAG:

```
# DAG Reset
Resume-ClusterNode $CurrentServer
Set-MailboxServer $CurrentServer -DatabaseCopyActivationDisabledAndMoveNow $False
Set-MailboxServer $CurrentServer -DatabaseCopyAutoActivationPolicy Unrestricted
Set-ServerComponentState $CurrentServer -Component HubTransport -State Active -Requester
Maintenance
```

Then services are restarted in order to make these changes:

```
# Reset services to get new settings
Restart-Service MSExchangeTransport
Restart-Service MSExchangeFrontEndTransport
```

As a final check, the script can change the component state of any component that is not Active to be Active:

```
#Final Check
$Component = (Get-ServerComponentState $CurrentServer | Where {$_.State -ne 'Active'}).Component
Foreach ($Line in $Component) {
    Set-ServerComponentState $CurrentServer -Component $Line -State Active -Requester Maintenance
}
```

Last, but not least, the script will show what components are active. If all are active, then the server should be good to go. If there are any non-active components, it warrants a check and review:

```
# Check if maintenance mode is over
Get-ServerComponentState $CurrentServer | ft Component,State –AutoSize
```

The script above, based off of Microsoft's guide, yet it has a couple of customizations that can be added is a check to see if the server is part of a DAG. If it is not, then skip the code section in the middle. First, we will query the Exchange Organization for servers belonging to DAGs:

```
$DAGServer = (Get-DatabaseAvailabilityGroup).Servers
```

We can then check to see if the $DAGServer variable is empty, meaning no DAGs are present. If DAGS are present PowerShell will continue (the variable will contain data), if not, it will skip the DAG section of the script:

```
If ($DAGServer -ne $Null) {
```

If there is a DAG, then we can cycle through each member of the DAG to see if the current server is a member:

```
Foreach ($Member in $DAGServer) {
    If ($CurrentServer -eq $Member) {
```

Once the correct server is found, the script then executes the code under the '# DAG Reset' comment as shown above.

A sample run-through of the script shows what removing maintenance mode would look like:

```
WARNING: Waiting for service 'Microsoft Exchange Transport (MSExchangeTransport)' to stop...
WARNING: Waiting for service 'Microsoft Exchange Transport (MSExchangeTransport)' to stop...
WARNING: Waiting for service 'Microsoft Exchange Transport (MSExchangeTransport)' to stop...
WARNING: Waiting for service 'Microsoft Exchange Transport (MSExchangeTransport)' to stop...
WARNING: Waiting for service 'Microsoft Exchange Transport (MSExchangeTransport)' to start...
WARNING: Waiting for service 'Microsoft Exchange Transport (MSExchangeTransport)' to start...
WARNING: Waiting for service 'Microsoft Exchange Transport (MSExchangeTransport)' to start...
WARNING: Waiting for service 'Microsoft Exchange Frontend Transport (MSExchangeFrontEndTransport)' to start...
```

At the end of the script all components appear to be active on the server once more:

```
Component                        State
---------                        -----
ServerWideOffline                Active
HubTransport                     Active
FrontendTransport                Active
Monitoring                       Active
RecoveryActionsEnabled           Active
AutoDiscoverProxy                Active
ActiveSyncProxy                  Active
EcpProxy                         Active
EwsProxy                         Active
ImapProxy                        Active
OabProxy                         Active
OwaProxy                         Active
PopProxy                         Active
PushNotificationsProxy           Active
RpsProxy                         Active
RwsProxy                         Active
RpcProxy                         Active
UMCallRouter                     Active
XropProxy                        Active
HttpProxyAvailabilityGroup       Active
ForwardSyncDaemon                Active
ProvisioningRps                  Active
MapiProxy                        Active
EdgeTransport                    Active
HighAvailability                 Active
SharedCache                      Active
MailboxDeliveryProxy             Active
RoutingUpdates                   Active
RestProxy                        Active
DefaultProxy                     Active
```

# Starting and Stopping Exchange Services

One of the more practical scripts for managing Exchange Server 2016 is one that will start and / or stop the services on an Exchange Server. This can be done via scripting, one for stopping and one for starting. If the need arises a menu could be constructed to either stop or start the services. First, a set of services is needed in order to proceed.

## Mailbox Server

To get a list of services with Microsoft Exchange in the name, a quick one-liner will do:

```
Get-Service -DisplayName "microsoft ex*" | ft -Auto
```

```
Status   Name                          DisplayName
------   ----                          -----------
Running  HostControllerService         Microsoft Exchange Search Host Controller
Running  MSComplianceAudit             Microsoft Exchange Compliance Audit
Running  MSExchangeADTopology          Microsoft Exchange Active Directory Topology
Running  MSExchangeAntispamUpdate      Microsoft Exchange Anti-spam Update
Running  MSExchangeCompliance          Microsoft Exchange Compliance Service
Running  MSExchangeDagMgmt             Microsoft Exchange DAG Management
Running  MSExchangeDelivery            Microsoft Exchange Mailbox Transport Delivery
Running  MSExchangeDiagnostics         Microsoft Exchange Diagnostics
Running  MSExchangeEdgeSync            Microsoft Exchange EdgeSync
Running  MSExchangeFastSearch          Microsoft Exchange Search
Running  MSExchangeFrontEndTransport   Microsoft Exchange Frontend Transport
Running  MSExchangeHM                  Microsoft Exchange Health Manager
Running  MSExchangeHMRecovery          Microsoft Exchange Health Manager Recovery
Stopped  MSExchangeImap4               Microsoft Exchange IMAP4
Stopped  MSExchangeIMAP4BE             Microsoft Exchange IMAP4 Backend
Running  MSExchangeIS                  Microsoft Exchange Information Store
Running  MSExchangeMailboxAssistants   Microsoft Exchange Mailbox Assistants
Running  MSExchangeMailboxReplication  Microsoft Exchange Mailbox Replication
Stopped  MSExchangeNotificationsBroker Microsoft Exchange Notifications Broker
Stopped  MSExchangePop3                Microsoft Exchange POP3
Stopped  MSExchangePOP3BE              Microsoft Exchange POP3 Backend
Running  MSExchangeRepl                Microsoft Exchange Replication
Running  MSExchangeRPC                 Microsoft Exchange RPC Client Access
Running  MSExchangeServiceHost         Microsoft Exchange Service Host
Running  MSExchangeSubmission          Microsoft Exchange Mailbox Transport Submission
Running  MSExchangeThrottling          Microsoft Exchange Throttling
Running  MSExchangeTransport           Microsoft Exchange Transport
Running  MSExchangeTransportLogSearch  Microsoft Exchange Transport Log Search
Stopped  MSExchangeUM                  Microsoft Exchange Unified Messaging
Running  MSExchangeUMCR                Microsoft Exchange Unified Messaging Call Router
Stopped  wsbexchange                   Microsoft Exchange Server Extension for Windows Server Backup
```

There are two ways to gather the names of the services in order to use it. Construct a CSV file to import:

```
$Services = Import-CSV "ExchangeSTOPServices.csv"
```

or query for the names of the services on the fly, in PowerShell and store the service names in a variable:

```
$Services = (Get-Service -DisplayName "microsoft ex*").Name
```

There is one problem with the above cmdlet and that is the fact that services that are set to 'Manual' and not Automatic, will also be started, which is not ideal. In order to work around this, the Get-CIMObject cmdlet can be used to filter for the same criteria as the Get-Service cmdlet, while adding the 'StartUpMode' criteria:

```
Get-CIMInstance Win32_Service | Where {$_.DisplayName -Match "microsoft ex*"} | Where {$_.
StartMode -eq 'Auto'} | ft Name,Startmode,State
```

```
name                           startmode state
----                           --------- -----
HostControllerService          Auto      Running
MSComplianceAudit              Auto      Running
MSExchangeADTopology           Auto      Running
MSExchangeAntispamUpdate       Auto      Running
MSExchangeCompliance           Auto      Running
MSExchangeDagMgmt              Auto      Running
MSExchangeDelivery             Auto      Running
MSExchangeDiagnostics          Auto      Running
MSExchangeEdgeSync             Auto      Running
MSExchangeFastSearch           Auto      Running
MSExchangeFrontEndTransport    Auto      Running
MSExchangeHM                   Auto      Running
MSExchangeHMRecovery           Auto      Running
MSExchangeIS                   Auto      Running
MSExchangeMailboxAssistants    Auto      Running
MSExchangeMailboxReplication   Auto      Running
MSExchangeNotificationsBroker  Auto      Stopped
MSExchangeRepl                 Auto      Running
MSExchangeRPC                  Auto      Running
MSExchangeServiceHost          Auto      Running
MSExchangeSubmission           Auto      Running
MSExchangeThrottling           Auto      Running
MSExchangeTransport            Auto      Running
MSExchangeTransportLogSearch   Auto      Running
MSExchangeUM                   Auto      Stopped
MSExchangeUMCR                 Auto      Running
```

```
$Services = (Get-CIMInstance Win32_Service | Where {$_.DisplayName -Match "microsoft ex*"} | Where {$_.StartMode -eq 'auto'}).Name
```

## Stop All Exchange Services (Non-Edge)

As can be seen by the screenshot below, stopping services requires that they be done in the correct order:

```
Stop-Service : Cannot stop service 'Microsoft Exchange Active Directory Topology
(MSExchangeADTopology)' because it has dependent services. It can only be stopped if the Force
flag is set.
At line:1 char:1
+ Stop-Service MSExchangeADTopology
+ ~~~~~~~~~~~~~~~~~~~~~~~~~~~~~~~~~~
    + CategoryInfo          : InvalidOperation: (System.ServiceProcess.ServiceController:ServiceCo
   ntroller) [Stop-Service], ServiceCommandException
    + FullyQualifiedErrorId : ServiceHasDependentServices,Microsoft.PowerShell.Commands.StopServic
   eCommand
```

## Sample Code

The first code iteration uses a CSV file which is not ideal, but more of an exercise in the capabilities of PowerShell. First, the services are stored in a CSV file, which was created prior to the running this script. The script will then loop through each entry and stop the services in order.

## Iteration #1 – Using a CSV File

```
$Services = Import-CSV "ExchangeSTOPServices.csv"
Foreach ($Line in $Services) {
  $Service = $Line.Service
  If ($Service -ne "MSExchangeADTopology") {
    Try {
      Stop-Service -Name $Service -ErrorAction STOP
    } Catch {
```

```
        Write-Host "Unable to stop the $Service" -ForegroundColor Red
      }
    } Else {
      Try {
        Stop-Service -Name $Service -ErrorAction STOP -Force
      } catch {
        Write-Host "Unable to stop the $service" -ForegroundColor Red
      }
    }
    Write-Host "The $service is now stopped." -ForegroundColor Cyan
  }
```

This version builds the list of services dynamically and the stops them based on the dynamic list:

**Iteration #2 – Using Variables**

```
$Services = (Get-CIMInstance Win32_Service | Where {$_.DisplayName -Match "microsoft ex*"} | Where {$_.StartMode -eq 'Auto'}).Name

Foreach ($Service in $Services) {

  If ($Service -ne "MSExchangeADTopology") {
    Try {
      Stop-Service -Name $Service -ErrorAction STOP
    } Catch {
      Write-Host "Unable to stop the $Service" -ForegroundColor Red
    }
  }
  Write-Host "The $Service is now stopped." -ForegroundColor Cyan
}

# Stop just the Exchange Active Directory Topology
Try {
  Stop-Service -Name "MSExchangeADTopology" -ErrorAction STOP -force
  Write-Host "The MSExchangeADTopology is now stopped." -ForegroundColor Cyan
} Catch {
  Write-Host "Unable to stop the MSExchangeADTopology" -ForegroundColor Red
}
```

# Start All Exchange Services (Non-Edge)

Now, with starting the services, the Exchange Active Directory Topology service needs to be started first due to other services depending on it.  One other criteria, is that only services that are set to Automatic start will be started as the services with a startup mode of manual were mostly likely not needed. Taking the code sample above for stopping the services, a similar script for starting services can be constructed like so:

**Iteration #1 - CSV File**

```powershell
$Services = (Get-Service -DisplayName "microsoft ex*").Name

Foreach ($Service in $Services) {
  Try {
    Start-Service -Name $Service -ErrorAction STOP
  } Catch {
    Write-Host "The $Service is could not be started." -ForegroundColor Red
  }
  Write-Host "The $Service is now started." -ForegroundColor Cyan
}
```

**Iteration #2 - Variable**

```powershell
$Services = (Get-CIMInstance Win32_Service | Where {$_.DisplayName -Match "microsoft ex*"} | Where {$_.StartMode -eq 'Auto'}).Name

Foreach ($Service in $Services) {
  try {
    Start-Service -Name $Service -ErrorAction STOP
  } catch {
    Write-Host "The $Service is could not be started." -ForegroundColor Red
  }
    Write-Host "The $Service is now started." -ForegroundColor Cyan
}
```

**Sample Run Through**

```
PS C:\> .\StartServices.ps1
WARNING: Waiting for service 'Microsoft Exchange Active Directory Topology (MSExchangeADTopology)' to start...
The MSExchangeADTopology is now started.
The MSExchangeAntispamUpdate is now started.
WARNING: Waiting for service 'Microsoft Exchange Compliance Service (MSExchangeCompliance)' to start...
WARNING: Waiting for service 'Microsoft Exchange Compliance Service (MSExchangeCompliance)' to start...
WARNING: Waiting for service 'Microsoft Exchange Compliance Service (MSExchangeCompliance)' to start...
The MSExchangeCompliance is now started.
WARNING: Waiting for service 'Microsoft Exchange DAG Management (MSExchangeDagMgmt)' to start...
The MSExchangeDagMgmt is now started.
WARNING: Waiting for service 'Microsoft Exchange Mailbox Transport Delivery (MSExchangeDelivery)' to start...
WARNING: Waiting for service 'Microsoft Exchange Mailbox Transport Delivery (MSExchangeDelivery)' to start...
WARNING: Waiting for service 'Microsoft Exchange Mailbox Transport Delivery (MSExchangeDelivery)' to start...
WARNING: Waiting for service 'Microsoft Exchange Mailbox Transport Delivery (MSExchangeDelivery)' to start...
The MSExchangeDelivery is now started.
WARNING: Waiting for service 'Microsoft Exchange Diagnostics (MSExchangeDiagnostics)' to start...
WARNING: Waiting for service 'Microsoft Exchange Diagnostics (MSExchangeDiagnostics)' to start...
WARNING: Waiting for service 'Microsoft Exchange Diagnostics (MSExchangeDiagnostics)' to start...
WARNING: Waiting for service 'Microsoft Exchange Diagnostics (MSExchangeDiagnostics)' to start...
The MSExchangeDiagnostics is now started.
WARNING: Waiting for service 'Microsoft Exchange EdgeSync (MSExchangeEdgeSync)' to start...
The MSExchangeEdgeSync is now started.
The MSExchangeFastSearch is now started.
WARNING: Waiting for service 'Microsoft Exchange Frontend Transport (MSExchangeFrontEndTransport)' to start...
WARNING: Waiting for service 'Microsoft Exchange Frontend Transport (MSExchangeFrontEndTransport)' to start...
WARNING: Waiting for service 'Microsoft Exchange Frontend Transport (MSExchangeFrontEndTransport)' to start...
WARNING: Waiting for service 'Microsoft Exchange Frontend Transport (MSExchangeFrontEndTransport)' to start...
The MSExchangeFrontEndTransport is now started.
WARNING: Waiting for service 'Microsoft Exchange Health Manager (MSExchangeHM)' to start...
WARNING: Waiting for service 'Microsoft Exchange Health Manager (MSExchangeHM)' to start...
WARNING: Waiting for service 'Microsoft Exchange Health Manager (MSExchangeHM)' to start...
The MSExchangeHM is now started.
The MSExchangeHMRecovery is now started.
WARNING: Waiting for service 'Microsoft Exchange IMAP4 (MSExchangeImap4)' to start...
WARNING: Waiting for service 'Microsoft Exchange IMAP4 (MSExchangeImap4)' to start...
```

** **Note** ** In the above Start and Stop scripts, notice that one service is getting special treatment.  As mentioned above this service is what all the other Exchange Server services are dependent on.  How do we know this?  Its dependent services can be discovered with PowerShell:

Get-Service -DisplayName "microsoft e*" | ft DisplayName,DependentServices

```
DisplayName                                          DependentServices
-----------                                          -----------------
Microsoft Exchange Search Host Controller            {}
Microsoft Exchange Compliance Audit                  {}
Microsoft Exchange Active Directory Topology         {MSExchangeUMCR, MSExchangeUM, MSExchangeTransportLogSea...
Microsoft Exchange Anti-spam Update                  {}
Microsoft Exchange Compliance Service                {}
Microsoft Exchange DAG Management                    {}
Microsoft Exchange Mailbox Transport Delivery        {}
Microsoft Exchange Diagnostics                       {}
Microsoft Exchange EdgeSync                          {}
Microsoft Exchange Search                            {}
Microsoft Exchange Frontend Transport                {}
Microsoft Exchange Health Manager                    {}
Microsoft Exchange Health Manager Recovery           {}
Microsoft Exchange IMAP4                             {}
Microsoft Exchange IMAP4 Backend                     {}
Microsoft Exchange Information Store                 {}
Microsoft Exchange Mailbox Assistants                {}
Microsoft Exchange Mailbox Replication               {}
Microsoft Exchange Notifications Broker              {}
Microsoft Exchange POP3                              {}
Microsoft Exchange POP3 Backend                      {}
Microsoft Exchange Replication                       {}
Microsoft Exchange RPC Client Access                 {}
Microsoft Exchange Service Host                      {}
Microsoft Exchange Mailbox Transport Submission      {}
Microsoft Exchange Throttling                        {}
Microsoft Exchange Transport                         {}
Microsoft Exchange Transport Log Search              {}
Microsoft Exchange Unified Messaging                 {}
Microsoft Exchange Unified Messaging Call Router     {}
Microsoft Exchange Server Extension for Windows Server B... {}
```

## Edge Transport Server

Now taking the same path we took on Mailbox Servers to handle an Edge Transport Server, a PowerShell one-liner needs to be run to get an idea what Exchange Server services are running on an Edge Transport server:

Get-CIMInstance Win32_Service | Where {$_.DisplayName -Match "microsoft ex*"} | Where {$_.StartMode -eq 'Auto'} | ft Name,Startmode,State

```
name                          startmode state
----                          --------- -----
ADAM_MSExchange               Auto      Running
MSExchangeAntispamUpdate      Auto      Running
MSExchangeDiagnostics         Auto      Running
MSExchangeEdgeCredential      Auto      Stopped
MSExchangeHM                  Auto      Running
MSExchangeHMRecovery          Auto      Running
MSExchangeServiceHost         Auto      Running
MSExchangeTransport           Auto      Running
MSExchangeTransportLogSearch  Auto      Running
```

Notice that there are a lot less services on an Edge Transport Server.   Also of note is that just like the Exchange Mailbox servers, there is a service that a lot of services are dependent on.  On the Edge server, it is the Microsoft Exchange ADAM service:

Get-Service -DisplayName "microsoft e*" | ft DisplayName,DependentServices

```
PS C:\> get-service -DisplayName "microsoft e*"  |ft displayname,dependentservices

DisplayName                                DependentServices
-----------                                -----------------
Microsoft Exchange ADAM                    {MSExchangeTransportLogSearch, MSExchangeTransport, MSEx...
Microsoft Exchange Anti-spam Update        {}
Microsoft Exchange Diagnostics             {}
Microsoft Exchange Credential Service      {}
Microsoft Exchange Health Manager          {}
Microsoft Exchange Health Manager Recovery {}
Microsoft Exchange Service Host            {}
Microsoft Exchange Transport               {}
Microsoft Exchange Transport Log Search    {}
```

Now, on to the task at hand.  Can the code that is used for Stopping and Starting services on a Mailbox Server be reused for the Edge Transport server?  Yes and no.  Stopping services needs to be modified so that the Topology services is exchanged for the ADAM service. Otherwise the stop AND start scripts are the same.

## STOP Services

**Sample Code**

```
$Services = (Get-CIMInstance Win32_Service | Where {$_.DisplayName -Match "microsoft ex*"} | Where {$_.Startmode -eq 'Auto'}).Name

Foreach ($Service in $Services) {

   If ($Service -ne "ADAM_MSExchange") {
     Try {
        Stop-Service -Name $Service -ErrorAction STOP
     } Catch {
        Write-Host "Unable to stop the $Service" -ForegroundColor Red
     }
   }
   Write-Host "The $Service is now stopped." -ForegroundColor Cyan
}

# Stop just the Exchange ADAM Service
Try {
   Stop-Service -Name "ADAM_MSExchange" -ErrorAction STOP -Force
   Write-Host "The ADAM_MSExchange is now stopped." -ForegroundColor Cyan
} Catch {
   Write-Host "Unable to stop the ADAM_MSExchange" -ForegroundColor Red
}
```

## Sample run of the script

```
The ADAM_MSExchange is now stopped.
The MSExchangeAntispamUpdate is now stopped.
The MSExchangeDiagnostics is now stopped.
The MSExchangeEdgeCredential is now stopped.
The MSExchangeHM is now stopped.
The MSExchangeHMRecovery is now stopped.
The MSExchangeServiceHost is now stopped.
WARNING: Waiting for service 'Microsoft Exchange Transport (MSExchangeTransport)' to stop...
The MSExchangeTransport is now stopped.
The MSExchangeTransportLogSearch is now stopped.
WARNING: Waiting for service 'Microsoft Exchange ADAM (ADAM_MSExchange)' to stop...
The ADAM_MSExchange is now stopped.
```

## START Services

### Sample Code

```
$Services = (Get-CIMInstance Win32_Service | Where {$_.DisplayName -Match "microsoft ex*"} | Where {$_.StartMode -eq 'Auto'}).Name

Foreach ($Service in $Services) {
  Try {
     Start-Service -Name $Service -ErrorAction STOP
  } Catch {
     Write-Host "The $Service is could not be started." -ForegroundColor Red
  }
  Write-Host "The $Service is now started." -ForegroundColor Cyan
}
```

# Database Management

Databases require maintenance, monitoring and more.  In this section we'll cover some ways to use PowerShell scripting management of those databases.

### Unhealthy Databases

Let's take a scenario where there are databases that are having issues.  How do we generate a quick report that can provide meaningful information on the databases?

### Script Code

First, we need to set some counters for Mounted, Healthy and Unhealthy database copies.

```
# Setting up counters for later
$Mounted=0
$Healthy=0
$UnHealthy=0
```

Descriptive line for user information:

```
 Write-Host "Checking database copies for ones that are in a 'failed' state........" -ForegroundColor Yellow
```

Next, we check the databases to see of any copies are unhealthy or unmounted:

```
$DatabaseCheck = Get-MailboxDatabase | Get-MailboxDatabaseCopyStatus | Where {($_.Status -ne "Mounted") -And ($_.Status -ne "Healthy")}
```

Start a loop, first part is if no unhealthy or unmounted databases were found:

```
If ($DatabaseCheck -eq $Null) {
```

This section is informational, informing

```
Write-Host "All database copies are 'healthy' or 'mounted'.  " -ForegroundColor Green -NoNewLine
Write-Host "There is no need for remediation." -ForegroundColor White
$DatabaseCheck2 = Get-MailboxDatabase | Get-MailboxDatabaseCopyStatus
```

Next another loop is started to count out the number of healthy and mounted databases:

```
Foreach ($Line in $DatabaseCheck2) {
    $Status = $Line.Status
    If ($Status -eq "Mounted") {$Mounted++}
    If ($Status -eq "Healthy") {$Healthy++}
}
```

Then these numbers are reported to the console:

```
Write-Host "Mounted database copies - " -ForegroundColor Cyan –NoNewLine
Write-Host "$Mounted" -ForegroundColor White
Write-Host "Healthy database copies - " -ForegroundColor Cyan –NoNewLine
Write-Host "$Healthy" -ForegroundColor White
$Total = $Healthy+$Mounted+$UnHealthy
Write-Host "------------------------------"
Write-Host "Total database copies   - " -ForegroundColor Cyan –NoNewLine
Write-Host "$Total" -ForegroundColor White
```

In this code section, any copies found are assumed to be unhealthy as that was the criteria defined before the loop:

```
} Else {
    Write-Host " "
    Write-Host "These database copies were found to be in an unhealthy state:" -ForegroundColor Cyan
    Write-Host " "
    Foreach ($Line in $DatabaseCheck) {
        $Name = $Line.Name
        $Status = $Line.Status
        Write-Host "The database copy " -ForegroundColor White -NoNewLine
        Write-Host "$name " -ForegroundColor red -NoNewLine
        Write-Host "is in a " -ForegroundColor white -NoNewLine
        Write-Host "$Status" -ForegroundColor Red -NoNewLine
        Write-Host " state.  Please remediate this as soon as possible." -ForegroundColor Yellow
        $UnHealthy++
}
```

Now, any database that did not have issue will be recorded in two variables - $Mounted and $Healthy:

```
Write-Host " "
Write-Host "Verifying how many copies are healthy" -ForegroundColor Yellow
Write-Host " "
$DatabaseCheck2 = Get-MailboxDatabase | Get-MailboxDatabaseCopyStatus
Foreach ($Line in $DatabaseCheck2) {
    $Status = $Line.Status
    If ($Status -eq "Mounted") {$Mounted++}
```

```
        If ($Status -eq "Healthy") {$Healthy++}
    }
```

In this section, a report is generated contain stats on how many healthy, mounted and unhealthy databases are:

```
        Write-Host "Unhealthy database copies - " -ForegroundColor Red -NoNewLine;
        Write-Host "$UnHealthy" -ForegroundColor White
        Write-Host "Mounted database copies - " -ForegroundColor Cyan -NoNewLine
        Write-Host "$Mounted" -ForegroundColor White
        Write-Host "Healthy database copies - " -ForegroundColor Cyan -NoNewLine
        Write-Host "$Healthy" -ForegroundColor White
        $Total = $Healthy+$Mounted+$UnHealthy
        Write-host "-----------------------------"
        Write-host "Total database copies  - " -ForegroundColor Cyan -NoNewLine
        Write-host "$total" -ForegroundColor White
        Write-host " "
    }
```

Putting this all together and run this on an Exchange Organization with issues and we see the results are concise:

```
Checking database copies for ones that are in a 'failed' state.......

These database copies were found to be in an unhealthy state:
The database copy DB01\EX03 is in a ServiceDown state.  Please remediate this as soon as possible.
The database copy DB02\EX03 is in a ServiceDown state.  Please remediate this as soon as possible.
The database copy DB03\EX03 is in a ServiceDown state.  Please remediate this as soon as possible.
The database copy DB16\EX03 is in a ServiceDown state.  Please remediate this as soon as possible.
The database copy DB17\EX03 is in a ServiceDown state.  Please remediate this as soon as possible.
The database copy DB18\EX03 is in a ServiceDown state.  Please remediate this as soon as possible.
The database copy DB19\EX03 is in a ServiceDown state.  Please remediate this as soon as possible.
The database copy DB20\EX03 is in a ServiceDown state.  Please remediate this as soon as possible.

Verifying how many copies are healthy

Unhealthy database copies - 22
Mounted database copies - 21
Healthy database copies - 12
-----------------------------
Total database copies  - 55
```

# Database Content Indexes

A database content index is used for client searches and its current state is important to end users.  The same is true for administrators as the content indexes on databases facilitate eDiscovery searches.  If the indexes are in a failed state, both the eDiscovery searches and client's searches will experience issues.

## How to check for a failed index? And fix it!

Exchange provides a couple of ways to check for corrupt indexes on databases.  One is to use the Exchange Admin Center or PowerShell.  With PowerShell we can check all databases at once versus only one at a time in the EAC.

**Example**

In this scenario, we have a medium environment of three servers and a few databases per server. Occasionally you've noticed that these databases have failed indexes and they need to be fixed. Instead of using the EAC to do this every time, we need to use PowerShell to handle this operation.

First we need to check a database for a failed index. How do we see this? Does the Get-MailboxDatabase cmdlet reveal any Index information? We can check by running this cmdlet:

```
Get-MailboxDatabase | ft Name,*index*
```

Unfortunately, this cmdlet shows only the database names and no index information:

```
Name
----
EX01-DB01
EX02-DB01
EX03-DB01
```

With a bit of research we find that Get-MailboxDatabaseCopyStatus will provide for the health of the content indexes:

```
Get-MailboxDatabaseCopyStatus | ft Name,ContentIndexState
```

```
Name                              ContentIndexState
----                              -----------------
EX02-DB01\EX02                              Healthy
```

This provides only the local database Content Index State. What if we need all of the Content Index States for all mailbox databases? What if we can pipe all the databases into this cmdlet to find the information?

```
Get-MailboxDatabase | Get-MailboxDatabaseCopyStatus | ft Name,ContentIndexState
```

```
Name                  ContentIndexState
----                  -----------------
EX01-DB01\EX01                  Healthy
EX02-DB01\EX02                  Healthy
EX03-DB01\EX03                  Healthy
```

Now we have a one-liner that can get the Index status. Other possible states are Failed and Suspended. Taking that code one-liner we can build a script to check for the failures and fix them.

**Script Code**

First the script checks to see what databases have unhealthy indexes and storing the names in a $IndexStatus variable:

```
Write-Host "Checking database content indexes now." -ForegroundColor Yellow
$IndexStatus=(Get-MailboxDatabase|Get-MailboxDatabaseCopyStatus|Where{$_.ContentIndexState
-ne "Healthy"})
```

If there are any databases with Content Indexes that are healthy (the $IndexStatus is not empty), then the script will display a message:

```
If ($IndexStatus -eq $Null) {
    Write-Host "No databases have failed content indexes!" -ForegroundColor Cyan
```

If there are any failed Content Indexes, then a new loop is started:

```
} Else {
    Foreach ($Line in $IndexStatus) {
```

Variables for the database Name and Content Index State are populated:

```
$Name = $Line.Name
$Status = $Line.ContentIndexState
```

A quick summary of failed databases are displayed to the PowerShell window:

```
Write-Host "The database " -ForegroundColor White -NoNewLine
Write-Host "$Name " -ForegroundColor Red -NoNewLine
Write-Host "content index status of " -ForegroundColor White -NoNewLine
Write-Host "$Status" -ForegroundColor Red -nonewline
Write-Host ".  Please remediate this as soon as possible." -ForegroundColor Yellow
}
```

Then the script will ask if you want to repair the databases:

```
Write-Host "Repair the failed content indexes? [y or n]" -ForegroundColor Cyan -NoNewLine
$answer = Read-Host
```

If the database index is in a failed state and a 'y' is entered, the content index will be rebuilt.  Below a Try..Catch code block is present in case the Update-MailboxDatabaseCopy cmdlet fails, an error message will display:

```
If ($Answer -eq "y") {
    Foreach ($Line in $IndexStatus) {
        $Identity = $Line.Name
        Try {
            Update-MailboxDatabaseCopy -Identity $Identity -CatalogOnly -ErrorAction STOP
        } Catch {
            Write-Host "The Content Index was not fixed for the $Identity database."
        }
    }
} Else {
    Write-Host "Make sure to repair your failed content indexes soon."  -ForegroundColor Yellow
}
```

A successful database repair would look like this:

```
[PS] C:\> .\failedindexes.ps1
Checking database content indexes now.
No databases have failed content indexes!
Fixing the failed content index for EX01\EX01-DB01.
Fixing the failed content index for EX02\EX01-DB02.
Fixing the failed content index for EX03\EX01-DB03.
```

The final script would then look like this:

```
Write-Host "Checking database content indexes now." -ForegroundColor Yellow
$IndexStatus =(Get-MailboxDatabase|Get-MailboxDatabasecopystatus|Where{$_.ContentIndexState
-ne "Healthy"})

if ($IndexStatus -eq $null) {
   write-host "No databases have failed content indexes!" -ForegroundColor Cyan
   write-host " "
} Else {
   ForEach ($Line in $IndexStatus) {
      $Name = $Line.Name
      $Status = $Line.ContentIndexState
      Write-Host "The database " -ForegroundColor White -NoNewLine
      Write-Host "$name " -ForegroundColor Red -NoNewLine
      Write-Host "content index status of " -ForegroundColor White -NoNewLine
      Write-Host "$Status" -ForegroundColor Red -NoNewLine
      Write-Host".  Please remediate this as soon as possible." -ForegroundColor Yellow
   }

   Write-Host "Repair the failed content indexes? [y or n]" -ForegroundColor Cyan -NoNewLine
   $Answer = Read-Host
   If ($Answer -eq "y") {
      ForEach ($Line in $IndexStatus) {
         $Identity = $Line.Name
         Try {
            Update-MailboxDatabaseCopy -Identity $Identity -CatalogOnly -ErrorAction STOP
         } Catch {
            Write-Host "The Content Index was not fixed for the $Identity database."
         }
      }
   } Else {
      Write-Host "Make sure to repair your failed content indexes soon."  -ForegroundColor Yellow
   }
}
```

**Activated Copies**

Databases in Database Availability Groups have a value called Activation Preference configured on them.  When a new database is added to a server, the Activation Preference is set to 1 for the current server.  A newly added copy for a database in a DAG is stamped with an Activation Preference of 2 and additional copies are incremented by one for each copy.  The Activation Preference can be changed to help tag a database to indicate which server is the preferred server for a mailbox database.

Forcing a database copy with an Activation Preference of 1 to be the mounted copy is not required. The value can be used by Exchange when for deciding which copy should be mounted and on what server.  In a production environment it also allows an engineer to decide which copy should be activated to be closer to users connecting to their mailboxes.  The value can also be set to load balance copies by deciding which databases should be mounted on a server and script PowerShell to monitor and move databases to the 'correct' server.   Here is a sample script for checking to see if the correct server has the 'correct' database copy mounted:

Script Sample

```
$DAG = Get-DatabaseAvailabilityGroup
Foreach ($Line in $DAG) {
   $DAGNAME = $Line.Name
   Write-Host "Examining the Database Availability Group $DAGName" -ForegroundColor Yellow
   # Get each database in each DAG
   $ActivationPreference = (Get-MailboxDatabase | Where {$_.MasterServerOrAvailabilityGroup -eq
   $DAGName})
   # Loop for each DAG
   Foreach ($Line2 in $ActivationPreference) {
      $Server = $Line2.Server
      $Database = $Line2.Name
      $Set = $Line2.ActivationPreference
      Foreach ($Line3 in $Set) {
         # Normalize variables for later use
         $Value = $Line3.Value
         $Server = $Line3.Key
         # Find the database copy with an Activation Preference of 1
         If ($Line4.Value -eq "1") {
            Write-Host "Server $Server with database $Database has the activation preference of $Value"
            # Find the mounted copy of the database
            $Mounted = Get-MailboxDatabase $Database
            $CurrentServer = $Mounted.Server.Name
            # Check to see if the copy mounted has an Activation Preference of 1
            If ($Server -ne $CurrentServer) {
               Write-Host "The server " -NoNewLine -ForegroundColor Cyan
               Write-Host $Currentserver -NoNewLine -ForegroundColor Red
               Write-Host " is not the correct server.  Please move the database to " -NoNewLine
               -ForegroundColor Cyan
               Write-host $Server -NoNewLine -ForegroundColor Red
               Write-Host " "
            }
         }
      }
   }
}
```

## Sample run through on multiple DAG servers:

```
Examining the Database Availability Group DAG01
Server W12EXMB01 with the database MBX01 has the activation preference of 1.
Server W12EXMB01 with the database MBX02 has the activation preference of 1.
Server W12EXMB01 with the database MBX03 has the activation preference of 1.
The Server W12EXMB01 is not the correct server.  Please move the database to W12EXMB02
Server W12EXMB01 with the database MBX04 has the activation preference of 1.
Server W12EXMB02 with the database MBX05 has the activation preference of 1.
Server W12EXMB02 with the database MBX06 has the activation preference of 1.
Examining the Database Availability Group DAG02
Server W12EXMB03 with the database MBX01 has the activation preference of 1.
Server W12EXMB03 with the database MBX01 has the activation preference of 1.
Server W12EXMB03 with the database MBX01 has the activation preference of 1.
Server W12EXMB04 with the database MBX01 has the activation preference of 1.
Server W12EXMB05 with the database MBX01 has the activation preference of 1.
The Server W12EXMB03 is not the correct server.  Please move the database to W12EXMB04
Server W12EXMB05 with the database MBX01 has the activation preference of 1.
Examining the Database Availability Group DAG03
Server W12EXMB06 with the database MBX01 has the activation preference of 1.
The Server W12EXMB07 is not the correct server.  Please move the database to W12EXMB06
Server W12EXMB06 with the database MBX01 has the activation preference of 1.
Server W12EXMB06 with the database MBX01 has the activation preference of 1.
Server W12EXMB07 with the database MBX01 has the activation preference of 1.
```

Notice that the name of the server, database and activation preference are listed.  There are also telltale signs of which database copies are not activated as planned.  In order to correct for this, a script could be written to move it from one Activation Copy to another, to rebalance the databases.

Keeping active databases on the correct server may be necessary to keep the load balanced.  Notice below that the Green and Active databases below have an AP (Activation Preference) of 1 and the Orange and Inactive Databases have an AP of 2:

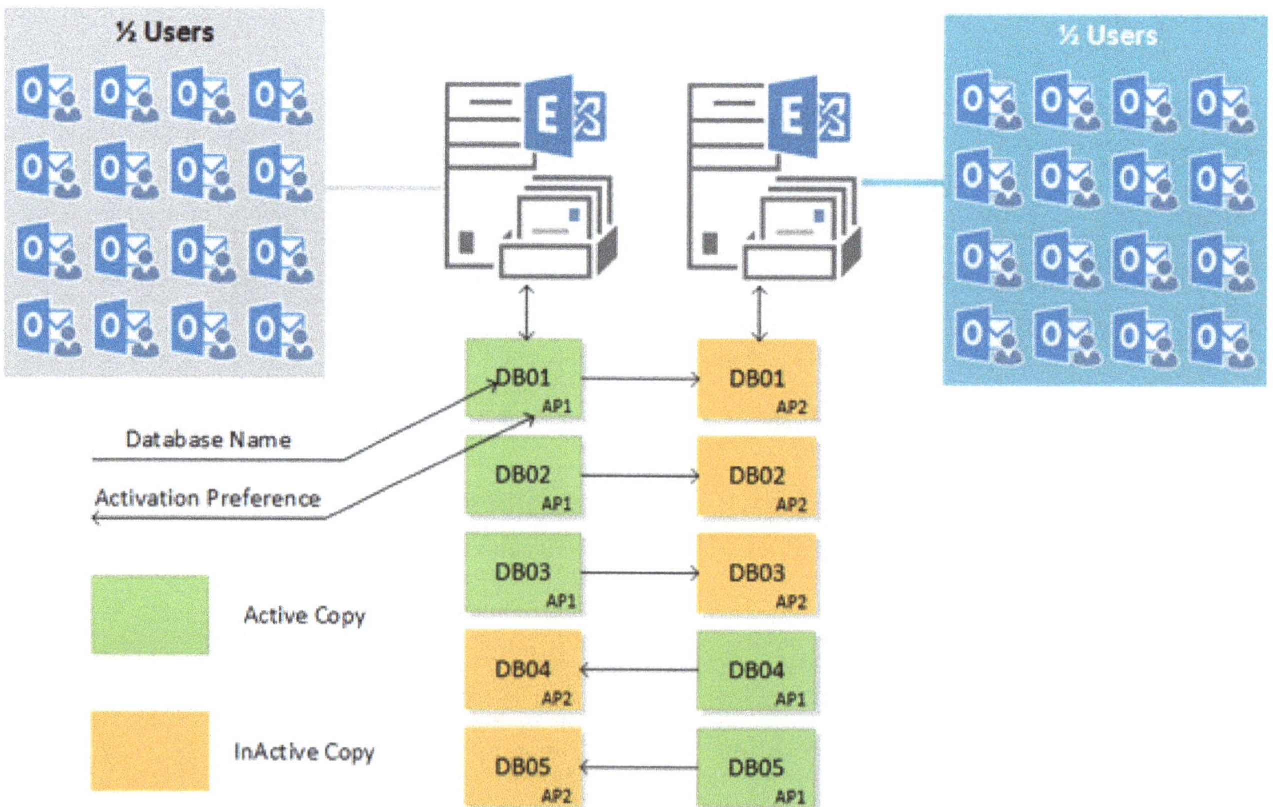

Imagine if the Active / Inactive copies are jumbled and don't match or another scenario when a server is rebooted and the databases that are active do not match the AP:

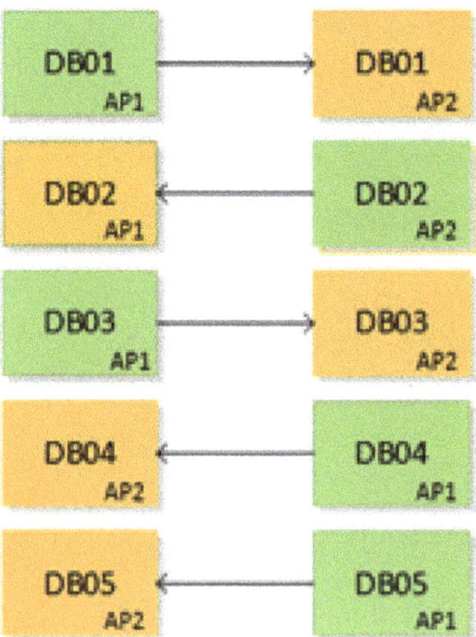

This scenario is what the script was made for because multiple database are in the wrong place which would be reported. Reporting on this could be considered a higher priority if the servers are in different locations and the database allocation should be as expected most if not all the time.

# Verifying Backups

Mailbox database backups are the first step in ensuring that an existing Exchange server can be rebuilt in the event of an accident. The databases contain all production mailboxes, so knowing the current state of the backups is a useful piece of information.

How can we see when the last backup was? Get-MailboxDatabase will help determine the current backup state:

Get-MailboxDatabase | ft Name,LastFullBackup -Auto

If the database has had a successful backup, why would the LastFullBackup date not display? The Get-MailboxDatabase cmdlet requires a '-Status' switch in order for the backup data to show:

Get-MailboxDatabase -Status | ft Name,LastFullBackup –Auto

If, while using the '–status' switch, the LastFullBackup is empty, we would want to run a complete backup immediately. Once the backup is completed, make sure the logs for the mailbox database have been truncated and 'Info' events are logged in the event viewer. A quick report can be generated with this script below, which provides for a good visible:

```
$Servers = Get-MailboxServer

Foreach ($Server in $Servers) {
    $Backups = $Null
    $Backups = Get-MailboxDatabase -Status -Server $Server -ErrorAction STOP -WarningAction STOP

    Write-Host "Server $Server backup status." -ForegroundColor Green
    Write-Host "-----------------------------" -ForegroundColor Green
    Write-Host " " # Formatting

    Foreach ($Backup in $Backups) {
        $Status = $Backup.LastFullBackup
        $Database = $Backup.Name
        If ($Status -ne $Null ) {
            Write-Host "The database $Databases last backup was on $Status. " -ForegroundColor White
        } Else {
            Write-Host "The database $Database had never been backed up." -ForegroundColor Yellow
        }
    }
    Write-Host " " # Formatting
}
```

Sample backup check for an Exchange 2016 server:

```
Server EX01 backup status.
---------------------------------
The database DB01's last backup was on 10/31/2016 02:00:20.
The database DB02's last backup was on 10/1/2016 06:10:20.
The database DB03's last backup was on 10/31/2016 11:00:20.
The database DB03 had never been backed up.
The database DB04 had never been backed up.
The database DB05 had never been backed up.
The database DB06 had never been backed up.
The database DB07 had never been backed up.
The database DB08 had never been backed up.
The database DB09 had never been backed up.
```

Note the different colors visually signify what databases were completely backed up and which were not.


## Backups, Suspended Copies and Log Files

Occasionally backups for your Exchange server can experience problems. Problems could be potentially be generated by a bad database copy (suspended or failed) which prevents logs for the database to build-up and possibly fill the hard drives up to where a disk is full and a database dismounts. PowerShell can be used to resolve these issues.

First, we need to check the status of all the mailbox databases:

```
Get-MailboxDatabase | Get-MailboxDatabaseCopyStatus | ft Name,Status,*QueueLength,ContentIn-
dexState –Auto
```

After reviewing the above screenshot, we can see that databases DB04 and DB06 have suspended copies. These suspended copies will hold up backups from truncating the backup logs from the previous backup. In order to resolve the issue, try the Resume-MailboxDatabaseCopy cmdlet.

First, we'll need to filter for suspended copies only:

```
Get-MailboxDatabase | Get-MailboxDatabaseCopyStatus | Where {$_.Status -eq "Suspended"}
```

```
Name          Status      CopyQueueLength    ReplayQueueLength    ContentIndexState
----          ------      ---------------    -----------------    -----------------
DB01\EX02     Mounted           0                    0                  Healthy
DB03\EX01     Mounted           0                    0                  Healthy
DB03\EX02     Healthy           0                    0                  Healthy
DB04\EX01     Mounted           0                    0                  Healthy
DB04\EX02     Suspended         0                    0                  Healthy
DB05\EX01     Mounted           0                    0                  Healthy
DB05\EX02     Healthy           0                    0                  Healthy
DB06\EX01     Mounted           0                    0                  Healthy
DB06\EX02     Suspended         0                    0                  Healthy
DB07\EX01     Mounted           0                    0                  Healthy
```

Once confirmed, we can take these results and pipe them to the Resume-MailboxDatabaseCopy as shown below:

```
Get-MailboxDatabase|Get-MailboxDatabaseCopyStatus|Where {$_.Status-eq "Suspended"}|Resume-
MailboxDatabaseCopy
```

No feedback will be given if successful. Rechecking mailbox copies using the below cmdlet show no more suspended copies:

```
Get-MailboxDatabase | Get-MailboxDatabaseCopystatus | Where {$_.Status -eq "Suspended"}
```

# Circular Logging

Circular logging is when Exchange actively reduces the amount of log files that are retained by a mailbox database. Instead of the log directory containing every log since the last backup, the log directory retains the bare minimum files that are needed for proper database operation. Using Circular Logging is not recommended for production databases on a normal day to day basis. Circular Logging should only be turned on for special cases:

- **Moving mailboxes** – reduces the size taken up by log during a move where the logs written essentially equal the data written to a database. Thus moving 20 GB of mailboxes creates ~20 GB of logs.
- **Clearing disk space** – backups have stopped working. Space is very limited. Turning on Circular Logging should be considered a last resort. Restoring backups would be a priority.
- **Journaling database** - if the mailboxes are cleaned out by a third party app or if the data is to be retained, then logs should be as well.

How can we manage the Circular Logging setting in PowerShell? Using PowerShell, check to see if the databases have a property for setting this:

Get-MailboxDatabase | ft Circ* -Auto

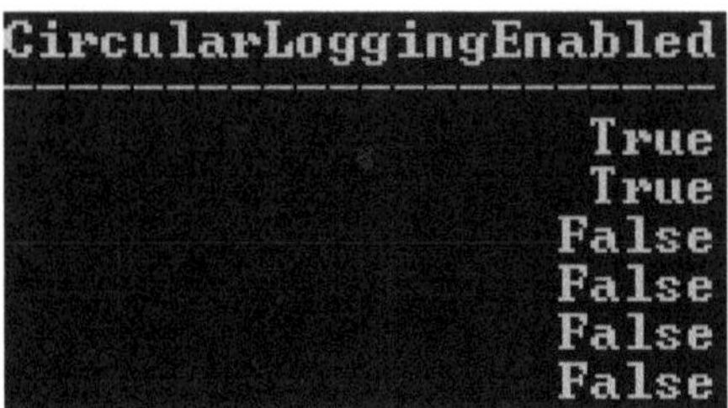

Now that we have the correct property, we can see which databases have this setting applied:

Get-MailboxDatabase | ft Name,Circ* -Auto

```
Name                              CircularLoggingEnabled
----                              ----------------------
DB02                                                True
Mailbox Database 0576450030                         True
Germany-Db                                         False
Italy-Db                                           False
Poland-Db                                          False
DB01                                               False
```

So removing and adding the CircularLoggingEnabled setting with the Set-MailboxDatabase setting.  If the setting is set to False, then this line will set it to true.  In a DAG, the databases will be updated automatically while single servers will need the databases dismounted (Dismount-Database) and remounted (Mount-Database):

Get-MailboxDatabase | Where {$_.CircularLoggingEnabled -eq $False} | Set-MailboxDatabase -CircularLoggingEnabled $True

The reverse scenario is if Circular Logging is enabled, this one-liner will disable the setting:

Get-MailboxDatabase | Where {$_.CircularLoggingEnabled -eq $True} | Set-MailboxDatabase -CircularLoggingEnabled $False

One item to remember for this section is that disabling this is not a good idea for a production environment.  Database logging is key in case a full recovery is needed with log replay.


## Monitoring Disk Space

Monitoring free disk space is an important part of managing your Exchange Servers. Querying disk space can be accomplished with CIM and WMI.  Doing some searching, we can find that disk drives are listed with the WIN32_VOLUME class.

Starting with a new query for disk drives, let's start with the basics of the class and server name:

Get-WMIObject Win32_Volume -Computer $Server

This provides a ton of disk properties (below is a small sample):

```
__GENUS           : 2
__CLASS           : Win32_Volume
__SUPERCLASS      : CIM_StorageVolume
__DYNASTY         : CIM_ManagedSystemElement
__RELPATH         : Win32_Volume.DeviceID="\\\\?\\Volume{1a13b53d-2570
__PROPERTY_COUNT  : 44
__DERIVATION      : {CIM_StorageVolume, CIM_StorageExtent, CIM_Logical
__SERVER          : 16-TAP-EX01
__NAMESPACE       : root\cimv2
__PATH            : \\16-TAP-EX01\root\cimv2:Win32_Volume.DeviceID="\\
Access            :
Automount         : True
Availability      :
BlockSize         : 4096
BootVolume        : False
Capacity          : 366997504
Caption           : \\?\Volume{1a13b53d-2570-11e6-80b1-806e6f6e6963}\
Compressed        : False
```

From the list of properties above, here are some that are quite useful:

- DriveLetter
- SystemName
- Caption
- FreeSpace
- Capacity

Pulling all of these into the same PowerShell cmdlet:

```
Get-WMIObject Win32_Volume -Computer $Server | ft DriveLetter,SystemName,Caption,FreeSpace,-
Capacity –Auto
```

```
DriveLetter SystemName  Caption                                                    FreeSpace    Capacity
                                                                                    ---------    --------
            16-TAP-EX01  \\?\Volume{1a13b53d-2570-11e6-80b1-806e6f6e6963}\           93380608    366997504
C:          16-TAP-EX01  C:\                                                      15708942336  107005079552
D:          16-TAP-EX01  D:\                                                                0    4268605440
```

The first drive is not a valid database drive (empty drive letter), so a filter should be put in place for an empty drive letter. The D: Drive is also an invalid drive, but we cannot filter by the amount of free space. Reviewing the properties of the D: Drive and C: Drive to see what the differences would be between then using WMI:

```
Get-WMIObject Win32_Volume -Computer $Server | ft DriveLetter,FileSystem -Auto
```

```
DriveLetter filesystem
----------- ----------
            NTFS
C:          NTFS
D:          UDF
```

In this case the D: Drive is a DVD Drive and the file format is UDF and not NTFS which is what Exchange Databases use. Using the original one-liner, we can now filter out the empty drive letter volumes as well as volumes of the UDF format.

```
Get-WMIObject Win32_Volume -Computer $Server | Where {($_.DriveLetter -ne $Null) -And ($_.
FileSystem -ne "udf")} | ft DriveLetter,SystemName,Caption,FreeSpace,Capacity –Auto
```

```
DriveLetter SystemName Caption  FreeSpace    Capacity
----------- ---------- -------  ---------    --------
E:          EX01       E:\      21661949952  75158777856
C:          EX01       C:\      11068751872  8579133849\6
```

The results need to be tweaked a bit further so that the FreeSpace and Capacity should be formatted in a better manner.  First, we can take the Freespace and format it into GB format:

```
@{Name="CapacityGB";Expression={"{0:N1}" -f($_.Capacity/1gb)}}
```

Then the Capacity will also be formatted into GB:

```
@{Name="FreeSpaceGB";Expression={"{0:N1}"-f($_.FreeSpace/1gb)}}
```

Each of these blocks perform a couple of different actions.

**Name** – Provides a new column header in the CSV file for results or when displayed in the PowerShell window.

**Expression** – Formats the data into a new format:
**{"{0:N1}"** – One decimal place rounding (a.k.a. precision)
**-f($_.freespace/1gb)** – Changes the format of the number into GB

From all the above information, we can pick these columns – SystemName, Caption, FreeSpace and Capacity, we can craft a EMI query like this:

```
Get-WMIObject Win32_Volume -Computer $Server | Where {$_.DriveLetter -ne $Null} | Select-Object SystemName,Caption,@{Name="FreeSpaceGB";Expression={"{0:N1}"-f($_.FreeSpace/1gb)}},@{Name="CapacityGB";Expression={"{0:N1}" -f($_.Capacity/1gb)}} | ft -Auto
```

```
systemname caption freespaceGB CapacityGB
---------- ------- ----------- ----------
EXO1       E:\     20.1        70.0
EXO1       C:\     10.3        79.9
EXO1       D:\     0.0         2.8
```

Now, we can take the same one-liner and craft a script to get the same information for all Exchange Servers:

**Sample Script for all Servers**

```
$Servers = (Get-ExchangeServer).Name

Foreach ($Server in $Servers) {
    Write-Host "Exchange Server $Server Freespace Report" -ForegroundColor Green
    $FreeSpace = Get-WMIObject Win32_Volume -Computer $Server |
    Where {($_.DriveLetter -ne $Null) -and ($_.FileSystem -ne "udf")} |
    Select-Object SystemName,Caption,@{Name="FreeSpaceGB";Expression={"{0:N1}"-f($_.
    FreeSpace/1gb)}},
    @{Name="CapacityGB";Expression={"{0:N1}" -f($_.capacity/1gb)}}
    Foreach ($Line in $FreeSpace) {
        $Free = $Line.FreeSpaceGB
        $All = $Line.CapacityGB
        $Percentage = ($Free/$All)*100
        $Percent = [Math]::Round($Percentage,2)
        Write-Host "The $Caption has $Percent % free disk space."
    }
}
```

## Sample Run Through on a DAG Cluster

```
Exchange Server 16-TAP-EX01 Freespace Report
The D:\ has 15.05 % free disk space.

Exchange Server 16-TAP-EX02 Freespace Report
The D:\ has 1 % free disk space.

Exchange Server 16-04-EDGE-01 Freespace Report
The D:\ has 72.92 % free disk space.
```

As we can see from the report above, we know that the middle server is having an issue with free disk space and should be investigated. Was the drive sized to small? Are the logs not truncating properly? Or did someone download files to the drive without removing them and allowing it to fill up?

## Managed Availability and Disk Space

Another method for monitoring disk space on Exchange 2016 servers is to use Managed Availability. Using Managed Availability, the disk space will get logged in the Event Log every hour. To configure this, we need to add a Global Monitoring Override. First, some examples from the PowerShell cmdlet:

```
Get-Help Add-GlobalMonitoringOverride -Examples
```

```
-------------------------- Example 1 --------------------------
This example adds a global monitoring override that disables the OnPremisesInboundProxy
probe for 30 days. Note that the value of Identity is case-sensitive.

Add-GlobalMonitoringOverride -Identity "FrontendTransport\OnPremisesInboundProxy"
-PropertyName Enabled -PropertyValue 0 -Duration 30.00:00:00 -ItemType Probe
```

```
-------------------------- Example 2 --------------------------
This example adds a global monitoring override that disables the
StorageLogicalDriveSpaceEscalate responder for all Exchange 2016 servers running version
15.01.0225.0422. Note that the value of Identity is case-sensitive.

Add-GlobalMonitoringOverride -Identity "MailboxSpace\StorageLogicalDriveSpaceEscalate"
-PropertyName Enabled -PropertyValue 0 -ItemType Responder -ApplyVersion "15.01.0225.0422"
```

Parameters that we need to figure out are (pulled from get-help Add-GlobalMonitoringOverride -full):

**ItemType** – Values are Probe, Monitor, Responder and Maintenance. We will need 'monitor'.
**Identity** – Contains these values <HealthSetName>\<MonitoringItemName> and in this case we want these values 'MailboxSpace\StorageLogicalDriveSpaceMonitor'.
**PropertyType** – MonitoringThreshold – this is when the alert is generated, so if disk space gets below a certain value.
**PropertyValue** – We'll set this to 5.
**ApplyVersion** – What version of Exchange the override applies too. This is the tricky one because if Exchange gets upgraded, this will need to be modified. The current version is 15.1.544.27 (CU 3).

Using these settings we can create a PowerShell one-liner:

```
Add-GlobalMonitoringOverride -Item Monitor –Identity MailboxSpace\
StorageLogicalDriveSpaceMonitor -PropertyName MonitoringThreshold -PropertyValue 5
-ApplyVersion 15.1.544.27
```

Running 'Get-GlobalMonitoringOverride | fl' provides verification of the monitoring settings:

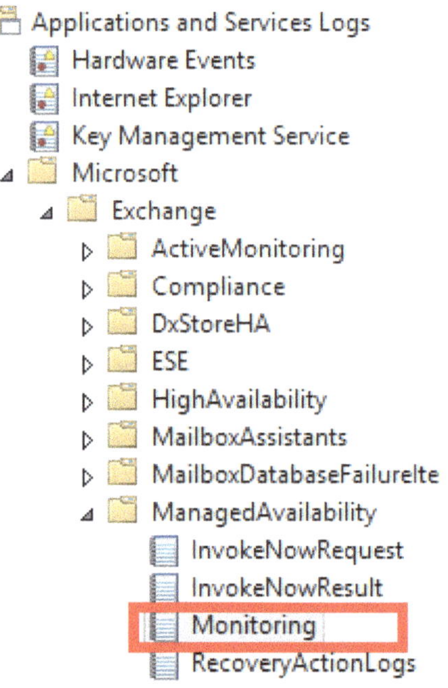


Events from the override will be placed under the ManagedAvailabilty – Monitoring log located here:



Sample disk space events look like this:

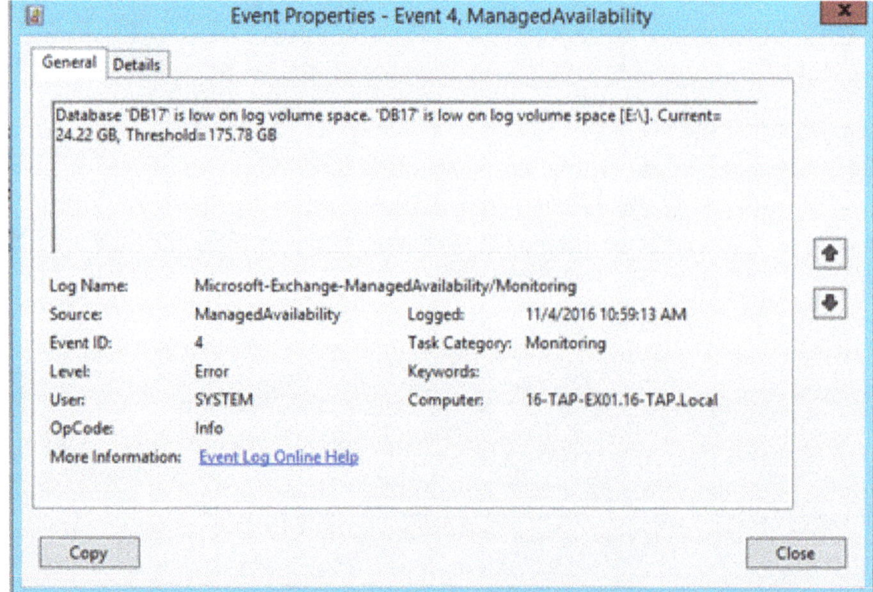

# Command Logging

PowerShell is very important to Exchange 2016 and even the Exchange Administration Console leverages PowerShell. The question is, can this be made visible? The answer is yes, it can. What benefits does this give to those who want to use PowerShell to maintain their Exchange Servers? For starters, when the PowerShell commands are revealed, insight may be gained into how to use the various switches and parameters when configuring an item in PowerShell.

That's great, but how do we turn it on? By logging into the Exchange Administration console, click on the Administrator drop down button and selecting the 'Show Command Logging' option.

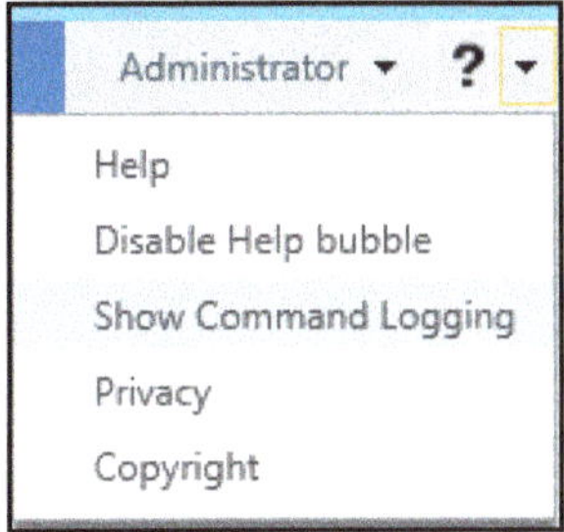


Once this is done, another windows will pop-up so have your pop-up blocker turned off. The window looks something like this:

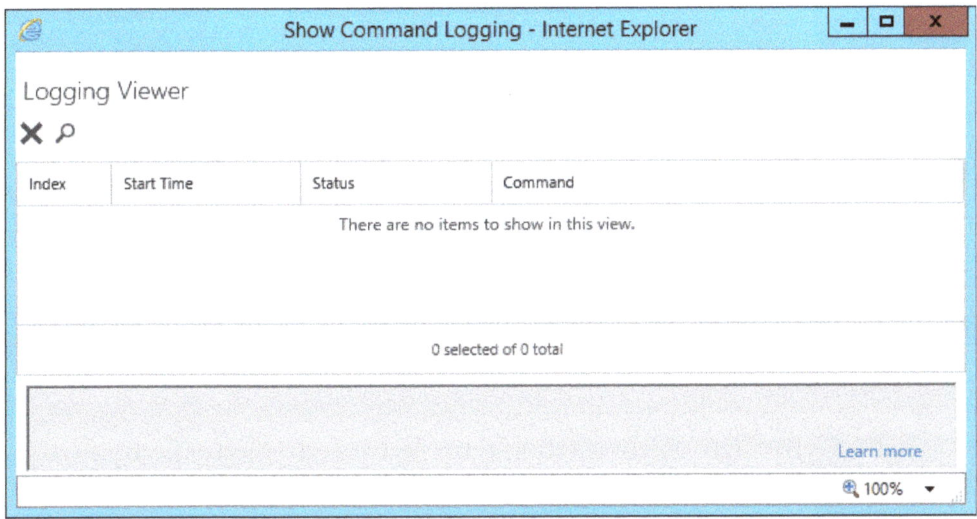


Notice that all boxes in the window are completely empty. To get commands to show here, we now need to manage our Exchange Server. Let's take for an example that I want to enable Circular Logging on databases for the purposes of migration or just clearing disk space (not recommended, backups should be used instead).

First, click on the Servers Tab in the management interface:

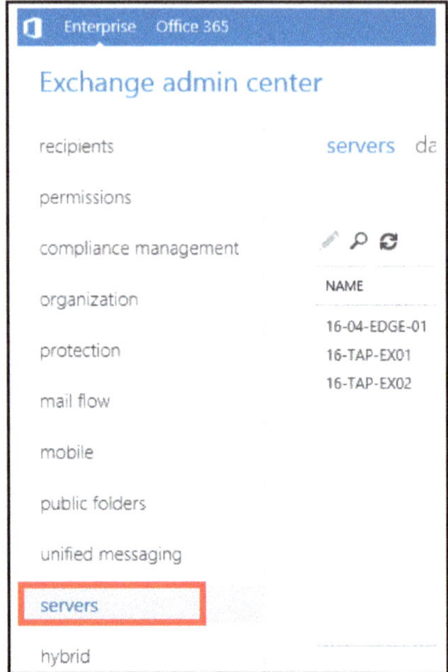

Then click on the databases tab:

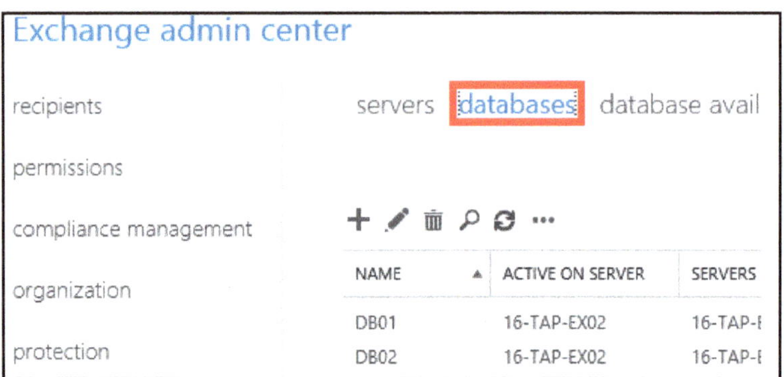

Then select a database and click on the Edit button.  Then click on Maintenance Tab (on the left) and then check circular logging checkbox at the bottom:

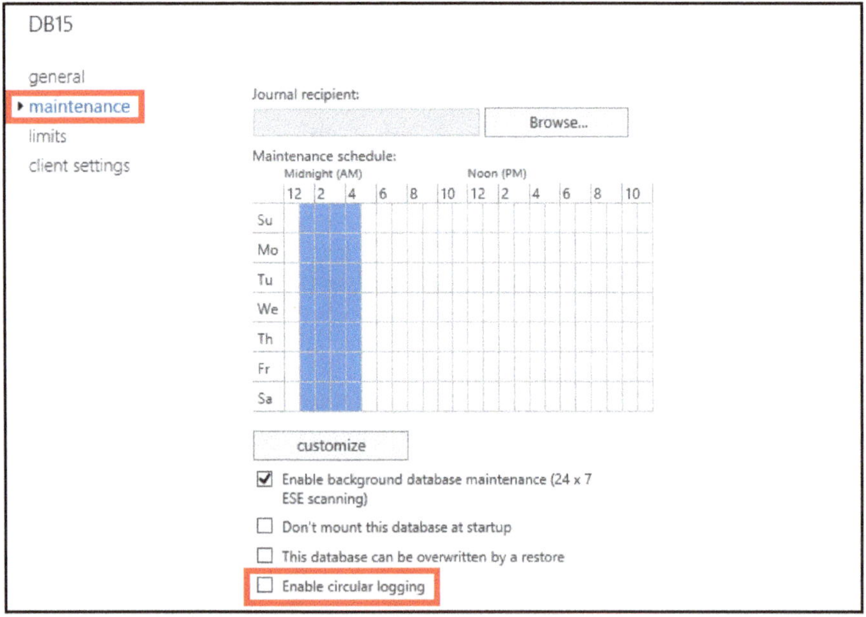

Once Circular Logging is checked, click Save and review the Command Logging window to see what actions were taken in PowerShell:

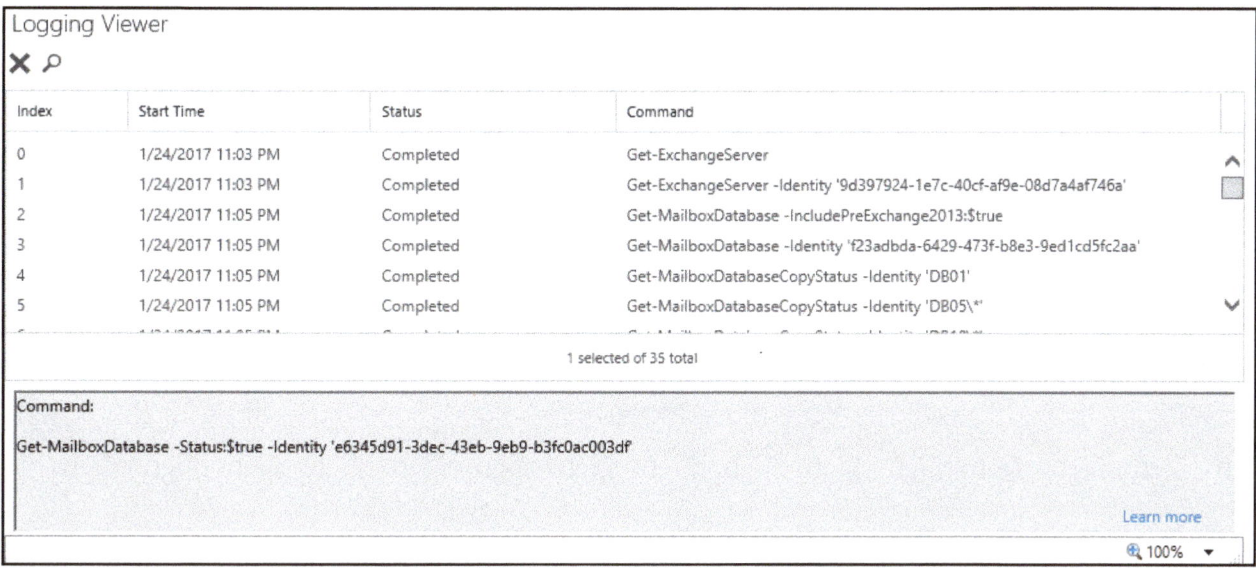

What can be gleaned from this information and how can an administrator use it to improve knowledge of Power-Shell?  First, take a look at the cmdlets that are listed.  Notice that that there are a lot of Get-MailboxDatabase cmdlets. One interesting one that sticks out from the window is this particular line:

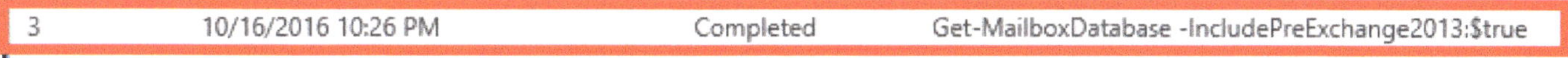

Notice the '-IncludePreExchange2013' switch that was included in the Get-MailboxDatabase.  Is the switch entirely self-evident?  Or is there more of an explanation in the Get-Help for this command?  Reviewing the Help file for the Get-MailboxDatabase reveals this:

-IncludePreExchange2013 <SwitchParameter>

The IncludePreExchange2013 switch parameter specifies whether to return information on Exchange 2010 mailbox databases. You don't need to specify a value with this switch.

Without this switch, the only databases that would be revealed would be the ones on Exchange Server 2013 and 2016.  So if you are moving from 2010 to 2016, this switch may be important for working with them in PowerShell. If more cmdlets are reviewed, we see that another command in the list is where the database is configured for Circular Logging and takes place in the form of a 'Set-MailboxDatabase' cmdlet:

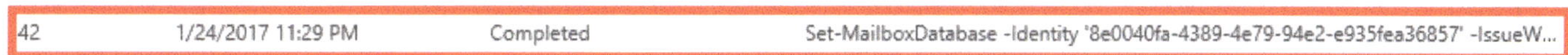

Notice that the cmdlet has been truncated above.  The entire cmdlet is revealed in the bottom window of the Command Logging box:

```
Command:

Set-MailboxDatabase -Identity '8e0040fa-4389-4e79-94e2-e935fea36857' -IssueWarningQuota '2040109466' -ProhibitSendReceiveQuota '2469606195'
-CircularLoggingEnabled:$false
```

The reason that this is useful is that this information can be copied and pasted outside of the Command Logging window:

```
Set-MailboxDatabase -Identity '8e0040fa-4389-4e79-94e2-e935fea36857' -IssueWarningQuota
'2040109466' -ProhibitSendReceiveQuota '2469606195' -CircularLoggingEnabled:$false
```

Now we have an example of how to enable Circular Logging in Exchange and build either a repeatable process or just use it in a singular way with databases we need to modify. The last tip is that ALL cmdlets that were run can be copies at once. Simply highlight all the entries you wish to copy in the Command Logging window like this:

**Logging Viewer**

✕ 🔍

| Index | Start Time | Status | Command |
|---|---|---|---|
| 37 | 1/24/2017 11:29 PM | Completed | Get-MailboxDatabaseCopyStatus -Identity 'Mailbox Database 0576450030*' |
| 38 | 1/24/2017 11:29 PM | Completed | Get-MailboxDatabase -Identity '8e0040fa-4389-4e79-94e2-e935fea36857' |
| 39 | 1/24/2017 11:29 PM | Completed | Get-MailboxDatabaseCopyStatus -Identity 'DB11' |
| 40 | 1/24/2017 11:29 PM | Completed | Get-MailboxDatabaseCopyStatus -Identity 'DB11*' |
| 41 | 1/24/2017 11:29 PM | Completed | Get-MailboxDatabase -Status:$true -Identity '8e0040fa-4389-4e79-94e2-e93... |
| 42 | 1/24/2017 11:29 PM | Completed | Set-MailboxDatabase -Identity '8e0040fa-4389-4e79-94e2-e935fea36857' -I... |
| 43 | 1/24/2017 11:29 PM | Completed | Get-MailboxDatabase -Status:$true -Identity '8e0040fa-4389-4e79-94e2-e93... |
| 44 | 1/24/2017 11:29 PM | Completed | Get-MailboxDatabase -Identity '8e0040fa-4389-4e79-94e2-e935fea36857' |
| 45 | 1/24/2017 11:29 PM | Completed | Get-MailboxDatabaseCopyStatus -Identity 'DB11' |

And the cmdlets are all revealed in the bottom half of the Command Logging window:

10 selected of 47 total

```
Get-MailboxDatabaseCopyStatus -Identity 'Mailbox Database 0576450030\*'

Get-MailboxDatabase -Identity '8e0040fa-4389-4e79-94e2-e935fea36857'

Get-MailboxDatabaseCopyStatus -Identity 'DB11'

Get-MailboxDatabaseCopyStatus -Identity 'DB11\*'

Get-MailboxDatabase -Status:$true -Identity '8e0040fa-4389-4e79-94e2-e935fea36857'
```

In the above example, 27 cmdlets were selected and all can be copied and pasted into Notepad, OneNote or your program of choice for analysis.

# Offline Address Book

The Offline Address Book (OAB) is a frozen in time copy of the GAL that existed when the OAB files were updated. These files are then downloaded on a daily basis by Outlook clients in cached mode. Changes that are made may not be seen in a cached Outlook client for up to two days. This can lead to some disconnect for end users who use cached Outlook, online Outlook and OWA. We can use PowerShell to enhance this experience and configure it to the environment.

## PowerShell

First, we need a list of cmdlets to work with the Offline Address Book:

    Get-Command *offline*

This provides a list of cmdlets that can be used to work with the Offline Address Book:

In addition to these commands, the 'Get-OabVirtualDirectory' cmdlet can be used for manipulating some settings, specifically Authentication, location and the Poll Interval. The Poll Interval is a server based update query to check for and update the OAB files. The default interval is 480 minutes (8 hours). One change that can be made to speed up OAB changes from reaching Outlook, which is to adjust the polling interval to something like 1 or 2 hours (specified in minutes):

    Get-OabVirtualDirectory | Set-OabVirtualDirectory –PollInterval 60

## Move-OfflineAddressBook

*Per Microsoft - 'This cmdlet is used for Exchange 2010 OAB Generation servers and cannot be used with Exchange 2013 or 2016.'*

## Update-OfflineAddressBook

Offline Address Books, depending on the environment, change quickly. This is especially true during an acquisition or even during summer hiring of temp workers. Using the 'Update-OfflineAddressBook' can help speed up the generation of the updates and allow Outlook to pick up the changes sooner. The cmdlet can also be used if a lot of entries were updated from say a mass change of Primary SMTP addresses to a new domain. If there is only one OAB in the environment, then this one-liner will work:

    Get-OfflineAddressBook | Update-OfflineAddressBook

If, however, there is more than one OAB, it would be more practical to isolate which OAB needs to be updated:

    Update-OfflineAddressBook –Identity "New OAB"

Once these commands are run, then the OAB is updated within Exchange. Check the Application Log if there are issues updating the OAB.

Exchange 2016's Offline Address Book uses a System Mailbox called 'SystemMailbox{bb558c35-97f1-4cb9-8ff7-d5 3741dc928c}' that is the OAB Generator Assistant. If the mailbox is available, the one-liner will update the address book and generate the Offline Address Book files. With no feedback in PowerShell. If there is an issue, check to make sure the System mailbox exists and its database is mounted.

## Set-OfflineAddressBook

What settings can be customized in the Address Book? First, we can review some examples from PowerShell:

```
Get-Help Set-OfflineAddressBook -Examples
```

```
-------------------------- Example 1 --------------------------
This example changes the name of the OAB.
Set-OfflineAddressBook -Identity "\Default Offline Address Book" -Name "My Offline Address Book"

-------------------------- Example 2 --------------------------
This example changes the arbitration mailbox that's responsible for generating the OAB.
Set-OfflineAddressBook -Identity "\Default Offline Address Book" -GeneratingMailbox OABGen2
```

Starting with the default address list:

```
Get-OfflineAddressBook | ft
```

```
Name                         Versions    AddressLists
----                         --------    ------------
Default Offline Address Book {Version4}  {\Default Global Address List}
```

We can see the default name and the Address Lists that fit in the OAB. Using the Set-OfflineAddressBook cmdlet, we can change the name to something more friendly as well as changing the mailbox that generates the OAB for Exchange. The new name will be "OAB For Exchange 2016" and the new mailbox will be 2016OAB.

```
Set-OfflineAddressBook –Identity "Default Offline Address Book" –GeneratingMailbox 2016OAB –
Name "OAB For Exchange 2016"
```

Make sure that the '2016OAB mailbox is created before running the above cmdlet. The mailbox also needs to be designated as an arbitration mailbox. The original mailbox can be found with this one-liner:

```
Get-Mailbox -Arbitration | Where {$_.PersistedCapabilities -Like "*oab*"} | ft Name,Servername
```

```
Name                                          ServerName
----                                          ----------
SystemMailbox{bb558c35-97f1-4cb9-8ff7-d53741dc928c} 16-tap-ex01
```

To create a new arbitration mailbox:

```
New-Mailbox -Arbitration -Name "2016 OAB" -Database DB02 -UserPrincipalName 2016OAB@16-tap.
local –DisplayName "2016 OAB Mailbox"
Set-Mailbox -Arbitration o2016OAB -OABGen $True
```

Then the generating mailbox can be moved. On the original information for the Address Book, we noticed that one Address List is connected. From the previous chapter, we created address lists. These can be added to this Offline Address Book or assigned to a new one. Let's take an example here where we've added these address lists:

Florida Users          Georgia Users          Alabama Users

A one-liner can be constructed to handle this:

```
Set-OfflineAddressBook "2016 OAB" –AddressLists "Florida Users"
```

Now the original "Default Global Address List" and the new address list "Florida Users" are included in the default Address List.

# 8     Mail Flow

**In This Chapter**

- Mail Flow Architecture
- Message Tracking Logs
- Transport Rules
- Accepted Domains
- Edge Transport Role
- Protocol Logging
- Test Cmdlets

The flow of e-mail is THE most important part of an Exchange 2016 Server. Without proper mail flow, the proper function Exchange servers in an organization breaks down. Potential problems with Exchange that would interrupt mail flow are a down server, a down Internet connection, firewall or antivirus issues. Being able to properly configure, maintain and troubleshoot SMTP in the messaging system is key.

The Exchange Admin Center (EAC) provides a way to configure mail flow features like send and receive connectors, transport rules, journaling and message tracking. However, the EAC is limited in many ways and some configuration options REQUIRE the use of PowerShell as no option is offered through EAC. Examples of this are message tracking log configuration and complete connector duplication (to another server). Connector duplication comes in handy for adding, replacing or upgrading server connectors.

This chapter will cover the various parts of Exchange mail flow from what the components are, the cmdlets used to configure them as well as cmdlets used to troubleshoot mail flow issues that could come up.

## Mail Flow Architecture

Beginning with Exchange Server 2013, Microsoft changed the architecture of the transport architecture with the consolidation of the Hub Transport Role (from Exchange 2007 and 2010) into the Mailbox Role. With the consolidation came a logical split of services and the creation of the FrontEnd and Hub Transport (or backend) from the single feature of mail flow:

FrontEnd Transport - this service functions as a stateless proxy for inbound and outbound external SMTP traffic.

Hub Transport - this service provides essentially the same features and functionality of the Hub Transport Role from Exchange Server 2010 - it handles mail flow routing, message categorization and message content inspection.

If setting up connectors for mail relay from scanners or applications, the FrontEnd Transport service is where the connector needs to be setup. If the connector is configured as a Hub Transport connector then possible mail flow issues could be created due to resource conflicts.

## Mail Flow Connectors

SMTP connectors are key to making mail flow functional in Exchange 2016. By default there are some built-in Receive Connectors, but no Send Connectors are present in the default Exchange 2016 installation. One thing about Send and Receive connectors is that they have different scopes or areas of responsibility. Receive Connectors are local to the server for which they are configured with a designated IP address to answer on, authentication types and more. Send Connectors however can be scoped for a single AD site or be used by multiple servers in different AD sites.

Let's explore the PowerShell cmdlets that can manage, report or modify connectors in Exchange:

```
Get-Command *connector*
```

```
CommandType     Name                                    ModuleName
-----------     ----                                    ----------
Function        Get-DeliveryAgentConnector              16-tap-ex01.16-tap.local
Function        Get-ForeignConnector                    16-tap-ex01.16-tap.local
Function        Get-IntraOrganizationConnector          16-tap-ex01.16-tap.local
Function        Get-ReceiveConnector                    16-tap-ex01.16-tap.local
Function        Get-SendConnector                       16-tap-ex01.16-tap.local
Function        New-DeliveryAgentConnector              16-tap-ex01.16-tap.local
Function        New-ForeignConnector                    16-tap-ex01.16-tap.local
Function        New-IntraOrganizationConnector          16-tap-ex01.16-tap.local
Function        New-ReceiveConnector                    16-tap-ex01.16-tap.local
Function        New-SendConnector                       16-tap-ex01.16-tap.local
Function        Remove-DeliveryAgentConnector           16-tap-ex01.16-tap.local
Function        Remove-ForeignConnector                 16-tap-ex01.16-tap.local
Function        Remove-IntraOrganizationConnector       16-tap-ex01.16-tap.local
Function        Remove-ReceiveConnector                 16-tap-ex01.16-tap.local
Function        Remove-SendConnector                    16-tap-ex01.16-tap.local
Function        Set-DeliveryAgentConnector              16-tap-ex01.16-tap.local
Function        Set-ForeignConnector                    16-tap-ex01.16-tap.local
Function        Set-IntraOrganizationConnector          16-tap-ex01.16-tap.local
Function        Set-ReceiveConnector                    16-tap-ex01.16-tap.local
Function        Set-SendConnector                       16-tap-ex01.16-tap.local
Application     ForefrontActiveDirectoryConnector.exe
```

Notice the last command on the list is actually an Application and that the Module Name is blank. In order to get just Exchange related cmdlets, use the Get-Excommad cmdlet like so to eliminate these results:

```
Get-Excommand | where {$_.Name -Like "*connector*"}
```

To confirm what connectors exist in Exchange 2016 to begin with, run the Get-*Connector cmdlets:

```
Get-SendConnector
```

```
[PS] C:\>Get-SendConnector
[PS] C:\>_
```

No Send Connectors exist by default, what about Receive Connectors?

```
Get-ReceiveConnector
```

```
Identity                                    Bindings                        Enabled
--------                                    --------                        -------
16-TAP-EX01\Default 16-EX01                 {0.0.0.0:2525, [::]:2525}       True
16-TAP-EX01\Client Proxy 16-EX01            {[::]:465, 0.0.0.0:465}         True
16-TAP-EX01\Default Frontend 16-EX01        {[::]:25, 0.0.0.0:25}           True
16-TAP-EX01\Outbound Proxy Frontend 16-EX01 {[::]:717, 0.0.0.0:717}         True
16-TAP-EX01\Client Frontend 16-EX01         {[::]:587, 0.0.0.0:587}         True
```

As you can see, there are a few default Receive Connectors in Exchange 2016 after it is installed. Note the FrontEnd connectors are noted as such, but the BackEnd ones do not display a specification for back or front end.

**Receive Connector Port Table**

| Connector | Port | Purpose |
| --- | --- | --- |
| Default <Server Name> | 2525 | Transport Service SMTP receive connector |
| Client Proxy <Server Name> | 465 | Transport Service client receive connector |
| Default FrontEnd <Server Name> | 25 | FrontEnd default receive connector from the Internet |
| Outbound Proxy FrontEnd <Server Name> | 717 | Outbound receive proxy for outbound emails |
| Client FrontEnd <Server Name> | 587 | FrontEnd connector for inbound client (SMTP) |

# Receive Connectors

Receive Connectors can also be used for mail relay of production applications or scanners. For example, with the appropriate Receive Connectors, notifications from applications can be delivered to a mailbox or general daily reports can also be delivered as well. A connector for this needs to be created carefully. If a new Hub Transport connector were created, instead of a FrontEnd connector, port conflicts occur and cause issues. When creating an Application Relay connector, we need to specify what IP addresses will connect to this connector versus the default connector. In other words, the more specific connector will be used for routing if the source IP address is matched versus the default connector which is listening for all connections.

## Connection Creation

Creating a Receive Connector for the application / scanner SMTP relaying should be configured with a couple of things in mind. First the Receive Connector needs to be a FrontEnd connector, not Hub Transport. Second, the connector requires a range or set of single IP addresses for the applications / scanners ready for the cmdlet. Lastly, a descriptive Display Name should be in hand as well. Optionally the connector can be bound to a certain IP, have a connection timeout, message size limits and more.

Here are the options from "Get-Help New-ReceiveConnector -Full":

```
NAME
    New-ReceiveConnector

SYNOPSIS
    This cmdlet is available only in on-premises Exchange Server 2016.

    Use the New-ReceiveConnector cmdlet to create a new Receive connector.

SYNTAX
    New-ReceiveConnector -Bindings <MultiValuedProperty> -RemoteIPRanges <MultiValuedProperty> -Name <String> [-Custom
    <SwitchParameter>] [-AdvertiseClientSettings <$true | $false>] [-AuthMechanism <None | Tls | Integrated |
    BasicAuth | BasicAuthRequireTLS | ExchangeServer | ExternalAuthoritative>] [-Banner <String>] [-BinaryMimeEnabled
    <$true | $false>] [-ChunkingEnabled <$true | $false>] [-Comment <String>] [-Confirm [<SwitchParameter>]]
    [-ConnectionInactivityTimeout <EnhancedTimeSpan>] [-ConnectionTimeout <EnhancedTimeSpan>] [-DefaultDomain
    <AcceptedDomainIdParameter>] [-DeliveryStatusNotificationEnabled <$true | $false>] [-DomainController <Fqdn>]
    [-DomainSecureEnabled <$true | $false>] [-EightBitMimeEnabled <$true | $false>] [-EnableAuthGSSAPI <$true |
    $false>] [-Enabled <$true | $false>] [-EnhancedStatusCodesEnabled <$true | $false>] [-ExtendedProtectionPolicy
    <None | Allow | Require>] [-Fqdn <Fqdn>] [-LongAddressesEnabled <$true | $false>] [-MaxAcknowledgementDelay
    <EnhancedTimeSpan>] [-MaxHeaderSize <ByteQuantifiedSize>] [-MaxHopCount <Int32>] [-MaxInboundConnection
    <Unlimited>] [-MaxInboundConnectionPercentagePerSource <Int32>] [-MaxInboundConnectionPerSource <Unlimited>]
    [-MaxLocalHopCount <Int32>] [-MaxLogonFailures <Int32>] [-MaxMessageSize <ByteQuantifiedSize>] [-MaxProtocolErrors
    <Unlimited>] [-MaxRecipientsPerMessage <Int32>] [-MessageRateLimit <Unlimited>] [-MessageRateSource <None |
    IPAddress | User | All>] [-OrarEnabled <$true | $false>] [-PermissionGroups <None | AnonymousUsers | ExchangeUsers
    | ExchangeServers | ExchangeLegacyServers | Partners | Custom>] [-PipeliningEnabled <$true | $false>]
    [-ProtocolLoggingLevel <None | Verbose>] [-RejectReservedSecondLevelRecipientDomains <$true | $false>]
    [-RejectReservedTopLevelRecipientDomains <$true | $false>] [-RejectSingleLabelRecipientDomains <$true | $false>]
    [-RequireEHLODomain <$true | $false>] [-RequireTLS <$true | $false>] [-Server <ServerIdParameter>]
    [-ServiceDiscoveryFqdn <Fqdn>] [-SizeEnabled <Disabled | Enabled | EnabledWithoutValue>] [-SuppressXAnonymousTls
    <$true | $false>] [-TarpitInterval <EnhancedTimeSpan>] [-TlsCertificateName <SmtpX509Identifier>]
    [-TlsDomainCapabilities <MultiValuedProperty>] [-TransportRole <None | Cafe | Mailbox | ClientAccess |
    EopBackground | UnifiedMessaging | HubTransport | Edge | All | Monitoring | CentralAdmin | CentralAdminDatabase |
    DomainController | WindowsDeploymentServer | ProvisionedServer | LanguagePacks | FrontendTransport | CafeArray |
    FfoWebService | OSP | OfficeDns | ManagementFrontEnd | ManagementBackEnd | SCOM | CentralAdminFrontEnd | NAT |
    DHCP | CM | TF | CY | TC | OC | PAUC>] [-WhatIf [<SwitchParameter>]] [<CommonParameters>]
```

Examples from Get-Help

```
This example creates the custom Receive connector Test with the following properties:

It listens for incoming SMTP connections on the IP address 10.10.1.1 and port 25.

It accepts incoming SMTP connections only from the IP range 192.168.0.1-192.168.0.24
New-ReceiveConnector -Name Test -Usage Custom -Bindings 10.10.1.1:25 -RemoteIPRanges 192.168.0.1-192.168.0.24
```

**Example**

New-ReceiveConnector -Name ApplicationRelay -Usage Custom -TransportRole FrontEndTransport
-RemoteIPRanges 10.0.0.1-10.0.0.5 -Bindings 10.0.1.25:25

```
Identity                              Bindings                          Enabled
--------                              --------                          -------
16-EX02\ApplicationRelay              {10.0.1.25:25}                    True
```

The new connector called "ApplicationRelay" is configured to be a FrontEndConnector, bound to 10.0.1.25, and which allows SMTP relay from devices with IP addresses of 10.0.0.1 to 10.0.0.5. When a device or application connects to Exchange to relay SMTP, the connection with the most specific IP Address will be the one to accept the connection. For Receive Connectors, this would be either the Default FrontEnd (all IP addresses) or a more specific relay connector like the example above. Protocol Logging is not on by default for the new connector; this setting should be enabled if the need for troubleshooting should arrive:

Set-ReceiveConnector -Identity "16-TAP-EX02\ApplicationRelay" -ProtocolLoggingLevel Verbose

## Send Connectors

Send Connectors can serve many purposes, but they are responsible for email that is outbound from Exchange to another system that accepts SMTP traffic. Sample uses for Send Connectors are external journaling, smart host routing (through a provider) or an internal server (SharePoint for example) that processes or stores emails for a specific purpose. There should be at least one Send Connector in most if not all Exchange Organizations. It is not uncommon for an Exchange Organization to have two or more Send Connectors serving different purposes. Let's walk through how to work with Send Connectors.

**PowerShell**

Get-Command –Noun SendConnector

```
CommandType     Name
-----------     ----
Function        Get-SendConnector
Function        New-SendConnector
Function        Remove-SendConnector
Function        Set-SendConnector
```

How can we create our first connector in Exchange? Let's review the Get-Help for the cmdlet:

Get-Help New-SendConnector –Examples

```
-------------------------- Example 1 --------------------------
It processes messages addressed only to Contoso.com and Fabrikam.com domains.
New-SendConnector -Internet -Name MySendConnector -AddressSpaces contoso.com,fabrikam.com

-------------------------- Example 2 --------------------------
$CredentialObject = Get-Credential

New-SendConnector -Name "Secure Email to Contoso.com" -AddressSpaces contoso.com -AuthenticationCredential
$CredentialObject -SmartHostAuthMechanism BasicAuth
```

From the above examples, we know that a name is required as well as the address space (domains) that the connector will be used to send email to.  Some other parameters we could use:

Connector Type:

- **Custom** – route email to all types of SMTP servers, especially non-Exchange servers
- **Partner** – route email to a trusted third party or partner company
- **Internal** – route the email to an internal resource (SharePoint for example)
- **Internet** – route the email to the Internet

SourceTransportServers:

- Which servers will send the SMTP messages to the destination

Routing Choice for SMTP Connections:

- **SmartHosts** – routes SMTP messages directly to a SMTP host
- **DNSRoutingEnabled** – routes SMTP messages based on MX records found in internal or Internet DNS zones

**Example**

For this example, we need to create two SMTP Send Connectors.  One is for a partner organization that requires TLS to always be used and another is for all other email to the Internet:

**Internet Mail Connector**
```
New-SendConnector –Name "Internet Email" -Custom –AddressSpaces *
```

**Partner Mail Connector**
```
New-SendConnector –Name "Big Corp Email" -Partner –AddressSpaces "BigCorp.Com" –RequireTLS $True
```

## Removing Connectors

Removing an existing connector is sometimes needed when an app or device is being retired.  PowerShell provides a cmdlet that allows for the removal of a connector.  To find out about this cmdlet, use the Get-Help:

```
Get-Help Remove-ReceiveConnector –Full
```

```
-------------------------------- EXAMPLE 1 --------------------------------

This example deletes the Receive connector Contoso.com Receive Connector.
Remove-ReceiveConnector "Contoso.com Receive Connector"
```

Using the above example, we can write a small one-liner to remove any old or test connectors that are no longer needed.  To remove the connector, the Remove-ReceiveConnector needs an identity of the connector to be removed.  The help file also provides information on what comprises an appropriate identity for the Receive Connector.

```
-Identity <ReceiveConnectorIdParameter>
    The Identity parameter specifies the GUID or connector name that represents a specific Receive connector. You can also inclu
```

Remove-ReceiveConnector "EX01\ApplicationRelay"

```
[PS] C:\>remove-ReceiveConnector "EX01\ApplicationRelay"

Confirm
Are you sure you want to perform this action?
Removing Receive connector "EX01\ApplicationRelay".
[Y] Yes  [A] Yes to All  [N] No  [L] No to All  [?] Help (default is "Y"): y
```

## Connector Reporting

In practical terms, a report on connectors would be good for server documentation and not much else.  A report like this would be just another page in an environment's documentation, providing a comprehensive look at the servers.  Connectors, both Send and Receive, have quite a few properties that could be documented.  Cherry picking properties is not advisable because a missed property could cause an issue on a rebuild of a connector.  So, a simple way to document a connector is to export all settings to a txt file.

### Example - Documenting One Connector

Get-ReceiveConnector ApplicationRelay | fl > C:\Documentation\Receive-ApplicationRelay.Txt

Part of the Receive-ApplicationRelay.txt file:

```
RunspaceId                             : 9398c684-23db-462f-a232-116b51487806
AuthMechanism                          : Tls
Banner                                 :
BinaryMimeEnabled                      : True
Bindings                               : {10.0.1.25:25}
ChunkingEnabled                        : True
DefaultDomain                          :
DeliveryStatusNotificationEnabled      : True
EightBitMimeEnabled                    : True
SmtpUtf8Enabled                        : False
BareLinefeedRejectionEnabled           : False
DomainSecureEnabled                    : False
EnhancedStatusCodesEnabled             : True
LongAddressesEnabled                   : False
OrarEnabled                            : False
SuppressXAnonymousTls                  : False
ProxyEnabled                           : False
AdvertiseClientSettings                : False
```

### Example – Document All Connectors

```
$Receive = (Get-ReceiveConnector).Name
Foreach ($Connector in $Receive) {
  Try {
    Get-ReceiveConnector -Identity $Connector -ErrorAction STOP | fl > "c:\documentation\receive-
    $Connector.txt"
    Write-Host "The Receive Connector $Connector has been documented." -ForegroundColor Cyan
  } Catch {
    Write-Host "The Receive Connector $Connector has not been documented." -ForegroundColor
    Red
  }
}

$Connector = $Null
$Send = (Get-SendConnector).Name
```

```
Foreach ($Connector in $Send) {
    Try {
        Get-ReceiveConnector -Identity $Connector -ErrorAction STOP | fl > "c:\documentation\Send-
        $Connector.txt"
        Write-Host "The Send Connector $Connector has been documented." -ForegroundColor Cyan
    } Catch {
        Write-Host "The Send Connector $Connector has not been documented." -ForegroundColor Red
    }
}
```

Using the Try and Catch along with Foreach loops the above script will document all Send and Receive Connectors. There is also some visual feedback as to which connectors are properly documented and which ones are not. Below is the visual output from the script:

```
The Receive Connector Client Proxy EX01 has been documented.
The Receive Connector Default EX01 has been documented.
The Receive Connector Default Frontend EX01 has been documented.
The Receive Connector Outbound Proxy Frontend EX01 has been documented.
The Receive Connector Client Frontend EX01 has been documented.
The Receive Connector Application 2 has been documented.
The Receive Connector Relay Test has been documented.
The Receive Connector Default EX03 has not been documented.
The Receive Connector Client Proxy EX03 has not been documented.
The Receive Connector Default Frontend EX03 has not been documented.
The Receive Connector Outbound Proxy Frontend EX03 has not been documented.
The Receive Connector Client Frontend EX03 has not been documented.
The Receive Connector ApplicationRelay has been documented.
The Send Connector Internet E-mail has not been documented.
The Send Connector To Office 365 has not been documented.
The Send Connector Outbound to Office 365 has not been documented.
```

## Hidden Connector(s)

Within Exchange Server 2016, there is a connector that exists outside the normal Get-ReceiveConnector and Get-SendConnector cmdlets. This connector exists to transfer emails between Exchange Servers and is only 'visible' or manageable through the Get-TransportService and Set-TransportService cmdlets. This is a change from previous versions of Exchange Server where the Get-TransportServer and Set-TransportServer were used but have now been deprecated. The connector does not have a lot that can be configured, in fact only two settings are visible with PowerShell and no connector is visible in the EAC. The Set-Transport service has quite a few options to pick from, more than can possibly be listed here. For our purposes the options available for the Set-TransportService and the internal connector have just two available options:

**IntraOrgConnectorProtocolLoggingLevel** - similar to the logging used on other connectors in Exchange. Two settings are available - None or Verbose.

**IntraOrgConnectorSmtpMaxMessagesPerConnection** - determines how many messages can be transmitted at a time on this connector - a 32 bit integer which is a number between 0 and 2,147,483,647.

This limited configuration of this connector is probably due to the fact that Microsoft considers the connector an "invisible intra-organization Send Connector". So, in terms of configuration, the protocol logging level is probably the most important and adjusting the Max Messages will only be needed if the connection becomes some sort of bottleneck. To adjust the settings for one server, use this cmdlet:

Set-TransportService -Identity ex01 -IntraOrgConnectorProtocolLoggingLevel Verbose

For all servers, simplify the cmdlet:

Get-TransportService | Set-TransportService -IntraOrgConnectorProtocolLoggingLevel Verbose

After changing the settings, no visible feedback results from the cmdlets. To verify the change was made, run the Get-TransportService cmdlet:

Get-TransportService | ft Name,IntraOrgConnectorProtocolLoggingLevel -Auto

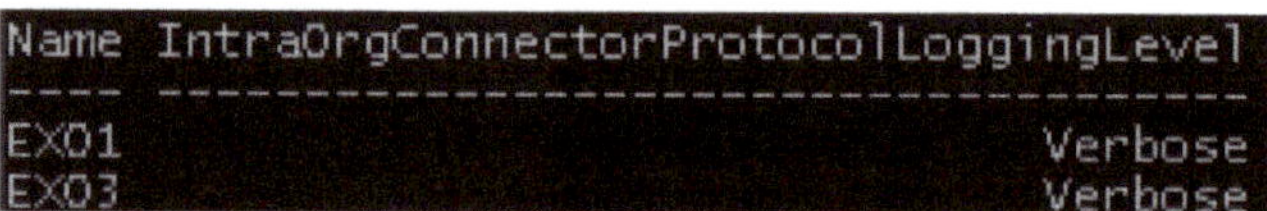


Once set, any connection made internally between Exchange servers will log their protocol connections in the same directory and log files as other protocol logging which logged here:

C:\Program Files\Microsoft\Exchange Server\V15\TransportRoles\Logs\FrontEnd\ProtocolLog\SmtpSend
C:\Program Files\Microsoft\Exchange Server\V15\TransportRoles\Logs\FrontEnd\ProtocolLog\SmtpReceive

Why is this useful? Of all the connections an Exchange server can make, the ones between Exchange servers should work… right? Well, yes and no. If there is anything or any device between the Exchange servers, the connection between the Exchange servers could fail. A misconfigured firewall could impede e-mail flow between physical sites. Reviewing the logs will reveal clues to what the issue is (or if a connection was made).

**Example**

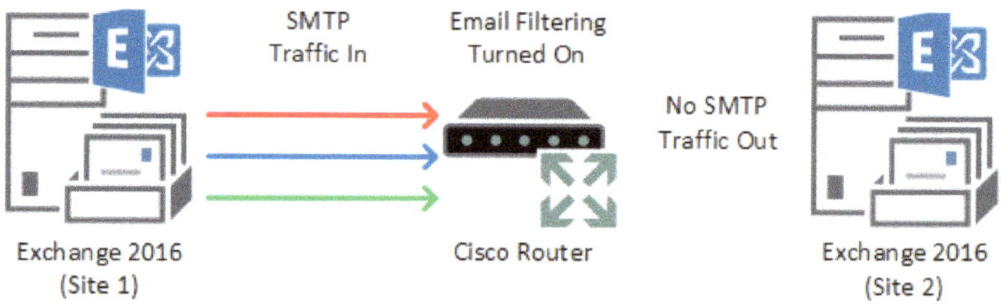


As shown in the diagram above, some devices (for example a Cisco router or firewall) have special filtering capabilities. These capabilities include filtering emails and other more specialized traffic. If the feature is turned on, email traffic between servers may not be delivered and the sending server does not receive an NDR or an indication that the SMTP traffic was delivered. So if there are items logged in the Send logs of one server and then nothing in the Receive logs of the destination server, then an intermediary device (firewall / router) should be investigated.

# Message Tracking Logs

## Configuration

Message tracking logs are a key component of Exchange's process of SMTP traffic. In older versions of Exchange, message tracking was optional and not configured by default. With newer versions of Exchange, Microsoft enabled message tracking and preconfigured some settings. Let's explore the PowerShell cmdlets that are needed to manage Message Tracking.

```
Get-Command *MessageTrack*
```

```
CommandType        Name
-----------        ----
Function           Get-MessageTrackingLog
Function           Get-MessageTrackingReport
Function           Search-MessageTrackingReport
```

Those cmdlets don't look promising.  Where else can we find the cmdlets needed to manage Message Tracking logs for Exchange Server?  A quick search via your favorite search engine:

**Search Terms** - change message tracking logs Exchange Server 2016

This reveals a link to a Microsoft TechNet article that points to configuring message tracking - https://technet.microsoft.com/en-us/library/aa997984(v=exchg.160).aspx/.  This link leads to two useful PowerShell cmdlets:

```
Get-TransportService
Set-TransportService
```

Let's take Set-TransportService cmdlet to see what we can gather from it.  Running Get-Help for the Set-TransportService cmdlet, we find there is a small set of settings that can be configured:

```
MessageTrackingLogEnabled <$True | $False>
MessageTrackingLogMaxAge <EnhancedTimeSpan>
MessageTrackingLogMaxDirectorySize <Unlimited>
MessageTrackingLogMaxFileSize <ByteQuantifiedSize>
MessageTrackingLogPath <LocalLongFullPath>
MessageTrackingLogSubjectLoggingEnabled <$True | $False>
```

In order to properly adjust these settings, we need the baseline settings.  Using the Get-TransportService cmdlet:

```
Get-TransportService | fl Messaget*
```

```
MessageTrackingLogEnabled                : True
MessageTrackingLogMaxAge                  : 30.00:00:00
MessageTrackingLogMaxDirectorySize        : 1000 MB (1,048,576,000 bytes)
MessageTrackingLogMaxFileSize             : 10 MB (10,485,760 bytes)
MessageTrackingLogPath                    : C:\Program Files\Microsoft\Exchange
                                            Server\V15\TransportRoles\Logs\MessageTracking
MessageTrackingLogSubjectLoggingEnabled  : True
```

As can be seen from the above settings, it appears that the default message tracking settings are 30 days, 1 GB in logs and Message Subject tracking is enabled.

## Change Message Tracking Log Settings

For this section we will examine a sample situation where it has been realized that the log sizing - 30 days and 1 GB - is not sufficient for being able to review the logs properly.  The logs are being overwritten in 10 days.  Per Microsoft's documentation on tracking logs, logs are overwritten if the message tracking logs reach a max age or if the log directory reaches its maximum size.  This means that the Exchange Server is generating 3 GB of logs a month.  There is a requirement to be able to review logs that are up to 45 days old.  This would require changing the max age from 30 days to 45 days and the max size from 1 GB to 4.5 GB.  These setting changes should be changed on each Exchange Server in the environment.

**Single Server Settings Change**

Get-TransportService 16-ex01 | Set-TransportService -MessageTrackingLogMaxAge 45
-MessageTrackingLogMaxDirectorySize 4500MB

The changes are now registered on the Exchange Server.

Get-TransportService | fl Messaget*

```
MessageTrackingLogEnabled                 : True
MessageTrackingLogMaxAge                  : 45.00:00:00
MessageTrackingLogMaxDirectorySize        : 4.395 GB (4,718,592,000 bytes)
MessageTrackingLogMaxFileSize             : 10 MB (10,485,760 bytes)
MessageTrackingLogPath                    : C:\Program Files\Microsoft\Exchange
                                            Server\V15\TransportRoles\Logs\MessageTracking
MessageTrackingLogSubjectLoggingEnabled   : True
```

**Modifying All Servers**

```
$Servers = (Get-TransportService).Name
Foreach ($Server in $Servers) {
   Try {
      Set-TransportService $Server -MessageTrackingLogMaxAge 45
      -MessageTrackingLogMaxDirectorySize 4500MB
   } Catch {
      Write-Host "Cannot change the message tracking log settings on $Server." -ForegroundColor Red
   }
}
```

```
MessageTrackingLogEnabled                 : True
MessageTrackingLogMaxAge                  : 45.00:00:00
MessageTrackingLogMaxDirectorySize        : 4.395 GB (4,718,592,000 bytes)
MessageTrackingLogMaxFileSize             : 10 MB (10,485,760 bytes)
MessageTrackingLogPath                    : C:\Program Files\Microsoft\Exchange
                                            Server\V15\TransportRoles\Logs\MessageTracking
MessageTrackingLogSubjectLoggingEnabled   : True
MessageTrackingLogEnabled                 : True
MessageTrackingLogMaxAge                  : 45.00:00:00
MessageTrackingLogMaxDirectorySize        : 4.395 GB (4,718,592,000 bytes)
MessageTrackingLogMaxFileSize             : 10 MB (10,485,760 bytes)
MessageTrackingLogPath                    : C:\Program Files\Microsoft\Exchange
                                            Server\V15\TransportRoles\Logs\MessageTracking
MessageTrackingLogSubjectLoggingEnabled   : True
```

No reboot or restart of services are required after making the changes.

## Querying Message Tracking Logs

Each Exchange 2016 Server has its own set of message tracking logs.  The tricky part can be when looking for a message is knowing where its ingress is into the Exchange messaging subsystem.  To begin querying for messages, we will start with one Exchange Server at a time, working our way up to all Exchange Servers in the environment. Depending on how many Exchange Servers there are and how many logs there are to review, this could impact the time it takes for the query to be completed.

First, let's get an example of how the cmdlet could be run:

```
Get-help Get-MessageTrackingLog -Examples
```

```
----------------------------- Example 1 -----------------------------
This example searches the message tracking logs on the Mailbox server named Mailbox01 for information about all
messages sent from March 13, 2015, 09:00 to March 15, 2015, 17:00 by the sender john@contoso.com.

Get-MessageTrackingLog -Server Mailbox01 -Start "03/13/2015 09:00:00" -End "03/15/2015 17:00:00" -Sender
"john@contoso.com"
```

Reviewing Example 1 we see that common criteria message tracking is start and stop dates, sender, recipients and server. Other possible criteria are EventId, Message Subject and ResultSize.

## Example

In this scenario all messages that were sent to the Administrator in the past month need to be found. This can either be done with just entering the current date and a date from 30 days ago, or a more programmatic approach could be taken. For this example we will go with option 2 with the reason being that the amount of days could then be altered for other scenarios making the script reusable. To get the dates we need, the Get-Date cmdlet will need to be used. The current date can be stored in a variable:

```
$CurrentDate = Get-Date
```

What about the date from 30 days ago? Get-Help Get-Date -Full or -examples do not contain any clues on how to handle this. A quick search with a search engine reveals that days can be added (and subtracted!) with an attribute called 'AddDays'. To go in reverse and subtract days, the value for AddDays needs to be negative:

```
$StartDate = (Get-Date).AddDays(-30)
```

These variables can now be placed into the cmdlet:

```
Get-MessageTrackingLog -Recipients administrator@domain.com -Start $StartDate -End
$CurrentDate -Server ex01
```

What if there were sixteen servers in the environment? We would not want to run this same cmdlet sixteen times. Let's construct a simple loop to handle this:

```
# Variable Definitions
$CurrentDate = Get-Date
$StartDate = (Get-Date).AddDays(-30)
$Servers = (Get-ExchangeServer).Name
$Recipient = "Administrator@Domain.Com"
$Failed = $False

Foreach ($Server in $Servers ) {
   Try {
      $Msg = Get-MessageTrackingLog -Recipients $Recipient -Start $StartDate -End $CurrentDate
      -Server $Server -ErrorAction STOP
   } Catch {
      Write-Host "The Exchange server $server could not be reached for tracking logs."
      -ForegroundColor Red
      $Failed = $True
   }
```

```
    # Check to see if the server failed and if any messages were found
    If ($Failed) {
        If ($Msg -eq $Null) {
            Write-Host "No messages were found on $Server." -ForegroundColor Yellow
        } Else {
            $Msg
        }
    } Else {
        $Failed = $False
    }
}
```

Script output:

```
Received                 Sender Address          Recipient Address       Subject
--------                 --------------          -----------------       -------
1/23/2017 11:48:49 PM    info@domain.com         dave@domain.com         Alert notification - AD change made
1/23/2017 11:48:49 PM    info@domain.com         damian@domain.com       Alert notification - AD change made
1/23/2017 12:12:52 AM    info@domain.com         dave@domain.com         Domain to expire
1/23/2017 12:12:52 AM    info@domain.com         damian@domain.com       Domain to expire
1/23/2017 12:12:52 AM    info@domain.com         it@domain.com           Domain to expire
1/22/2017 10:52:58 PM    info@domain.com         dave@domain.com         Alert notification - Disk Space
1/22/2017 10:52:58 PM    info@domain.com         damian@domain.com       Alert notification - Disk Space
1/22/2017 10:52:58 PM    info@domain.com         it@domain.com           Alert notification - Disk Space
1/22/2017 8:53:07 PM     info@domain.com         dave@domain.com         Rights Changes
1/22/2017 8:53:07 PM     info@domain.com         damian@domain.com       Rights Changes
1/22/2017 8:53:07 PM     info@domain.com         it@domain.com           Rights Changes
1/21/2017 7:57:36 PM     info@domain.com         dave@domain.com         RDP Server Changes
1/21/2017 7:57:36 PM     info@domain.com         damian@domain.com       RDP Server Changes
1/21/2017 7:57:36 PM     info@domain.com         it@domain.com           RDP Server Changes
1/21/2017 4:45:23 AM     william@littlebox.com   damian@domain.com       Your order at Littlebox.com
1/21/2017 4:45:23 AM     william@littlebox.com   damian@domain.com       Your order at Littlebox.com
1/20/2017 8:59:40 PM     info@domain.com         dave@domain.com         Alert Notification - Password Policy Cha
1/20/2017 8:59:40 PM     info@domain.com         damian@domain.com       Alert Notification - Password Policy Cha
1/20/2017 8:59:40 PM     info@domain.com         it@domain.com           Alert Notification - Password Policy Cha
```

The $Servers variable stores just the names of the Exchange 2016 Servers and $Recipients stores all recipients who received messages.  The Try and Catch section of code looks for the messages, but will display an error if an Exchange server could not be reached.  If a server cannot be reached, an error message is generated:

```
The Exchange server EX03 could not be reached for tracking logs.
```

After finding all of those messages, let's narrow it down to messages where the EventID is not 'Deliver'.  Changing the query line to add a filter for the EventId (see Chapter 2).

```
Get-MessageTrackingLog -Recipients Administrator@Domain.Com -Start $StartDate -End $CurrentDate
-Server Ex01 | Where {$_.Eventid -ne "Deliver"} | ft -Auto
```

```
EventID   Source   Sender                 Recipients                      MessageSubject
-------   ------   ------                 ----------                      --------------
FAIL      DNS      damian@domain.com      administrator@domain.com        Important Notice - Password Policy Change
FAIL      DNS      damian@domain.com      administrator@domain.com        Testing mail flow - is there a problem?
FAIL      DNS      damian@domain.com      administrator@domain.com        RDP server changes
FAIL      DNS      damian@domain.com      administrator@domain.com        Rights changes
```

# Transport Rules

Transport rules can be used for so many purposes.  These rules are usually created in the EAC, however, there are some rules that are easier to create in PowerShell due to the amount of options available.  Let's start with what is available outside of PowerShell.

Within the EAC there are some pre-canned templates for Transport rules:

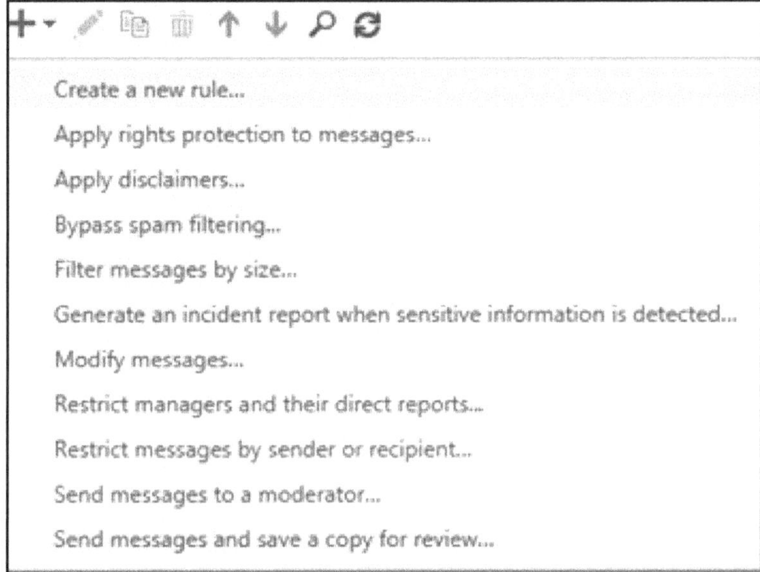

While these rule templates make life easier for making certain rules, PowerShell provides for additional configuration options not available in the web interface.  With this thought in mind, this section will cover the Transport Rule PowerShell cmdlets.   First, start with what cmdlets are available for Transport Rules:

Get-Command –Noun TransportRule

```
CommandType          Name
-----------          ----
Function             Disable-TransportRule
Function             Enable-TransportRule
Function             Get-TransportRule
Function             New-TransportRule
Function             Remove-TransportRule
Function             Set-TransportRule
```

** **Note** ** In the above PowerShell cmdlet, a difference technique is used to find a cmdlet.  The term we are searching for in the PowerShell cmdlet is in the noun (right of the hyphen) portion of the PowerShell cmdlet.  We can use the '-Noun' parameter to find cmdlets with the 'TransportRule' phrase in the noun.

Let's now examine these cmdlets in the context of some real-world scenarios.

## Example 1

In this scenario the legal department has requested a disclaimer to be placed at the bottom of each email.  The disclaimer has to contain text that was provided.  Other requirements for the disclaimer are that it must only be applied once to a message, it can be applied to only external emails, it needs to be in HTML format and contain images that provide link backs to the company's Facebook sites.  PowerShell can be used to create a

Disclaimer rule:

```
New-TransportRule -SentToScope 'NotInOrganization' -ApplyHtmlDisclaimerLocation 'Append'
-ApplyHtmlDisclaimerText 'This email is for its intended recipient.  If you are not the recipient,
please delete this email immediately.' -ApplyHtmlDisclaimerFallbackAction 'Wrap' -Name 'Legal
Required Disclaimer' -StopRuleProcessing:$false -Mode 'Enforce'  -RuleErrorAction 'Ignore'
-SenderAddressLocation 'Header'  -ExceptIfSubjectOrBodyContainsWords 'This email is for its
intended recipient'
$Logo = '<br><div style="color:#675C53; letter-spacing: 2px; line-height: 125%;"><a href="https://
www.facebook.com"> <img src="https://www.facebookbrand.com/img/assets/asset.f.logo.lg.png
"></a><br></div>'

New-TransportRule -Name 'FaceBook_logo' -Comments 'Contoso Signature - Logo' -FromMemberOf
'signature@contoso.com' -ApplyHtmlDisclaimerText $Logo -ApplyHtmlDisclaimerLocation Append
-ApplyHtmlDisclaimerFallbackAction Wrap -ExceptIfHeaderContainsWords 'This email is for its
intended recipient' -Enabled $False -Priority 11
```

To keep track of the rule being applied, PowerShell provides a switch for the one parameter of the New-TransportRule that is not available in the EAC called "log an event with message".  This used to be in the GUI, but it is no longer available. To log the event, add the switch like this:

```
-LogEventText 'Disclaimer added to the outbound message.'
```

The limitation of this switch is that it can only be run on an Edge Transport server, otherwise if its run on a server with the mailbox server an error will be generated:

```
A specified parameter isn't valid on a server with the Hub Transport role installed.
    + CategoryInfo          : InvalidArgument: (LogEventText:String) [New-TransportRule], ArgumentException
    + FullyQualifiedErrorId : [Server=16-TAP-EX02,RequestId=159a0903-64c6-4ed2-8fac-a65df3616ca8,TimeStamp=1/11/2017 5
   :35:00 PM] [FailureCategory=Cmdlet-ArgumentException] 6643FC8A,Microsoft.Exchange.MessagingPolicies.Rules.Tasks.Ne
  wTransportRule
    + PSComputerName        : 16-tap-ex02.16-tap.local
```

When the rule is triggered, an event is generated in the Application Log, Event 4000, with the event text contained in the body of the error message.


**Example 2**

Your company has decided to block all ZIP attachments in emails from external senders.  The rule should also send the original email to an email address of "Damian@16-tap.com" and delete it prior to delivery.

```
New-TransportRule -Name "ZIP Block"  -AttachmentNameMatchesPatterns zip
-GenerateIncidentReport "Damian@16-tap.com" -IncidentReportOriginalMail IncludeOriginalMail
-DeleteMessage $True -SetAuditSeverity Medium
```


Options needed for this new transport rule:

**AttachmentNameMatchesPatterns** - the name of the attachment to be found with the rule - in this case it will be 'zip'
**GenerateIncidentReport** - destination email address for incident reports when the rule matches its criteria
**IncidentReportOriginalMail** - specifies the message properties that are included in the incident report
**SetAuditSeverity** - defines a severity assigned to the message and logged into the message tracking logs

Incident report looks like the below image, notice the Rule Hit at the bottom of the screenshot for 'ZIP Block'. Below is an example of real spam being blocked because of the ZIP attachment:

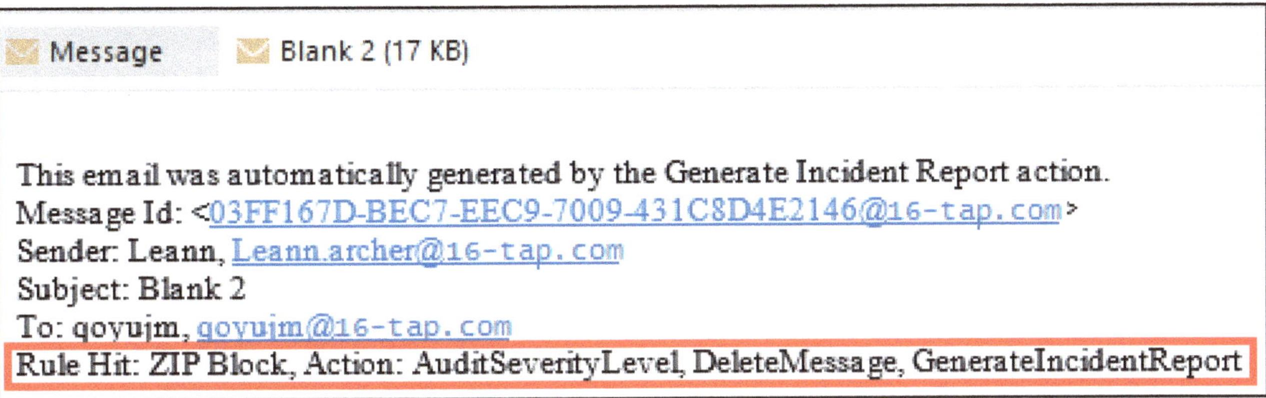


The original email is an attachment in this case 'Blank 2' is the original message with the ZIP file.

# Accepted Domains

Accepted Domains are domains for which Exchange will answer SMTP deliveries for. If a domain is not defined and an email delivery is attempted for that domain, it will not be delivered. Defining these domains is important. In addition to defining the domain, it is also ideal to have Postmaster email addresses defined as well:

## Postmaster Check

RFC822 specifies that the Postmaster address be valid for an organization. The standard does not specify whether or not the email address is attached to one mailbox or simply as an alias for any number of mailboxes in Exchange. To find a mailbox that has the Postmaster@Domain.Com address attached to it, simply use the Get-Mailbox cmdlet:

> RFC stands for Request for Comments. These documents are considered to be official documents by the IETF and ISOC. First created in 1969 as an informal process for keeping track of changes in ARPANET, they eventually morphed into a set of standards that are to be adhered to for system interoperability on the Internet.

```
Get-Mailbox Postmaster@domain.com
```

If a mailbox is found, then this requirement from RFC 822 has been satisfied. However, what if there is more than one domain in the environment? First, a list of accepted domains is needed:

```
Get-Command –Noun AcceptedDomain
```

```
CommandType          Name
-----------          ----
Function             Get-AcceptedDomain
Function             New-AcceptedDomain
Function             Remove-AcceptedDomain
Function             Set-AcceptedDomain
```

From the above results we can choose Get-AcceptedDomain as our seed cmdlet. As always, make sure to store the output from the Get-AcceptedDomain cmdlet with a variable. However, in this scenario the script does not need all information about an accepted domain, only the name of the domain is needed. How do we get this property?

Well, let's examine the output of Get-AcceptedDomain cmdlet:

```
Name                    DomainName              DomainType          Default
----                    ----------              ----------          -------
16-TAP.Local            16-TAP.Local            Authoritative       True
```

From that cmdlet, the property is appropriately name 'Domain Name'. So, using a variable for store, the Get-AcceptedDomain cmdlet and the 'DomainName' property, the following one-liner is assembled:

```
$AcceptedDomains = (Get-AcceptedDomain).DomainName
```

For processing more than one domain, a Foreach loop will be used:

```
Foreach ($Domain in $AcceptedDomains) { }
```

Now, for each domain, the verification check is for 'postmaster@domain.com'. In order to do this, first the script needs to assemble the postmaster address:

```
$Postmaster = 'Postmaster@'+$Domain
```

Now with the correct address, the script can check for a mailbox with this address. The Get-Mailbox cmdlet is the best option for this. All that is needed is the email address, which was just assembled for the Postmaster mailbox:

```
$Check = Get-Mailbox $Postmaster
```

However, what if the mailbox does not exist? There will be a need for error handling. In order to do so, results from a Get-Mailbox cmdlet for the constructed Postmaster address are stored in a variable. If the variable is empty, then a negative response is written to the screen. If the Postmaster mailbox is found, a positive response is displayed.

```
$Check = Get-Mailbox $Postmaster -ErrorAction SilentlyContinue
If (!$Check) {
   Write-Host $Postmaster" does not exist." -ForegroundColor Yellow
} Else {
   Write-Host $Postmaster" does exist" -ForegroundColor Cyan
}
```

Assemble all the code together to get this:

```
$AcceptedDomains = (Get-AcceptedDomain).DomainName
Foreach ($Domain in $AcceptedDomains) {
   $PostMaster = 'Postmaster@'+$Domain
   $Check = Get-Mailbox $Postmaster -ErrorAction SilentlyContinue
   If (!$Check) {
      Write-Host $Postmaster" does not exist." -ForegroundColor Yellow
   } Else {
      Write-Host $Postmaster" does exist" -ForegroundColor Cyan
   }
}
```

In the below testing, the two domains listed in Exchange do not have a Postmaster address defined and thus generate yellow text, a warning to add these addresses.

```
Postmaster@mmcug.com does not exist.
Postmaster@Test123.Local does not exist.
```

To rectify this, either create a Postmaster mailbox that has both these aliases assigned to it, create one Postmaster mailbox per domain or add the aliases to an existing account, preferably in IT.

## Adding Accepted Domains

Accepted Domains in Exchange can be used for many purposes - public facing domain, testing and even for internal applications mail routing.  Reviewing the PowerShell cmdlet help for New-AcceptedDomain:

```
Get-Help New-AcceptedDomain -Examples
```

```
NAME
    New-AcceptedDomain

SYNOPSIS
    This cmdlet is available only in on-premises Exchange Server 2013.

    Use the New-AcceptedDomain cmdlet to create an accepted domain in your organization. An a

    -------------------------- EXAMPLE 1 --------------------------



    This example creates the new authoritative accepted domain Contoso.


    New-AcceptedDomain -DomainName Contoso.com -DomainType Authoritative -Name Contoso
```

For adding a new domain, the criteria needed for the cmdlet is the Domain Name, Type and Display Name:

```
New-AcceptedDomain -Name Test -DomainName Test123.Local -DomainType Authoritative
```

| Name | DomainName | DomainType | Default |
| ---- | ---------- | ---------- | ------- |
| Test | Test123.Local | Authoritative | False |

Now a new Authoritative (non-relay domain) has been added to Exchange Server 2016.

## Removing Accepted Domains

Over time, some Exchange Organizations get bloated with excess SMTP domains perhaps from test purposes, acquisitions or any number of other reasons.  Removing domains from Exchange is just as easy as adding them via PowerShell.  From the previous section, we know that there is a cmdlet called Remove-AcceptedDomain.  Examples can be found using the -example switch if unsure how to use it.

```
Get-Help Remove-AcceptedDomain -Examples
```

```
NAME
    Remove-AcceptedDomain

SYNOPSIS
    This cmdlet is available only in on-premises Exchange Server 2013.

    Use the Remove-AcceptedDomain cmdlet to remove an accepted domain. When you remove an

    -------------------------- EXAMPLE 1 --------------------------


    This example removes the accepted domain Contoso.

    Remove-AcceptedDomain Contoso
```

From the help example above, the removal of a domain in PowerShell should be a simple one-liner. However, the criteria for removal is not the name of the domain, but a friendly name or display name of the domain in Exchange. Picking one domain simply requires the '| where' filter:

Get-AcceptedDomain | Where {$_.DomainName -eq "test123.local"}

Now that the domain we wish to remove has been verified, the same one-liner can be piped to the Remove-AcceptedDomain.

Get-AcceptedDomain | Where {$_.DomainName -eq "test123.local"} | Remove-AcceptedDomain

```
[PS] C:\>get-AcceptedDomain | where {$_.DomainName -eq "test123.local"} | Remove-AcceptedDomai

Confirm
Are you sure you want to perform this action?
Removing Accepted Domain "Test".
[Y] Yes  [A] Yes to All  [N] No  [L] No to All  [?] Help (default is "Y"): a
```

That's it, the Accepted Domain is no longer present in Exchange.

# Edge Transport Role

The Edge Transport Role is one of the least deployed roles in Exchange Server. That does not diminish its importance or potential. The Edge Transport Role can serve many functions in a messaging environment. It can help keep SPAM at bay, rewrite addresses and provide Hybrid mail flow between on-premises and Office 365 mail servers.

This Exchange Server Role is the only one that is supported to be deployed in the DMZ. This same role is also not deployed into the production domain and typically deployed in a workgroup. The exception to this is if there is a group of these Edge Transport servers, a domain could be created and maintained for the purposes of a common login, Group Policy and more, for all Edge Transport servers.

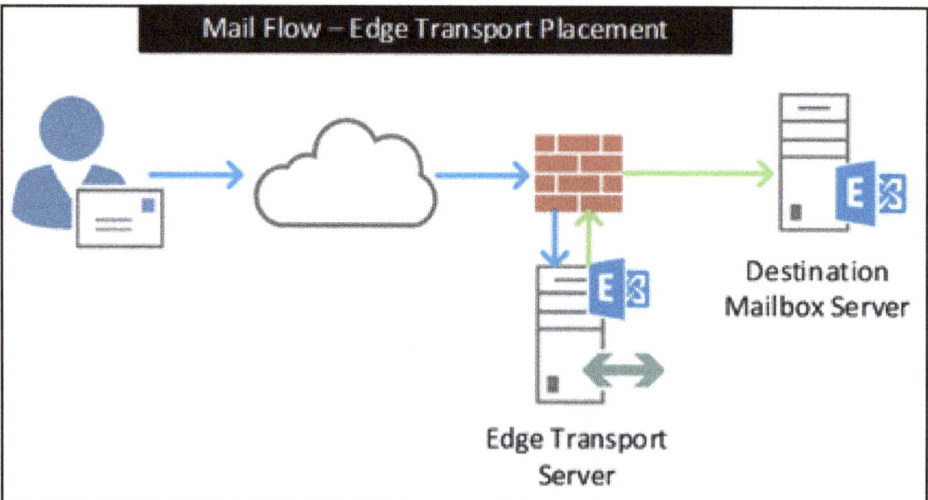


When it comes to PowerShell and the Edge Transport server, there are quite a few items that can be configured. It's

also important to note that using PowerShell is the ONLY method to manage the Edge Transport Role in Exchange Server 2016.

## Edge Subscription

Once the Edge Transport Role has been installed, one of the first things that needs to be configure will be an Edge Subscription. Think of the Edge Subscription as a link between the backend Mailbox Servers and the Edge Transport server(s) which is in the DMZ and not part of the domain. The Edge Subscription will configure the SMTP connectors so that email can flow from the Internet, through the Edge servers to the Mailbox server as well as the connectors necessary for outbound email to flow from the Mailbox server to the Edge Transport server and to the Internet.

First, creating the Edge Subscription, find the relevant PowerShell cmdlet:

```
Get-Command *edgesub*
```

```
CommandType        Name
-----------        ----
Function           Get-EdgeSubscription
Function           New-EdgeSubscription
Function           Remove-EdgeSubscription
```

```
Get-Help New-EdgeSubscription -Examples
```

```
-------------------------- Example 1 --------------------------

This example creates the Edge Subscription file. It should be run on your Edge Transport server.
New-EdgeSubscription -FileName "c:\EdgeServerSubscription.xml"

-------------------------- Example 2 --------------------------
This example imports the Edge Subscription file generated in Example 1 to the Active Directory site
Default-First-Site-Name. Importing the Edge Subscription file completes the Edge Subscription process. You must
run this command on the Mailbox server.

The first command reads the data from the Edge Subscription file and stores it in a temporary variable as a
byte-encoded data object. The second command completes the Edge subscription process.

[byte[]]$Temp = Get-Content -Path "C:\EdgeServerSubscription.xml" -Encoding Byte -ReadCount 0

New-EdgeSubscription -FileData $Temp -Site "Default-First-Site-Name"
```

When an Edge Subscription XML file is created, make sure to read the warning message to understand what an Edge Subscription entails - manually configured items such as accepted domains, classifications, domains and send connectors will be removed. These items will be modified from internal server(s) (mailbox servers) after the Edge Sync begins.

```
Confirm
If you create an Edge Subscription, this Edge Transport server will be managed via EdgeSync replication. As a result,
any of the following objects that were created manually will be deleted: accepted domains, message classifications,
remote domains, and Send connectors. After creating the Edge Subscription, you must manage these objects from inside
the organization and allow EdgeSync to update the Edge Transport server. Also, the InternalSMTPServers list of the
TransportConfig object will be overwritten during the synchronization process.
 EdgeSync requires that this Edge Transport server is able to resolve the FQDN of the Mailbox servers in the Active
Directory site to which the Edge Transport server is being subscribed, and those Mailbox servers be able to resolve the
 FQDN of this Edge Transport server. You should complete the Edge Subscription inside the organization in the next
"1440" minutes before the bootstrap account expires.
[Y] Yes  [A] Yes to All  [N] No  [L] No to All  [S] Suspend  [?] Help (default is "Y"): y
```

Sample XML File for Edge Subscription:

```xml
<?xml version="1.0"?>
<EdgeSubscriptionData xmlns:xsd="http://www.w3.org/2001/XMLSchema" xmlns:xsi="http://www.w3.org/2001/XMLSchema
    <EdgeServerName>16-04-EDGE-01</EdgeServerName>
    <EdgeServerFQDN>16-04-EDGE-01.16-04.local</EdgeServerFQDN>
    <EdgeCertificateBlob>CwAAAAEAAAAmAAAATQBpAGMAcgBvAHMAbwBmAHQAIABFAHgAYwBoAGEAbgBnAGUAUAAAADAAAAAQAAABQAAADnDGM
    <ESRAUsername>CN=ESRA.16-04-EDGE-01,CN=Services,CN=Configuration,CN={54A4DB9B-1CF9-4155-8D31-9745F9AB632D}</
    <ESRAPassword>dyyhABvIEP4=OYfoyN(W</ESRAPassword>
    <EffectiveDate>636067778837061980</EffectiveDate>
    <Duration>864000000000</Duration>
    <AdamSslPort>50636</AdamSslPort>
    <ServerType>â\»à ƒç ³à ƒç ³à ƒç ³à ƒç ³à ƒç„ a„ ˆâ¥ˆ â± â±µà¥€â… â^ â¤â^ â¶â½â½â½â¶¶¶¶¶¶"Œ<
    <ProductID />
    <VersionNumber>1942061522</VersionNumber>
    <SerialNumber>Version 15.1 (Build 30466.34)</SerialNumber>
</EdgeSubscriptionData>
```

This XML file needs to be copied to a mailbox server and be imported to finalize the Edge Subscription:

```
[PS] C:\>[byte[]]$Temp = Get-Content -Path "C:\EdgeServerSubscription.xml" -Encoding Byte -ReadCount 0
[PS] C:\>New-EdgeSubscription -FileData $Temp -Site "Default-First-Site-Name"

Name              Site                    Domain
----              ----                    ------
16-04-EDGE-01     16-TAP.Local/Conf...    16-04.local
WARNING: EdgeSync requires that the Mailbox servers in Active Directory site Default-First-Site-Name be
able to resolve the IP address for 16-04-EDGE-01.16-04.local and be able to connect to that host on port
50636.
```

After the Edge Subscription is in place, send some test messages and verify delivery with MessageTracking logs, examine message headers for the hops taken inbound and outbound by emails to and from Exchange 2016. If the message is not delivered, examine protocol logs on the internal servers first. Note that Port 50636 needs to be opened to the Edge Transport Server as well as Port 25 for SMTP traffic. Refer to https://technet.microsoft.com/en-us/library/bb331973(v=exchg.160).aspx for more information.

## Address Rewriting

This feature can be invaluable in certain scenarios with Exchange. Being able to rewrite addresses is valuable in scenarios like acquisitions (transitioning time for domain changes), partners who need to act like they are part of your company or consolidation of internal domains or groups. First, let's start with the discovery of PowerShell cmdlets needed for this:

```
Get-Command *addressr*
```

```
CommandType        Name
-----------        ----
Cmdlet             Get-AddressRewriteEntry
Cmdlet             New-AddressRewriteEntry
Cmdlet             Remove-AddressRewriteEntry
Cmdlet             Set-AddressRewriteEntry
```

Next, use the cmdlets to create a new address entry:

```
Get-Help New-AddressRewriteEntry -Examples
```

```
------------------------- Example 1 -------------------------
This example creates an address rewrite entry that rewrites the email address david@contoso.com to
david@northwindtraders.com in outbound mail. Because the OutboundOnly parameter is not set to $true, inbound mail
sent to david@northwindtraders.com is rewritten back to david@contoso.com.

New-AddressRewriteEntry -Name "Address rewrite entry for david@contoso.com" -InternalAddress david@contoso.com
-ExternalAddress david@northwindtraders.com
```

```
------------------------ Example 2 ------------------------
This example creates an address rewrite entry that rewrites all email addresses in the contoso.com domain to
northwindtraders.com in outbound mail. Because the OutboundOnly parameter is not set to $true, inbound mail sent
to northwindtraders.com recipients is rewritten back to contoso.com.
New-AddressRewriteEntry -Name "Address rewrite entry for all contoso.com email addresses" -InternalAddress
contoso.com -ExternalAddress northwindtraders.com
```

```
------------------------ Example 3 ------------------------
This example creates an address rewrite entry that rewrites all email addresses in the contoso.com domain and all
subdomains to northwindtraders.com. However, email addresses in research.contoso.com and corp.contoso.com are not
rewritten. Because this address rewrite entry affects a domain and all subdomains (*.contoso.com), address
rewriting occurs on outbound mail only.

New-AddressRewriteEntry -Name "Address rewrite entry for contoso.com and all subdomain email addresses"
-InternalAddress *.contoso.com -ExternalAddress northwindtraders.com -ExceptionList
research.contoso.com,corp.contoso.com -OutboundOnly $true
```

## Scenario 1

The company you work for has acquired a few companies over the years and is looking to add a new address rewrite policy for a newly acquired company. The current parent company domain is BigCorp.Com and the newly acquired company has an email domain of LittleBox.Com. The desire is to rewrite all email addresses for the LittleBox.Com address as BigCorp.Com addresses. Using Example 2, the cmdlet would look like this:

> New-AddressRewriteEntry –Name "LittleBox to BigCorp address rewrite." -InternalAddress LittleBox.com –ExternalAddress BigCorp.Com

With this address rewrite entry, any mailbox user with an @littlebox.com address exits the organization as @bigcorp.com:

| Internal Email Address | External Email Address |
| --- | --- |
| damian@littlebox.com | damian@bigcorp.com |
| david@littlebox.com | david@bigcorp.com |

When an email exits the Edge Transport server, the address is rewritten. By default, a reply email that comes back through the Edge Transport server and the address is rewritten back to the original domain. To ensure that happens, the Address Rewrite Entry needs to have the 'OutboundOnly' property set to the default value of 'False' as seen below:

Get-AddressRewriteEntry

```
InternalAddress    : littlebox.com
ExternalAddress    : BigCorp.Com
ExceptionList      : {}
OutboundOnly       : False
AdminDisplayName   :
ExchangeVersion    : 0.1 (8.0.535.0)
Name               : LittleBox to BigCorp address rewrite
DistinguishedName  : CN=LittleBox to BigCorp address rewr:
                     Configuration,OU=MSExchangeGateway
Identity           : CN=LittleBox to BigCorp address rewr:
                     Configuration,OU=MSExchangeGateway
Guid               : 611908d4-63fd-405a-b736-45edb7f58dd7
ObjectCategory     : CN=ms-Exch-Address-Rewrite-Entry,CN=!
                     D>
ObjectClass        : {top, msExchAddressRewriteEntry}
WhenChanged        : 8/14/2016 6:16:25 PM
WhenCreated        : 8/14/2016 6:16:25 PM
WhenChangedUTC     : 8/15/2016 1:16:25 AM
WhenCreatedUTC     : 8/15/2016 1:16:25 AM
OrganizationId     :
Id                 : CN=LittleBox to BigCorp address rewr:
                     Configuration,OU=MSExchangeGateway
OriginatingServer  : localhost
IsValid            : True
ObjectState        : Unchanged
```

Notice in the Address Rewrite Entry above, that there is also a setting for exceptions. This setting is to be used for subdomains that may not need to have an address rewritten. Take for example our fictitious LittleBox.Com domain. If there are a couple of subdomains that do not need to be process, the –ExceptionList parameter is made explicitly for that purpose. Here is an example of this exception:

New-AddressRewriteEntry -Name LittleBox -InternalAddress LittleBox.Com -ExternalAddress BigCorp.Com -ExceptionList "rnd.littlebox.com,marketing.littlebox.com" -OutboundOnly $True

```
InternalAddress     : littlebox.com
ExternalAddress     : bigcorp.com
ExceptionList       : {rnd.littlebox.com,marketing.littlebox.com}
OutboundOnly        : True
AdminDisplayName    :
ExchangeVersion     : 0.1 (8.0.535.0)
Name                : LittleBox
```

In the same scenario, at the end of the acquisition when all the mailboxes have had their primary SMTP address changed to the BigCorp.Com, the Address Rewrite Entry could be removed:

Get-AddressRewriteEntry | Remove-AddressRewriteEntry

```
Confirm
Are you sure you want to perform this action?
Removing the address rewrite entry "611908d4-63fd-405a-b736-45edb7f58dd7".
[Y] Yes  [A] Yes to All  [N] No  [L] No to All  [S] Suspend  [?] Help (default is "Y"): y
[PS] C:\>
```

**Scenario 2**

In another scenario a small consulting firm needs to hire subcontractors in order to work on larger projects or projects that are not in their normal skill set. In this scenario, individual address rewrite entries will need to be created in order to handle the new contractors that are going to work as members of the consulting firm. The address rewrite entries will take care of the external access and then the Exchange Servers will route with connectors to the appropriate destination.

New-AddressRewriteEntry -Name "Address rewrite entry for JohnSmith@DiffBox.Com" -InternalAddress JohnSmith@DiffBox.Com -ExternalAddress JohnSmith@LittleBox.Com

Similar to the entire domain address rewrite, this entry ensures that outbound messages from JohnSmith@DiffBox.Com will be rewritten to JohnSmith@LittleBox.Com.

**Configuring Anti-Spam Features**

The Edge Transport server has 10 built-in anti-spam and filtering agents present to handle message hygiene. A smaller subset of these options are also available on the Mailbox Role. How do we find these agents and configure them for proper operation? The anti-spam filters are known as Transport Agents in Exchange:

Get-Command *TransportAgent

```
CommandType         Name
-----------         ----
Cmdlet              Disable-TransportAgent
Cmdlet              Enable-TransportAgent
Cmdlet              Get-TransportAgent
Cmdlet              Install-TransportAgent
Cmdlet              Set-TransportAgent
Cmdlet              Uninstall-TransportAgent
```

First, let's start with what Transport Agents that are present on the Exchange 2016 Server:

Get-TransportAgent

```
Identity                                      Enabled        Priority
--------                                      -------        --------
Connection Filtering Agent                    True           1
Address Rewriting Inbound Agent               True           2
Edge Rule Agent                               True           3
Content Filter Agent                          True           4
Sender Id Agent                               True           5
Sender Filter Agent                           True           6
Recipient Filter Agent                        True           7
Protocol Analysis Agent                       True           8
Attachment Filtering Agent                    True           9
Address Rewriting Outbound Agent              True           10
```

Now that we have a list of agents, how can these be configured for a production environment? First, a list of PowerShell cmdlets is needed:

Get-command *filter*

```
Cmdlet          Get-AttachmentFilterEntry
Cmdlet          Get-AttachmentFilterListConfig
Cmdlet          Get-ContentFilterConfig
Cmdlet          Get-ContentFilterPhrase
Cmdlet          Get-MalwareFilteringServer
Cmdlet          Get-RecipientFilterConfig
Cmdlet          Get-SenderFilterConfig
Cmdlet          Set-AttachmentfilterListConfig
Cmdlet          Set-ContentFilterConfig
Cmdlet          Set-MalwareFilteringServer
Cmdlet          Set-RecipientFilterConfig
Cmdlet          Set-SenderFilterConfig
```

**Connection Filtering Agent**

The anti-spam agent with the highest priority is the Connection Filtering Agent. This Agent provides filters based off of the connecting servers IP Address. The following is a list of the kinds of settings that can be set for that filter:

- **IP Block List** – IP addresses that will be blocked from connecting to Exchange following a RCPT TO
- **IP Allow List** – A server that connects from this IP will bypass the anti-spam processing in Exchange
- **IP Block List Providers** – an external resource used as a reference of sending mail servers that will be blocked
- **IP Allow List Providers** - an external resource used as a reference of sending mail servers that will be allowed

There are four cmdlets that can be used to add IP Allow IPs and Providers and IP Block IPs and Providers, which correspond appropriately with the list above:

Add-IPBlockListEntry
Add-IPBlockListProvider
Add-IPAllowListEntry
Add-IPAllowListProvider

Here are some sample configuration cmdlets for this particular Transport Agent on the Edge Transport server using the above cmdlets:

```
Add-IPAllowListEntry -IPAddress 157.166.168.213
Add-IPAllowListProvider -Name "Spamhaus" -LookupDomain swl.spamhaus.org -AnyMatch $True
Add-IPBlockListEntry –IPAddress 157.166.168.210
Add-IPBlockListProvider –Name "Spamhaus Blocking" –LookupDomain sbl.spamhaus.org -AnyMatch
$True
```

The first command will allow connections from 157.166.168.213 and the second cmdlet will depend on the DNS Whitelist of the Spamhaus service to allow sender connections. The third cmdlet will block connections from the IP address of 157.166.168.210 and the fourth cmdlet will block IPs based on the DNS Block list from the Spamhaus service.

Reporting on these settings requires the use of the 'Get' version of the 'Add' cmdlets above (while selecting certain fields):

```
Get-IPAllowListProvider | ft Id, LookupDomain, Priority, Enabled, Anymatch –Auto
```

| Id | LookupDomain | Priority | Enabled | AnyMatch |
|---|---|---|---|---|
| Spamhaus | swl.spamhaus.org | 1 | True | True |

```
Get-IPAllowListEntry
```

| Identity | IPRange | ExpirationTime | HasExpired |
|---|---|---|---|
| 1 | 157.166.168.213 | 12/31/9999 3:59:59 PM | False |

```
Get-IPBlockListEntry
```

| Identity | IPRange | ExpirationTime | HasExpired | IsMachineGenerated |
|---|---|---|---|---|
| 2 | 157.166.168.210 | 12/31/9999 3:59:59 PM | False | False |

```
Get-IPBlockListProvider | ft Id, LookupDomain, Priority, Enabled, Anymatch -Auto
```

| Id | LookupDomain | Priority | Enabled | AnyMatch |
|---|---|---|---|---|
| Spamhaus Blocking | sbl.spamhaus.org | 1 | True | True |

**Note** ** Some cmdlets had to use *'–Auto'* to properly format the results.

The Connection Filter IP settings can provide a way, through the whitelist and blacklist providers, of maximizing filtering with very little work. The downside is that some companies IPs get put on a list which can cause mail flow issues between your servers and theirs. This conundrum is the double edge sword of protection. However, a good provider will help limit the number of bad connections to your server which will help to reduce the number of SPAM messages making it into Exchange.

**Address Rewriting Inbound and Agents**

These agents have already been discussed in an earlier section.

## Edge Rule Agent

This agent's function is to processes transport rules on the Edge Transport Service. If this Agent is enabled, rules can be processed on the Edge Transport Server. If this is disabled, those rules will not apply, after the connection filter and the address rewrite agents. To verify the agent is available, we need to filter the current Transport Agents as there is no special cmdlet to configure this Agent other than disable or enable:

```
Get-TransportAgent -Identity "Edge Rule Agent" | ft Identity,Enabled,Priority,Isvalid,ObjectState -Auto
```

```
Identity            Enabled Priority IsValid ObjectState
--------            ------- -------- ------- -----------
Edge Rule Agent     True           3 True            New
```

If you intend to use Transport rules, make sure to keep this service enabled and if no rules will be put in place, then turning it off won't prevent mail flow in Exchange:

```
Disable-TransportAgent -Identity "Edge Rule Agent"
```

```
Confirm
Are you sure you want to perform this action?
Disabling Transport Agent "Edge Rule Agent".
[Y] Yes  [A] Yes to All  [N] No  [L] No to All  [S] Suspend  [?] Help (default is "Y"): y
WARNING: The following service restart is required for the change(s) to take effect : MSExchangeTransport
```

### Content Filter Agent

The content filter agent is used for analyzing the content of emails entering Exchange. This can be accomplished with bad and good word lists. PowerShell cmdlets for the Content Filter Agent are:

**Add-ContentFilterPhrase** – similar to any anti-spam solution, phrases can be used as a filtering mechanism, like profanity or other undesirable works. The same phrase can also be determined to be a good word that is allowed to bypass filtering.

#### Blocking Phrase
```
Add-ContentFilterPhrase -Phrase "Free credit report" -Influence BadWord
```

```
Influence   : BadWord
Phrase      : Free credit report
Identity    : Free credit report
IsValid     : True
ObjectState : New
```

#### Allowed Phrase
```
Add-ContentFilterPhrase -Phrase "Project Undercorver" -Influence GoodWord
```

```
Influence   : GoodWord
Phrase      : Project Undercorver
Identity    : Project Undercorver
IsValid     : True
ObjectState : New
```

**Get-ContentFilterConfig** – Displays the current configuration of the filtering agent on the Edge Transport Server.

The default settings for an Exchange 2016 Edge Transport Server are:

```
Name                                   : ContentFilterConfig
RejectionResponse                      : Message rejected as spam by Content Filtering.
OutlookEmailPostmarkValidationEnabled  : True
BypassedRecipients                     : {}
QuarantineMailbox                      :
SCLRejectThreshold                     : 7
SCLRejectEnabled                       : True
SCLDeleteThreshold                     : 9
SCLDeleteEnabled                       : False
SCLQuarantineThreshold                 : 9
SCLQuarantineEnabled                   : False
BypassedSenders                        : {}
BypassedSenderDomains                  : {}
Enabled                                : True
ExternalMailEnabled                    : True
InternalMailEnabled                    : False
```

**Get-ContentFilterPhrase** – will display the currently phrases defined, though none are defined by default.  Check the phrases that were added in Exchange from the previous cmdlets (by default the cmdlet would not provide results):

```
Influence   : GoodWord
Phrase      : Project Undercorver
Identity    : Project Undercorver
IsValid     : True
ObjectState : New

Influence   : BadWord
Phrase      : Free credit report
Identity    : Free credit report
IsValid     : True
ObjectState : New
```

**Remove-ContentFilterPhrase** – allows the removal of an existing phrase.

Remove-ContentFilterPhrase -Phrase "Free credit report"

```
Confirm
Are you sure you want to perform this action?
Removing content filter phrase "Free credit report".
[Y] Yes  [A] Yes to All  [N] No  [L] No to All  [S] Suspend  [?] Help (default is "Y"): y
```

**Set-ContentFilterConfig** – Allows the change of the filtering configuration.

Reviewing the above Get-ContentFilterConfig results, we can see there are quite a few settings that can be adjusted. Notice that the SCL Delete and the SCL Quarantine are both disabled and only the SCL Reject setting is enabled.  Microsoft recommends leaving the values at the default unless messages are being blocked too often or not enough messages are being blocked.  Here are some sample uses of the cmdlet.

First, the cmdlet can be used to bypass filtering by email address or domain:

Set-ContentFilterConfig –ByPassedSenders John@TechCenter.Com
Set-ContentFilterConfig –ByPassedSenderDomains Geek.Com

The settings will replace any previous entries, so be careful when using this setting in this manner, or use the hashtable @{Add=} or @{Remove} to add or remove entries. Verify the Content Filter Configuration prior to adding or removing entries.

Second, the cmdlet can be used to adjust SCL levels for the Reject, Delete or Quarantine thresholds.  The use of the SCL Delete Threshold should be used sparingly because if the SCL Threshold is reached then the message is deleted without notification and no protocol notification is provided for the source.  A better way to handle messages with SCL Thresholds is to set just the Reject and Quarantine Thresholds, which retains the message, but delivers it to a quarantine mailbox.  Assuming an organization has had too much spam, let's adjust the Reject and Quarantine SCLs as well as add the Quarantine mailbox:

```
Set-ContentFilterConfig -SCLRejectThreshold 7 -SCLQuarantineThreshold 5 -SCLQuarantineEnabled
$True -QuarantineMailbox damian@16-tap.com
```

```
Name                                  : ContentFilterConfig
RejectionResponse                     : Message rejected as spam by Content Filtering.
OutlookEmailPostmarkValidationEnabled : True
BypassedRecipients                    : {}
QuarantineMailbox                     : damian@16-tap.local
SCLRejectThreshold                    : 7
SCLRejectEnabled                      : True
SCLDeleteThreshold                    : 9
SCLDeleteEnabled                      : False
SCLQuarantineThreshold                : 5
SCLQuarantineEnabled                  : True
BypassedSenders                       : {John@TechCenter.Com}
BypassedSenderDomains                 : {Geek.Com}
Enabled                               : True
ExternalMailEnabled                   : True
InternalMailEnabled                   : False
```

Now when messages are stamped with an SCL of 5 or 6, the message will be delivered to the Quarantine mailbox and if the message is stamped with a higher SCL, the message will be rejected, but in no scenario the email addresses.

## SenderID Agent

The SenderID Agent uses the SPF record of the sending domain and a process defined in RFC 4407.  The intent is to determine the reputation of the sender before accepting email from that server.  Let's review the default settings to see what can be changed or might be useful:

```
Get-SenderIDConfig
```

```
SpoofedDomainAction  : StampStatus
TempErrorAction      : StampStatus
BypassedRecipients   : {}
BypassedSenderDomains : {}
Name                 : SenderIdConfig
Enabled              : True
ExternalMailEnabled  : True
InternalMailEnabled  : False
```

Notice that the agent for SenderID is only enabled for external emails and not internal emails.  This is a default configuration and normally should not be changed.  One part of the Agent filtering that can be tweaked is the BypassedRecipients and BypassedSenderDomains.  These settings are similar to the Content Filtering settings.  Using PowerShell to change these settings:

```
Set-SenderIdConfig -BypassedRecipients John@TechCenter.Com -BypassedSenderDomains Geek.Com
```

Verifying the configuration changes:

```
Get-SenderIDConfig
```

```
SpoofedDomainAction  : StampStatus
TempErrorAction      : StampStatus
BypassedRecipients   : {John@TechCenter.Com}
BypassedSenderDomains : {Geek.Com}
Name                 : SenderIdConfig
Enabled              : True
ExternalMailEnabled  : True
InternalMailEnabled  : False
```

The difference between this and the previous filter is that even if the senders domain or server is flagged with a SenderID reputation issue, the email domain Geek.Com and the email address of John@TechCenter.Com will be allowed through.

## Sender Filter Agent

The Sender filter relies on the MAIL FROM: field in the SMTP header of an email. The Sender filter is commonly used to block blank senders (BlankSenderBlockingEnabled) as well as specific senders. However, entire domains and even their subdomains can be blocked depending on the need or SPAM attack occurring.

PowerShell cmdlets for this Agent are:

```
Get-Command *SenderFilter*
```

```
CommandType          Name
-----------          ----
Cmdlet               Get-SenderFilterConfig
Cmdlet               Set-SenderFilterConfig
```

Now we'll check the baseline or default configuration for this agent:

```
Get-SenderFilterConfig
```

```
Name                          : SenderFilterConfig
BlockedSenders                : {}
BlockedDomains                : {}
BlockedDomainsAndSubdomains   : {}
Action                        : Reject
BlankSenderBlockingEnabled    : False
RecipientBlockedSenderAction  : Reject
Enabled                       : True
ExternalMailEnabled           : True
InternalMailEnabled           : False
```

Let's configure the Sender Filter for a bad domain, block blank senders, change the action to Delete instead of the default action which is Reject, while also changing the action from Reject to StampStatus:

```
Set-SenderFilterConfig –BlockedDomains BobsSpamService.Com –BlankSenderBlockingEnabled $True
–Action StampStatus –RecipientBlockedSenderAction Delete
```

Verify the changes with Get-SenderFilterConfig:

```
Name                          : SenderFilterConfig
BlockedSenders                : {}
BlockedDomains                : {BobsSpamService.Com}
BlockedDomainsAndSubdomains   : {}
Action                        : StampStatus
BlankSenderBlockingEnabled    : True
RecipientBlockedSenderAction  : Delete
Enabled                       : True
ExternalMailEnabled           : True
InternalMailEnabled           : False
```

The blank sender blocking is one of the most useful parts of this agent. Remember to turn this on as it is a SPAM attack vector.

**Recipient Filter Agent**

The Recipient Filter is used with Connection filtering to determine if messages need to be blocked if on the block list or if the Recipient Validation is enabled and the mailbox does not exist.  Proper configuration of the Recipient Filter means (1) Enabling the agent, (2) Add recipients to block, (3) Configure ADAM for lookup and (4) Configure tarpitting.

PowerShell cmdlets for this Agent are:

```
Get-RecipientFilterConfig
Set-RecipientFilterConfig
```

Now we'll check the baseline or default configuration for this Agent:

```
Get-RecipientFilterConfig
```

```
Name                        : RecipientFilterConfig
BlockedRecipients           : {}
RecipientValidationEnabled  : False
BlockListEnabled            : False
Enabled                     : True
ExternalMailEnabled         : True
InternalMailEnabled         : False
```

For this configuration, we'll enable the blocking of email to the administrator mailbox and allow recipient validation:

```
Set-RecipientFilterConfig –BlockedRecipients Administrator@tap-16.com –BlockListEnabled $True –
RecipientValidationEnabled $True
```

Validating the configuration:

```
Get-RecipientFilterConfig
```

```
Name                        : RecipientFilterConfig
BlockedRecipients           : {Administrator@tap-16.com}
RecipientValidationEnabled  : True
BlockListEnabled            : True
Enabled                     : True
ExternalMailEnabled         : True
InternalMailEnabled         : False
```

**Protocol Analysis Agent**

Works in conjunction with the Sender reputation configuration (see above).

**Attachment Filtering Agent**

This Agent can filter a message based on the type or file extension of messages coming inbound.  By default quite a few attachments types are defined, being blocked by the Edge Transport Role and stripped from the email message inbound from the Internet.

PowerShell cmdlets for the Attachment Filter:

```
CommandType          Name
-----------          ----
Cmdlet               Add-AttachmentFilterEntry
Cmdlet               Get-AttachmentFilterEntry
Cmdlet               Get-AttachmentFilterListConfig
Cmdlet               Remove-AttachmentFilterEntry
Cmdlet               Set-AttachmentfilterListConfig
```

By default, quite a few file types are already configured to be blocked:

Get-AttachmentFilterEntry

```
[PS] C:\>Get-AttachmentFilterEntry |ft -auto

      Type Name                        Identity                             IsValid ObjectState
      ---- ----                        --------                             ------- -----------
ContentType application/x-msdownload   ContentType:application/x-msdownload    True Unchanged
ContentType message/partial           ContentType:message/partial             True Unchanged
ContentType text/scriptlet            ContentType:text/scriptlet              True Unchanged
ContentType application/prg           ContentType:application/prg             True Unchanged
ContentType application/msaccess      ContentType:application/msaccess        True Unchanged
ContentType text/javascript           ContentType:text/javascript             True Unchanged
ContentType application/x-javascript  ContentType:application/x-javascript    True Unchanged
ContentType application/javascript    ContentType:application/javascript      True Unchanged
ContentType x-internet-signup         ContentType:x-internet-signup           True Unchanged
ContentType application/hta           ContentType:application/hta             True Unchanged
  FileName *.xnk                       FileName:*.xnk                          True Unchanged
  FileName *.wsh                       FileName:*.wsh                          True Unchanged
  FileName *.wsf                       FileName:*.wsf                          True Unchanged
  FileName *.wsc                       FileName:*.wsc                          True Unchanged
  FileName *.vbs                       FileName:*.vbs                          True Unchanged
  FileName *.vbe                       FileName:*.vbe                          True Unchanged
  FileName *.vb                        FileName:*.vb                           True Unchanged
  FileName *.url                       FileName:*.url                          True Unchanged
  FileName *.shs                       FileName:*.shs                          True Unchanged
  FileName *.shb                       FileName:*.shb                          True Unchanged
  FileName *.sct                       FileName:*.sct                          True Unchanged
  FileName *.scr                       FileName:*.scr                          True Unchanged
  FileName *.scf                       FileName:*.scf                          True Unchanged
```

The agent configured (default settings):

Get-AttachmentFilterListConfig

```
Name                 : Transport Settings
RejectResponse       : Message rejected due to unacceptable attachments
AdminMessage         : This attachment was removed.
Action               : Strip
ExceptionConnectors  : {}
AttachmentNames      : {ContentType:application/x-msdownload, ContentTyp
                       ContentType:application/prg, ContentType:applicat
                       ContentType:application/x-javascript, ContentType
                       ContentType:x-internet-signup, ContentType:applic
                       FileName:*.wsf, FileName:*.wsc, FileName:*.vbs, F
```

We can add another file extension to this list.  In this scenario, we are blocking OpenOffice docs (ODT):

Add-AttachmentFilterEntry -Name *.odt -Type FileName

```
Type        : FileName
Name        : *.odt
Identity    : FileName:*.odt
IsValid     : True
ObjectState : Unchanged
```

Now the Edge Transport Role will block files with the ODT extension.

Instead of stripping the file from the email, there are other options (from the help file):

```
-Action <Reject | Strip | SilentDelete>
```

The SilentDelete will remove the attachment and the email from being delivered, while the Reject action will simply reject the message and stamp it with the reject message.

You may want to customize the 'RejectMessage' and the 'AdminMessage' for example if you are given a requirement from your legal department.  Here's how:

```
Set-AttachmentFilterListConfig –RejectResponse "This message has been rejected due to a file type that is not allowed per our Legal department.  Please resend with a different file format."  -AdminMessage "This document type is not allowed per Legal.  Please try a different format for the document."
```

Get-AttachmentFilterListConfig now shows the below, matching the changes that were made:

```
Name                 : Transport Settings
RejectResponse       : This message has been rejected due to a file type that is not allowed per our Legal department.
                       Please resend with a different file format.
AdminMessage         : This document type is not allowed per Legal.  Please try a different format for the document.
Action               : Strip
ExceptionConnectors  : {}
AttachmentNames      : {FileName:*.odt, ContentType:application/x-msdownload, ContentType:message/partial,
                       ContentType:text/scriptlet, ContentType:application/prg, ContentType:application/msaccess,
                       ContentType:text/javascript, ContentType:application/x-javascript,
                       ContentType:application/javascript, ContentType:x-internet-signup, ContentType:application/hta,
                       FileName:*.xnk, FileName:*.wsh, FileName:*.wsf, FileName:*.wsc, FileName:*.vbs...}
AdminDisplayName     :
```

# Protocol Logging

In Exchange Server 2016, there are two types of 'logging' enabled for SMTP connectors - Protocol Logging and Message Tracking.  By default Message Tracking is enabled, but Protocol Logging is not enabled.  The two types of logging perform a different function in Exchange.  Protocol logs are there for keeping track of the SMTP protocol communications step by step from the initial connection, transmission of the emails and the closing of the connection with the remote host:

```
#Software: Microsoft Exchange Server
#Version: 15.0.0.0
#Log-type: SMTP Receive Protocol Log
#Date: 2016-08-13T00:00:10.254Z
#Fields: date-time,connector-id,session-id,sequence-number,local-endpoint,remote-endpoint,event,data,context
2016-08-12T23:59:43.111Z,16-TAP-EX02\Default Frontend 16-TAP-EX02,08D3C2BB3FFCDE87,0,127.0.0.1:25,127.0.0.1:51302,+,,
2016-08-12T23:59:43.111Z,16-TAP-EX02\Default Frontend 16-TAP-EX02,08D3C2BB3FFCDE87,1,127.0.0.1:25,127.0.0.1:51302,>,"220 16-TAP-EX02.16-TAP.Local Micro
2016-08-12T23:59:43.111Z,16-TAP-EX02\Default Frontend 16-TAP-EX02,08D3C2BB3FFCDE87,2,127.0.0.1:25,127.0.0.1:51302,<,EHLO,
2016-08-12T23:59:43.111Z,16-TAP-EX02\Default Frontend 16-TAP-EX02,08D3C2BB3FFCDE87,3,127.0.0.1:25,127.0.0.1:51302,>,250  16-TAP-EX02.16-TAP.Local Hello
2016-08-12T23:59:43.111Z,16-TAP-EX02\Default Frontend 16-TAP-EX02,08D3C2BB3FFCDE87,4,127.0.0.1:25,127.0.0.1:51302,<,QUIT,
2016-08-12T23:59:43.111Z,16-TAP-EX02\Default Frontend 16-TAP-EX02,08D3C2BB3FFCDE87,5,127.0.0.1:25,127.0.0.1:51302,>,221 2.0.0 Service closing transmiss
2016-08-12T23:59:43.111Z,16-TAP-EX02\Default Frontend 16-TAP-EX02,08D3C2BB3FFCDE87,6,127.0.0.1:25,127.0.0.1:51302,-,,Local
2016-08-13T00:01:01.270Z,16-TAP-EX02\Default Frontend 16-TAP-EX02,08D3C2BB3FFCDE88,0,192.168.0.126:25,192.168.0.126:51376,+,,
2016-08-13T00:01:01.270Z,16-TAP-EX02\Outbound Proxy Frontend 16-TAP-EX02,08D3C2BB3FFCDE89,0,192.168.0.126:717,192.168.0.126:51377,+,,
2016-08-13T00:01:01.270Z,16-TAP-EX02\Default Frontend 16-TAP-EX02,08D3C2BB3FFCDE88,1,192.168.0.126:25,192.168.0.126:51376,>,"220 16-TAP-EX02.16-TAP.Loc
```

The log sample above shows a sample connection being made on an Exchange 2016 Server.  Notice the initial lines show the connection with the remote server.  Then there is an exchange of certificates for TLS capabilities.  After that the Mail From, Receipt To are exchanged, the message is delivered and the connection is closed.

If there is an issue with an email being delivered, this is a good place to begin for troubleshooting emails after reviewing message tracking logs.  While there is not real PowerShell script or cmdlet for searching the data, a search of the contents can be done with PowerShell.  The hard part is knowing what to look for.  In cases like this, it is usually easier to examine this file manually until the error message is found.  Then once an error message is found, then the search can be performed for reporting purposes.

** **Note** ** Outside of PowerShell, LogParser and LogParser Studio have potential to help sort out log files from the various Exchange 201 services.

https://technet.microsoft.com/en-us/scriptcenter/dd919274.aspx
https://gallery.technet.microsoft.com/Log-Parser-Studio-cd458765

**Example**

*2016-08-13T12:29:44.767Z,16-TAP-EX02\AppRelay,08D3C2BB3FF-CE7E5,15,192.168.0.126:25,192.168.0.171:25158,>,530 5.7.57 SMTP; Client was not authenticated to send anonymous mail during MAIL FROM*

Notice the error message about Authentication. With this error message PowerShell can search for this information in the SMTP Protocol Logs. What field should be examined in the Protocol Log? Data. This was determined by opening the file in Excel using comma delimitation:

| #Fields: date-time | connector-id | session-id | seque | local-endpoin | remote-endpoint | event | data |
|---|---|---|---|---|---|---|---|
| 2016-08-12T23:59:43.111Z | 16-TAP-EX02\Default Fi | 08D3C2BB3F | 0 | 127.0.0.1:25 | 127.0.0.1:51302 | + | |
| 2016-08-12T23:59:43.111Z | 16-TAP-EX02\Default Fi | 08D3C2BB3F | 1 | 127.0.0.1:25 | 127.0.0.1:51302 | > | 220 16-TAP-EX02.16-TAP.Local Micr |
| 2016-08-12T23:59:43.111Z | 16-TAP-EX02\Default Fi | 08D3C2BB3F | 2 | 127.0.0.1:25 | 127.0.0.1:51302 | < | EHLO |
| 2016-08-12T23:59:43.111Z | 16-TAP-EX02\Default Fi | 08D3C2BB3F | 3 | 127.0.0.1:25 | 127.0.0.1:51302 | > | 250 16-TAP-EX02.16-TAP.Local Hell |
| 2016-08-12T23:59:43.111Z | 16-TAP-EX02\Default Fi | 08D3C2BB3F | 4 | 127.0.0.1:25 | 127.0.0.1:51302 | < | QUIT |

Remember that with the transport services in Exchange Server 2016, there is a FrontEnd Transport Server and a Transport Service. The FrontEnd is what answers most SMTP connections coming to an Exchange Server. Some connections will also go to the Transport Service (known on the backend as the old Hub Transport service from Exchange 2007 and 2010). We will need cmdlets to find the logs files.

```
[PS] C:\>get-command *transport*

CommandType          Name
-----------          ----
Function             Disable-TransportAgent
Function             Disable-TransportRule
Function             Enable-TransportAgent
Function             Enable-TransportRule
Function             Export-TransportRuleCollection
Function             Get-FrontendTransportService
Function             Get-MailboxTransportService
Function             Get-NetTransportFilter
```

The cmdlet we need is the Get-FrontEndTransportService. With this cmdlet we can find where the Protocol logs are for the FrontEnd Transport service and thus review each log file for the phrase "*not authenticated*".

This script is modeled after the POP3 and IMAP scripts from Chapter 10. Here is the script that can parse the logs:

```
# Define Variables
$Content = @()
$Phrase = "not authenticated"

# Get all Exchange 2016 Servers
$Servers = (Get-ExchangeServer).Name
```

```
Foreach ($Server in $Servers) {
  # Get files for parsing
  $ReceiveProtocolLogPath = (Get-FrontendTransportService $Server).ReceiveProtocolLogPath
  $Location = $ReceiveProtocolLogPath.PathName
  $Path = "\\$Server`\$($Location.Replace(':','$'))"
  $Files = Get-ChildItem $Path
  Foreach ($File in $Files) {
    # Get the file name
    $Name = $File.Name
    # Import the file into a variable
    $Content = Get-Content $Path"\"$Name
    # Read each line, skip lines that start with '#' and look for lines with a phrase
    Foreach ($Line in $Content) {
      If ($Line -Like "#") {
      } Else {
        If ($Line -Match $Phrase) {
          Write-Host "$Line" -ForegroundColor Yellow
        }
      }
    }
  }
}
```

Key changes here were made in order to parse the Protocol Log files instead:

- Changed the cmdlet use for the query - Get-FrontendTransportService
- An additional line was added to parse out the path for the files as the ReceiveProtocolLogPath is a multi-value property - extracted PathName
- Change the loop to use the $Phrase variable which stores the words to be queried
- Had the script write the results to the PowerShell Window for ease of reporting

End results look something like this:

```
2016-08-13T12:28:34.674Z,16-TAP-EX02\AppRelay,08D3C2BB3FFCE7DF,14,192.168.0.126:25,192.168.0.171:25038,*,Tarpit for '0.00:00:05' due to '530 5.7.57 SMTP; Client
was not authenticated to send anonymous mail during MAIL FROM',
2016-08-13T12:28:39.690Z,16-TAP-EX02\AppRelay,08D3C2BB3FFCE7DF,15,192.168.0.126:25,192.168.0.171:25038,>,530 5.7.57 SMTP; Client was not authenticated to send a
nonymous mail during MAIL FROM,
2016-08-13T12:29:39.751Z,16-TAP-EX02\AppRelay,08D3C2BB3FFCE7E5,14,192.168.0.126:25,192.168.0.171:25158,*,Tarpit for '0.00:00:05' due to '530 5.7.57 SMTP; Client
was not authenticated to send anonymous mail during MAIL FROM',
2016-08-13T12:28:34.674Z,16-TAP-EX02\AppRelay,08D3C2BB3FFCE7DF,14,192.168.0.126:25,192.168.0.171:25038,*,Tarpit for '0.00:00:05' due to '530 5.7.57 SMTP; Client
was not authenticated to send anonymous mail during MAIL FROM',
2016-08-13T12:28:39.690Z,16-TAP-EX02\AppRelay,08D3C2BB3FFCE7DF,15,192.168.0.126:25,192.168.0.171:25038,>,530 5.7.57 SMTP; Client was not authenticated to send a
nonymous mail during MAIL FROM,
2016-08-13T12:29:39.751Z,16-TAP-EX02\AppRelay,08D3C2BB3FFCE7E5,14,192.168.0.126:25,192.168.0.171:25158,*,Tarpit for '0.00:00:05' due to '530 5.7.57 SMTP; Client
was not authenticated to send anonymous mail during MAIL FROM',
```

This script provided six results of bad authentication attempts on two Exchange 2016 Servers.

PowerShell cmdlets can also turn on Protocol Logging as well as manipulate other settings on the various connectors or log files.  Modify log locations:

```
Set-TransportService "Application Relay" -ReceiveProtocolLogPath "d:\receive\protocol\"
Set-FrontEndTransportService "Application Relay" -ReceiveProtocolLogPath "d:\receive\protocol\"
```

Modify verbose settings on the connectors:

```
Set-ReceiveConnector "Application Relay" -ProtocolLoggingLevel Verbose
Set-ReceiveConnector "Application Relay" -ProtocolLoggingLevel None
Set-SendConnector "Internet Email" -ProtocolLoggingLevel Verbose
Set-SendConnector "Internet Email" -ProtocolLoggingLevel None
```

# Test Cmdlets

As with many other features or functions in Exchange, test cmdlets are useful for confirming functionality of said feature or function. When it comes to SMTP traffic, there is a set of two cmdlets that are appropriate for testing mail flow:

```
Test-Mailflow
Test-SmtpConnectivity
```

** **Note** ** Outside of PowerShell, Microsoft provides a website called Remote Connectivity Analyzer which can be found at https://testconnectivity.microsoft.com/. This site provides for many Exchange tests, among these tests are mail flow tests. Test cmdlets focused on client access services like Outlook, ActiveSync, POP and more require a Microsoft provided be run (and run as an Administrator) New-TestCASConnectivityUser.ps1.

## Test Mailflow

The Test-Mailflow cmdlet provides a quick test of the recipient address to see if the destination can be reached. First, start with the get-help of the cmdlet to see what kinds of tests could be run in Exchange Server 2016:

```
Get-Help Test-Mailflow -Examples
```

```
------------------------ EXAMPLE 1 ------------------------
This example tests message flow from the server name Mailbox1 to the server named Mailbox2. Note that you need
while connected to Mailbox1.

Test-Mailflow Mailbox1 -TargetMailboxServer Mailbox2
```

```
------------------------ EXAMPLE 2 ------------------------
This example tests message flow from the local Mailbox server where you're running this command to the email address
Test-Mailflow -TargetEmailAddress john@contoso.com
```

For the first example, a test of a single internal email address to Exchange:

```
Test-Mailflow -TargetEmailAddress damian@16-tap.local
```

The cmdlet generates a quick summary of results from the SMTP test to this single email address:

```
[PS] C:\>Test-Mailflow -TargetEmailAddress damian@16-tap.local

RunspaceId          : 27a8fb00-0f5e-4d8f-84ab-f676fefbfb0e
TestMailflowResult  : Success
MessageLatencyTime  : 00:00:26.6848138
IsRemoteTest        : True
Identity            :
IsValid             : True
ObjectState         : New
```

Now, if a Test-Cmdlet finds an issue, an error message will be generated:

```
[PS] C:\> Test-Mailflow 16-tap-ex01 -TargetMailboxServer 16-tap-ex02
Database is dismounted.
    + CategoryInfo          : InvalidData: (:) [Test-Mailflow], RecipientTaskException
    + FullyQualifiedErrorId : [Server=16-TAP-EX02,RequestId=ac118776-e9fd-408c-82b1-2c1faef5a708,TimeStamp:
   ientTaskException] C5B3053A,Microsoft.Exchange.Monitoring.TestMailFlow
    + PSComputerName        : 16-tap-ex02.16-tap.local
```

Another type of error could show up if there is a mail flow problem:

```
[PS] C:\Downloads> Test-Mailflow 16-tap-ex02 -TargetMailboxServer 16-tap-ex01


RunspaceId          : 27a8fb00-0f5e-4d8f-84ab-f676fefbfb0e
TestMailflowResult  : *FAILURE*
MessageLatencyTime  : 00:00:00
IsRemoteTest        : True
Identity            :
IsValid             : True
ObjectState         : New
```

## Test-SmtpConnectivity

The test-smtpconnectivity cmdlet can bulk examine all the receive connectors to see if SMTP connectivity can be verified for each connector.

```
Get-help Test-SMTPConnectivity -Examples
```

```
------------------------------ Example 1 ------------------------------
This example verifies SMTP connectivity for all Receive connectors on the Mailbox server named Mailbox01

Test-SmtpConnectivity Mailbox01
```

```
------------------------------ Example 2 ------------------------------
This example verifies SMTP connectivity for all Receive connectors on all Mailbox servers in the organization.

Get-TransportService | Test-SmtpConnectivity
```

Sample results from Test-SMTPConnectivity:

```
[PS] C:\Downloads>get-transportservice | Test-SmtpConnectivity

ReceiveConnector                Binding              EndPoint                              StatusCode
Default 16-EX01                 0.0.0.0:2525         192.168.0.125:2525                    Success
Default 16-EX01                 0.0.0.0:2525         [fe80::15cc:8c1c:5205:70a8]:2525      Success
Default 16-EX01                 [::]:2525            192.168.0.125:2525                    Success
Default 16-EX01                 [::]:2525            [fe80::15cc:8c1c:5205:70a8]:2525      Success
Client Proxy 16-EX01            [::]:465             192.168.0.125:465                     Success
Client Proxy 16-EX01            [::]:465             [fe80::15cc:8c1c:5205:70a8]:465       Success
Client Proxy 16-EX01            0.0.0.0:465          192.168.0.125:465                     Success
Client Proxy 16-EX01            0.0.0.0:465          [fe80::15cc:8c1c:5205:70a8]:465       Success
Default Frontend 16-EX01        [::]:25              192.168.0.125:25                      Success
Default Frontend 16-EX01        [::]:25              [fe80::15cc:8c1c:5205:70a8]:25        Success
Default Frontend 16-EX01        0.0.0.0:25           192.168.0.125:25                      Success
Default Frontend 16-EX01        0.0.0.0:25           [fe80::15cc:8c1c:5205:70a8]:25        Success
Outbound Proxy Frontend 16-EX01 [::]:717             192.168.0.125:717                     Success
Outbound Proxy Frontend 16-EX01 [::]:717             [fe80::15cc:8c1c:5205:70a8]:717       Success
Outbound Proxy Frontend 16-EX01 0.0.0.0:717          192.168.0.125:717                     Success
Outbound Proxy Frontend 16-EX01 0.0.0.0:717          [fe80::15cc:8c1c:5205:70a8]:717       Success
Client Frontend 16-EX01         [::]:587             192.168.0.125:587                     Success
Client Frontend 16-EX01         [::]:587             [fe80::15cc:8c1c:5205:70a8]:587       Success
Client Frontend 16-EX01         0.0.0.0:587          192.168.0.125:587                     Success
Client Frontend 16-EX01         0.0.0.0:587          [fe80::15cc:8c1c:5205:70a8]:587       Success
Default 16-EX02                 0.0.0.0:2525         192.168.0.126:2525                    Success
Default 16-EX02                 0.0.0.0:2525         [fe80::c0dc:f380:cca:c2e3]:2525       Success
Default 16-EX02                 [::]:2525            192.168.0.126:2525                    Success
Default 16-EX02                 [::]:2525            [fe80::c0dc:f380:cca:c2e3]:2525       Success
Client Proxy 16-EX02            [::]:465             192.168.0.126:465                     Success
Client Proxy 16-EX02            [::]:465             [fe80::c0dc:f380:cca:c2e3]:465        Success
Client Proxy 16-EX02            0.0.0.0:465          192.168.0.126:465                     Success
Client Proxy 16-EX02            0.0.0.0:465          [fe80::c0dc:f380:cca:c2e3]:465        Success
```

This cmdlet is very handy for verifying that the Receive Connectors on both servers are working as expected.

**Further Reading on Mail Flow**

https://msdn.microsoft.com/en-us/library/aa998825(v=exchg.160).aspx
https://technet.microsoft.com/en-us/library/aa996349(v=exchg.160).aspx
https://technet.microsoft.com/en-us/library/jj150491(v=exchg.160).aspx

# 9 Mail Flow - Compliance



In the previous chapter we covered some of the basics of the SMTP protocol in Exchange 2016 and how we can work with it in PowerShell. This chapter will cover the more advanced components of SMTP in Exchange 2016 – message hygiene, Data Loss Prevention (DLP), journaling and Rights Management. Some of the things that will be configured or managed with PowerShell may require additional licensing in Exchange. Some of these features are considered premium and will require an enterprise user CAL to be properly licensed to use the feature.

This chapter covers enterprise level features that are more likely to be used by larger messaging environments. Generally larger environments dictate more strict compliance requirements rather than smaller environments. Legal departments tend to be larger and more structured with policies in place for protecting all forms of communication and email is heavily regulated.

DLP is an interesting feature that was introduced into Exchange Server 2013 and continued in Exchange Server 2016. This features allows for more advanced transport rules for processing emails containing potentially sensitive information in them. Additional knowledge of Regular Expressions (RegEx) and compliance regulations may be needed in order to make the most of this feature. RegEx allows for more complex transport criteria.

The journaling feature is a feature commonly used in Exchange. Typically journaling is used for compliance, business continuity or discovery purposes. Messages can be journaled locally or externally depending on the need. Best practices for journaling will be covered as well.

Rights Management is a particularly interesting feature that also requires outside servers to make the feature work with Exchange. While Rights Management will be covered with respect to Exchange 2016 the build-out of the Rights Management infrastructure will not be covered detail. Sample diagrams will be provided. Some configuration tips will also be included for Rights Management, but no detailed installation or configuration will be provided.

Lastly, message hygiene, covered in the previous chapter, will be covered more in this chapter. Best practices for this feature in Exchange 2016 will be covered as well.

# Message Hygiene

Message hygiene is a nebulous topic, but one of importance from an administration and user perspective. For administrators reducing the amount of spam or malware that enters Exchange makes for less supports calls, fixing or troubleshooting issues with email. For the end user, a reduced amount of bad messages makes for a better experience. In Chapter 8, as part of this books coverage of message hygiene, the Edge Transport Role was covered and this role includes many message hygiene features. This chapter will cover this topic a bit more with a brief explanation of external controls for message hygiene, agents on the mailbox servers, malware filter and finally managing it all with PowerShell.

## External Controls

In order to block spam prior to the message being delivered to any Exchange Mailbox or Edge Transport servers, there are some additional things we can enable to help control message hygiene.

- **DKIM** – Allows a recipient of a message to verify the sender of the message. Requires a third party product like PowerMTA, DkimX or a DKIM Transport / Signing Agent. Signs the email with a digital signature that is verifiable with via the signers public key.
- **DMARC** – A Special TXT DNS record used by servers on how to handle DKIM or SPF failures.
- **SPF Record** – A special DNS record that provides a list of valid SMTP servers for your domain.
- **Message hygiene appliances or services** – There are many third party vendors available for message hygiene.

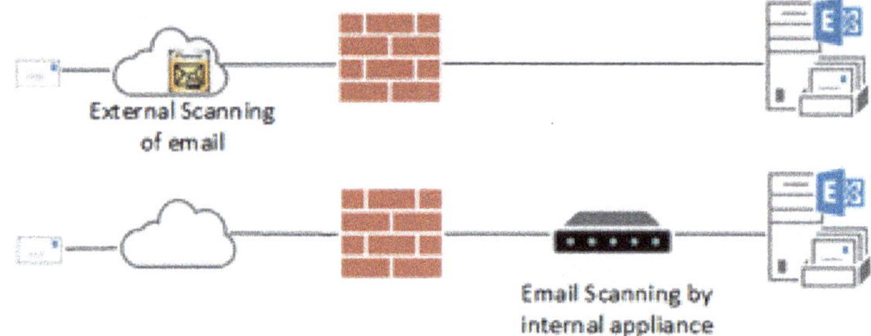


**Note** None of the above can be configured with PowerShell, but these items should be on your list to begin protecting Exchange 2016. DKIM and DMARC require outside products and are not native to Exchange 2016.

## Mailbox Server Agents

Like the Edge Transport Role, the Mailbox server role also has agents for message hygiene. The agents are not as numerous as what the Edge Transport Role has on them. The most important missing agent is the Connection Filtering agent which prevents the use of Real-time Black Lists (RBL) which are most effective in message hygiene. The agents on mailbox role servers are not enabled by default, been the case with previous versions of Exchange. The agents that are available on this role are:

- Sender Filter agent
- Sender ID agent
- Content Filter agent
- Protocol Analysis agent (sender reputation)

Enabling these agents requires a pre-built Microsoft PowerShell script:

```
& $env:ExchangeInstallPath\Scripts\Install-AntiSpamAgents.ps1
```

After the script is run, the Transport service needs to be restarted to initiate the newly configured agents.

```
Restart-Service MSExchangeTransport
```

Once that is complete, make sure to change the global configuration settings for the Exchange Transport to include all internal mail servers so as to not have any messages blocked by the newly configured agents. For example, if you have three internal SMTP servers that need to bypass the agents and they have IP Addresses of 172.20.1.55, 172.20.1.56 and 172.20.1.57:

```
Set-TransportConfig -InternalSMTPServers @{Add="172.20.1.55","172.20.1.56","172.20.1.57"}
```

Once the settings are configured, verify them with a Get-TransportConfig cmdlet:

```
Get-TransportConfig | fl InternalSMTPServers
```

## Managing Transport Agents

If there is no Edge Transport server present, then configuring these agents on the Mailbox servers is one option. All of these agents were detailed with PowerShell cmdlets in Chapter 8, the agents can be configured the same way. See page 179 for configuring these agents. That being said, the agents that can be configured on the Mailbox server only are not as effective as what is provided to the Edge Transport server. A better option would be to use a third party appliance or service to handle these features more effectively.

# Data Loss Prevention

Data Loss Prevention (DLP) is a growing feature request among many types of organizations. The draw for these companies is that the DLP provides another line of defense for loss of corporate sensitive data. Key among features built into Exchange Server's DLP are the predefined sensitive data types provided by Microsoft and that DLP can be customized for an environment with templates and policy tips. For the end user, DLP is invisible for some scenarios, for example when administrators are testing rules, when a DLP policy stops a message from either reaching the end user or exiting Exchange DLP is only visible when a Policy Tip is configured to make the end user aware of the information that was being sent out.

** **Note** ** DLP is a premium feature of Exchange Server 2016 and requires an Enterprise CAL.

## Features of DLP

- 80+ Sensitive Data Types
- Policy Tips – for OWA and Outlook
- Document Fingerprinting
- Coordinates with Transport Rules
- Customization – Templates
- 'Test Mode' – without affecting users

## DLP PowerShell

First, we'll start with the cmdlets that are available for DLP:

```
Get-Command *DLP*
```

```
CommandType        Name
----------         ----
Function           Export-DlpPolicyCollection
Function           Get-DlpPolicy
Function           Get-DlpPolicyTemplate
Function           Import-DlpPolicyCollection
Function           Import-DlpPolicyTemplate
Function           New-DlpPolicy
Function           Remove-DlpPolicy
Function           Remove-DlpPolicyTemplate
Function           Set-DlpPolicy
```

Exchange Server 2016 has no DLP policies defined by default. With a brand new installation of Exchange 2016 this can be verified with 'Get-DLPPolicy'. The same cmdlet can also be used later for verifying DLP policies.

## DLP Templates

DLP Templates are one of the building blocks for DLP in Exchange Server 2016. To begin with the process, first use a template that is custom created or a Microsoft template. A DLP Policy is built based on that Template and then the DLP Policy is used in a Transport Rule.

With Exchange Server 2016, Microsoft has included a few DLP Templates to speed up deployment of DLP:

```
Get-DlpPolicyTemplate | ft –Auto
```

Creating Custom DLP Templates can be done with PowerShell or with an XML editor as there is no option to do so in the EAC. Whichever way the template is created it can be imported into Exchange with PowerShell. Looking at the cmdlets above, the Import-DLPPolicyTemplate looks like the cmdlet to do the job. What cmdlet examples are there:

```
Get-Help Import-DLPPolicyTemplate -Examples
```

```
---------------------------- Example 1 ----------------------------

This example imports the DLP policy template file C:\My Documents\External DLP Policy
Template.xml.

Import-DlpPolicyTemplate -FileData ([Byte[]]$(Get-Content -Path "C:\My Documents\External DLP
Policy Template.xml" -Encoding Byte -ReadCount 0))
```

From the above example, we see that an XML file is needed in order to create/import a DLP Template into Exchange. Creating an XML file takes a bit of time and is somewhat complicated. These XML files can be created with a PowerShell script that has a series of questions. This script was written by one of the authors of the book and can be found here:

https://justaucguy.wordpress.com/2015/01/27/dlp-custom-xml-generation-script/

In practical terms, creating a one-off XML file is easier if you can use the Microsoft help and TechNet pages that are provided. Skipping forward, assuming an XML file has been created (BigBox-PII.XML) we can import the template using the example above for guidance.

```
Import-DlpPolicyTemplate -FileData ([Byte[]]$(Get-Content -Path "C:\DLPTemplate\BigBox-PII.xml"
-Encoding Byte -ReadCount 0))
```

Once the template is created, we can proceed to the creating of a DLP Policy based off of this template. There is no real limit to the number of templates that can be created. The advantage of a custom XML for a custom template is that a RegEx query can be used to query for custom criteria – bank account numbers, custom card numbers, etc. The process for DLP rules is the same from here on whether the XML file is a custom or predefined template.

## DLP Policies

DLP policies are built off of either the built in templates provided by Microsoft (see above) or custom templates like the one created in the example on the previous page. Transport Rules use DLP policies as matching criteria for SMTP messages traversing through an Exchange Server. Pre-canned templates exist for more common data types (financial data for Canada, UK or the US).

Creating a new DLP Policy with PowerShell requires the 'New-DLPPolicy' cmdlet. Here is an example of the cmdlet:

```
Get-Help New-DLPPolicy –Examples
------------------------- Example 1 -------------------------
This example creates a new DLP policy named Contoso PII with the following values:

The DLP policy is enabled and set to audit only.

The DLP policy is based on the existing "U.S. Personally Identifiable Information (PII) Data"
DLP policy template.
New-DlpPolicy –Name "Contoso PII" –Template "U.S. Personally Identifiable Information (PII)
Data"
```

Other options that are available for configuring a new DLP Policy that should be considered are:

- **Mode <Audit | AuditAndNotify | Enforce>** - How the policy notifies the end users
- **State <Enabled | Disabled>** - Policies are enabled by default

Sample Policy creations of these two new DLP policies will be based off of an existing Microsoft templates ("Japan Financial Data") and a template we created in the previous section ("Big Box PII"):

```
New-DlpPolicy -Name "Big Box Personal Info" -Template "Big Box PII"
New-DlpPolicy -Name "Japanese Subsidiary Finance Data" -Template "Japan Financial Data"
```

The Japanese DLP Policy did generate a notification when it was created:

Once created, verifying the policies is the next step:

```
Get-DLPPolicy | ft -Auto
```

| Name | Publisher | State | Mode |
|------|-----------|-------|------|
| Japanese Subsidiary Finance Data | Microsoft | Enabled | Audit |
| Big Box PII | Data Big Box | Enabled | Audit |

Now there are two DLP policies that can be called by Transport Rules to affect messages that meet the policy's criteria.

## Policy Tips

Policy Tips are like any other Exchange Server Tips (MailTips is one example) that provide a visual indicator of a problem or something that the end user (the message sender) should be aware of. DLP policy tips will work in either Outlook or OWA. For Outlook, make sure that the latest version of Outlook 2013 or 2016 are used in order to get the most out of the tips. Outlook can cache DLP information and any changes that are made may show up immediately. Previous versions of Outlook do not work with Policy Tips, nor a standalone installation of Outlook.

** **Note** ** Policy tips do not work if the full Office Suite is also not installed. Standalone Outlook will not work with policy tips - https://support.microsoft.com/en-us/kb/2823263.

With regards to PowerShell and Policy Tips, the wording of the tip can be customized and the tip can be turned on or off depending on the scenario. For example, a DLP Policy, tied to a Transport Rule that looks for sensitive data, can be flagged for 'Testing with no Policy Tips'. To configure the rule, we need to look at options for this rule ('mode' parameter):

Get-Help Set-TransportRule –Full

```
-Mode <Audit | AuditAndNotify | Enforce>
    The Mode parameter specifies in which mode this rule will operate. Valid values include:

    * Audit The rule is turned on, and what would have happened if the rule was enforced is
      logged in message tracking logs. Exchange doesn't take any action that impacts the
      delivery of the message.
    * AuditAndNotify The rule is turned on, and it operates the same way it would in Audit
      mode, but notifications are also enabled.
    * Enforce The rule is turned on, and all actions specified in the rule are taken.
    The default value is Enforce.

    Required?                       false
    Position?                       Named
    Default value
    Accept pipeline input?          False
    Accept wildcard characters?     false
```

Using the switch '-Mode Audit' and no Policy Tips would be visible to the end user. For either '-Mode AuditAnd-Notify' or '-Mode Enforce', policy tips would be visible in the mail client if a message matches the rule (and the associated DLP Policy). Policy Tips can also be customized. If, instead of the pre-canned tips, there is a need for a custom message for end users, these can be done with PowerShell. First, what cmdlets are available:

Get-Command *PolicyTip*

```
CommandType         Name
-----------         ----
Function            Get-PolicyTipConfig
Function            New-PolicyTipConfig
Function            Remove-PolicyTipConfig
Function            Set-PolicyTipConfig
```

First, we start with what is already configured for Policy Tips:

Get-PolicyTipConfig

As expected, no results are to be found. We will need to create our own set of Policy Tips to notify end users with these custom messages.

Get-Help New-PolicyTipConfig –Examples

The most important parameter is '-Value' as it determines what the end message will be provided to the end user. Notice that the second example provides a URL for the end user. This might be more appropriate if there is a fully fleshed out policy for these restricted attachments or PII. When creating a new Policy Tip, the name of the tip needs to reference two criteria: the locale and the action to be performed. A working example for the English language would be:

-Name "en\NotifyOnly"

If for example the wrong name is chosen, then a lot of errors are generated:

```
Name must be in the form locale\action where action can be: "zh-CHS, en, fr, de, ja, zh-CHT, it, ko, pt, ru, es, ar,
cs, da, nl, fi, el, he, hu, no, pl, pt-PT, sv, tr, ro, th, fil-PH, hi, id, lv, ms, uk, vi, bg, hr, et, lt, sr, sk, sl,
eu, ca, zh-HK, fa, gl, is, kk, sr-Cyrl-CS, ur, af, sq, am-ET, hy, as-IN, bn-IN, bn-BD, bs-Cyrl-BA, bs-Latn-BA, ka, gu,
ha-Latn-NG, ig-NG, iu-Latn-CA, ga-IE, xh-ZA, zu-ZA, kn, km-KH, qut-GT, rw-RW, sw, kok, ky, lo-LA, lb-LU, mk, ms-BN,
ml-IN, mt-MT, mi-NZ, mr, ne-NP, nn-NO, or-IN, ps-AF, pa, quz-PE, nso-ZA, tn-ZA, si-LK, ta, tt, te, uz, cy-GB, wo-SN,
yo-NG" and locale can be: "NotifyOnly, RejectOverride, Reject, Url". If action is URL, then name must be "Url" with
no locale.
    + CategoryInfo          : InvalidArgument: (:) [New-PolicyTipConfig], NewPolicyTipConfigInvalidNameException
    + FullyQualifiedErrorId : [Server=16-TAP-EX02,RequestId=c29978a8-adbe-4cc1-b8B1-30fd2474b531,TimeStamp=8/30/2016 2
   :16:59 AM] [FailureCategory=Cmdlet-NewPolicyTipConfigInvalidNameException] D715A4C9,Microsoft.Exchange.Management.
   PolicyNudges.NewPolicyTipConfig
    + PSComputerName         : 16-tap-ex02.16-tap.local
```

A complete cmdlet would look like this:

New-PolicyTipConfig -Name en\NotifyOnly -Value 'This message contains private information that should not be shared outside of this company.'

To verify the cmdlet worked:

Get-PolicyTipConfig | ft –Auto

```
Identity       Value
--------       -----
en\NotifyOnly  This message contains private information that should not be shared outside of thi...
```

Other possible actions are RejectOverride and Reject.  Reject will block the message completely whereas RejectOverride allows for an override if the user puts "Override" in the subject line of the message.

New-PolicyTipConfig -Name en\RejectOverride -Value 'This message contains private information that should not be shared outside of this company.'


# Document Fingerprinting

DLP's Document Fingerprinting feature allows for DLP to search for very specific content that is sent through e-mail, in this case a matching attachment.  The fingerprint is basically a hash of the properties of the document in question.  The document itself is not stored in Exchange.  Outlook will also evaluate a document locally and the document is not sent over the wire between Exchange and Outlook.  The process is similar to creating a template, with the source being a document to import.  Then build Transport Rules around the document to restrict, allow or log when a rule processes the e-mail.  Below is a scenario which will provide a better idea as to what can be done with this, and what PowerShell can provide.


### Scenario

HR has some confidential forms that are to be used internally by the company.  They've provided IT with three forms that need to prevent from being emailed to anyone external to the organization.  First, place a copy of the document on the Exchange server so that it can be imported for creating the DLP Policy.  Any form or document to be 'fingerprinted' should be blank so that no information interferes with the evaluation.

For PowerShell cmdlets, start with Get-Content (used to store the file in a variable) and then use New-FingerPrint to create the fingerprint based off the content from the Get-Content variable.  Follow this by creating a new Data Classification to be used by Transport Rules later.

There are three forms to be protected:

- EmployeePII-Form.docx
- Employee-Review-2016.docx
- Termination-RequestForm.docx

Next, store the document content in a variable in preparation for Transport Rules to use the content. Let's walk through the process of taking these documents and creating Transport Rules to handle them:

Import each individual document into a separate variable to be used by New-Fingerprint:

```
$HRDoc1 = Get-Content "C:\Documents\HR\EmployeePII-Form.docx" -Encoding Byte
$HRDoc2 = Get-Content "C:\Documents\HR\Employee-Review-2016.docx" -Encoding Byte
$HRDoc3 = Get-Content "C:\Documents\HR\Termination-RequestForm.docx" -Encoding Byte
```

Notice that the documents are encoded as a 'byte' type document. According to the help file on the 'Get-Help' cmdlet, there are a few data types that can be used:

ASCII, BigEndianUnicode, Byte, String, Unicode, UTF7, UTF8 and Unknown.

In choosing a Word document (which is a binary file) we need to choose 'byte' for the encoding to properly ingest the hash from the file. The 'Get-Content' cmdlet does have other parameters, but for the purposes of fingerprinting itself, no others are required. Simply put in a location of the file and what encoding to use for the document for fingerprinting and store that in a variable.

Create a fingerprint based off the document stored in each variable:

```
$HRDoc1_Fingerprint = New-Fingerprint -FileData $HRDoc1 -Description "Employee PII Form"
$HRDoc2_Fingerprint = New-Fingerprint -FileData $HRDoc2 -Description "Employee Review 2016"
$HRDoc3_Fingerprint = New-Fingerprint -FileData $HRDoc3 -Description "Termination Request Form"
```

** No cmdlet can query fingerprints that were created, to see the fingerprints raw data, you can simply 'dump' the variable contents to the PowerShell window:

```
$HRDoc1_Fingerprint | fl
```


```
Description   : Employee PII Form
ShingleCount  : 20
Value         : fz382n/99+z//vdfsu/9Rv/G3/7G+vZT11Pu/v/v+//F2s9v/td9//X6sxN/dtfbz6rv3v/+9fy6U9f8W/9/9v/+3sr9xsf7+2d/Xt/P
                919/bM+K/7//3ePvktyX/cff/3f3/H92/Preiu/+3/N//XXs/27v3vrX/ftdW390/leh//9275517ebj375/+/5ff17/9///f3v7d/9/
                x8f9TtX7f/9v/etv/7//b9b6//67F+7e//5/7LP9f7//3vt37/p5f+fvs1/v//GTH//rd38919/v7v/Mf/7v/v6q1s3//+/+357fc7p/
                vv3o/fvur/n3/+dTz67039bc1/qf/7r+v/P/TnHs0v377/3m3/9//PbM5do6/c76f+7+yu93j9/XvN3bk9w7////72//619f/7j6U9/u
                Pf3v////6//uyv10x00z+Xn87Nrv7vXe3fydF3/c/qrb3X9//1eP//3eu+z/9n/M17x/f8//58/T7H/+vn/W+ut/7+fUuHfs/z3/b/P9
                9kP37Kn991P7U++eD//7/M7j3md970/PxueW738//e78f924y91//n897293/P3/xdrbW/1W/e5/v5NT//992/+azPr/35nfn////rX
                3Nrv/v/P5uudX3/978//vf6q5sO58+vn+uzPR/9DxPrde7pf996P+f3u+//ez/vX/1/9U+36//9/259/+9fu+s////Z/Tv/vW/9933/9
                S/99/tf8n9/rZ61919/P+v/v//6zy/Hu5fvnZ3//79//37vff/7nzcb6/e9/f/Zjf27vzrl/f04f/85/z80/2eba8u7WR+7Kffv/vfXa
                uzus/392/Wb/ulv/9ez/3jr/3pr9Uv//x97/995D7//T7P9b/z//XLOT9szr6btfj/9r/+/0c+7z7Nza/frfy8Tf/z0b/1/7/X///v9/
                3bx/v/+T7+9/TN3b19P/7n/97fr/dv/u+//3/7Eb2/3HQ7WX0+3jzZ79e//P95L/eP2+/9/78zfevszfo+m23PTa/+7Hd3+973d9X8d7
                vlefy+9/++9/396KrH/90//0f/z/9/9+nRvrycP572//fn/9z8rr5+h9bX/9RvW4zd77d+ZDj//fvJ/df/z9bv/e/f7d+///i9l/vep9
                78//Rtv/f1v/zN7e/Nov//3b7n33x3///vqj+8+eff3/Z/H8/87+9837a//uitEX785L/9/bf37/ftMzS///fLvL/3+67n3+/vvf3/7X
                +/79/+/ut8u+3//76v//X/+///3/Pf38nv1fW/t//mf/91/77v792/175sf/3p3z/vv02sZH/fp/v/f///1//vdvM+3/Pr39M3///vM/3
                ffz/+Gv/8/n/9rpf9/z/zu/9fv+r/7Gzf3bN+v7+f+y9U/f3f//t+9NT+3fHb//+c+x7/Z/JF73Z1/9mPH39dv/037f//tX83/vv73/s
                t+/9Rv73/dv9//7//3fvut/HxN/9z5r93d7//s/+/3z/d/d70/3r79db+vf/dv92795/P+/6v/uU2/v/17x/fv/T5/p/e8v/x/r75/93
                /Uv1/P9v/33P6Wr/783//+vn3/raz0bP/fj7/7Pb/Xab7ubLF7/3H//e/97/f37/t9x/9vvf+///R978//b/dv/+//b/b50bxtrc/vtv
                txd/9tz/zpre3+/P/r5/P8za31t/9/038+/v/2/9/6r/9+76+t+r/33/3+rfb8f6+99/duvv3o77dx//1/zHzfp3+te613//9bzzkz//
                /opu/f/b7/f//O/n1xPU2n9/f3399k//3nt/7s//u937/X93f35z7P7a++zf+Pz/9fz/7n/+/Ufv/1//1tt/PXv/y//v/75/z/+397L
                f9y//97b/2y+f8/ae/30vlv///9///078706n9c//9//iz/8e6RG9+e+/+T+wv/v8uTX//bmXv/7t/bd/7/bu/O+2f91v/+u/fn2197
                t9n2zPbz/XuDyZ/Nf37vzvTaL///3v/Pa/9/zn97rX27/P/2x/uv/75f//bUvP24z8p/f/66f261n+99/fzf+y//9fz1/H/2/3/9+/v8
                /73Pnvv/1N//zF//72f//dX83fvu38/0f8zv76Ptk/zn359zxt7f7v3sfz3/P3/+f/b3/n9M//7/fn/9j+vP+g//29vX+vfs36r/XtZj
                37h/PWr9j9nxv95Lf////7t6us1v/f////+H39Un99dfzW3vtnff7/d50f/2zvb/9H7+/7/1v////7//X6/9z/d+Tf7+7fi/z9v5N//3vu
                dez//v9Xvv/9dn+9++99/MbH7frPyrObqn1//dI/97/7e3/+08+6d5P5//zeyu/0k937/5Le/33vf+/0z5p/fs+uf3723v/ef25/++/u
                19x//P5H19+737/XS///7t/M6+/1+/n9av272Xfu9v/zzfPs/+//zv//xuPd2n/vi/r//9Xf37fn99bt5f//+/ef/v91v9nj//9+Prf
                ++fr5/9v/2e5+/nsq//vzvf+51f3M9be3t730/T/0+n/Zvtfa/+off7b+v/9U3v//3/9Rvt//45/f3+9P/29/87n+1/03/1unbOf////
                f7/e24vrtvz+///e9v/dvP98///Pjv7qkft//P3m7s6D2f9//3z/f19b1t+Us3/s/39/v87Hf/64//9/f96610//8v7v9/9u/+a3F/9G
                79//9n9fdex/W/7f///eQ1/b93c=
```

The New-Fingerprint cmdlet has even less options than the Get-Content cmdlet and examples from the cmdlet use only the two parameters chosen above – FileData and Description. FileData references the document stored in the variable.

Now that the Fingerprint has been created, it can be used by the New-DataClassification cmdlet to create a data classification for a Transport Rule:

```
New-DataClassification -Name "HR Confidential Form 1" -Fingerprints $HRDoc1_Fingerprint
-Description "Message contains confidential employee information."

New-DataClassification -Name "HR Confidential Form 2" -Fingerprints $HRDoc2_Fingerprint
-Description "Message contains confidential employee information."

New-DataClassification -Name "HR Confidential Form 3" -Fingerprints $HRDoc3_Fingerprint
-Description "Message contains confidential employee information."
```

The New-DataClassification cmdlet can be used to create individual classifications or it can group multiple Fingerprints together into one classification as the parameter used for this is 'Fingerprints' not 'Fingerprint'. Make sure to separate multiple Fingerprints with a comma.

** **Note** ** Document fingerprints can also be added to existing data classifications using the Set-DataClassification cmdlet and the –Fingerprints parameter:

```
Set-DataClassification -Name "HR Confidential Form 3" -Fingerprints $HRDoc3_Fingerprint
```

To verify the Fingerprints were successful in being converted to an Exchange Data Classifications, run the following:

```
Get-DataClassification
```

```
Name                                   LocalizedName                          Publisher               ClassificationType
----                                   -------------                          ---------               ------------------
Croatia Identity Card Number           Croatia Identity Card Number           Microsoft Corporation               Entity
Czech National Identity Card Number    Czech National Identity Card Number    Microsoft Corporation               Entity
Greece National ID Card                Greece National ID Card                Microsoft Corporation               Entity
South Africa Identification Number     South Africa Identification Number     Microsoft Corporation               Entity
HR Confidential Form 1                  HR Confidential Form 1                 16-TAP                         Fingerprint
HR Confidential Form 2                  HR Confidential Form 2                 16-TAP                         Fingerprint
HR Confidential Form 3                  HR Confidential Form 3                 16-TAP                         Fingerprint
```

Notice the header fields of Invariant Name, Localized Name, Publisher and Classification Type. The other Data Classification entries show the Publisher to be Microsoft and the Classification Type to be Entity. Can we change ours to something more meaningful? First, what other cmdlets are available for Data Classifications:

```
Get-Command *DataClass*
```

```
Name                            Category
----                            --------
Get-DataClassification          Cmdlet
New-DataClassification          Cmdlet
Remove-DataClassification       Cmdlet
Set-DataClassification          Cmdlet
Test-DataClassification         Cmdlet
```

Upon reviewing the parameters for these cmdlets reveals that this cannot be changed. The Classification type is set once a Fingerprint is used. The publisher simply matches the name of the server it was created on.

Continuing on the Fingerprints are created and stored as new Data Classifications. This Data Classification can be used by a Transport Rule to block these emails (and their attachments) from leaving Exchange.

New-TransportRule -Name 'Notify :External Recipient BigBox confidential' -RejectMessageReasonText 'This file is restricted and may not be emailed outside the company.' -NotifySender $Null -Mode Enforce -SentToScope NotInOrganization -MessageContainsDataClassification @{Name=' HR Confidential Form 1'}

New-TransportRule -Name 'Notify :External Recipient BigBox confidential #2' -RejectMessageReasonText 'This file is restricted and may not be emailed outside the company.' -NotifySender $Null -Mode Enforce -SentToScope NotInOrganization -MessageContainsDataClassification @{Name=' HR Confidential Form 2'}

New-TransportRule -Name 'Notify :External Recipient BigBox confidential #3' -RejectMessageReasonText 'This file is restricted and may not be emailed outside the company.' -NotifySender $Null -Mode Enforce -SentToScope NotInOrganization -MessageContainsDataClassification @{Name=' HR Confidential Form 3'}

Verify Transport Rules were created:

Get-TransportRule

```
Name                                          State     Mode       Priority Comments
----                                          -----     ----       -------- --------
Notify :External Recipient BigBox confide...  Enabled   Enforce    3
Notify :External Recipient BigBox confide...  Enabled   Enforce    4
Notify :External Recipient BigBox confide...  Enabled   Enforce    5
```

How does this work in practice?  First, a message created in OWA is created with one of the three HR documents attached and addresses to an external recipient:

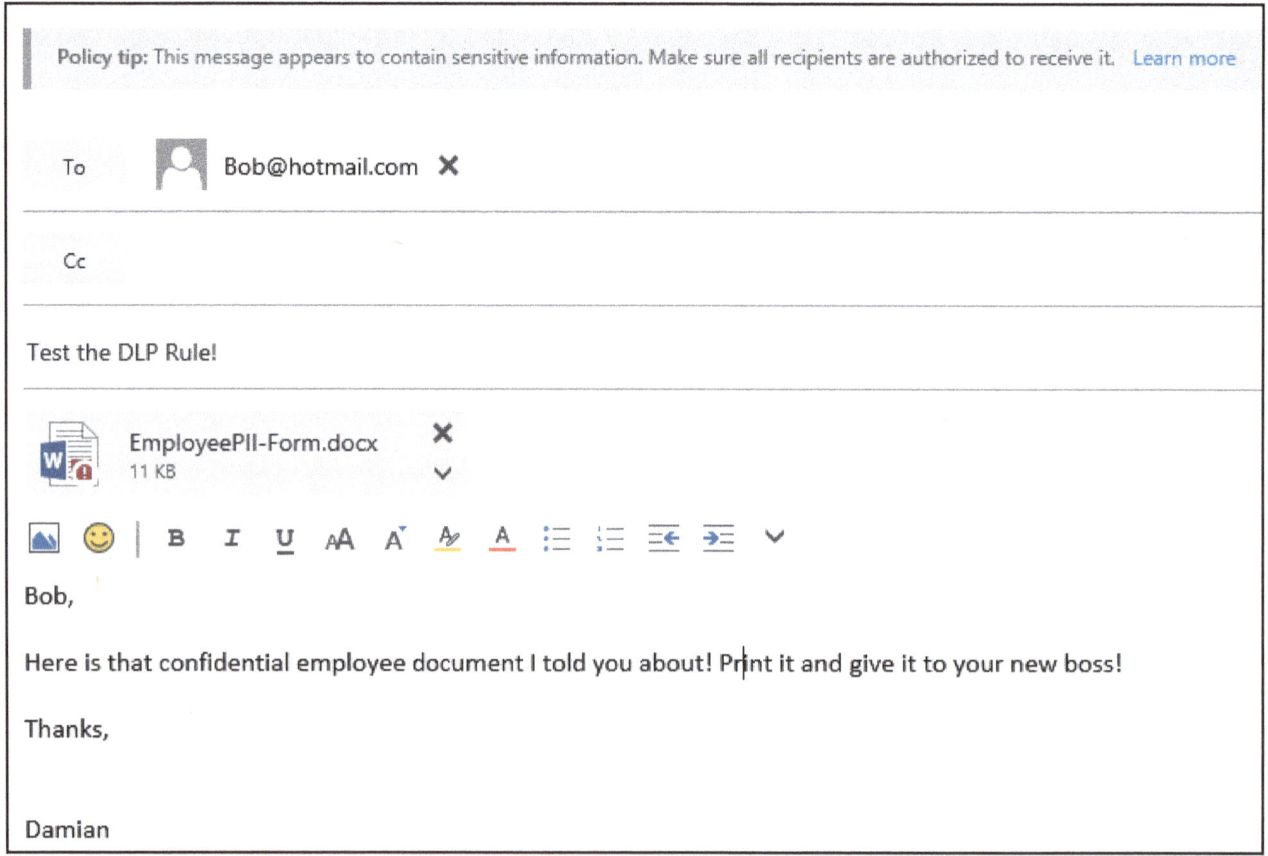

Notice the Policy Tip at the top of the email as well as the fact that the document itself has a red exclamation point to indicate that it has been recognized by its content. If a user is unsure why this is occurring, there is a 'Learn More' button at the top which provides this tidbit (as well as an option for feedback). The option show is based on which Action was chosen in the Policy Tip.

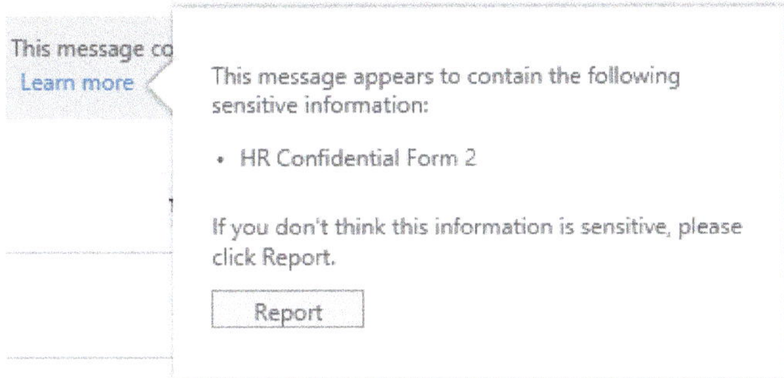


After the message is sent, an NDR is generated:

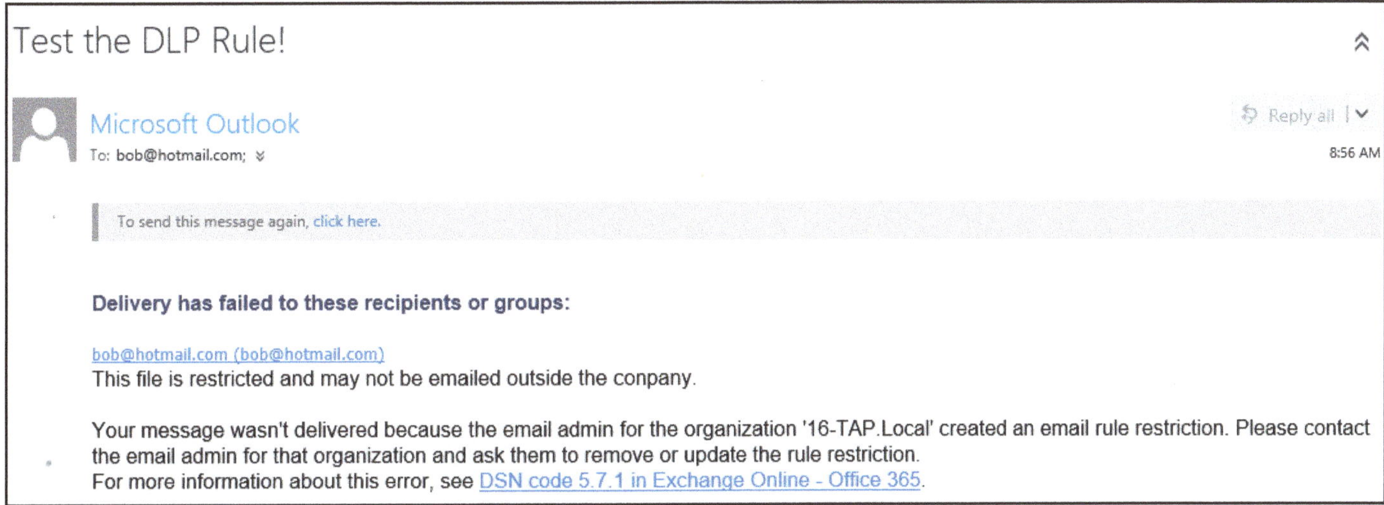


Going back to PowerShell, how can these DLP flagged messages be tracked? More importantly, how can a meaningful report be generated for management to show the effectiveness of the rules?

Examining the Message Tracking Logs, we need criteria to create a list of blocked messages. Taking the example above, start by reviewing all messages that were sent to 'bob@hotmail.com':

```
Get-MessageTrackingLog -Start "8/27/16" -Recipient Bob@hotmail.com | ft
```

```
EventId          Source       Sender                   Recipients
-------          ------       ------                   ----------
HAREDIRECT       SMTP         Administrator@16-t...    {Bob@hotmail.com}
RECEIVE          SMTP         Administrator@16-t...    {Bob@hotmail.com}
AGENTINFO        AGENT        Administrator@16-t...    {Bob@hotmail.com}
TRANSFER         ROUTING      Administrator@16-t...    {Bob@hotmail.com}
HARECEIVE        SMTP         Administrator@16-t...    {bob@hotmail.com}
HADISCARD        SMTP         Administrator@16-t...    {bob@hotmail.com}
```

Running the same cmdlet with '| fl' instead of '| ft –auto' reveals that there may be some useful information:

```
ServerIp                 :
ServerHostname           : 16-TAP-EX02
SourceContext            : ExplicitlyDiscarded
ConnectorId              :
Source                   : SMTP
EventId                  : HADISCARD
InternalMessageId        : 5205500362875
```

However, using any criteria fails to provide sufficient information for finding just these messages. For example, filtering for an EventID of 'HADiscard' ends up with internal heath status information:

Hardly the information that we are looking for.

What other criteria can be used? There is a curious field near the bottom called 'EventData' and inside that field there are a few references to 'Rule' in the properties. The 'Rule' looks like a GUID, perhaps the ID of the rule we are looking for?

If that is true, we could use PowerShell to find the Transport Rule by the GUID [picking one from EventData (in red rectangles)]:

```
Get-TransportRule -Identity 4fca7be8-a5ee-4f61-93ca-1295e9c5cae5
```

The rule looks correct, and now a Message Tracking Log trace will be done with that criteria and a report created:

```
Get-MessageTrackingLog -Start "8/27/16" -Recipients bob@hotmail.com | Where {$_.EventData -Match "4fca7be8-a5ee-4f61-93ca-1295e9c5cae5"}
```

The above is one of the messages that were caught by this Transport Rule.

What other ways can the Document Fingerprinting feature be used? Maybe in a set of documents that should never leave HR or be sent in email or some intellectual property documents (patent forms) that should never leave R&D or never even be sent through email. These scenarios can also be controlled via the Document Fingerprinting feature. Each scenario should be created with its own unique fingerprint, data classification and Transport Rules to keep track of each particular scenario in a company. This will make troubleshooting much easier if issues or discrepancies occur (document is updated or message is or is not delivered).

## Test Mode

The advantage of test mode for DLP Policies, templates and rules is that an IT department can create the DLP policies and Transport Rules driven by Legal, HR, management, auditors and government regulation to test the policy without an end users knowledge.  Doing so will allow IT to validate a rules effectiveness to test parameters as well as to validate a rules effect on the end users.  The later could be done with an auditing report that allows IT to query what messages would have been touched by what Transport Rules and thus blocked or redirected or whatever action is desired.  This allows for real time data collection of messages to determine the effectiveness.

To change the setting in PowerShell, use the following:

Get-TransportRule "Name of Rule" | Set-TransportRule -Mode Audit

With auditing in place, messages processed by this rule will have an EventID of 'AgentInfo' and have rules applied, but the message will not be rejected.  Look for the rule with Mode=Audit, like so:

```
[TRA, ETRP|ruleId=6e43c1fe-1271-4bdf-b8aa-f04e4ec06ff2|st=2016-08-27T17:14:36.00000000Z|ExecW=
0|ExecC=0], [TRA, ETRP|ruleId=0def4c2f-3ece-4cdc-a08a-323210d04398|st=2016-08-27T17:14:37.000
0000Z|ExecW=0|ExecC=0], [TRA, ETRP|ruleId=b596965f-98a9-4eaf-b719-03083a9375bb|st=2016-08-27T
17:14:37.00000000Z|ExecW=0|ExecC=0], [TRA, ETRP|ruleId=b0461b52-2bb3-475a-957e-2f54fb791f4a|st
=2016-08-27T17:14:37.00000000Z|ExecW=0|ExecC=0], [TRA, ETRP|ruleId=14df3fca-db10-4304-b784-c8d
9dd053ff3|st=2016-08-27T17:14:37.00000000Z|ExecW=0|ExecC=0], [TRA,
ETR|ruleId=cac2c318-d0ae-4c50-b01d-b3256a9d31f5|st=8/27/2016 6:44:03
PM|action=RejectMessage|sev=1|mode=Audit]...>
: Email
: 15.01.0466.033
```

Now the rule can be tested with production and reports produces for the rule requestor.


# Journaling

Journaling is the process of making a copy of an email and storing it in a location routed via an email address.  A message can be journaled to a local database or an external service.  Either method is supported using the Journaling rule cmdlets below.  Messages can be journaled for compliance or for business continuity.  Business continuity is one of the features external services tote as a reason to use their product.


## PowerShell

For journaling, a small subset of cmdlets is available for managing Journal rules in Exchange Server 2016:

Get-Command *journ*

```
CommandType     Name
-----------     ----
Function        Disable-JournalRule
Function        Enable-JournalRule
Function        Export-JournalRuleCollection
Function        Get-JournalRule
Function        Import-JournalRuleCollection
Function        New-JournalRule
Function        Remove-JournalRule
Function        Set-JournalRule
```

By default, there are no Journal rules configured by default which can be confirmed by running 'Get-JournalRule' in a new Exchange Server environment.   To begin exploring PowerShell journaling, create some Journaling rules using the 'New-JournalRule' cmdlet.  See below for an example:

**New-JournalRule**

*Commonly Used Options*

**JournalEmailAddress**
**Name** - Name of the new Journal Rule
**Enabled** <$true | $false> - Whether the rule is enabled or not
**Recipient** <SmtpAddress>
**Scope** <Internal | External | Global>
- Global - Global rules process all email messages that pass through a Transport service.
- This includes email messages that were already processed by the external and internal rules.
- Internal - Internal rules process email messages sent to and received by recipients in your organization.
- External - External rules process email messages sent to recipients or from senders outside your organization.

**Sample One-Liner**

New-JournalRule -Name "Personal Data (US)" -JournalEmailAddress "US Journal Mailbox" -Scope Global -Recipient USJournaling@BigBox.Com -Enabled $True

**Example Usage**

As the email administrator of the legal department determined that with a new implementation of an Exchange 2016 server environment, all messages need to be journaled.  The reason for the journaling is to comply with the current government regulations for email retention.

New-JournalRule -Name "Test" -JournalEmailAddress "JournalingMailbox@16-tap.local" -Scope Global -Enabled $True

**Script Scenario**

You work for a company with 12,000 users.  There are offices all over the world with major concentrations of users in the US and Europe.  There are different compliance requirements for the different regions.

All the users from Europe need to be journaled for new compliance regulations, separate from current archiving and business continuity of the US branch.  The users are in three different countries, each on different Exchange servers - Poland, Italy and Germany.  Each of these groups comprise of about 1,000 workers.  The legal department wants each group to be journaled to a local database.   Your IT manager wants separate rules and a way to track the configuration.  HR provides a complete list of users to help verify that the correct employees are being journaled.

Here are the steps that need to be taken in order to make this possible:

- Assign user a custom attribute - this can be used for a query when assigning
- Create a journaling database on each server
- Turn on circular logging - reduces the size of the database on the disk
- Create mailbox local to the region - keeps traffic local
- Add the journal rule for each user with the custom attribute, which makes this a custom journal rule and thus requires an enterprise Client Access License (CAL)

Active Directory is not organized by geographical location, but by business unit, so trying to get lists of users by Organizational Unit (OU) will not provide valid results.  Mailboxes may not be in the correct OU and users need to be tagged by country.

Knowing this we need some sort of reference point for the script to pull users from. What attribute on the user account and what attribute should be used to be queried later?

Take a look at the help for the Set-Mailbox cmdlet looking for valid parameters:

```
Get-Help Set-Mailbox -full
```

In the list of attributes that can be used is a set of custom attributes:

```
CustomAttribute1 to 15
```

The CustomAttribute1 to CustomAttribute15 parameters allow the configuration of custom attributes. You can use these attributes to store additional custom information.

For simplicity's sake, set the attribute value to a regional code:

```
1 for Germany
2 for Italy
3 for Poland
```

Using the list of users from the CSV file provided by HR, assign a region code to each mailbox in the CSV file. Like so:

```
$Csv = Import-Csv "c:\downloads\MailboxList.csv"

Foreach ($Line in $Csv) {
    Get-Mailbox $Line.Mailbox | Set-Mailbox -CustomAttribute1 $Line.Region
}
```

**CSV File Format**

```
Mailbox,Region
Damian,1
DStork,2
TestUser01,3
TUser02,1
```

Next, let's create a new mailbox database for journaling (see Chapter 7 of Server Management for cmdlets):

```
# Create Journaling database for the German Exchange Server
New-MailboxDatabase -Name "Journaling-Germany-Db" -Server SRV-GB-EX01 -EdbFilePath D:\
Databases\Journaling\Journaling.EDB -LogFolderPath E:\Logs\Journaling -IsExcludedFromProvisioning
$True -AutoDagExcludeFromMonitoring $True

# Create Journaling database for the Italian Exchange Server
New-MailboxDatabase -Name "Journaling-Italy-Db" -Server SRV-IT-EX01 -EdbFilePath D:\Databases\
Journaling\Journaling.EDB -LogFolderPath E:\Logs\Journaling -IsExcludedFromProvisioning $True
-AutoDagExcludeFromMonitoring $$True

# Create Journaling database for the Polish Exchange Server
New-MailboxDatabase -Name "Journaling-Poland-Db" -Server SRV-PO-EX01 -EdbFilePath D:\Databases\
Journaling\Journaling.EDB -LogFolderPath E:\Logs\Journaling -IsExcludedFromProvisioning $True
-AutoDagExcludeFromMonitoring $True
```

**Options Chosen** - Options below were chosen because the database is a journaling database
*IsExcludedFromProvisioning* - no new mailboxes are automatically added to the database – set this to $true
*AutoDagExcludeFromMonitoring* - suppresses error messages related to a database not having a copy in a DAG environment – set this to $true

**Sample Results**

| Name | Server | Recovery | ReplicationType |
| --- | --- | --- | --- |
| Journaling-Italy-Db | 16-TAP-EX01 | False | None |

### Good Reference

https://blogs.technet.microsoft.com/scottschnoll/2014/06/27/keeping-up-to-date-with-whats-happening-with-set-mailboxdatabase-ii/

After the databases are created, PowerShell can be used to enable circular logging and then dismount and remount the database. Then the script will provide an option to restart the Information Store service (best practice Microsoft).

### Script

Breaking down the script requirements, the script functions on a simple yes/no basis. If the question to restart the service is 'y', then the service is restarted and if the answer is 'n' then the script notifies you that the service needs to be restarted. The reason for this setup is that if a database is created during the day you probably will not want to restart the IS service.

For the question, using 'read-host –prompt' allows for a text question and an answer right after.

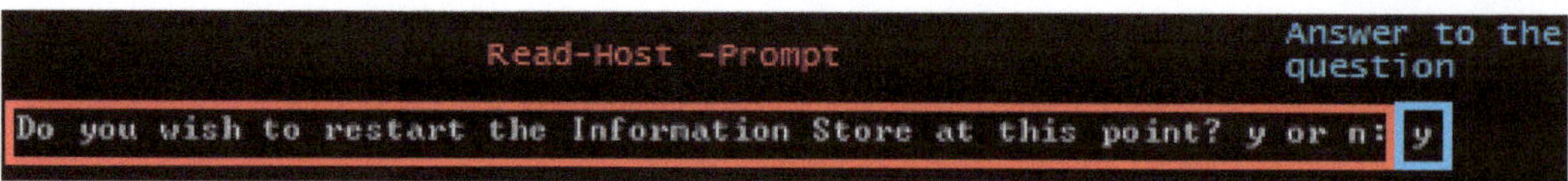

The IF..ELSE code block handles the 'what to do' with the answer given. There is no built-in error checking, but the script is relatively simple:

```powershell
# Restart IS
$Answer = Read-Host -Prompt "Do you wish to restart the Information Store at this point? [y or n]"
If ($Answer -eq 'y') {
    Get-Service MSExchangeIS | Restart-Service
} Else {
    Write-Host "Make sure to restart the Exchange Information Store for memory management."
    -ForegroundColor Cyan
}
```

```
[PS] C:\>.\Restart.ps1
Do you wish to restart the Information Store at this point? y or n: y
WARNING: Waiting for service 'Microsoft Exchange Information Store (MSExchangeIS)' to start...
WARNING: Waiting for service 'Microsoft Exchange Information Store (MSExchangeIS)' to start...
WARNING: Waiting for service 'Microsoft Exchange Information Store (MSExchangeIS)' to start...
[PS] C:\Downloads>.\Restart.ps1
Do you wish to restart the Information Store at this point? y or n: n
Make sure to restart the Exchange Information Store for memory management.
```

Create a mailbox on each regional database:

```powershell
# Create Journaling mailbox on the German Exchange Server
New-Mailbox -Shared -Name "Journaling-Germany" -DisplayName "Journaling-Germany" -Alias
Journaling-Germany -Database "Journaling-Germany-Db"

# Create Journaling mailbox on the Italian Exchange Server
New-Mailbox -Shared -Name "Journaling-Italy" -DisplayName "Journaling-Italy" -Alias Journaling-Italy
-Database "Journaling-Italy-Db"

# Create Journaling mailbox on the Polish Exchange Server
New-Mailbox -Shared -Name "Journaling-Poland" -DisplayName "Journaling-Poland" -Alias Journaling-
Poland -Database "Journaling-Poland-Db"
```

These same one-liners can be simplified into a single line of code:

```powershell
'Germany','Italy','Poland'|%{New-Mailbox-Shared-Name "Journaling-$_"-DisplayName "Journaling-$_"
-Alias "Journaling-$_" -Database "Journaling-$_-Db" }
```

What this line does is specify a series of values which when read in with the '%' (an alias for ForEach-Object) and places the value into the '$_' variable. Thus this one line will run three times, one for each value provided at the beginning of the line.

### Sample Output

```
Name                        Alias                   ServerName      ProhibitSendQuota
----                        -----                   ----------      -----------------
Journaling-Germany          Journaling-Germany      16-tap-ex02     Unlimited
```

Create a new Journal Rule and Dynamic Distribution List (DDL) for emails to recipients from a certain region to a certain journaling database:

```
# Create Dynamic list of users and a journal rule that uses that group
New-DynamicDistributionGroup -Name GermanyJournaling -RecipientFilter {(CustomAttribute1 -eq "1")}
$smtp = ((Get-DynamicDistributionGroup GermanJournaling).PrimarySmtpAddress).Address

New-JournalRule -Name "Journaling for Germany mailboxes" -JournalEmailAddress "Journaling-Germany" -Scope Global -Recipient $Smtp -Enabled $True

# Create Dynamic list of users and a journal rule that uses that group
New-DynamicDistributionGroup -Name ItalyJournaling -RecipientFilter {(CustomAttribute1 -eq "2")}
$smtp = ((Get-DynamicDistributionGroup ItalyJournaling).PrimarySmtpAddress).Address

New-JournalRule -Name "Journaling for Italy mailboxes" -JournalEmailAddress "Journaling-Italy" -Scope Global -Recipient $Smtp -Enabled $True

# Create Dynamic list of users and a journal rule that uses that group
New-DynamicDistributionGroup -Name PolandJournaling -RecipientFilter {(CustomAttribute1 -eq "3")}
$smtp = ((Get-DynamicDistributionGroup PolandJournaling).PrimarySmtpAddress).Address

New-JournalRule -Name "Journaling for Poland mailboxes" -JournalEmailAddress "Journaling-Poland" -Scope Global -Recipient $smtp -Enabled $True
```

**Sample Output**

```
Name                 : Journaling for German Users
Recipient            : GermanJournaling@16-tap.local
JournalEmailAddress  : Journaling-Germany@16-tap.local
Scope                : Global
Enabled              : True
```

With the above setup, any email that goes to a user who is in the Dynamic Distribution List for a particular country will have their messages journaled to a local journaling database.


## Best Practices (and the PowerShell to configure them…)

When working with the journaling process there are a few things to remember for the configuration of Journaling in Exchange Server 2016 (and any other version of Exchange up to this point):

- Journal Recipient is hidden from the Global Address List (GAL)
- Journal mailbox is on its own database and the database is on separate disks
- Journal mailbox database should be excluded from automatic provisioning and excluded from DAG monitoring

For the above best practices, items 2 and 3 were taken care of in the creation of the database and mailbox. A separate database was created, it was placed on its own disk drives (separate from other databases), it was excluded from automatic provisioning (-IsExcludedFromProvisioning $true) and the database will not generate errors about not having a secondary copy in a DAG environment (-AutoDagExcludeFromMonitoring $true).

This leaves hiding the mailbox from view.  We do not want end users sending emails to this user or being about to see the user in the Global Address List (GAL).  Since the rest of the configuration process is complete, we can now hide the mailbox from the GAL (note the wildcard in the name of the mailbox this will get all mailboxes that begin with 'journal'):

Get-Mailbox Journal* | Set-Mailbox -HiddenFromAddressListsEnabled $True

**Before**

**After**

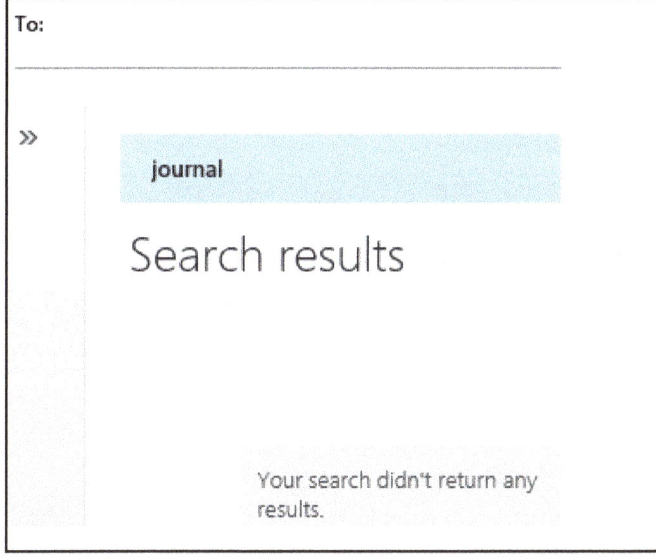

## Journaling Verification

Now that the Journaling is in place, how can we verify that journaling is working as expected? There are a few places where we can verify the proper operation of the journaling setup can be verified – contents of the journaling mailbox (if journaling is kept internal), Message Tracking Logs or Mailbox Statistics:

*Mailbox Contents*

The easiest method is to grant an administrator 'Full Access' to the mailbox and then open the mailbox in

Outlook to verify the contents of the mailbox. The mailbox can also be opened in OWA. Once open an administrator can verify that journaling messages appeared.

*Mailbox Statistics*

Using mailbox statistics to determine the usage of the Journaling mailbox is not the most insightful way to figure out whether or not the journaling rule is working as expected, but it can provide one vital statistic – does the item count of the mailbox go up. If the mailbox is hidden, then emails destined for it should be ones that were generated by the journaling process. To see the changes, use the Get-MailboxStatistics cmdlet to monitor the item count for the mailbox increment over time. For this one, we can script something small that will run each hour to see how many emails appear in the mailbox over time [in this example every hour for 48 hours]:

```
# Check the statistics on the mailbox each hour, every hour for the next 48 hours
$Hours = 0
Do {
    Write-Host "Mailbox statistics @ $Hours hours."
    Get-Mailbox Journal* | Get-MailboxStatistics -WarningAction 0| ft DisplayName,ItemCount
    Start-Sleep 3600
    $Hours = $Hours++
} While ($Hours -lt 48)
```

Using a Do…While loop, the code visually indicates the hour the script is on. Then the script will report back the item counts for any mailbox with the name 'journal' in the front of it. Notice there is a '-warningaction 0' (a.k.a. SilentlyContinue) for Get-MailboxStatistics; without this, a mailbox that has not been logged into (typically a mailbox like this) will receive a warning message to that affect:

```
WARNING: The user hasn't logged on to mailbox '16-TAP.Local/Users/Journaling-Germany'
('4e88519a-48d3-47a8-acc1-b00607d0b001'), so there is no data to return. After the user logs on, this warning will no
longer appear.
```

The switch will suppress this warning message. After the mailbox statistics displays the current item counts, the script sleeps for an hour. When it starts back up, the hour counter increments by one and so on for 48 hours.

*Message Tracking*

Following in the footsteps of Chapter 8, a review of tracking logs can provide information on how many messages are getting delivered to a journaling mailbox like so:

```
Get-MessageTrackingLog -start 8/25/16 -ResultSize Unlimited | Where {$_.Recipients -Match "Journal*"}
| ft TimeStamp, EventId, Recipients, Sender -Auto
```

Results will look like something like this:

```
Timestamp                 EventId    Recipients                              Sender
---------                 -------    ----------                              ------
8/25/2016 2:22:02 AM RECEIVE    {Journaling-Germany@16-tap.local} MicrosoftExchange329e71
8/25/2016 2:22:02 AM AGENTINFO  {Journaling-Germany@16-tap.local} MicrosoftExchange329e71
8/25/2016 2:22:02 AM SEND       {Journaling-Germany@16-tap.local} MicrosoftExchange329e71
8/25/2016 2:22:32 AM RECEIVE    {Journaling-Germany@16-tap.local} MicrosoftExchange329e71
8/25/2016 2:22:32 AM AGENTINFO  {Journaling-Germany@16-tap.local} MicrosoftExchange329e71
8/25/2016 2:22:32 AM SEND       {Journaling-Germany@16-tap.local} MicrosoftExchange329e71
8/25/2016 2:23:03 AM RECEIVE    {Journaling-Germany@16-tap.local} MicrosoftExchange329e71
8/25/2016 2:23:03 AM AGENTINFO  {Journaling-Germany@16-tap.local} MicrosoftExchange329e71
8/25/2016 2:23:03 AM SEND       {Journaling-Germany@16-tap.local} MicrosoftExchange329e71
```

## Reporting on Journaling Rules

Knowing what rules are in place can be important if there is a need to troubleshoot a journaling process, especially if there is an external product or process that is analyzing these messages.  Understanding what destination email address is being used to journal for what recipient(s).  'Get-JournalRule' is the cmdlet to provide the needed information:

Get-JournalRule | ft Name, Recipient, JournalEmailAddress, Scope, Enabled –Auto

```
Name                          Recipient                   JournalEmailAddress              Scope  Enabled
----                          ---------                   -------------------              -----  -------
Journaling for German Users   GermanJournaling@16-tap.local  Journaling-Germany@16-tap.local  Global    True
Journaling for Poland mailboxes PolandJournaling@16-tap.local Journaling-Poland@16-tap.local  Global    True
```

## Disabling Rules

Why disable a Journaling Rule? Normally the disabling of Journaling Rules is done when the original need has past or a new rule needs to be created or if a different destination server or to who to journal.  The Disable-Journal cmdlet is the cmdlet for the job.  First we need to use the Get-JournalRule on the rule to be disabled and then pipe '|' that journal rule to the 'Disable-JournalRule' cmdlet:

Get-JournalRule "Journaling for German Users" | Disable-JournalRule

```
Confirm
Are you sure you want to perform this action?
Disabling journal rule "Journaling for German Users".
[Y] Yes  [A] Yes to All  [N] No  [L] No to All  [?] Help (default is "Y"): y
```

After disabling the rule, verify that the rule is disabled:

Get-JournalRule

```
Name                : Journaling for German Users
Recipient           : PolandJournaling@16-tap.local
JournalEmailAddress : Journaling-Poland@16-tap.local
Scope               : Global
Enabled             : False
```

Enabled is now set to 'False'.

If the rule needs to be re-enabled, simply use the same process as the Disable-JournalRule:

Get-JournalRule "Journaling for German Users" | Enable-JournalRule

This cmdlet does not provide any feedback, only by running Get-JournalRule will you be able to verify if the rule is enabled again.

## Removing Rules

Removing a rule is similar to disabling the Journaling Rule – use the Get-JournalRule and pass that information along to the Remove-JournalRule:

Get-JournalRule "Journaling for German Users" | Remove-JournalRule

```
Confirm
Are you sure you want to perform this action?
Removing journal rule "Journaling for German Users".
[Y] Yes  [A] Yes to All  [N] No  [L] No to All  [?] Help (default is "Y"): y
```

# Rights Management

Rights management in Exchange 2016 relies on Active Directory Right Management Services (ADRMS) as an additional security feature that can be added.  Exchange refers to RMS as Information Rights Services or IRM.  This is important to remember because PowerShell in Exchange uses IRM and not RMS, which is key to knowing what PowerShell cmdlets are available.  In order to enable Rights Management in Exchange Server 2016, a Windows Server 2012 (R2) needs to be setup and configured for RMS in Active Directory.   This new server needs to have the Active Directory Rights Management role installed on it.

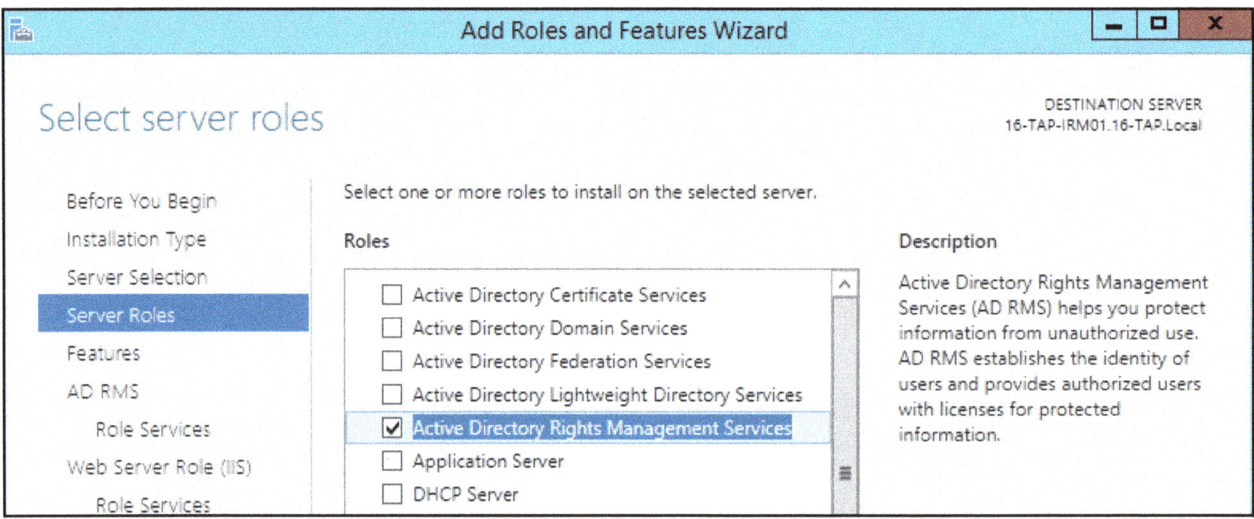


This book will not cover the installation or configuration of a Rights Management infrastructure, but suffice it to say that a single RMS server will be sufficient to provide Exchange with what it needs.  However, a redundant architecture can be configured (see below):

## Sample RMS Architecture

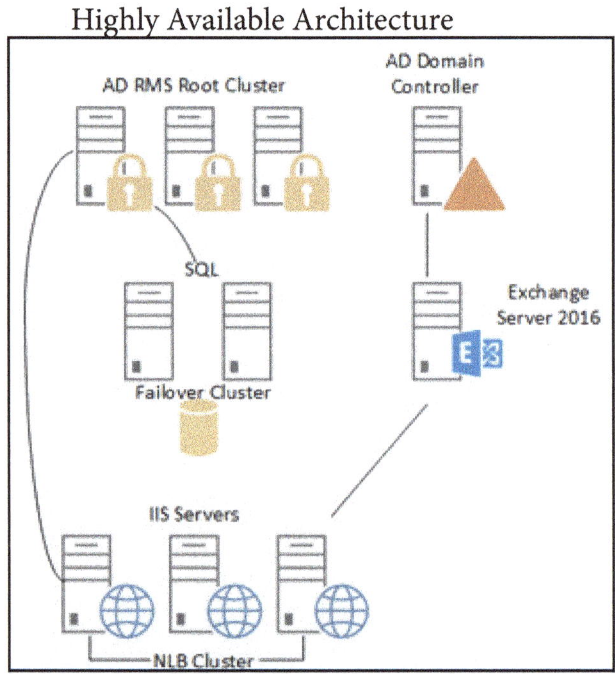


Once the RMS infrastructure is in place, we can configure Exchange Server to work in conjunction with it.

## PowerShell

Get-Command *irm*

```
CommandType          Name
----------           ----
Alias                irm -> Invoke-RestMethod
Function             Get-IRMConfiguration
Function             Set-IRMConfiguration
Function             Test-IRMConfiguration
```

First explore the current IRM configuration on an Exchange 2016 server.

Get-IRMConfiguration

```
InternalLicensingEnabled            : False
ExternalLicensingEnabled            : False
JournalReportDecryptionEnabled      : True
ClientAccessServerEnabled           : True
SearchEnabled                       : True
TransportDecryptionSetting          : Optional
EDiscoverySuperUserEnabled          : True
RMSOnlineKeySharingLocation         :
RMSOnlineVersion                    :
ServiceLocation                     :
PublishingLocation                  :
LicensingLocation                   : {}
```

Notice that by default that IRM is enabled for client access on the Exchange server. However notice that no licensing is enabled or that the IRM configuration is published. Below is a list of parameters that can be configured for IRM:

Get-Help Set-IRMConfiguration -Full

**Parameters**

ClientAccessServerEnabled <$true | $false> - this option turns on IRM for OWA and ActiveSync
Confirm [<SwitchParameter>]
DomainController <Fqdn>
EDiscoverySuperUserEnabled <$true | $false> -
ExternalLicensingEnabled <$true | $false> - enable or disable IRM for messages sent to external recipients
Force <SwitchParameter>
InternalLicensingEnabled <$true | $false> -
JournalReportDecryptionEnabled <$true | $false>
LicensingLocation <MultiValuedProperty>
PublishingLocation <Uri>
RefreshServerCertificates <SwitchParameter>
RMSOnlineKeySharingLocation <Uri>
SearchEnabled <$true | $false>
TransportDecryptionSetting <Disabled | Optional | Mandatory>

When further customizing the IRM configuration, the following setting should also be considered:

**EDiscoverySuperUserEnabled** – If this is set to true, users with eDiscovery privileges can access IRM protected emails

**SearchEnabled** – On by default, it enables OWA to search for IRM messages

**ExternalLicensingEnabled** - Allows for the use of RMS on external emails

**InternalLicensingEnabled** – Allows for the use of RMS on internal emails

**JournalReportDecryptionEnabled** – If journaling is present in Exchange, any IRM messages that are journaled have an unencrypted copy stored with the Journal message

For a scenario where internal messages should be protected by IRM and legal needs to perform legal discovery on emails that are IRM protected, the IRM configuration should be updated like so:

Set-IRMConfiguration –EDiscoverySuperUserEnabled $True –InternalLicensingEnabled $True

Once configured, RMS is ready to use internally and templates and configuration within RMS should be configured.  Both internal and external licensing can be enabled in the same configuration if need be.

Set-IRMConfiguration –InternalLicensingEnabled $True – ExternalLicensingEnabled $False

In addition to configuring the IRM settings, the same settings can be tested / verified using the Test-IRMConfiguration Cmdlet.  To test the configuration for external recipients, the following syntax can be used:

Test-IRMConfiguration -Recipient damian@geek.com -Sender damian@BigCorp.Com

The test will go through a series of steps:

```
Checking Exchange Server ...
    - PASS: Exchange Server is running in Enterprise.
Loading IRM configuration ...
    - PASS: IRM configuration loaded successfully.
Retrieving RMS Certification Uri ...
    - PASS: RMS Certification Uri: https://adrms.16-tap.local/_wmcs/certification.
Verifying RMS version for https://adrms.16-tap.local/_wmcs/certification ...
    - WARNING: Failed to verify RMS version. IRM features require AD RMS on Windows Server 200
article 973247 (http://go.microsoft.com/fwlink/?linkid=3052&kbid=973247) or AD RMS on Windows
```

And a final result at the end:

```
OVERALL RESULT: PASS with warnings on disabled features
```

## Outlook Protection Rules

Transport Rules can be created to utilize RMS to protected messages at the Exchange Server level.  However, Outlook Protection Rules will protect messages at the Outlook level even before the email has left the Outlook client.  PowerShell cmdlets for Outlook Protection Rules:

Get-Command *OutlookProt*

```
CommandType          Name
-----------          ----
Function             Disable-OutlookProtectionRule
Function             Enable-OutlookProtectionRule
Function             Get-OutlookProtectionRule
Function             New-OutlookProtectionRule
Function             Remove-OutlookProtectionRule
Function             Set-OutlookProtectionRule
```

Like many other protections in Exchange, there are no Outlook rules by default which can be verified with the Get-OutlookProtectionRule cmdlet.  In order to get started let's review the New-OutlookProtectionRule examples:

```
Get-Help New-OutlookProtectionRule –Examples
```

```
-------------------------- Example 1 --------------------------

This example applies the AD RMS template Template-Contoso to messages sent to the SMTP address Joe@contoso.com.
New-OutlookProtectionRule -Name "Project Contoso" -SentTo Joe@contoso.com -ApplyRightsProtectionTemplate
"Template-Contoso"
```

Other parameters to consider when working with Outlook Protection Rules are –ApplyRightsProtectionTemplate, SentTo, SentToScope, UserCanOverride and enabled.  A sample command would look like this:

```
New-OutlookProtectionRule -Name "R and D" -SentTo Sam@HotMail.Com
-ApplyRightsProtectionTemplate "Big Box – Outlook Rule 1" -UserCaOoverride $False
```

## Mobile Protection

Mobile protection via IRM is enabled when the 'ClientAccessServerEnabled' setting is configured for $true:

```
Set-IRMConfiguration –ClientAccessServerEnabled $True
```

Now ActiveSync devices can be protected as well.  Microsoft also recommends that certain settings for the Microsoft ActiveSync policy should also be configured:

**DevicePasswordEnabled** - $True
**RequireDeviceEncryption** - $True
**AllowNonProvisionableDevices** - $False

Depending on the name of the ActiveSync policy being applies to your mobile devices, the one-liners to make these changes might be a bit different.  In the case below, we will modify the default policy to these settings:

```
Get-MobileDeviceMailboxPolicy | Where {$_.IsDefault -eq "True"} | Set-MobileDeviceMailboxPolicy
-PasswordEnabled $True -RequireDeviceEncryption $True -AllowNonProvisionableDevices $False
```

If IRM is not enabled on the mobile device policy, that should be enabled as well:

```
Get-MobileDeviceMailboxPolicy | Where {$_.IsDefault -eq "True"} | Set-MobileDeviceMailboxPolicy –
IRMEnabled $True
```

Last configuration items:

Add the Federation mailbox (a system mailbox created by Exchange 2013 and Exchange 2010 Setup) to the super users group in AD RMS.  This can be done with a simple one-liner:

```
Add-DistributionGroupMember ADRMSSuperUsers -Member FederatedEmail.4c1f4d8b-8179-4148-
93bf-00a95fa1e042
```

Mobile devices users can now perform the following actions:

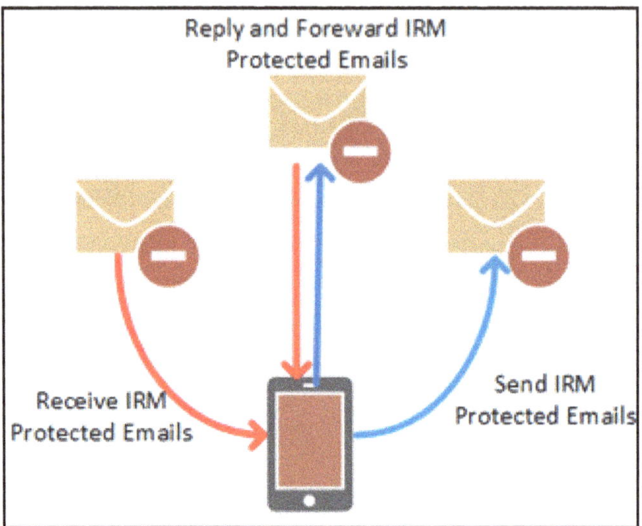


Same Message tracking applies to mobile devices as would have been present with OWA and Outlook client emails.

## IRM Logging

The Transport Service contains a configuration for IRM logging.  These settings can be verified with a Get-TransportService command like so:

```
Get-TransportService | ft IRM* -Auto

Name              IrmLogEnabled IrmLogMaxAge IrmLogMaxDirectorySize
----              ------------- ------------ ----------------------
16-TAP-EX01                True 90.00:00:00  1.221 GB (1,310,720,000 bytes)
16-TAP-EX02                True 90.00:00:00  1.221 GB (1,310,720,000 bytes)
16-04-EDGE-01              True 30.00:00:00  Unlimited
```

```
IrmLogMaxFileSize          IrmLogPath
-----------------          ----------
10 MB (10,485,760 bytes)   C:\Program Files\Microsoft\Exchange Server\V15\Logging\IRMLogs
10 MB (10,485,760 bytes)   C:\Program Files\Microsoft\Exchange Server\V15\Logging\IRMLogs
10 MB (10,485,760 bytes)
```

Browsing to the log directory for IRM logs and we see there are a two types of files that can be examined:

```
Name
----
w3wp_MSExchangeOWAAppPool_IRMLOG20160813-1.LOG
w3wp_MSExchangeOWAAppPool_IRMLOG20160827-1.LOG
w3wp_MSExchangePowerShellAppPool_IRMLOG20160827-1.LOG
```

Opening up the last file, we find that the RMS server in AD was discovered to be used in Exchange:

```
w3wp_MSExchangePowerShellAppPool_IRMLOG20160827-1.LOG - Notepad

hange Server

hager Log
30.753Z
re,event-type,tenant-id,server-url,data,context,transaction-id
DrmInitialization,Success,,,MSDRM.DLL version: 6.3.9600.17415,,00000000-0000-0000-0000-000000000000
```

This file is used to log all IRM RMS transactions run from PowerShell, while other IRM log files present are for OWA transactions. When in use, up to four total log file types are present:

- Log for Transport transactions for RMS
- Log for Search and Index requests for RMS transactions
- Log for OWA RMS transactions
- Log for PowerShell RMS transactions

These logs make a good place to begin a search for any issues with Exchange and RMS.

One thing to note is that the logs are rather small at 250 MB in size. The age of the logs is also set to a relatively short timeframe of 30 days. A recommended setting, especially on a busy server, it may be necessary to adjust the max age to 90 days and the size to something over 1 GB in size. To change this, the Set-TransportService needs to be utilized:

```
Get-TransportService | Set-TransportService -IrmLogMaxAge 90.00:00:00 -IrmLogMaxDirectorySize 1250MB
```

For the Edge Transport Role, the command needs to be run locally:

```
You can't use this command to configure an Edge Transport server on a machine that is on your
internal network. You must perform this operation directly on the Edge Transport server.
    + CategoryInfo          : InvalidOperation: (:) [Set-TransportService], CannotSetEdgeTr...erOn
  AdException
    + FullyQualifiedErrorId : [Server=16-TAP-EX02,RequestId=0b3ca335-9689-4042-9848-c4f36032ad00,T
  imeStamp=1/16/2017 3:50:05 AM] [FailureCategory=Cmdlet-CannotSetEdgeTransportServerOnAdExcepti
 on] 1ABD3ACD,Microsoft.Exchange.Management.SystemConfigurationTasks.SetTransportService
    + PSComputerName        : 16-tap-ex02.16-tap.local
```

Once the cmdlet is run locally on the Edge Transport server, the new results are listed below:

```
Get-TransportService 16-04-edge-01 | Set-TransportService -IrmLogMaxAge 90.00:00:00
-IrmLogMaxDirectorySize 1250MB
```

# 10  IMAP and POP

---

In This Chapter

- POP3
- Discovering POP3 Connections
- IMAP4
- POP3 and IMAP4 Reporting

---

## POP3

POP3 is still commonly used by ISP's (Internet Service Providers) as a means for mail clients to retrieve mail from a mail server.  POP3 utilizes port 110 (unencrypted, not secure or opportunistic TLS) or port 995 (secure, encrypted) for connecting to a server, so the client could potentially use either a secure or an insecure connection when retrieving emails.  Generally speaking, Outlook users with an Exchange mailbox do not use POP3 nor is it recommended.  MAPI, RPC over HTTP or MAPI over HTTP are the preferred methods to access a mailbox.  POP3 is either used by older clients, clients on Operating Systems other than Windows or by applications that retrieve mail for a special purpose.

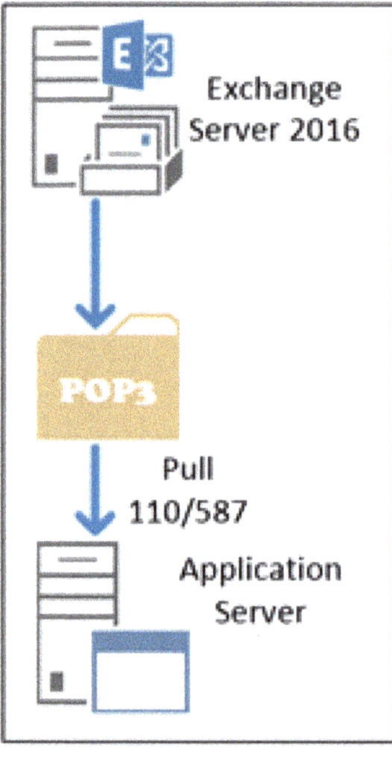


POP3 was created quite a long time ago and is beginning to show its age in the form of negative.  The perception is that the number of apps or clients that connect using this method is declining.  Here is a short list of limitations:

1. Download and Delete:  POP3 clients initiate a download of messages from the server.  Once downloaded the emails are removed from the server that hosts the emails.  While some ISP's and POP3 providers have put in delays for when messages are removed, the messages will be removed and the only copy will be the local copy.
2. Limited client connectivity as only one device can download the emails.

For the purposes of scripting, we may not care about these deficiencies.  Most Exchange engineers work with POP3 in three scenarios (1) setting up the initial configuration which means deciding on a login method, security (or no security) and then testing with the application needing the connection, (2) troubleshooting an existing POP3 setup or (3) checking for POP3 connections to see if that service needs to be moved to the new servers a client is deploying.

The below scenario will cover the third scenario and build a script to look at the POP3 logs.  By examining the POP3 logs of an Exchange server, we can see if the service is being used and even report back what servers or clients are using POP3 to pull email from the Exchange server.

# Discovering POP3 Connections

**Scenario** - Migrating email from Exchange 2010 to Exchange 2016 (based on real world experiences)
**Goal** - Discover if apps are using POP3
**Why?** - Make sure all services are moved to 2016


## How to accomplish the goal?

For our scenario we need to discover what applications, servers or computers are attempting to connect to Exchange 2010 so we can replicate these connections in Exchange 2016.  First we need to start out with what we know about Exchange 2010's POP3 and IMAP feature.  We know there are two services that Exchange uses to allow client connections.  First one is called 'Microsoft Exchange POP3' and the second service is called 'Microsoft Exchange IMAP4'.   We need to first check to see if these services are running on the server.  We can do this with the Services. msc MMC console or we can do it with PowerShell.

Discovering properties on these services is easy with PowerShell:

```
[PS] C:\>Get-Service "microsoft exchange IMAP4"

Status    Name               DisplayName
------    ----               -----------
Running   MSExchangeImap4    microsoft exchange IMAP4


[PS] C:\>Get-Service "microsoft exchange POP3"

Status    Name               DisplayName
------    ----               -----------
Running   MSExchangePop3     microsoft exchange POP3
```

How do we know what PowerShell cmdlet to use? Using what we was discussed previously in the book, we can run:

```
Get-Command *Service
```

> ** **Note** ** The use of the '*' wildcard symbol which confers any amount and type of characters before the word 'service'.

This will give us a list of PowerShell cmdlets with the word 'service' in it.  Here is the list of cmdlets we can use:

```
CommandType       Name
-----------       ----
Function          _CheckServicesStarted
Function          Disable-ServiceEmailChannel
Function          Enable-ServiceEmailChannel
Function          Get-EdgeSyncServiceConfig
Function          Get-ServiceAvailabilityReport
Function          Get-ServiceStatus
Function          Get-WebServicesVirtualDirectory
Function          New-EdgeSyncServiceConfig
Function          New-WebServicesVirtualDirectory
Function          Remove-WebServicesVirtualDirectory
Function          Set-EdgeSyncServiceConfig
Function          Set-WebServicesVirtualDirectory
Function          Test-OutlookWebServices
Function          Test-ServiceHealth
Function          Test-WebServicesConnectivity
Function          Update-FileDistributionService
```

We can further improve our cmdlet search by just looking for GET cmdlets as these are informational:

Get-Command Get-*Service*

This gives us GET cmdlets with the word 'service' in it:

```
CommandType         Name
Function            Get-EdgeSyncServiceConfig
Cmdlet              Get-Service
Function            Get-ServiceAvailabilityReport
Function            Get-ServiceStatus
Function            Get-WebServicesVirtualDirectory
```

From the above list we want 'Get-Service'.   If you don't know the exact name of the service, try to perform similar search as we did for the Get-Service cmdlet, using the keyword 'POP':

Get-Service *Pop*

On the Exchange 2010 server, one service is returned from the above query:

```
[PS] C:\>get-service *pop*

Status     Name                DisplayName
------     ----                -----------
Running    MSExchangePop3      Microsoft Exchange POP3
```

These cmdlets establish that POP3 services are running on the server. How do we find configuration settings which will lead us to connection information?  To find the command for POP settings, try:

Get-Command *Pop*

Which displays these relevant cmdlets:

```
CommandType         Name
Function            Get-PopSettings
Function            Set-PopSettings
Function            Test-PopConnectivity
Cmdlet              Pop-Location
```

**TIP:** Different ways to display settings for POP3:

FT presents the settings for POP3:

```
UnencryptedOrTLSBindings   SSLBindings
------------------------   -----------
{[::]:110, 0.0.0.0:110}    {[::]:995, 0.0.0.0:995}
```

While FL presents the settings for POP3 as a list:

```
RunspaceId                     : ec18349d-5b90-4b4f-93f6-fc8d2274542d
Name                           : 1
ProtocolName                   : POP3
MaxCommandSize                 : 512
MessageRetrievalSortOrder      : Ascending
UnencryptedOrTLSBindings       : {[::]:110, 0.0.0.0:110}
SSLBindings                    : {[::]:995, 0.0.0.0:995}
InternalConnectionSettings     : {16-02-EX02.16-02.local:995:SSL, 16-0:
ExternalConnectionSettings     : {}
X509CertificateName            : 16-02-EX02
Banner                         : The Microsoft Exchange POP3 service i:
LoginType                      : SecureLogin
```

The command needed to find POP3 settings is:

Get-PopSettings

We need detailed information from each cmdlet.  In order to get this, we need to add '| fl' to the end of each cmdlet.  For POP3 the log location is revealed (in this particular Exchange installation) to be:

```
EnforceCertificateErrors             : False
LogFileLocation                      : C:\Program Files\Microsoft\Exchange Server\V14\Logging\Pop3
LogFileRollOverSettings              : Daily
```

Make sure that Protocol logging (a verbose log of all connections on a particular protocol) is enabled, this is not a default setting.  To enable logging forPOP3 run this PowerShell cmdlet:

Set-PopSettings -ProtocolLogEnabled $True

Don't forget to restart the POP service, otherwise the log directories don't get created:

Restart-Service MSExchangePOP3

If there are log files in the directory, PowerShell can parse these files looking for relevant values.  First we need to get the location of the files to work with:

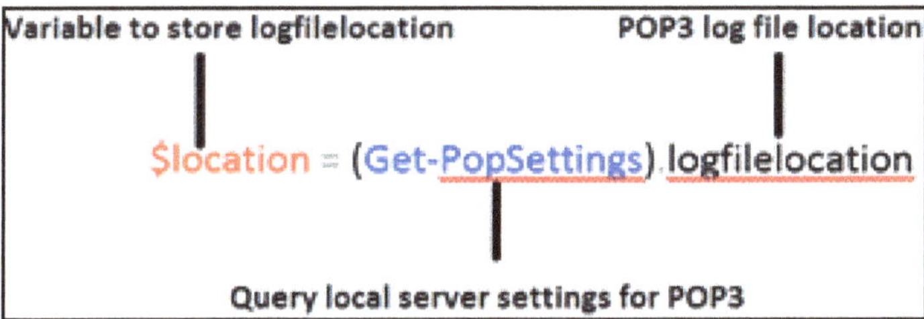


** The .logfilelocation is a specific property retrieved by Get-PopSettings

Once we have the location of the POP3 log files, we can get a full list of the files using the Get-ChildItem cmdlet (which provides 'child' items under a specified folder):

Get-ChildItem $Location

The above cmdlet, using the file location stored in $location and provides this result:

```
        Directory: C:\Program Files\Microsoft\Exchange Server\V14\Logging\Pop3


Mode                LastWriteTime       Length Name
----                -------------       ------ ----
-a---         1/24/2016     4:25 PM        855 Pop320160123-1.LOG
-a---         1/24/2016     3:28 PM        857 Pop320160124-1.LOG
```

However, we need to be able to store the above information and analyze each of the POP3 log files for the CIP (Client IP Address).  We will store the results in a variable called $files:

$Files = Get-ChildItem $Location

We now have a list of files to work with.  With PowerShell we can use the Foreach loop to examine each file.  Code to execute on each file will be placed in the brackets '{ }'.

Foreach ($File in $Files) { }

Once in the loop, we need to get the name of the file from the current line in the $files array:

$Name = $File.Name

** .name is a property of the file

We now have the file location ($location) and the name of the current POP3 file ($name) and need to store this into the $Csv variable so we can search each line for the CIP value:

$Csv= Import-Csv (Join-Path $Location $Name)

The $csv variable will have a lot of lines to review, so we can loop using the Foreach command to review each line in the current POP3 log file:

Foreach ($Line in $Csv) {

The POP3 log files contain some commented lines, with '#' at the very beginning of the lines.  PowerShell can ignore these lines with some help:

If ($Line -Like "#") { }

The above line looks for a line with '#' in it and skips it.  This process will happen as we loop through each line in the CSV.  Below is a sample version of an Exchange 2010 POP3 log file.  Notice the lines with a '#' in front of them:

If the line in the CSV file does not have a '#' in front of it, we can process it.  To do so we can use an 'Else {' code section.  This new section of code to work with lines with no '#' in front of it.

Else {

Here we are isolating the CIP (Client IP) value.  The $info variable will store the CIP value in the current line of the current log file:

$Info = $Line.Cip

** **Note** ** How variables store data:

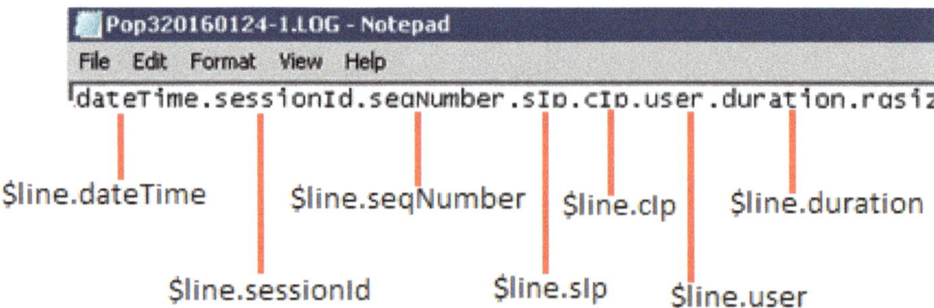


Part of troubleshooting the script is to remove bugs or workaround that data that is ingested into variables. In this case, $info has a value of CIP for the first line.  This line effectively says if $info does not have a value of 'cip' then do these steps.

```
If ($Info -ne "Cip") {
```

This line will loop through all the values in the $info variable. Without this step, we would receive an error about indexing a null array as well a perform a certain operation on the data.

```
Foreach ($Value in $Info) {
```

While working on this section of code, an error was generated in testing:

```
You cannot call a method on a null-valued expression.
At C:\Downloads\testpop2.ps1:28 char:29
+                             $ID = $value.Split([char]0x003A)
+                             ~~~~~~~~~~~~~~~~~~~~~~~~~~~~~~~~~~~~~~~~~~~
    + CategoryInfo          : InvalidOperation: (:) [], RuntimeException
    + FullyQualifiedErrorId : InvokeMethodOnNull

Cannot index into a null array.
At C:\Downloads\testpop2.ps1:29 char:29
+                             $CIP = $ID[0]
+                             ~~~~~~~~~~~~~~~
    + CategoryInfo          : InvalidOperation: (:) [], RuntimeException
    + FullyQualifiedErrorId : NullArray

You cannot call a method on a null-valued expression.
```

PowerShell ran into an issue and the solution is to loop through the variable as it is an array of values. The 'Cannot index into a null array' is the clue. The fact that the variable is an array provides an opportunity to work with the data better in a loop. The Foreach loop will allow PowerShell to go through each line and process it correctly.

This line will allow us to split the $value variable into chunks, using the ':' character as the splitting point. 0x003A stands for the ':' character.

```
$ID = $Value.Split([Char]0x003A)
```

Data in the $Value variable prior to splitting:

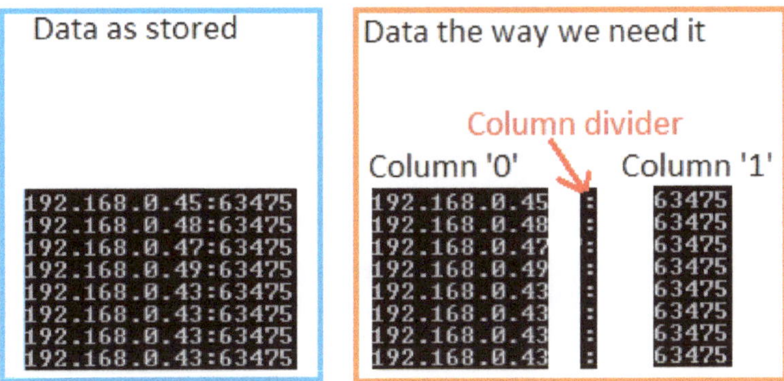



$ID[0] is the first value stored in the $ID array.

```
$CIP = $ID[0]
```

This data looks like this:

```
192.168.0.45
192.168.0.48
192.168.0.47
192.168.0.49
192.168.0.43
192.168.0.43
192.168.0.43
192.168.0.43
```

Here were are combining all of the values found in $Cip and storing them in an array called $CipResults:

    $CipResults += $Cip

Because we are storing variables in the $CipResults variable, we also need to define the variable as an array. It is not uncommon to have to define this after a script is almost complete especially if the data type to be stored in a variable are not known. The best practice is to place these lines at the top of the script:

    $CipResults = @()

After the script reads all the POP3 log files and stores the information in a variable (this part could take time depending on the number of log files and size of the files that were are searching through). PowerShell can now display a list of the CIP values:

    $CipResults | Sort -Unique

This line will take the values in $CipResults find all unique values and sort them. If for example, if the data set looked like this:

    192.168.0.43,192.168.0.43,192.168.0.43,192.168.0.45,192.168.0.46,192.168.0.46,192.168.0.43,192.168.0.47

You would see this displayed at the end:

    192.168.0.43    192.168.0.45    192.168.0.46    192.168.0.47

## Final Script

```
# Define Variables
$CipResults = @()
# Get Files for parsing
$Location = (Get-PopSettings).LogfileLocation
$Files = Get-ChildItem $Location
# Loop for each file to get IP Addresses
Foreach ($File in $Files) {
  $Name = $File.Name
  $Csv= Import-Csv (Join-Path $location $name)
  Foreach ($Line in $Csv) {
    If ($Line -Like "#") { }
    Else {
      # Get the Client IP
      $Info = $Line.Cip
      If ($Info -ne "Cip") {
        Foreach ($Value in $Info) {
          # Client IP also contains the port number which we will remove here
          $ID = $Value.Split([Char]0x003A)
          $CIP = $ID[0]
          $Cipresults += $cip
        }
      }
    }
  }
}
```

```
# Optional - Remove Duplicates
Write-host "List of IP Addresses that connect to the POP3 Service of all the Exchange 2010 Servers."
$cipResults | Sort -Unique
```

Results produced by the script:

```
List of IP Addresses that connect to the POP3 Service of all the Exchange 2010 Servers
192.168.0.43
192.168.0.45
192.168.0.47
192.168.0.48
192.168.0.49
```

## Limitations and How to Overcome Them

The PowerShell script used for determining POP3 Connections is written to query one local server. What if the Exchange organization contains a large number of servers? In a large migration, that could be a problem. Do we want to run the script separately on each server? Or do we want to use PowerShell to handle multiple queries? How do we overcome this problem?

First, since this scenario is built off Exchange 2010 (in a migration to Exchange 2016), we'll assume we need to check each Exchange 2010 server for the same information. A common solution when dealing with a large number of servers is running a loop with the code run against each server. There are exceptions, but in general expanding the same code to be run against multiple objects is one of the main advantages of PowerShell. First, a list of Exchange Servers is needed in order to know what servers are being queried in the script:

```
Get-ExchangeServer
```

```
Name                Site                    ServerRole   Edition      AdminDisplayVersion
----                ----                    ----------   -------      -------------------
LAB20-EX2010        LAB20.LOCAL/Confi...    Mailbox,...  Standard...  Version 14.3 (Bu...
LAB20-EX2010-2      LAB20.LOCAL/Confi...    Mailbox,...  Standard...  Version 14.3 (Bu...
LAB20-EX2016        LAB20.LOCAL/Confi...    Mailbox,...  Standard...  Version 15.1 (Bu...
```

Unfortunately we get all Exchange Servers even the Exchange Server 2016 servers. We need to filter those servers out and leave only 2010 servers behind. Exchange 2010 Servers have the value of "Version 14.3 (Bu...)" for the AdminDisplayVersion property (last column in the above screenshot). To get just those Exchange 2010 servers the Get-ExchangeServer cmdlet, is used and a filter is employed to get the results for that property, with that value:

```
Get-ExchangeServer | Where {$_.AdminDisplayVersion -Like "Version 14*"}
```

```
Name                Site                    ServerRole   Edition      AdminDisplayVersion
----                ----                    ----------   -------      -------------------
LAB20-EX2010        LAB20.LOCAL/Confi...    Mailbox,...  Standard...  Version 14.3 (Bu...
LAB20-EX2010-2      LAB20.LOCAL/Confi...    Mailbox,...  Standard...  Version 14.3 (Bu...
```

Now that the list contains just Exchange 2010 servers the 'Name' property is all we need. Refining the results again, we place brackets '( )' around the previous one-liner which allow us to pick a property from the servers, in this case 'name':

```
(Get-ExchangeServer | Where {$_.AdminDisplayVersion -Like "Version 14*"}).Name
```

Next will be to store the server names in a variable called '$Servers':

```
$Servers = (Get-ExchangeServer | Where {$_.AdminDisplayVersion -Like "Version 14*"}).Name
```

Then a loop is necessary to process a series of PowerShell cmdlets for each Exchange 2010 server name stored in $Server. The loop will read in the $servers variable and store the current line of values in a variable called $server (notice the singular vs plural). Inside the loop there will be code for the POP3 log analysis.

```
Foreach ($Server in $Servers) { … insert code here .. }
```

The next step is to integrate the $server variable into the script so that each time the Foreach loop reads another name, the correct settings can be read for the server. Not only do we need to do that, but the file name path will need to be adjusted to a UNC path in order to be read properly:

** **Note** ** new multi-server script shown below:

**New Code**
Get all Exchange 2010 servers

```
# Define Variables
$cipresults = @()

# Get all Exchange 2010 servers
$servers = (Get-ExchangeServer | where {$_.admindisplayversion -like "Version 14*"}).name

foreach ($server in $servers) {    Loop to handle multiple servers

    # Get Files for parsing
    $location = (Get-PopSettings -server $server).logfilelocation
    $path = "\\$Server\$($location.Replace(':','$'))"
    $files = get-childitem $path

    foreach ($file in $files) {
        $name = $file.name
        $csv = import-csv $path"\"$name
        foreach ($line in $csv) {
            if ($line -like "#") {
            } else {

# Get the Client IP
                $info = $line.cip
                if ($info -ne "cip") {
                    foreach ($value in $info) {
                        if ($value -ne $null) {

# Client IP also contains the port number which we will remove here
                            $ID = $value.Split([char]0x003A)
                            $CIP = $ID[0]
                            $cipresults += $cip
                        }
                    }
                }
            }
        }
    }
}
```

**New Code**
Change path to UNC Path

The results will work the same as the single server script in that multiple servers can now be queried.

Last limitation is there is the 'X' Factor that we do not know how many or how large the POP3 log files would be. For a typical migration, the last 30 days for connection detection should be sufficient. In this case we would only review logs that are <= 30 days old. To handle this, we would set a time limit using the Get-Date cmdlet and subtracting 30 days from the current date. We reuse the $path variable which refers to the file location on a remote server.

```
$Limit = (Get-Date).AddDays(-30)
Get-ChildItem $Path -Recurse | ? {-Not $_.PSIsContainer -And $_.CreationTime -lt $limit} | Remove-Item
```

## Conclusion for this Script

While the above script was written for Exchange Server 2010, it was written for a migration to Exchange Server 2016. The same code in the final script works on 2010, on 2013 and on 2016. This was verified in multiple test labs prior to putting this code in our book.

Summary of Cmdlets Used:

```
Get-ExchangeServer
Get-POPSettings
Get-ChildItem
Import-Csv
Write-Host
```

# IMAP4

We've covered POP3, but now IMAP4 deserves attention as we are more likely to find clients connecting with IMAP4 versus POP3. In the POP3 section we were able to track down the logs and write a script to find any client connections using that protocol. Let's see what it takes to accomplish the same task with IMAP4. We will skip some of the above steps as we've 'worked out the kinks' in the way the script needs to run.

IMAP is a more modern protocol and tends to be the protocol used by mail servers that are not Exchange Servers. IMAP also operates in a different manner than the previous POP3 protocol. It does not download email from the mail server and delete it from the server. This allows for multiple clients (think multiple computers and mobile devices) to connect to the same email account and not have to worry about mail being missing. In our BYOD and multiple device age, the IMAP4 protocol provides a superior end user experience to POP3.

IMAP uses ports 143 (insecure, unencrypted or opportunistic TLS) and 993 (secure and encrypted). Commonly an ISP's (like Google) uses IMAP, as do many mail servers that run on Mac servers, Exchange server and Office 365 can enable it as well.

Similar to POP3, most engineers deal with IMAP4 for initial setup, troubleshooting and migrations. Like POP3, we will start with discovering IMAP4 connections.

## Script Reusability

IMAP is similar enough in Exchange that the script used for POP3 can be re-used to handle IMAP4 logs on the same Exchange servers. After reviewing the code for the script, the only lines that needed to be changes were:

```
$Location = (Get-POPSettings -Server $Server).LogFileLocation
```

Which becomes:

```
$Location = (Get-IMAPSettings -Server $Server).LogFileLocation
```

And then the description line at the bottom of the script:

```
Write-Host "List of IP Addresses that connect to the POP3 Service of all the Exchange 2010 Servers."
```

Which becomes:

```
Write-Host "List of IP Addresses that connect to the IMAP4 Service of all the Exchange 2010 Servers."
```

Really, that was it. The rest of the lines in the script dealt with querying server names, parsing log files and summarizing results. The similarities were key in the area of log files that POP3 and IMAP4 use. This very little effort was needed to create two completed scripts, which report on two different protocol connections for Exchange Servers.

### IMAP4 Script Code

```
# Define Variables
$CipResults = @()
# Get Files for parsing
$Location = (Get-IMAPSettings).LogFileLocation
$Files = Get-ChildItem $Location
# Loop for each file to get IP Addresses
Foreach ($File in $Files) {
   $Name = $File.Name
   $Csv = Import-Csv $Location"\"$Name
   Foreach ($Line in $Csv) {
     If ($Line -Like "#") { }
     Else {
# Get the Client IP
        $Info = $Line.Cip
        If ($Info -ne "cip") {
           Foreach ($Value in $Info) {
# Client IP also contains the port number which we will remove here
              $ID = $Value.Split([Char]0x003A)
              $CIP = $ID[0]
              $CipResults += $Cip
     }
    }
   }
  }
}

# Optional - Remove Duplicates
Write-Host "List of IP Addresses that connect to the IMAP4 Service of all the Exchange 2010 Servers."
$CipResults | Sort -Unique
```

Results for the IMAP version of the script:

```
List of IP Addresses that connect to the IMAP4 Service of all the Exchange 2010 Servers
192.168.0.217
```

# POP3 and IMAP4 Reporting

While finding the connections made by clients or servers to Exchange Servers can be useful for long term maintenance or documenting settings for these services. The documentation can be as simple as a formatted list report created in PowerShell as complex as a complete export of settings with these settings extracted and then reformatted into an HTML report for server documentation purposes.

## POP3 Setting

Going back to the beginning of this chapter we know we can run these commands to begin our analysis:

```
Get-Service *Pop*
Get-POPSettings
```

The Get-Service command is good, but it is not nearly detailed enough for providing information.  Using WMI or CIM queries are a better bet as more information is stored:

```
Get-WmiObject Win32_Service -Property *  | Where {$_.Name -Like "*pop*"} | Select *
```

** Notice the use of the 'Win32_Service' class in the above command.  To find the appropriate class see the WMI/CIM chapter.

```
PSComputerName              : 16-01-EX01
Name                        : MSExchangePop3
Status                      : OK
ExitCode                    : 1077
DesktopInteract             : False
ErrorControl                : Normal
PathName                    : "C:\Program Files\Microsoft\Exchange
                              Server\V15\FrontEnd\PopImap\Microsoft.Exchange.Pop3Service.exe"
ServiceType                 : Own Process
StartMode                   : Manual
__GENUS                     : 2
__CLASS                     : Win32_Service
__SUPERCLASS                : Win32_BaseService
__DYNASTY                   : CIM_ManagedSystemElement
__RELPATH                   : Win32_Service.Name="MSExchangePop3"
__PROPERTY_COUNT            : 25
__DERIVATION                : {Win32_BaseService, CIM_Service, CIM_LogicalElement, CIM_ManagedSystemElement}
__SERVER                    : 16-01-EX01
__NAMESPACE                 : root\cimv2
__PATH                      : \\16-01-EX01\root\cimv2:Win32_Service.Name="MSExchangePop3"
AcceptPause                 : False
AcceptStop                  : False
Caption                     : Microsoft Exchange POP3
CheckPoint                  : 0
CreationClassName           : Win32_Service
Description                 : Provides Post Office Protocol version 3 service to clients. If this service is stopped,
                              clients can't connect to this computer using the POP3 protocol.
DisplayName                 : Microsoft Exchange POP3
InstallDate                 :
ProcessId                   : 0
ServiceSpecificExitCode     : 0
Started                     : False
StartName                   : LocalSystem
State                       : Stopped
SystemCreationClassName     : Win32_ComputerSystem
SystemName                  : 16-01-EX01
TagId                       : 0
WaitHint                    : 0
Scope                       : System.Management.ManagementScope
Path                        : \\16-01-EX01\root\cimv2:Win32_Service.Name="MSExchangePop3"
Options                     : System.Management.ObjectGetOptions
ClassPath                   : \\16-01-EX01\root\cimv2:Win32_Service
Properties                  : {AcceptPause, AcceptStop, Caption, CheckPoint...}
SystemProperties            : {__GENUS, __CLASS, __SUPERCLASS, __DYNASTY...}
Qualifiers                  : {dynamic, Locale, provider, UUID}
Site                        :
Container                   :
```

While the amount of information may seem overwhelming, the get-wmiobject command enables us to pick the needed details. Take some time to review each line as this information may come handy with future queries.  The service account, if there is a service account, is shown as "StartName" and the path to the executable that is linked to the service on the server is listed as "PathName".

Get-WmiObject Win32_Service -Property * | Where {$_.Name -Like "*pop*"} | Select Caption, SystemName, StartMode, State, StartName, PathName | fl

This cmdlet reveals some key information about the POP3 services on an Exchange 2016 server:

```
caption     : Microsoft Exchange POP3
SystemName  : 16-01-EX01
StartMode   : Manual
State       : Stopped
StartName   : LocalSystem
pathname    : "C:\Program Files\Microsoft\Exchange Server\V15\FrontEnd\PopImap\Microsoft.Exchange.Pop3Service.exe"

caption     : Microsoft Exchange POP3 Backend
SystemName  : 16-01-EX01
StartMode   : Manual
State       : Stopped
StartName   : NT AUTHORITY\NetworkService
pathname    : "C:\Program Files\Microsoft\Exchange Server\V15\ClientAccess\PopImap\Microsoft.Exchange.Pop3Service.exe"
```

Next the 'Get-PopSettings | fl' one-liner will provide the remaining information on POP3 for the Exchange server:

```
RunspaceId                        : c8be5ab8-e4e3-4541-9e98-368576651c9d
Name                              : 1
ProtocolName                      : POP3
MaxCommandSize                    : 512
MessageRetrievalSortOrder         : Ascending
UnencryptedOrTLSBindings          : {[::]:110, 0.0.0.0:110}
SSLBindings                       : {[::]:995, 0.0.0.0:995}
InternalConnectionSettings        : {16-TAP-EX02.16-TAP.Local:995:SSL,
                                    16-TAP-EX02.16-TAP.Local:110:TLS}
ExternalConnectionSettings        : {}
X509CertificateName               : 16-TAP-EX02
Banner                            : The Microsoft Exchange POP3 service is ready.
LoginType                         : SecureLogin
AuthenticatedConnectionTimeout    : 00:30:00
PreAuthenticatedConnectionTimeout : 00:01:00
MaxConnections                    : 2147483647
MaxConnectionFromSingleIP         : 2147483647
MaxConnectionsPerUser             : 16
MessageRetrievalMimeFormat        : BestBodyFormat
ProxyTargetPort                   : 1995
CalendarItemRetrievalOption       : iCalendar
OwaServerUrl                      :
EnableExactRFC822Size             : False
LiveIdBasicAuthReplacement        : False
SuppressReadReceipt               : False
ProtocolLogEnabled                : False
EnforceCertificateErrors          : False
LogFileLocation                   : C:\Program Files\Microsoft\Exchange Server\V15\Logging\Pop3
LogFileRollOverSettings           : Daily
LogPerFileSizeQuota               : 0 B (0 bytes)
ExtendedProtectionPolicy          : None
EnableGSSAPIAndNTLMAuth           : True
Server                            : 16-TAP-EX02
AdminDisplayName                  :
ExchangeVersion                   : 0.10 (14.0.100.0)
DistinguishedName                 : CN=1,CN=POP3,CN=Protocols,CN=16-TAP-EX02,CN=Servers,CN=Exchange
                                    Administrative Group (FYDIBOHF23SPDLT),CN=Administrative
                                    Groups,CN=TAP,CN=Microsoft
                                    Exchange,CN=Services,CN=Configuration,DC=16-TAP,DC=Local
Identity                          : 16-TAP-EX02\1
```

Depending on what the POP3 server is used for or what clients are connecting, settings can be chosen for documentation purposes.  Here is a sample of the above services:

```
[PS] C:\>Get-PopSettings | fl server,protocolname,x509*,logint*,logfile1*,unen*,SSL*,*authe*


Server                            : 16-01-EX01
ProtocolName                      : POP3
X509CertificateName               : 16-01-EX01
LoginType                         : SecureLogin
LogFileLocation                   : C:\Program Files\Microsoft\Exchange Server\V15\Logging\Pop3
UnencryptedOrTLSBindings          : {[::]:110, 0.0.0.0:110}
SSLBindings                       : {[::]:995, 0.0.0.0:995}
AuthenticatedConnectionTimeout    : 00:30:00
PreAuthenticatedConnectionTimeout : 00:01:00
```

If there are multiple Exchange 2016 servers present, the above one-liner's won't be as useful because they commands only run locally and not globally against a larger environment. That is, unless these commands are modified to handle more than one server. Several available options present themselves in order to solve this conundrum.

**(1) Loop**
$Servers = Get-ExchangeServer

Foreach ($Server in $Servers) {
    Get-PopSettings -Server $Server | fl Server, ProtocolName,x509*,logint*,logfilel*,unen*,SSL*,*authe*
}

**(2) One liner**
Get-ExchangeServer | Get-PopSettings | fl Server, ProtocolName, x509*, logint*, logfilel*, unen*, SSL*, *authe*

Both of these methods create the same results in the end:

```
Server                            : 16-01-EX01
ProtocolName                      : POP3
X509CertificateName               : 16-01-EX01
LoginType                         : SecureLogin
LogFileLocation                   : C:\Program Files\Microsoft\Exchange Server\V15\Logging\Pop3
UnencryptedOrTLSBindings          : {[::]:110, 0.0.0.0:110}
SSLBindings                       : {[::]:995, 0.0.0.0:995}
AuthenticatedConnectionTimeout    : 00:30:00
PreAuthenticatedConnectionTimeout : 00:01:00

Server                            : 16-01-EX02
ProtocolName                      : POP3
X509CertificateName               : 16-01-EX02
LoginType                         : SecureLogin
LogFileLocation                   : C:\Program Files\Microsoft\Exchange Server\V15\Logging\Pop3
UnencryptedOrTLSBindings          : {[::]:110, 0.0.0.0:110}
SSLBindings                       : {[::]:995, 0.0.0.0:995}
AuthenticatedConnectionTimeout    : 00:30:00
PreAuthenticatedConnectionTimeout : 00:01:00
```

If a POP3 connection is failing, use this command to review the LoginType and X509 certificate, as well as the Unencrypted and SSL bindings. If your POP3 application does not require a secure login, the options needs to change 'Set-POPSettings':

**Before:**

```
UnencryptedOrTLSBindings    SSLBindings              LoginType       X509CertificateName
------------------------    -----------              ---------       -------------------
{[::]:110, 0.0.0.0:110}     {[::]:995, 0.0.0.0:995}  PlainTextLogin  16-02-EX02
```

Run this command to change the LoginType (to handle the different connection type):

    Set-PopSettings -LoginType PlaintextLogin

**After:**

```
UnencryptedOrTLSBindings    SSLBindings              LoginType       X509CertificateName
------------------------    -----------              ---------       -------------------
{[::]:110, 0.0.0.0:110}     {[::]:995, 0.0.0.0:995}  SecureLogin     16-02-EX02
```

Remember to utilize Get-Help <command name> -Full in order to get information on what options are available for a particular PowerShell cmdlet.

HINT for converting single server queries to multiple server queries:

Converting a PowerShell cmdlet to query more than one Exchange Server:

Replace the server name "ex01" with $server, the loop will use the name in $server instead.

```
Get-POPSettings "ex01" | fl server,protocolname,x.509*,logint*,logfile1*,unen*,SSL*,*authe*
```

```
$servers = (Get-ExchangeServer).name
foreach ($server in $servers) {

}
```

Code shell that can be used for single server querying PowerShell cmdlets.

After changing the server name to the variable and inserting the code into the loop, the results looks like this:

```
$servers = (Get-ExchangeServer).name
foreach ($server in $servers) {
    Get-POPSettings $server | fl server,protocolname,x.509*,logint*,logfile1*,unen*,SSL*,*authe*
}
```

## IMAP4 Setting

IMAP4 in Exchange Server 2016 contains a similar set of cmdlets and configuration data to POP3.  As such, we can use very similar cmdlets to work on the IMAP4 like POP3.

```
Get-Service *IMAP*
Get-IMAPSettings
```

We know from the POP3 section that the Get-Service command is good, but it is not nearly detailed enough for providing information.  Using WMI or CIM queries are a better bet as more information is provided when compared to the *-Service cmdlets, such as checking the startup mode of services (StartMode):

```
Get-WmiObject Win32_Service -Property *  | Where {$_.Name -Like "*imap*"} | Select *
```

```
Name                      : MSExchangeImap4
Status                    : OK
ExitCode                  : 1077
DesktopInteract           : False
ErrorControl              : Normal
PathName                  : "C:\Program Files\Microsoft\Exchange Server\V15\FrontEnd\PopImap\Microsoft.Exchange.Imap4Service.exe"
ServiceType               : Own Process
StartMode                 : Manual
__GENUS                   : 2
__CLASS                   : Win32_Service
__SUPERCLASS              : Win32_BaseService
__DYNASTY                 : CIM_ManagedSystemElement
__RELPATH                 : Win32_Service.Name="MSExchangeImap4"
__PROPERTY_COUNT          : 25
__DERIVATION              : {Win32_BaseService, CIM_Service, CIM_LogicalElement, CIM_ManagedSystemElement}
__SERVER                  : 16-01-EX01
__NAMESPACE               : root\cimv2
__PATH                    : \\16-01-EX01\root\cimv2:Win32_Service.Name="MSExchangeImap4"
AcceptPause               : False
AcceptStop                : False
Caption                   : Microsoft Exchange IMAP4
CheckPoint                : 0
CreationClassName         : Win32_Service
Description               : Provides Internet Message Access Protocol service to clients. If this service is stopped, clients won't
                            computer using the IMAP4 protocol.
DisplayName               : Microsoft Exchange IMAP4
InstallDate               :
ProcessId                 : 0
ServiceSpecificExitCode   : 0
Started                   : False
StartName                 : LocalSystem
State                     : Stopped
SystemCreationClassName   : Win32_ComputerSystem
```

Just like POP3, we can use the Get-WmiObject command to help pick the needed details. The service account, if there is a service account, is shown as "StartName" and the path to the executable that is linked to the service on the server is listed as "PathName".

Get-WmiObject Win32_Service -Property * | Where {$_.Name -Like "*imap*"} | Select Caption, SystemName, StartMode, State, StartName, PathName | fl

This cmdlet reveals some key information about the IMAP4 services on an Exchange 2016 server:

```
Caption     : Microsoft Exchange IMAP4
SystemName  : 16-TAP-EX02
StartMode   : Manual
State       : Stopped
StartName   : LocalSystem
PathName    : "C:\Program Files\Microsoft\Exchange
              Server\V15\FrontEnd\PopImap\Microsoft.Exchange.Imap4Service.exe"

Caption     : Microsoft Exchange IMAP4 Backend
SystemName  : 16-TAP-EX02
StartMode   : Manual
State       : Stopped
StartName   : NT AUTHORITY\NetworkService
PathName    : "C:\Program Files\Microsoft\Exchange
              Server\V15\ClientAccess\PopImap\Microsoft.Exchange.Imap4Service.exe"
```

Next the 'Get-IMAPSettings | fl' cmdlet provides the remaining information on IMAP4 for the Exchange server:

```
RunspaceId                        : c8be5ab8-e4e3-4541-9e98-368576651c9d
ProtocolName                      : IMAP4
Name                              : 1
MaxCommandSize                    : 10240
ShowHiddenFoldersEnabled          : False
UnencryptedOrTLSBindings          : {[::]:143, 0.0.0.0:143}
SSLBindings                       : {[::]:993, 0.0.0.0:993}
InternalConnectionSettings        : {16-TAP-EX02.16-TAP.Local:993:SSL,
                                    16-TAP-EX02.16-TAP.Local:143:TLS}
ExternalConnectionSettings        : {}
X509CertificateName               : 16-TAP-EX02
Banner                            : The Microsoft Exchange IMAP4 service is ready.
LoginType                         : SecureLogin
AuthenticatedConnectionTimeout    : 00:30:00
PreAuthenticatedConnectionTimeout : 00:01:00
MaxConnections                    : 2147483647
MaxConnectionFromSingleIP         : 2147483647
MaxConnectionsPerUser             : 16
MessageRetrievalMimeFormat        : BestBodyFormat
ProxyTargetPort                   : 1993
CalendarItemRetrievalOption       : iCalendar
OwaServerUrl                      :
EnableExactRFC822Size             : False
LiveIdBasicAuthReplacement        : False
SuppressReadReceipt               : False
ProtocolLogEnabled                : False
EnforceCertificateErrors          : False
LogFileLocation                   : C:\Program Files\Microsoft\Exchange Server\V15\Logging\Imap4
LogFileRollOverSettings           : Daily
LogPerFileSizeQuota               : 0 B (0 bytes)
ExtendedProtectionPolicy          : None
EnableGSSAPIAndNTLMAuth           : True
Server                            : 16-TAP-EX02
AdminDisplayName                  :
ExchangeVersion                   : 0.10 (14.0.100.0)
DistinguishedName                 : CN=1,CN=IMAP4,CN=Protocols,CN=16-TAP-EX02,CN=Servers,CN=Exchang
                                    e Administrative Group (FYDIBOHF23SPDLT),CN=Administrative
                                    Groups,CN=TAP,CN=Microsoft
                                    Exchange,CN=Services,CN=Configuration,DC=16-TAP,DC=Local
Identity                          : 16-TAP-EX02\1
Guid                              : 8f8b1db8-dcc4-4edf-914e-132bc59b77a4
ObjectCategory                    : 16-TAP.Local/Configuration/Schema/ms-Exch-Protocol-Cfg-IMAP-Ser
                                    ver
ObjectClass                       : {top, protocolCfg, protocolCfgIMAP, protocolCfgIMAPServer}
WhenChanged                       : 7/7/2016 6:28:21 AM
WhenCreated                       : 7/7/2016 6:28:18 AM
WhenChangedUTC                    : 7/7/2016 11:28:21 AM
WhenCreatedUTC                    : 7/7/2016 11:28:18 AM
OrganizationId                    :
```

Depending on what the IMAP4 server is used for or what clients are connecting, settings can be chosen for documentation purposes:

```
[PS] C:\>Get-IMAPSettings -Server $server | fl server,protocolname,x509*,logint*,logfilel*,unen*,SSL*,*authe*

Server                              : 16-01-EX02
ProtocolName                        : IMAP4
X509CertificateName                 : 16-01-EX02
LoginType                           : SecureLogin
LogFileLocation                     : C:\Program Files\Microsoft\Exchange Server\V15\Logging\Imap4
UnencryptedOrTLSBindings            : {[::]:143, 0.0.0.0:143}
SSLBindings                         : {[::]:993, 0.0.0.0:993}
AuthenticatedConnectionTimeout      : 00:30:00
PreAuthenticatedConnectionTimeout   : 00:01:00
```

Just like we did with POP3, if there are multiple Exchange 2016 servers are present, the above one-liner's won't be as useful because the commands only run locally and not globally against a larger environment. That is, unless these commands are modified to handle more than one server. Several available options present themselves in order to solve this conundrum.

**(1) Loop**
```
$Servers = Get-ExchangeServer
Foreach ($Server in $Servers) {
    Get-IMAPSettings -Server $Server | fl Server, ProtocolName, x509*, Logint*, Logfilel*, Unen*, SSL*, *Authe*
}
```

**(2) One liner**
```
Get-ExchangeServer | Get-IMAPSettings | fl Server, ProtocolName, X509*, Logint*, Logfilel*, Unen*, SL*, *Authe*
```

Both of these methods create the same results in the end:

```
Server                              : 16-01-EX01
ProtocolName                        : IMAP4
X509CertificateName                 : 16-01-EX01
LoginType                           : SecureLogin
LogFileLocation                     : C:\Program Files\Microsoft\Exchange Server\V15\Logging\Imap4
UnencryptedOrTLSBindings            : {[::]:143, 0.0.0.0:143}
SSLBindings                         : {[::]:993, 0.0.0.0:993}
AuthenticatedConnectionTimeout      : 00:30:00
PreAuthenticatedConnectionTimeout   : 00:01:00

Server                              : 16-01-EX02
ProtocolName                        : IMAP4
X509CertificateName                 : 16-01-EX02
LoginType                           : SecureLogin
LogFileLocation                     : C:\Program Files\Microsoft\Exchange Server\V15\Logging\Imap4
UnencryptedOrTLSBindings            : {[::]:143, 0.0.0.0:143}
SSLBindings                         : {[::]:993, 0.0.0.0:993}
AuthenticatedConnectionTimeout      : 00:30:00
PreAuthenticatedConnectionTimeout   : 00:01:00
```

If an IMAP4 connection is failing, use this command to review the LoginType and X509 certificate, as well as the Unencrypted and SSL bindings. If your IMAP4 application does not require a secure login, the options needs to change.

# Testing POP3 and IMAP Connections

Exchange Server 2016 includes a series of test-xxx cmdlets that enable an Exchange admin to test various parts of Exchange to make sure they are functional. Utilizing these cmdlets would allow the construction of a server health script.

After prepping the environment for testing, the Test-IMAPConnectivity cmdlet will now generate results. The results would quickly show what mailboxes have IMAP and which have POP3 enabled. On Exchange 2016 servers, POP3 and IMAP4 are disabled and the test cmdlets reveal this configuration:

**IMAP4**

```
[PS] C:\>Test-ImapConnectivity -ClientAccessServer:16-01-ex01 |ft -auto

CasServer   LocalSite                Scenario                Result   Error
---------   ---------                --------                ------   -----
16-01-EX01  Default-First-Site-Name  Test IMAP4 Connectivity Failure  Service 'MSExchangeIMAP4' is not running.
```

**POP3**

```
C:\>Test-popConnectivity -ClientAccessServer:16-01-ex01 |ft -auto

erver  LocalSite                Scenario               Result   Error
-----  ---------                --------               ------   -----
1-EX01 Default-First-Site-Name  Test POP3 Connectivity Failure  Service 'MSExchangePOP3' is not runn
```

In a troubleshooting scenario, this cmdlet could verify that a service is up and connections are good. If one user reports an issue, the command can be tailored to that one user. To do so, specifying credentials will enable the test cmdlet to connect to the POP3 or IMAP4 services with those credentials, effectively impersonating the user (place this at the end of the IMAP4 and POP3 one-liners above:

> -MailboxCredential:(Get-Credential 16-01.local\administrator)

If this command succeeds and the user still cannot connect, comparing the settings on the application being used to the service settings is key. Specifically looking at the Login Type. Some applications will not handle 'SecureOnly' (the encrypted version of POP3 or IMAP4) well at all.


## IMAP4 and POP3 – User Settings


One of the often forgotten PowerShell cmdlets is Get-CASMailbox. Seems like an odd cmdlet, but it turns out to be very convenient. The Get-CASMailbox can be quite useful in providing information on what protocols a user with a mailbox can use to connect to an Exchange 2016 server - but on a mailbox level and not a server level. In the above screenshot, all mailboxes are enabled for EAS (ActiveSync), OWA, POP, IMAP and MAPI. If one were to run a simple one-liner like this:

Get-Mailbox | Get-CASMailbox

```
[PS] C:\>get-mailbox | get-casmailbox

Name              ActiveSyncEnabled OWAEnabled  PopEnabled  ImapEnabled  MapiEnabled
----              ----------------- ----------  ----------  -----------  -----------
Administrator     True              True        True        True         True
DiscoverySearchMa... True            True        True        True         True
extest_628b03ba937b4 True            True        True        True         True
```

Wait. What? Get-CASMailbox? CAS did stand for Client Access Server, a role that existed in Exchange Server 2013? However, this command is used for some special operations on mailboxes in Exchange Server. In some sense it is a holdover purely based on its name. The command is useful for managing mailboxes in Exchange 2016.


Get-CASMailbox can also reveal other properties of a mailbox like:

- OWAMailboxPolicy
- OWAforDevicesEnabled
- ECPEnabled
- MapiHttpEnabled

- UniversalOutlookEnabled
- EwsEnabled
- EwsAllowOutlook
- EwsAllowMacOutlook
- EwsAllowEntourage
- EwsApplicationAccessPolicy
- EwsAllowList
- EwsBlockList
- ShowGalAsDefaultView
- … and more ….

How can these properties be utilized?  Let's take a scenario where a company has put in place a policy that restricts the use of certain protocols with their new Exchange 2016 servers.  IT wants to restrict POP3 and IMAP access.  There is a small subset of users that require the use of these protocols and IT wants to limit IMAP and POP protocols.  Lastly, we need to accomplish these goals with PowerShell and it needs to be scalable.

## Where To Start

Each protocol will have two groups of users – those that have access and those that do not.  The first step would be to group users that should have access as this group will be the easiest to build and maintain rather than trying to maintain a group of those to block access to a resource.   In Active Directory, create a group called "POP3 Access" and another call "IMAP Access".   We then add users who will have access to these resources like so: (using Active Directory Users and Computers).

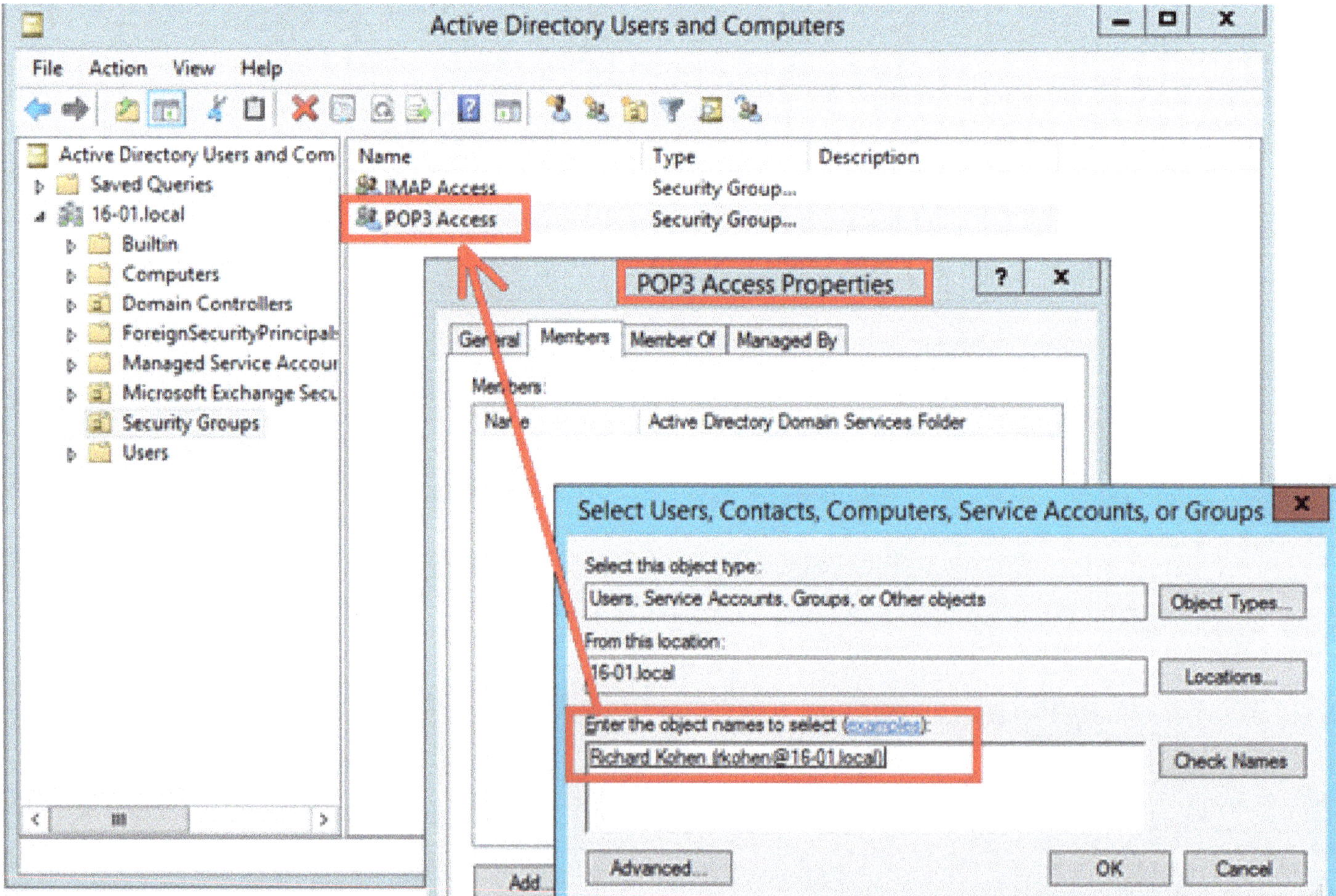

Now that the groups are populated with users a script will be needed to enforce these access conditions. What is needed in order to build the script?

1.  Need to store this user list in a variable to determine access or use the group name in the script as the determining factor for access in the script.
2.  What access should be granted or denied depending on members?
3.  What commands we can use to query this information in Exchange?
4.  What commands we can use to add or remove access to the resource?
5.  How often do we would want to reinforce this action?

## PowerShell Cmdlet Determination

*Storing the names of users who need access or using the group name?*
Using a group name is far easier than storing the list of names. The reason to do this is if PowerShell were to cycle through each mailbox to determine access, it would be easier to see if they are a member of a group (single comparison) versus comparing a list of uses (multiple comparisons). The single comparison method is much faster. Storing the group name in a variable is step one in the script build:

    $POP3AccessGroup = "POP3 Access"

*What access should be granted or denied depending on group membersip?*
In this case, the requirement was to allow certain user's access to POP3 and block all other users from using POP3. Going back to the Get-CASMailbox cmdlet, 'OWA Enabled' is an option that can be configured on a mailbox. Get CASMailbox has a set-command for changing settings – Set-CASMailbox. Not knowing what options that can be configured, I can run a 'get-help set-casmailbox –full' to see what options can be changed, while specifically looking for POP3 and IMAP4:

```
[PS] C:\>Get-Help Set-CASMailbox -Full

NAME
    Set-CASMailbox

SYNOPSIS
    This cmdlet is available in on-premises Exchange Server 2016 and in the cloud-based service.
    Some parameters and settings may be exclusive to one environment or the other.

    Use the Set-CASMailbox cmdlet to configure client access settings on a mailbox. For example,
    you can configure settings for Microsoft Exchange ActiveSync, Microsoft Outlook, Outlook on
    the web, POP3, and IMAP4.

    For information about the parameter sets in the Syntax section below, see Exchange cmdlet
    syntax.

SYNTAX
    Set-CASMailbox -Identity <MailboxIdParameter> [-ActiveSyncAllowedDeviceIDs
    <MultiValuedProperty>] [-ActiveSyncBlockedDeviceIDs <MultiValuedProperty>]
    [-ActiveSyncDebugLogging <$true | $false>] [-ActiveSyncEnabled <$true | $false>]
    [-ActiveSyncMailboxPolicy <MailboxPolicyIdParameter>] [-Confirm [<SwitchParameter>]]
    [-DisplayName <String>] [-DomainController <Fqdn>] [-ECPEnabled <$true | $false>]
    [-EmailAddresses <ProxyAddressCollection>] [-EwsAllowEntourage <$true | $false>]
    [-EwsAllowList <MultiValuedProperty>] [-EwsAllowMacOutlook <$true | $false>] [-EwsAllowOutlook
    <$true | $false>] [-EwsApplicationAccessPolicy <EnforceAllowList | EnforceBlockList>]
    [-EwsBlockList <MultiValuedProperty>] [-EwsEnabled <$true | $false>] [-IgnoreDefaultScope
    <SwitchParameter>] [-ImapEnabled <$true | $false>] [-ImapEnableExactRFC822Size <$true |
    $false>] [-ImapForceICalForCalendarRetrievalOption <$true | $false>]
    [-ImapMessagesRetrievalMimeFormat <TextOnly | HtmlOnly | HtmlAndTextAlternative |
    TextEnrichedOnly | TextEnrichedAndTextAlternative | BestBodyFormat | Tnef>]
    [-ImapSuppressReadReceipt <$true | $false>] [-ImapUseProtocolDefaults <$true | $false>]
    [-IsOptimizedForAccessibility <$true | $false>] [-MAPIBlockOutlookExternalConnectivity <$true
    | $false>] [-MAPIBlockOutlookNonCachedMode <$true | $false>] [-MAPIBlockOutlookRpcHttp <$true
    | $false>] [-MAPIBlockOutlookVersions <String>] [-MAPIEnabled <$true | $false>]
    [-MapiHttpEnabled <$true | $false>] [-Name <String>] [-OWAEnabled <$true | $false>]
    [-OWAforDevicesEnabled <$true | $false>] [-OwaMailboxPolicy <MailboxPolicyIdParameter>]
    [-PopEnabled <$true | $false>] [-PopEnableExactRFC822Size <$true | $false>]
    [-PopForceICalForCalendarRetrievalOption <$true | $false>] [-PopMessagesRetrievalMimeFormat
    <TextOnly | HtmlOnly | HtmlAndTextAlternative | TextEnrichedOnly |
    TextEnrichedAndTextAlternative | BestBodyFormat | Tnef>] [-PopSuppressReadReceipt <$true |
```

Looking closely at the options we see IMAPEnabled and POPEnabled. Both have two settings - $True and $False. We can set these values for each mailbox on the Exchange 2016 Servers.

With the base command figured out, the next step is to use these cmdlets to set the access for all mailboxes or for some mailboxes based off of group membership.  How can group membership be verified?

*What commands we can use to query this information in Exchange?*

First, get a list of groups a user is in using the 'memberof' property:

```
$MemberOf = (Get-ADUser -Identity (Get-Mailbox Administrator).Alias -Properties Memberof).
MemberOf
```

*What commands we can use to add or remove access to the resource?*

As discussed above, one PowerShell cmdlet and two parameters will allow for the changing of access to IMAP or POP:

```
Set-CASMailbox –IMAPEnabled $True
Set-CASMailbox –POPEnabled $True
```

$False would be used to disable access to those not in the AD Group.

**Putting it together**

Then, using the names of the groups stored in $MemberOf, check for any groups that match our POP3 Access groups and then set POP3access:

```
If ($MemberOf -Like "*POP3 Access*") { Set-CasMailbox $Alias –POPEnabled $True}
```

Putting these pieces together, we can create a script like this: (note we are excluding the Discovery mailbox as well)

```
$Mailboxes = Get-Mailbox | where {$_.Name -NotLike "DiscoverySearchMailbox*"}
ForEach ($Mailbox in $Mailboxes) {
    # Get all groups a user is a 'member of'
    $MemberOf = (Get-ADUser -Identity (Get-Mailbox $Mailbox).Alias -Properties MemberOf).MemberOf

    # If the user is in the POP Access group enable access and if not ('Else'), disable access
    If ($MemberOf -Like "*POP3 Access*") {
        Set-CasMailbox $Mailbox –POPEnabled $True
    } Else {
        Set-CasMailbox $Mailbox –POPEnabled $False
    }
}
```

** **Note** ** The POP3 Access lines can be compressed into one line where the $True or $False value from $MemberOf could be applied to the PopEnabled value for the mailbox:

```
Set-CasMailbox $mailbox –POPEnabled ($MemberOf -like "*POP3 Access*")
```

Prior to running the above script, validate who has the setting enabled or disabled: (*note what mailboxes are disabled*)

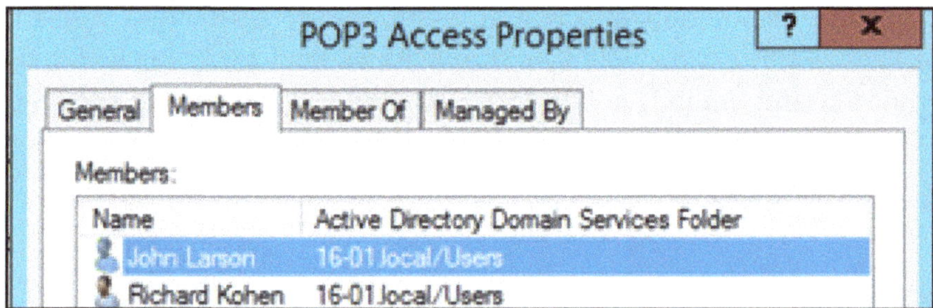

The POP Access group has these members:

After the script is run, ONLY John and Richard would get POP3 access, all others remain disabled ($False).

As expected, the results produced are what IT had given as a task. Now, to do the same for IMAP, the script has a couple of lines changes:

```
$Mailboxes = Get-Mailbox | Where {$_.Name -NotLike "DiscoverySearchMailbox*"}
ForEach ($Mailbox in $Mailboxes) {
    # Get all groups a user is a 'member of'
    $MemberOf = (Get-ADUser -Identity (Get-Mailbox $Mailbox).Alias -Properties MemberOf).MemberOf
    # If the user is in the IMAP Access group enable access and if not ('Else'), disable access
    If ($MemberOf -like "*IMAP Access*") {
        Set-CasMailbox $Mailbox –IMAPEnabled $True
    } Else {
        Set-CasMailbox $Mailbox –IMAPEnabled $False
    }
}
```

Before the script:

After the script:

```
Name                            ActiveSyncEnabled  OWAEnabled  PopEnabled  ImapEnabled  MapiEnabled
----                            -----------------  ----------  ----------  -----------  -----------
Administrator                   True               True        False       True         True
extest_628b03ba937b4            True               True        False       False        True
John Larson                     True               True        True        True         True
Richard Kohen                   True               True        True        False        True
```

How often we would want reinforce this action?

Once the script is created, we would then need to decide how and when to enforce these settings. Running the script weekly and daily would be ideal from a restrictive access view. The script can be deployed as a cleanup tool or enforcement tool using the Windows scheduler, setting up jobs to handle these changes on a weekly or daily basis.

# 11            Users

**In This Chapter**

- Types of Objects
- Creating Users
- Enabling Mailbox
- Deleting Users
- Modifying Users
- Converting Types
- Reporting

There is a saying in IT that the perfect network doesn't have any pesky users. While it's true admin work would be much easier without users, it completely defeats the purpose of having a network at all. In fact, users should be a key focus point of your network because they are the ones that create the company and make sure it is creating revenue. Which in turn pays for the network and your salary; at least in most cases.

So, users are fundamental in your network and obviously, the topic of this chapter. In this chapter, we will discuss creating and managing users along with all the secondary configuration options that will benefit your users, network and your admin responsibilities.

While the Exchange Admin Center offers a great deal of configuration options regarding the creation, management, etc. of users, you will hopefully see the major benefits of PowerShell when requiring bulk creation and changes. Knowing what is possible with Exchange Management Shell (EMS) might have some impact on how best to provision your users, your use of attributes and other conventions. It might be prudent to review those practices.

## Types of Objects

There are different types of objects that this chapter will address:

- User Mailbox
- Mail Enabled User
- Mail Contact
- Linked Mailboxes
- Resource Mailbox
- Archive Mailbox
- Public Folder Mailbox
- Shared Mailbox
- Remote Mailbox

A **User Mailbox** is an AD user with a mailbox. This is different from a **Mail User** that can log in, but has no mailbox, and will only forward to another email address.  A **Mail Contact** is an object that represents an email address in another environment, but is not security enabled and therefore cannot login.

Comparable in most respects to the User Mailbox, the **Linked Mailbox** is a mailbox that resides in another AD Forest than the AD user account, which is used to authenticate to gain access.

**Resource Mailboxes** have a disabled user account, like a User Mailbox they also calendar but it is designed for resource reservations like rooms and/or equipment. There are two types of resource mailboxes: Room and Equipment. These have a few different attributes and additional features to support planning meetings or equipment information.

A **Shared Mailbox** has a disabled user account. The idea is that normal user mailboxes get permission to access email and send as that mailbox, with all the data stored in that mailbox and not across different mailboxes. Useful for general email addresses like info@company.com etc., in which several people require access and send permissions.

With Modern Public Folders introduced in Exchange Server 2013, the infrastructure has changed radically and Public Folder data is no longer stored in a separate database, but in **Public Folder Mailboxes** in mailbox databases. The user experience has not changed however.

An **Archive Mailbox** is an additional mailbox linked to the user's primary mailbox, with the distinct difference that the Archive mailbox is only available via Outlook Desktop (ProPlus) and Outlook Web App (OWA) edition when connected to Exchange. This means that no offline access is available per design, it is meant primarily as a PST replacement.


# Creating Users

To explain the intricacies of creating users who will be able to send and receive email, we should look a little into how Active Directory (or AD) works and how Exchange leverages it.

### Mailbox or Mail Enabled User

There are two kinds of users possible, mailbox or mail enabled. The first is a user account that can be authenticated by the Active Directory and has a mailbox connected to it. This means the user can send and receive email, manage calendars, contacts, etc. All that information is stored in Exchange Databases.

A mail enabled user (or mail user for short) can also be authenticated by the Active Directory, but does not have a mailbox. Their user object does have a email address and a forwarding address, most likely to a mailbox in another environment (i.e partner company).  If anyone sends an email to this user, Exchange will forward the email to the forwarding address. For instance, if you are an IT consultant with multiple customers, it's reasonable to not have to maintain multiple mailboxes. This way users of each environment can find you in the Address List and send email, you on the other hand will get all email in one mailbox depending on your forwarding address. Nice to know: that will also limit the need for Exchange Client Access Licenses.

**New Mailbox**

You can directly create a new mailbox without the need to create an Active Directory (AD) user first, it will be automatically created. However, the options available to you are mostly limited to things related to Exchange, for instance a home path cannot be configured in the same action. You will probably need to configure the user with AD cmdlets if so required.

Use the following command to create an AD user immediately with a mailbox. These are the minimum required parameters:

```
New-Mailbox -Name "Dom Rigel" -UserPrincipalName Dom.Rigel@Contoso.Com -Password
$SecurePassword
```

** **Note** ** When using spaces in the Name field, you are required to use quotation marks if there is a space. The UserPrincipalName should obviously be valid for the AD Forest/Domain (you might need to add UPN suffixes) and preferably should correspond to the primary SMTP address the account will be using.

You can define the password via a prompt:

```
$SecurePassword = Read-Host -Prompt "Enter password" -AsSecureString
```

or a pre-determined value:

```
$PlainPassword = "Th1sSho4ldB3Secr3t"
$SecurePassword = $PlainPassword | ConvertTo-SecureString -AsPlainText -Force
```

In both cases the passwords must adhere to the password policy in place. The first method is fine for single changes. The latter is ideal for bulk additions of mailboxes. Obviously, you can also define a randomly generated unique password for each new mailbox, which is from a security perspective preferable.

Now, this was a New-Mailbox cmdlet with the minimum of required parameters, but almost certainly not a good fit for your environment. Why not? Some of the more obvious reasons are:

- The user is created in the Users container, which could mean that the incorrect security setting, Email Address Policy will be used, etc.
- The alias and SAMAccountName values are derived from the local part (before the @) of the UserPrincipalName (which is mandatory), thus in this example dom.rigel.
- Users do not require to reset password on next logon.
- Other attributes are not automatically filled, such as FirstName, LastName etc., which could have an effect on for instance Email Address Policies.
- Adds the mailbox to a randomly chosen mailbox database, unless that database has been limited from this automatic provisioning.

You can create the object in a specific OU with the -OrganizationalUnit parameter:

```
New-Mailbox "Dom Rigel" -OrganizationalUnit "Contoso.Com/Lab/Users"
```

You can explicitly define alias and SAMAccountName:

```
New-Mailbox -Alias Dom.Rigel -SamAccountName Dom.Rigel
```

The Alias and SamAccountName can be different from each other. The SamAccountName can also be different than the UserPrincipalName (UPN), in most cases it will differ as the maximum used length from SamAccount-Name is 20 characters, as the local part (before the @) of the UPN could be 64 characters at maximum (following the same RFC822 as for SMTP email addresses). If you do not specify the Alias, Exchange will generate one from the Name value. It does convert it to valid input (i.e. replacing invalid characters, removing spaces).

To make it mandatory for users to change their password after their first logon:

    New-Mailbox "Dom Rigel" -ResetPasswordOnNextLogon $True

To define FirstName, LastName etc. at account creation:

    New-Mailbox "Dom Rigel" -FirstName Dom -LastName Rigel

To explicitly define a mailbox database (in this case DB01):

    New-Mailbox "Dom Rigel" -Database DB01

Additional parameters are:

*PrimarySmtpAddress* – Which defines the primary SMTP address or reply address for that mailbox. Do note that when using this parameter, the Email Address Policy (EAP) setting EmailAddressPolicyEnabled is set to $False which means no EAP is applied on this account. This can be useful if you don't want this account to have all the SMTP addresses applied from an EAP, for instance with Shared Mailboxes. Or this mailbox will be used for a very specific purposes requiring only the set address.

*AccountDisabled* – When creating the mailbox and logon account, security policies might dictate you to disable the Active Directory account until it's ready for use (maybe additional security settings are required) or when the actual user is allowed to use it. For these circumstance, you can use this switch, but no value is required (i.e. $False isn't needed).

*ResetPasswordOnNextLogon* - With New-Mailbox a new logon account is also created as such compliancy and legal rules or just simple security regulations might require a user changes their password after the supplied ones has been used, to ensure that only the end user knows the password in normal circumstances. When creating the account, the admin has to enter a valid password but that means at least one other person in the organization knows the password. To prevent these situations, use -ResetPasswordOnNextLogon $True; the default is $False.

There are several types of policies available in Exchange, you can set specific (custom) policies with the following aptly named policy parameters:

- ActiveSyncMailboxPolicy
- AddressBookPolicy
- RetentionPolicy
- RoleAssignmentPolicy
- SharingPolicy
- ThrottlingPolicy

Name, DisplayName, FirstName, LastName are all values that have a special relationship together. These values are used by other users or even admins to identify the correct mailbox to the real-world user. Especially in large organizations it is prudent to have a good naming convention in place, also planning for all deviations that will happen. No naming convention will incorporate every possible situation, especially if your users have very different cultural naming standards and practices.

Name is a mandatory value, which becomes part of the DistinguishedName field, when creating a mailbox and must be a unique value within an Organization Unit (OU). DisplayName is the name of the mailbox, visible in admin tools, address lists and Outlook. When not specified, the value of the Name parameter is copied, which is a mandatory value.

FirstName and LastName were already discussed, but it still important to point out that these values can be used in your Email Address Policy. So, even though they are not mandatory, it might help with your Email Address Policies or help your users find the correct person within your (Exchange) organization.

You can further specify the user's Office and Phone parameters. These are, by default, visible in address lists etc., so make sure that privacy regulations in your country/region are followed. Note that you can filter based on Office locations when using RecipientFilter with many Exchange cmdlets.

Also note that although an AD User is created, there is no way to add home or profile paths at creation of the AD user etc. You'd have to either create the AD user beforehand with desired values and enable the mailbox later (see below how to do that) or use the New-Mailbox cmdlet and set the preferred values on the AD user using Set-ADUser or ADU&C later. If not everybody in your organization will get an (on-premises) mailbox, the first option could be the best fit.

Furthermore, not even all Exchange related values can be set when creating the mailbox, it is highly likely that you must use other cmdlets to completely configure the mailbox account to your organizations requirements and/or liking.

# Enabling Mailbox

If your user(s) already have an Active Directory account, some parameters are already configured via other means. This way you only must concentrate on Exchange specific attributes and thus cmdlet parameters.

You can mailbox enable a user with at least these parameters:

```
Enable-Mailbox -Identity Sjon.Lont
```

In this case Identity can be the Name, Display Name or other types of values, that can uniquely identify the target user account. Note that when not specifying other parameters the default values are used, the same when using the New-Mailbox cmdlets.

The cmdlet further behaves the same as the New-Mailbox cmdlet, with the distinct difference the AD account and the mandatory values are already provided.

## Enabling Archive Mailbox

You can enable the Archive Mailbox on an existing mailbox user with an archive switch:

```
Enable-Mailbox Dom.Rigel -Archive -ArchiveDatabase DB01 -ArchiveName "Dom Rigel Archive"
```

The ArchiveDatabase specifies explicitly where to put the Archive mailbox. If not specified it will be placed in the same database as the normal mailbox of the user. The ArchiveName specifies the name that identifies the Archive mailbox, otherwise the default naming is used, which is "In-Place Archive – " before the mailbox display name.

You can also create a new mailbox immediately with an archive by adding the -Archive switch to New-Mailbox or Enable-Mailbox.

The default archive quota and archive quota warning are 100 GB and 90GB. You can change those values with Set-Mailbox after the archive mailbox has been created:

```
Set-Mailbox Dom.Rigel -ArchiveQuota 10GB -ArchiveWarningQuota 9GB
```

Do not forget to apply the appropriate Retention Policy, which can be specified when Archive enabling the user with the -RetentionPolicy parameter.

## Linked Mailboxes

What if you have multiple Active Directory Forests? One way to provide mailboxes is to have an Exchange Environment in each AD Forest. However, unless specific additional configuration has been made, those environments are somewhat isolated. Things such as a shared Address List, permissions, availability etc. are possible, but add complexity to your environment.

Consolidating each environment into one centralized Exchange environment results in a simpler and thus easier manageable service. But due to technical or other restrictions, it might be required that the AD user remains in their forest.

There are several options here, a second set of credentials for the mailbox user and AD user, a second set of credentials synced to keep the state the same (using Microsoft Identity Manager for instance). Another option is the topic of this section: the linked mailbox.

The linked mailbox is a mailbox with a disabled user account in the Exchange environment (i.e. the resource forest). However, the AD User from another AD Forest (i.e. the account forest, with a trust between them) is linked to that account. Thus, creating the capability to connect to a mailbox.

You can create a linked mailbox with either the New-Mailbox or Enable-Mailbox cmdlet, depending whether the AD account already exists. You are required to add a domain controller and admin credentials of the account forest.

```
$RemoteCred = Get-Credential accountforest\administrator
New-Mailbox -Name "Sjon Lont" -LinkedDomainController dc.accountforest.com -LinkedMasterAccount
accountforest\Sjon.Lont -LinkedCredential $RemoteCred
```

You are required to provide the name, just like New-Mailbox always requires. The LinkedDomainController is a DC from the account forest, the LinkedMasterAccount is the account from the accountforest that should have ownership of the mailbox and LinkedCredential are the admin credentials required to affect changes in the account forest. You run this in the resource forest with credentials that have the required access to Exchange.

This will create a disabled user account in the resource forest, you can use all other parameters to configure this disabled user account. For instance, placing these accounts in a specific Organizational Unit.

Although it's not used for authentication, the properties are however used within Exchange for address lists, policies etc. So, consider this account practically the same as every other account. Note that changes made to the account in the account forest are not automatically reflected in the resource forest. Depending on the situation (short term due to merging for instance) you might want to invest in Microsoft Identity Manager or other automation/IdM synchronization solutions.

### New Mail Contacts

Mail enabled contacts are a way to create entries in the Global Address List that users can use to email often used addresses outside of your environment. For instance, if you have a Shared Service Desk supplier, you can create a mail contact with a recognizable name and an internal email address which also contains a forwarding address.

To create a contact:

```
New-MailContact -Name "Richard Deck" -ExternalEmailAddress R.Deck@Outlook.Com
```

Note that the contact will get an SMTP address according Email Address Policy settings, however the ExternalEmailAddress is the primary address and all email sent to the contact will be forwarded to the external address.

To delete a contact:

```
Remove-MailContact "Richard Deck"
```

# Deleting Users

There are two options: deleting the mailbox or deleting the user account including the mailbox. It depends on your own requirements and situations which of the two options is valid.

To remove the mailbox and NOT the user:

```
Disable-Mailbox -Identity Dom.Rigel
```

Note that you must confirm this with an explicit 'Yes'. You can prevent that by adding the -Confirm:$False option. Another consideration is that if the user also has an Archive mailbox, this too will be disabled and marked for deletion from the database (depending on your Exchange retention settings for mailboxes).

To remove the mailbox AND the user:

```
Remove-Mailbox -Identity Dom.Rigel -Confirm:$False
```

Alternatively, it's also possible to change the type of a user mailbox to Shared to keep the data and email flow available. See later in this chapter on how to do this.

# Modifying Users

There is one constant, and that is that things change. This is definitely the case for users. A lot can be changed via Exchange Management Shell and it's probable that a lot of settings are never changed or will require being changed.

But when it comes to modifying mailbox users, there are several things to consider. Most importantly, there is no single cmdlet that can modify everything on a mailbox. You must use the correct cmdlet for the required changes you want to make.

For an overview of all the attributes that (might) be subject to any modification, see the Reporting section later in this chapter. In that overview the Get-* cmdlets are used, but obviously to change the attributes you should use the Set-* variant or in some cases (like permissions) the option to use Add-* or Remove-* is also an option.

It's not the goal of this book to review every possible modification available, we will show what we feel are the most important and common modifications.

## User

The user object is where it all starts, whether it has a mailbox or is only mail-enabled. You can set multiple Exchange relevant attributes with Set-User such as Office, Phone, CustomAttributes, etc., and change AD specific ones like SAMAccountname or User Principal Name (UPN):

```
Set-User -Identity Gene.Ricks@Contoso.Com -UserPrincipalName Gene.Ricks@Contoso.Com
```

## Mailbox

There are several cmdlets that configure options on a (user) mailbox, most of those features are set with Set-Mailbox. There are other cmdlets that set other very specific settings, so if this cmdlet doesn't provide what you want to change you might have to use another cmdlet.

Why not in one cmdlet? Some of the settings control specific user settings that a user should have access to. Because of that everything is controlled in one way or another with PowerShell and Role Based Access Control (RBAC), it's sometimes easier to have a separate cmdlet for specific settings that are also configurable by users. It makes it easier to control those permissions (via Role Assignments with RBAC).

Settings on the mailbox include some email flow control such as addresses, forwarding or size/delivery restrictions, storage or quota settings and some policies. Others include junk email handling, OWA configuration (including features other than what is set via OWA Mailbox policies) and regional settings.

We will discuss some cmdlets in more detail below, in a per cmdlet way instead of a per scenario way.

### Set-Mailbox

One example to change the email flow settings is to set a forwarding address to another user:

```
Set-Mailbox -Identity Gene.Ricks@Contoso.Com -DeliverToMailboxAndForward:$True
-ForwardingAddress Ann.Pels@Contoso.Com
```

Above we set this to an SMTP address, for which there must be a matching Active Directory object for it; a mailbox, mail user or mail contact. If you needed to forward a message to an external SMTP address the Forwarding-SmtpAddress property would be set instead.

With delivery restrictions, you can control what email is accepted or not.

```
Set-Mailbox -Identity Gene.Ricks@Contoso.Com -RequireSenderAuthenticationEnabled:$True
-AcceptMessagesOnlyFromSendersOrMembers @('Ann.Ples@Contoso.Com')
-RejectMessagesFromSendersOrMembers @('Mike.Soft@Contoso.Com')
```

With RequireSenderAuthenticationEnabled only accounts in your Exchange Organization can email this mailbox (this is enabled for distribution groups by default). You can also configure users or groups to be accepted or rejected explicitly, in this example email from Ann Ples is accepted and from Mike Soft is rejected. Note that those are multi valued properties.

Another setting is the mailbox quota's, mainly the IssueWarningQuota, ProhibitSendQuota and ProhibitSendReceiveQuota settings. There are also quota's when using auditing and Litigation/In-Place hold, but the principle is the same. The big difference is that most mailboxes will use the default Database quota settings, but in case you need to override those settings you have to set them on the mailbox:

```
Set-Mailbox -Identity Gene.Ricks@Contoso.Com -IssueWarningQuota '10737418240' -ProhibitSendQuota
'11811160064' -ProhibitSendReceiveQuota '12884901888' -UseDatabaseQuotaDefaults:$False
```

In this example the mailbox quotas are respectively 10GB, 11GB and 12GB, the normal input is in MB (megabytes) however you can explicitly state whether you use MB or GB etc.:

```
Set-Mailbox -Identity Gene.Ricks@Contoso.Com -IssueWarningQuota 10GB
```

Do not forget to set the parameter UseDatabaseQuotaDefaults to $False when specifying mailbox level quotas.

If you require to retain deleted items longer than the default 14 days set on the mailbox database:

```
Set-Mailbox -Identity Gene.Ricks@Contoso.Com -UseDatabaseRetentionDefaults:$false
-RetainDeletedItemsFor '31' -RetainDeletedItemsUntilBackup:$true
```

In this example the database retention defaults are disabled; the deleted items are retained for user recovery for 31 days. Additionally, these items are retained until a successful backup was performed after those 31 days.

For setting additional SMTP addresses see example Adding/Removing an email address later in this chapter.

### Set-MailboxAutoReplyConfiguration

Configuration of the Out of Office (OOF) replies, including scheduling, inside and outside organization message. Basically, every possible setting the user can set. See Enabling and configure Out of Office settings by the admin for an example.

### Set-MailboxJunkEmailConfiguration

Configure the User Junk folder with specifics in addition to what the user has configured via OWA/Outlook.

```
Set-MailboxJunkEmailConfiguration -Identity Gene.Ricks@Contoso.Com -TrustedSendersAndDomains
fabrikam.com
```

The above will add the fabrikam.com domain as a trusted sender and Exchange will handle those domains differently (however if you have valid spam filtering software, their settings probably take precedence).

**Set-MailboxRegionalConfiguration**

Configures regional settings on a specific mailbox, such as time zone, date format, language etc.. Users will be prompted the first time they log in OWA or it will be configured depending on the client. However, as an admin you can provision these settings.

See Setting Regional setting in this chapter for an example.

## OWA

There are some settings specifically for OWA. The user can change these settings, but as in other similar examples it might be required to provision some settings for users.

```
Set-MailboxMessageConfiguration
```

Configures the behavior of OWA for a specific mailbox. For instance; the automatic addition of a signature, always show the 'From:' field when composing messages, conversation order and whether ReplyAll is the default response:

```
Set-MailboxMessageConfiguration -Identity Gene.Ricks@Contoso.Com -AutoAddSignature
$True -AlwaysShowFrom $True -ConversationSortOrder ChronologicalNewestOnTop
-IsReplyAllTheDefaultResponse $False
```

**Set-MailboxSpellingConfiguration**

Set the spelling language in OWA, force check before sending the email and whether to ignore uppercase and mixed digits:

```
Set-MailboxSpellingConfiguration  -Identity  Gene.Ricks@Contoso.Com  -CheckBeforeSend  $True
-IgnoreUpperCase $True -IgnoreMixedDigits $True -DictionaryLanguage Dutch
```

## Calendar

Calendar settings can be changed to affect the way calendar invites are processed or to set time zones for instance. While you can configure calendar settings for user mailboxes during provisioning, you will likely have to perform these actions more often for Room and Equipment Mailboxes as users can change most of these settings themselves.

**Set-MailboxCalendarConfiguration**

Can change calendar configurations and is available to the user, but also the admins so they can provision certain settings for the users. Such as WorkDays/WorkingHours, the first week of the year, timezones and such. Some customization are for OWA only as Outlook (or other clients) have their own settings that supersede these.

```
Set-MailboxCalendarConfiguration -Identity Gene.Ricks@Contoso.Com –WeekStartDay Monday
```

Sets the first day of the week to Monday, instead of the default Sunday.

### Set-MailboxCalendarFolder

This cmdlet is only relevant when sharing a calendar with a federated Exchange organization or when Internet Publishing is allowed. You can reset the published URLs, change the date range of what is published and disable the sharing. You can only do this for you own mailbox, unless you change the Role Assignment.

```
Set-MailboxCalendarFolder administrator:\Calendar -PublishEnabled $True -DetailLevel Limited
```

### Set-CalendarProcessing

The cmdlet Set-CalenderProcessing configures the way Exchange will handle meeting requests. As previously stated, users can configure these settings themselves and some settings are not relevant for user mailboxes. However, they are for Room and Equipment mailboxes which can turn them into automatic booking systems. You can use the same principal for inactive mailboxes, previously owned by users and setting to refuse every meeting request.

```
Set-CalendarProcessing -Identity Auditorium -ProcessExternalMeetingMessages $True
-AutomateProcessing AutoAccept -AddOrganizerToSubject $True -AddAdditionalResponse $True
-AdditionalResponse "Your request has been accepted."
```

This example configures the Room mailbox Auditorium to process External meeting requests (coming from outside of the Exchange organization), automatically accepts the requests, changes the Subject to the name of the organizer and will reply with a customized response to the organizer.

You can set additional options like whether users can set a reoccurring meeting, maximum meeting duration and delegates that have to give approval.

### Client Access

All client access related settings are performed with Set-CASMailbox. You can disable/enable and configure specific protocols, such as IMAP/POP or OWA, ActiveSync and Exchange Web Services (EWS). Basically, everything mailbox client connection related (with the exception of SMTP) can be configured.

```
Set-CASMailbox -Identity Gene.Ricks@Contoso.Com -PopEnabled $False -ImapEnabled $False
-EwsAllowEntourage $False -ActiveSyncEnabled $False
```

In this example, POP, IMAP, ActiveSync are disabled and EWS Entourage support (an Outlook for MacOS predecessor) is not allowed. Note that IMAP and POP are default enabled, but the service is by default disabled on every Exchange server. Thus, if an application or user requires either one of the protocols the services must be enabled and started. It's a best practice to disable these protocols or to not publish the ports to the Internet as a way of increasing security.

## Policies

Policies are an easy way to ensure users get the right configuration and is preferable to changing each specific user. There are several policies available:

- Throttling
- OWA Mailbox
- Retention

- RoleAssignmentPolicy
- SharingPolicy
- Mobile Device

Throttling policies regulate the amount of resources a mailbox can use up in order to prevent one mailbox causing performance issues on the server(s) and for other users.

OWA Mailbox policies regulate the Outlook Web App capabilities available to the user, the default has every feature enabled. For instance, Offline Mode is one often disabled feature in the default policy or other custom policies.

Retention policies give users and admins the option to regulate the retention of items in their mailbox or specific folders. When the mailbox is Archive enabled Retention policies (with the "Move to Archive") are commonly used, but an Archive mailbox is not required for their use.

Role assignments are part of Role Based Access Control (RBAC), the security model within Exchange. These policies regulate what users can carry out what actions on what objects, such as updating a distribution group for instance.

Sharing policies regulate sharing of calendar information within federated Exchange organizations or via Internet Calendar Publishing.

Mobile Device policies configure the security settings and features on connected mobile devices, via Exchange ActiveSync or the Outlook for iOS/Android app. Most commonly a mandatory PIN is set via these policies.

Obviously to assign or to change policies, the policies must exist. Assigning or changing the assigned policy on a mailbox is done via the Set-Mailbox or Set-CASMailbox cmdlet:

**Throttling policy:**

```
Set-Mailbox -Identity Gene.Ricks@Contoso.Com -ThrottlingPolicy HeavyEWSUsage
```

**OWA Mailbox policy:**

```
Set-CASMailbox -Identity Gene.Ricks@Contoso.Com -OwaMailboxPolicy NoOfflineOWA
```

**Retention Policy:**

```
Set-Mailbox -Identity Gene.Ricks@Contoso.Com -RetentionPolicy AutoCleanDeletedItems
```

**Role Assignment policy:**

```
Set-Mailbox -Identity Gene.Ricks@Contoso.Com -RoleAssignmentPolicy EditSubsetGroups
```

**Sharing policy:**

```
Set-Mailbox -Identity Gene.Ricks@Contoso.Com -SharingPolicy InternetSharing
```

**ActiveSync Mailbox policy:**

```
Set-CASMailbox -Identity Gene.Ricks@Contoso.Com -ActiveSyncMailboxPolicy HighSecurity
```

See Chapter 12 for more information on managing non-user objects. For Mobile Device policies check Chapter 13.

## Permissions

These are different levels of permissions possible on Exchange mailboxes:

- Full Access
- Send As
- Send On Behalf
- Folder Permissions

To add Full Access permissions, use Add-MailboxPermission:

```
Add-MailboxPermission -user Mike.Soft -identity Ann.Ples -AccessRights FullAccess -InheritanceType All
-Automapping $False
```

In this case Mike Soft will be granted full access on Ann Ples' Mailbox, additionally this permission will be granted to all folders within the mailbox. The setting Automapping controls whether Ann's mailbox is automatically added in Mike's Outlook (via AutoDiscover), in this case by setting it to $false it will not. When the Automapping feature is not configured it is default True (which is also the case when using the Exchange Admin Center).

This will not grant Send-As permissions, that is actually an Active Directory permission and can be set via:

```
Add-ADPermission -Identity Ann.Ples -User Mike.Soft -AccessRights ExtendedRight -ExtendedRights
"Send As"
```

In this example user Mike has been granted Send As permissions to Ann's Mailbox. Do note that Mike has to change the 'From:' value in Outlook to Ann's email address.

In cases where it is required that the actual sender is still visible, Send on Behalf is the best option. This must be configured with the Set-Mailbox cmdlet:

```
Set-Mailbox –Identity Ann.Ples -GrantSendOnBehalfTo Mike.Soft
```

In this example Mike has been granted Send on Behalf permissions. As with Send-As, Mike must change the 'From:' value in Outlook to make use of this permission. However, the recipient will now see the actual sender even if replies are sent back to the main mailbox (Ann's).

In some cases, Full Access is too broad therefore it is good to be able to set permissions on specific folders. Folder Permissions are set via the user itself in Outlook or OWA, but admins can use:

```
Add-MailboxFolderPermission -Identity Ann.Ples:\Inbox -User Mike.Soft -AccessRights Owner
```

In this example, Mike gets Owner permissions on the Inbox folder inside Ann's Mailbox. There are quite a lot of different permissions possible, be sure to read up on them at Technet. Note that the Calendar folder has two additional permission roles specifically for availability visibility.

In this example, the Add-MailboxFolderPermission was used which adds permissions and lets previously set (not inherited) permissions as is. Use the Set-MailboxFolderPermission to edit previously assigned permissions, and Remove-MailboxFolderPermissions to remove permissions.

```
[PS] C:\>Add-MailboxFolderPermission -Identity Ann.Ples:\Inbox -User GeneRicks -AccessRights Owner

FolderName              User                    AccessRights
----------              ----                    ------------
Inbox                   Gene Ricks              {Owner}


[PS] C:\>Set-MailboxFolderPermission -Identity Ann.Ples:\Inbox -User GeneRicks -AccessRights Editor
[PS] C:\>Get-MailboxFolderPermission -Identity Ann.Ples:\Inbox

FolderName              User                    AccessRights
----------              ----                    ------------
Inbox                   Default                 {None}
Inbox                   Anonymous               {None}
Inbox                   Gene Ricks              {Editor}


[PS] C:\>Remove-MailboxFolderPermission -Identity Ann.Ples:\Inbox -User GeneRicks

Confirm
Are you sure you want to perform this action?
Removing mailbox folder permission on "Ann.Ples:\Inbox" for user "Gene Ricks".
[Y] Yes  [A] Yes to All  [N] No  [L] No to All  [?] Help (default is "Y"):
[PS] C:\>
[PS] C:\>Get-MailboxFolderPermission -Identity Ann.Ples:\Inbox

FolderName              User                    AccessRights
----------              ----                    ------------
Inbox                   Default                 {None}
Inbox                   Anonymous               {None}
```

Note that the Well-Known folders (like Inbox, Calendar, Sent Items etc.) will change with regional settings set by the user (via OWA) or by language settings of Outlook when first connecting to their Mailbox. This might pose a challenge if you want to automate specific settings on those Well-Known folders. Luckily the FolderType is a constant and that value will tell you what kind of folder it is. Custom made folders (a second calendar for instance) have the folder type of "User Created".  Use the following PowerShell one-liner in order to find the specific name of the Well-Known Calendar folder:

```
Get-Mailbox <Mailbox>|Get-MailboxFolderStatistics|Where {$_.FolderType -eq "Calendar"}
```

The value of the FolderType can be Inbox, Contacts, Sent Items, Deleted Items etc.. You can list this for a specific mailbox with:

```
Get-Mailbox <mailbox> |Get-MailboxFolderStatistics| Select FolderType
```

## Often Requested Changes

Below is a comprehensive list of often performed changes.

### Enabling and configure Out of Office settings by the admin

Even with all the options available to a user to configure the Out of Office (OOF, which is an abbreviation for Out of Facility, harking back to early Exchange years when its predecessor was used internally), you might get requests to set this. Luckily this is relatively easily done:

```
Set-MailboxAutoReplyConfiguration -Identity Ann.Ples -AutoReplyState Enabled -InternalMessage "I'm currently out of office"
```

This is the simplest configuration, there are options to set a message for external users (i.e. not in the Exchange organization), setting a time period when the OOF status has to be enabled, automatically declining meeting request etc. Basically, every setting available to the user, when using a recent version of Outlook or OWA. However, for an admin this example will probably be sufficient in most cases.

## Regional Setting

In some cases you want to set regional settings for a user, so that the user has an even more fluid first logon experience and isn't bothered by questions about language etc.. Especially valid if your organization is set in a single language region etc..

You can set the specific regional settings with:

```
Set-MailboxRegionalConfiguration -Identity "Hans de Vries" -Language nl-nl -DateFormat "dd-MM-yy"
-LocalizeDefaultFolderName -TimeZone "W. Europe Standard Time"
```

In this example the user will have Netherlands Dutch language settings in OWA and in Outlook, the LocalizeDefaultFolderName parameter will change the well known folders like Inbox and Calendar to the localized versions (respectively 'Postvak IN' and 'Kalender' in this case). The latter could be important when you have scripts to set Calendar folder permissions or require to migrate to a non-Exchange environment via PST. Furthermore, the date format has been set to correspond with the region and the time zone has been set to West Europe.

### Adding/Removing an Email Address

Even with Email Address Policies it is possible that the naming convention doesn't provide the required SMTP address. Or the account requires additional SMTP addresses or the user changed his or her name.

You can add email addresses with the Set-Mailbox cmdlet with the EmailAddresses parameter. However, if you use this parameter the value will replace all of the configured address (only to be added again by the Email Address Policy). Therefore you need to use a little different syntax:

```
Set-Mailbox Ann.Ples -EmailAddresses @{Add="smtp:Ann.Ples@Contoso.Com"}
```

In this example the Ann.Ples@Contoso.Com address is added to other addresses on the Ann Ples mailbox. Note the small caps type "smtp". If you change this to capital letters, this will become the Primary SMTP address. However, this could be overruled by any active Email Address Policy.

Removing an email address is achieved by using Remove instead of the Add:

```
Set-Mailbox Ann.Ples -EmailAddresses @{Remove="smtp:Ann.Ples@Contoso.Com"}
```

In both cases, other SMTP addresses configured on the mailbox are not removed.

## Converting Mailbox Types

There are times you might have to change the type of the (user) object to another; types being user, resource or shared. Sometimes, converting a mail user to a full mailbox enabled user is required or when mergers have been completed Linked mailboxes might have to be converted to user mailboxes. This quickly summarizes the options and some of the things you should consider.

### Converting Mail User to User Mailbox

There are situations that might require you to convert a mail user to a mailbox user.

This is simply done by using the Enable-Mailbox cmdlet, working the same way as if you are mailbox-enabling an existing user. The ExternalEmailAddress is retained as an extra SMTP address which may or may not need to be removed.

```
[PS] C:\>New-MailUser -Name "Pete Blanket"

cmdlet New-MailUser at command pipeline position 1
Supply values for the following parameters:
ExternalEmailAddress: pblanket@outlook.com

Name                                          RecipientType
----                                          -------------
Pete Blanket                                  MailUser


[PS] C:\>Enable-mailbox "Pete Blanket"

Name                      Alias               ServerName          ProhibitSendQuota
----                      -----               ----------          -----------------
Pete Blanket              PeteBlanket         116-ex01            Unlimited
```

## Converting User Mailbox to Shared Mailbox

This might be useful when a person leaves the organization, but you are required to keep the data intact due to legal and/or compliance regulations. By converting the mailbox from user mailbox to shared, you disable the AD account (lowering the risk of breaches), give access to others within the company and you are still able to keep the mail flow intact.

You can convert mailbox types with the Set-Mailbox cmdlet:

```
Set-Mailbox -Identity PeteBlanket -Type Shared
```

You can change the type of mailboxes to Resources (Room, Equipment), Shared or UserMailboxes in this way with the Set-Mailbox cmdlet. Valid values are:

- Regular
- Room
- Equipment
- Shared

When changing the type of the mailbox, do not forget that additional configuration specifics for the new mailbox type is required depending on your organizational needs.

## Converting Linked Mailbox to User Mailbox

To convert a linked mailbox to a normal user mailbox (because of a merger etc.) is quite easy, you must remove the LinkedMasterAccount value and set it to $null on the disabled mailbox user:

```
Set-User -Identity Pete.Blanket -LinkedMasterAccount $Null
```

However, there are some caveats such as removed permissions that might require some additional work depending on how accounts where migrated. See this excellent blog post on this subject: The Good, the Bad and sIDHistory: https://ingogegenwarth.wordpress.com/2015/04/01/the-good-the-bad-and-sidhistory

# Reporting

In this section, we will give some attention towards reporting on user mailboxes. This is discussed in more depth in Chapter 16 - Reporting, but there are some specifics that warrant a mention in this chapter.

## General Remarks

It's prudent to check with every update if there are any new commands or new attributes exposed in the Get cmdlets. Especially when new features are added, you'd expect to find some way of configuring those features. However, as Exchange is developed with Office 365 (or specifically Exchange Online) in mind you might encounter attributes that are of no use on-premises (or vice versa). You can ignore those.

When you have a lot of objects, do not forget to add the -ResultSize parameter to your cmdlet preferably with "Unlimited" as a value, otherwise only 1000 objects are returned. You will get a warning, but within a script you might miss that and it could result in incomplete processing or reporting of your environment. For testing purposes, you could use this to limit the number of objects returned and thus speed up your script.

```
WARNING: By default, only the first 1000 items are returned. Use the ResultSize parameter to specify the number of
items returned. To return all items, specify "-ResultSize Unlimited". Be aware that, depending on the actual number of
items, returning all items can take a long time and consume a large amount of memory. Also, we don't recommend storing
the results in a variable. Instead, pipe the results to another task or script to perform batch changes.
```

## Cmdlets

Let's see the relevant cmdlets, what kind of information they reveal and in some instances, some extra useful information. Do note that some cmdlets are not that obvious. Check the screenshots for some formatting suggestions, some -Identity fields are sometimes a bit more complex than just adding user identity values. Also, some cmdlets show more interesting information when you pipe the cmdlet to Format-List (FL in short), this has been used in the examples but is not required when using a script (as PowerShell returns objects not text).

### Get-User

Lists attributes such as phone, address names etc. from active directory users, whether they are mail- or mailbox enabled or not. The focus is the Active Directory user object rather than the mailbox.

```
Get-User -Identity Gene.Ricks@Contoso.Com | FL
```

```
[PS] C:\>Get-User -Identity Gene.Ricks@contoso.com | FL

RunspaceId                     : 75ebeb44-7a0c-4c1e-8909-46edbe6fee1d
IsSecurityPrincipal            : True
SamAccountName                 : genericks
Sid                            : S-1-5-21-3301277859-669238010-861383530-1147
SidHistory                     : {}
UserPrincipalName              : Gene.Ricks@Contoso.com
ResetPasswordOnNextLogon       : False
CertificateSubject             : {}
RemotePowerShellEnabled        : True
WindowsLiveID                  :
MicrosoftOnlineServicesID      :
NetID                          :
ConsumerNetID                  :
UserAccountControl             : NormalAccount
OrganizationalUnit             : lab2016.com/Lab
IsLinked                       : False
LinkedMasterAccount            :
ExternalDirectoryObjectId      :
SKUAssigned                    :
IsSoftDeletedByRemove          : False
IsSoftDeletedByDisable         : False
WhenSoftDeleted                :
PreviousRecipientTypeDetails   : None
UpgradeRequest                 : None
UpgradeStatus                  : None
UpgradeDetails                 :
UpgradeMessage                 :
UpgradeStage                   :
```

```
MailboxProvisioningConstraint  :
MailboxProvisioningPreferences : {}
InPlaceHoldsRaw                 : {}
MailboxRelease                  : None
ArchiveRelease                  : None
AccountDisabled                 : False
AuthenticationPolicy            :
StsRefreshTokensValidFrom       :
MailboxLocations                : {1;bcf374a7-c2c0-4aac-8cb0-878eb64dc6dd;Primary;lab2016.com;34a3b448-8aa2-4400-88a0-96
                                  33d33325e5, 1;e0d97326-52bf-4e58-b48b-c6602c3e934f;MainArchive;lab2016.com;34a3b448-8a
                                  a2-4400-88a0-9633d33325e5}
AssistantName                   :
City                            :
Company                         :
CountryOrRegion                 :
Department                      :
DirectReports                   : {}
DisplayName                     : Gene Ricks
Fax                             :
FirstName                       : Gene
GeoCoordinates                  :
HomePhone                       :
Initials                        :
IsDirSynced                     : False
LastName                        : Ricks
Manager                         :
MobilePhone                     :
Notes                           :
Office                          :
OtherFax                        : {}
OtherHomePhone                  : {}
OtherTelephone                  : {}
Pager                           :
Phone                           :
PhoneticDisplayName             :
PostalCode                      :
PostOfficeBox                   : {}
RecipientType                   : UserMailbox
RecipientTypeDetails            : UserMailbox
SimpleDisplayName               :
StateOrProvince                 :
StreetAddress                   :
Title                           :
UMDialPlan                      :
UMDtmfMap                       : {emailAddress:436374257, lastNameFirstName:742574363, firstNameLastName:436374257}
AllowUMCallsFromNonUsers        : SearchEnabled
WebPage                         :
TelephoneAssistant              :
WindowsEmailAddress             : Gene.Ricks@contoso.com
UMCallingLineIds                : {}
SeniorityIndex                  :
VoiceMailSettings               : {}
Identity                        : lab2016.com/Lab/Gene Ricks
IsValid                         : True
ExchangeVersion                 : 0.20 (15.0.0.0)
Name                            : Gene Ricks
DistinguishedName               : CN=Gene Ricks,OU=Lab,DC=lab2016,DC=com
Guid                            : d4d83f76-c223-4177-b072-1844f3947eb2
ObjectCategory                  : lab2016.com/Configuration/Schema/Person
ObjectClass                     : {top, person, organizationalPerson, user}
WhenChanged                     : 1/17/2017 11:34:31 PM
WhenCreated                     : 8/7/2016 4:35:59 PM
WhenChangedUTC                  : 1/17/2017 10:34:31 PM
WhenCreatedUTC                  : 8/7/2016 2:35:59 PM
OrganizationId                  :
Id                              : lab2016.com/Lab/Gene Ricks
OriginatingServer               : L16-DC01.lab2016.com
ObjectState                     : Changed
```

## Get-Mailbox

Lists mailbox enabled objects, these can be of RecipientTypeDetail UserMailbox, Shared, Linked, Room or Equipment. The focus of this cmdlet is settings directly related to the mailbox functionality.

Most interesting attributes are those related to quotas of not only the user mailbox but all kinds of quotas, mailflow handling, auditing, and the custom attributes.

```
Get-Mailbox -Identity Gene.Ricks@Contoso.Com | fl
```

```
[PS] C:\>Get-Mailbox -Identity Gene.Ricks@contoso.com | fl

RunspaceId                              : 75ebeb44-7a0c-4c1e-8909-46edbe6fee1d
Database                                : DB02
MailboxProvisioningConstraint           :
MessageCopyForSentAsEnabled             : False
MessageCopyForSendOnBehalfEnabled       : False
MailboxProvisioningPreferences          : {}
UseDatabaseRetentionDefaults            : True
RetainDeletedItemsUntilBackup           : False
DeliverToMailboxAndForward              : False
IsExcludedFromServingHierarchy          : False
IsHierarchyReady                        : True
IsHierarchySyncEnabled                  : True
HasSnackyAppData                        : False
LitigationHoldEnabled                   : False
SingleItemRecoveryEnabled               : False
RetentionHoldEnabled                    : False
EndDateForRetentionHold                 :
StartDateForRetentionHold               :
RetentionComment                        :
RetentionUrl                            :
LitigationHoldDate                      :
LitigationHoldOwner                     :
LitigationHoldDuration                  : Unlimited
ManagedFolderMailboxPolicy              :
RetentionPolicy                         : Default MRM Policy
AddressBookPolicy                       :
CalendarRepairDisabled                  : False
ExchangeGuid                            : bcf374a7-c2c0-4aac-8cb0-878eb64dc6dd
MailboxContainerGuid                    :
UnifiedMailbox                          :
MailboxLocations                        : {1;bcf374a7-c2c0-4aac-8cb0-878eb64dc6dd;Primary;lab2016.com;34a3b448-8aa2-4400
                                          -88a0-9633d33325e5, 1;e0d97326-52bf-4e58-b48b-c6602c3e934f;MainArchive;lab2016
                                          .com;34a3b448-8aa2-4400-88a0-9633d33325e5}
AggregatedMailboxGuids                  : {}
ExchangeSecurityDescriptor              : System.Security.AccessControl.RawSecurityDescriptor
ExchangeUserAccountControl              : None
AdminDisplayVersion                     : Version 15.1 (Build 396.30)
MessageTrackingReadStatusEnabled        : True
ExternalOofOptions                      : External
ForwardingAddress                       :
ForwardingSmtpAddress                   :
RetainDeletedItemsFor                   : 14.00:00:00
IsMailboxEnabled                        : True
Languages                               : {en-US}
OfflineAddressBook                      :
ProhibitSendQuota                       : Unlimited
ProhibitSendReceiveQuota                : Unlimited
RecoverableItemsQuota                   : 30 GB (32,212,254,720 bytes)
RecoverableItemsWarningQuota            : 20 GB (21,474,836,480 bytes)
CalendarLoggingQuota                    : 6 GB (6,442,450,944 bytes)
DowngradeHighPriorityMessagesEnabled    : False
ProtocolSettings                        : {IMAP4§0§§§§§§§§§§§, POP3§0§§§§§§§§§§§, RemotePowerShell§1}
RecipientLimits                         : Unlimited
ImListMigrationCompleted                : False
SiloName                                :
IsResource                              : False
IsLinked                                : False
IsShared                                : False
IsRootPublicFolderMailbox               : False
LinkedMasterAccount                     :
ResetPasswordOnNextLogon                : False
ResourceCapacity                        :
ResourceCustom                          : {}
ResourceType                            :
RoomMailboxAccountEnabled               :
SamAccountName                          : genericks
SCLDeleteThreshold                      :
SCLDeleteEnabled                        :
SCLRejectThreshold                      :
SCLRejectEnabled                        :
SCLQuarantineThreshold                  :
SCLQuarantineEnabled                    :
SCLJunkThreshold                        :
SCLJunkEnabled                          :
AntispamBypassEnabled                   : False
ServerLegacyDN                          : /o=2016 Organization/ou=Exchange Administrative Group
                                          (FYDIBOHF23SPDLT)/cn=Configuration/cn=Servers/cn=L16-EX01
ServerName                              : l16-ex01
UseDatabaseQuotaDefaults                : False
IssueWarningQuota                       : 10 GB (10,737,418,240 bytes)
RulesQuota                              : 256 KB (262,144 bytes)
Office                                  :
UserPrincipalName                       : Gene.Ricks@Contoso.com
UMEnabled                               : False
MaxSafeSenders                          :
MaxBlockedSenders                       :
NetID                                   :
ReconciliationId                        :
WindowsLiveID                           :
MicrosoftOnlineServicesID               :
ThrottlingPolicy                        : EASConcurrencyLimit
RoleAssignmentPolicy                    : Default Role Assignment Policy
DefaultPublicFolderMailbox              :
EffectivePublicFolderMailbox            :
SharingPolicy                           : Default Sharing Policy
RemoteAccountPolicy                     :
MailboxPlan                             :
ArchiveDatabase                         : DB02
ArchiveGuid                             : e0d97326-52bf-4e58-b48b-c6602c3e934f
ArchiveName                             : {In-Place Archive - Gene Ricks}
```

```
JournalArchiveAddress                     :
ArchiveQuota                              : 100 GB (107,374,182,400 bytes)
ArchiveWarningQuota                       : 90 GB (96,636,764,160 bytes)
ArchiveDomain                             :
ArchiveStatus                             : None
ArchiveState                              : Local
DisabledMailboxLocations                  : False
RemoteRecipientType                       : None
DisabledArchiveDatabase                   :
DisabledArchiveGuid                       : 00000000-0000-0000-0000-000000000000
QueryBaseDN                               :
QueryBaseDNRestrictionEnabled             : False
MailboxMoveTargetMDB                      :
MailboxMoveSourceMDB                      :
MailboxMoveFlags                          : None
MailboxMoveRemoteHostName                 :
MailboxMoveBatchName                      :
MailboxMoveStatus                         : None
MailboxRelease                            :
ArchiveRelease                            :
IsPersonToPersonTextMessagingEnabled      : False
IsMachineToPersonTextMessagingEnabled     : True
UserSMimeCertificate                      : {}
UserCertificate                           : {}
CalendarVersionStoreDisabled              : False
ImmutableId                               :
PersistedCapabilities                     : {}
SKUAssigned                               :
AuditEnabled                              : False
AuditLogAgeLimit                          : 90.00:00:00
AuditAdmin                                : {Update, Move, MoveToDeletedItems, SoftDelete, HardDelete, FolderBind,
                                            SendAs, SendOnBehalf, Create}
AuditDelegate                             : {Update, SoftDelete, HardDelete, SendAs, Create}
AuditOwner                                : {}
WhenMailboxCreated                        : 8/7/2016 4:35:59 PM
SourceAnchor                              :
UsageLocation                             :
IsSoftDeletedByRemove                     : False
IsSoftDeletedByDisable                    : False
IsInactiveMailbox                         : False
IncludeInGarbageCollection                : False
WhenSoftDeleted                           :
InPlaceHolds                              : {}
GeneratedOfflineAddressBooks              : {}
AccountDisabled                           : False
StsRefreshTokensValidFrom                 :
DataEncryptionPolicy                      :
AuditStorageStartTimeUTC                  :
AuditStorageEndTimeUTC                    :
AuditStorageState                         : None
Extensions                                : {}
HasPicture                                : False
HasSpokenName                             : False
IsDirSynced                               : False
AcceptMessagesOnlyFrom                    : {lab2016.com/Users/Ann Ples}
AcceptMessagesOnlyFromDLMembers           : {}
AcceptMessagesOnlyFromSendersOrMembers    : {lab2016.com/Users/Ann Ples}
AddressListMembership                     : {\Mailboxes(VLV), \All Mailboxes(VLV), \All Recipients(VLV), \Default Global
                                            Address List, \All Users}
Alias                                     : GeneRicks
ArbitrationMailbox                        :
BypassModerationFromSendersOrMembers      : {}
OrganizationalUnit                        : lab2016.com/Lab
CustomAttribute1                          :
CustomAttribute10                         :
CustomAttribute11                         :
CustomAttribute12                         :
CustomAttribute13                         :
CustomAttribute14                         :
CustomAttribute15                         :
CustomAttribute2                          :
CustomAttribute3                          :
CustomAttribute4                          :
CustomAttribute5                          :
CustomAttribute6                          :
CustomAttribute7                          :
CustomAttribute8                          :
CustomAttribute9                          :
ExtensionCustomAttribute1                 : {}
ExtensionCustomAttribute2                 : {}
ExtensionCustomAttribute3                 : {}
ExtensionCustomAttribute4                 : {}
ExtensionCustomAttribute5                 : {}
DisplayName                               : Gene Ricks
EmailAddresses                            : {SMTP:Gene.Ricks@contoso.com, smtp:GeneRicks@lab2016.com}
GrantSendOnBehalfTo                       : {}
ExternalDirectoryObjectId                 :
HiddenFromAddressListsEnabled             : False
LastExchangeChangedTime                   :
LegacyExchangeDN                          : /o=2016 Organization/ou=Exchange Administrative Group
                                            (FYDIBOHF23SPDLT)/cn=Recipients/cn=fe795a5da3254110a79c1b8aa19e1085-Gene R
MaxSendSize                               : Unlimited
MaxReceiveSize                            : Unlimited
ModeratedBy                               : {}
ModerationEnabled                         : False
PoliciesIncluded                          : {841c7d03-236e-4c1a-a588-a4314d868573, {26491cfc-9e50-4857-861b-0cb8df22b5d7}}
PoliciesExcluded                          : {}
EmailAddressPolicyEnabled                 : True
PrimarySmtpAddress                        : Gene.Ricks@contoso.com
RecipientType                             : UserMailbox
RecipientTypeDetails                      : UserMailbox
RejectMessagesFrom                        : {lab2016.com/Users/Mike.Soft}
RejectMessagesFromDLMembers               : {}
RejectMessagesFromSendersOrMembers        : {lab2016.com/Users/Mike.Soft}
```

```
RequireSenderAuthenticationEnabled     : True
SimpleDisplayName                      :
SendModerationNotifications            : Always
UMDtmfMap                              : {emailAddress:436374257, lastNameFirstName:742574363,
                                         firstNameLastName:436374257}
WindowsEmailAddress                    : Gene.Ricks@contoso.com
MailTip                                :
MailTipTranslations                    : {}
Identity                               : lab2016.com/Lab/Gene Ricks
IsValid                                : True
ExchangeVersion                        : 0.20 (15.0.0.0)
Name                                   : Gene Ricks
DistinguishedName                      : CN=Gene Ricks,OU=Lab,DC=lab2016,DC=com
Guid                                   : d4d83f76-c223-4177-b072-1844f3947eb2
ObjectCategory                         : lab2016.com/Configuration/Schema/Person
ObjectClass                            : {top, person, organizationalPerson, user}
WhenChanged                            : 1/18/2017 12:12:29 AM
WhenCreated                            : 8/7/2016 4:35:59 PM
WhenChangedUTC                         : 1/17/2017 11:12:29 PM
WhenCreatedUTC                         : 8/7/2016 2:35:59 PM
OrganizationId                         :
Id                                     : lab2016.com/Lab/Gene Ricks
OriginatingServer                      : L16-DC01.lab2016.com
ObjectState                            : Unchanged
```

## Get-MailboxAutoReplyConfiguration

Configuration of the Out of Office (OOF) replies, including scheduling, and inside and outside organization message. Basically, every possible setting the user (or an admin) has set. With this you can check whether an OOF has been set.

Get-MailboxAutoReplyConfiguration -Identity Gene.Ricks@Contoso.Com

```
[PS] C:\>Get-MailboxAutoReplyConfiguration -Identity Gene.Ricks@contoso.com


RunspaceId                         : 75ebeb44-7a0c-4c1e-8909-46edbe6fee1d
AutoDeclineFutureRequestsWhenOOF   : False
AutoReplyState                     : Disabled
CreateOOFEvent                     : False
DeclineAllEventsForScheduledOOF    : False
DeclineEventsForScheduledOOF       : False
EventsToDeleteIDs                  :
EndTime                            : 1/19/2017 12:00:00 AM
ExternalAudience                   : All
ExternalMessage                    :
InternalMessage                    :
DeclineMeetingMessage              :
OOFEventSubject                    :
StartTime                          : 1/18/2017 12:00:00 AM
MailboxOwnerId                     : lab2016.com/Lab/Gene Ricks
Identity                           : lab2016.com/Lab/Gene Ricks
IsValid                            : True
ObjectState                        : Unchanged
```

## Get-CalendarProcessing

Display the way Exchange will process meeting invites on the mailbox at hand. In most cases for user mailboxes the default settings will be adequate, however for Room, Equipment and maybe Shared mailboxes changes may be required. Due to privacy regulations, it might be required to remove the subject of a meeting from a room mailbox. Or you want to limit the way users are booking a meeting with a room mailbox.

Get-CalendarProcessing -Identity Gene.Ricks@Contoso.Com | fl

```
[PS] C:\>Get-CalendarProcessing -Identity Gene.Ricks@contoso.com | fl

RunspaceId                             : 75ebeb44-7a0c-4c1e-8909-46edbe6fee1d
AutomateProcessing                     : AutoUpdate
AllowConflicts                         : False
BookingWindowInDays                    : 180
MaximumDurationInMinutes               : 1440
AllowRecurringMeetings                 : True
EnforceSchedulingHorizon               : True
ScheduleOnlyDuringWorkHours            : False
ConflictPercentageAllowed              : 0
MaximumConflictInstances               : 0
ForwardRequestsToDelegates             : True
DeleteAttachments                      : True
DeleteComments                         : True
RemovePrivateProperty                  : True
DeleteSubject                          : True
AddOrganizerToSubject                  : True
DeleteNonCalendarItems                 : True
TentativePendingApproval               : True
EnableResponseDetails                  : True
OrganizerInfo                          : True
ResourceDelegates                      : {}
RequestOutOfPolicy                     : {}
AllRequestOutOfPolicy                  : False
BookInPolicy                           : {}
AllBookInPolicy                        : True
RequestInPolicy                        : {}
AllRequestInPolicy                     : False
AddAdditionalResponse                  : False
AdditionalResponse                     :
RemoveOldMeetingMessages               : True
AddNewRequestsTentatively              : True
ProcessExternalMeetingMessages         : False
RemoveForwardedMeetingNotifications    : False
MailboxOwnerId                         : lab2016.com/Lab/Gene Ricks
Identity                               : lab2016.com/Lab/Gene Ricks
IsValid                                : True
ObjectState                            : Changed
```

**Get-MailboxCalendarConfiguration**

This cmdlet shows the configuration of the calendar specific settings, such as the time zone, working hours and such. You could use this to check whether users are correctly provisioned per their actual regional location or other considerations.

Most of these features influence Outlook Web App, although some are also valid for other clients. The Events-FromEmailEnabled* and Weather* settings are for Exchange online only (as some other features which are mention on the TechNet page for this cmdlet).

Note that this cmdlet does not change any calendar processing settings. See Get-CalendarProcessing for those settings.

```
Get-MailboxCalendarConfiguration -Identity Gene.Ricks@Contoso.Com | fl
```

```
[PS ] C:\>Get-MailboxCalendarConfiguration -Identity Gene.Ricks@contoso.com | fl


RunspaceId                                  : 75ebeb44-7a0c-4c1e-8909-46edbe6fee1d
WorkDays                                    : Weekdays
WorkingHoursStartTime                       : 08:00:00
WorkingHoursEndTime                         : 17:00:00
WorkingHoursTimeZone                        : W. Europe Standard Time
WeekStartDay                                : Sunday
ShowWeekNumbers                             : False
FirstWeekOfYear                             : FirstDay
TimeIncrement                               : ThirtyMinutes
RemindersEnabled                            : True
ReminderSoundEnabled                        : True
DefaultReminderTime                         : 00:15:00
WeatherEnabled                              : FirstRun
WeatherUnit                                 : Default
WeatherLocations                            : {}
WeatherLocationBookmark                     : 0
AgendaMailEnabled                           : False
SkipAgendaMailOnFreeDays                    : True
EventsFromEmailEnabled                      : True
ReportEventsCreatedFromEmailEnabled         : True
FlightEventsFromEmailEnabled                : True
DiningEventsFromEmailEnabled                : True
HotelEventsFromEmailEnabled                 : True
RentalCarEventsFromEmailEnabled             : True
EntertainmentEventsFromEmailEnabled         : True
PackageDeliveryEventsFromEmailEnabled       : True
UseBrightCalendarColorThemeInOwa            : False
CalendarFeedsPreferredLanguage              :
CalendarFeedsPreferredRegion                :
CalendarFeedsRootPageId                     :
Identity                                    : lab2016.com/Lab/Gene Ricks
IsValid                                     : True
ObjectState                                 : New
```

## Get-MailboxCalendarFolder

The cmdlet shows settings specifically targeted at sharing or publishing Calendar folder data of the user. It shows the period that data is visible, including the detail level for anonymous users. This is only the case when the calendar is shared, which is defined by the PublishEnabled attribute and the existence of publishing URLs.

Get-MailboxCalendarFolder -Identity Gene.Ricks@Contoso.Com:\Calendar

```
[PS ] C:\>Get-MailboxCalendarFolder -Identity Gene.Ricks@contoso.com:\Calendar


RunspaceId           : 75ebeb44-7a0c-4c1e-8909-46edbe6fee1d
Identity             : lab2016.com/Lab/Gene Ricks:\Calendar
PublishEnabled       : False
PublishDateRangeFrom : ThreeMonths
PublishDateRangeTo   : SixMonths
DetailLevel          : FullDetails
SearchableUrlEnabled : False
PublishedCalendarUrl :
PublishedICalUrl     :
IsValid              : True
ObjectState          : Unchanged
```

The same user now with a shared calendar:

```
[PS] C:\>Get-MailboxCalendarFolder -Identity Gene.Ricks@contoso.com:\Calendar


RunspaceId            : 75ebeb44-7a0c-4c1e-8909-46edbe6fee1d
Identity              : lab2016.com/Lab/Gene Ricks:\Calendar
PublishEnabled        : True
PublishDateRangeFrom  : ThreeMonths
PublishDateRangeTo    : SixMonths
DetailLevel           : FullDetails
SearchableUrlEnabled  : False
PublishedCalendarUrl  : http://webmail.lab2016.com/owa/calendar/bcf374a7c2c04aac8cb0878eb64dc6dd@contoso.com/83e503
                        746da92845517b865a92022133761078705316121/calendar.html
PublishedICalUrl      : http://webmail.lab2016.com/owa/calendar/bcf374a7c2c04aac8cb0878eb64dc6dd@contoso.com/83e503
                        746da92845517b865a92022133761078705316121/calendar.ics
IsValid               : True
ObjectState           : Unchanged
```

## Get-MailboxFolder

View information on folders in your own mailbox.

> Get-MailboxFolder Administrator:\Inbox | fl

```
[PS] C:\>Get-MailboxFolder Administrator:\Inbox | fl


RunspaceId                    : 75ebeb44-7a0c-4c1e-8909-46edbe6fee1d
Name                          : Inbox
Identity                      : lab2016.com/Lab/Administrator:\Inbox
ParentFolder                  : lab2016.com/Lab/Administrator:\
FolderStoreObjectId           : LgAAAAN7VD+w641T7GvhTzEiIoHAQBshNj4uY5HTr5Lys/Q+gXeAAAAAAEMAAAB
FolderSize                    : 62136
HasSubfolders                 : False
FolderClass                   : IPF.Note
FolderPath                    : {Inbox}
AssociatedDumpsterFolders     :
DefaultFolderType             : Inbox
ExtendedFolderFlags           :
MailboxOwnerId                : lab2016.com/Lab/Administrator
IsValid                       : True
```

Do note that you require the correct permissions on the mailbox, otherwise an error will be show stating that the mailbox doesn't exist. It's already trying to get information on the root folder and because you don't have access it will think it doesn't exist.

The default permissions are set via the Role Based Access Control role MyBaseOptions, this means that even an administrator can only use this cmdlet on their own mailbox, but will get this error when trying to query others. This obviously limits the use of this cmdlet for reporting.

```
The specified mailbox  Gene.Ricks@Contoso.Com\Inbox doesn't exist.
    + CategoryInfo          : NotSpecified: (:) [Get-MailboxFolder], ManagementObjectNotFoundExcep
   tion
    + FullyQualifiedErrorId : [Server=L16-EX01,RequestId=93e85a5d-0e0e-4210-b8dd-16577b1fd465,T
   imeStamp=12/17/2016 3:04:26 PM] [FailureCategory=Cmdlet-ManagementObjectNotFoundException] 701B
   F26B,Microsoft.Exchange.Management.StoreTasks.GetMailboxFolder
    + PSComputerName        : L16-EX01.LAb2016.Com
```

## Get-MailboxFolderPermission

Used to view folder permissions within mailboxes. You must specify the correct folder path, which for the default/well-known folders in Exchange is dependent on the regional settings of the mailbox that create these folders at first login. So, the default Calendar folder might be named different in Spanish.

Also, note that the calendar folder permissions have additional AccessRights available; AvailabilityOnly and LimitedDetails. Both influence the visibility of specific information of meetings (subject and location is also shown with LimitedDetails).

```
Get-MailboxFolderPermission -Identity Gene.Ricks@Contoso.Com:\Inbox
```

```
[PS] C:\>Get-MailboxFolderPermission -Identity Gene.Ricks@contoso.com:\Inbox

FolderName              User                    AccessRights
----------              ----                    ------------
Inbox                   Default                 {None}
Inbox                   Anonymous               {None}


[PS] C:\>Get-MailboxFolderPermission -Identity Gene.Ricks@contoso.com:\Calendar

FolderName              User                    AccessRights
----------              ----                    ------------
Calendar                Default                 {AvailabilityOnly}
Calendar                Anonymous               {None}
```

### Get-MailboxFolderStatistics

View information on specific folders in a mailbox. This includes the folder size, number of items. For more information, you can add the -IncludeAnalysis switch, which can help with troubleshooting.

It will return values that would otherwise remain empty, the reason being that it can take a while for the analysis to complete. The values however, can help with troubleshooting or reporting.

```
Get-MailboxFolderStatistics -Identity Gene.Ricks@Contoso.Com -FolderScope Inbox -IncludeAnalysis
```

This would result into something like this excerpt:

```
TopSubject                     : [Outlook junk mail report] isthis sapm is this spam?
TopSubjectSize                 : 30.29 KB (31,015 bytes)
TopSubjectCount                : 1
TopSubjectClass                : REPORT.IPM.Note.NDR
TopSubjectPath                 : \Top of Information Store\Inbox
TopSubjectReceivedTime         : 12/9/2016 1:02:52 AM
TopSubjectFrom                 : Microsoft Outlook
TopClientInfoForSubject        : \ \
TopClientInfoCountForSubject   : 1
```

Another parameter that might provide useful information for troubleshooting or reporting is the IncludeOldestAndNewestItems parameter. As the name suggests, you will then receive more information on the oldest and newest items in the specified mailbox.

```
Get-MailboxFolderStatistics -Identity Gene.Ricks@Contoso.Com -FolderScope Inbox
-IncludeOldestAndNewestItems
```

This would result into this:

```
[PS] C:\>Get-MailboxFolderStatistics -Identity Gene.Ricks@contoso.com -FolderScope Inbox -IncludeOldestAndNewes

RunspaceId                          : 75ebeb44-7a0c-4c1e-8909-46edbe6fee1d
Date                                : 11/30/2016 3:45:29 PM
Name                                : Inbox
FolderPath                          : /Inbox
FolderId                            : LgAAAADXjYS++nXBT6C97g9pIfWIAQD4U12FBhXPTIB1Aj/NSCkyAAAAAAEMAAAB
FolderType                          : Inbox
ContentFolder                       : True
ContentMailboxGuid                  : bcf374a7-c2c0-4aac-8cb0-878eb64dc6dd
Movable                             : False
RecoverableItemsFolder              : False
AssociatedIPMFolderPath             :
ItemsInFolder                       : 5
DeletedItemsInFolder                : 0
FolderSize                          : 44.58 KB (45,654 bytes)
ItemsInFolderAndSubfolders          : 5
DeletedItemsInFolderAndSubfolders   : 0
FolderAndSubfolderSize              : 44.58 KB (45,654 bytes)
CurrentSchemaVersion                :
OldestItemReceivedDate              : 12/6/2016 8:01:05 PM
NewestItemReceivedDate              : 12/9/2016 1:02:52 AM
OldestDeletedItemReceivedDate       :
NewestDeletedItemReceivedDate       :
```

```
OldestItemLastModifiedDate          : 12/6/2016 8:01:05 PM
NewestItemLastModifiedDate          : 12/9/2016 1:02:52 AM
OldestDeletedItemLastModifiedDate   :
NewestDeletedItemLastModifiedDate   :
ManagedFolder                       :
DeletePolicy                        :
ArchivePolicy                       :
TopSubject                          :
TopSubjectSize                      : 0 B (0 bytes)
TopSubjectCount                     : 0
TopSubjectClass                     :
TopSubjectPath                      :
TopSubjectReceivedTime              :
TopSubjectFrom                      :
TopClientInfoForSubject             :
TopClientInfoCountForSubject        : 0
SearchFolders                       :
AuditAuxMailboxGuid                 :
AuditFolderStubSize                 :
Identity                            : Gene.Ricks@contoso.com\Inbox
IsValid                             : True
ObjectState                         : New
```

Note that you do not supply a folder path, but rather a folder type with the FolderScope parameter. With this all folders of the same type are returned and not just one specific folder.

Valid input values for FolderScope are:

| | |
|---|---|
| All | Calendar |
| Contacts | ConversationHistory |
| DeletedItems | Drafts |
| Inbox | JunkEmail |
| Journal | LegacyArchiveJournals |
| ManagedCustomFolder | NonIpmRoot |
| Notes | Outlook |
| Personal | RecoverableItems |
| RssSubscriptions | SentItems |
| SyncIssues | Tasks |

The ManagedCustomFolder value returns output for all managed custom folders. The RecoverableItems value returns output for the Recoverable Items folder and the Deletions, DiscoveryHolds, Purges, and Versions subfolders. Also see TechNet.

If you require information regarding statistics of the whole mailbox, see Get-MailboxStatistics.

**Get-MailboxJunkEmailConfiguration**

Use this cmdlet to see the User Junk Mail folder configuration for a specific mailbox, including any blocked or trusted email addresses or domains. This can be useful to determine whether your central anti-spam solutions requires some tweaking.

```
Get-MailboxJunkEmailConfiguration -Identity Gene.Ricks@Contoso.Com
```

```
[PS] C:\>Get-MailboxJunkEmailConfiguration -Identity Gene.Ricks@contoso.com

RunspaceId                      : 75ebeb44-7a0c-4c1e-8909-46edbe6fee1d
Enabled                         : True
TrustedListsOnly                : False
ContactsTrusted                 : False
TrustedSendersAndDomains        : {fabrikam.com}
BlockedSendersAndDomains        : {henk@wingtoys.com}
TrustedRecipientsAndDomains     : {fabrikam.com}
MailboxOwnerId                  : lab2016.com/Lab/Gene Ricks
Identity                        : lab2016.com/Lab/Gene Ricks
IsValid                         : True
ObjectState                     : Unchanged
```

In this case the user has blocked a Wingtoys address.

**Get-MailboxMessageConfiguration**

Shows the configuration of Outlook Web App for a specific mailbox.

```
Get-MailboxMessageConfiguration -Identity Gene.Ricks@Contoso.Com
```

```
[PS] C:\>Get-MailboxMessageConfiguration -Identity Gene.Ricks@contoso.com

RunspaceId                      : 75ebeb44-7a0c-4c1e-8909-46edbe6fee1d
AfterMoveOrDeleteBehavior       : OpenNextItem
NewItemNotification             : All
EmptyDeletedItemsOnLogoff       : False
AutoAddSignature                : True
AutoAddSignatureOnReply         : False
SignatureText                   :
SignatureHtml                   :
AutoAddSignatureOnMobile        : True
SignatureTextOnMobile           :
UseDefaultSignatureOnMobile     : True
DefaultFontName                 : Calibri
DefaultFontSize                 : 3
DefaultFontColor                : #000000
DefaultFontFlags                : Normal
AlwaysShowBcc                   : False
AlwaysShowFrom                  : True
DefaultFormat                   : Html
ReadReceiptResponse             : DoNotAutomaticallySend
PreviewMarkAsReadBehavior       : OnSelectionChange
PreviewMarkAsReadDelaytime      : 5
ConversationSortOrder           : ChronologicalNewestOnTop
ShowConversationAsTree          : False
HideDeletedItems                : False
SendAddressDefault              :
EmailComposeMode                : Inline
CheckForForgottenAttachments    : True
AreFlaggedItemsPinned           : False
IsReplyAllTheDefaultResponse    : False
KeyboardShortcutsMode           : Owa
LinkPreviewEnabled              : True
FeatureMCSignatureEnabled       : False
ShowPreviewTextInListView       : True
GlobalReadingPanePosition       : Right
IsFavoritesFolderTreeCollapsed  : False
IsMailRootFolderTreeCollapsed   : False
MailFolderPaneExpanded          : True
ShowSenderOnTopInListView       : True
ShowReadingPaneOnFirstLoad      : False
NavigationPaneViewOption        : Default
MailboxOwnerId                  : lab2016.com/Lab/Gene Ricks
Identity                        : lab2016.com/Lab/Gene Ricks
IsValid                         : True
ObjectState                     : Unchanged
```

## Get-MailboxPermission

Shows the permissions set on the specific mailbox. Note that these are not permissions on the subsequent folders. The IsInherited column indicates whether the permission is inherited from a higher source from the Active Directory (AD) configuration as Mailbox permissions are actually AD permissions.

> Get-MailboxPermission -Identity Gene.Ricks@Contoso.Com

```
[PS] C:\>Get-MailboxPermission -Identity Gene.Ricks@contoso.com

Identity              User                AccessRights                                                      IsInherited Deny
lab2016.com/Lab/G...  NT AUTHORITY\SELF   {FullAccess, ReadPermission}                                      False       False
lab2016.com/Lab/G...  LAB2016\Administr... {FullAccess}                                                     False       False
lab2016.com/Lab/G...  LAB2016\Administr... {FullAccess}                                                     True        True
lab2016.com/Lab/G...  LAB2016\Domain Ad... {FullAccess}                                                     True        True
lab2016.com/Lab/G...  LAB2016\Enterpris... {FullAccess}                                                     True        True
lab2016.com/Lab/G...  LAB2016\Organizat... {FullAccess}                                                     True        True
lab2016.com/Lab/G...  NT AUTHORITY\SYSTEM {FullAccess}                                                      True        False
lab2016.com/Lab/G...  NT AUTHORITY\NETW... {ReadPermission}                                                 True        False
lab2016.com/Lab/G...  LAB2016\Administr... {FullAccess, DeleteItem, ReadPermission, ChangePermissio...     True        False
lab2016.com/Lab/G...  LAB2016\Domain Ad... {FullAccess, DeleteItem, ReadPermission, ChangePermissio...     True        False
lab2016.com/Lab/G...  LAB2016\Enterpris... {FullAccess, DeleteItem, ReadPermission, ChangePermissio...     True        False
lab2016.com/Lab/G...  LAB2016\Organizat... {FullAccess, DeleteItem, ReadPermission, ChangePermissio...     True        False
lab2016.com/Lab/G...  LAB2016\Public Fo... {ReadPermission}                                                 True        False
lab2016.com/Lab/G...  LAB2016\Delegated.. {ReadPermission}                                                  True        False
lab2016.com/Lab/G...  LAB2016\Exchange ... {FullAccess, ReadPermission}                                    True        False
lab2016.com/Lab/G...  LAB2016\Exchange ... {FullAccess, DeleteItem, ReadPermission, ChangePermissio...     True        False
lab2016.com/Lab/G...  LAB2016\Managed A... {ReadPermission}                                                 True        False
```

If you require only the permissions of a specific user, you can use the -User parameter.

> Get-MailboxPermission -Identity Gene.Ricks@Contoso.Com -User Administrator

```
[PS] C:\>Get-MailboxPermission -Identity Gene.Ricks@contoso.com -User Administrator

Identity              User                AccessRights                                                      IsInherited Deny
lab2016.com/Lab/G...  LAB2016\Administr... {FullAccess}                                                     False       False
lab2016.com/Lab/G...  LAB2016\Administr... {FullAccess}                                                     True        True
lab2016.com/Lab/G...  LAB2016\Administr... {FullAccess, DeleteItem, ReadPermission, ChangePermissio...     True        False
```

In some cases, you only want to report on non-inherited permissions i.e. directly assigned mailbox permissions, which are the permissions set if you use Exchange cmdlets. You can do that by filtering using the Where cmdlet.

> Get-MailboxPermission -Identity Gene.Ricks@Contoso.Com | Where {$_.IsInherited -eq $False}

```
[PS] C:\>Get-MailboxPermission -Identity Gene.Ricks@contoso.com | Where {$_.IsInherited -eq $False}

Identity              User                AccessRights                                                      IsInherited Deny
lab2016.com/Lab/G...  NT AUTHORITY\SELF   {FullAccess, ReadPermission}                                      False       False
lab2016.com/Lab/G...  LAB2016\Administr... {FullAccess}                                                     False       False
```

## Get-MailboxRegionalConfiguration

Use this cmdlet to extract regional settings on a specific mailbox, such as timezone, date format, language etc..

> Get-MailboxRegionalConfiguration -Identity Gene.Ricks@Contoso.Com | fl

```
[PS] C:\>Get-MailboxRegionalConfiguration -Identity Gene.Ricks@contoso.com | fl


RunspaceId                            : 75ebeb44-7a0c-4c1e-8909-46edbe6fee1d
DateFormat                            : M/d/yyyy
Language                              : en-US
DefaultFolderNameMatchingUserLanguage : False
TimeFormat                            : h:mm tt
TimeZone                              : W. Europe Standard Time
Identity                              : lab2016.com/Lab/Gene Ricks
IsValid                               : True
ObjectState                           : New
```

The *DefaultFolderNameMatchingUserLanguage* indicates whether the default (or Well-Known folders such as Inbox) are localized, if True, those folders names are in the language indicated. This has an impact when you use specific cmdlets that target specific folders, for instance folder permissions.

**Get-MailboxSpellingConfiguration**

Retrieve spelling configuration set by the user for Outlook Web App.

Get-MailboxSpellingConfiguration -Identity Gene.Ricks@Contoso.Com

```
[PS] C:\>Get-MailboxSpellingConfiguration -Identity Gene.Ricks@contoso.com

RunspaceId           : 75ebeb44-7a0c-4c1e-8909-46edbe6fee1d
CheckBeforeSend      : False
DictionaryLanguage   : EnglishUnitedStates
IgnoreUppercase      : False
IgnoreMixedDigits    : False
Identity             : lab2016.com/Lab/Gene Ricks
IsValid              : True
ObjectState          : New
```

**Get-MailboxStatistics**

Will show you statistics of a specific mailbox, such as the database name, size, number of items, the last logged on user etc. (although if this interests you, you should turn on auditing on those mailboxes for more detail information).

Get-MailboxStatistics -Identity Gene.Ricks@Contoso.Com | fl

```
[PS] C:\>Get-MailboxStatistics -Identity Gene.Ricks@contoso.com | fl

RunspaceId                        : 75ebeb44-7a0c-4c1e-8909-46edbe6fee1d
MoveHistory                       :
AssociatedItemCount               : 18
DeletedItemCount                  : 0
ItemCount                         : 8
TotalDeletedItemSize              : 0 B (0 bytes)
TotalItemSize                     : 80.01 KB (81,932 bytes)
MessageTableTotalSize             : 1.625 MB (1,703,936 bytes)
MessageTableAvailableSize         : 1.438 MB (1,507,328 bytes)
AttachmentTableTotalSize          : 576 KB (589,824 bytes)
AttachmentTableAvailableSize      : 448 KB (458,752 bytes)
OtherTablesTotalSize              : 960 KB (983,040 bytes)
OtherTablesAvailableSize          : 448 KB (458,752 bytes)
CurrentSchemaVersion              : 0.135
DisconnectDate                    :
DisconnectReason                  :
DisplayName                       : Gene Ricks
LastLoggedOnUserAccount           :
LastLogoffTime                    : 12/7/2016 6:11:49 AM
LastLogonTime                     : 12/7/2016 6:06:48 AM
LegacyDN                          : /o=2016 Organization/ou=Exchange Administrative Group
                                    (FYDIBOHF23SPDLT)/cn=Recipients/cn=fe795a5da3254110a79c
MailboxGuid                       : bcf374a7-c2c0-4aac-8cb0-878eb64dc6dd
OwnerADGuid                       : d4d83f76-c223-4177-b072-1844f3947eb2
MailboxType                       : Private
MailboxTypeDetail                 : UserMailbox
ObjectClass                       : Unknown
StorageLimitStatus                :
MailboxTableIdentifier            :
Database                          : DB02
ServerName                        : L16-EX01
DatabaseName                      : DB02
IsDatabaseCopyActive              : True
IsClutterEnabled                  : False
IsQuarantined                     : False
QuarantineDescription             :
QuarantineLastCrash               :
QuarantineEnd                     :
QuarantineFileVersion             :
ExternalDirectoryOrganizationId   : 00000000-0000-0000-0000-000000000000
IsEncrypted                       : False
```

```
DataEncryptionPolicyId                          :
KeyVersionID                                    :
AdvancedDataEncryptionDetails                   :
IsArchiveMailbox                                : False
IsMoveDestination                               : False
MailboxMessagesPerFolderCountWarningQuota       :
MailboxMessagesPerFolderCountReceiveQuota       :
DumpsterMessagesPerFolderCountWarningQuota      :
DumpsterMessagesPerFolderCountReceiveQuota      :
FolderHierarchyChildrenCountWarningQuota        :
FolderHierarchyChildrenCountReceiveQuota        :
FolderHierarchyDepthWarningQuota                :
FolderHierarchyDepthReceiveQuota                :
FoldersCountWarningQuota                        :
FoldersCountReceiveQuota                        :
NamedPropertiesCountQuota                       : 16384
SystemMessageSize                               : 0 B (0 bytes)
SystemMessageCount                              : 0
SystemMessageSizeWarningQuota                   : 4.5 GB (4,831,838,208 bytes)
SystemMessageSizeShutoffQuota                   : 5 GB (5,368,709,120 bytes)
DatabaseIssueWarningQuota                       : 1.899 GB (2,039,480,320 bytes)
DatabaseProhibitSendQuota                       : 2 GB (2,147,483,648 bytes)
DatabaseProhibitSendReceiveQuota                : 2.3 GB (2,469,396,480 bytes)
Identity                                        : bcf374a7-c2c0-4aac-8cb0-878eb64dc6dd
MapiIdentity                                    : bcf374a7-c2c0-4aac-8cb0-878eb64dc6dd
OriginatingServer                               : 116-ex01.lab2016.com
IsValid                                         : True
ObjectState                                     : Unchanged
```

## Get-CASMailbox

Retrieve client access settings on a specific mailbox, such as what kind of protocols are enabled on this mailbox and the specific configuration of those protocols

Get-CASMailbox -Identity Gene.Ricks@contoso.com

```
[PS] C:\>Get-CASMailbox -Identity Gene.Ricks@contoso.com

Name          ActiveSyncEnabled OWAEnabled      PopEnabled      ImapEnabled     MapiEnabled
----          ----------------- ----------      ----------      -----------     -----------
Gene Ricks    False             True            False           False           True
```

Get-CASMailbox -Identity Gene.Ricks@contoso.com | fl

```
[PS] C:\>Get-CASMailbox -Identity Gene.Ricks@contoso.com | fl

RunspaceId                              : 75ebeb44-7a0c-4c1e-8909-46edbe6fee1d
EmailAddresses                          : {SMTP:Gene.Ricks@contoso.com, smtp:GeneRicks@lab2016.com}
LegacyExchangeDN                        : /o=2016 Organization/ou=Exchange Administrative Group
                                          (FYDIBOHF23SPDLT)/cn=Recipients/cn=fe795a5da3254110a79c1b8aa19e1085-Gene R
LinkedMasterAccount                     :
PrimarySmtpAddress                      : Gene.Ricks@contoso.com
SamAccountName                          : genericks
ServerLegacyDN                          : /o=2016 Organization/ou=Exchange Administrative Group
                                          (FYDIBOHF23SPDLT)/cn=Configuration/cn=Servers/cn=L16-EX01
ServerName                              : 116-ex01
DisplayName                             : Gene Ricks
ActiveSyncAllowedDeviceIDs              : {}
ActiveSyncBlockedDeviceIDs              : {}
ActiveSyncMailboxPolicy                 : VIP_temp
ActiveSyncMailboxPolicyIsDefaulted      : False
ActiveSyncDebugLogging                  : False
ActiveSyncEnabled                       : False
HasActiveSyncDevicePartnership          : False
ExternalImapSettings                    :
InternalImapSettings                    :
ExternalPopSettings                     :
InternalPopSettings                     :
ExternalSmtpSettings                    :
InternalSmtpSettings                    :
OwaMailboxPolicy                        :
OWAEnabled                              : True
OWAforDevicesEnabled                    : True
ECPEnabled                              : True
PopEnabled                              : False
PopMessageDeleteEnabled                 : False
PopUseProtocolDefaults                  : True
PopMessagesRetrievalMimeFormat          : BestBodyFormat
PopEnableExactRFC822Size                : False
PopSuppressReadReceipt                  : False
PopForceICalForCalendarRetrievalOption  : False
ImapEnabled                             : False
ImapUseProtocolDefaults                 : True
ImapMessagesRetrievalMimeFormat         : BestBodyFormat
ImapEnableExactRFC822Size               : False
ImapSuppressReadReceipt                 : False
```

```
MAPIEnabled                                 : True
MapiHttpEnabled                             :
MAPIBlockOutlookNonCachedMode               : False
MAPIBlockOutlookVersions                    :
MAPIBlockOutlookRpcHttp                     : False
MAPIBlockOutlookExternalConnectivity        : False
UniversalOutlookEnabled                     : True
EwsEnabled                                  :
EwsAllowOutlook                             :
EwsAllowMacOutlook                          :
EwsAllowEntourage                           : False
EwsApplicationAccessPolicy                  :
EwsAllowList                                :
EwsBlockList                                :
ShowGalAsDefaultView                        : True
Identity                                    : lab2016.com/Lab/Gene Ricks
IsValid                                     : True
ExchangeVersion                             : 0.20 (15.0.0.0)
Name                                        : Gene Ricks
DistinguishedName                           : CN=Gene Ricks,OU=Lab,DC=lab2016,DC=com
Guid                                        : d4d83f76-c223-4177-b072-1844f3947eb2
ObjectCategory                              : lab2016.com/Configuration/Schema/Person
ObjectClass                                 : {top, person, organizationalPerson, user}
WhenChanged                                 : 1/18/2017 12:12:29 AM
WhenCreated                                 : 8/7/2016 4:35:59 PM
WhenChangedUTC                              : 1/17/2017 11:12:29 PM
WhenCreatedUTC                              : 8/7/2016 2:35:59 PM
OrganizationId                              :
Id                                          : lab2016.com/Lab/Gene Ricks
OriginatingServer                           : L16-DC01.lab2016.com
ObjectState                                 : Changed
```

# 12 Non-User Objects

---

In This Chapter

- Shared Mailboxes
- Resource Mailboxes
- Public Folder Mailboxes
- Distribution Groups
- Group Moderation
- Putting It All Together

---

In the previous chapter, we covered user mailboxes and their management with PowerShell. While most Exchange operations involve these user mailboxes, there are other non-user objects that need to be managed as well. These objects serve a variety of purposes in Exchange and include objects like Shared Mailboxes, Resource Mailboxes, Public Folder Mailboxes and Distribution Groups.

Shared Mailboxes provide a common mailbox for a group of users to access. They also provide a common address for sending emails out as a single email address. They can be used by departments as a shared inbox or calendar for departmental operations.

Resource Mailboxes can be used for various reasons, from rooms, to equipment to other resources that an organization may want to keep track of. Examples of resources are Rooms and Equipment mailboxes. Room Lists can also be created and managed with PowerShell.

Public Folder Mailboxes are used by Exchange to store Public Folder data. Gone are the days of Public Folder databases with SMTP replicas and separate management. With modern Public Folders replication occurs within a Database Availability Group (DAG) and provides a more stable access method than before. With PowerShell we can still manage settings for Public Folders, but we need to be cognizant of the underlying architecture in order to properly manage Public Folders for Exchange 2016.

Distribution Groups are used for mass mailing, for updates meant for a group or for granting access to a group of people to mail objects in Exchange. With PowerShell we can manipulate the characteristics of these groups, add and remove members and more. Groups can also be moderated to control the flow of messages and to prevent information overload or improper emails from being sent to groups.

# Shared Mailboxes

Shared Mailboxes are commonly used by organizations as either a central place for group emails to be delivered or as a single mailbox to be used as a public customer facing presence where a group of users can send as a single user. Some examples are Customer Service mailboxes like 'Help Desk' where the customers are internal users and 'Support' where the clients are external people that have purchased a company's product. Another user would be a 'Faxes' mailbox that would be used as a central location for all faxes coming into an organization could be received and then forwarded on to the appropriate internal recipients. Additionally a shared mailbox could be used for solely a group calendar which for example could be used by marketing management and users to keep track of when people will be in the office or maybe when marketing events are occurring.

## PowerShell

Like the previous chapter explained, creating a new user in PowerShell is done using the New-Mailbox PowerShell cmdlet. When creating a new shared mailbox, a special parameter needs to be used in order for the mailbox to be designated as a shared mailbox. The '-Shared' parameter is all that is needed in order for this to occur.

### Example

In this example, the IT Manager has decided he wants the Help Desk to respond to emails from a single mailbox so that all communications are funneled through a central mailbox. The manager wants this because this ensures that end users reply to the Help Desk emails and not individuals. Because schedules for Help Desk workers vary greatly, a central mailbox will allow for other Help Desk employees to be able to pick up an existing case if the original Help Desk employee was off work due to scheduling or sickness.

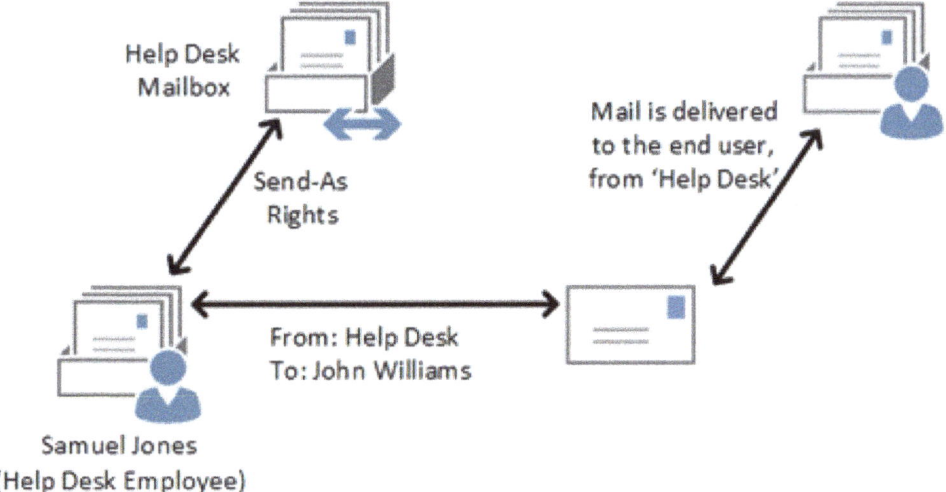


Now we need to create the mailbox and then assign Full Mailbox and Send-As rights to all users in the Help Desk Active Directory group. First, let's create the shared mailbox:

```
New-Mailbox -Shared -Name "Help Desk" -DisplayName "Help Desk"
```

| Name | Alias | ServerName | ProhibitSendQuota |
| --- | --- | --- | --- |
| Help Desk | HelpDesk | ex02 | Unlimited |

The Help Desk shared mailbox is now in Exchange and we need to assign rights to the mailbox for the Help Desk users to be able to send as the shared mailbox. For this part, there are two options for assigning the correct permissions for the Help Desk users. Either the rights can be assigned on a per-user or a per-group basis. For a group like the Help Desk, it would be more appropriate to use a group as the Help Desk group is likely to have a higher turnover rate than other groups. The other reason to use a group is that it is far easier to assign rights with groups than users. That way when a new Help Desk user is hired, in order to grant rights to the Shared Mailbox, all the admin has to do is to add the user to the group instead of using PowerShell to assign the rights.

## PowerShell

How can permissions be added to mailboxes in Exchange via PowerShell? First, let's check for appropriate PowerShell cmdlets with the 'Permissions' keyword in them:

```
Get-Command *Permission*

CommandType        Name
-----------        ----
Function           Add-ADPermission
Function           Add-MailboxFolderPermission
Function           Add-MailboxPermission
Function           Add-PublicFolderClientPermission
Function           Get-ADPermission
Function           Get-MailboxFolderPermission
Function           Get-MailboxPermission
Function           Get-NfsSharePermission
Function           Get-PublicFolderClientPermission
Function           Grant-NfsSharePermission
Function           Remove-ADPermission
Function           Remove-MailboxFolderPermission
Function           Remove-MailboxPermission
Function           Remove-PublicFolderClientPermission
Function           Revoke-NfsSharePermission
Function           Set-MailboxFolderPermission
```

As we can see above, there are a few cmdlets that are useful for manipulating mailbox permissions. In particular, the Add-MailboxPermission cmdlet looks like what we need to handle this. Reviewing the examples for the cmdlet, Example 3 appears to be what is needed for this example.

```
------------------------- Example 3 -------------------------
Add-MailboxPermission -Identity JeroenC -User 'Mark Steele' -AccessRights FullAccess -InheritanceType All
-AutoMapping $false
```

Now if the Help Desk users are all in a group called "Help Desk Users", we can first add the FullAccess permission as seen above to the Help Desk Mailbox:

```
Add-MailboxPermission –Identity "Help Desk" –User "Help Desk" –AccessRights FullAccess –
InheritanceType All
```

** **Note** ** The group needs to be a security type group, not a distribution type group.

The 'InheritanceType' parameter is used to make sure the permissions are applied to all folders in the mailbox. We now need to assign the Send-As permissions. However, the Add-MailboxPermission cmdlet does not have an option for that. The available permissions are:

| | | |
|---|---|---|
| FullAccess | ExternalAccount | DeleteItem |
| ReadPermission | ChangePermission | ChangeOwner |

Notice that Send-As is not included in the above list. So if this is not a mailbox level permission, where else can rights be assigned? They can be assigned at the AD Object Level. Reviewing the previous list of PowerShell cmdlets, we see there is an 'Add-ADPermission' cmdlet that look promising. So, if we review the examples from PowerShell we see that there is an example for Send-As permissions:

```
---------------------------- EXAMPLE 1 ----------------------------
Add-ADPermission -Identity "Terry Adams" -User AaronPainter -AccessRights ExtendedRight -ExtendedRights "Send As"
```

Going back to our need to add the Send-As rights for Help Desk Users on the Help Desk mailbox, we get the following:

> Add-ADPermission –Identity "Help Desk" –User "Help Desk Users" -AccessRights ExtendedRight
> -ExtendedRights "Send As"

Although the parameter above is 'User' it can be used for groups as well. Now users from the Help Desk can send as the Help desk and not themselves:

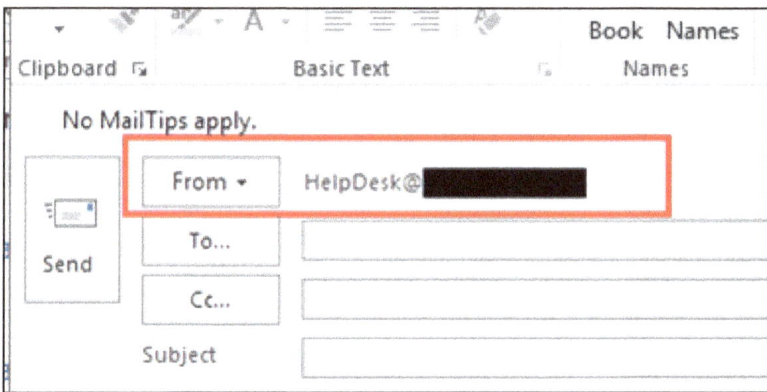


## Example

In another scenario, the IT Department has received a request to produce a list of all shared mailboxes and a list of who has permissions for each mailbox. The rights that should be reported on are Send-As and Full Mailbox permissions. As we saw from the previous example, assigning these rights takes two PowerShell cmdlets (Add-ADPermission and Add-MailboxPermission). We can safely assume that a pair of cmdlets will also be needed to query these. One more criteria we need to consider – whether or not the right was assigned directly (not inherited) by an Administrator or if the right was inherited and not assigned by an admin. From the request, it appears there is no distinction, just a report of the rights that are assigned on a mailbox. As such we will just look for 'Full Access' and 'Send-As' permission on the mailbox.

First, let's start with the mailbox permission set with Add-MailboxPermission. From the previous page (top) we see a cmdlet called Get-MailboxPermission. For this environment, we will use a mailbox called "Help Desk" which has these permissions assigned to it, as our way to work out our PowerShell for all mailboxes.

First, let's see what PowerShell can reveal to us:

> Get-Mailbox "Help Desk" | Get-ADPermission | FT –Auto

```
Identity                          User                              Deny  Inherited
--------                          ----                              ----  ---------
16-TAP.Local/Users/Help Desk NT AUTHORITY\SELF                      False False
16-TAP.Local/Users/Help Desk NT AUTHORITY\Authenticated Users       False False
16-TAP.Local/Users/Help Desk NT AUTHORITY\SYSTEM                     False False
16-TAP.Local/Users/Help Desk S-1-5-32-548                           False False
16-TAP.Local/Users/Help Desk 16-TAP\Domain Admins                   False False
16-TAP.Local/Users/Help Desk Everyone                               False False
16-TAP.Local/Users/Help Desk NT AUTHORITY\SELF                      False False
16-TAP.Local/Users/Help Desk NT AUTHORITY\SELF                      False False
16-TAP.Local/Users/Help Desk NT AUTHORITY\SELF                      False False
16-TAP.Local/Users/Help Desk NT AUTHORITY\SELF                      False False
16-TAP.Local/Users/Help Desk NT AUTHORITY\SELF                      False False
16-TAP.Local/Users/Help Desk NT AUTHORITY\SELF                      False False
16-TAP.Local/Users/Help Desk NT AUTHORITY\Authenticated Users       False False
16-TAP.Local/Users/Help Desk NT AUTHORITY\Authenticated Users       False False
```

From that one-liner we don't see the permissions assigned to the mailbox.  If we run the same one-liner with '| fl'
our results now look like this:

```
User                 : Everyone
Identity             : 16-TAP.Local/Users/Help Desk
Deny                 : False
AccessRights         : {ExtendedRight}
IsInherited          : False
Properties           :
ChildObjectTypes     :
InheritedObjectType  :
InheritanceType      : None

User                 : NT AUTHORITY\SELF
Identity             : 16-TAP.Local/Users/Help Desk
Deny                 : False
AccessRights         : {ReadProperty, WriteProperty}
IsInherited          : False
Properties           : {Personal-Information}
ChildObjectTypes     :
InheritedObjectType  :
InheritanceType      : All

User                 : NT AUTHORITY\SELF
Identity             : 16-TAP.Local/Users/Help Desk
Deny                 : False
AccessRights         : {ExtendedRight}
IsInherited          : False
Properties           :
ChildObjectTypes     :
InheritedObjectType  :
InheritanceType      : All
```

Notice the red rectangles above.  Send-As is an Extended right.  Some properties in AD are expandable in the sense
that the revealed value, like the one above, can hide more detail.  The cmdlet below uses a filter on ExtendedRights
to just show them:

```
Get-Mailbox "Help Desk" | Get-ADPermission | Where {$_.AccessRights -eq "ExtendedRight"} | FT -Auto
```

```
Identity                          User                                         Deny  Inherited
--------                          ----                                         ----  ---------
16-TAP.Local/Users/Help Desk Everyone                                          False False
16-TAP.Local/Users/Help Desk NT AUTHORITY\SELF                                 False False
16-TAP.Local/Users/Help Desk NT AUTHORITY\SELF                                 False False
16-TAP.Local/Users/Help Desk NT AUTHORITY\SELF                                 False False
16-TAP.Local/Users/Help Desk BUILTIN\Backup Operators                          False False
16-TAP.Local/Users/Help Desk 16-TAP\Help Desk Users                            False False
16-TAP.Local/Users/Help Desk 16-TAP\Exchange Windows Permissions               False True
16-TAP.Local/Users/Help Desk 16-TAP\Exchange Windows Permissions               False True
```

What if we were to wrap the above one-liner in brackets like '()' and select ExtendedRight:

```
(Get-Mailbox "Help Desk" | Get-ADPermission | Where {$_.AccessRights -eq "ExtendedRight"}).
ExtendedRight
```

This returns no results. What went wrong? Well, when the rights were assigned, we used ExtendedRights, plural, to assign the rights. So let's try it again with the plural version with ExtendedRights:

```
| Get-ADPermission | where {$_.AccessRights -eq "ExtendedRight"}).ExtendedRights
```

```
RawIdentity
-----------
User-Change-Password
Send-As
Receive-As
User-Change-Password
Send-As
Send-As
User-Change-Password
User-Force-Change-Password
```

Now we have a set of rights. But we don't know any other information. How can we get that so we understand what is assigned to who? Select-Object. We can use that to select which properties we want to display:

```
Get-Mailbox "Help Desk" | Get-ADPermission | Where {$_.AccessRights -eq "ExtendedRight"} | Select-Object Identity, User, ExtendedRights
```

```
Identity                          User                               ExtendedRights
--------                          ----                               --------------
16-TAP.Local/Users/Help Desk      Everyone                           {User-Change-Password}
16-TAP.Local/Users/Help Desk      NT AUTHORITY\SELF                  {Send-As}
16-TAP.Local/Users/Help Desk      NT AUTHORITY\SELF                  {Receive-As}
16-TAP.Local/Users/Help Desk      NT AUTHORITY\SELF                  {User-Change-Password}
16-TAP.Local/Users/Help Desk      BUILTIN\Backup Operators           {Send-As}
16-TAP.Local/Users/Help Desk      16-TAP\Help Desk Users             {Send-As}
16-TAP.Local/Users/Help Desk      16-TAP\Exchange Windows Permissions {User-Change-Password}
16-TAP.Local/Users/Help Desk      16-TAP\Exchange Windows Permissions {User-Force-Change-Password}
```

If we desire cleaner results, ones with just users that are not SELF or any built, we could apply a filter to the 'User' attribute as well:

```
Get-Mailbox "Help Desk" | Get-ADPermission | Where {$_.AccessRights -eq "ExtendedRight"} | Select-Object Identity,User,ExtendedRights | Where {($_.User -NotLike "*SELF") -And ($_.User -NotLike "BUILTIN*") -And ($_.User -NotLike "EVERYONE")}
```

```
Identity                          User                               ExtendedRights
--------                          ----                               --------------
16-TAP.Local/Users/Help Desk      16-TAP\Help Desk Users             {Send-As}
16-TAP.Local/Users/Help Desk      16-TAP\Exchange Windows Permissions {User-Change-Password}
16-TAP.Local/Users/Help Desk      16-TAP\Exchange Windows Permissions {User-Force-Change-Password}
```

This narrows out the SELF, BuiltIn and Everyone. Now we have results for one mailbox and can query all shared mailboxes:

```
Get-Mailbox -Filter {RecipientTypeDetails -eq "SharedMailbox"} | Get-ADPermission | Where {$_.AccessRights -eq "ExtendedRight"} | Select-Object Identity, User, ExtendedRights | Where {($_.User -NotLike "*SELF") -And ($_.User -NotLike "BUILTIN*") -And ($_.User -NotLike "EVERYONE")}
```

Simply removing the single mailbox query and adding a filter for the RecipientTypeDetails matching "SharedMailbox". We end up getting the same results above, but for all Shared Mailboxes.

# Resource Mailboxes

There are two types of Resource Mailboxes in Exchange 2016 – Room and Equipment. The room mailbox is generally used to designate rooms that will be used by more than two people for meeting purposes. Whether these are large or small conference rooms, stand up only spaces or maybe even the lunch room, the purpose of a room mailbox is to provide a central scheduling place for users within Exchange. Calendars on room mailboxes operate differently than calendars for regular users and can be tweaked to handle different booking scenarios (AutoBooking and restricted hours) in an organization. A resource mailbox is generally used for items that can be checked out for a certain time period like projects, or TVs or maybe even vehicles for a company.

## Equipment Mailboxes

Examples of equipment mailboxes are projectors, cars, laptops and more. By creating a mailbox in Exchange your users will be able to use their own mailbox calendar to book or request the booking of equipment that may be used for example in a client presentation. By its definition equipment should be portable or something that one of your users can transport.

### Example

For this example we have a sale department with a hundred sales people that constantly travel to client sites to help present new products or to inform potential clients about the services your company provides. These sales people use a series of projectors for their presentations. The projectors range from the small travel projectors to the larger, more professional and higher quality projectors. The sales people and IT management would like to create these as objects in Exchange so that the sales people can check them out. The idea is that instead of constantly asking about the availability of equipment, the sales people would be able to confirm availability and schedule meetings with the equipment to secure the projects for a certain amount of hours / days.

Some of the projectors (the larger ones) require the approval of Sales Managers. The reason is that the larger projectors are expensive company property and need to be properly tracked. Some have gone missing over the years due to mismanagement.

### PowerShell

Creating a mailbox for the projects is the same as creating a user mailbox, with the exception of a –Equipment parameter being added to designate the mailbox as an equipment mailbox:

```
New-Mailbox –Name "Portable Projector 1" –Equipment
```

```
Name                      Alias                ServerName    ProhibitSendQuota
----                      -----                ----------    -----------------
Portable Projector 1      PortableProjector1   ex02          Unlimited
```

Now that the mailbox is in Exchange we can modify some settings. For the smaller projectors, we need to make sure that they are available for AutoBooking and restrict to only be bookable by the Sales Department. How do we do this? Set-CalendarProcessing. This cmdlet can be used with any mailbox. It is especially useful for Equipment, Shared and Room mailboxes.

Let's review some examples from the cmdlet:

```
------------------------------ Example 1 ------------------------------
Set-CalendarProcessing -Identity "Conf 212" -AutomateProcessing AutoAccept -DeleteComments $true
-AddOrganizerToSubject $true -AllowConflicts $false


------------------------------ Example 3 ------------------------------
Set-CalendarProcessing -Identity "5th Floor Conference Room" -AutomateProcessing AutoAccept -AllBookInPolicy $true
```

From these examples, we can use the bottom example for our cmdlet to enable resource mailbox scheduling and make sure to include this parameter:

    –AutomateProcessing AutoAccept

The request also stated that only users in the Sales Department can reserve the equipment.  Reviewing examples from the same cmdlet we see that there is an option to do this as well:

```
----------------------- Example 6 --------------------------
Set-CalendarProcessing -Identity "Car 53" -AutomateProcessing AutoAccept -BookInPolicy
"ayla@contoso.com","tony@contoso.com"
```

Reviewing Get-Help for Set-CalendarProcessing, the BookInPolicy states that:

*"The BookInPolicy parameter specifies a comma-separated list of users who are allowed to submit in-policy meeting requests to the resource mailbox. Any in-policy meeting requests from these users are automatically approved."*

By default all users should be blocked from automatically booking a room.   Putting together the two parameters, we get:

    Set-CalendarProcessing "Portable Projector 1" –AutomateProcessing AutoAccept –BookInPolicy "Sales Dept"

Now when someone from the Sales Department wants to book this projector they can.  Now, if we want to restrict all projectors with the word 'Projector' in the name to just the Sales Department we first need a way to get a list of all of these projectors:

    Get-Mailbox -Filter {(RecipientTypeDetails -eq "EquipmentMailbox") -and (Name -Like "*projector*")}

The '–filter' parameter allows for the result set of 'Get-Mailbox' to be shrunk to only mailboxes that are Equipment and have 'projector' in the name.


## Equipment Mailbox Management

When all the equipment mailboxes are created, a report on the equipment mailboxes can be generated with:

    Get-Mailbox -Filter {RecipientTypeDetails -eq "EquipmentMailbox"}

Using the above one-liner, we can now perform mass manipulation on a group of mailboxes based solely on the type of mailbox specified.  For example, if we create a new database in Exchange called "Resources" and move all the mailboxes to that database, this is simply done like so:

    Get-Mailbox -Filter {RecipientTypeDetails -eq "EquipmentMailbox"} | New-MoveRequest
    -TargetDatabase "DB02"

```
DisplayName                   StatusDetail              TotalMailboxSize        TotalArchiveSize
-----------                   ------------              ----------------        ----------------
Portable Projector 1          WaitingForJobPickup       0 B (0 bytes)
```

## Room Mailboxes

Room mailboxes are by far the most used and configured of the resource mailboxes in Exchange. Room mailboxes need more care and maintenance to get them into useful order. Rooms can be large or small and designated as such in the capacity property. They can even be organized into lists. Let's see what we can do with rooms with PowerShell:

### Example

Take for example a large organization that has a dozen locations in the US and Asia. Each of these locations has dozens of rooms. IT Management has been given the directive to create a series of rooms for each location. The naming of the rooms needs to be easy for end users to interpret which location and / or what floor a room is on. Groups of rooms should also be created if possible in order to help the end user find an appropriate room or even just an available room in a quick manner. First, we need to create all of the rooms. For this scenario we will use this list of locations:

| US | Asia |
|---|---|
| Orlando | Tokyo |
| Dallas | Taipei |
| San Diego | Seoul |
| Denver | Shanghai |
| New York | Singapore |
| Seattle | Hong Kong |

For the sake of this book, we will concentrate on one site in the US and one site in Asia to work on creating and configuring these rooms per management's requirements. We will use PowerShell to create the rooms and then configure booking options for each room. In order to facilitate the creation of the rooms, a CSV file is prepopulated with details such as the region the room it's in, what city, the floor the room is on, a description, capacity and phone number. The same CSV file is below:

```
Region,City,Floor,Description,Capacity,Phone
US,Orlando,1,SW,20,"+1 (407) 220-1212"
US,Orlando,1,SE,20,"+1 (407) 220-1213"
US,Orlando,1,NW,20,"+1 (407) 220-1214"
US,Orlando,1,NE,25,"+1 (407) 220-1215"
US,Orlando,1,Large,50,"+1 (407) 220-1216"
US,Orlando,2,SW,20,"+1 (407) 220-2212"
US,Orlando,2,SE,15,"+1 (407) 220-2213"
US,Orlando,2,NW,20,"+1 (407) 220-2214"
US,Orlando,2,NE,20,"+1 (407) 220-2215"
US,Orlando,2,Large,40,"+1 (407) 220-2216"
US,Orlando,3,SW,20,"+1 (407) 220-3212"
US,Orlando,3,SE,20,"+1 (407) 220-3213"
US,Orlando,3,NW,20,"+1 (407) 220-3214"
US,Orlando,3,NE,20,"+1 (407) 220-3215"
US,Orlando,3,Small,5,"+1 (407) 220-3216"
US,Orlando,4,SW,15,"+1 (407) 220-4212"
US,Orlando,4,SE,15,"+1 (407) 220-4213"
US,Orlando,4,NW,25,"+1 (407) 220-4214"
US,Orlando,4,NE,20,"+1 (407) 220-4215"
US,Orlando,4,Small,10,"+1 (407) 220-4216"
US,Orlando,5,Amphitheater,100,"+1 (407) 220-5212"
US,Orlando,5,"Standing Room",75,"+1 (407) 220-5213"
US,Orlando,5,NW,25,"+1 (407) 220-5214"
US,Orlando,6,Executive,10,"+1 (407) 220-6212"
Asia,Seoul,10,SW,15,+82-02-505-1212
Asia,Seoul,10,SE,15,+82-02-505-1213
Asia,Seoul,10,NW,15,+82-02-505-1214
Asia,Seoul,10,NE,15,+82-02-505-1215
Asia,Seoul,10,Large,30,+82-02-505-1216
Asia,Seoul,10,Small,5,+82-02-505-1217
Asia,Seoul,15,SW,20,+82-02-505-2212
Asia,Seoul,15,SE,15,+82-02-505-2213
Asia,Seoul,15,NW,20,+82-02-505-2214
Asia,Seoul,15,NE,15,+82-02-505-2215
Asia,Seoul,15,Large,50,+82-02-505-2216
Asia,Seoul,16,SW,15,+82-02-505-3212
Asia,Seoul,16,SE,15,+82-02-505-3213
```

Now that a list of rooms is stored in a CSV file we can create a script that will read each line in the CSV file and create a room based off this information.

**Sample Script**

First section reads in the CSV we created above:

```
$Rooms = Import-CSV C:\Scripting\RoomList.csv
```

Next, using a Foreach loop, the $Rooms variable is looped to go through each line:

```
Foreach ($Room in $Rooms) {
    $Region = $Room.Region
    $City = $Room.City
    $Floor = $Room.Floor
    $Location = "$Region-$City"
    $Capacity = $Room.Capacity
    $Phone = $Room.Phone
    $Description = $Room.Description
    $Roomname = "$City"+"-Floor-"+"$Floor"+"-"+"$Description"
```

Once the variable and values for the room are set, the New-Mailbox cmdlet is used to create the rooms as needed in the organization:

```
# Create mailbox with criteria from CSV file
    New-Mailbox -Room -Name $RoomName -Phone $Phone -ResourceCapacity $Capacity -Office
    $Location
}
```

A sample run shows the rooms being created:

```
Name                        Alias                       ServerName   ProhibitSendQuota
----                        -----                       ----------   -----------------
Orlando-Floor-1-SW          Orlando-Floor-1-SW          ex02         Unlimited
Orlando-Floor-1-SE          Orlando-Floor-1-SE          ex02         Unlimited
Orlando-Floor-1-NW          Orlando-Floor-1-NW          ex02         Unlimited
Orlando-Floor-1-NE          Orlando-Floor-1-NE          ex02         Unlimited
Orlando-Floor-1-Large       Orlando-Floor-1-L...        ex02         Unlimited
Orlando-Floor-2-SW          Orlando-Floor-2-SW          ex02         Unlimited
Orlando-Floor-2-SE          Orlando-Floor-2-SE          ex02         Unlimited
Orlando-Floor-2-NW          Orlando-Floor-2-NW          ex02         Unlimited
Orlando-Floor-2-NE          Orlando-Floor-2-NE          ex02         Unlimited
Orlando-Floor-2-Large       Orlando-Floor-2-L...        ex02         Unlimited
Orlando-Floor-3-SW          Orlando-Floor-3-SW          ex02         Unlimited
Orlando-Floor-3-SE          Orlando-Floor-3-SE          ex02         Unlimited
Orlando-Floor-3-NW          Orlando-Floor-3-NW          ex02         Unlimited
Orlando-Floor-3-NE          Orlando-Floor-3-NE          ex02         Unlimited
Orlando-Floor-3-Small       Orlando-Floor-3-S...        ex02         Unlimited
Orlando-Floor-4-SW          Orlando-Floor-4-SW          ex02         Unlimited
Orlando-Floor-4-SE          Orlando-Floor-4-SE          ex02         Unlimited
Orlando-Floor-4-NW          Orlando-Floor-4-NW          ex02         Unlimited
Orlando-Floor-4-NE          Orlando-Floor-4-NE          ex02         Unlimited
Orlando-Floor-4-Small       Orlando-Floor-4-S...        ex02         Unlimited
Orlando-Floor-5-Amphit...   Orlando-Floor-5-A...        ex02         Unlimited
Orlando-Floor-5-Standi...   Orlando-Floor-5-S...        ex02         Unlimited
Orlando-Floor-5-NW          Orlando-Floor-5-NW          ex02         Unlimited
Orlando-Floor-6-Executive   Orlando-Floor-6-E...        ex02         Unlimited
Seoul-Floor-10-SW           Seoul-Floor-10-SW           ex02         Unlimited
Seoul-Floor-10-SE           Seoul-Floor-10-SE           ex02         Unlimited
Seoul-Floor-10-NW           Seoul-Floor-10-NW           ex02         Unlimited
Seoul-Floor-10-NE           Seoul-Floor-10-NE           ex02         Unlimited
Seoul-Floor-10-Large        Seoul-Floor-10-Large        ex02         Unlimited
Seoul-Floor-10-Small        Seoul-Floor-10-Small        ex02         Unlimited
Seoul-Floor-15-SW           Seoul-Floor-15-SW           ex02         Unlimited
```

# Room Lists

Once rooms have been created in Exchange, a new feature can be used called Room Lists.  Think of Room Lists as groups of rooms that are logically put together by location.

## PowerShell

Let's start out by looking for cmdlets that we can use to manage these lists.  As a forewarning, it's not located where you think:

```
Get-Command *Room*
Get-Command *List*
```

Neither reveal any useful information.  So how do I get the right cmdlet?  Use a Search Engine.

**Search Terms:** Exchange PowerShell Room Lists

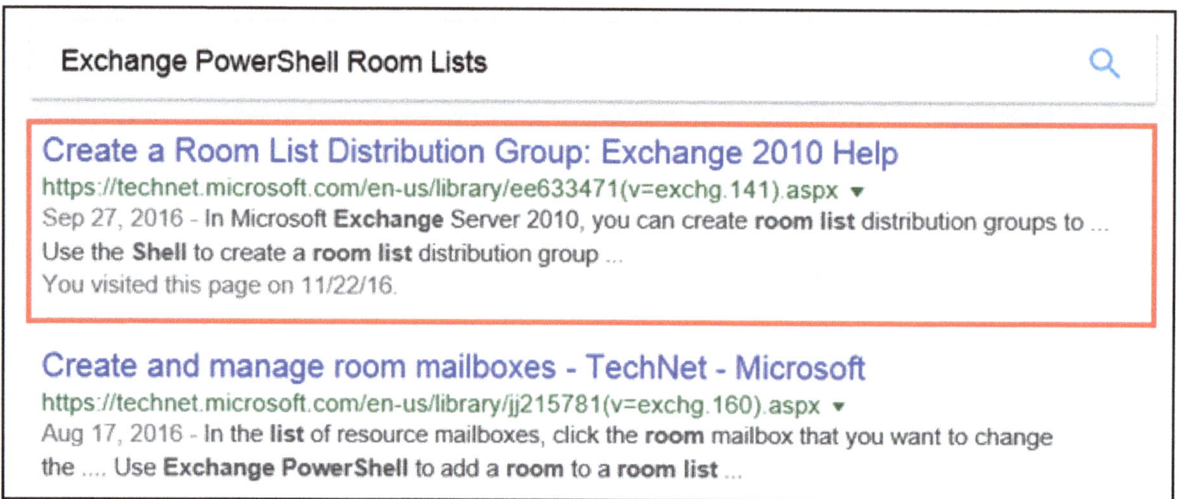


So according to the results list above, a Room List can be created as part of a Distribution Group creation.   Reviewing the Get-Help for New-DistributionGroup you will see the 'RoomList' parameter:

```
-RoomList <SwitchParameter>
    The RoomList switch specifies that all members of this distribution group are room mailboxes. You don't need
    to specify a value with this switch.

    You can create a distribution group for an office building in your organization and add all rooms in that
    building to the distribution group. Room list distribution groups are used to generate a list of building
    locations for meeting requests in Outlook 2010 or later. Room lists allow a user to select a building and get
    availability information for all rooms in that building, without having to add each room individually.
```

So the Room List parameter allows for a group of rooms to be stored as members of a Distribution Group and seen by the client as a grouping of Rooms.

## PowerShell

Using the rooms we created above, let's see if we can create a list of all room mailboxes in Orlando.  Now, it would be nice if the New-DynamicDistributionGroup had a switch for Room Lists, but it does not.  So any rooms added will be a manual process.

First, we can store all Rooms that start with Orlando in a variable called $Members:

    $Members = Get-Mailbox -Filter {Name -Like "Orlando*"} | Where {$_.RecipientTypeDetails -eq "RoomMailbox"}

After that, a new Distribution Group can be created with the –RoomList parameter and members added from the $Members variable:

    New-DistributionGroup -Name "Orlando Meeting Rooms" -DisplayName "Orlando Meeting Rooms" -RoomList -Members $Members

Verifying that the group has all the room mailboxes in it:

    Get-DistributionGroupMember -Identity "Orlando Meeting Rooms"

Now when a new meeting is created and 'Add Rooms' is chosen, the List appears instead of each individual room:

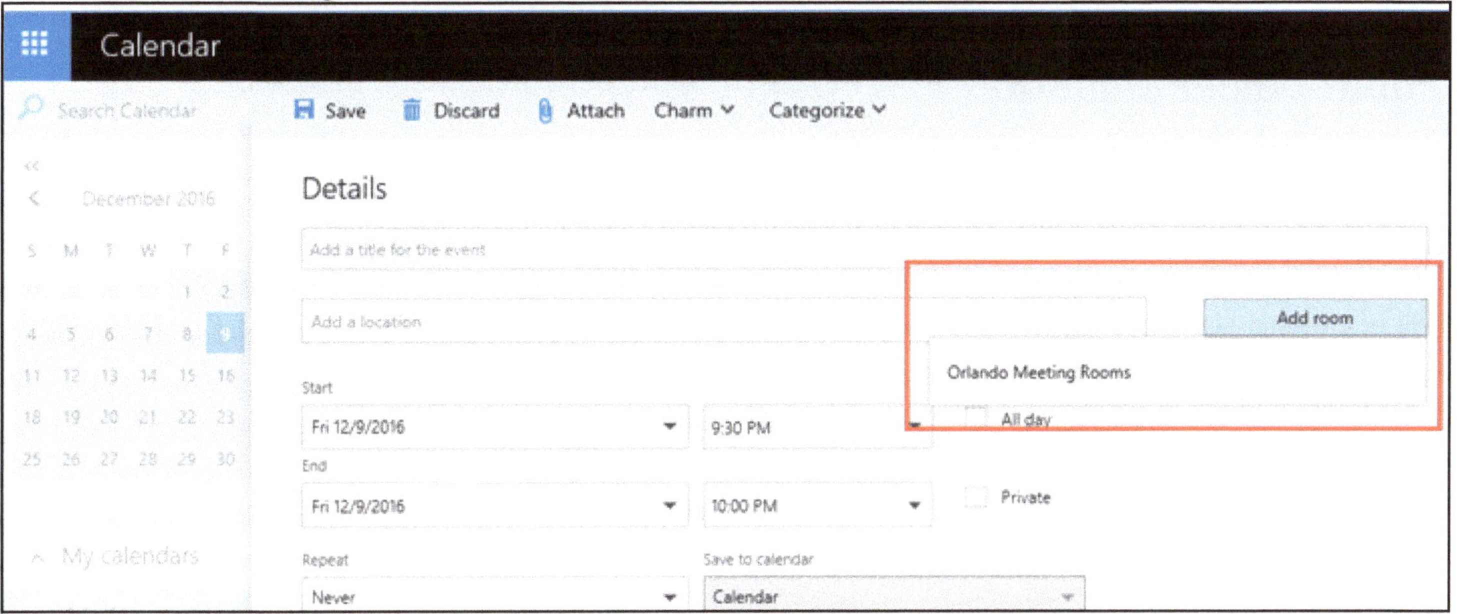


New room lists will begin to populate and display when the 'Add Rooms' button is used:

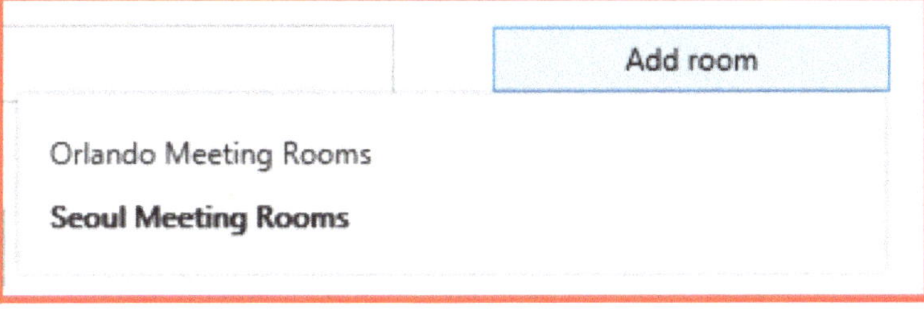

Clicking on the Seoul Room List, a list of available rooms appears for the user:

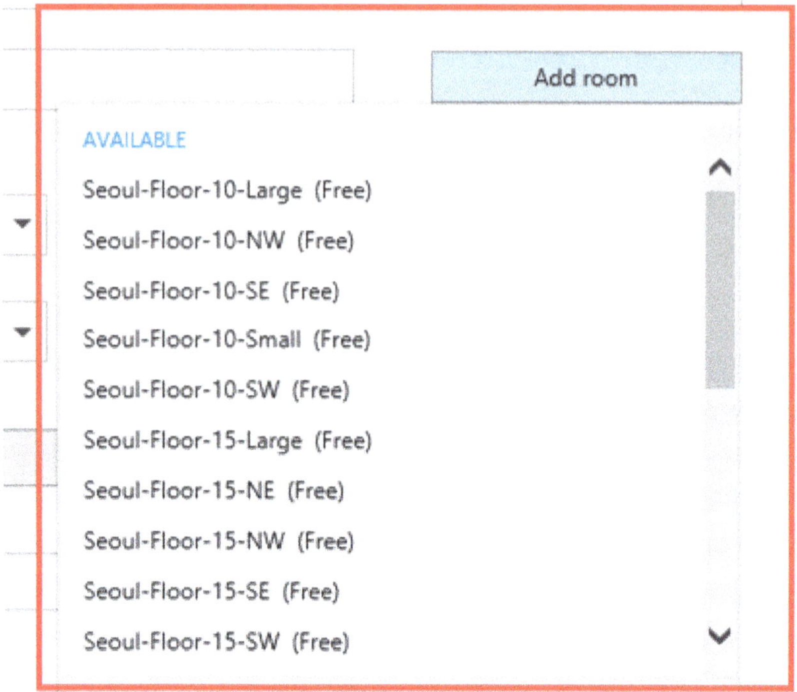


Room Lists can become very useful in organizations with either a lot of rooms, or a highly organized set of rooms and their names.  Regular Distribution Groups can also be converted into Room Lists as well.

# Public Folder Mailboxes

With the change in Public Folder architecture, it is now important to work with Public Folder Mailboxes which are the core underlying structure of Public Folders.  PowerShell can help us manage these folders.  Exchange 2016 introduced a new paradigm for the way Public Folders operate.  Instead of a database for Public Folders, a series of mailboxes in a regular mailbox database store all the Public Folder data, including the hierarchy.  The reasoning was that Public Folder replication was notoriously problematic and used SMTP to make copies on other Public Folder Databases.  This had the potential to clog up SMTP queues.   Now Public Folder data can be replicated within the DAG infrastructure and have true high availability.

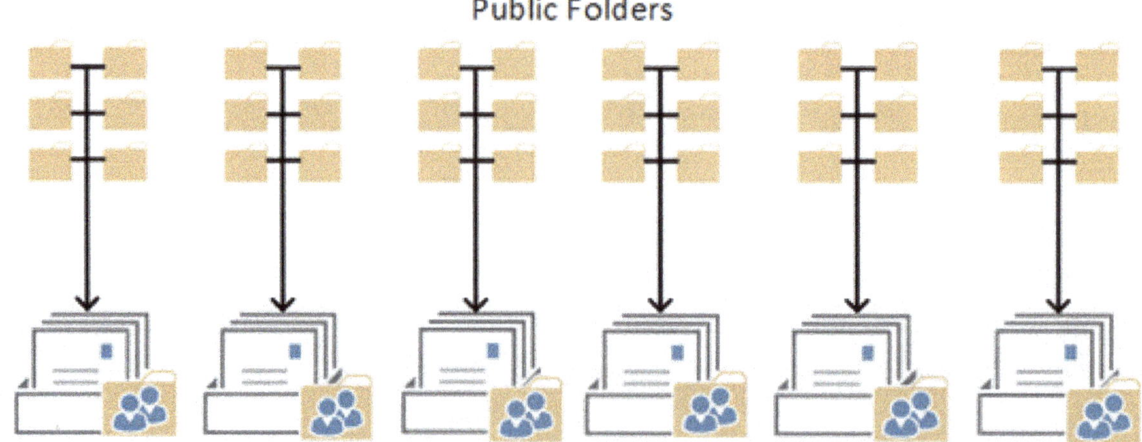


Public Folder Mailboxes – Responsible for content and hierarchy

**PowerShell**

First, we'll explore what PowerShell cmdlets are available for Public Folders:

Get-Command *PublicFolder*

```
CommandType     Name
-----------     ----
Function        Add-PublicFolderClientPermission
Function        Disable-MailPublicFolder
Function        Enable-MailPublicFolder
Function        Get-MailPublicFolder
Function        Get-PublicFolder
Function        Get-PublicFolderClientPermission
Function        Get-PublicFolderDatabase
Function        Get-PublicFolderItemStatistics
Function        Get-PublicFolderMailboxDiagnostics
Function        Get-PublicFolderMailboxMigrationRequest
Function        Get-PublicFolderMailboxMigrationRequestStatistics
Function        Get-PublicFolderMigrationRequest
Function        Get-PublicFolderMigrationRequestStatistics
Function        Get-PublicFolderMoveRequest
Function        Get-PublicFolderMoveRequestStatistics
Function        Get-PublicFolderStatistics
Function        New-PublicFolder
Function        New-PublicFolderMigrationRequest
Function        New-PublicFolderMoveRequest
Function        New-SyncMailPublicFolder
Function        Remove-PublicFolder
Function        Remove-PublicFolderClientPermission
Function        Remove-PublicFolderMailboxMigrationRequest
Function        Remove-PublicFolderMigrationRequest
Function        Remove-PublicFolderMoveRequest
Function        Remove-SyncMailPublicFolder
Function        Resume-PublicFolderMailboxMigrationRequest
Function        Resume-PublicFolderMigrationRequest
Function        Resume-PublicFolderMoveRequest
Function        Set-MailPublicFolder
Function        Set-PublicFolder
Function        Set-PublicFolderMailboxMigrationRequest
Function        Set-PublicFolderMigrationRequest
Function        Set-PublicFolderMoveRequest
Function        Suspend-PublicFolderMigrationRequest
Function        Suspend-PublicFolderMoveRequest
Function        Update-PublicFolderMailbox
```

What we see from the above is that there is no direct cmdlet for creating a Public Folder mailbox. We know that Public Folders require Public Folder mailboxes, so what about the New-Mailbox cmdlet? Is there a parameter for this?

Get-Help New-Mailbox –Full

```
-PublicFolder <SwitchParameter>
    The PublicFolderswitch specifies that the mailbox is a public folder mailbox. You don't need to specify a
    value with this switch. This switch is required onlyif you're creating a public folder mailbox.

    Public folder mailboxes are specially designed mailboxes that store the hierarchy and content of public
    folders. The first public folder mailbox created in your Exchange organization is called the primary hierarchy
    mailbox. It contains the writeable copy of the hierarchy of public folders for the organization and public
    folder content. There can be only one writeable copy of the public folder hierarchy in your organization. All
    other public folder mailboxes are called secondary public folder mailboxes and contain a read-only copy of the
    hierarchy and the content for public folders.
```

Public Folder mailboxes can be created with a simple one-liner that requires only two parameters – the first is '-PublicFolder' and the second is '-name':

New-Mailbox –PublicFolder –Name "Public Folder 1"

```
[PS] C:\>new-mailbox -PublicFolder -name "Public Folder 1"
[PS] C:\>_
```

Remember that when running this cmdlet without specifying a database, the mailbox will be placed in a random database by Exchange. If, for example, all Public Folders mailboxes should be places in a particular database be sure to specify it like so:

New-Mailbox –PublicFolder –Name "Public Folder 1" –Database "DB01"

To verify that the mailbox was created, simple run:

Get-Mailbox -PublicFolder

```
[PS] C:\>Get-Mailbox -PublicFolder

Name                          Alias              ServerName       ProhibitSendQuota
----                          -----              ----------       -----------------
Public Folder 1               PublicFolder1      ex02             Unlimited
Public Folder 2               PublicFolder2      ex02             Unlimited
```

Once mailboxes have been created, Public Folder(s) can be created in order to store data. The cmdlet we need is New-PublicFolder. What examples does Microsoft provide us:

```
-------------------------- Example 1 --------------------------
New-PublicFolder -Name Marketing

-------------------------- Example 2 --------------------------
New-PublicFolder -Name FY2013 -Path \Legal\Cases
-------------------------- Example 3 --------------------------
New-PublicFolder -Name Support -Mailbox North_America
```

First, we will create a Root Public Folder to hold other Public Folders for the IT Department.

New-PublicFolder -Name 'IT Department' -Path '\'

Then we can create sub-Public Folders under the root of 'IT Department'.

New-PublicFolder -Name 'Testing' -Path '\IT Department'

You can keep creating folders like, or via a script, as needed.


# Distribution Groups

Distribution Groups in Exchange 2016 come in two different varieties – Dynamic and Static. Static groups are ones were the membership needs to be added or removed manually with PowerShell, Exchange EAC or Active Directory Users and Computers. A Dynamic Distribution Group builds its membership based on a set of criteria you define and thus the members that appear in the group are dynamic. This means that, based on the criteria for a group, if a user no longer meets that criteria, the user does not appear as a member of the group. If a user object is modified to meet the criteria again, it will then appear as a member of the group again. The distinction is also important in PowerShell as there exists two different sets of cmdlets for each group type.

## PowerShell

First, let's review what cmdlets are available for distribution groups (dynamic or static):

```
Get-Command *Distribution*
CommandType       Name
-----------       ----
Function          Add-DistributionGroupMember
Function          Disable-DistributionGroup
Function          Enable-DistributionGroup
Function          Get-DistributionGroup
Function          Get-DistributionGroupMember
Function          Get-DynamicDistributionGroup
Function          New-DistributionGroup
Function          New-DynamicDistributionGroup
Function          Remove-DistributionGroup
Function          Remove-DistributionGroupMember
Function          Remove-DynamicDistributionGroup
Function          Set-DistributionGroup
Function          Set-DynamicDistributionGroup
Function          Update-DistributionGroupMember
```

Now that we have a list of PowerShell cmdlets to use, let's use the New-DistributionGroup cmdlet to create some groups for Exchange:

```
Get-Help New-DistributionGroup –Examples
```

```
----------------------- Example 1 -----------------------

New-DistributionGroup -Name Managers"Managers" -Type "Security"
You use the Add-DistributionGroupMember cmdlet to add members after you create the group.

----------------------- Example 2 -----------------------

New-DistributionGroup -Name "ITDepartment" -Members
chris@contoso.com,michelle@contoso.com,laura@contoso.com,julia@contoso.com
```

The examples given by PowerShell are rather basic and if more options are desired, then make sure to run:

```
Get-Help New-DistributionGroup -Full
```

Some sample options that can be chosen for the group are:

**RequireSenderAuthenticationEnabled** – This parameter determines if only internal users can send emails to the group or if external senders are allowed.

**OrganizationalUnit** – Use this parameter if you wish to specify an OU to place the group. Especially useful if your Active Directory structure is highly organized.

**MemberJoinRestriction** – If the group membership needs to be controlled, use this option to set 'ApprovalRequired' which will allow the membership to be managed.

**MemberDepartRestriction** – Conversely, the opposite of the above option, this is for users wishing to leave a group, the same controls can be put into place as those wishing/needing to join a group.

**ManagedBy** – Assigns a user the role of managing the group for approvals, removals, approve moderation requests and more.


## Management

In Exchange, Distribution Groups can be used for many purposes. Whether they are used to represent parts of a company (e.g. All Users, North American Users and Paris Users). Or for a specific notification for IT (e.g. Alerts), they all need to be managed and maintained. In most organizations there will be group sprawl with groups going unused or forgotten and even completely emptied of all users without removal. Proper management and pruning of these extraneous groups allows for more efficient management. For the scenario below we'll explore a couple of items that can be managed for groups.

**Example**

In this scenario, we have an environment that has grown from Exchange 2000 and steadily updated Exchange to Exchange 2016. The company has also grown from 50 users to well over 2,000 users through organic growth and acquisitions. Now the messaging team has decided to do some cleanup. There are 1,000 distribution groups that have been created over the past 15 years by various administrators. No one in the organization can say for sure which groups are needed and which are not.

In this scenario, we need to evaluate two criteria – number of members in a group and if any emails have gone to the group. The first is relatively easy as we simply need to query each group to see if it contains members. For the second, determining mail flow to groups requires a bit of legwork and keeping track of active groups.

From the list of cmdlets above, we see there is a cmdlet specifically for distribution group members. What do the examples for this cmdlet provide to help us query for empty groups:

```
--------------------------- Example 1 ---------------------------
Get-DistributionGroupMember -Identity "Marketing USA"
```

Not much to go on with the included examples for the cmdlet. However, when the cmdlet is run against a distribution group in Exchange, it reveals the members of that particular group. For our scenario, we have 1,000 distribution groups to query and get members from. This will require each group name to be piped from Get-DistributionGroup to the Get-DistributionGroupMember cmdlet in a Foreach loop. Two loops will be needed as each group type (dynamic and regular) need to be handled separately.

To determine which groups are empty, we first need to get a complete list of groups and store the groups in a variable:

```
$DistributionGroups = Get-DistributionGroup -ResultSize Unlimited
```

Once a list of groups is stored in $DistributionGroups we can now go through each group in a Foreach loop:

```
Foreach ($Group in $DistributionGroups) {
```

Notice the naming of variables was done for ease of keeping track of the current context, whether it's all groups ($DistributionGroups) or the current group in the list ($Group). In addition, we'll use a variable as a counter to keep track of distribution groups with no members ($N) – we'll set this to 0 before the Foreach loop.

For the next line we query the current Distribution Group in the loop for members:

```
$Members = Get-DistributionGroupMember -Identity $Group.DisplayName
```

Then, using an IF statement, the $Empty variable is checked to see if it is empty:

```
If ($Members -eq $Null) {
```

If this variable has no value assigned, then no members were found that are in the current group. This is reported to the PowerShell window with the Write-Host statement. The $N++ is an incremental counter:

```
Write-Host "The group $Group is an empty Distribution Group." -ForegroundColor Yellow
$N++
  }
}
```

At the very end of the script we'll check to see if $N is equal to zero and if it is, then no empty groups have been found:

```
If ($N -eq 0) {
    Write-Host "No empty Distribution Groups were found." -ForegroundColor Cyan
}
```

If there are no empty groups, then the script will report that:

```
-- Empty Distribution Group report --

No empty Distribution Groups were found.



-- Empty Dynamic Distribution Group report --

No empty Dynamic Distribution Groups were found.
```

When there are groups present with no members, the script will report them like so:

```
-- Empty Distribution Group report --
The group Sales Dept is an empty Distribution Group.
```

Dynamic Groups require a slightly different tactic. The line that queries for members has to be different because a dynamic group doesn't have actual members, virtual membership is calculated at query time for these groups.

**Regular group members**
```
$Members = Get-DistributionGroupMember -Identity $Group.DisplayName
```

**Dynamic group members**
```
$GroupDetails = Get-DynamicDistributionGroup $Group.DisplayName
$Members = Get-Recipient -RecipientPreviewFilter $GroupDetails.RecipientFilter
```

Note, the RecipientFilter is used to find all recipients that match the filter on the dynamic group.


**Complete Script Code – Empty Distribution Groups**

```
# Get a list of all empty distribution groups
$DistributionGroups = Get-DistributionGroup -ResultSize Unlimited
Write-Host "-- Empty Distribution Group report --" -ForegroundColor Green
Write-Host " "
$N = 0

 Foreach ($Group in $DistributionGroups) {
   $Members = Get-DistributionGroupMember -Identity $Group.DisplayName
   If ($Members -eq $Null) {
```

```
        Write-Host "The group $Group is an empty Distribution Group." -ForegroundColor Yellow
        $N++
    }
}

If ($N -eq 0) {
    Write-Host "No empty Distribution Groups were found." -ForegroundColor Cyan
}
```

Script Code – Empty Dynamic Distribution Groups

```
CLS
$DynamicDistribution = Get-DynamicDistributionGroup
Write-Host "-- Empty Dynamic Distribution Group report --" -ForegroundColor Green
Write-Host " "
$N = 0

Foreach ($Group in $DynamicDistribution) {
    $Members = Get-Recipient -RecipientPreviewFilter $Group.RecipientFilter
    If ($Members -eq $Null) {
        Write-Host "The group $Group is an empty Dynamic Distribution Group." -ForegroundColor Yellow
        $N++
    }
}

If ($N -eq 0) {
    Write-Host "No empty Dynamic Distribution Groups were found." -ForegroundColor Cyan
}
```

## Unused Distribution Groups

This task is a bit more complicated. The goal is to find any distribution group that has not been used for a certain amount of time. Defining that time interval is the hard part. Is a group inactive at 30 days? 90 days? 180 days? 365 days? For the sake of argument, we will define a group as inactive if it has not received email after six months or around 180 days.

What criteria can be used to determine if a group is not active? Well, what is active? We defined it above as email to the group in the past x months. To evaluate this criteria, we need to trace email messages that are being delivered or sent to them. As distribution groups are not mailboxes, we cannot review the contents of a mailbox. A valid option for tracking these messages would be to review the Message Tracking Logs on Exchange servers to see if anything was logged by that server. One thing to keep in mind is if there are multiple servers, all servers will need to be reviewed.

If we are looking for messages to these groups and the messages need to be sent in the past six months, how do we find out what the retention period for Message Tracking logs?

Get-Command *MessageTracking*

```
CommandType       Name
-----------       ----
Function          Get-MessageTrackingLog
Function          Get-MessageTrackingReport
Function          Search-MessageTrackingReport
```

None of these cmdlets look correct. Let's take a look at the servers. Specifically the Transport layer configuration. What cmdlets exist for the Transport layer:

Get-Command Get-Transport*

```
CommandType       Name
-----------       ----
Function          Get-TransportAgent
Function          Get-TransportConfig
Function          Get-TransportPipeline
Function          Get-TransportRule
Function          Get-TransportRuleAction
Function          Get-TransportRulePredicate
Function          Get-TransportServer
Function          Get-TransportService
```

Of these cmdlets, the bottom two are the ones used to find the message tracking settings. The only difference between the two is that 'Get-TransportServer' is being depreciated and Microsoft wants the administrator to use Get-TransportService (or any cmdlets with TransportService vs TransportServer) to be used in the future. This is because the Hub Transport Role has been removed with the introduction of Exchange 2016.

```
WARNING:  The Get-TransportServer cmdlet will be removed in a future version of Exchange. Use the
Get-TransportService cmdlet instead. If you have any scripts that use the Get-TransportServer
cmdlet, update them to use the Get-TransportService cmdlet.  For more information, see
http://go.microsoft.com/fwlink/p/?LinkId=254711.
```

Using the Get-TransportService cmdlet, we can see what the message tracking log settings are for a particular server:

Get-TransportService –Server <server name>

```
MessageTrackingLogEnabled                 : True
MessageTrackingLogMaxAge                  : 45.00:00:00
MessageTrackingLogMaxDirectorySize        : 4.395 GB (4,718,592,000 bytes)
MessageTrackingLogMaxFileSize             : 10 MB (10,485,760 bytes)
MessageTrackingLogPath                    : C:\Program Files\Microsoft\Excha
MessageTrackingLogSubjectLoggingEnabled   : True
```

From the settings above we can see that the default retention period for Message Tracking Logs on a server is 45 days. Our requirements are 180 days. For smaller environments, adjusting the retention to 180 days might be feasible. The real restriction for tracking logs is disk space. The higher the days are set, the greater possibility there is that a large amount of space may be required and thus the Directory Size for Message Tracking Logs may need to be increased. For larger environments, increase the amount of days higher may not be ideal because of this.

For this example, let's assume that the Exchange servers are very busy and it is impractical to set the logs files larger than 90 days. The assumption is that at six months of no emails, the group is considered inactive. We will thus examine the Message Tracking Logs on a monthly basis. In order to keep track of the activity of the groups, we can either record it in a CSV file or change an Active Directory property on the group. The second option is a cleaner option and something that can be queried by an outside script. It also does not rely on file shares, permissions or any other issues that may complicate the CSV file access and querying.

## Building the Script

First we'll need to set some baselines for dates in the script to be referenced later during queries:

```
# Production Dates
$Current = Get-Date
$OneMonth = ((Get-Date).AddMonths(-1))
```

Next, we'll need to configure some arrays to be used later in the scripts:

```
# Variables
$ActiveGroups2 = @()
$ActiveGroups = @()
$InactiveGroups = @()
$AllGroups = @()
$Smtp = @()
```

Later in the script, we'll need to run some Active Directory PowerShell cmdlets and in order to do so the Active Directory PowerShell module will need to be loaded:

```
# Load AD Module for PowerShell
Import-Module ActiveDirectory
```

Now that we've established the beginning of the script, we now need to review the Message Tracking Logs to determine if any messages for a particular group have been sent through the Exchange Servers. First, we'll need a list of all servers that can send and receive emails:

```
$Servers = Get-TransportService
```

Now that the Exchange 2016 servers are stored in the $Servers variable, we can examine each servers tracking logs for messages to those groups:

```
Foreach ($Name in $Servers) {
```

This next line is a long one. First of note is that $ActiveGroups2 is an array and we use the '+=' to add active groups to the list. Using the Get-MessageTrackingLog cmdlet, we specifically look for the EVENTID of 'Expand' as this relates specifically to Distribution Groups. The 'Start' and 'Stop' parameters are used to define the past month and up to the present. All results are sorted by the RelatedRecipientAddress, which is also a trait of Distribution Groups. All of the results are grouped here with 'Group-Object', again by RelatedRecipientAddress. This eliminates all duplicate groups and leaves a single line for each group found. Lastly the groups are sorted by name:

```
$ActiveGroups2 += (Get-MessageTrackingLog -Server $Name.Name -EventId Expand -ResultSize
Unlimited -Start $OneMonth -End $Current | Sort-Object RelatedRecipientAddress | Group-Object
RelatedRecipientAddress | Sort-Object Name | Select-Object Name)
}
```

Once out of this loop, all active groups are stored in $ActiveGroups and is out of order.  Now we need to sort the contents of this variable one more time:

```
$ActiveGroups2 = $ActiveGroups2 | Sort-Object Name | Group-Object Name
```

Once this is complete, we need to get just the name of each group found to be active:

```
Foreach ($Line in $ActiveGroups2) {
    $ActiveGroups += $Line.Name
}
```

In order to see which groups were not active, a list of all groups needs to be gathered as well.  In order to properly compare active and inactive groups, a common property needs to be used.  When we examined the logs for email to distribution groups, the SMTP address for the group was stored in a variable.  In the below line, the $AllGroups2 variable retrieves the primary SMTP address and store it labeled 'Name':

```
$AllGroups2 = Get-DistributionGroup -ResultSize Unlimited | Select-Object -Property @{Label="Name";
Expression={$_.PrimarySmtpAddress}}
```

We then need to store all the groups names in $AllGroups for comparing later to ActiveGroups:

```
Foreach ($Line in $AllGroups2) {
    $AllGroups += $Line.Name
}
```

Next, we take $ActiveGroups (groups who we found messages for in the Message Tracking Logs) and $AllGroups. The Compare-object cmdlet can be used for this:

```
DESCRIPTION
    The Compare-Object cmdlet compares two sets of objects. One set of objects is the "reference set," and the other
    set is the "difference set."

    The result of the comparison indicates whether a property value appeared only in the object from the reference set
    (indicated by the <= symbol), only in the object from the difference set (indicated by the => symbol) or, if the
    IncludeEqual parameter is specified, in both objects (indicated by the == symbol).

    NOTE:  If the reference set or the difference set is null ($null), Compare-Object generates a terminating error.
```

```
$InactiveGroups2 = Compare-Object $ActiveGroups $AllGroups
```

Once a list of Inactive Groups has been determined, we need to pull the results out of the comparison variable and stored in $InactiveGroups":

```
Foreach ($Line in $InactiveGroups2) {
    $Smtp2=$Line.InputObject
    $Address=$Smtp2.Local+"@"+$Smtp2.Domain
    $InactiveGroups += $Address
}
```

Now we have gotten to the whole point of the script and we can mark which groups are inactive and which ones are active.  Active groups will have 'CustomAttribute10' set to 0.  This indicates the number of months a group has been inactive, which in this case is '0':

```
# Set custom attribute 10 for active groups to 0
Foreach ($Line in $ActiveGroups) {
    Set-DistributionGroup -Identity $Line -CustomAttribute10 0 -WarningAction SilentlyContinue
}
```

Next, inactive groups will have the 'CustomAttribute10' incremented by 1.  This indicates an additional inactive month for the group.  In order to do so, the initial 'CustomAttribute10' value needs to be read from the group.

```
Foreach ($Line in $InactiveGroups){
  [String]$Email = $Line
  [Int]$Number = (Get-DistributionGroup -Identity $Email).CustomAttribute10
  $Number += 1
  Set-DistributionGroup -Identity $Email -CustomAttribute10 $Number
}
```

In addition to this, reports could be generated on what groups are active and inactive like so:

```
Foreach ($Group In $DG) {
  $CustomAttribute10 = $Group.CustomAttribute10
  If ($CustomAttribute10 -eq 0) {
    Write-Host "$Group is Active" -ForegroundColor Green
  } Else {
    Write-Host "$Group is Inactive" -ForegroundColor Yellow
  }
}
```



In addition, email notifications could be generated to notify group managers and / or IT admins as to groups that are no longer active.

# Group Moderation

Emails to groups sometimes need to be moderated.  Examples of this moderation occur with groups that contain C level management which may not want emails from just anyone in the company.  Dynamic Groups such as 'All Employees' are also ones that should be controlled to prevent mass emails of 'ReplyAll' which can cause havoc or even embarrassment in the organization.  Depending on the size of the organization, message approvers could be a single individual or a group of users responsible for this task.

## PowerShell

To see what can be done in PowerShell, we can review the Get-Help for the Set-DistributionGroup:

```
Get-Help Set-DistributionGroup
```

```
Set-DistributionGroup -Identity <DistributionGroupIdParameter> [-AcceptMessagesOnlyFrom <MultiValuedProperty>] [-Accept
<MultiValuedProperty>] [-AcceptMessagesOnlyFromSendersOrMembers <MultiValuedProperty>] [-Alias <String>] [-Arbitration
[-BypassModerationFromSendersOrMembers <MultiValuedProperty>] [-BypassNestedModerationEnabled <$true | $false>] [-Bypas
<SwitchParameter>] [-Confirm [<SwitchParameter>]] [-CreateDTMFMap <$true | $false>] [-CustomAttribute1 <String>] [-Cust
[-CustomAttribute11 <String>] [-CustomAttribute12 <String>] [-CustomAttribute13 <String>] [-CustomAttribute14 <String>
[-CustomAttribute2 <String>] [-CustomAttribute3 <String>] [-CustomAttribute4 <String>] [-CustomAttribute5 <String>] [-C
[-CustomAttribute7 <String>] [-CustomAttribute8 <String>] [-CustomAttribute9 <String>] [-DisplayName <String>] [-Domai
<ProxyAddressCollection>] [-EmailAddressPolicyEnabled <$true | $false>] [-ExpansionServer <String>] [-ExtensionCustomAt
[-ExtensionCustomAttribute2 <MultiValuedProperty>] [-ExtensionCustomAttribute3 <MultiValuedProperty>] [-ExtensionCustom
[-ExtensionCustomAttribute5 <MultiValuedProperty>] [-ForceUpgrade <SwitchParameter>] [-GenerateExternalDirectoryObjectI
[-GrantSendOnBehalfTo <MultiValuedProperty>] [-HiddenFromAddressListsEnabled <$true | $false>] [-IgnoreDefaultScope <Sw
[-IgnoreNamingPolicy <SwitchParameter>] [-MailTip <String>] [-MailTipTranslations <MultiValuedProperty>] [-ManagedBy <
[-MaxReceiveSize <Unlimited>] [-MaxSendSize <Unlimited>] [-MemberDepartRestriction <Closed | Open | ApprovalRequired>
Open | ApprovalRequired>] [-ModeratedBy <MultiValuedProperty>] [-ModerationEnabled <$true | $false>] [-Name <String>]
[-RejectMessagesFrom <MultiValuedProperty>] [-RejectMessagesFromDLMembers <MultiValuedProperty>] [-RejectMessagesFromSe
<MultiValuedProperty>] [-ReportToManagerEnabled <$true | $false>] [-ReportToOriginatorEnabled <$true | $false>] [-Requ
<$true | $false>] [-RoomList <SwitchParameter>] [-SamAccountName <String>] [-SendModerationNotifications <Never | Inter
[-SendOofMessageToOriginatorEnabled <$true | $false>] [-SimpleDisplayName <String>] [-UMDtmfMap <MultiValuedProperty>]
[-WindowsEmailAddress <SmtpAddress>] [<CommonParameters>]
```

From the above list of parameters we see there are two parameters for handling moderation of distribution groups. Reviewing the detailed description of these parameters we can get an understanding of what they are used for:

```
-ModeratedBy <MultiValuedProperty>
    The ModeratedBy parameter specifies one or more moderators for this recipient. A moderator
    approves messages sent to the recipient before the messages are delivered. A moderator
    must be a mailbox, mail user, or mail contact in your organization. You can use any value
    that uniquely identifies the moderator.
```

```
-ModerationEnabled <$true | $false>
    The ModerationEnabled parameter specifies whether moderation is enabled for this
    recipient. Valid value are:

    * $true Moderation is enabled for this recipient. Messages sent to this recipient must be
      approved by a moderator before the messages are delivered.
    * $false Moderation is disabled for this recipient. Messages sent to this recipient are
      delivered without the approval of a moderator. This is the default value.
    You use the ModeratedBy parameter to specify the moderators.
```

Combined, these two values enable control of message flow to a particular group.  Below is an example of how to configure moderation on a Distribution Group called 'Sales Dept':

```
Set-DistributionGroup "Sales Dept" -ModerationEnabled $true -ModeratedBy "Damian"
```

Note that when this is set, a Mail Tip might be displayed for users in OWA or Outlook depending on other configuration settings:



## Controlling Group Mail Flow

If moderators are not desired, other controllers can be put in place such as restricting who can send to the group or if external senders can send to an internal group.  Restrictions as to who can send to the group or who are blocked from sending to the group can also be set if so desired.

To control these settings we can review the list of parameters from the last section. The appropriate settings are as follows:

AcceptMessagesOnlyFrom

AcceptMessagesOnlyFromDLMembers

AcceptMessagesOnlyFromSendersOrMembers

RejectMessagesFrom

RejectMessagesFromDLMembers

RejectMessagesFromSendersOrMembers

Depending on what the desired restrictions are for a group, we can pick from the above list to configure these restrictions.

## Example 1

Take for example a company that has a group specifically for Sales. The Sales Department would like to restrict emails so that only users within the Sale Group can email the Sales Group distribution list. From the above parameters, it appears that either 'AcceptMessagesOnlyFrom' or 'AcceptMessagesOnlyFromDLMembers' would work. However, the restriction is for only group members so 'AcceptMessagesOnlyFromDLMembers' would be the ideal option for this scenario. Reviewing the parameter from Get-Help we can see that his acts like an Access Control List (ACL) on a distribution group:

```
-AcceptMessagesOnlyFromDLMembers <MultiValuedProperty>
    The AcceptMessagesOnlyFromDLMembers parameter specifies who is allowed to send messages to
    this recipient. Messages from other senders are rejected.
```

```
Set-DistributionGroup "Sales Dept" –AcceptMessagesOnlyFromDLMembers "Sales Dept"
```

When a message is sent to the group from someone outside the group they will now receive a Mail Tip:

You don't have permission to send to Sales Dept. Remove recipient

The end user also received an NDR:

**Delivery has failed to these recipients or groups:**

Sales Dept (SalesDept@Domain.Com)
Your message couldn't be delivered because you don't have permission to send to this distribution list. Ask the owner of the distribution list to grant you permission and then try again.

Users in the Sales Deptartment group will not receive a mail tip and will be the only ones who can send to this distribution group.

## Example 2

In another example a group has been created for C Level Executives and the directive from IT Management is that only direct reports may send emails to this new group. The group is called 'Company Executives' for this example.

We can then use PowerShell to get a list of the direct reports for each C Level executive:

First, we clear the array variable we will use to store the users allowed to send to this group:

```
$TeamMembers = @()
```

Next store the group name in a variable for use in the script:

```
$Group = "Company Executives"
```

Then all the members of the group are also stored in a variable. In order to do this, we use the Get-DistributionGroup and feed this to the Get-DistributionGroupMember command to get the members of $Group:

```
$Members = Get-DistributionGroup $Group | Get-DistributionGroupMember
```

Then a Foreach loop will read through each line in $Members to get all members and their direct reports:

```
Foreach ($Member in $Members) {
```

Within this loop, we first get the distinguishedName of each member and add it to $TeamMembers:

```
$TeamMembers += $Member.DistinguishedName
```

Next, the distinguishedName of all users with that manager are added to $TeamMembers:

```
$TeamMembers += (Get-ADUser -Properties * -Filter {Manager -eq $Member.DistinguishedName}).
DistinguishedName
}
```

With the $TeamMembers variable now storing all members of the group, their direct reports, and the loop finished, we need to remove any duplicates from $TeamMembers:

```
$TeamMembers = $TeamMembers | Select -Unique
```

Then the AcceptMessagesOnlyFrom parameter is set for the group with the $DirectReports:

```
Set-DistributionGroup $Group -AcceptMessagesOnlyFrom $DirectReports
```

Once set, we can verify the users are correctly configured:

```
Get-DistributionGroup "Company Executives" | ft AcceptMessagesOnlyFrom
```

```
AcceptMessagesOnlyFrom
----------------------
{16-TAP.Local/Users/Test User01, 16-TAP.Local/Users/Dave Stork, 16-TAP.Local/Users/Damian Scoles}
```

# Putting It All Together

Combining some knowledge from Chapter 11 and this chapter, we'll write a script that can provide a useful reporting script on mailboxes and groups within Exchange 2016. Let's take a typical environment that has user, shared, room, equipment and public folder mailboxes. There are also regular and dynamic distribution groups. You'd like to have a quick report that was generated by PowerShell that was able to display the number of mailboxes of each type, number of groups by type and the sizes of each mailbox category.

In the below script, we can use Get-Mailbox, Get-DistributionGroup, Get-DynamicDistributionGroup and Get-MailboxStatistics to do this. For finding each mailbox type, we look for a value called "RecipientTypeDetails". Why use that? Because it provides the mailbox differentiation information we need.

## Script Code

This first section uses the 'Get-Mailbox' cmdlet to get a list of mailboxes. The '-filter' parameter allows for a filter based on one mailbox property, which in our case is 'RecipientTypeDetails'. This attribute was chosen because it stores the type of mailbox the object is. Next, the ().**Count** bracket is used in order to get a count of whatever is returned from within the parentheses:

```
# Get mailbox and group counts per type
$DistributionGroupCount = (Get-DistributionGroup).Count
$DynDistributionGroupCount = (Get-DynamicDistributionGroup).Count
$AllMailboxCount = (Get-Mailbox).Count
$UserMailboxCount = (Get-Mailbox -Filter {RecipientTypeDetails -eq "UserMailbox"}).Count
$SharedMailboxCount = (Get-Mailbox -Filter {RecipientTypeDetails -eq "SharedMailbox"}).Count
$PublicFolderMailboxCount = (Get-Mailbox -PublicFolder).Count
$EquipmentMailboxCount = (Get-Mailbox -Filter {RecipientTypeDetails -eq "EquipmentMailbox"}).Count
$RoomMailboxCount = (Get-Mailbox -Filter {RecipientTypeDetails -eq "RoomMailbox"}).Count
```

Next, each mailbox type is processed with the Get-MailboxStatistics cmdlet to get statistical information on the mailboxes. The 'TotalItemSize' value is the size of the mailbox and using the '.Value.ToMB()' converts the value to MB. These values are also stored in variables like the first section of code, to be used in the reporting section, which will follow:

```
$PublicFolderMailboxUsage = ((Get-Mailbox -PublicFolder | Get-MailboxStatistics).TotalItemSize.Value.ToMB() | Measure-Object -Sum).Sum
$SharedMailboxUsage = ((Get-Mailbox -Filter {RecipientTypeDetails -eq "SharedMailbox"} | Get-MailboxStatistics).TotalItemSize.Value.ToMB() | Measure-Object -Sum).Sum
$UserMailboxUsage = ((Get-Mailbox -Filter {RecipientTypeDetails -eq "UserMailbox"} | Get-MailboxStatistics).TotalItemSize.Value.ToMB() | Measure-Object -Sum).Sum
$EquipmentMailboxUsage = ((Get-Mailbox -Filter {RecipientTypeDetails -eq "EquipmentMailbox"} | Get-MailboxStatistics).TotalItemSize.Value.ToMB() | Measure-Object -Sum).Sum
$RoomMailboxUsage = ((Get-Mailbox -Filter {RecipientTypeDetails -eq "RoomMailbox"} | Get-MailboxStatistics).TotalItemSize.Value.ToMB() | Measure-Object -Sum).Sum
```

For this last section of the script a visual report will be displayed in the PowerShell window which will give mailbox and group counts as well as the sizes of each type of mailbox in Exchange:

```
Write-Host "Number of Mailboxes found:" -ForegroundColor Green
Write-Host "-------------------------" -ForegroundColor Green
Write-Host "User Mailboxes: $UserMailboxCount." -ForegroundColor White
Write-Host "Shared Mailboxes: $SharedMailboxCount." -ForegroundColor White
Write-Host "Room Mailboxes: $RoomMailboxCount." -ForegroundColor White
Write-Host "Equipment Mailboxes: $EquipmentMailboxCount." -ForegroundColor White
Write-Host "Public Folder Mailboxes: $PublicFolderMailboxCount." -ForegroundColor White
Write-Host " " # Blank line for formatting
Write-Host "Number of Distribution Groups" -ForegroundColor Green
Write-Host "Distribution Groups: $DistributionGroupCount." -ForegroundColor White
Write-Host "Dynamic Distribution Groups: $DynDistributionGroupCount." -ForegroundColor White
Write-Host " " # Blank line for formatting
Write-Host "Mailbox Usage Stats" -ForegroundColor Green
Write-Host "User Mailboxes are $UserMailboxUsage MB in size." -ForegroundColor White
Write-Host "Shared Mailboxes are $SharedMailboxUsage MB in size." -ForegroundColor White
Write-Host "Equipment Mailboxes are $EquipmentMailboxUsage MB in size." -ForegroundColor White
Write-Host "Public Folder Mailboxes are $PublicFolderMailboxUsage MB in size." -ForegroundColor White
```

A quick run of the script generates a little concise report for Exchange:

```
Number of Mailboxes found:
--------------------------
User Mailboxes: 26.
Shared Mailboxes: 3.
Room Mailboxes: 1.
Equipment Mailboxes: 1.
Public Folder Mailboxes: 1.

Number of Distribution Groups
Distribution Groups: 8.
Dynamic Distribution Groups: 3.

Mailbox Usage Stats
User Mailboxes are 18713 MB in size.
Shared Mailboxes are 0 MB in size.
Equipment Mailboxes are 0 MB in size.
Public Folder Mailboxes are 0 MB in size.
```

# 13 Mobile Devices



Since the introduction of Exchange ActiveSync (EAS) in Exchange 2003 SP1, it has seen adoption over the years leading up to the current status that practically every mobile device has EAS capabilities.

There have been improvements every major build of Exchange Server, not just features but also in regards to access complacency and security. Regarding management, the adoption of PowerShell has been a welcome improvement, making admin control a lot easier than before.

To recap the whole process: A user has a device and a mailbox on Exchange Server 2016. The user wants to access their mailbox from that device and it has EAS capabilities. The user enters his or hers email address and their corresponding password. In a lot of cases the connection is successful and a pop-up appears warning you about security policies that have to be implemented. After accepting the user can now access mail, calendar, contacts and sometime additional features like Tasks or setting the Out of Office reply.

There are variants when used with conditional access from Office 365 Mobile Device Management (MDM)/Intune or other MDM solutions or when certificate based authentication is required.

In the background, a device partnership has been made between the users' mailbox and the device, which is manageable (locking, remote wiping etc.) belonging to the users and admin's capabilities. What is available depends on device capabilities and support.

In this chapter, we will go through device access, device policies, managing devices and some reporting. It's important to note that as with Exchange Server 2016, some cmdlets have been renamed from ActiveSync to MobileDevice, as the focus for Microsoft seems to be the Outlook app on iOS and Android and Outlook Mail app on Windows 10, which use some elements of EAS but leverage Exchange Web Services in some instances.

# Server Configuration

## EAS Virtual Directory

The ActiveSync Virtual Directory (vDir) is the object that holds the internal and external URLs and the authentication method. Each Exchange server has one virtual directory for ActiveSync. So be sure to configure all vDirs correctly.

To list all servers with an ActiveSync Virtual Directory (all Exchange 2016 servers, and Client Access Servers in legacy Exchange for coexistence with 2016) but in a fast way, use:

```
Get-ActiveSyncVirtualDirectory -ADPropertiesOnly
```

The ADPropertiesOnly switch prevents the download of each server's related IIS Metabase information and only returns the information stored in Active Directory. This will return the standard information in a much faster way than without this switch.

In order to set the internal and external URL for ActiveSync, use:

```
Set-ActiveSyncVirtualDirectory -Identity "SERVER\Microsoft-Server-ActiveSync (Default Web Site)" -InternalUrl https://eas.contoso.com/Microsoft-Server-ActiveSync -ExternalUrl https://eas.contoso.com/Microsoft-Server-ActiveSync
```

Note the distinct syntax for identity, first the server name followed by the vDir name. The internal and external URL require the Fully Qualified Domain Name of the URL and the server path. Please note the https at the beginning, if only http (the unencrypted variety) is used the devices try to connect without encryption.

If the configuration of the virtual directory has been corrupted, it might be required to recreate the virtual directory. Exchange Admin Center which provides a refresh button, but if you want somewhat more control you can do this via PowerShell as well.

```
Remove-ActiveSyncVirtualDirectory -Identity "SERVER\Microsoft-Server-ActiveSync (Default Web Site)"
```

Or somewhat more easy:

```
Get-ActiveSyncVirtualDirectory -Server SERVER | Remove-ActiveSyncVirtualDirectory
```

And to recreate a default ActiveSync Virtual Directory:

```
New-ActiveSyncVirtualDirectory -Server SERVER
```

Do not forget to re-configure the URLs and authentication requirements.

## Testing

Testing ActiveSync can be done via:

```
Test-ActiveSyncConnectivity
```

That will use the Extest account. If you want to test ActiveSync for a specific user, you have to save the credentials in a variable and then present the variable to the test:

```
$Cred = Get-Credential
Test-ActiveSyncConnectivity -MailboxCredential $Cred
```

This will show something like this:

```
[PS] C:\>$cred = Get-Credential

cmdlet Get-Credential at command pipeline position 1
Supply values for the following parameters:
Credential
[PS] C:\>Test-ActiveSyncConnectivity -MailboxCredential $Cred

CasServer   LocalSite      Scenario        Result  Latency(MS) Error
116-ex01    Default-Fi...  Options         Failure             [System.Net.WebExcept...
```

In this case the ActiveSync test failed for the test user. Use the command again with Format-List (FL) to investigate further.


# EAS Policies

The most important thing regarding EAS, are the EAS Mailbox policies that define what features are available (such as Camera, downloads from the Store, etc.) and the level of security (password policy, remote wipe options). This is configured in the Mobile Device Mailbox Policy, which is assigned to mailboxes. You can have multiple policies which can be assigned to different mailboxes. However, an assigned EAS Mailbox policy will be valid for all devices that have a device partnership with that specific account; you cannot have a different policy on the same mailbox for different devices.

## Managing Mobile Device Mailbox Policies

The basis of controlling devices with Exchange is the Mobile Device Mailbox policy, previously known as the Exchange ActiveSync (EAS) Mailbox policy. The policy defines specific security settings the device might have to support and implement, and the user has to accept them in order to gain access to their mailbox.

You can have multiple policies in your organization, to cater different security policies. But a user (or mailbox) can only have one policy applied, which is valid for all devices connected to the mailbox.

For those who are wondering about users that have multiple mailboxes configured on their device: the policies are applied cumulative with the most restrictive setting being applied over less restrictive settings or undefined settings.

### Listing

To get a listing of current Mobile Device mailbox policies you use:

```
Get-MobileDeviceMailboxPolicy
```

You would see at least the Default policy and its values in raw output:

```
[PS] C:\>Get-MobileDeviceMailboxPolicy

RunspaceId                             : c01b70d6-15b9-454a-88d9-c8710ed75c41
AllowNonProvisionableDevices           : True
AlphanumericPasswordRequired           : False
AttachmentsEnabled                     : True
DeviceEncryptionEnabled                : False
RequireStorageCardEncryption           : False
PasswordEnabled                        : False
PasswordRecoveryEnabled                : False
DevicePolicyRefreshInterval            : Unlimited
AllowSimplePassword                    : True
MaxAttachmentSize                      : Unlimited
WSSAccessEnabled                       : True
UNCAccessEnabled                       : True
MinPasswordLength                      :
MaxInactivityTimeLock                  : Unlimited
MaxPasswordFailedAttempts              : Unlimited
PasswordExpiration                     : Unlimited
PasswordHistory                        : 0
IsDefault                              : True
AllowApplePushNotifications            : True
AllowMicrosoftPushNotifications        : True
AllowGooglePushNotifications           : True
AllowStorageCard                       : True
AllowCamera                            : True
RequireDeviceEncryption                : False
AllowUnsignedApplications              : True
AllowUnsignedInstallationPackages      : True
AllowWiFi                              : True
AllowTextMessaging                     : True
AllowPOPIMAPEmail                      : True
AllowIrDA                              : True
RequireManualSyncWhenRoaming           : False
AllowDesktopSync                       : True
AllowHTMLEmail                         : True
RequireSignedSMIMEMessages             : False
RequireEncryptedSMIMEMessages          : False
```

** **Note** ** The cmdlet Get-ActiveSyncMailboxPolicy does the same as Get-MobileDeviceMailboxPolicy, but is deprecated and will be removed in a future version of Exchange.

## Creating and Assigning

You can create additional Mobile Device policies via:

    New-MobileDeviceMailboxPolicy -Name "VIP"

```
[PS] C:\>New-MobileDeviceMailboxPolicy -Name VIP

RunspaceId                             : c01b70d6-15b9-454a-88d9-c8710ed75c41
AllowNonProvisionableDevices           : False
AlphanumericPasswordRequired           : False
AttachmentsEnabled                     : True
DeviceEncryptionEnabled                : False
RequireStorageCardEncryption           : False
PasswordEnabled                        : False
PasswordRecoveryEnabled                : False
DevicePolicyRefreshInterval            : Unlimited
AllowSimplePassword                    : True
MaxAttachmentSize                      : Unlimited
WSSAccessEnabled                       : True
UNCAccessEnabled                       : True
MinPasswordLength                      :
MaxInactivityTimeLock                  : Unlimited
MaxPasswordFailedAttempts              : Unlimited
PasswordExpiration                     : Unlimited
PasswordHistory                        : 0
IsDefault                              : False
AllowApplePushNotifications            : True
AllowMicrosoftPushNotifications        : True
AllowGooglePushNotifications           : True
AllowStorageCard                       : True
AllowCamera                            : True
RequireDeviceEncryption                : False
AllowUnsignedApplications              : True
AllowUnsignedInstallationPackages      : True
AllowWiFi                              : True
AllowTextMessaging                     : True
AllowPOPIMAPEmail                      : True
AllowIrDA                              : True
RequireManualSyncWhenRoaming           : False
AllowDesktopSync                       : True
AllowHTMLEmail                         : True
RequireSignedSMIMEMessages             : False
RequireEncryptedSMIMEMessages          : False
```

Without any parameters configured a default configuration will be used.

You can add values at creation or adjust values after creating the policy. Example:

```
Set-MobileDeviceMailboxPolicy -Identity "VIP"  -DeviceEncryptionEnabled $True
```

This will require Device Encryption on our previously created policy.

If a policy isn't required anymore, you can remove it:

```
Remove-MobileDeviceMailboxPolicy -Identity "VIP"
```

Be sure that the policy isn't assigned to any mailbox or are assigned to another policy, otherwise the mailboxes will revert to the Default policy. You can define the default Mobile Device mailbox policy in the policy itself (only one can be the default, obviously):

```
Set-MobileDeviceMailboxPolicy -Identity "VIP" -IsDefault $True
```

Assigning the MobileDevice Mailbox policy is done via Set-CASMailbox:

```
Set-CASMailbox JanCrichton@contoso.com -ActiveSyncMailboxPolicy "VIP"
```

And if required you can assign a specific policy to all mailboxes, however you could just use the Default policy. It's probably more common to have most mailboxes use the default policy and assign specific policy to specific users. One way is to use groups to determine who would require a certain policy:

```
(Get-Group -Identity "VIP").Members | Set-CASMailbox -ActiveSyncMailboxPolicy "VIP"
```

Now, this is just one possible way but it should give you an idea how to use and assign multiple Mobile Device Mailbox Policies.

**Note:** The cmdlets New-ActiveSyncMailboxPolicy, Set-ActiveSyncMailboxPolicy, Remove-ActiveSyncMailboxPolicy are the same as respectivly New-MobileDeviceMailboxPolicy, Set-MobileDeviceMailboxPolicy, Remove-MobileDeviceMailboxPolicy but are deprecated and will be removed in a future version of Exchange.

## Best Practices

It depends on your organization and your stance on types of supported devices (non-managed or highly managed with conditional access), but most organizations agree on basic security:

### Allow Non-Provisionable Devices

Allows devices to synchronize, even if it's clear that they cannot apply certain policies; for instance Device Encryption. This is basically the "Best Effort" setting; if the device supports a set feature, it has to enable it. If the device does not support a feature, it will still be allowed to sync despite possible lower security. Disable (default) when you want to have a strict adherence to the device policy. But to enable it use:

```
Set-MobileDeviceMailboxPolicy -Identity Default -AllowNonProvisionableDevices $True
```

### Required Password

With this setting a password is required. This means a user has to input a password or PIN at boot time and to unlock the device. In this way, access to company data can be protected. There are different choices to be made, a numeric PIN or alphanumeric password.

```
Set-MobileDeviceMailboxPolicy -Identity Default -PasswordEnabled:$True
```

You can set the minimal amount of characters required for the PIN:

```
Set-MobileDeviceMailboxPolicy -Identity Default -MinPasswordLength 4
```

In this case the PIN has a minimum of four numbers. You can have a forced minimum password length with a maximum of 16 (so passwords need to be at least sixteen, if so configured). However, four or six are common.

What about fingerprint access? This feature is dependent on the device OS as to how that is handled. In iOS you are require to enter the PIN the first time at start up and then fingerprint authentication via TouchID is possible. With Android, it's very dependent on how it's implemented, however a lot of pattern locks weren't possible when requiring a PIN. Consider this when configuring this setting.

You can force an alphanumeric password, such as on Desktops.

```
Set-MobileDeviceMailboxPolicy -Identity Default -AlphanumericPasswordRequired:$True
```

If enabled, you can set the amount of complex characters, ranging from one to four.

```
Set-MobileDeviceMailboxPolicy -Identity Default -MinPasswordComplexCharacters 4
```

Where MinPasswordComplexCharacters can be one of the following values:

1. Digits only
2. Digits and lower case letters
3. Digits, lower case letters, and upper case letters
4. Digits, lower case letters, upper case letters, and special characters

However, on most mobiles a value of four is not very user friendly and it's not very common, but due to more combinations and complexity of these kinds of passwords it does provide extra security. But you won't make many friends with those kind of requirements (unless you'll only allow devices with a physical or large on-screen keyboard).

Other ways to increase password security, is to limit the reuse of old passwords:

```
Set-MobileDeviceMailboxPolicy -Identity Default -PasswordHistory 2
```

With two in this example the previous two passwords are remembered and blocked from being reused and with zero no passwords are remembered. Determining an ideal number is dependent on how often the device password has to change. You can control that by adding a password age limit:

```
Set-MobileDeviceMailboxPolicy -Identity Default -PasswordExpiration '90.00:00:00'
```

The value syntax is DD.HH:MM:SS, or days, hours, minutes and seconds.

As with Outlook clients, you will need to find a balance between user friendliness and security.

## Encrypted Device and Memory Card

These settings will make encryption mandatory for the device itself. Nowadays most modern mobile OS have device encryption enabled per default, but if it is not it might require the device to perform a reboot and additional configuration time. However, this will mean that the complete device is encrypted, which means any sensitive company data is secure from malicious attempts to access this when locked.

```
Set-MobileDeviceMailboxPolicy -Identity Default -RequireDeviceEncryption:$True
```

Some devices offer to extend the storage capacity via memory cards. Some OS's allow applications and their data to be moved to the memory card or data from within the app is stored on the card. When the card is not encrypted, that data is readable for anyone that has access to the card. For instance, when the device is stolen or lost. An encrypted card will prevent unintentional data leaks. However, some devices require the card to be formatted when encryption was not set initially. This could mean data loss. Warn your users when enabling this option, which you can in this way:

```
Set-MobileDeviceMailboxPolicy -Identity Default -RequireStorageCardEncryption:$True
```

### Lock Device After x Minutes

Same idea with automatic locks on desktop computers, requiring users to authenticate in order to continue their session. Adds security when the device is (temporarily) left unattended or lost, narrowing the window the device and its data is accessible. With mobile devices, often a PIN is allowed for easily accessing the device. Some apps lock only the access to the app with a PIN, while most lock the whole device.

```
Set-MobileDeviceMailboxPolicy -Identity "VIP" -MaxInactivityTimeLock '00:15:00'
```

This example will lock the device after fifteen minutes of inactivity. In most cases this value is the same as the desktop lock policy, which makes sense as users are already use to those kinds of mechanism and makes explaining somewhat easier.

### Wipe Device After x Failed Attempts

To prevent hammering and brute force attempts by just guessing the password and trying endlessly, this policy adds a self-destruct mechanism to the device or data in the app (depending on various mobile OS and other parameters).

```
Set-MobileDeviceMailboxPolicy -Identity "VIP" -MaxPasswordFailedAttempts 8
```

In this example the device will be wiped after eight failed attempts to access the contents of the device by trying to guess the password, this is an anti-hammering feature which can be useful when devices end up in the wrong hands. It does not require a connection to Exchange, so this will work even when the device has no Internet connection. This also means that an admin cannot override it remotely. The valid range is four to sixteen attempts.

Be sure that users are informed about this feature and its consequences when configured. Especially if the device is not company owned, it will surely contain personal data (like photos) which will most likely also be wiped. I've had cases that devices where wiped because their young children got hold of their device and pushed the screen buttons over and over, accidentally activating this feature.

**Disable camera etc.**

Additional options are to disable certain hardware features of the device, such as Bluetooth, the camera or other requirements. Do note that these (and some other settings) require the use of an Exchange Enterprise Client Access License in addition to the Exchange Standard Client Access License.

This example would disable the camera (if present) on the device:

```
Set-MobileDeviceMailboxPolicy -Identity Default -AllowCamera:$False
```

In some cases, it even makes camera apps unavailable (for sure in iOS).

There are a lot more configurations possible, it depends on your requirements and the capabilities of the devices you require to adhere to these policies. Be sure to test these policies out with test devices before deploying to your users.

# Managing Devices

## Device Access ABQ

One of the improvements introduced in Exchange Server 2010 is Device Access Rules, sometimes referred to as ABQ which stands for Allow, Block or Quarantine.

This way it's possible to either block or quarantine specific types of devices. Perhaps a specific DeviceOS has issues (which has happened in the past with iOS 6.x for instance) or you want to limit access to devices that are supported by your organization.

With Block, devices are permanently prohibited access to Exchange; you'd have to resolve the limitation (for instance DeviceOS version due to an update) and remove the blocked partnership and try again. As with Quarantine the partnership does not have to be removed from the mailbox, just the blocking issue has to be resolved (for instance updating the device OS to a supported version).

You can add a block with New-ActiveSyncDeviceAccessRule:

```
New-ActiveSyncDeviceAccessRule -QueryString "iOS 9.0.2 13A452" -Characteristic DeviceOS
-AccessLevel Quarantine
```

As you can see, there are several parameters involved. Starting at the back is the AccessLevel; in this example the access rule will set the access level to Quarantine, other options are Allow or Block. This means that when the blocking issue has been resolved, the user can connect again without removing the partnership, resulting in a sort of temporary ban. For instance, if your organization doesn't support a certain Device OS version because of known bugs (iOS has had some in the past), you should use this option.

The Characteristic parameter can be used to configure the specific device identifier which has to be handled by the Access rule, valid values are DeviceModel, DeviceType, DeviceOS, UserAgent and XMWSLHeader. Those values can be extracted from Exchange when those devices already have made successful partnership with the Exchange mailbox, use:

```
Get-MobileDevice | Format-List DeviceOS, DeviceModel, DeviceType, DeviceUserAgent
```

Which will result in something like this:

```
PS C:\> Get-MobileDevice | Format-List DeviceOS,DeviceModel,DeviceType,DeviceUserAgent


DeviceOS        : iOS 9.0.2 13A452
DeviceModel     : iPad2C1
DeviceType      : iPad
DeviceUserAgent : Apple-iPad2C1/1301.452

DeviceOS        : Windows Phone 10.0.10149
DeviceModel     : RM-1034_1032
DeviceType      : WP8
DeviceUserAgent : MSFT-WP/10.0.10149

DeviceOS        : Windows Phone 8.10.14219
DeviceModel     : RM-1045_1064
DeviceType      : WP8
DeviceUserAgent : MSFT-WP/8.10.14219
```

DeviceOS is the actual OS version and build, DeviceModel the specific model, DeviceType the major type (Android, iPad, iPhone etc.) and finally DeviceUserAgent. DeviceUserAgent is the same as UserAgent. The XMWSL-Header is a new characteristic and its values aren't found in Exchange, but you'd probably can find them in your Exchange's IIS logs. However, most of the times DeviceOS is used with ABQ.

Alternatively, you could get (some) device information via Get-ActiveSyncDeviceClass:

```
Get-ActiveSyncDeviceClass | Ft *device*
```

Which provides this kind of output:

```
PS C:\> Get-ActiveSyncDeviceClass |  Ft *device*

DeviceType   DeviceModel
----------   -----------
WP8          RM-1045_1064
WindowsMail  Venue 8 Pro 5830
WP8          RM-1104_15250
iPad         iPad2C1
WindowsMail  Rampage Formula
WindowsMail  Surface 3
WindowsMail  Dell Inc. Precision M4700 Precision M4700
WP8          RM-1034_1032
WindowsMail  Virtual Machine
Outlook      Outlook for iOS and Android
WindowsMail  WindowsMail
```

The values have to be configured via the QueryString parameter. Note that this is a string value and does not support Regex, wildcards or partial matches; it has to be exact. This also means that for every Characteristic type you will require a separate Device Access rule. If you haven't found the correct values, you'd have to wait on users to connect or fall back to the Internet for those values.

Removing a device class is possible, this can be required if you want a lean list. This could be the case because you now require limited access to only a specific set of devices after allowing all device classes.

```
Remove-ActiveSyncDeviceClass -Identity "WindowsMail§Virtual Machine"
```

Another option available is to change the default ActiveSync behavior with Set-ActiveSyncOrganizationSettings. You can set the default DefaultAccessLevel to Allow, Block or Quarantine. The default is Allow, setting it to Quarantine is probably the next user friendly setting. You can enable email requests via the multi valued property AdminMailRecipients, and add extra clarification in the email message users get when their devices are blocked/ quarantined with OtaNotificationMailInsert (when a device update is required) and UserMailInsert (to add additional information in the notification mail).

As you can see in the above example the DeviceOS and DeviceUserAgent are version dependent. This means that you might have to add an additional rule if the DeviceOS changes. Therefore, you could focus on DeviceType if you want to regulate the different types of devices (no Windows Phone, just iPhones or something like this). However, you will probably already see some of the caveats of ABQ, if so you might want to invest in real MDM solutions.

** **Note** ** The cmdlet Get-ActiveSyncDevice does the same as Get-MobileDevice, but is deprecated and will be removed in a future version of Exchange.

In order to check whether there is already a Device Access Rule in place, use:

    Get-ActiveSyncDeviceAccessRule

This would give you output like this (if there is a rule present):

```
PS C:\> Get-ActiveSyncDeviceAccessRule


RunspaceId          : 21d04711-9245-4a26-a70c-5c001f6add7f
QueryString         : iPhone5C2
Characteristic      : DeviceModel
AccessLevel         : Quarantine
Name                : iPhone5C2 (DeviceModel)
AdminDisplayName    :
ExchangeVersion     : 0.10 (14.0.100.0)
DistinguishedName   : CN=iPhone5C2 (DeviceModel),CN=Mobile Mailbox Se
Identity            : iPhone5C2 (DeviceModel)
Guid                : 17206491-3464-42e8-b426-78dad24b8360
ObjectCategory      : EURPR04A002.prod.outlook.com/Configuration/Sche
ObjectClass         : {top, msExchDeviceAccessRule}
WhenChanged         : 1-2-2014 06:45:55
WhenCreated         : 1-2-2014 06:45:30
WhenChangedUTC      : 1-2-2014 05:45:55
WhenCreatedUTC      : 1-2-2014 05:45:30
OrganizationId      : EURPR04A002.prod.outlook.com/Microsoft Exchange
Id                  : iPhone5C2 (DeviceModel)
OriginatingServer   : AM3PR04A002DC12.EURPR04A002.prod.outlook.com
IsValid             : True
ObjectState         : Unchanged
```

In this case the access rule will Quarantine certain iPhone models.

When there is no requirement for the Device Access Rule anymore, you can remove it via:

    Remove-ActiveSyncDeviceAccessRule -Identity "iPhone5C2 (DeviceModel)"

Or when the requirements change, you can change the AccessLevel to another value.

    Set-ActiveSyncDeviceAccessRule -Identity "iPhone5C2 (DeviceModel)" -AccessLevel "Allow"

However, after changing this AccessLevel, you might have to manually check whether all devices are now adhering to the new access level.

## Default Access Level

But what if you only want to allow one specific device (because it's company owned) and block every other device? Even with multiple device access rules you cannot be certain only the specific devices have access to your Exchange organization.

Luckily you can set a default access level for mobile devices. To see the current configuration use:

    Get-ActiveSyncOrganizationSetting

Which gives you an unformatted output, like below (with default values):

```
[PS] C:\>Get-ActiveSyncOrganizationSettings

RunspaceId                         : f72910e9-7020-40ff-8060-289aedf26258
DefaultAccessLevel                 : Allow
UserMailInsert                     :
AllowAccessForUnSupportedPlatform  : False
AdminMailRecipients                : {}
OtaNotificationMailInsert          :
DeviceFiltering                    :
Name                               : Mobile Mailbox Settings
IsIntuneManaged                    : False
OtherWellKnownObjects              : {}
AdminDisplayName                   :
ExchangeVersion                    : 0.10 (14.0.100.0)
DistinguishedName                  : CN=Mobile Mailbox Settings,CN=2016 Organization,CN=Microsoft
                                     Exchange,CN=Services,CN=Configuration,DC=lab2016,DC=com
Identity                           : Mobile Mailbox Settings
Guid                               : 9d2ae890-9616-4e49-bd42-e655109c8182
ObjectCategory                     : lab2016.com/Configuration/Schema/ms-Exch-Mobile-Mailbox-Settings
ObjectClass                        : {top, msExchMobileMailboxSettings}
WhenChanged                        : 4/29/2015 3:53:54 PM
WhenCreated                        : 4/29/2015 3:53:54 PM
WhenChangedUTC                     : 4/29/2015 1:53:54 PM
WhenCreatedUTC                     : 4/29/2015 1:53:54 PM
OrganizationId                     :
Id                                 : Mobile Mailbox Settings
OriginatingServer                  : L16-DC01.lab2016.com
IsValid                            : True
ObjectState                        : Unchanged
```

Changing the values can be done via:

    Set-ActiveSyncOrganizationSettings -DefaultAccessLevel Quarantine -UserMailInsert "Contact IT for access"

This will set the default access toward Quarantine and will send a mail to the user with additional information.

Do note, that you can then allow the specific device on a user level (without affecting other similar devices) or create a specific Device Access rule, which overrule the Organization settings. This is why if you already have users connecting with ActiveSync devices and you need to implement (or change) the default access level, in order to prevent current devices to be unable to access Exchange you have to create separate device access rules allowing those devices (if so required).

## Allowing a Blocked/Quarantined Device

If a device has been blocked or quarantined, an admin can override this. You have to use the Set-CASMailbox in order to achieve this:

```
Set-CASMailbox -ActiveSyncAllowedDeviceIDs @('2FA6AB45DD32ECF337F603CBC6393ECB') -Identity JanCrichton@contoso.com
```

Identity is the UserMailbox containing the specific device and with ActiveSyncAllowdDeviceIDs you can add devices in the allowed list. This is a multi-valued property as indicated by the formatting. Take that into account when the user has multiple devices that have had a block or quarantine.

The value is the specific device ID. This is found via the Get-MobileDevice cmdlet:

```
Get-MobileDevice | ft FriendlyName, DeviceID
```

Which results into this:

## Getting Devices for a Mailbox

Mobile and ActiveSync devices are objects stored in the AD under an ExchangeActiveSyncDevices object under the user's account. To manage an individual device, you must have the full distinguished named (DN) path of the object. A DN can be something like:

```
lab2016.com/Lab/Jan Crichton/ExchangeActiveSyncDevices/WindowsMail§FCC88BEB8E0A665D7FB83BA17BB340A9
```

If you want get devices for a specific user, use the Get-MobileDevice command with the -Mailbox parameter added with the correct identity:

```
Get-MobileDevice -Mailbox JanCrichton@contoso.com | ft FriendlyName, DeviceID, Identity
```

Which would result into something like this:



Note that in this example you also see a TestActiveSyncConnectivity "device", this is the Managed Availability test probe.

## Device Wipe

The most drastic security measure in order to prevent data leakage is of course the remote wipe. This feature has been available in EAS from the beginning and enables either the user or the admin to completely wipe the device and reset it toward a factory default. In recent years, some OSs or apps implemented a partial wipe, deleting only the account info and downloaded data for that app. Due to the rise of using your personal device for business purposes, the fact that EAS could wipe your device and all of your personal data became more and more controversial.

Some DeviceOS's or the app that are used only wipe the data obtained via the EAS synchronization and not for instance your precious pets or children's photos. Do note that they report a successful wipe, but do not assume that the compete device has been reset to factory defaults. Saved attachments may be present on external storage, encrypted or not encrypted (depending on device policies). So, if you need guarantees, managing your devices via ActiveSync is probably not adequate and you should investigate Mobile Device Management (MDM) such as Microsoft System Center Configuration Manager (SCCM) with or without Microsoft Intune, or use the Office 365 MDM solution. There are also third party solutions like AirWatch and MobileIron.

A user can also initiate a remote wipe from webmail (OWA), but an admin can do so as well using the Clear-MobileDevice cmdlet, using the full Identity value:

```
Clear-MobileDevice -Identity "contoso.com/Users/Jill Smith/ExchangeActiveSyncDevices/
iPhone§ApplF2LJPJK5F8H5" -NotificationEmailAddresses Jill@Contoso.Com
```

Please note that Identity defines the specific mobile device, not the mailbox ID as a user can easily have multiple (active) devices partnered with their mailbox. A notification email address is optional, but it can be a helpful indicator for the end-user as to what just happened.

The next time the device connects to Exchange via ActiveSync, the device notices the wipe request and will adhere according how the app or OS would handle it normally. This also means you get confirmation whether the wipe request was received.

Another consideration is when you want to re-introduce the previously wiped device to Exchange, the wipe command still stands and will wipe the device again as soon as you connect it to Exchange.

You can cancel the wipe request by adding the Cancel switch to the command:

```
Clear-MobileDevice -Identity "contoso.com/Users/Jill Smith/ExchangeActiveSyncDevices/
iPhone§ApplF2LJPJK5F8H5" -Cancel
```

Another option is to remove the device partnership. However, if the device was lost and in the hands of a malicious person, keeping wipe request in place even will be more secure way to remove data from the device and to prevent unsolicited access to Exchange. If your credentials are compromised, the device will be wiped again immediately after they connect to Exchange (if the device still matches the same partnership, a software update might break that relationship).

Note: The cmdlet Clear-ActiveSyncDevice does the same as Clear-MobileDevice, but is deprecated and will be removed in a future version of Exchange. The same is valid for Get-ActiveSyncDeviceStatistics which has its equivalent in Get-MobileDeviceStatistics.

## Removing a Device

There might be reasons to remove a mobile device, for instance if there are too many stale partnerships it can prevent users adding a new device; the device limit is per default 10.

You can remove the device with same cmdlet as with removing the wipe command.

```
Remove-MobileDevice -Identity "contoso.com/Users/Jill Smith/ExchangeActiveSyncDevices/
iPhone§ApplF2LJPJK5F8H5" -NotificationEmailAddresses jill@contoso.com
```

**Note:** The cmdlet Remove-ActiveSyncDevice does the same as Remove-MobileDevice, but is deprecated and will be removed in a future version of Exchange.

## ActiveSync Device Limit

Since Exchange 2010 there has been a device limit of 10 ActiveSync devices for each mailbox. In normal cases that should be more than enough, however if a user switches devices frequently (because of device or app testing) they might get hit by this as stale device partnerships are still counted towards the total of 10.

Best thing is to remove the mobile devices that aren't being used anymore, but for those who do really require more than 10 devices you can change this. The setting is stored in the default Global Throttling policy. You can see the (ActiveSync) settings via:

```
Get-ThrottlingPolicy | FL *EAS*
```

Which would give you something like this:

```
[PS] C:\>Get-ThrottlingPolicy | FL *EAS*

EasMaxConcurrency                 : 10
EasMaxBurst                       : 480000
EasRechargeRate                   : 1800000
EasCutoffBalance                  : 600000
EasMaxDevices                     : 100
EasMaxDeviceDeletesPerMonth       : Unlimited
EasMaxInactivityForDeviceCleanup  : Unlimited
```

The parameter we're interested in is the EasMaxConcurrency setting, which is 10 per default. However, it is a best practice to leave default policy settings as is and create a separate Throttling policy in which the new values are defined. You then can assign the Throttling policy to those users requiring more than 10 devices concurrently.

Creating a new Throttling policy with a new threshold value:

```
New-ThrottlingPolicy -Name EASConcurrencyLimit -EasMaxConcurrency 15
```

Assigning the new Throttling policy to Gene Ricks mailbox:

```
Set-Mailbox -Identity Gene.Ricks@Contoso.Com -ThrottlingPolicy EASConcurrencyLimit
```

The result is this:

```
[PS] C:\>New-ThrottlingPolicy -Name EASConcurrencyLimit -EasMaxConcurrency 15

Name                                      ThrottlingPolicyScope                 IsServiceAccount
----                                      ---------------------                 ----------------
EASConcurrencyLimit                       Regular                               False
[PS] C:\>Set-Mailbox -Identity gene.ricks@contoso.com -ThrottlingPolicy EASConcurrencyLimit
[PS] C:\>
```

## Autoblocking Thresholds

Autoblocking thresholds are not a part of device access rules, as these are best comparable with Throttling policies specific for ActiveSync in general. If it's detected that a specific device misbehaves, the Device Autoblock feature can temporarily block devices from accessing Exchange.

You can see the currently configured values with:

Get-ActiveSyncDeviceAutoblockThreshold

```
[PS] C:\>Get-ActiveSyncDeviceAutoblockThreshold | FT *behavior*, DeviceBlockDuration -AutoSize

          BehaviorType BehaviorTypeIncidenceLimit BehaviorTypeIncidenceDuration DeviceBlockDuration
          ------------ -------------------------- ----------------------------- -------------------
      UserAgentsChanges                          0 00:00:00                      00:00:00
        RecentCommands                           0 00:00:00                      00:00:00
               Watsons                           0 00:00:00                      00:00:00
          OutOfBudgets                           0 00:00:00                      00:00:00
          SyncCommands                           0 00:00:00                      00:00:00
 EnableNotificationEmail                         0 00:00:00                      00:00:00
       CommandFrequency                          0 00:00:00                      00:00:00
```

The example below has some formatting for readability. The values are the default values:

You can change these values:

Set-ActivesyncDeviceAutoblockThreshold -Identity "Watsons" -BehaviorTypeIncidenceLimit 5 -BehaviorTypeIncidenceDuration 01:00:00 -DeviceBlockDuration 01:00:00 -AdminEmailInsert "Your device had too many errors and is temporarily blocked"

BehaviorTypeIncidenceLimit is the number of times the specified behavior is allowed to occur before the block occurs, another option is to configure the BehaviorTypeIncidenceDuration which specifies with which intervals in minutes the behavior must occur in order for the device to become blocked.

Additional available parameters are the DeviceBlockDuration which is the amount of time the device won't be able to sync with Exchange. Another is AdminEmailInsert, which is the text sent to the device user explaining why their device has been (temporarily) blocked and could provide information on how long this block will last and other information.

This provides a way to cope with devices that have a problematic implementation of ActiveSync. You can determine the specific BehaviorType from IIS logs on your Exchange servers or other ways of (network) monitoring that is able to inspect HTTPS packets.

# Reporting

To get a feel of where your company data resides, it's common to create an overview of clients (and especially mobile devices). What kind of device types, device OS builds, what was the last sync, etc. can be useful information to check on your BYOD implementation or perhaps even choosing a third party Mobile Device Management (MDM) solution. You may want to know what you have and whether you can manage them with a certain third-party product. Or maybe you just are a numbers geek and just want to know!

These examples tend to use Format-Table (or FT) to modify output. However, there's a lot more (potentially) useful information in the output, so check that out and experiment with it.

### Types of devices/OS etc.

If you require a list of used Devicetypes (in order to build a device access rule for instance), use the following:

```
(Get-MobileDevice -ResultSize Unlimited).Devicetype | Sort-Object |Get-Unique
```

If you want a list with all devices DeviceOS's, use the following:

```
(Get-MobileDevice -ResultSize Unlimited).DeviceOS|Select $_.DeviceOS -Unique
```

The ResultSize parameter is used in case there are more than 1,000 devices connected to Exchange.

### Stale partnerships (last sync)

You might want to create a list with all devices and their last successful synchronization, using this cmdlet you can:

```
Get-MobileDevice|Get-MobileDeviceStatistics|FTDeviceFriendlyName,DeviceID,LastSyncAttemptTime,
LastSuccessSync -Auto
```

This will give you all devices and their sync times. However, you might want to sort it on the sync date:

```
Get-MobileDevice|Get-MobileDeviceStatistics|Sort ($_.LastSuccessSync) | FT DeviceFriendlyName,
DeviceID, LastSyncAttemptTime, LastSuccessSync -Auto
```

Note, both of these cmdlets may take a while to produce results.

As it stands now it will be sorted with the oldest date first in the table. Note that the ResultSize hasn't been added, which might be required if you have more than a thousand devices.

## Blocked/Quarantined Devices

Each device has a DeviceAccessState which shows whether the device has been Blocked or Quarantined. This makes it simple to make a list:

```
Get-Mobiledevice -Filter {DeviceAccessState -ne "Allowed"} | FT FriendlyName, DeviceAccessState,
UserDisplayName -Auto
```

In this case the Get-MobileDevice cmdlet has a filter option, so we can use it to filter out what we don't want to see. In this case Allowed devices.

## Wiped Devices

This information is stored in the device statistics. To see whether devices have been successfully wiped, use this:

Get-MobileDevice | Get-MobileDeviceStatistics | Where {$_.Status -eq "DeviceWipeSucceeded"}

You can see something like this:

```
[PS] C:\>Get-MobileDevice|Get-MobileDeviceStatistics | Where {$_.Status -eq "DeviceWipeSucceeded"}

RunspaceId                      : 75ebeb44-7a0c-4c1e-8909-46edbe6fee1d
FirstSyncTime                   : 1/17/2017 5:43:36 PM
LastPolicyUpdateTime            : 1/17/2017 5:58:11 PM
LastSyncAttemptTime             : 1/17/2017 5:54:44 PM
LastSuccessSync                 : 1/17/2017 5:54:44 PM
DeviceType                      : WindowsMail
DeviceID                        : 2FA6AB45DD32ECF337F603CBC6393ECB
DeviceUserAgent                 : MSFT-WIN-3/10.0.10586
DeviceWipeSentTime              : 1/17/2017 5:58:11 PM
DeviceWipeRequestTime           : 1/17/2017 5:55:09 PM
DeviceWipeAckTime               : 1/17/2017 5:58:11 PM
LastPingHeartbeat               :
RecoveryPassword                : ********
DeviceModel                     : Virtual Machine
DeviceImei                      :
DeviceFriendlyName              : WINDOWS10VMB
DeviceOS                        : Windows 10.0.10586
DeviceOSLanguage                : English
DevicePhoneNumber               :
MailboxLogReport                :
DeviceEnableOutboundSMS         : False
DeviceMobileOperator            : OperatorName
Identity                        : lab2016.com/Lab/Jan
                                  Crichton/ExchangeActiveSyncDevices/WindowsMail§2FA6AB45DD32ECF337F603CBC6393ECB
Guid                            : 5b2a216c-9466-4f93-9a44-e0cec9f174d2
IsRemoteWipeSupported           : True
Status                          : DeviceWipeSucceeded
StatusNote                      : To sync with the server, you need to remove this partnership from the list after th
                                  wipe completes successfully. For security reasons, your device will continue wiping
                                  data if you try to synchronize again.
DeviceAccessState               : Blocked
DeviceAccessStateReason         : Policy
DeviceAccessControlRule         :
DevicePolicyApplied             : VIP_temp
DevicePolicyApplicationStatus   : AppliedInFull
LastDeviceWipeRequestor         : Administrator@contoso.com
ClientVersion                   : 14.1
NumberOfFoldersSynced           : 6
SyncStateUpgradeTime            :
ClientType                      : EAS
```

Note the different moments in time when the wipe request was requested, sent and actually performed by the device (if you trust the device or app being accurate). You can also see the Wipe requester, in this case the Administrator.

## ActiveSync Enabled/Disabled Accounts

If you limit access to ActiveSync, it might be helpful to have an overview which mailboxes have this protocol (or client access protocols) enabled or not. You can see this as such:

Get-Mailbox | Get-CasMailbox -ProtocolSettings

Which will show this:

```
[PS] C:\>Get-Mailbox | Get-CasMailbox -ProtocolSettings

Name              ActiveSyncEnabled OWAEnabled         PopEnabled         ImapEnabled         MapiEnabled

Administrator     True              True               True               True                True
DiscoverySear...  True              True               True               True                True
Jeff Withers      False             True               True               True                True
Damian Scoles     False             True               True               True                True
Journaling Ma...  True              True               True               True                True
```

So, to only show ActiveSync disabled accounts the syntax would be:

Get-Mailbox | Get-CASMailbox -ProtocolSettings | Where {$_.ActiveSyncEnabled -eq $False}

Which would result in:

```
[PS] C:\>Get-Mailbox | Get-CASMailbox -ProtocolSettings | Where {$_.ActiveSyncEnabled -eq $False}

Name               ActiveSyncEnabled OWAEnabled      PopEnabled    ImapEnabled    MapiEnabled

Jeff Withers       False             True            True          True           True
Damian Scoles      False             True            True          True           True
Dave Stork         False             True            True          True           True
James Forth        False             True            True          True           True
Help Desk          False             True            True          True           True
```

## ActiveSync Log

If you require actual connectivity data from ActiveSync devices, you can let Export-ActiveSyncLog parse through your servers IIS logs and provide you with several CSV's with useful information, such as Usernames and how much bandwidth they are using, error codes etc. You have to provide an IIS log which will be parsed:

Export-ActiveSyncLog -Filename "C:\inetpub\logs\LogFiles\W3SVC2\u_ex160814.log" -StartDate "8/01/2016 12:00AM" -EndDate "8/15/2016 10:00PM" -OutputPath "c:\temp\"

This would give you:

```
[PS] C:\>Export-ActiveSyncLog -Filename "C:\inetpub\logs\LogFiles\W3SVC2\u_ex160814.log" -S
tartDate "8/01/2016 12:00AM" -EndDate "8/15/2016 10:00PM" -OutputPath "c:\temp\"

Mode              LastWriteTime           Length Name
----              -------------           ------ ----
darhs           12/31/1600    6:00 PM            Users.csv
darhs           12/31/1600    6:00 PM            Servers.csv
darhs           12/31/1600    6:00 PM            Hourly.csv
darhs           12/31/1600    6:00 PM            StatusCodes.csv
darhs           12/31/1600    6:00 PM            PolicyCompliance.csv
darhs           12/31/1600    6:00 PM            UserAgents.csv
```

The downside is that you can analyze only one IIS log at a time, which makes this somewhat limited for reporting and/or troubleshooting. If this kind of information interests you or even required, check out Log Parser and Log Parser Studio. A free tool from Microsoft and with the additional pre-made queries in Log Parser Studio, you can analyze multiple log files, also from other servers.

## Overview of Deprecated Cmdlets

As some notes have stated, some cmdlets referencing ActiveSync are deprecated, meaning that they are no longer maintained and will be removed in a future Exchange version. While it might not impact you at this moment, it is advisable to already become familiar with the new cmdlets and update any of your scripts to reflect this. This will prevent unnecessary surprises after upgrading your servers.

| Deprecated cmdlet | New cmdlet |
|---|---|
| Clear-ActiveSyncDevice | Clear-MobileDevice |
| Get-ActiveSyncDevice | Get-MobileDevice |
| Get-ActiveSyncMailboxPolicy | Get-MobileDeviceMailboxPolicy |
| Get-ActiveSyncDeviceStatistics | Get-MobileDeviceStatistics |
| New-ActiveSyncMailboxPolicy | New-MobileDeviceMailboxPolicy |
| Remove-ActiveSyncMailboxPolicy | Remove-MobileDeviceMailboxPolicy |
| Set-ActiveSyncMailboxPolicy | Set-MobileDeviceMailboxPolicy |

<table>
<tr><td>**14**</td><td># Migrations</td></tr>
</table>



# Introduction

It's very unlikely that there is no Exchange admin that has not or will not have to move one or more mailboxes from one Exchange database to another. While some scenarios are quite easy, there are some scenarios that require some more planning, reporting and so on.

With the introduction of Exchange 2010, Microsoft also improved the one element that would grow into an almost impossible task: Mailbox moves. The revolutionary change in Exchange 2010 made it possible to move mailbox data while the user still could access and modify his/her data: Online Mailbox Move. New incoming mail is queued in mail queues until the mailbox is available again (i.e. when it's successfully moved or has failed).

With the trend of growing average mailbox sizes, this was a necessary step. Otherwise it could mean that a migration would take too long to perform in a single big bang, meaning that you have to migrate mailboxes in stages and maintain a coexistence environment until the last mailbox has been moved. It was also a major step towards making Office 365 more accessible to migrate to and more flexible for Microsoft on managing servers and databases. Just consider moving mailboxes like in Exchange 2003, hoping that every mailbox has moved before your maintenance window closes… <shivers>.

Luckily this has changed, and as Exchange 2016 can only coexist with Exchange 2010 and 2013, earlier versions of Exchange won't be an issue. However, the option is still there with the -ForceOffline switch in the New-MoveRequest cmdlet. You shouldn't have to use it under normal conditions, however from time to time a mailbox is fickle and can only move via an Offline move.

Now, most of the move mailbox options are available from within the Exchange Admin Center in one way or another. But in our experience, EAC is probably fine for simple migrations or the incidental move of one mailbox. If you migrate your server environment from one major build to another, it's almost impossible to ignore PowerShell. Those migrations are far more complex and full of caveats, that it mostly always requires the use of custom PowerShell cmdlets and scripts.

But, before delving more into the PowerShell of (Online) Mailbox moves we shall explain the fundamentals of Mailbox moves since Exchange 2010.

# Basics

Although Exchange 2016 creates Migration Batches (more on that later) automatically even when moving one single mailbox, the basis of a mailbox migration is the New-MoveRequest cmdlet. The name is telling; you request the system to move a mailbox. Why is that? Well, it could be the source or more importantly the target server is not in good health before or during the move. The Mailbox Replication service (present on each server in 2016) can decide that the move is too impactful or too risky and stalls the move.

Exchange is responsible for a successful mailbox move to be not to impactful on client experience, due to performance loss (a move does cost extra resources) and preventing data loss during a move.

Another benefit is that an Exchange server can reboot and the mailbox moves can resume after the server has rebooted, or another server will continue the move requests. This is possible since all move requests are stored in arbitration mailboxes (system mailboxes, hidden from normal view) and another server could process them, if the servers are in a Database Availability Group (DAG). Or when a move fails for whatever reason, if you can resolve the issue you can restart the (online) move again. Or you could temporarily suspend any moves when you perceive any issues in your Exchange environment and after resolving those issues, continue at your leisure.

This means the mailbox migrations are a lot more robust and flexible for admins than in previous versions of Exchange (2007 and earlier). You can prepare, pre-stage the data and if necessary troubleshoot your migration long before completing the mailbox moves to the target servers. That moment that is traditionally prone to errors and requiring some aftercare normally.  With online mailbox moves, these efforts will often be limited to client issues, rather than (also) server issues.

## Migration Batch

As mentioned previously when using the web based Exchange Admin Center, even when you move one single mailbox it will create a Migration Batch. Migration Batches are bulk mailbox moves, which makes those bulk moves more easy to handle: Stopping or suspending them will stop/suspend all moves part of the batch.

Creating a most basic new batch:

```
New-MigrationBatch -Local -Name "Batch01" -CSVData ([System.IO.File]::ReadAllBytes("C:\scripting\
batch01.csv")) -TargetDatabases "DB21"
```

The parameter Local indicates a move within the same Exchange environment (or AD Forest). Name is the identifier and CSVData is a CSV file with the mailboxes required to move with this Migration Batch. TargetDatabases is the target database.  The only column required in the CSV is "EmailAddress", where each mailbox to be migrated should have at least their email address listed, one per line.  For information on the format of the input CSV file see:  https://technet.microsoft.com/en-us/library/dn170437(v=exchg.150).aspx

Although in this example there is only one database defined, it is possible to enter multiple target databases usable for this Migration Batch. You can do this by using the parameter formatting:

```
-TargetArchiveDatabases @("DB21","DB22","DB23")
```

However, you do not have control over which mailbox will end up in which database and it does not take mailbox sizes or current mailbox database sizes into account which means you could end up with uneven distributed databases.

So, that's the basic command, but let's take a look at the other often used cmdlets and parameters. To know what's already present as a Migration Batch, you'd have to list them with Get-MigrationBatch:

```
[PS] C:\>Get-MigrationBatch

Identity                        Status              Type                        TotalCount
--------                        ------              ----                        ----------
DB01 to DB02                    Completed           ExchangeLocalMove           2
Select Users                    Created             ExchangeLocalMove           3
```

With the AutoComplete parameter, you tell Exchange the mailboxes in the Migration Batch may be completed immediately when all the data has been moved of a specific mailbox. With the parameter AutoStart the batch will start at creation, if you do not use this you will have to start the batch manually with:

Start-MigrationBatch -Identity "<batchname>"

```
[PS] C:\>Start-MigrationBatch -Identity "Select Users"
[PS] C:\>
[PS] C:\>Get-MigrationBatch

Identity                        Status              Type                        TotalCount
--------                        ------              ----                        ----------
DB01 to DB02                    Completed           ExchangeLocalMove           2
Select Users                    Syncing             ExchangeLocalMove           3
```

You can see the status has (eventually) changed to Syncing, after starting the Migration Batch.

In optimal situations, there are no corrupt items in mailboxes, however based on years of experience there can be many unexpected corruptions that may make an object unreadable or unable to be migrated. Sometimes you can repair those objects, but it is not always practical. Luckily you can configure the Migration Batch to accept a number of corrupt items that will be skipped and thus lost, with the BadItemLimit parameter.

Not only can corrupt items stall a mailbox move, also large items that are over the set MaxReceiveSize value in the organization can halt a move. The LargeItemLimit specific the number of "violations" that are acceptable, but note that those items are not migrated and thus this can also lead to data/items being lost. You could consider increasing the MaxReceiveSize (and MaxSendSize), using Set-TransportConfig, in the organization or probably better these specific values on the mailbox in the source Exchange environment. Mailbox limits, like these, will stay in effect after the migration, because they are stored in the AD and replicated to Office 365 or the target forest normally. The BadItemLimit and LargeItemLimit parameters are available in the Exchange Admin Center as well, but if you require the use of Exchange PowerShell, these parameters are often a good practice to include. Note that the LargeItemLimit parameter is not valid for local moves, those within the same Exchange organization.

**Example of the BadItemLimit parameter:**

New-MigrationBatch -Local -Name "Batch01" -CSVData ([System.IO.File]::ReadAllBytes("C:\scripting\batch01.csv")) -TargetDatabases "DB21" -BadItemLimit 10

When your environment contains Archive mailboxes in Exchange Server, it might be required to move the primary mailbox separate from the Archive mailbox, you can configure that with the PrimaryOnly or ArchiveOnly parameter. For instance, when you require only Archive mailboxes moved:

```
New-MigrationBatch -Local -Name "Archivebatch01" -CSVData ([System.IO.File]::ReadAllBytes("C:\
scripting\Archivebatch01.csv")) -ArchiveOnly
```

You can use the latter one with the TargetArchiveDatabases parameter when you migrate only archive mailboxes. If you have multiple databases as a target, you can use the same syntax as with TargetDatabases:

```
-TargetArchiveDatabases @("DB21","DB22","DB23")
```

Whenever you don't use AutoComplete with your Migration Batch, the batch will automatically synchronize each mailbox every 24 hours. If for whatever reason you do not want this to happen (you expect some performance issues during those synchronization moments for instance), you should use parameter AllowIncrementalSyncs with the value $False.  Note that this will result in a longer completion duration wich lowers the benefits of an online move.

There are guidelines for the CSV files in order to work correctly with Migration Batches. One requirement is a column with header EmailAddress that will contain the (primary) SMTP address of the mailbox you want to move. Other columns are optional, but when configured will overrule the settings made with MigrationBatch cmdlets. Optional column names are: TargetDatabase, TargetArchiveDatabase, BadItemLimit and/or MailboxType. The first three will act like previously described, MailboxType however will determine whether the primary, archive mailbox or both are moved (with the values PrimaryOnly, ArchiveOnly and PrimaryAndArchive).

A valid CSV would look like this:

```
EmailAddress, TargetDatabase, TargetArchiveDatabase, BadItemLimit, MailboxType
Manager@contoso.com, DB01, DB02, 10, PrimaryAndArchive
Admin1@contoso.com, DB04, DB04, 10, Primary
```

In this example: Manager primary mailbox will be moved to DB01, the Archive mailbox to DB02. Ten bad items are accepted. Admin1 primary mailbox will be moved to DB04, the Archive mailboxes will remain on it's current location. Ten bad items are accepted. See also this site for more info on CSV configuration for Migration Batches:

https://technet.microsoft.com/en-us/library/dn170437(v=exchg.160).aspx

If you get CSV files with some extra columns with attributes not used for mailbox migrations, you could use AllowUnknownColumnsInCsv in order to let Exchange ignore those and only focus on the Identity values.

For those who require regular updates, via email, on the status of the Migration Batch, use the NotificationEmails parameter. It's a multi-valued string and entries should be delimited with commas. Like so:

```
New-MigrationBatch -Local -Name Batch01 -CSVData ([System.IO.File]::ReadAllBytes("C:\scripting\
batch01.csv")) -NotificationEmails admin1@contoso.com, manager@contoso.com
```

Did you forgot a parameter or do you need to change a specific value? Know that you can change certain parameter values of existing Migration Batches with Set-MigrationBatch. For instance:

```
Set-MigrationBatch -Identity Batch01 -BadItemLimit 10 -AllowIncrementalSyncs $False
```

Not all values can be changed, for a full overview of the available Set-MigrationBatch parameters check out: https://technet.microsoft.com/en-us/library/jj218662(v=exchg.160).aspx

For a full overview of the New-MigrationBatch parameters, what they do and when you should use them check out this page: https://technet.microsoft.com/en-us/library/jj219166(v=exchg.160).aspx

Other Migration Batch cmdlets are:

### Start-MigrationBatch

- Starts a previously defined Migration Batch.
- https://technet.microsoft.com/en-us/library/jj219165(v=exchg.160).aspx

### Stop-MigrationBatch

- Stops a Migration Batch immediately, although already migrated (and potentially completed) mailboxes are left untouched.
- https://technet.microsoft.com/en-us/library/jj219168(v=exchg.160).aspx

### Complete-MigrationBatch

- Finalizes the mailbox migration process. After this command has been entered, a last incremental synchronization will be performed and after that the user client will use the new mailbox location.
- https://technet.microsoft.com/en-us/library/jj218648(v=exchg.160).aspx

### Remove-MigrationBatch

- Removes a non-running or completed Migration Batch. You can only have 100 Migration Batches at a time, so at some point it may be required to clean up old batches.
- https://technet.microsoft.com/en-us/library/jj219167(v=exchg.160).aspx

### Get-MigrationConfig

- Too see the maximum number of batches or concurrent migrations.

### Set-MigrationConfig

- Too change migration configuration settings, such as the maximum number of batches. You can change that from 100 to 200 with:
- Set-MigrationConfig -MaxNumberOfBatches 200

## Move Requests

Migration Batches create the actual move requests, the actual objects that controls each mailbox move. The batch is there to easily manage move requests in bulk. However, knowing how to control separate move requests is paramount in most successful mailbox migrations.

First, a simple move request command in Exchange PowerShell would look like:

```
New-MoveRequest -Identity "<Mailbox ID>" -TargetDatabase <DB ID>
```

In this case the Identity value can be different, but we tend to use the Active Directory User Principal Name (UPN) or the primary email address (often they are the same). They are both unique values, user friendly and most objects have an attribute with either of them.

The Database parameter value, while optional, is the target database, the location you want the mailbox to reside. This can be any database in the Exchange Organization and thus Active Directory Forest (cross-forest migrations are discussed below). If you do not specify the target database, Exchange will select a healthy mounted mailbox database randomly, which has not set the IsExcludedFromProvisioning parameter to $False. This database IsExcludedFromProvisioning parameter is only checked if the CheckInitialProvisioningSetting switch is included with the move request.

The move request will be queued immediately and when the source server is ready the move will begin. During this time the user can still work up until the last percentages. On those last moments, the mailbox moved is finalized; its locked so further changes can't be made to it, the last changes are performed and synchronized, and changes are made in both the source and target Active Directory, if different. There are also a couple of different ways to delay the move finalization that are covered later.

Depending on your source and target servers, the user may have to restart Outlook after their mailbox move is finalized, in order for the Outlook profile to be updated to the new target environment. When users are prompted to restart Outlook was changed with Exchange 2013. With 2013 and higher, the server name value stored in Outlook is actually a unique identifier based on the Mailbox ID and the AD domain name and no longer a "server" name. This way Outlook does not have to be restarted as that ID will never change and clients should be connecting to normally a single normally load balanced DNS entry that can point to any Exchange 2016 server. For mailboxes being moved from Exchange 2010 or 2013, the Outlook protocol may also be updated from MAPI/RPC to a HTTPS based connection, using Outlook Anywhere.

Do note, that you cannot manage move requests not part of a Migration Batch via the Exchange Admin Center, so you will have to use Exchange PowerShell to manage the mailbox moves done directly with New-MoveRequest.

This principle of Online Mailbox moves makes migrations a lot more flexible and less prone to risks.  For instance, to create a Move-Request that will be suspended before it completes, add the SuspendWhenReadyToComplete switch:

```
New-MoveRequest -Identity "<Mailbox ID>" -SuspendWhenReadyToComplete
```

It will stop the progress at 95%. This value is not an actual representation of the amount of data migrated, it's just Exchange's internal way of telling you it's practically done. By default, the move request will also perform an incremental sync every 24 hours.

So, now we have a Move-Request that is suspended. Can we do anything useful with it? Well, yes! With Set-MoveRequest we can change some of the parameters of the move, without stopping and restarting the move from the start! Better yet, even if the move has failed we can still change parameters and restart the move. When it's an Online move (read: from Exchange 2010 or higher) it will restart at the point of failure.

A lot of parameters available within New-MoveRequest are the same as with the New-MigrationBatch cmdlet. This is logical as the Migration Batch in its turn creates a move request per mailbox and subsequently passes on the specified parameter to the move request.

To control the amount of acceptable corrupted objects, before a move fails, you use BadItemLimit with an integer indicating how many failed objects are acceptable. If you have a value of 51 or higher (meaning you accept skipping 50 corrupted objects before the mailbox move fails and stops), you have to add the additional AcceptLargeDataLoss switch otherwise the move will fail. This is an additional safety measure to prevent you from accidentally accepting a data loss of more than 50 items.

In addition, the LargeItemLimit should be used to indicates the number of objects that are allowed to be skipped, that are larger than the message receive limits set on the target. The default message size limit is only valid for mailboxes that inherit the default database limits on the target database, otherwise message size limits set on the mailbox will be used. Another possible reason for failure, is when there are items already in the mailbox that exceed the limits, which existed before specific mailbox item size limits were set.

An alternative to the LargeItemLimit parameter is the AllowLargeItems switch, which is specific for move requests and is not available with Migration Batches. When the AllowLargeItems switch has been added to a New-MoveRequest, Exchange will move all items that exceed the size limits set on target databases or mailbox limits. Both AllowLargeItems and LargeItemLimit should not be used together, the LargeItemLimit will cause the move to fail once the threshold specified has been reached even with the AllowLargeItems switch included. So you cannot use both parameters at the same time since this will result in a failed mailbox move when not expected.

If you have Archive mailboxes you can also control the migration of the primary or archive mailbox separate from each other. The same switches and parameters that control these behaviors are also present. For a description see our section within New-MigrationBatch. The switches and parameters are:

* ArchiveOnly
* ArchiveTargetDatabase
* PrimaryOnly
* TargetDatabase

Every Migration Batch will have a name, but move requests can also have a Batch name defined by using the parameter BatchName. This is a way to easily bulk manage multiple similar move requests. For instance, if you create multiple move-requests with the same Batch name, you can reference that parameter value. For instance, you've created multiple move requests like so:

```
New-MoveRequest -Identity walter.pinkman@contoso.com -BatchName "Logistics"
New-MoveRequest -Identity jesse.white@contoso.com -BatchName "Logistics"
```

Now you can find them via:

```
Get-MoveRequest -BatchName "Logistics"
```

Subsequently you can pipe the output to other cmdlets, for instance Get-MoveRequestStatistics:

```
Get-MoveRequest -BatchName "Logistics" | Get-MoveRequestStatistics
```

If you've created a Migration Batch, the move request batch name attribute does not correspond exactly with the Migration Batch name value. To give distinction between move requests created via a Migration Batch or a manual action, Migration Batches have the batch name prepended with "MigrationService:". So, if you have any need to investigate specific move requests created via a Migration Batch with the name "Batch01", you could use the following syntax:

```
Get-MoveRequest -BatchName "MigrationService:Batch01"
```

Obviously, you can pipe this to other commands. In this case:

```
Get-MoveRequest -BatchName "MigrationService:Batch01" | Get-MoveRequestStatistics
```

Unlike Migration Batches, you can set the priority of a move request. This way you can control the order of processing the queue of move requests, but other factors, like server health, status, etc. will also affect move request. Possible values are:

- Lowest
- Lower
- Low
- Normal (Default)
- High
- Higher
- Highest
- Emergency

Therefore, if needed in your organization, a specific mailbox can be requested to be moved ahead of others by changing the priority of its move request. Note that it only influences the processing order of the queue. It does not affect requests that are in progress. An example:

    New-MoveRequest -Identity "<Mailbox ID>" -Priority Higher

An example for existing (queued) move requests:

    Set-MoveRequest -Identity "<Mailbox ID>" -Priority Lower

Another way to influence the impact of your mailbox moves after initial pre-staging has completed, is the frequency of incremental synchronizations. The default value is every 24 hours. The format looks like, where dd:hh:mm:ss stands for days (dd), hours (hh), minutes (mm) and seconds (ss):

    New-MoveRequest -Identity "<Mailbox ID>" -IncrementalSyncInterval <dd.hh:mm:ss>

For instance, you create a move request and set it to sync every 12 hours with the IncrementalSyncInterval parameter:

    New-MoveRequest -Identity "<Mailbox ID>" -IncrementalSyncInterval 00.12:00:0

Normally adjusting the interval is probably not required, however it makes sense if you want specific batches to be started and completed after specific moments in time. You can adjust the sync frequency to suit your needs. You can schedule the start time of a move request with the parameter StartAfter and you can also schedule the completion of a move with the parameter CompleteAfter.

The date value format is dependent on the regional settings of the server and specifically the Short Date value. In this example the format is M/d/yyyy, which translates as 5/23/2016.

    New-MoveRequest -Identity <mailboxid> -StartAfter 5/23/2016

You can also add a specific time, which uses the short time notation in your regional settings. You have to add quotes to the value when you do so:

    New-MoveRequest -Identity <mailboxid> -CompleteAfter "6/19/2016 9:59"

They can also be combined into one cmdlet:

    New-MoveRequest -Identity <mailboxid> -StartAfter 6/10/2016 -CompleteAfter "6/19/2016 9:59" –
    IncrementalSyncInterval 00:01:00:00

This will start the move request on the 10th of June 2016 and will complete it nine days later at 9:59 (AM in this case, a 24 hour notation was configured in regional settings). It will sync every one hour after the initial synchronization has finished.

The use of the StartAfter and CompleteAfter parameters is recommended by Microsoft. However, there is no specific technical reason to use these verse just manually complete the mailbox moves. Usage of either options to complete moves is dependent on your specific requirements. I personally like to manually perform the completion of moves, mostly because some organizations have a GO/NOGO moment just before completion.

You can find the date and time short formats in Control Panel>Region:

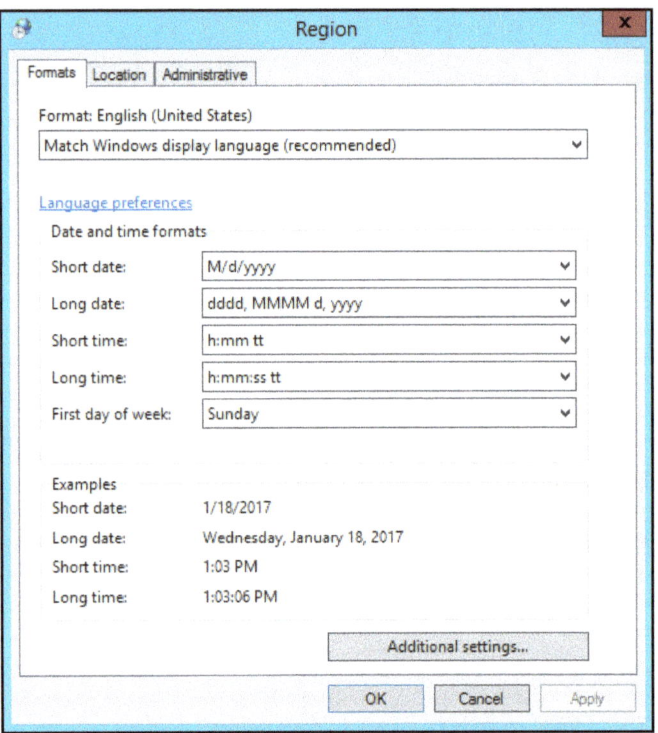

Two other switches, PreventCompletion and SuspendWhenReadyToComplete, also prevent the completion of the move request. Both of these switches suspend the mailbox move, at 95%, like the CompleteAfter switch. But both of these switches require manually finishing/resuming the mailbox move for it to be completed. Therefore, Microsoft recommends using the CompleteAfter switch to make sure the mailbox moves are completed at some point and not forgotten about.

If you want to create move requests, but be certain that they are not immediately queued and potentially started, you can use the Suspend switch.

When a move request has completed (with or without errors), the requests will be saved up to 30 days and then removed from the system. If you require shorter/longer duration, you can specify this with CompletedRequestAgeLimit. The value is an integer and represents the amount of days:

```
Set-MoveRequest -Identity <Mailbox ID> -CompletedRequestAgeLimit 120
```

This will retain the completed move request for 120 days.

In some specific cases, it is possible you cannot migrate a mailbox with an online move. In such cases, one thing that might help is to explicitly force an offline move. This will cause the mailbox to be locked as soon as the move request has reached the InProgress status. Unfortunately, this means users cannot access the mailbox until the offline mailbox move has completed.

```
New-MoveRequest -Identity <Mailbox ID> -ForceOffline
```

For a full overview of the parameters, what they do and when you should use them check out this page: https://technet.microsoft.com/en-us/library/dd351123(v=exchg.160).aspx

Other cmdlets regarding move requests are:

### Get-MoveRequest

- Listing current move requests.
- https://technet.microsoft.com/en-us/library/dd335227(v=exchg.160).aspx

### Remove-MoveRequest

- Removing a move request.
- https://technet.microsoft.com/en-us/library/dd335149(v=exchg.160).aspx

### Resume-MoveRequest

- Resume a suspended move request. Either due to when the SuspendWhenReadyToComplete switch has been set or the Suspend-MoveRequest cmdlet.
- https://technet.microsoft.com/en-us/library/ee332320(v=exchg.160).aspx

### Set-MoveRequest

- Change specific attributes of a move request, for instance when it has failed due to too many bad items.
- https://technet.microsoft.com/en-us/library/ee332314(v=exchg.160).aspx

### Suspend-MoveRequest

- Suspending a move request in queue or when in progress. Restart the move with Resume-MoveRequest.
- https://technet.microsoft.com/en-us/library/ee332310(v=exchg.160).aspx

## Cross-Forest Moves

There are situations that you will not use the same Active Directory (AD) Forest for the source and target of a mailbox move. Most commonly this is due to organization reasons (mergers, acquisitions, divestitures, etc.) or due to policy and technical requirements (shared resource forest). Luckily you can migrate mailboxes from one AD forest to another with built-in mechanisms.

The requirements for source and target versions of Exchange is the same as when migrating within the same Active Directory forest, so for Exchange 2016 this would require a minimum of Exchange 2010 with the correct patch level.

**Example steps, more may be required for your environment:**

1. Open ports between the two environments
2. Ensure two-way name resolution, servers must be able to resolve FQDN and NETBIOS names of servers in the other forest: DNS or Host file
3. Create an Active Directory forest trust
4. Enable the Mailbox Replication Service proxy (MRSProxyEnabled) in the target (or source depending if the migration is a push or pull migration) Exchange environment
5. Create Mail enabled user objects in target forest based on Mailbox enabled user objects in source forest
   - Either with PrepareMoveRequest.ps1 and ADMT, or a combination, or other tools (Microsoft Identity Manager and 3rd party ones)
6. Add a targetdomain SMTP address on the target mail user object
   - Usually with an Email Address Policy, but sometimes you have to manually or script add the targetdomain addresses
7. Create a move request

The Prepare-MoveRequest.ps1 script is key. It will create and prepare a target user object for the cross-forest mailbox move. It will copy important attributes from the source objects and sets them correctly on the target object. Especially the LegacyExchangeDN, which is a critical attribute, that has to be added as an X500 address on the target object. Otherwise users will get NDR when trying to email users in the other forest.

You have to have credentials of both the source and target AD forest, represented with $RemoteCredentials and $LocalCredentials variables.

A typical syntax is:

```
./Prepare-MoveRequest.ps1 -Identity "joe@fabrikam.com" -RemoteForestDomainController remotedc.
fabrikam.com -RemoteForestCredential $RemoteCredentials -LocalForestDomainController localdc.
contoso.com -LocalForestCredential $LocalCredentials
```

This will connect to the remote domain controller with your remote credentials stored in the $RemoteCredentials variable and connect with your local domain controller with the $LocalCredentials credentials. In this example, the remote forest is the source Exchange environment and local is the target AD forest. You perform this command preferably in the target environment.

This will create a mail user in the target AD forest, similar to the mailbox user in the source AD forest. Address book related properties and proxy address are copied to the target mail user, in addition the legacyExchangeDN is added to the target mail user object as an x500 address. Adding this address will prevent name resolution related problems, which include issues that come up with Outlook's nickname cache and replying to emails sent and received while the mailboxes were still in the source environment. Internally, Exchange uses this attribute as a unique identify for all mail enabled objects, therefore if this value doesn't exist in the new environment it will lead to message delivery issues. For more details on the legacyExchangeDN attribute see this article: https://eightwone.com/2013/08/12/legacyexchangedn-attribute-myth/.

If an account from another, trusted, forest should be the owner of the mailbox add the LinkedMailUser switch. To have all new mail user objects created in a specific OU use TargetMailUserOU switch. Sometimes issues can come up with the email address policies in the target forest for the newly made objects, you can disable support on the new object via the DisableEmailAddressPolicy switch.

If an existing object should be updated, the OverWriteLocalObject switch should be used with the Prepare-MoveRequest script. This will tell it to overwrite the mail related attributes on the existing object with the values from the source object.

This only covers part of the Exchange preparation needed, which in part can also be performed with ADMT, MIM/FIM/ILM or other AD object synchronization solutions. Additional steps are required for mail flow between the Exchange organization, calendar sharing, and more.

For more information about doing cross-forest moves, see this article series, which is on Exchange 2010 but the vast majority of steps are the same with Exchange 2016: https://blogs.technet.microsoft.com/meamcs/2011/06/10/exchange-2010-cross-forest-migration-step-by-step-guide-part-i

# Checking Migration Status and Reports

During the mailbox move or pre-staging, you undoubtedly want to monitor the progress and catch any problematic moves. Also in this case the EAC provides basic information that might not be enough for large batch moves.

Even if using Exchange 2016 Migration Batches, each mailbox is represented by a Move Request. The Migration Batches are a way to easily manage those multiple move request.

## Status

To see the status of current Migration Batches, use:

Get-MigrationBatch

```
[PS] C:\>Get-MigrationBatch

Identity                        Status              Type                        TotalCount
--------                        ------              ----                        ----------
DB01 to DB02                    Completed           ExchangeLocalMove           2
Select Users                    Created             ExchangeLocalMove           3
```

That only tells us information about Migration Batches and not real info on specific mailbox statuses. You would need Get-MoveRequest for this.

In order to get statistics from a list of all MoveRequest independent of their state, you can use:

Get-MoveRequest -ResultSize Unlimited | Get-MoveRequestStatistics

However, you can achieve a more granular view by adding the status:

Get-MoveRequest -ResultSize Unlimited -MoveStatus Completed | Get-MoveRequestStatistics

```
[PS] C:\>Get-MoveRequest -ResultSize Unlimited -MoveStatus Completed | Get-MoveRequestStatistics

DisplayName         StatusDetail        TotalMailboxSize            TotalArchiveSize        PercentComplete
-----------         ------------        ----------------            ----------------        ---------------
Administrator       Completed           58.47 KB (59,873 bytes)                             100
Jan Crichton        Completed           2.678 KB (2,742 bytes)                              100
```

This will show each move that has the InProgress status equal to Completed. The status options are AutoSuspended, Completed, CompletedWithWarning, CompletionInProgress, Failed, InProgress, None, Queued, and Suspended. Most are evident, however AutoSuspended are those requests that have finished the pre-staging and were given the SuspendWhenReadyToComplete parameter in the Move-Request.

If you want to limit your selection to a specific Migration Batch, you can add the BatchName:

    Get-MoveRequest -ResultSize Unlimited -BatchName "<batchname>" | Get-MoveRequestStatistics

Note that the BatchName value in New-MoveRequest, created directly, are different than the MigrationBatch value created by EAC and the New-MigrationBatch cmdlet, Exchange adds "MigrationService:" to the latter. So, in order to find all move-request from a previously created MigrationBatch named "DB01 to DB02", use:

    Get-MoveRequest -ResultSize Unlimited -BatchName "MigrationService:DB01 to DB02" | Get-MoveRequestStatistics

```
[PS] C:\>Get-MoveRequest -ResultSize Unlimited -BatchName "MigrationService:DB01 to DB02"| Get-MoveRequestStatistics

DisplayName              StatusDetail            TotalMailboxSize           TotalArchiveSize          PercentComplete
-----------              ------------            ----------------           ----------------          ---------------
Administrator            Completed               58.47 KB (59,873 bytes)                                           100
Jan Crichton             Completed               2.678 KB (2,742 bytes)                                            100
```

Obviously, you can get it even more granular if you add the MoveStatus:

    Get-MoveRequest -ResultSize Unlimited -BatchName "<batchname>" -MoveStatus Completed | Get-MoveRequestStatistics

## Reporting

If there are any move requests that have failed, you need to know what the cause of the failure is. Most cases involve too many corrupt/bad items or too many large items, where the limits have been reached. Before increasing those limits, you'd probably want to know whether these are important items or not, for instance a calendar item from five years back is probably not crucial and can be skipped. But sometimes it's an important mail with attachments, you might want to try and extract that object via other means if possible (Outlook perhaps). Or you could decide to perform a New-MailboxRepairRequest on the source mailbox.

Luckily you can investigate each move request's detailed reporting, you can retrieve that report via:

    Get-MoveRequestStatistics -Identity "<move request>" -IncludeReport

However, you won't see that report unless specifically made visible: Via piping to Format-List or (cmdlet).Report:

    Get-MoveRequestStatistics -Identity "<move request>" -IncludeReport | fl

```
[PS] C:\>Get-MoveRequestStatistics -Identity "Jan Crichton" -IncludeReport | FL Report

Report : 5/25/2016 5:10:44 PM [L16-EX01] '' created move request.
         5/25/2016 5:10:53 PM [L16-EX01] The Microsoft Exchange Mailbox Replication service 'L16-EX01.lab2016.com'
         (15.1.396.30 caps:03FFFF) is examining the request.
         5/25/2016 5:10:54 PM [L16-EX01] Connected to target mailbox '364180a1-ec52-44a4-a383-d570da49140b (Primary)',
         database 'DB02', Mailbox server 'L16-EX01.lab2016.com' Version 15.1 (Build 396.0).
         5/25/2016 5:10:54 PM [L16-EX01] Connected to source mailbox '364180a1-ec52-44a4-a383-d570da49140b (Primary)',
         database 'DB01', Mailbox server 'L16-EX01.lab2016.com' Version 15.1 (Build 396.0).
         5/25/2016 5:10:54 PM [L16-EX01] Request processing started.
         5/25/2016 5:10:54 PM [L16-EX01] Source mailbox information:
         Regular Items: 1, 2.678 KB (2,742 bytes)
         Regular Deleted Items: 0, 0 B (0 bytes)
         FAI Items: 0, 0 B (0 bytes)
         FAI Deleted Items: 0, 0 B (0 bytes)
         5/25/2016 5:10:54 PM [L16-EX01] Cleared sync state for request 364180a1-ec52-44a4-a383-d570da49140b due to
         'CleanupOrphanedMailbox'.
         5/25/2016 5:10:57 PM [L16-EX01] Stage: CreatingFolderHierarchy. Percent complete: 10.
```

```
(Get-MoveRequestStatistics -Identity "<move request>" -IncludeReport).report
```

```
[PS] C:\>(Get-MoveRequestStatistics -Identity "Jan Crichton" -IncludeReport).Report|FL Entries

Entries : {5/25/2016 5:10:44 PM [L16-EX01] '' created move request., 5/25/2016 5:10:53 PM [L16-EX01] The Microsoft
          Exchange Mailbox Replication service 'L16-EX01.lab2016.com' (15.1.396.30 caps:03FFFF) is examining the
          request., 5/25/2016 5:10:54 PM [L16-EX01] Connected to target mailbox '364180a1-ec52-44a4-a383-d570da49140b
          (Primary)', database 'DB02', Mailbox server 'L16-EX01.lab2016.com' Version 15.1 (Build 396.0)., 5/25/2016
          5:10:54 PM [L16-EX01] Connected to source mailbox '364180a1-ec52-44a4-a383-d570da49140b (Primary)', database
          'DB01', Mailbox server 'L16-EX01.lab2016.com' Version 15.1 (Build 396.0)., 5/25/2016 5:10:54 PM [L16-EX01]
          Request processing started., 5/25/2016 5:10:54 PM [L16-EX01] Source mailbox information:
          Regular Items: 1, 2.678 KB (2,742 bytes)
          Regular Deleted Items: 0, 0 B (0 bytes)
          FAI Items: 0, 0 B (0 bytes)
          FAI Deleted Items: 0, 0 B (0 bytes), 5/25/2016 5:10:54 PM [L16-EX01] Cleared sync state for request
          364180a1-ec52-44a4-a383-d570da49140b due to 'CleanupOrphanedMailbox'., 5/25/2016 5:10:57 PM [L16-EX01]
          Stage: CreatingFolderHierarchy. Percent complete: 10., 5/25/2016 5:11:02 PM [L16-EX01] Initializing folder
          hierarchy from mailbox '364180a1-ec52-44a4-a383-d570da49140b (Primary)': 24 folders total., 5/25/2016
          5:11:02 PM [L16-EX01] Folder creation progress: 0 folders created in mailbox
          '364180a1-ec52-44a4-a383-d570da49140b (Primary)'., 5/25/2016 5:11:03 PM [L16-EX01] Folder hierarchy
          initialized for mailbox '364180a1-ec52-44a4-a383-d570da49140b (Primary)': 23 folders created., 5/25/2016
          5:11:03 PM [L16-EX01] Stage: CreatingFolderHierarchy. Percent complete: 10., 5/25/2016 5:11:05 PM [L16-EX01]
          Stage: CreatingInitialSyncCheckpoint. Percent complete: 15., 5/25/2016 5:11:05 PM [L16-EX01] Initial sync
          checkpoint progress: 0/24 folders processed. Currently processing mailbox
          '364180a1-ec52-44a4-a383-d570da49140b (Primary)'., 5/25/2016 5:11:05 PM [L16-EX01] Initial sync checkpoint
          completed: 23 folders processed., 5/25/2016 5:11:06 PM [L16-EX01] Stage: LoadingMessages. Percent complete:
          20....}
```

As you can see, they provide the same information.

To export that to a text file, you can use the Export-Csv cmdlet:

```
Get-MoveRequestStatistics -Identity "<move request>" -IncludeReport | Export-CSV -Encoding UTF8
-Path "<filename>"
```

The encoding ensures any non-ASCII characters are presented correctly (such as in DisplayName values, etc.). The Path is the path and filename of the export file.

If you require bulk export of reports, a Foreach loop is required. The basic principle would be:

```
$MoveRequests = Get-MoveRequest -ResultSize Unlimited

Foreach ($MoveRequest in $MoveRequests){
(Get-MoveRequestStatistics -Identity $MoveRequest.Identity -IncludeReport).Report | Export-CSV
-Encoding UTF8 -Path "$MoveRequest.txt"}
```

First all move requests are stored in a variable. Then for each request, the Get-MoveRequestStatistics cmdlet is performed on them. That cmdlet retrieves the move statistics report, which is then exported to an TXT file (in CSV format) with the DisplayName of the mailbox as a file name.

Obviously, there are variants possible, depending on your requirements. Most importantly you can select specific move requests by adding more filters. Check the beginning of the chapters on how to leverage Get-MoveRequest in order to get the reports you need. Be sure to also check out our chapter on Reporting with PowerShell.


# Public Folder Migrations

Yes, Public Folders just won't die on us… Starting in Exchange 2013, the way Public Folder data is stored has changed dramatically. From a separate type of database (Public Folder Database as opposed to Mailbox Database), data is now stored in Public Folder Mailboxes inside Mailbox Databases. End-user experience hasn't changed, but the administration is somewhat different and more importantly the migration from legacy Public Folders to Modern Public Folders is very different.

Simply put, the move is akin to the Mailbox Move-Request; the mailbox replication service is responsible for synchronizing PF data across PF mailboxes. This is initially staged online, which means users can continue to view/edit PFs during this stage. After the initial stage, incremental syncs are performed until the moment of switchover and a relatively short downtime of Public Folders.

The process is best described in this TechNet Article:

> *Use batch migration to migrate public folders to Exchange 2013 from previous versions:*
>
> https://technet.microsoft.com/en-us/library/dn912663(v=exchg.160).aspx

If you are still on Exchange 2007 or 2010 and want to migrate Public Folders to Office 365/Exchange Online, use this:

> *Use batch migration to migrate legacy public folders to Office 365 and Exchange Online:*
>
> https://technet.microsoft.com/en-us/library/dn874017(v=exchg.150).aspx

As of early 2017, there is no Microsoft provided way to migrate from Exchange 2013 or 2016 Public Folder, aka Modern Public Folders, to Office 365/Exchange Online; currently the only way to migrate them directly is to use a third party tool.

For some real-world experiences these blog posts are most helpful:

**Legacy Public Folders to Exchange 2013 Migration Tips**
https://dirteam.com/dave/2014/06/30/migrating-legacy-public-folders-to-exchange-2013-tips/

**Exchange Server 2010 to 2013 Migration – Moving Public Folders**
http://exchangeserverpro.com/exchange-server-2010-2013-migration-moving-public-folders/

More details on migrations of mailbox and Public Folder are outside the scope of this book, so be sure to check those articles and others on these topics.

# 15                Hybrid

**In This Chapter**

- Connecting to Office 365
- Azure Active Directory Recycle Bin
- Licensing
- IdFix
- UPN and Primary SMTP Address Updates

As it turns out neither Exchange Server nor Office 365 is an island unto itself. Microsoft has worked hard to construct a platform that is flexible and scalable. As such, it only makes sense to build a Hybrid interface between the two systems. Sometimes this interconnection needs PowerShell to properly manage. Exchange 2010 and Exchange 2013 both have Hybrid options which allow for Exchange on-premises to coexist with Office 365. Exchange 2016 continues this trend and allows for a Hybrid organization with Exchange Online. In fact, Microsoft has recently enhanced its Hybrid Configuration Wizard software to be independent of the Exchange Server.

When it comes to PowerShell, Exchange 2016 and Exchange Online there are lot of similarities as they are both running the same code base. Because the systems provide for different features and are coded to handle things slightly differently for a hosted versus a non-hosted environment, there will be some nuances for what is allowed on-premises versus what is allowed in the hosted Exchange Online service.

For this chapter, we assume that coexistence has been configured between Exchange on-premises and Exchange Online. Since the book is written for Exchange 2016, the PowerShell cmdlets will focus on the functionality it brings. However, most of the cmdlets, scripts and one-liners will work with Exchange 2013 as well.

**Notes**
- If moving from a non-Exchange mail system, install Exchange prior to installing Azure AD Sync.
- Make sure User Principal Names (UPN) match the Primary SMTP address.
- Installing an Exchange server in most scenarios, because using ADSI Edit to managed mail attributes is not supported.

# Connecting to Office 365

Connecting PowerShell to Office 365 requires the proper version of Windows PowerShell Snap-in to handle the connection.  Make sure the management computer needs to be Windows 7+ and have PowerShell 2.0 and .Net 4.5.

Office 365 has many connection points in order to manage its various services. These connection points are URLs that PowerShell uses in order to execute remote PowerShell cmdlets and scripts.  Here is a sample of the connection points available (a.k.a. Connection URIs):

| Service | ConnectionURI |
| --- | --- |
| Exchange Online | https://ps.outlook.com/powershell/ |
| SharePoint Online | https://domainhost-admin.sharepoint.com |
| Security and compliance | https://ps.compliance.protection.outlook.com/powershell-liveid/ |

In order to connect to these services, PowerShell need additional modules in order for the connections to be successful.  The current download for the Azure PowerShell module is located here -https://aka.ms/webpi-azps

The installation package is part of a larger product called 'Microsoft Web Platform Installer 5.0':

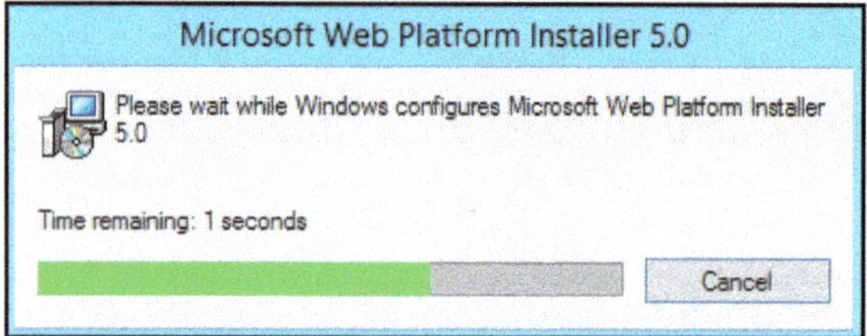

The install process for the Module is completed by clicking 'Install' and 'I Accept':

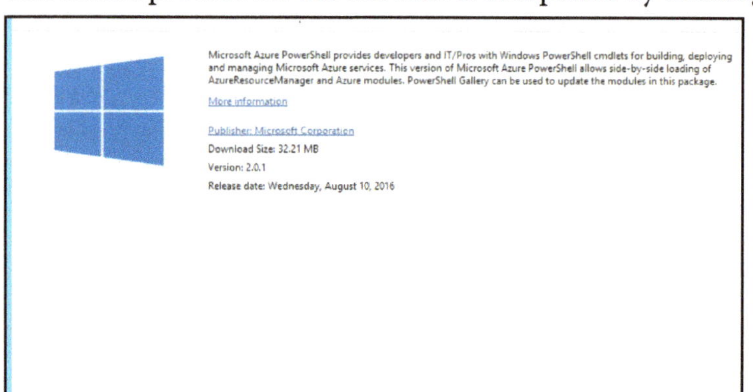

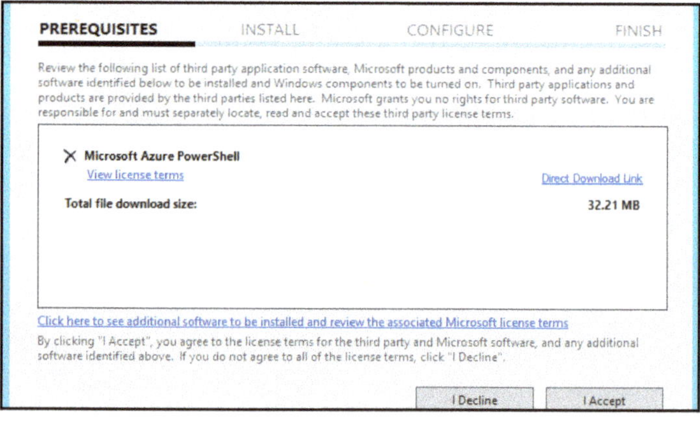

Then wait for the install to complete and click finish.  The module is now installed.

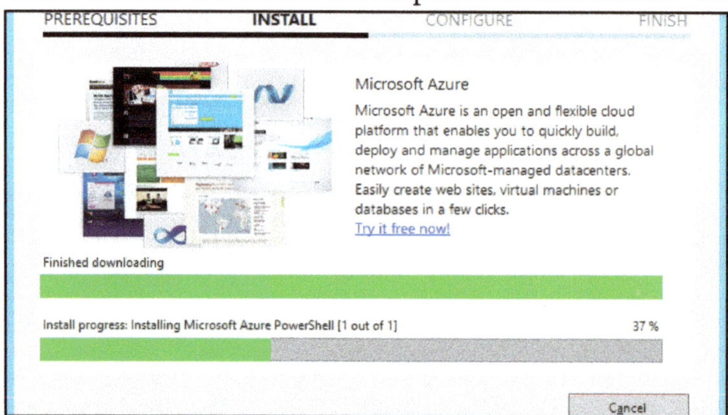

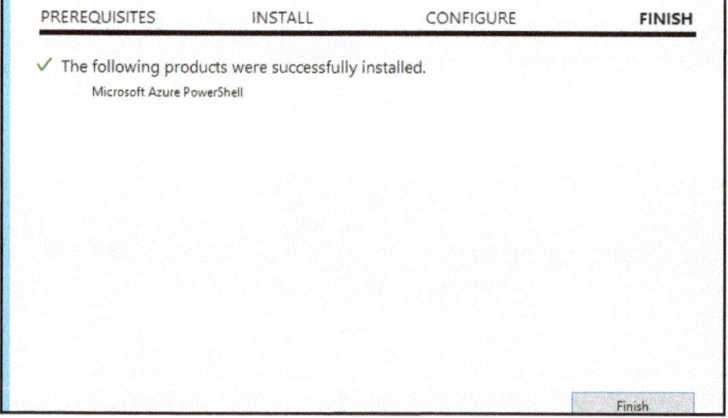

## PowerShell Cmdlets

In order to connect, to Exchange Online via PowerShell, a series of cmdlets needs to be run. Make sure to start Windows PowerShell as an Administrator. First, Exchange Online credentials should be stored in a variable:

```
$Office365Cred = Get-Credential
```

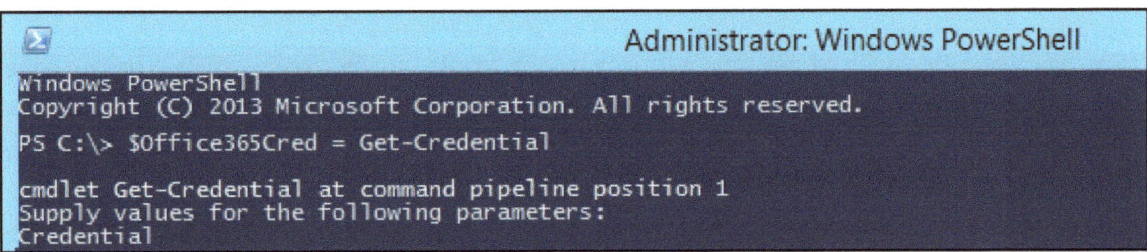



A pop-up is displayed which needs to be filled with credentials for an account with proper rights in the tenant:

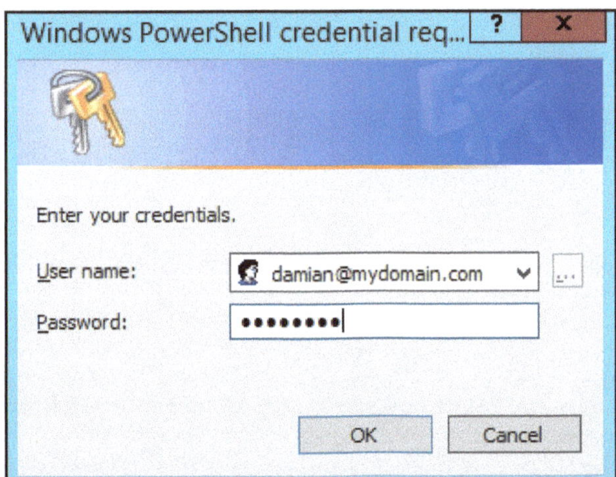



These credentials are then used as part of the PowerShell session parameters. These are again stored in a variable for a set of connection parameters:

```
$Session = New-PSSession -ConfigurationName Microsoft.Exchange -ConnectionUri https://ps.outlook.com/powershell/ -Credential $Office365Cred -Authentication Basic -AllowRedirection
```

The $Session variables are then fed into the Import-PSSession cmdlet:

```
PS C:\> $Session = New-PSSession -ConfigurationName Microsoft.Exchange -ConnectionUri https://ps.outlook.com/powershell/
 -Credential $Office365Cred -Authentication Basic -AllowRedirection
WARNING: Your connection has been redirected to the following URI:
"https://ps.outlook.com/PowerShell-LiveID?PSVersion=4.0 "
```

```
Import-PSSession $Session
```

```
PS C:\> Import-PSSession $Session
WARNING: The names of some imported commands from the module 'tmp_ffz2bqqb.u40' include unapproved verbs that might
make them less discoverable. To find the commands with unapproved verbs, run the Import-Module command again with the
Verbose parameter. For a list of approved verbs, type Get-Verb.

ModuleType Version    Name                            ExportedCommands
---------- -------    ----                            ----------------
Script     1.0        tmp_ffz2bqqb.u40                {Add-AvailabilityAddressSpace, Add-DistributionGroupMember...


PS C:\> _
```

Once the connection has been established, PowerShell can be used to work with objects that are synced to Azure AD. The caveat is that if the object is synced from an on-premises Active Directory, then some attributes may not be manageable.

## Office 365 Cmdlets

Now that a connection has been established, we need to figure out what cmdlets are available in the tenant. In PowerShell a group of cmdlets can be filtered based off the server name. For an Office 365 tenant, there is no 'server' to filter for. However, there is a name revealed after the Import-PSSession is established, in this example 'tmp_ffz2bqqb.u40', that can be queried, but this name will vary on each connect.

```
ModuleType Version   Name                ExportedCommands
---------- -------   ----                ----------------
Script     1.0       tmp_ffz2bqqb.u40    {Add-AvailabilityAddressSpace, Add-DistributionGroupMember...
```

Cmdlets can then be found with this filter:

```
Get-Command | Where {$_.ModuleName -eq 'tmp_ffz2bqqb.u40'}
```

```
CommandType     Name                                      ModuleName
-----------     ----                                      ----------
Function        Add-AvailabilityAddressSpace              tmp_ffz2bqqb.u40
Function        Add-DistributionGroupMember               tmp_ffz2bqqb.u40
Function        Add-MailboxFolderPermission               tmp_ffz2bqqb.u40
Function        Add-MailboxPermission                     tmp_ffz2bqqb.u40
Function        Add-ManagementRoleEntry                   tmp_ffz2bqqb.u40
Function        Add-PublicFolderClientPermission          tmp_ffz2bqqb.u40
Function        Add-RecipientPermission                   tmp_ffz2bqqb.u40
Function        Add-RoleGroupMember                       tmp_ffz2bqqb.u40
Function        Add-UnifiedGroupLinks                     tmp_ffz2bqqb.u40
Function        Clear-ActiveSyncDevice                    tmp_ffz2bqqb.u40
Function        Clear-MobileDevice                        tmp_ffz2bqqb.u40
Function        Clear-TextMessagingAccount                tmp_ffz2bqqb.u40
Function        Compare-TextMessagingVerificationCode     tmp_ffz2bqqb.u40
Function        Complete-MigrationBatch                   tmp_ffz2bqqb.u40
Function        Disable-App                               tmp_ffz2bqqb.u40
```

## Connect to Azure Active Directory

After connecting to your tenant, there is an additional connection that can be made with the 'Connect-MSOLService' cmdlet. The cmdlet provides a connection to the Microsoft Azure Active Directory for your tenant. The connection allows access to user objects in your tenant. To connect, either pass stored credentials with a variable or just type in 'Connect-MSOLService' and enter credentials into the pop-up box that is presented.

Microsoft has also added a Multi-Factor Authentication (MFA) option for connecting to various PowerShell resources in Office 365. These include Exchange Online, Azure, Azure Resource Manager and more. Consider enabling this for an additional security layer for your Office 365 tenant.

** **Note** ** What's available for PowerShell MFA could change at any time, verify what works before trying to connect with this method.

## Managing Office 365 Mailboxes from On-Premises PowerShell

In an Exchange Hybrid environment mailboxes, can exists on-premises and in the Office 365 tenant. In addition to regular mailboxes, archive mailboxes also can exist on-premises or in Office 365. The mailbox and archive mailbox can also be on the same service (Exchange or Exchange Online). PowerShell cmdlets exist to configure and manage these objects:

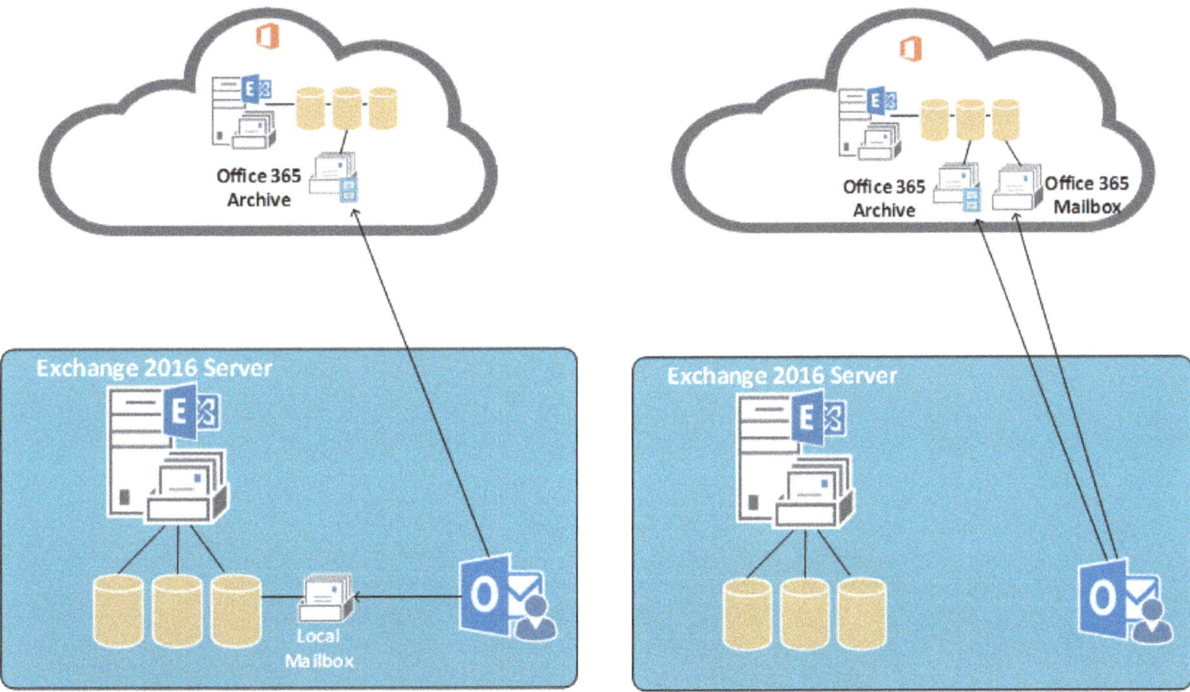


To manage the 'hybrid' environment, let's look for cmdlets on the Exchange 2016 server. What cmdlets exist that are based off a single keyword, 'Remote'? Here is a list of the cmdlets with the keyword:

```
Get-Command *Remote* | ft -Auto
```

```
CommandType       Name                    ModuleName
-----------       ----                    ----------
Function          Disable-RemoteMailbox   16-tap-ex02.16-tap.local
Function          Enable-RemoteMailbox    16-tap-ex02.16-tap.local
Function          Get-RDRemoteApp         RemoteDesktop
Function          Get-RDRemoteDesktop     RemoteDesktop
Function          Get-RemoteDomain        16-tap-ex02.16-tap.local
Function          Get-RemoteMailbox       16-tap-ex02.16-tap.local
Function          New-RDRemoteApp         RemoteDesktop
Function          New-RemoteDomain        16-tap-ex02.16-tap.local
Function          New-RemoteMailbox       16-tap-ex02.16-tap.local
Function          Remove-RDRemoteApp      RemoteDesktop
Function          Remove-RemoteDomain     16-tap-ex02.16-tap.local
Function          Remove-RemoteMailbox    16-tap-ex02.16-tap.local
Function          Set-RDRemoteApp         RemoteDesktop
Function          Set-RDRemoteDesktop     RemoteDesktop
Function          Set-RemoteDomain        16-tap-ex02.16-tap.local
Function          Set-RemoteMailbox       16-tap-ex02.16-tap.local
ExternalScript    RemoteExchange.ps1
Application       SystemPropertiesRemote.exe
```

To further narrow this down for our purposes of managing from the local server:

```
Get-Command *remote* | Where {$_.ModuleName -eq "16-tap-ex02.16-tap.local"}
```

```
CommandType          Name                     ModuleName
----------           -----                    -----------
Function             Disable-RemoteMailbox    16-tap-ex02.16-tap.local
Function             Enable-RemoteMailbox     16-tap-ex02.16-tap.local
Function             Get-RemoteDomain         16-tap-ex02.16-tap.local
Function             Get-RemoteMailbox        16-tap-ex02.16-tap.local
Function             New-RemoteDomain         16-tap-ex02.16-tap.local
Function             New-RemoteMailbox        16-tap-ex02.16-tap.local
Function             Remove-RemoteDomain      16-tap-ex02.16-tap.local
Function             Remove-RemoteMailbox     16-tap-ex02.16-tap.local
Function             Set-RemoteDomain         16-tap-ex02.16-tap.local
Function             Set-RemoteMailbox        16-tap-ex02.16-tap.local
```

Most of the cmdlets needed for managing mailboxes will have 'RemoteMaibox' in the name.

A remote mailbox is a mailbox in Office 365 whose user account is a mail enabled user that resides in Active Directory. The mailbox is recognized in the Exchange 2016 EAC under Recipients - Mailboxes. PowerShell can be used to manage these mailboxes with the cmdlets we found above. To query for mailboxes in Exchange 2016 that are remote mailboxes, use the Get-RemoteMailbox cmdlet which is distinct from the Get-Mailbox cmdlet which shows only the mailboxes that are on-premises. All queries and cmdlets run against the local AD object.

When it comes to archive mailboxes, management depends on where the mailbox is. If the mailbox is on-premises and the archive is in Office 365 then the Get-Mailbox cmdlet would display the archive properties. The properties of the online archive appear on the local mailbox:

Get-Mailbox | fl Archive*

```
ArchiveGuid            : 78ccc49c-d236-4efb-8af9-331ed1641964
ArchiveName            : {In-Place Archive }
ArchiveQuota           : 100 GB (107,374,182,400 bytes)
ArchiveWarningQuota    : 90 GB (96,636,764,160 bytes)
ArchiveDomain          : domian.mail.onmicrosoft.com
ArchiveStatus          : None
```

---

**NOTE**

One key factor of having archive mailboxes in the Office 365 tenant is that in order for archiving to work properly a mailbox called 'FederatedEmail.4c1f4d8b-8179-4148-93bf-00a95fa1e042' needs to exist and be accessible. If this mailbox is missing, then Hybrid mail flow could become compromised. Specifically messages that need to be delivered to an archive mailbox in Office 365 will cause the transport service on an Exchange server to crash. To fix this issue, the arbitration mailbox may need to be recreated.

Following Microsoft's article on recreating system mailboxes, make sure to run these two steps:

From the Exchange media that matches your Exchange 2016 build:

    Setup.com /PrepareAD

This will create missing system mailboxes in Exchange. However these will then need to be enabled in Active Directory. Run the following cmdlet to enable the Federated mailbox:

    Enable-Mailbox –Arbitration "FederatedEmail.4c1f4d8b-8179-4148-93bf-00a95fa1e042"

Now messages destined for the archive mailboxes in Office 365 will be delivered.

**Example 1**

For this scenario, user mailboxes are moving from Exchange 2010/2013 and there is a desire or requirement to move all mailboxes. An Exchange 2016 server be used as the management server. The Hybrid Configuration Wizard is used to configure this server as the connection point between Exchange on-premises and Exchange Online. Active Directory is currently at the Windows 2008 R2 level for the domain and forest functional level. Once all of the Exchange Server 2010 servers have been patched to the latest Update Rollup, Exchange 2016 can be installed. The new Exchange 2016 server will now serve as the organizations "hybrid" server for the Office 365 deployment. In this example, the cmdlets for managing Office 365 mailboxes should only be used if there are issues with the moved accounts.

**Cmdlets For Management**
Get-RemoteMailbox
Set-RemoteMailbox
New-RemoteMailbox

What are these cmdlets used for? Get-RemoteMailbox can be used for documentation of mailboxes in Office 365. Here are some examples from Microsoft on the proper usage of these cmdlets.

Some practical examples:

```
------------------------------ Example 1 ------------------------------
This example returns a summary list of all remote mailboxes in your organization.
Get-RemoteMailbox
```

```
------------------------------ Example 2 ------------------------------
Get-RemoteMailbox -Identity laura@contoso.com | Format-List
```

```
------------------------------ Example 3 ------------------------------
Get-RemoteMailbox -Credential $Credentials
```

**Example 1** would be used to get basic mailbox information:
Get-RemoteMailbox | ft SamAccountName, UserPrincipalName, RemoteRoutingAddress

```
SamAccountName  UserPrincipalName      RemoteRoutingAddress
--------------  -----------------      --------------------
Damian          Damian@domain.com      SMTP:damian@domain.onmicrosoft.com
```

**Example 2** would be used to get any information on litigation, retention, and InPlace mailbox holds:
Get-RemoteMailbox | ft SamAccountName, LitigationHoldEnabled, RetentionHoldEnabled, InPlaceHolds -Auto

```
SamAccountName  LitigationHoldEnabled  RetentionHoldEnabled  InPlaceHolds
--------------  ---------------------  --------------------  ------------
Damian                          False                 False  {}
```

**Example 3** covers some other critical mailbox settings:
Get-RemoteMailbox | ft SamAccountName, ArchiveState, SingleItemRecoveryEnabled, HiddenFromAddressListsEnabled -Auto

```
SamAccountName  ArchiveState  SingleItemRecoveryEnabled  HiddenFromAddressListsEnabled
--------------  ------------  -------------------------  -----------------------------
Damian                  None                      False                          False
```

Set-RemoteMailbox is used for changing settings on mailboxes. Perhaps the Remote Routing email address is incorrect and needs to be changed:

Set-RemoteMailbox "Damian Scoles" –RemoteRoutingAddress damian@tenant.onmicrosoft.com

New-RemoteMailbox is used for creating a mailbox that has a local Active Directory user and a mailbox in Exchange Online. Some examples by Microsoft are show below:

Get-Help New-RemoteMailbox –Examples

```
----------------------- Example 1 -----------------------
$Credentials = Get-Credential

Then run the New-RemoteMailbox cmdlet to create the mail user.

New-RemoteMailbox -Name "Kim Akers" -Password $Credentials.Password -UserPrincipalName kim@corp.contoso.com

After the new mail user is created, directory synchronization synchronizes the new mail user to the service and
the associated mailbox is created.

----------------------- Example 2 -----------------------
$Credentials = Get-Credential

Then run the New-RemoteMailbox cmdlet to create the mail user.

New-RemoteMailbox -Name "Kim Akers" -Password $Credentials.Password -UserPrincipalName kim@corp.contoso.com
-OnPremisesOrganizationalUnit "corp.contoso.com/Archive Users" -Archive
```

In practical terms, using this PS cmdlet is the simplest environment to manage from end to end as all servers are Exchange and PowerShell can be used against all servers, whether Exchange 2010, 2016 or Exchange Online.

## Example 2

For this scenario, a company uses a non-Exchange Server mail system for their email system. Company employees with email may or may not have user objects in Active Directory. For a migration scenario where the company is moving to Office 365, all users in the email system will get Active Directory Accounts. HR provides a list of employees in CSV format with some basic information about the employees. IT Management wants the employees listed in the CSV file to have AD object because they will have mailboxes in Office 365. The company's main corporate SMTP domain is @contoso.com. This address needs to be assigned as a UPN and the users need to have this set as their email address in Exchange as a mail user.

Exchange 2016 is installed at the latest CU release available. Once Exchange 2016 is installed, the Active Directory accounts will be created. Once all Active Directory accounts are created, all the users in the CSV file will need to have AD accounts created, be mail enabled, accounts synchronized to Office 365, accounts converted into Remote Mailboxes in EXO, then the mailbox data can be migrated from the third-party email system to Exchange Online.

First, we need to start with the CSV file that was provided by HR. The fields and a data sample look something like this:

```
FirstName,LastName,Alias,PrimarySMTPAddress,Title
Damian,Scoles,dscoles,dscoles@contoso.com,ITGuy
David,Stork,dstork,dstork@contoso.com,ITManager
```

… and so on …

Next, a script is needed to simply add users from the CSV. A crucial component is that we need to make sure that the user account does not exist. This will be done with two verification steps - alias and user principal name. The user principal name will match the primary SMTP address.

**Script # 1** - Add Users to Active Directory

First store the CSV file from HR in a variable called $csv using the Import-CSV cmdlet.

```
# Read in the CSV file
$CSV = Import-CSV "c:\downloads\Mail-System-List.csv"
```

Now that the values are stored in a $CSV variable, a loop can be created with each line of the CSV, which can be accessed with a $line variable.

```
Foreach ($Line in $Csv) {
```

With the loop started, the script will clear and set variables needed for the loop. For this script, two variables (UPN and Alias) have their values reset. Then the DisplayName variable is populated with the values of the First and Last name variables.

```
# Variable configuration / reset
$LastName = $$Line.Last
$FirstName = $Line.First
$NoAlias = $Null
$NoUPN = $Null
$DisplayName = "$FirstName $LastName"
```

Next the script needs to check for users in Active Directory using aliases. Note that the test will be performed in with Try {} Catch {} code block. If the Get-ADUser finds a user in AD then the rest of the script will be skipped because the $NoAlias variable (set to $Null at the beginning of the loop) cannot pass the test posed by 'If ($NoAlias)'. Thus the script skips to the ELSE section of the IF...ELSE code block:

```
# Verification Step One - Alias
Try {
   $User = Get-ADUser -Identity $Line.Alias -ErrorAction STOP
} Catch {
   $NoAlias = $True
}
```

If the $NoAlias variable is set to $True (no user found), then the next part of the script is initiated. Another Try {} Catch {} section is used, this time the code tries to match the UPN of a user account. If no user match is found, then $NoUPN becomes $True as well:

```
If ($NoAlias) {
   # Verification Step Two - UPN
   Try {
      $User = Get-ADUser -UserPrincipalName $Line.PrimarySMTPAddress -ErrorAction STOP
   } Catch {
      $NoUPN = $True
   }
}
```

Now if the script has passed both tests ($NoUPN = $True and $NoAlias = $True) then another Try {} Catch {} section is used to create the user.  If the user is created, no error message occurs.  If the creation fails, then an error message is displayed:

```
If ($NoUPN) {
    Try {
    New-ADUser -Name $Line.Alias -GiveName $FirstName -Surname -$LastName -Title $Line.Title
    -Displayname $DisplayName -ErrorAction STOP
    } Catch {
    Write-Host "Could not create the new user in Active Directory." -ForeGroundColor Red
}
```

Lastly, if those tests fail, a message appears that states the user exists and a user will not be created.

```
    } Else {
        Write-Host "The user already exists in Active Directory and was not created." -ForegroundColor
        Yellow
    }
}
```

> **Alternative Example**
>
> If all the users that were in AD prior to running the above script were already mail enabled, and they would show up in Exchange as a mailuser, the New-MailUser cmdlet could be used instead of New-ADUser. The reason for that is New-MailUser allows for the creation of an Active Directory object (Mail User) and allow Exchange to manage it directly. This would skip the need for step one and two. The reason we are not using this method in the book is so that you, the end user of PowerShell, understand the full process of object creation from nothing to a Remote Mailbox.

Now that the users are created, we need to log onto the Exchange 2016 server to enable all user objects from the CSV as Mail Users.  If you have a large Active Directory environment you may have to wait for replication to finish.

** **Note**** The above script could be enhanced to make a complete report of new users created as well as a report of what users that were found in Active Directory.  See the Reporting Chapter 16 for steps on how to create reports.

**Part Two**

For this next step we need to mail enable all users that have mailboxes in the third party messaging system.  These users are all listed in the same CSV from HR.  The reason we need to mail enable them is so that they can be managed from the Hybrid server.  After the users are mail enabled and after they are moved to the cloud, you can proceed to the third script which will explain how to convert a mail user to a mail enabled user.

```
Get-Help Enable-MailUser –Examples
```

```
-------------------------------- Example 1 --------------------------------

This example mail-enables user John with the external email address john@contoso.com.
Enable-MailUser -Identity John -ExternalEmailAddress john@contoso.com
```

For the below script sample, the HR's CSV file is read into the $CSV variable and then a Foreach loop is used to go through each line.  A Try{} Catch {} code block is used to mail enable the user and if it fails an error message is displayed.

**Script # 2** - Mail Enable All Users in CSV

```
# Read in the HR CSV file
$CSV = Import-CSV "c:\downloads\Mail-System-List.csv"
Foreach ($Line in $Csv) {
   $DisplayName = "$First $Last"
   # Mail Enable the User
   Try {
      Enable-MailUser -Identity $Line.Alias -ExternalEmailAddress $Line.PrimarySMTPAddress
   } Catch {
      Write-Host "Could not mail enable the user object for $DisplayName."
   }
}
```

Results of the script:

```
[PS] C:\Downloads>.\MailEnable-Test.ps1

Name                                    RecipientType
----                                    -------------
William Tell                            MailUser
Benjamin Franklin                       MailUser
```

For this script a couple of new cmdlets will be used for Remote Mailbox creation:

### Get-Help New-MailUser –Examples

```
---------------------------- Example 1 ----------------------------
New-MailUser -Name "Ed Meadows" -ExternalEmailAddress ed@tailspintoys.com -MicrosoftOnlineServicesID
ed@tailspintoys -Password (ConvertTo-SecureString -String 'P@ssw0rd1' -AsPlainText -Force)

---------------------------- Example 2 ----------------------------
$password = Read-Host "Enter password" -AsSecureString
New-MailUser -Name "Ed Meadows" -ExternalEmailAddress ed@tailspintoys.com -UserPrincipalName ed@contoso
-Password $password
```

### Get-Help Enable-RemoteMailbox –Examples

```
---------------------------- Example 1 ----------------------------
Enable-RemoteMailbox "Kim Akers" -RemoteRoutingAddress "kima@contoso.mail.onmicrosoft.com
After the user is mail-enabled, directory synchronization synchronizes the mail-enabled user to the service and
the associated mailbox is created.

---------------------------- Example 2 ----------------------------
Enable-RemoteMailbox "Kim Akers" -RemoteRoutingAddress "kima@contoso.mail.onmicrosoft.com -Archive
```

## Example Summary

So what did we learn in these examples?   We learned that in order to properly manage Office 365 mailboxes that have accounts in the on-premises Active Directory, we need to satisfy a few requirements.  First is that all mailboxes will need an Active Directory user account.  Then the users are mail enabled and they show up in the Exchange Administration Console as mail enabled users.  Finally, the users are converted to Remote Mailboxes.  The last step can only be performed once the mailbox has moved off the old platform.

# Azure Active Directory Recycle Bin

Azure AD has a Recycle Bin (similar to on-premises Active Directory) for objects that are removed from the tenant. These objects stay in the Recycle Bin for 30 days and then the objects are removed permanently. There are no direct PowerShell cmdlets (like Get-RecycleBin) for the Recycle Bin in Office 365. In order to find objects, the Get-MSOLUser cmdlet has a switch for this:

```
-ReturnDeletedUsers [<SwitchParameter>]
    If set, only users in the recycling bin will be deleted.

    Required?                       false
    Position?                       named
    Default value
    Accept pipeline input?          false
    Accept wildcard characters?     false
```

The 'ReturnDeletedUsers' will provide a list of users that were removed and are now awaiting for permanent deletion:

```
UserPrincipalName           DisplayName          isLicensed
-----------------           -----------          ----------
jdoe@domain.com             John Doe             False
hcastille@domain.com        Harold Castille      True
bhope@domain.com            Bob Hope             False
thill@domain.com            Thomas Hill          False
```

These same users can be removed with the Remove-MSOLUsers. Let's go through the process for an Office 365 tenant. Users that were recently deleted can be found in the Deleted Users tab under Users in the Office 365 interface:

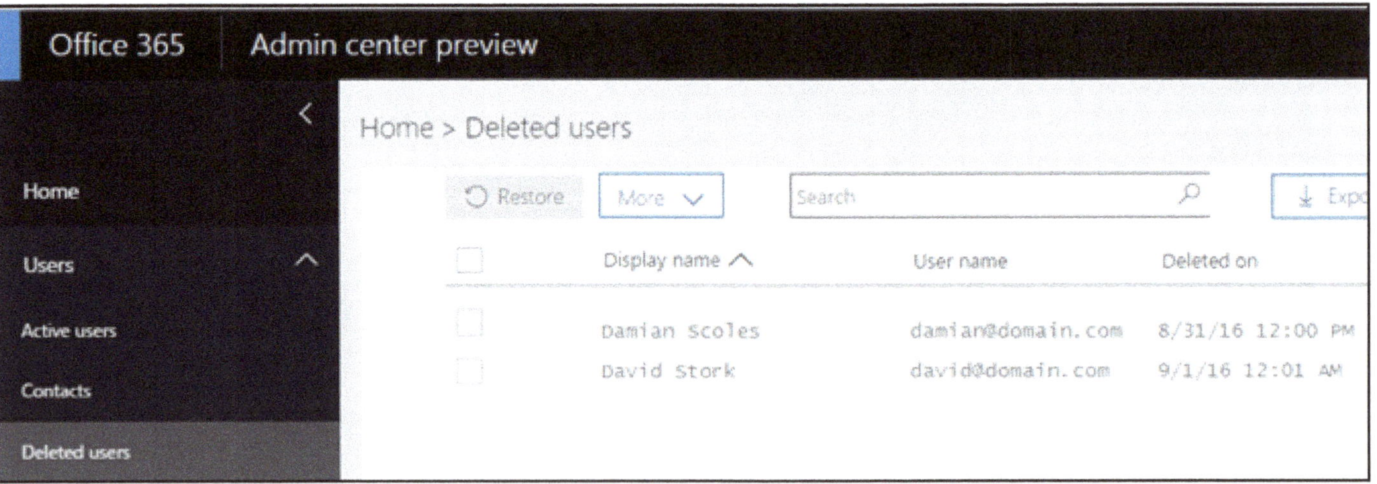


In order to properly remove users from the Recycle Bin, we first need the UPN and Object ID. The UPN is needed to verify which user will be deleted while the Object ID is actually used by PowerShell to remove the users [Don't forget to run Connect-MSOLService first]:

Get-MsolUser -ReturnDeletedUsers | Select UserPrincipalName, ObjectId

```
UserPrincipalName           Objectid
-----------------           --------
jdoe@domain.com             105856af-663a-49a8-bdad-efe8947ef70a
hcastille@domain.com        1b0ed587-4cf4-4e46-b5c5-5efab200007c
bhope@domain.com            866e6c23-629d-4239-aed9-c731173811dc
thill@domain.com            98fab817-b97b-436e-8854-47638b1af079
```

## Example 1

Removing only one user from the Recycle Bin can be done with a one-liner.  The only criteria needed as mentioned above, is the ObjectID from the list of objects in the Recycle Bin.

```
Remove-MsolUser -RemoveFromRecycleBin -ObjectId 98fab817-b97b-436e-8854-47638b1af079
```

```
PS C:\> Remove-MsolUser -RemoveFromRecycleBin -ObjectId 98fab817-b97b-436e-8854-47638b1af0

Confirm
Continue with this operation?
[Y] Yes  [N] No  [S] Suspend  [?] Help (default is "Y"): y
```

Then verify that the user is removed:

```
Get-MsolUser -ReturnDeletedUsers | select UserPrincipalName, ObjectId
```

```
UserPrincipalName        Objectid
-----------------        --------
jdoe@domain.com          105856af-663a-49a8-bdad-efe8947ef70a
hcastille@domain.com     1b0ed587-4cf4-4e46-b5c5-5efab200007c
bhope@domain.com         866e6c23-629d-4239-aed9-c731173811dc
```

## Example 2

Removing all users in the Recycle Bin requires a query to get the objects stored in the Recycle Bin and then a cmdlet to remove these objects.  Is this example the ObjectID does not need to be specified as we are removing all items.

```
Get-MsolUser -ReturnDeletedUsers | Remove-MsolUser -RemoveFromRecycleBin
```

```
PS C:\> Get-MsolUser -ReturnDeletedUsers | Remove-MsolUser -RemoveFromRecycleBin
Confirm
Continue with this operation?
[Y] Yes  [N] No  [S] Suspend  [?] Help (default is "Y"): y

Confirm
Continue with this operation?
[Y] Yes  [N] No  [S] Suspend  [?] Help (default is "Y"): y

Confirm
Continue with this operation?
[Y] Yes  [N] No  [S] Suspend  [?] Help (default is "Y"): y
```

Then verify that the user is removed:

```
Get-MsolUser -ReturnDeletedUsers | select UserPrincipalName, ObjectId
```

```
PS C:\> Get-MsolUser -ReturnDeletedUsers | select UserPrincipalName, ObjectId
PS C:\> _
```

**Result** – empty Recycle Bin.

# Licensing

Another case for using PowerShell in managing your Office 365 tenant is mass licensing manipulation. While the Portal for your tenant will allow for mass changes, the manipulation that it is capable is also limited. Only 100 accounts can be modified at any one time. If there is a need to adjust more at one time, then PowerShell is required to make the changes successful. PowerShell is especially useful if more complex changes are required – licensing determined by groups or granular licensing is needed.

First and foremost, what PowerShell cmdlets are available for these changes? Make sure a connection is opened up via the Windows PowerShell Azure Module – connect to the tenant and then the MSOL Service.

```
Get-Command *licen*
```

```
CommandType          Name
-----------          ----
Function             Get-LicenseVsUsageSummaryReport
Cmdlet               New-MsolLicenseOptions
Cmdlet               New-MsolLicenseOptions
Cmdlet               Set-MsolUserLicense
Cmdlet               Set-MsolUserLicense
```

Starting with the first cmdlet can provide some information about license usage:

```
Get-LicenseVsUsageSummaryReport | ft -Auto
```

```
Date                 TenantGuid                     Workload  NonTrialEntitlements  TrialEntitlements  ActiveUsers
----                 ----------                     --------  --------------------  -----------------  -----------
9/7/2016 12:00:00 AM                                EXO       395                   0                  0
9/7/2016 12:00:00 AM                                LYO       375                   0                  0
9/7/2016 12:00:00 AM                                SPO       375                   0                  3
9/7/2016 12:00:00 AM                                Yammer    375                   0                  1
```

Where would licensing be stored? Maybe the information is stored in the properties of a user account in Azure AD. To get all the properties from a user account in Azure AD, the Get-MSOLUser cmdlet can be used for this:

```
Get-MsolUser -UserPrincipalName damian@domain.com | fl
```

Deep in the properties for this user we can see that there is an Enterprise License installed for the tenant this user account is in:

```
LastName                          : Scoles
LicenseReconciliationNeeded       : False
Licenses                          : {Domain:ENTERPRISEPACK}
```

However, the licenses assigned are not granular and we need to find out what options can be set via PowerShell. Cutting to the chase, the cmdlet needed is not as obvious:

```
Get-MsolAccountSku
```

The cmdlet only has one parameter "TenantID" and one example, which is just the base cmdlet. What information will this provide us?

```
ExtensionData     : System.Runtime.Serialization.ExtensionDataObject
AccountName       : Domain
AccountObjectId   : a59a9dcf-a1c7-4dfa-b98c-d9b0fc4a8fd2
AccountSkuId      : Domain:ENTERPRISEPACK
ActiveUnits       : 375
ConsumedUnits     : 63
LockedOutUnits    : 0
ServiceStatus     : {Microsoft.Online.Administration.ServiceStatus, Microsoft.Online.Administration.ServiceStatus,
                    Microsoft.Online.Administration.ServiceStatus, Microsoft.Online.Administration.ServiceStatus...}
SkuId             : 6fd2c87f-b296-42f0-b197-1e91e994b900
SkuPartNumber     : ENTERPRISEPACK
```

Notice the information in the red rectangle, the information is repeating and not detailed. PowerShell has a tendency to oversimplify values when it cannot display them properly. That is the same case here. We will use PowerShell on the ServiceStatus value to reveal all of its contents.

First, capture the field in a variable:

```
$ServiceStatus = (Get-MsolAccountSku | Where {$_.SkuPartNumber -eq "ENTERPRISEPACK"}).
ServiceStatus
```

Then display the variable in a table format:

```
$ServiceStatus | ft
```

```
ServicePlan                                         ProvisioningStatus
-----------                                         ------------------
PROJECTWORKMANAGEMENT                                Success
SWAY                                                Success
INTUNE_O365                                         PendingInput
YAMMER_ENTERPRISE                                   Success
RMS_S_ENTERPRISE                                    Success
OFFICESUBSCRIPTION                                  Success
MCOSTANDARD                                         Success
SHAREPOINTWAC                                       Success
SHAREPOINTENTERPRISE                                Success
EXCHANGE_S_ENTERPRISE                               Success
```

The same information can be displayed for a single mailbox:

```
$Upn = "damian@domain.com"
(Get-MsolUser -User $Upn).Licenses[0].ServiceStatus
```

The above PowerShell is handy to validate any individual changes.

From the above Service Plans, a determination of what can be licensed is shown below:

| Service Plan | What License Does this Apply to? |
| --- | --- |
| PROJECTWORKMANAGEMENT | Office 365 Planner Preview |
| SWAY | Sway |
| INTUNE_O365 | Intune |
| YAMMER_ENTERPRISE | Yammer |
| RMS_S_ENTERPRISE | Rights Management Service |
| OFFICESUBSCRIPTION | Office ProPlus |
| MCOSTANDARD | Lync Online (Plan 2) |
| SHAREPOINTWAC | Office Online |
| SHAREPOINTENTERPRISE | SharePoint Online (Plan 2) |
| EXCHANGE_S_ENTERPRISE | Exchange Online |

The above chart can be found at the below Microsoft link. The Service Plans on the left are the ones that would be referenced in with PowerShell scripts - https://blogs.technet.microsoft.com/treycarlee/2014/12/09/powershell-licensing-skus-in-office-365/.

Now that we have the license options for this particular license SKU, how can these options be turned on and off for the users in Office 365? The most common method is to create what is called a 'Disabled Plan' which is essentially a set of options above that need to be unlicensed from a user account. Instead of enabling what is needed,

PowerShell will need to disable what is unneeded. The reason for this will be apparent in the below script and available parameters.

### Sample Script – Disable Licenses

```
# Read Users from CSV list
$Users = Import-Csv "c:\Scripting\UserList.csv"
```

An array of disabled Service Plans is created and stored in the $DisabledOptions:

```
#Set disabled Options
$DisabledOptions = @()
$DisabledOptions += "SHAREPOINTENTERPRISE"
$DisabledOptions += "MCOSTANDARD"
$DisabledOptions += "OFFICESUBSCRIPTION"
$DisabledOptions += "SHAREPOINTWAC"
$DisabledOptions += "PROJECTWORKMANAGEMENT"
$DisabledOptions += "SWAY "
$DisabledOptions += "INTUNE_O365"
$DisabledOptions += "RMS_S_ENTERPRISE"
```

Then a loop is used to process each user in the CSV file:

```
# Loop each account to set location and license options.
Foreach ($Line in $Users) {
```

Then PowerShell checks for the user's location and if the same account is licensed:

```
$Upn = $Line.Upn
$Location = (Get-MsolUser -UserPrincipalName $Upn).UsageLocation
$Licensed = (Get-MsolUser -UserPrincipalName $Upn).IsLicensed
```

For this section, if the location is not set, a location of 'US' will be configured:

```
If ($Location -eq $Null) {
    Set-MsolUser -UserPrincipalName $Upn -UsageLocation "US"
}
```

Next, if the user is not licensed, this block will add a valid license to the user:

```
If ($Licensed -eq $False) {
    Set-MsolUserLicense -UserPrincipalName $Upn -AddLicenses "<tenantname>:ENTERPRISEPACK"
}
```

Note: "<tenantname>" should be replaced with the Office 365 tenant name. This can be obtained using Login-AzureRmAccount, which will prompt for credentials and then reveal the tenant information:

```
Environment            : AzureCloud
Account                : Damian@domain.onmicrosoft.com
TenantId               : ########-####-####-####-############
SubscriptionId         :
SubscriptionName       :
CurrentStorageAccount  :
```

A valid set of license options is stored in the $LicenseOptions variable:

> $LicenseOptions = New-MsolLicenseOptions –AccountSkuId "<tenantname>:ENTERPRISEPACK" –DisabledPlans $DisabledOptions

The license options are then applied to the user account:

> Set-MsolUserLicense –User $Upn –LicenseOptions $LicenseOptions
> $Status = (Get-MsolUser -User $Upn).Licenses[0].ServiceStatus

After the script completes, the current licensing options for the user account can be verified with PowerShell first:

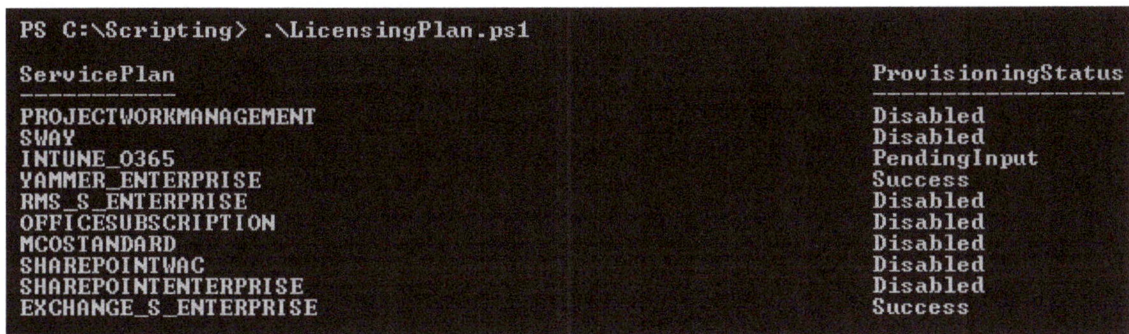


The results can also be verified in the Office 365 console:

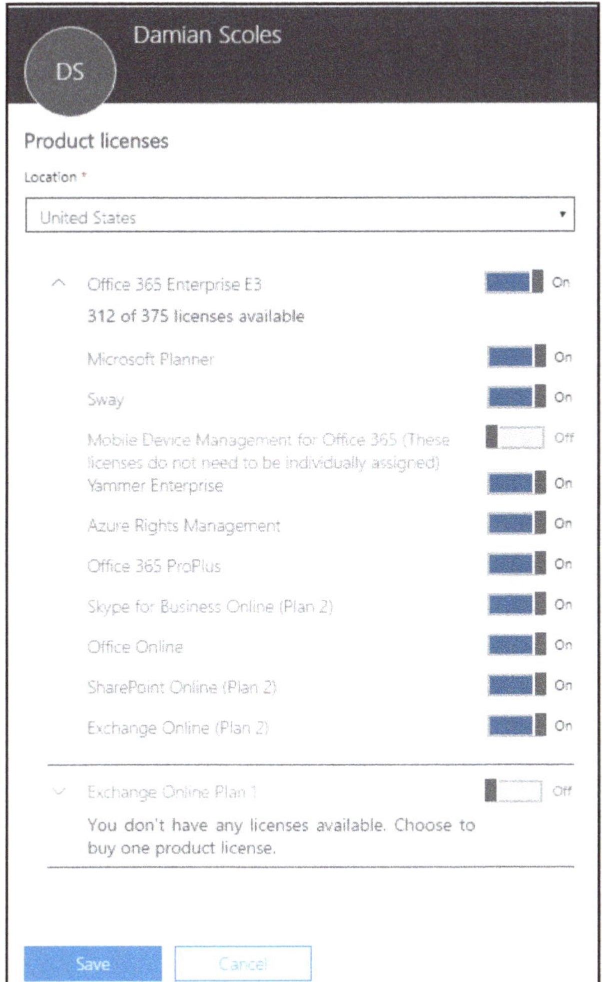

Why is this the solution? Unfortunately the licensing for Office 365 does not work in a cumulative manner or allow the option to choose which options to enable. For Office 365, Microsoft requires the licensing to be applied in a subtractive manner. For example with an E3 license (previous page) there are essentially 10 sub-licenses. By default, assigning an E3 license will enable all of these sub-licenses. However, if there are users that are only required to have Exchange Online, the other nine need to be disabled and instead of just enabling the Exchange Online license.

The option to select and unselect license options is important as need changes, user roles change, and organizational app needs change and so on. Being able to add or remove individual licenses are important for maintaining strict access to apps that may only be necessary for a particular user's job function.

**Sample Script 2**

Take the same scenario where licenses need to be adjusted. IT management has decided that there will be licensing tiers to make sure that users only have access to applications that are required for them to do their jobs. The list of requirements is divided into four different licensing groups. Here are the requirements (by group):

| Warehouse | Marketing | InfoWorkers | IT |
| --- | --- | --- | --- |
| EXCHANGE_S_ENTERPRISE | SWAY | INTUNE_O365 | PROJECTWORKMANAGEMENT |
| SHAREPOINTWAC | YAMMER_ENTERPRISE | YAMMER_ENTERPRISE | SWAY |
|  | RMS_S_ENTERPRISE | RMS_S_ENTERPRISE | INTUNE_O365 |
|  | OFFICESUBSCRIPTION | OFFICESUBSCRIPTION | YAMMER_ENTERPRISE |
|  | MCOSTANDARD | MCOSTANDARD | RMS_S_ENTERPRISE |
|  | SHAREPOINTWAC | SHAREPOINTWAC | OFFICESUBSCRIPTION |
|  | SHAREPOINTENTERPRISE | SHAREPOINTENTERPRISE | MCOSTANDARD |
|  | EXCHANGE_S_ENTERPRISE | EXCHANGE_S_ENTERPRISE | SHAREPOINTWAC |
|  |  |  | SHAREPOINTENTERPRISE |
|  |  |  | EXCHANGE_S_ENTERPRISE |

In order to make this work properly, Active Directory Groups need to be assigned and then the licensing can be applied in a per group manner. First, the group assignment needs to occur in order to prepare for assigning licenses on a per group basis.

**Sample Source CSV File**

```
SamAccountNameGroup
Administrator,IT
Guest,Warehouse
Krbtgt,Marketing
Damian,IT
```

**Sample Script Code**

```powershell
# Read Users from CSV list
$Users = Import-Csv "c:\Scripting\GroupsToUsers.csv"

Foreach ($Line in $Users) {
    # 'normalize' variables
    $Member = $Line.SamAccountName
    $Group = $Line.Group

    # Add user to the group listed in the CSV file
    Try {
        Add-ADGroupMember -Identity $Group -Member $Member -ErrorAction STOP
        Write-Host "Successfully added $Member to the group $Group." -ForegroundColor Cyan
    } Catch {
        Write-Host "Could not add $Member to the group $Group." -ForegroundColor Yellow
    }
}
```

When run, the users are added to their respective groups:

```
PS C:\Scripting> .\UsersToGroups.ps1
Successfully added Administrator to the group IT.
Successfully added Guest to the group warehouse.
Successfully added krbtgt to the group Marketing.
Successfully added damian to the group IT.
Successfully added dstork to the group IT.
Successfully added tuser01 to the group Marketing.
Successfully added tuser02 to the group warehouse.
Successfully added adrms to the group IT.
Successfully added jton to the group Marketing.
Successfully added jforth to the group Marketing.
Successfully added jwithers to the group Marketing.
Successfully added GlenJohn to the group IT.
Successfully added wtell to the group Marketing.
Successfully added bfranklin to the group warehouse.
```

Now the groups have been populated, the disabled plans can be created – one per AD group:

```powershell
# Disabled Options for Warehouse workers
$DisabledOptionsWH = @()
$DisabledOptionsWH += "SWAY"
$DisabledOptionsWH += "YAMMER_ENTERPRISE"
$DisabledOptionsWH += "RMS_S_ENTERPRISE"
$DisabledOptionsWH += "OFFICESUBSCRIPTION"
$DisabledOptionsWH += "MCOSTANDARD"
$DisabledOptionsWH += "SHAREPOINTENTERPRISE"
$DisabledOptionsWH += "EXCHANGE_S_ENTERPRISE"
$DisabledOptionsWH += "SHAREPOINTENTERPRISE"
$DisabledOptionsWH += "PROJECTWORKMANAGEMENT"
```

```
# Disabled Options for Marketing
$DisabledOptionsMKT = @()
$DisabledOptionsMKT += "PROJECTWORKMANAGEMENT"

# Disabled Options for Information Workers
$DisabledOptionsIW = @()
$DisabledOptionsIW += "PROJECTWORKMANAGEMENT"
$DisabledOptionsIW += "SWAY"

# Disabled Options for Information Technology
# None - all active at this time
```

After the licensing options are configured, the user lists need to be created so that licenses can be assigned by group membership:

```
# Store group members into variables
$IW = Get-ADGroup "IT" | Get-AdGroupMember
$Marketing = Get-ADGroup "Marketing" | Get-AdGroupMember
$Warehouse = Get-ADGroup "Warehouse" | Get-AdGroupMember
```

Next the connection to Office 365 need to be established:

```
# Connect to Office 365
Write-host "Enter the password for Office 365 administrative rights." -ForegroundColor Cyan
Read-Host -SssecureString | ConvertFrom-SecureString | Out-File "c:\scripting\securestring.txt"
$Password = cat "c:\scripting\securestring.txt" | ConvertTo-SecureString
$UserName = "<UPN of Global Admin>"
$O365Cred = New-Object -TypeName System.Management.Automation.PSCredential -ArgumentList $Username, $Password
$Session = New-PSSession -ConfigurationName Microsoft.Exchange -ConnectionUri https://ps.outlook.com/powershell/ -Credential $O365Cred -Authentication Basic -AllowRedirection
Import-PSSession $Session
```

Then a connection to the Microsoft Azure Active Directory tenant needs to be established:

```
# Connect to MSOL Service
Connect-MsolService -Credential $O365Cred
```

After all the connections are made (Office 365 and MSOL Service) and the variables are populated with the users to be configured for proper licensing, a licensing code block will be run for each group (a repeat of previous code):

```
# Set licensing for Information Workers
Foreach ($Line in $IW) {

    # Set variables
    $Upn = $Line.UserPrincipalName
    $Location = (Get-MsolUser -UserPrincipalName $Upn).UsageLocation
    $Licensed = (Get-MsolUser -UserPrincipalName $Upn).IsLicensed

    # Set location to United States
```

```
    If ($Location -eq $Null) {
        Set-MsolUser -UserPrincipalName $Upn -UsageLocation "US"
    }

    # Assign full license to start with
    If ($Licensed -eq $False) {
        Set-MsolUserLicense -UserPrincipalName $Upn -AddLicenses "<tenantname>:ENTERPRISEPACK"
    }

    # Remove 'excess' license options
    $LicenseOptions = New-MsolLicenseOptions –AccountSkuId "<tenantname>:ENTERPRISEPACK" –
    DisabledPlans $DisabledOptions
    Set-MsolUserLicense –User $Upn –LicenseOptions $LicenseOptions
}
```

Repeat the same code above, simply switching out this one line for each group to be configured:

```
    Foreach ($Line in $IW) {
```

Which becomes:

```
    Foreach ($Line in $Marketing) {
```

And:

```
    Foreach ($Line in $Warehouse) {
```

Now all users have their licensing configured per IT Management.


# IdFix

For Hybrid environments with an on-premises Active Directory and Azure AD free edition, one of the key component of a user's identity is the User Principal Names (UPNs) for all users. The UPN is important for accessing resources in a Hybrid environment. Microsoft recommends that the UPN and the Primary SMTP address match. This recommendation is so that the end user does not experience pop-ups and is able to connect to resources without issue.

In order to validate or verify that this is correctly configured, Microsoft provides a tool called IdFix. This utility will analyze the various attributes in Active Directory and determine if there are any potential issues with connecting to an Office 365 tenant. The tool can be downloaded from here as of the writing of this book:

https://www.microsoft.com/en-us/download/details.aspx?id=36832

Any errors that are found by this tool should be remediated prior to a directory sync tool being installed and synching data to Office 365 – Azure AD Connect for example. Once the tool is downloaded, it can be run just by double-clicking on the executable:

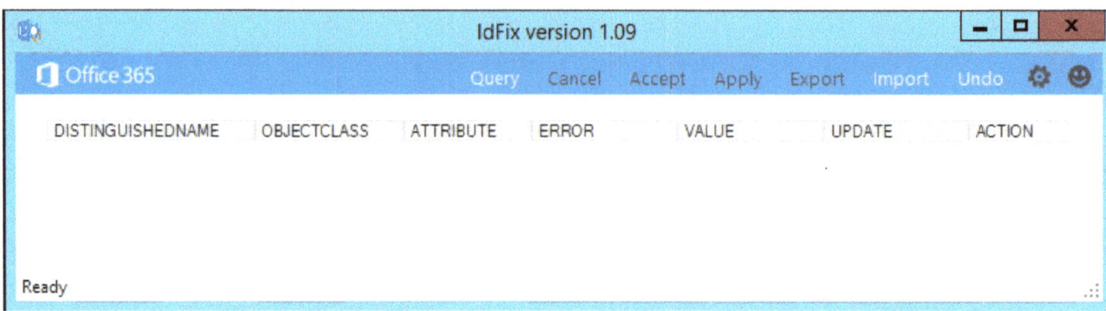

Click Query to see if there are any issues that need to be resolved:

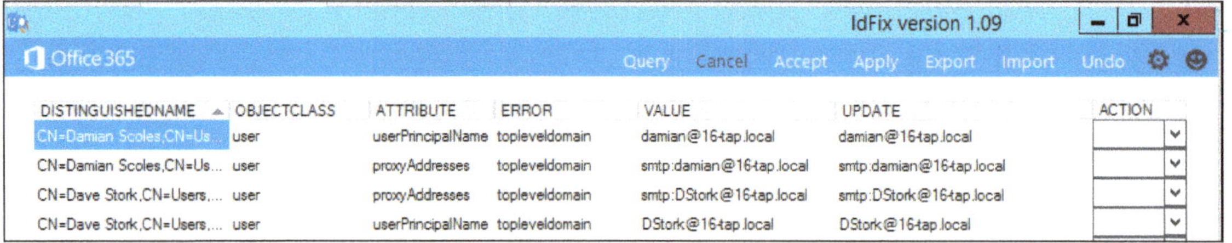

These results can be exported as a CSV file. Simply click 'Export' and select a location to export the results to a CSV file. Since IdFix can export the results in a CSV format, the CSV file can be used with PowerShell later. The CSV file can be used as a data source for correcting user issues with PowerShell. Let's take the IdFix CSV file and use it to correct any user objects with an invalid User Principal Name. The script needs to read in the CSV file, run a loop to process all the entries and the correct only those invalid entries matching that criteria. The CSV file contains the following fields [As seen above]:

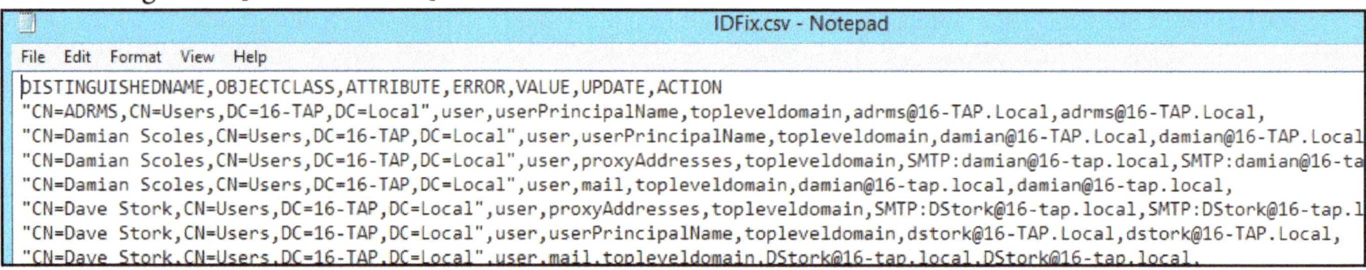

DISTINGUISHEDNAME          OBJECTCLASS               ATTRIBUTE
ERROR                      VALUE                     UPDATE
ACTION

For the below example, the UserPrincipalName needs to be updated to match the primary SMTP address:

**Example Script – Fix UserPrincipalName**

This code section will start an error log file and populate header information of the file:

```
# Get date for the file name
$Date = Get-Date -Format "MM.dd.yyyy-hh.mm-tt"
# Create a file for errors
$ErrorFileName = "C:\Downloads\IdFix\$date-Errors.txt"
$ScriptErrors = "This is the error file for problems creating or modifying users on $date.`r
`n------------------------------------------------------------------- `r`n" | Out-File -FilePath $ErrorFileName
```

The CSV file is imported for the loop below:

```
# Import the CSV File
$Csv = Import-Csv "c:\downloads\idfix\idfix.csv"

Foreach ($Line in $Csv) {
```

First, only lines with the Objectclass of 'User' to proceed:

```
If ($Line.OBJECTCLASS -eq "User") {
```

Then, examining the same line, the script looks for an 'Attribute' value of UserPrincipalName and allows it to proceed:

```
If ($Line.Attribute -eq "UserPrincipalName") {
```

This section verifies the identity of the user, so that the correct mailbox can be modified:

```
$User = $Line.DISTINGUISHEDNAME
Try {
    $Address = (Get-Mailbox $user -ErrorAction STOP).PrimarySmtpAddress
} Catch {
    $ScriptErrors = "User $User mailbox was not found." | Out-File -FilePath $ErrorFileName
}
```

Sets the Primary SMTP address to be applied to the user to correct the error:

```
$PrimarySMTPAddress = $Address.Address
```

This code section sets the user properties correctly to fix the issues found in the IdFix report:

```
Try {
    Set-ADUser -Identity $User -UserPrincipalName $PrimarySmtpAddress
} Catch {
    $ScriptErrors = "Unable to change the UPN for the user $user" | Out-File -FilePath $ErrorFileName
}
```

Post script run, an IdFix query is run again:

| DISTINGUISHEDNAME ▲ | OBJECTCLASS | ATTRIBUTE | ERROR | VALUE | UPDATE |
| --- | --- | --- | --- | --- | --- |
| CN=Damian Scoles,CN=Us... | user | proxyAddresses | topleveldomain | smtp:damian@16-tap.local | smtp:damian@16-tap.local |
| CN=Dave Stork,CN=Users,... | user | proxyAddresses | topleveldomain | smtp:DStork@16-tap.local | smtp:DStork@16-tap.local |

For the next error on the list, there is an issue with one of the defined proxy addresses that are on all accounts in Active Directory.  To change this, the default address policy may need to be removed and then the offending proxy address can be removed.

### Example Script – Remove Bad SMTP Addresses

The purpose of the script is to query only users that have ProxyAddress issues (as found in the CSV file from IdFix).  After those values are filtered, the script will attempt to remove the offending SMTP address from the ProxyAddresses on a user account.  Any errors encountered will be appended to a log file for later review.  The script code is below.

This section grabs the current date and stores the value in a particular format in the $Date variable:

```
# Get date for the file name
$Date = Get-Date -Format "MM.dd.yyyy-hh.mm-tt"
```

A logging file gets created, with a unique name and is populated with a header for reference:

```
# Create a file for errors
$ErrorFileName = "C:\Downloads\IdFix\$date-ProxyErrors.txt"
$ScriptErrors = "This is the error file for problems creating or modifying users on $Date.`r
`n------------------------------------------------------------------ `r`n" | Out-File -FilePath $ErrorFileName
```

Then the IdFix CSV file is imported into the $CSV variable:

```
# Import the CSV File
$Csv = Import-Csv "c:\downloads\idfix\idfix.csv"
```

This loop has some complicated steps and each will be reviewed and split for clarity. First the $CSV file is used for a Foreach loop, with each line in the CSV loaded into the $Line variable:

```
Foreach ($Line in $Csv) {
```

Since the script is for user objects only, the first IF…THEN loop is started to filter for only user objects:

```
If ($Line.OBJECTCLASS -eq "User") {
```

Since the script then looks for the ProxyAddresses issues, another IF…THEN loop is started to filter for this:

```
If ($Line.Attribute -eq "ProxyAddresses") {
```

Variables are set for the loop, two are pulled from the $CSV and one is $Null for each loop. The $BadSMTP address variable will store the value that needs to be removed. The reset of these variables is to make sure no data is retained for each loop:

```
$Fail = $Null
$User = $Line.DISTINGUISHEDNAME
$BadSMTP = $Line.Value
```

In order to remove an address, the EmailAddressPolicyEnabled value needs to be $False.

```
Try {
    $PolicyApplied = (Get-Mailbox $User -ErrorAction STOP).EmailAddressPolicyEnabled
} Catch {
    $ScriptErrors = "User $user mailbox was not found." | Out-File -FilePath $ErrorFileName
}
```

If the Policy is enabled, this loop will set the 'EmailAddressPolicyEnabled' value to $False, in preparation for removing the bad SMTP Address:

```
If ($PolicyApplied) {
    # Email Address is applied - Remove the policy and then remove the address
    Try {
        Set-Mailbox $User -EmailAddressPolicyEnabled $False -ErrorAction STOP
    } Catch {
        $ScriptErrors = "The EmailAddressPolicyEnabled property for $user cannot be changed." | Out-File
        -FilePath $ErrorFileName
```

```
            $Fail = $True
    }
```

The next IF…ELSE code section looks to see if the policy change failed.  If it did not, then the address can be removed.  To remove the value, first a Get-ADUser cmdlet needs to be used with the –identity and –property parameters.  The results of this cmdlet are piped ('|') to a Set-ADUser cmdlet.  Notice that there is a –Remove parameter.  This allows PowerShell to remove a particular value from a property on an AD Object.

```
If ($Fail -ne $True) {
    Try {
        Get-ADUser -identity $User -property * | Set-ADUser -remove @{'ProxyAddresses' = $BadSMTP}
    } Catch {
        $ScriptErrors = "Cannot remove $BadSMTP from the mailbox of $User." | Out-File -FilePath
        $ErrorFileName
    }
}
```

The purpose of this code section is to make the change if the EmailAddressPolicy is NOT enabled by default.  The code is separate because there are no blockers to removing a bad Proxy Address:

```
    } Else {
        # Email Address is not applied - Remove the address
        Try {
            Get-ADUser -identity $User -property * | Set-ADUser -Remove @{'ProxyAddresses' = $BadSMTP}
        } Catch {
            $ScriptErrors = "Cannot remove $BadSMTP from the mailbox of $User." | Out-File -FilePath
            $ErrorFileName
        }
}
```

Note in the Try..Catch code, there's code to export an error message to a logging file.  No output should be seen if the script runs successfully.  If IdFix is run again, the proxy address errors should be gone.  If they are not, check the logging file for details.

New IdFix Query – very clean, error count is low after these two scripts were run:

| DISTINGUISHEDNAME ▲ | OBJECTCLASS | ATTRIBUTE | ERROR | VALUE | UPDATE |
|---|---|---|---|---|---|
| CN=Migration.8f3e7716-20… | user | userPrincipalName | topleveldomain | Migration.8f3e7716-2011-43e4-96b1-aba62d229136@16-TAP.Local | Migration.8f3e7716-2011-43e4-9 |

# UPN and Primary SMTP Address Updates

In a Hybrid environment, it is sometimes necessary to change UPNs or Primary SMTP addresses. An example of this more complex Hybrid scenario, a company is consolidating email domains to a brand new SMTP domain. In doing so, the UPNs and Primary SMTP addresses for all users need to be from LittleBox.Com to BigBox.Com.

**Example Script – Changing UPN and SMTP Addresses**

```
# Import the AD Module
Import-Module ActiveDirectory

# Import the CSV File
$Users = Import-CSV "c:\scripting\mailboxusers.csv"
$Domain = 'BigBox.Com'

Foreach ($Line in $Users) {
        $Alias = $Line.Alias
        $Primary = $Alias+'@'+$Domain
        Get-Mailbox $Alias |Set-Mailbox -PrimarySmtpAddress $Primary -UserPrincipalName $Primary
        Get-AdUser $Alias | Set-ADUser -EmailAddress $Primary
}
```

This script needs to be run from a PowerShell console that has the Exchange Server cmdlets due to the Set-Mailbox cmdlet. This PowerShell Console can be on an Exchange Server or on a management workstation.

# 16     Reporting

**In This Chapter**

- Screenshots
- TXT Files
- CSV Files
- HTML Files
- Delivery Methodologies
- File Copy

When managing systems like Exchange Server, often the concentration of work to manage these is reviewing the configuration with Get cmdlets or making configuration changes with Set cmdlets. Of course there are other cmdlets starting with New, Remove, and so on. Either way the daily tasks such as adding mailboxes, changing settings on the server, looking for issues and scouring through logs will take up the majority of time and little time is given to documenting an environment or being proactive and producing daily reports.

PowerShell makes creating reports easy and while there are third party products that can produce canned results, they are not usually as flexible as PowerShell. With PowerShell, an administrator can choose the parameters to be reported on, the formatting and delivering method. Scripts can also be scheduled and contain error correction as needed depending on the intended results.

In this chapter, we will explore various reporting formats like TXT, CSV, HTML, and more. Delivery methods will also be explored and ways to schedule the reports. Real world scenarios will be used to help illustrate the usefulness of each method as well as the possibilities that each of these formats will provide.

# Screenshots

The simplest method for using PowerShell to document an Exchange Server 2016 environment is to use screenshots to capture script results. The advantages to this method are that it is quick, simple and somewhat flexible. The disadvantages are that the results are harder to manipulate post screenshot and not as flexible for generating good documentation.

Using programs like the Windows Snipping Tool, OneNote, SnagIt and others can make quick snapshots of your PowerShell Script results. However, since this is a PowerShell book, I would only recommend using these tools as enhancements for documentation or reports that were created in PowerShell.

Let's explore other options for creating documentation via PowerShell.

# TXT Files

PowerShell provides a variety of ways to export results from cmdlets or scripts thus making results accessible for later review. One of these methods includes exporting any and all results to a text file.

Exporting the output can be done with a couple different methods. One is to use the '>' symbol and specifying a TXT file name for output. The second method for exporting the results via the Out-File cmdlet. The below examples will explore both of these options for real world scenarios.

First, reporting the statistics for mailboxes in an Exchange Server environment requires a couple of cmdlets to gather the data. Get-Mailbox, which is piped to Get-MailboxStatistics to derive the numbers needed for an accurate report of all mailbox sizes. In addition to these cmdlets, some formatting has been inserted for attributes that are reported on. Note that Select-Object is being used to facilitate this:

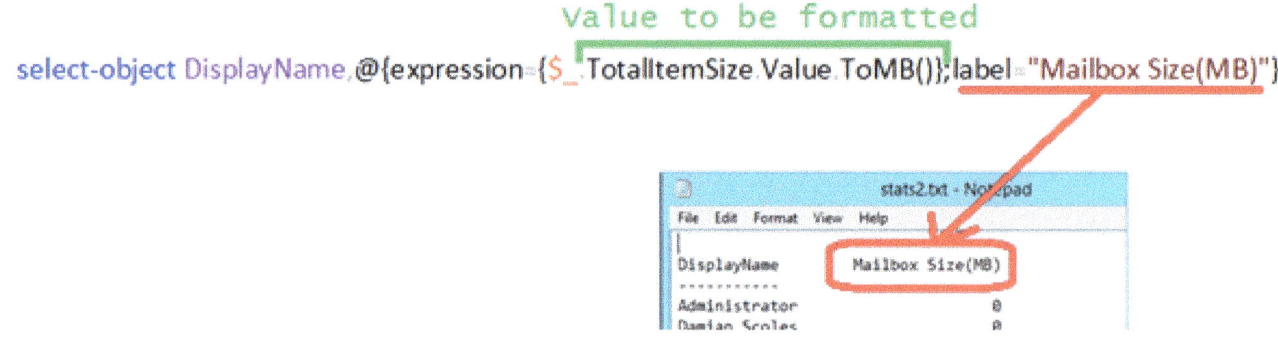



## Example – '>'

```
Get-Mailbox | Get-MailboxStatistics | Select-Object DisplayName,@Expression={$_.TotalItemSize.Value.
ToMB()};Label="Mailbox Size(MB)"} | ft -Auto > C:\downloads\stats2.txt
```

** **Note** ** The '>' symbol can be used to create or overwrite an existing file, while using '>>' will append to an existing file.

This cmdlet drops the results of this cmdlet to a local text file:

```
                          stats2.txt - Notepad
 File   Edit   Format   View   Help

 |
 DisplayName              Mailbox Size(MB)
 -----------              ----------------
 Administrator                          0
 Damian Scoles                          0
 Journaling Mailbox                     0
 Dave Stork                             0
```

**Example** – 'Out-File'-

Similar to the '>' output symbol, the Out-File provides a method for exporting results of the cmdlet to a TXT file. However, Out-File provides more options for formatting the actual output; including Encoding, NoClobber, as well as width of the output.

```
Get-Mailbox | Get-MailboxStatistics | Select-Object DisplayName,@{Expression={$_.TotalItemSize.
Value.ToMB()};Label="Mailbox Size(MB)"} | ft -Auto | Out-File -FilePath C:\downloads\stats2-OF.txt
-NoClobber
```

This PowerShell cmdlet drops the results to a local text file:

```
                          stats2-OF.txt - Notepad
 File   Edit   Format   View   Help

 |
 DisplayName              Mailbox Size(MB)
 -----------              ----------------
 Administrator                          0
 Damian Scoles                          0
 Journaling Mailbox                     0
 Dave Stork                             0
 Test User01                            0
 Test User02                            0
 Journaling-Germany                     1
```

Notice that in terms of actual output or formatting, the text file is exactly the same for either '>' or 'Out-File'. The true differentiator will be the usage of NoClobber and Encoding. While Encoding was not used for this example, it is an available option. The –NoClobber is useful as it will prevent the overwriting a file by the output of this cmdlet. This is useful for running reports that may need to be reviewed later and having a script overwrite a file would make data analysis later impossible.

**Example** – Out-File – 2

The first example was a bit simple, based off a single cmdlet. In this example a script will be written to produce a report of the mailbox statistics on multiple servers, sorted by size, and arranged by server, then exported to a TXT file for reporting:

```powershell
# Get all mailbox servers
$ExchangeServers = Get-MailboxServer

# Start new text file
$ServerHeadline = "All Server Mailbox Statistics. `r`n---------------------------- `r`n" | Out-File -FilePath C:\
downloads\AllServerStats.txt

Foreach ($Server in $ExchangeServers) {
    # Get Mailbox Statistics from the current server
    $ServerHeadline = "These are the results from the $Server server. `r`n" | Out-File -Filepath C:\
    downloads\AllServerStats.txt -Append
    Get-Mailbox -Server $Server | Get-MailboxStatistics | Select-Object DisplayName, @{Expression={$_.
    TotalItemSize.Value.ToMB()};Label="Mailbox Size(MB)"} | ft -Auto | Out-File -FilePath C:\downloads\
    AllServerStats.txt -append
    $ServerHeadline = "`r`n" | Out-File -FilePath C:\downloads\AllServerStats.txt -Append
}
```

Contents of the resulting TXT file are:

```
All Server Mailbox Statistics.
-----------------------------

These are the results from the 16-TAP-EX01 server.


DisplayName    Mailbox Size(MB)
-----------    ----------------
Administrator                 1
Jim Tom                       0




These are the results from the 16-TAP-EX02 server.


DisplayName        Mailbox Size(MB)
-----------        ----------------
Damian Scoles                     2
Journaling Mailbox                0
Dave Stork                        0
Test User01                       0
Test User02                       0
Journaling-Germany                3
```

## Explanation of the Script

In the first part of the script, lines are added to title the TXT file with 'All Mailbox Statistics', followed by a carriage return and then a line of '-' to create an underline and then this line is followed by another carriage return. Note that the switch –append is not used. This is because the file needs to start fresh, with no content for the header, otherwise the 'header' would go to the bottom of the file and is then not a header.

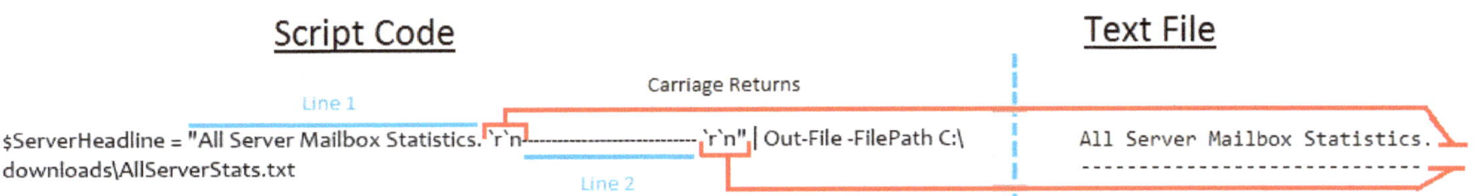



The next section (inside the Foreach loop), a line is added to declare which server is being analyzed in this part of the script. Than a carriage return is added. The '–append' is added to the Out-File cmdlet to make sure that this is added underneath the header.

Next, a section of code is needed to add the Mailbox Statistics (just like the previous one liner In Example – Out-File):

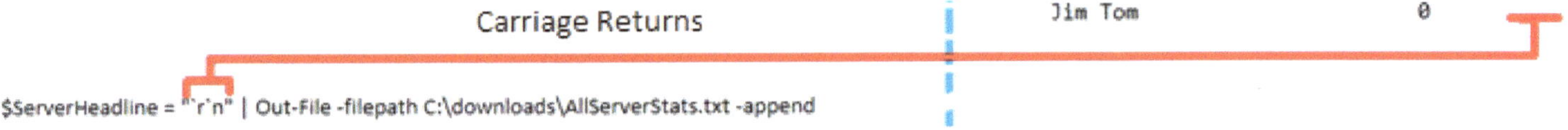



This part called out in line below, adds an additional carriage return after the mailbox statistics is purely for formatting and making room for the next server.



From the script above and the previous Out-File and '>' methodology, exporting the results of PowerShell can be used for reporting and can be formatted to your liking. The Out-File cmdlet is not a complex cmdlet and provides an easy way to create documentation or create a starting point for further reporting on an Exchange Server environment. The caveat is that it cannot be easily utilized for producing additional reports and these TXT reports are essentially just screen scrapes. The next section of this chapter, on CSV files, provides that next step of exporting data to a file that can be used for future reports and even as input to other systems or spreadsheets easily.

# CSV Files

A CSV file can be constructed by using Export-CSV cmdlet in PowerShell. CSV files are a good data format for tables since their format can be used for future scripts. CSV file data is also similar in format to the format of an array of arrays used in PowerShell. They're typically used as either a temporary data storage for a script for further processing, used by a different script or just to document values found in Exchange. In terms of documenting an Exchange messaging environment CSV files are useful for creating large data tables to be analyzed/reported on. They can also easily be imported into Excel and other tools for further data analysis and usage.

In terms of real world examples, CSV files can be used to document things such as:

- **Mailbox Statistics** – name, number of items, database, server, mailbox size, quotas and more

- **Exchange Server Information** – name, site, role, version, mailboxes on a server, etc.
- **Transport Settings** – tracking logs, protocol logs and more
- **Mailbox Information** – name, database, UPN, primary SMTP address, SIP Address and more
- **SMTP Connectors** – server, connector name, connector type, Remote IPs, authentication and scoping

All of the examples above are good examples of what can be contained in these CSV files. How do we use PowerShell to create a CSV file? Let's go through some practical examples of how to create files and use the data that is contained in the CSV file.

** **Note** ** The CSV delimiter value could be different depending on your region. Another sample delimiters is ';' which is used in German and Dutch language regions.

**Example 1**

For this example, we have a project where IT Management has decided to upgrade Exchange 2010 to Exchange 2016 while also providing a hybrid environment for possible Office 365 mailboxes for subsidiary companies or off-shore workers. In preparing for this project, as the Exchange administrator you need to gather a list of all mailboxes with the following data – Display Name, SAM Account Name, UPN, Primary SMTP Address and other values. This information will be stored as a CSV file for future work – UPN and/or Primary SMTP address corrections.

First, the main cmdlet for gathering information on Exchange Server mailboxes is 'Get-Mailbox'. However, does this cmdlet provide all the criteria we are looking for on the mailboxes? Yes. Here is the cmdlet we need to cover all mailboxes:

```
Get-Mailbox | ft Name, SamAccountName, UserPrincipalName, PrimarySMTPAddress,
HiddenFromAddressListsEnabled, ArchiveDatabase
```

** **Note** ** In most environments, the use of the -ResultSize Unlimited parameter should be used so that the the number of results returned will not be capped at 1000.

In a typical environment, this cmdlet will gather all user mailboxes in Exchange. At least one extraneous mailbox will show up in the report and it is the Discovery Mailbox. In order to eliminate this from the report we need to make an exception. The easiest way to make that exception is to use the filtering techniques used in Chapter 2. Here is the filter to be used:

```
| Where {$_.Name -NotMatch "Discovery"}
```

This will exclude the Discovery Mailbox. The full one liner is:

```
Get-Mailbox|Where{$_.Name-NotMatch"discovery"}|ft Name,SamAccountName,UserPrincipalName,
PrimarySMTPAddress, HiddenFromAddressListsEnabled, ArchiveDatabase
```

**Before**

```
Name                                    SamAccountName              UserPrincipalName
----                                    --------------              -----------------
Administrator                           Administrator               Administrator@16-TAP.Local
DiscoverySearchMailbox {D919BA05-46A6-... SM_68c96b52ffb74d289       DiscoverySearchMailbox {D91
Damian Scoles                           damian                      damian@16-TAP.Local
Journaling Mailbox                      Journaling                  Journaling@16-TAP.Local
```

**After**

```
Name                                    SamAccountName              UserPrincipalName
----                                    --------------              -----------------
Administrator                           Administrator               Administrator@16-TAP.Local
Damian Scoles                           damian                      damian@16-TAP.Local
Journaling Mailbox                      Journaling                  Journaling@16-TAP.Local
```

Now that we have all the mailbox properties lined up, the data needs to be exported to a CSV file.  What cmdlets are available for CSV export?  What cmdlets have 'CSV' in them:

Get-Command *csv*

```
Function        Stop-PcsvDevice
Cmdlet          ConvertFrom-Csv
Cmdlet          ConvertTo-Csv
Cmdlet          Export-Csv
Cmdlet          Import-Csv
Application     csvde.exe
Application     Microsoft.Exchange.Edge
```

Export-Csv has several useful parameters for exporting the data from the above one-liner and export it to a usable CSV file:

| | | |
|---|---|---|
| Append | InputObject | UseCulture |
| Delimiter | NoClobber | LiteralPath |
| Encoding | NoTypeInformation | |
| Force | Path | |

## Example 2

In this example there is a need to monitor mailbox growth over time.  In order to do so, the Get-MailboxStatistics cmdlet will be used in conjunction with the Export-CSV cmdlet to create CSV files every day which when combined together will then provide historical data.  Each file will be tagged with a date (no time stamp) and the files created must not be overwritten.  Using a similar process to Example 1 where the results of a cmdlet are exported to a CSV file. The additional criteria is that a different file be generated and placed in a shared folder:

```
$Date = Get-Date -Format "yyyy-MM-dd"
Get-Mailbox | Get-Mailboxstatistics -WarningAction 0 | Select-Object DisplayName, @{Expression={$_.
TotalItemSize.Value.ToMB()};Label="Mailbox Size(MB)"}, ItemCount | Export-Csv $Date-MailboxStat.
csv -NoClobber -NoType
```

This code is saved as a script and then scheduled to run once per day.  The 'NoClobber' switch makes sure that none of the files are overwritten when the new daily file is generated.  The 'NoType' switch makes sure that the format is clean for the CSV file.

Exporting the CSV file without using –NoType, results in the CSV file containing bad data (in the red rectangle):

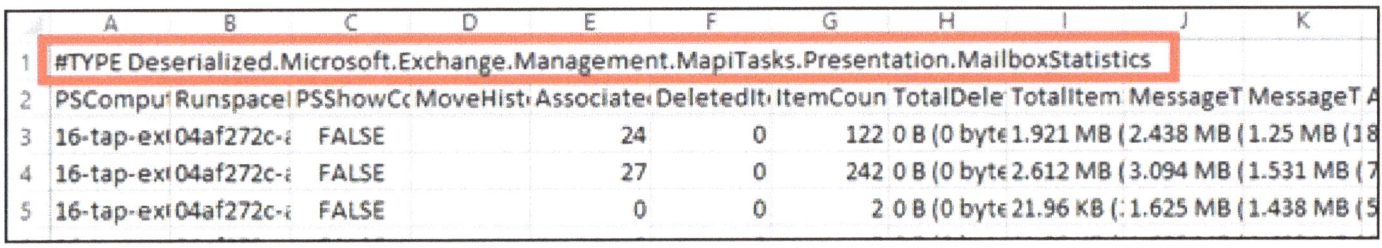

| | A | B | C | D | E | F | G | H | I | J | K |
|---|---|---|---|---|---|---|---|---|---|---|---|
| 1 | #TYPE Deserialized.Microsoft.Exchange.Management.MapiTasks.Presentation.MailboxStatistics | | | | | | | | | | |
| 2 | PSCompu | Runspace | PSShowCc | MoveHist | Associate | DeletedIt | ItemCoun | TotalDele | Totalitem | MessageT | MessageT A |
| 3 | 16-tap-ex | 04af272c-& | FALSE | | 24 | 0 | 122 | 0 B (0 byte | 1.921 MB ( | 2.438 MB ( | 1.25 MB (18 |
| 4 | 16-tap-ex | 04af272c-& | FALSE | | 27 | 0 | 242 | 0 B (0 byte | 2.612 MB ( | 3.094 MB ( | 1.531 MB (7 |
| 5 | 16-tap-ex | 04af272c-& | FALSE | | 0 | 0 | 2 | 0 B (0 byte | 21.96 KB (: | 1.625 MB ( | 1.438 MB (5 |

Exporting the CSV file with the –NoType parameter removes this unneeded data:

| | A | B | C | D | E | F | G | H |
|---|---|---|---|---|---|---|---|---|
| 1 | PSComputerName | RunspaceId | PSShowComputerNa | MoveHistory | Associate | DeletedIt | ItemCoun | TotalD |
| 2 | 16-tap-ex02.16-tap.l | 04af272c-a74c-4 | FALSE | | 24 | 0 | 122 | 0 B (0 |
| 3 | 16-tap-ex02.16-tap.l | 04af272c-a74c-4 | FALSE | | 27 | 0 | 242 | 0 B (0 |
| 4 | 16-tap-ex02.16-tap.l | 04af272c-a74c-4 | FALSE | | 0 | 0 | 2 | 0 B (0 |

Then the Get-Date cmdlet is stored in the $Date variable which is used to tag the file name. Key to that cmdlet is the formatting of the date to year-month-day (i.e. 2016-08-16).

To Schedule PowerShell scripts, store the scripts in a secure location – isolated by NTFS permissions and placed on a share that is also locked down by permissions. Then the scheduled task will also need stored credentials to run.

The data is stored into a CSV file as such:

```
"DisplayName","Mailbox Size(MB)","ItemCount"
"Administrator","1","122"
"Damian Scoles","2","242"
"Journaling Mailbox","0","2"
"Dave Stork","0","2"
```

This data could now be used to create charts for trending data, in Excel for example. Imported one day of data into Excel, a data set would look like this:

| DisplayName | Mailbox Size(MB) | ItemCount |
|---|---|---|
| Administrator | 1 | 122 |
| Damian Scoles | 2 | 242 |
| Journaling Mailbox | 0 | 2 |
| Dave Stork | 0 | 2 |

# HTML Files

When it comes to creating reports, HTML provides the most flexible platform for customization, creativity and informational overload. Visually speaking, HTML is excellent with the customization allowing for reports that are more visually presentable to the consumer of the report. This is important because, the reports should be useable and read by the recipient of the report. Reports should be meaningful, containing real data that the recipient can readily understand and not ignore because it's just a table of numbers.

The most useful and information oriented HTML reports contain good coloring, column sizing, spacing and more. In this section on HTML reporting three types of reports will be covered:

- Quick HTML Report
- Some Formatting Present
- Advanced Formatting

The first involves using just the Set-Content and ConvertTo-Html, basic, quick and easy.  While the second involves some basic options for formatting using CSS and the ConvertTo-Html  cmdlet.  The last option is to use headers, table formatting and multiple sections of information put into an HTML file, using variables to assemble the content.

## Quick HTML Reports

Get-Mailbox | Get-MailboxStatistics  | Sort-Object TotalItemSize -Descending | ConvertTo-Html DisplayName, @{Label="TotalItemSize(MB)";Expression={$_.TotalItemSize.Value.ToMB()}} | Set-Content c:\test.html

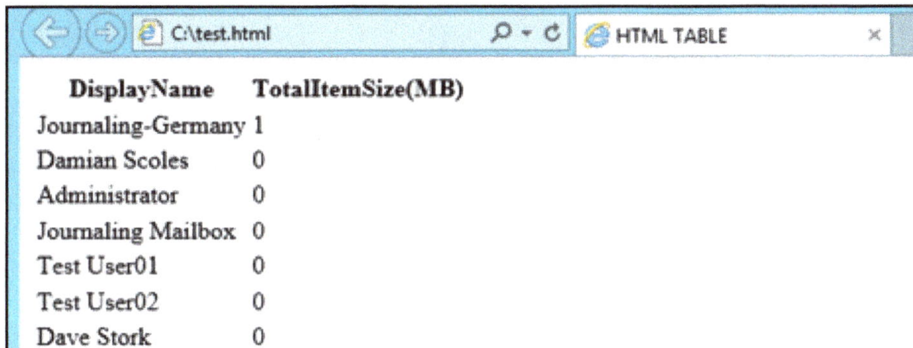


The above one-liner does the following:

| Code Section | What it does |
|---|---|
| Get-Mailbox | Finds all mailboxes in Exchange |
| \| Get-MailboxStatistics | Pipes the mailboxes into the Get-MailboxStatistics cmdlet |
| \| Sort-Object TotalItemSize -Descending | Sorts the Size by MB (descending order) |
| \| ConvertTo-Html DisplayName, @{label="TotalItemSize(MB)";expression={$_.TotalItemSize.Value.ToMB()}} | Formats the table columns and values |
| \| set-content c:\test.html | This last part takes the values |

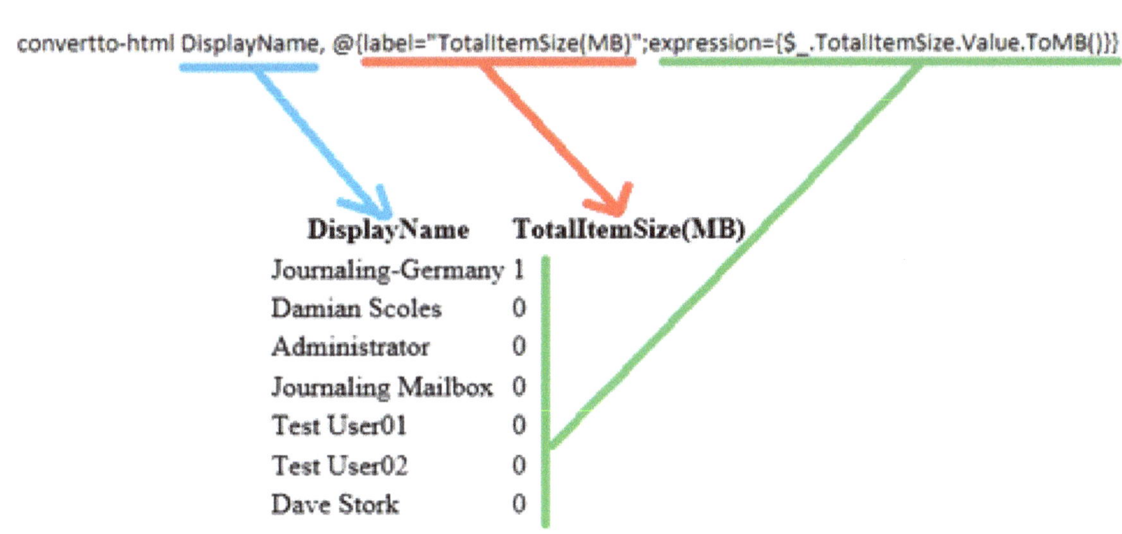

As can be seen by the resulting HTML table, the results are really basic.  For quick reports that needs low effort, this report fits that need.  HTML table can have as many fields as needed.  Take for an example where a list of Domain Controllers as part of documentation for the Exchange Server environment.  A typical one-line report allows for a formatted table of the results to be created:

Get-ADDomainController -Filter * | ft Name, OperatingSystem, OperatingSystemVersion, Ipv4Address, Forest -Auto

```
name       operatingsystem                          operatingsystemversion ipv4address    forest
----       ---------------                          ---------------------- -----------    ------
16-LG-DC01 Windows Server 2012 R2 Standard 6.3 (9600)                      192.168.0.186 16-lg.local
16-LG-DC02 Windows Server 2012 R2 Standard 6.3 (9600)                      192.168.0.187 16-lg.local
16-LG-DC03 Windows Server 2012 R2 Standard 6.3 (9600)                      192.168.0.188 16-lg.local
16-LG-DC04 Windows Server 2012 R2 Standard 6.3 (9600)                      192.168.0.189 16-lg.local
```

Taking this same PowerShell one-liner and adding ConvertTo-Html, a portable document can be created and stored as part of an overall documentation of the IT infrastructure (including Exchange and Active Directory):

Get-ADDomainController -Filter * | Select-Object Name, OperatingSystem, OperatingSystemVersion, Ipv4Address, Forest | ConvertTo-Html Name, OperatingSystem, OperatingSystemVersion, Ipv4Address, Forest | Set-Content c:\test2.html

**Resulting HTML file:**

| name | operatingsystem | operatingsystemversion | ipv4address | forest |
|---|---|---|---|---|
| 16-LG-DC01 | Windows Server 2012 R2 Standard 6.3 (9600) | | 192.168.0.186 | 16-lg.local |
| 16-LG-DC02 | Windows Server 2012 R2 Standard 6.3 (9600) | | 192.168.0.187 | 16-lg.local |
| 16-LG-DC03 | Windows Server 2012 R2 Standard 6.3 (9600) | | 192.168.0.188 | 16-lg.local |
| 16-LG-DC04 | Windows Server 2012 R2 Standard 6.3 (9600) | | 192.168.0.189 | 16-lg.local |

Similar to the first HTML example, a portable HTML file is now available for IT to keep as a reference in case there are any issues.  However, the formatting lacks quite a bit of finish – no header, no grid marking columns and rows.

Next, let's add some polish to these HTML reports.


## Adding Polish – Refining HTML Reports

Creating better HTML reports start with formatting and refining the look of the HTML output itself.  This requires several features of HTML - CSS Styling, headers and possibly a footer as well.  Each of these will provide value to the final file when it is delivered or printed out for documentation.

In this first example, the report generated will have a Header, Title and more added to it.  At the very top of the HTML report will be this block of text.  The colorful 'rectangles' refer back to the sections of code that made them possible:

```
$InitialUserInfo = $InitialUserCSV | ConvertTo-Html -Fragment -As Table -PreContent "<h2>Current User Attributes Before Import</h2>" | Out-String
$InitialReport = ConvertTo-Html -Title "Current State - User Data" -Head "<h1>PowerShell Reporting</h1><br>This report was run: $(Get-Date)" -Body
```

Starting with the first line and 'ConvertTo-Html' portion of this one-liner, notice the following parameters that are being used:

- **Fragment** - Defined because this section of code refers to only part of the HTML header being constructed
- **As Table** - Formatting the output as a table
- **PreContent** - Wording of this section of the HTML header

On the second line, starting with 'ConvertTo-Html' again, there are these parameters populated:

- **Title** – The title as seen in a browser window
- **Head** – Words to appear at the top of the spreadsheet

When coding the next part of the script, displayed in the next section, needs to include a CSS code section, for formatting the overall colors of the chart and other options.  The value of the $CSS variable are stored between a pair of ' ' (single quotes).  This example uses a black and white coloring scheme.  <TD> sections are Black with White text and <TD> sections are White with Black text:

```
$Css='<style>table{margin:auto; width:98%};Body{background-color:Cyan; Text-align:Center;};th{background-color:black; color:white;};td{background-color:white; color:Black; Text-align:Center;};</style>'
```

The last line of the full code, which exists outside the configuration of the HTML file, is to actually export the HTML code to a text file:

```
$Report | Out-File $Filepath
```

**Complete Coded Section**

```
$FilePath = "c:\Downloads\report.html"
$Css='<style>table{margin:auto; width:98%};Body{background-color:Cyan; Text-align:Center;};th{background-color:black; color:white;};td{background-color:white; color:Black; Text-align:Center;};</style>'
$UserCSV = Get-AdUser -Filter * -Properties * | Select-Object GivenName, Initials, Surname, DisplayName, EmployeeID, Company, Division, Office, Department, Title
$UserCSV | Export-CSV c:\Downloads\InitialUserState-$date.csv -NoType
$UserInfo = $UserCSV | ConvertTo-Html -Fragment -As Table -PreContent "<h2>Current User Attributes Before Import</h2>" | Out-String
$Report = ConvertTo-Html -Title "Current State - User Data" -Head "<h1>PowerShell Reporting</h1><br>This report was ran: $(Get-Date)" -Body "$UserInfo $Css"
$Report | Out-File $FilePath
```

Sample results from this:

# PowerShell Reporting

This report was ran: 09/06/2016 18:00:34

## Current User Attributes Before Import

| GivenName Initials | Surname | DisplayName |
| --- | --- | --- |
| Damian | Scoles | Damian Scoles |
| Journaling | Mailbox | Journaling Mailbox |
| Dave | Stork | Dave Stork |

## Detailed, Complex HTML Reporting

For the last section on HTML reporting, the creation of complex, detailed and visually appealing HTML files are what would have a wow factor or just considered more 'accessible' with color coding. This section will concentrate on creating a full HTML report with coloring, multiple charts, legends and more. For this scenario we'll use a report of certain values for Exchange Server that should be configured a certain way. The report will contain the role, version, Operating System and more.

Caveats to this approach are that you must know HTML. Whole books have been written about HTML. Consider the next few pages a primer on how to combine HTML and PowerShell into one. Feel free to use snippets of code for your own scripts. This will make the script building process go quicker and allow one to explore the code to create more personalized reports.

First, a destination HTML file needs to be declared for holding the information to be gathered with PowerShell. To provide information on this code line, a comment will be included just above the file declaration line:

```
$HTMLReport = "c:\downloads\Book-Server-Specs.html"
```

Next we'll need to begin building HTML files. This section starts with the variable which will store all information that will be exported to a HTML file:

```
$Output="<html><body>
```

Next, define the font for the header to be applied to the Header and the Subheader (if needed) – the two headers are defined with <h1> and <h3>:

```
<Font Size=""1"" face=""Calibri,Sans-Serif"">
<H1 Align=""Center"">Exchange Server Configuration</H1>
<H3 Align=""Center"">Generated $((Get-Date).ToString())</H3>
</Font>
```

After the header has been created, a table is defined for the display of the data that will be gathered with PowerShell cmdlets – border is applied ("1") and some room around each cell ("3") is added.  Also notice that there are double quotes around values, this is because it is being stored within a variable.  This section is then closed off with a quote to end stop populating the $Output variable for now:

```
<Table Border=""1"" CellPadding=""3"" Style=""Font-Size:8pt;Font-Family:Arial,Sans-Serif"">
<tr bgcolor=""#3498db "">"
```

The HTML file now has a defined header with labels.  After that, table headers need to be defined.  Make sure there is one <th> per column (closed with '</th>') and value that will be displayed.  For this block four columns are defined for the four values.  Two lines are used for readability, four lines could be used or even one long line could be used:

```
# Build Server Table Headers
$Output += "<th Colspan=""10000""><Font Color=""#ffffff"">Exchange Server</Font></th><th
Colspan=""10000""><Font Color=""#ffffff"">Exchange Server Version</Font></th>"

$Output += "<th colspan=""10000""><Font Color=""#ffffff"">OS Version</Font></th><th
Colspan=""10000""><Font Color=""#ffffff"">Databases</Font></th></tr>"
```

** **Note** ** this section is ended with '</tr>' which will start a new section and a new line.

For the next section of the script, each Exchange Server needs to have these values queries: name, Exchange Server version, Operating System version and the number of databases on that server.  First, it gathers the server names and use the names list (stored in a variable called $ExchangeServers) to process each server in the Foreach loop:

```
$ExchangeServers = (Get-ExchangeServer).Name

# Build the Data Table
Foreach ($Server in $ExchangeServers) {
```

Once the loop is started, the first data gathered is the version of Exchange (we already have the server name, which is column 1).  For the value of this exercise, only Exchange Server versions are valid – Preview, RTM, CU1 and CU2:

```
# Get Exchange Versions
$Ver = (Get-ExchangeServer $Server).AdminDisplayVersion
Foreach ($Line in $Ver) {
   If ($Line -Match 15.1) {
      If ($Line -Match "466.34") {$Version =  "Exchange Server 2016 CU2";$Found = $True}
      If ($Line -Match "396.30") {$Version =  "Exchange Server 2016 CU1";$Found = $True}
      If ($Line -Match "225.42") {$Version =  "Exchange Server 2016 RTM";$Found = $True}
      If ($Found -ne $True) {
      $Version = "Exchange Server 2016 Preview or previous"
   }
}
```

After setting the name of the server and Exchange Server version, these can be placed into a column for the table.  The column is started with '<td>' and ended with '</td>'.  In between this will be the variable value for the server name and version of Exchange.  Also defined are the width of the column (10000), the alignment of the text (center) and the font color (#000000).  The variable also is defined as '$Output +=' as this will append these lines to the

$Output variable:

```
$Output += "<td Colspan=""10000"" Align=""Center""><Font Color=""#000000"">$Server</Font></
td>"
$Output += "<td Colspan=""10000"" Align=""Center""><Font Color=""#000000"">$Version</font></
td>"
```

Next, the Operating System version will also be queried, this time with a WMI and stored in the $OSVer variable. This is limited to Windows Server 2012 and 2012 R2 because this is where Exchange Server can be installed on:

```
#OS Version
$OS = (Get-WmiObject -Class Win32_OperatingSystem -ComputerName $Server).Version
If ($OS -Match "6.3") {$OSVer = "Windows Server 2012 R2"}
If ($OS -Match "6.2") {$OSVer = "Windows Server 2012"}
```

The next column is created, in the same manner and settings as previous columns:

```
$Output += "<td Colspan=""10000"" Align=""Center""><Font Color=""#000000"">$OSVer</Font></
td>"
```

In the last column will be the number of databases present on an Exchange mailbox server. To accomplish this, a Try and Catch section is set up in case a server has no databases. If databases are found, the number is stored in the $Count variable. If no databases are found "N/A" is stored in this variable. Notice at the end of the $Output variable line, that a </TR> is there. This is used to start another new line for the next server to go into the chart:

```
# Databases
Try{
    $Count = (Get-MailboxDatabase -Server $Server -ErrorAction STOP).Count
} Catch {
    $Count = "N/A"
}
    $Output += "<td Colspan=""10000"" Align=""Center""><Font Color=""#000000"">$Count</Font></
    tr>"
}
```

At the end of the script, the $Output variable is closed up with "</body></html>" which closes off these sections in HTML.

```
# Ending the HTML FILE
$Output+="</body></html>"
```

Then the variable is exported to an HTML file:

```
# Export the Outlook variable to the HTML Report
$Output | Out-File $HTMLReport
```

The end result of the HTML script, looks like this:

### Exchange Server Configuration

Generated 9/4/2016 6:49:19 PM

| Exchange Server | Exchange Server Version | OS Version | Databases |
|---|---|---|---|
| 16-TAP-EX01 | Exchange Server 2016 CU2 | Windows Server 2012 R2 | 2 |
| 16-TAP-EX02 | Exchange Server 2016 CU2 | Windows Server 2012 R2 | 4 |
| 16-04-EDGE-01 | Exchange Server 2016 CU2 | Windows Server 2012 R2 | N/A |

Notice that some cells have a color assigned to them and that the table has defined columns. These column borders can be removed by changing its definition here - <table border=""0"">:

### Exchange Server Configuration

Generated 9/4/2016 6:48:30 PM

| Exchange Server | Exchange Server Version | OS Version | Databases |
|---|---|---|---|
| 16-TAP-EX01 | Exchange Server 2016 CU2 | Windows Server 2012 R2 | 2 |
| 16-TAP-EX02 | Exchange Server 2016 CU2 | Windows Server 2012 R2 | 4 |
| 16-04-EDGE-01 | Exchange Server 2016 CU2 | Windows Server 2012 R2 | N/A |

If for instance, additional table need to be added to this HTML file, simply add some lines like this:

```
$Output += "<BR><BR>"
```

Then add a new table the same way as the previous section.

```
Complete Script:
# HTML File name
$HTMLReport = "c:\downloads\Book-Server-Specs.html"

# Create the HTML Header for the report
$Output="<Html>
<Body>
<Font Size=""1"" face=""Calibri,Sans-Serif"">
<H1 Align=""Center"">Exchange Server Configuration</h1>
<H3 Align=""Center"">Generated $((Get-Date).ToString())</h3>
</Font>
<Table Border=""1"" CellPadding=""3"" Style=""Font-Size:8pt;Font-Family:Arial,Sans-Serif"">
<tr Bgcolor=""#3498db "">"

# Build Server Table Headers
$Output += "<th Colspan=""10000""><Font Color=""#ffffff"">Exchange Server</Font></th><th
colspan=""10000""><font color=""#ffffff"">Exchange Server Version</Font></th>"
$Output += "<th colspan=""10000""><Font Color=""#ffffff"">OS Version</Font></th><th
colspan=""10000""><Font Color=""#ffffff"">Databases</Font></th></tr>"
$ExchangeServers = (Get-ExchangeServer).Name
```

```powershell
# Build the Data Table
Foreach ($Server in $ExchangeServers) {

    # Get Exchange Versions
    $Ver = (Get-ExchangeServer $Server).AdminDisplayVersion
    Foreach ($Line in $Ver) {
        If ($Line -Match 15.1) {
            If ($Line -Match "466.34") {$Version = "Exchange Server 2016 CU2";$found = $True}
            If ($Line -Match "396.30") {$Version = "Exchange Server 2016 CU1";$found = $True}
            If ($Line -Match "225.42") {$Version = "Exchange Server 2016 RTM";$found = $True}
            If ($Found -ne $True) {
            $Version = "Exchange Server 2016 Preview or previous"
        }
        }
    }
    $Output += "<td Colspan=""10000"" Align=""Center""><Font Color=""#000000"">$Server</Font></td>"
    $Output += "<td Colspan=""10000"" Align=""Center""><Font Color=""#000000"">$Version</Font></td>"

    #OS Version
    $OS = (Get-WmiObject -class Win32_OperatingSystem -ComputerName $Server).Version
    If ($OS -Match "6.3") {$OSVer = "Windows Server 2012 R2"}
    If ($OS -Match "6.2") {$OSVer = "Windows Server 2012"}
    $Output += "<td Colspan=""10000"" Align=""Center""><Font Color=""#000000"">$OSVer</Font></td>"

    # Databases
    Try{
        $Count = (Get-MailboxDatabase -Server $Server -ErrorAction STOP).Count
    } Catch {
        $Count = "N/A"
    }
    $Output += "<td Colspan=""10000"" Align=""Center""><Font Color=""#000000"">$Count</Font></tr>"
}

# Ending the HTML FILE
$Output+="</Body></Html>"

# Export the Outlook variable to the HTML Report
$Output | Out-File $HTMLReport
```

# Delivery Methodologies

Once a report has been created and validated, a delivery method might need to be chosen.  One of the most common delivery mechanism is email, but a file copy could also be employed.  For this section on delivery we will go through both options to see how this can be done via PowerShell to deliver the report to their destination.

## SMTP Delivery

Sending a report created in PowerShell via Exchange is probably the most common delivery method for PowerShell reporting.  Email delivery requires a few things:

- IP Address or FQDN of the Exchange Server to relay email through
- The location of the source document to be sent
- Determine if the file is to be attached or inserted into the body of an email
- The destination email address
- The sender email address
- Subject line of the email messages

Each of these parameters will fit into a variable to be defined and then placed into the section of code that handles the email sending.  First, how do we send an email in PowerShell?  Well, let's search for the cmdlet:

```
Get-Command *Message
```

```
Cmdlet                    Protect-CmsMessage
Cmdlet                    Send-MailMessage
Cmdlet                    Unprotect-CmsMessage
```

There is a cmdlet called Send-MailMessage, which looks appropriate for our task at hand.  Reviewing the parameters of the cmdlet using 'Get-Help Send-MailMessage –full' and comparing them to the list of items needed for the report to be sent:

| | |
|---|---|
| **-Attachments** | The location of the source document to be sent |
| **-Body** | Determine if the file is to be attached or inserted into the body of an email |
| **-BodyAsHtml** | Would be used if sending the report in the body of the email |
| **-From** | The sender email address |
| **-SmtpServer** | IP Address or FQDN of the Exchange Server to relay email through |
| **-Subject** | Subject line of the email messages. |
| **-To** | The destination email address |

Now that the parameters are known, variables can be defined and placed into the cmdlet to send the email:

```
$Date = Get-Date -Format U
$Attachment = "\\FileServer01\ReportShare\ExchangeReport-2016-07-22-html"
$Body = "The report was created on $Date."
$From = "Reporting@Domain.Com"
$To = "ItDistributionGroup@Domain.Com"
$SMTPServer = "10.1.1.1"
$Subject = "Exchange Report from $Date"
```

Incorporating all the variables above and using them for the Send-MailMessage cmdlet, the cmdlet looks like this:

```
Send-MailMessage -To $To -From $From -Subject $Subject -Attachment $Attachment -Body $Body
-SmtpServer $SmtpServer
```

Make sure to configure relays correctly to relay emails like this or an error might occur:

```
Send-MailMessage : Mailbox unavailable. The server response was: 5.7.54 SMTP; Unable to relay
recipient in non-accepted domain
At line:1 char:1
+ Send-MailMessage -To $To -From $From -Subject $Subject -SmtpServer $SmtpServer
+ ~~~~~~~~~~~~~~~~~~~~~~~~~~~~~~~~~~~~~~~~~~~~~~~~~~~~~~~~~~~~~~~~~~~~~~~~~~~~~~~~~
    + CategoryInfo          : InvalidOperation: (System.Net.Mail.SmtpClient:SmtpClient) [Send-Mail
   Message], SmtpFailedRecipientException
    + FullyQualifiedErrorId : SmtpException,Microsoft.PowerShell.Commands.SendMailMessage
```

When a successful email is sent, it would arrive (as seen below) with the HMTL document attached:

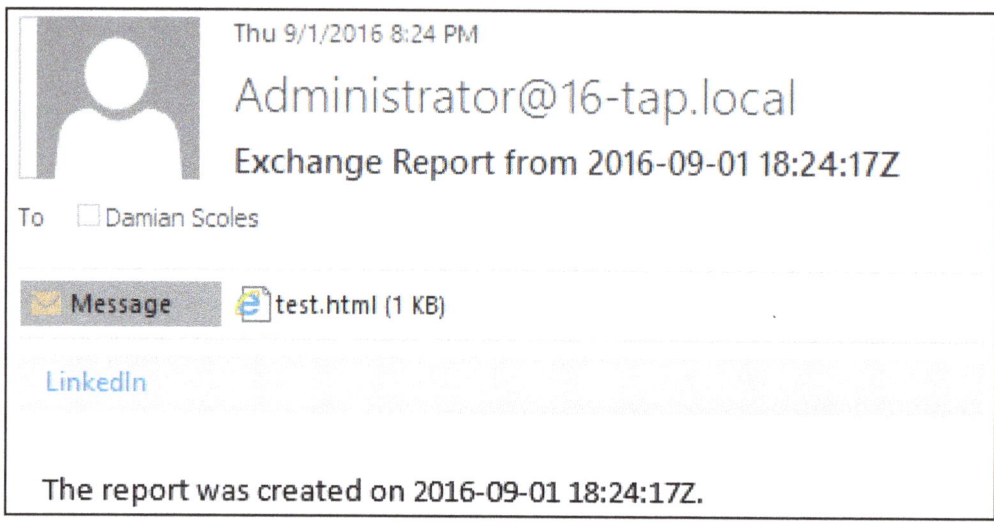


If, however, the report needed to be in the body of the message, the script would be changed as follows:

```
$Body = Get-Content "\\16-tap-EX02.16-tap.local\c$\downloads\report.html" –Raw
Send-MailMessage -To $To -From $From -Subject $Subject -Attachment $Attachment -Body $Body
-SmtpServer $SmtpServer -BodyAsHTML
```

We included the -Attachment also, in addition to replacing the body with the same HTML code. The $body variable stores the HTML file since it the message body will be the HTML file and the -RAW switch will help facilitate that. The email arrives in the destination mailbox as so, with the HTML document pasted into the body of the message.  The left side is the email delivered to the mailbox and on the right is the original HTML file (for comparison):

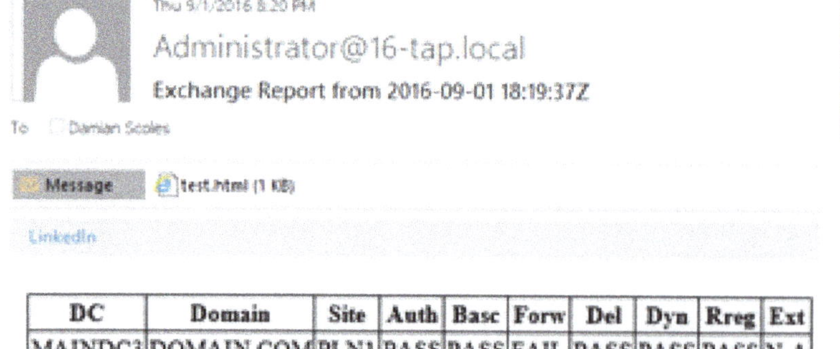


| DC | Domain | Site | Auth | Basc | Forw | Del | Dyn | Rreg | Ext |
|---|---|---|---|---|---|---|---|---|---|
| MAINDC3 | DOMAIN.COM | PLN1 | PASS | PASS | FAIL | PASS | PASS | PASS | N-A |
| MAINDC4 | DOMAIN.COM | PLN1 | PASS | PASS | FAIL | PASS | PASS | FAIL | N-A |
| MAINDC1 | DOMAIN.COM | RAT1 | PASS | PASS | PASS | PASS | PASS | PASS | N-A |
| MAINDC1 | DOMAIN.COM | PAR1 | PASS | PASS | PASS | PASS | PASS | PASS | N-A |

| DC | Domain | Site | Auth | Basc | Forw | Del | Dyn | Rreg | Ext |
|---|---|---|---|---|---|---|---|---|---|
| MAINDC3 | DOMAIN.COM | PLN1 | PASS | PASS | FAIL | PASS | PASS | PASS | N-A |
| MAINDC4 | DOMAIN.COM | PLN1 | PASS | PASS | FAIL | PASS | PASS | FAIL | N-A |
| MAINDC1 | DOMAIN.COM | RAT1 | PASS | PASS | PASS | PASS | PASS | PASS | N-A |
| MAINDC1 | DOMAIN.COM | PAR1 | PASS | PASS | PASS | PASS | PASS | PASS | N-A |

# File Copy

Copying reports to a central location can be a solid alternative to sending all reports through email. By doing so, these files are accessible and possibly kept indefinitely for historical reporting. What cmdlets can be used for moving files to file servers? The BITS Transfer service would be ideal for moving files. This was used in a previous Chapter 3. What cmdlets are available for this service?

Get-Help *BITS*

```
Name                       Category   Module

Add-BitsFile               Cmdlet     BitsTransfer
Complete-BitsTransfer      Cmdlet     BitsTransfer
Get-BitsTransfer           Cmdlet     BitsTransfer
Remove-BitsTransfer        Cmdlet     BitsTransfer
Resume-BitsTransfer        Cmdlet     BitsTransfer
Set-BitsTransfer           Cmdlet     BitsTransfer
Start-BitsTransfer         Cmdlet     BitsTransfer
Suspend-BitsTransfer       Cmdlet     BitsTransfer
```

Reviewing the list above, what cmdlets from this list are needed for transferring files from place to place? Start-BitsTransfer will copy a file from a source to a destination. This cmdlet is similar to a file copy daemon on steroids. Start-BitsTransfer has quite a few options to choose for running the cmdlet:

-Asynchronous
-Authentication - Basic, Digest, NTLM or Negotiate
-Credential
-Description
-Destination
-DisplayName
-Priority - High, Normal and Low
-ProxyAuthentication:
    Basic, Digest, NTLM, Negotiate or Password
-ProxyBypass
-ProxyCredential
-ProxyList
-ProxyUsage:
    System Default, NoProxy, AutoDetect or OverRide
-RetryInterval - default is 600 seconds
-RetryTimeout - default is 1209600 seconds (14 Days)
-Source
-Suspended
-TransferPolicy
-TransferType
-UseStoredCredential

Depending on the destination and how to file needs to be transferred, BITS could be the ideal solution. It is useful if a large number of large files need to be transferred as BITS will dynamically associate bandwidth with a file transfer, run in the background and handle transfers even with network interruptions. In Chapter 3, this cmdlet is used in the script built to download files for use on servers. In the case of documentation, the cmdlets can now be used to move these documentation files to a central location.

In order copy files to a central location, there is a need to define the source files that need to be moved, where the files will be moved to and if any sort of logging, authentication or priority needs to be assigned to these jobs. Retry intervals can be configured if the files are pulled from a source over a slow or notoriously high latency connection and to adjust for these connections 'RetryInterval' and/or 'RetryTimeout'.

## Example

For this example the requirement for the script is to pull locally run results files like CSV, HTML and or text files from five different global locations. These results will deposited on one server and stored for analysis by the global IT team located in the US global headquarters. Locations and destinations are known, for three of the five links are to overseas locations are low latency. Two other links are high latency and need to be accounted for. Let's begin by focusing on the low latency links and work our way out to the high latency link. The jobs should log if possible, the transfer jobs should be described accurately. No special authentication is needed.

### *Low Latency*

For the low latency links, the source and destination options are a given and are filled with the source and destination files. The priority is defined in case this needs adjustments later. To help identify the BITS Transfer, a description and name are given to the processes transferring files. Here are the three Bits Transfer PowerShell one-liners for this process:

```
Start-BITSTransfer –Displayname "Exchange HTML From GB" –Description "Exchange Information –
British Servers" -Priority Normal -Source \\GB-SRV-EXMBX01\Reporting\*.html –Destination \\US-SRV-
FS01\Reporting\Exchange
```

```
Start-BITSTransfer –Displayname "Exchange HTML From Poland" –Description "Exchange Information
– Polish Servers" -Priority Normal -Source \\POL-SRV-EXMBX01\Reporting\*.html –Destination \\US-SRV-
FS01\ Reporting\Exchange
```

```
Start-BITSTransfer –Displayname "Exchange HTML From Canada" –Description "Exchange Information
– Canadian Servers" -Priority Normal -Source \\CAN-SRV-EXMBX01\Reporting\*.html –Destination \\US-
SRV-FS01\Reporting\Exchange
```

With the above cmdlets, all files are being copied to the same root folder and not a specific folder for each server. It is assumed that all files are unique and identifiable from the location that they come from. For example each set of files could be prefaced with a location and then the current date. This helps identity where and when these files are generated.

### *High Latency*

For higher latency links, the same criteria above is used, with the addition of higher Retry Internal and Timeout. This is done because of the higher latency of the links. These values would be tweaked over time to adjust for any issues on these links.

```
Start-BITSTransfer –Displayname "Exchange HTML From China" –Description "Exchange Information
– Chinese Servers" -Priority High -RetryInterval 900 -RetryTimeout 2419200 -Source \\CH-SRV-EXMBX01\
Reporting\*.html –Destination \\US-SRV-FS01\Reporting\Exchange
```

```
Start-BITSTransfer –Displayname "Exchange HTML From SA" –Description "Exchange Information
– South African Servers" -Priority High -RetryInterval 900 -RetryTimeout 2419200 -Source \\SA-SRV-
EXMBX01\Reporting\*.html –Destination \\US-SRV-FS01\Reporting\Exchange
```

In summary, the BITS Transfer process can be used to move files between destinations with some advantages over a regular file copy.  BITS transfer jobs that error or timeout can be examined with the Get-BITSTransfer cmdlet. There are policies that could be applied if necessary to manipulate the file transfer as well.  For large file transfers the BITS Transfer can be monitored and manipulated while in flight (Set-BITSTransfer) and Get-BITSTransfer.

<table><tr><td>17</td><td># Troubleshooting</td></tr></table>

---

**In This Chapter**

- Breaking up the Script
  - Pause and Sleep
- Write-Host
- Comments
- Event Logging
- PowerShell ISE
- Debugging
- Catch and Try
- ErrorAction
- Transcript
- Deciphering Error Messages
- Access Denied
- Variables
- Arrays
- Conclusion

---

## An Intro to Troubleshooting

We're now at the point in the book where you, the reader, should be more comfortable with writing scripts for Exchange Server 2016.  You should be able to write scripts that manage, manipulate, and report on your Exchange 2016 servers.  Hopefully you've begun writing scripts for your Exchange Server 2016 environment by now and are familiar with the various cmdlets at your disposal.  As you've begun doing this, no doubt you have had issues with your scripts.  From infamous red text of cmdlets failing to getting results that were not quite what you expect.  This is where troubleshooting comes into play.

Troubleshooting PowerShell can be complicated by many factors. These factors include troubleshooting code you did not write, different variable data types, null variables when expecting a result and more.  In order to tackle an issue, it is helpful to understand the end goal of the script that is being written.  If the goal is simply to run a few PowerShell cmdlets and expect results, then there might not be a lot to troubleshoot and when there is a more complex goal, it might require a method to do so.

Let's explore some of the many options for troubleshooting scripts.

# Breaking up the Script

PowerShell scripts can vary greatly in length.  A very complex script can go well over a thousand lines and can go much higher.  Troubleshooting something this complex may require different techniques depending what errors or problems are noted.  One technique of many, is to break the script apart to find the problem. This could be a simple as commenting out whole sections of code or copying a whole section of code and copying that to a new script to run for testing.

Take for example a script that will modify Active Directory User Attributes to keep the GAL accurate and in the same script generates a before and after report in HTML with a copy of the results in a CSV file as well.  The script has five distinct parts – the header (script description), the before report, the section that makes the changes, the part that reports on the change that was made, and the body of the script which defines variables and runs each function.

## Pause and Sleep

PAUSE in PowerShell allows you to stop the scripts actions for a period of time while you examine what is either displayed in the PowerShell window or maybe the objects that were modified (AD, Exchange, etc.).  Once results have been confirmed or an error noted, then PowerShell can be stopped with a BREAK key or let it complete depending on the script.  I have used the Pause key for scripts that run too quickly for results or error messages to be seen. The key with Pause is that it requires user interaction to allow the script to continue processing.

SLEEP in PowerShell temporarily pauses the PowerShell script.  Essentially allowing for the same functionality as PAUSE, with the notable exception that the SLEEP command is time based and after the time parameter has expired, the PowerShell script will continue:

```
#Pause and Sleep

$N = 1
Write-Host "Number counts."
Pause

Do {

    Write-Host "This is the number $."
    If ($N -eq 5) {Sleep 5;Write-Host "Sleep for 5 successful." -ForegroundColor Cyan}
    If ($N -eq 10) {Sleep 2;Write-Host "Sleep for 2 successful." -ForegroundColor Cyan}
    If ($N -eq 15) {Sleep 7;Write-Host "Sleep for 7 successful." -ForegroundColor Cyan}
    $N++

} While ($N -lt 20)

Write-Host "Twenty numbers."
```

```
[PS] C:\>.\NumberCounts.ps1
Number counts.
Press Enter to continue...:
This is the number 0.
This is the number 1.
This is the number 2.
This is the number 3.
This is the number 4.
Sleep for 5 successful.
This is the number 5.
This is the number 6.
This is the number 7.
This is the number 8.
This is the number 9.
Sleep for 2 successful.
This is the number 10.
This is the number 11.
This is the number 12.
This is the number 13.
This is the number 14.
Sleep for 7 successful.
This is the number 15.
This is the number 16.
This is the number 17.
This is the number 18.
This is the number 19.
Twenty numbers.
[PS] C:\>_
```

Explanation of the script:

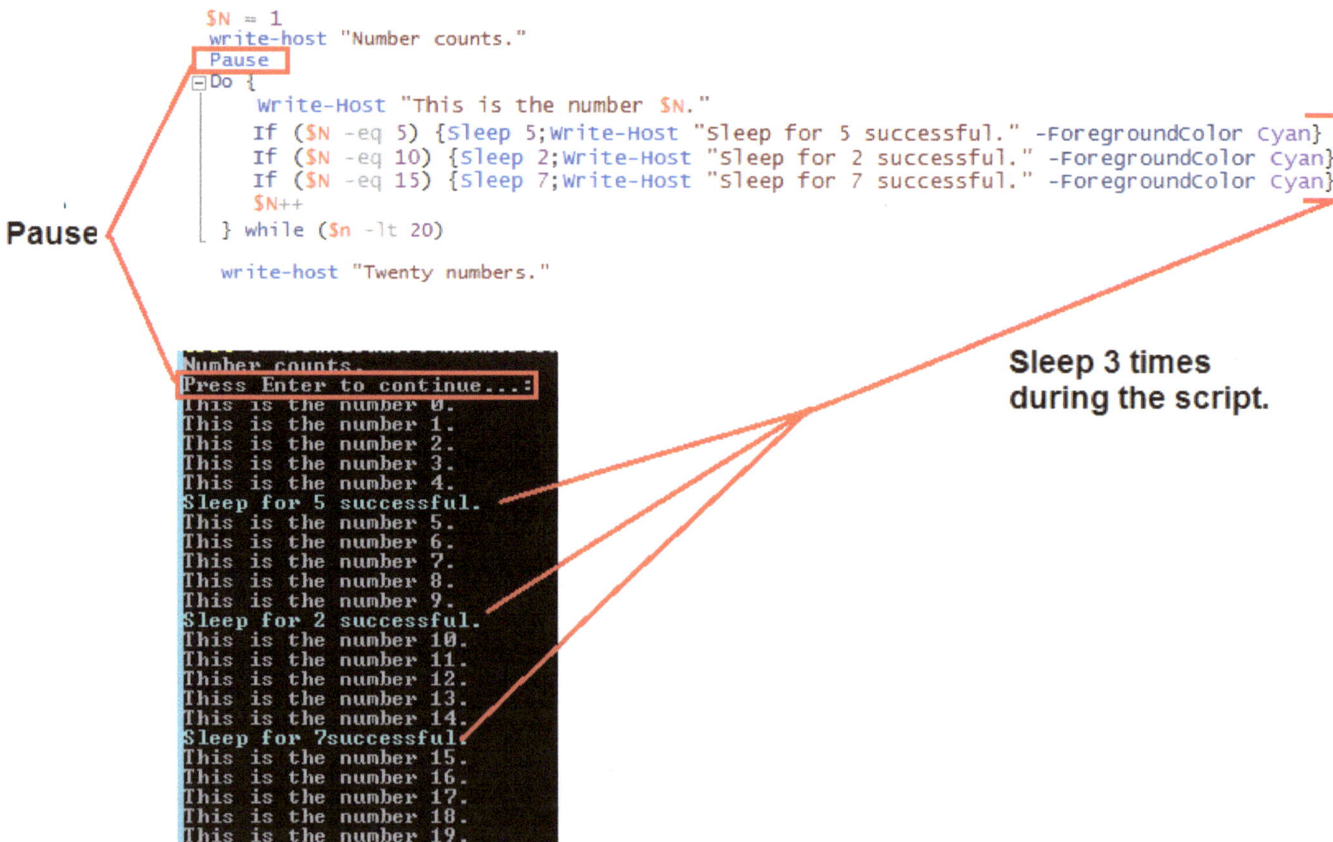


The pauses in a script can help isolate sections of the script for troubleshooting. This method could be used inside of a function that does not seem to be working, to pausing between each function or pausing after a certain block of code runs.  It would be best to use multiple pauses as it will help to isolate the cause of errors to a smaller section of code.

# Write-Host

Write-host tells PowerShell to each contents of variables, display strings of text and more.  The cmdlet can be an excellent troubleshooting tool for PowerShell and it can be used to display information for troubleshooting.

Take for example working on a large script that may have generated an error some effort may be needed to figure out where the error was generated in the script.  Using write-host, lines of code can be inserted into the script to display a number.  A series of these the script can be broken up numerically so when the script breaks a numerical indicator will help determine the code causing the issue.  With a more complex script, it may take several iterations.

**Script Text**

```
Write-Host "Start of the script"
$Servers = Get-ExchangeServer
$N = 2
$Sites = @()
Write-Host "STEP 1 Complete"
Foreach ($Server in $Servers) {
    $Name = $Server.Site
    Write-Host "The server $Server is in the $Name site!"
    Write-Host "STEP $N Complete"
    $Sites += $Name
    $N++
}
Write-Host "End of the script on STEP #$N"
```

**Explanation of the Script**

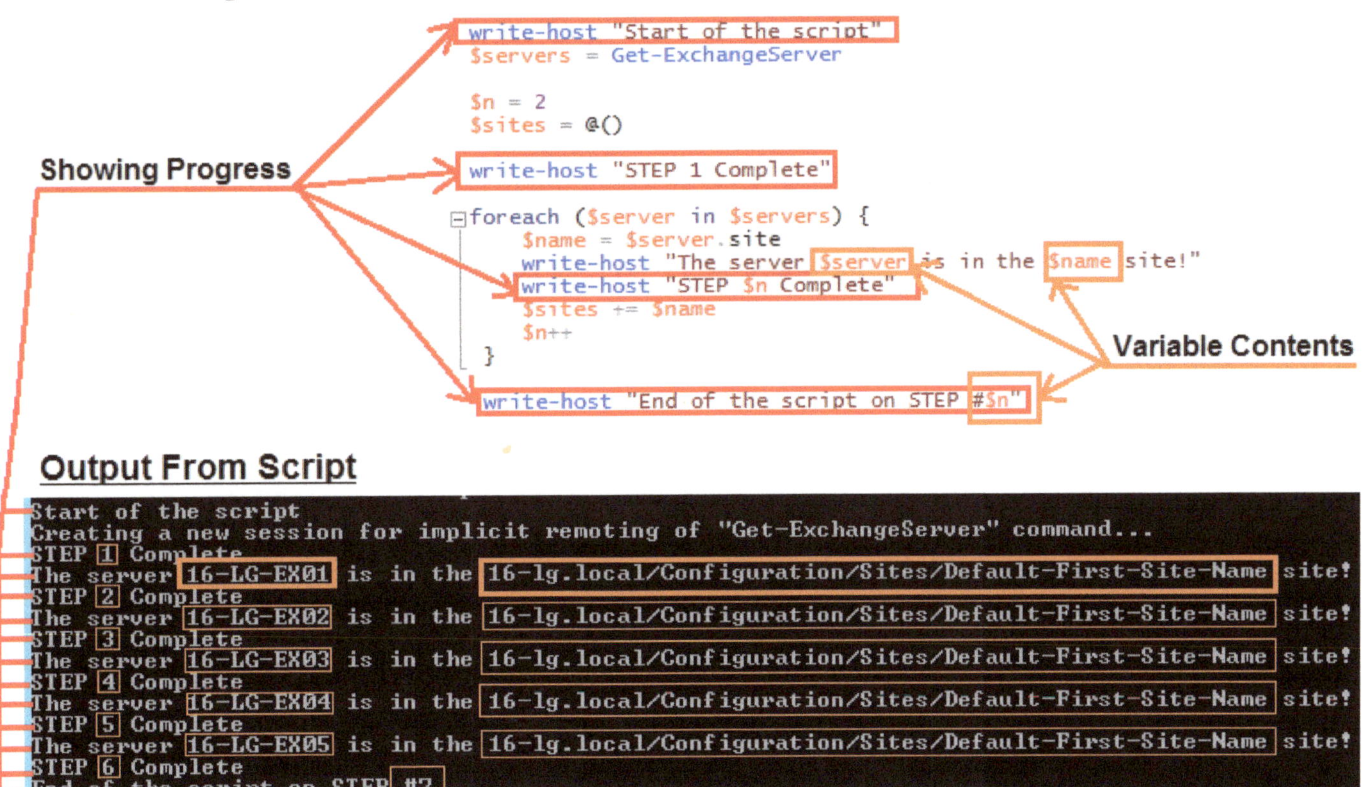

# Comments

In previous chapters, comments were added to scripts for various reasons – a script description header and code line documentation and for blocking out lines of code.  For this chapter, the latter options will be most of use for troubleshooting.  Comments in this text are simply blockers for preventing certain sections of code from executing.

### Line Changes

For the first example the comment ('#') symbol can be used to save the contents of an old line in case the replacement line fails to work properly or to remove a line no longer needed or to remove a line from execution in case it is causing an issue.

### Example Code

```powershell
$Reg = Get-Service -Name "Remote Registry"
If ($Reg.Status -ne "Running") {
   $StartUpMode = (Get-WmiObject Win32_Service | Where-Object {$_.Name -eq "RemoteRegistry"}).
   StartMode
   If ($StartUpMode -eq "Disabled") {
      Set-Service -Name RemoteRegistry -StartupType Automatic
      Start-Service -Name "Remote Registry"
      $StatusReg = (Get-Service -Name "Remote Registry").Status
   }
   Start-Service -Name "Remote Registry"
   $StatusReg = (Get-Service -Name "Remote Registry").Status
   If ($StatusReg -ne "Running"){
      Write-Host "FAILED - " -ForegroundColor Red -NoNewLine
      Write-Host "the Remote Registry service won't start." -ForegroundColor Red
      $Failed ++
      $FailedTests += "[Remote Registry Service]"
   } Else {
      Write-Host "PASSED - " -ForegroundColor Green -NoNewLine
      Write-Host "the Remote Registry Service is running." -ForegroundColor White
      $Passed++
   }
}
```

A successful run would look like this:

```
PS C:\downloads\report> .\RemoteRegistry.ps1
PASSED - the Remote Registry Service is running.
```

Now imagine if the code were written close to the above, but maybe we had some misspelled words or maybe we want to get rid of certain steps, commenting out a line could help simply the script or block out bad code or allow one to copy a line to rewrite a different way, while retaining the original code for backup.

An example of this would be the line 'Set-Service -Name RemoteRegistry -StartupType Automatic'. Maybe the name for the PowerShell cmdlet was mistyped and an error occurred or a section of code needs to be removed because we don't want the service to be started, but only have the script notify because it's being run during the day.

Scripts like the above are built in blocks based on function. Then the script is assembled using these code blocks. Perhaps after the blocks are assembled an error occurs. One way to troubleshoot the script would be to comment ('#') out a script block to see if that alleviates the issue.

The script run with the misspelled cmdlet:

```
Set-Services : The term 'Set-Services' is not recognized as the name of a cmdlet, function, script
file, or operable program. Check the spelling of the name, or if a path was included, verify that
the path is correct and try again.
At line:1 char:1
+ Set-Services
+ ~~~~~~~~~~~~
    + CategoryInfo          : ObjectNotFound: (Set-Services:String) [], CommandNotFoundException
    + FullyQualifiedErrorId : CommandNotFoundException
```

Commenting out the first line:

    # Set-Services -Name RemoteRegistry -StartupType Automatic'

Then rewrite the line:

    Set-Service -Name RemoteRegistry -StartupType Automatic'

Now the code block runs successfully. The old line was kept as a backup in case a recoded line fails again with a bad switch or invalid variable.

Comments would also come in handy when converting a script that is designed for a single mailbox, server or whatever to a script that can handle all mailboxes, servers or whatever in an environment. This requires some variable changes, a loop and a few other code changes. If this conversion process fails, comments could be used to remove the Foreach loop, variable changes and more and enabling troubleshooting of the new code.


## Example

Similar to the first two examples, CIM/WMI queries may fail for different reasons. A script that built on CIM queries that has to query non-domain computers, failures are sure to occur. A '#' comment could be placed in from of the CIM line and a WMI line could be built off of it:

## Code sample

    # (Get-CIMInstance -ComputerName $Name -ClassName Win32_PhysicalMemory -ErrorAction Stop |
    Measure-Object -Property Capacity -Sum).Sum/$GB
    (Get-WMIObject -Computer $Name -Class Win32_PhysicalMemory -ErrorAction Stop | Measure-Object
    -Property Capacity -Sum).Sum/$GB

Now if the script needs to query both domain and workgroup computers, using Try {} Catch {} will resolve this issue.

**** Note ** See page 163 for an example of Try {} and Catch {}**

# Event Logging

Event logs on Windows Servers serve many purposes. They range from an informational message about when a service started to a problem with a physical disk. Event message categories are information, warning, error and critical, all serving a purpose. PowerShell has several commands for working with event logs.

Following the practices of previous chapters, finding commands that relate to Event Logs is a simple search:

    Get-Command *EventLog*

The Get-Command provides a short list of PowerShell cmdlets for event log manipulation:

```
CommandType         Name
-----------         ----
Cmdlet              Clear-EventLog
Cmdlet              Get-EventLog
Cmdlet              Limit-EventLog
Cmdlet              New-EventLog
Cmdlet              Remove-EventLog
Cmdlet              Show-EventLog
Cmdlet              Write-EventLog
```

For troubleshooting, the Write-EventLog cmdlet is key to providing a log of when events occurred, what occurred and more. The cmdlet could be used for a manually run script or even for a scheduled task. The fact that an event could be written at each stage of a script could providing important information on how long a section took to run, current values of variables and what completed and what did not. Total runtime for the script could be calculated from a start and end event logged on the server.

## Example 1

Referring back to the requirements script from Chapter 3, the Write-EventLog cmdlet could be used to record a successful completion of a prerequisite installation. Prior to writing events to the Event Logs, we will need to define what is being written and where:

    New-EventLog –LogName Application –Source "UPN Script"

This code will now allow a new event log entry with the source of "UPN Script" to be added to the Application Log.

### Sample Code

```
Write-EventLog -LogName application -EntryType Information -EventId 2016 -Source "UPN Script"
-Message "Hotfix 2919355 is installed."
Write-EventLog -LogName application -EntryType Information -EventId 2016 -Source "UPN Script"
-Message ".Net 4.6.1 is installed."
Write-EventLog -LogName application -EntryType Information -EventId 2016 -Source "UPN Script"
-Message "UCM 4.0 is installed."
Write-EventLog -LogName application -EntryType Information -EventId 2016 -Source "UPN Script"
-Message "Windows features are installed."
```

Integrating this code into the prerequisite code would just require the insertion of the Write-EventLog line as the last line in an installation function code block. The events would register like this in the Application Event log:

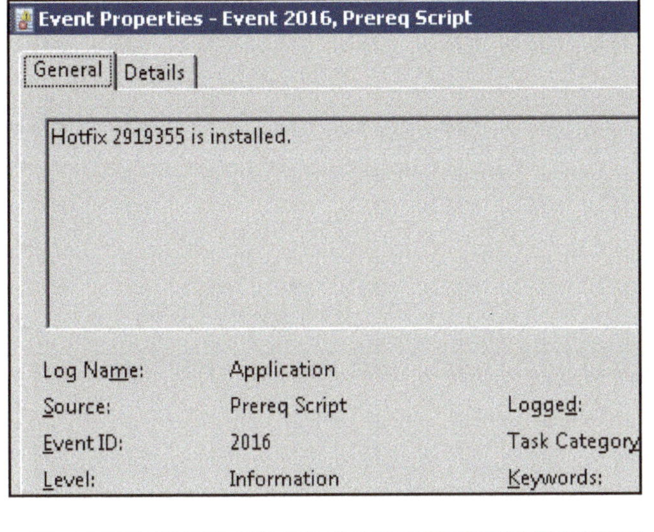


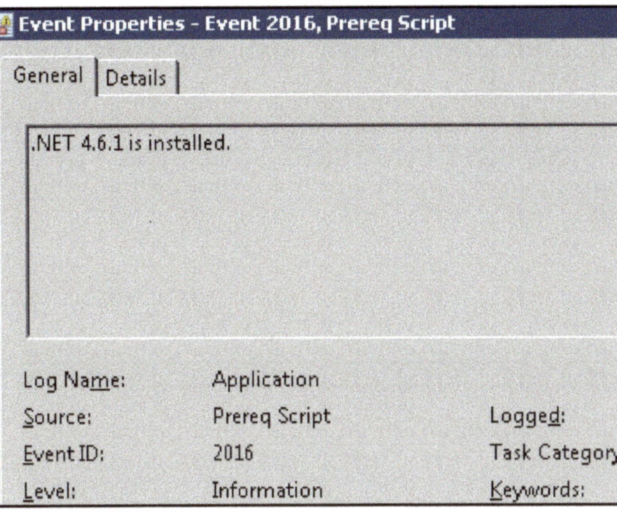


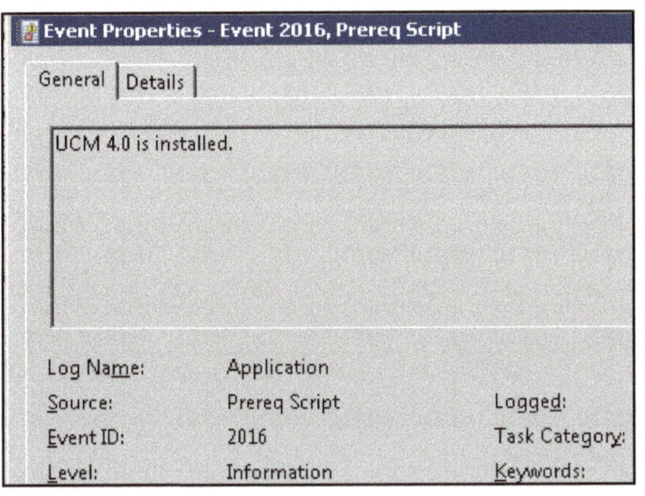


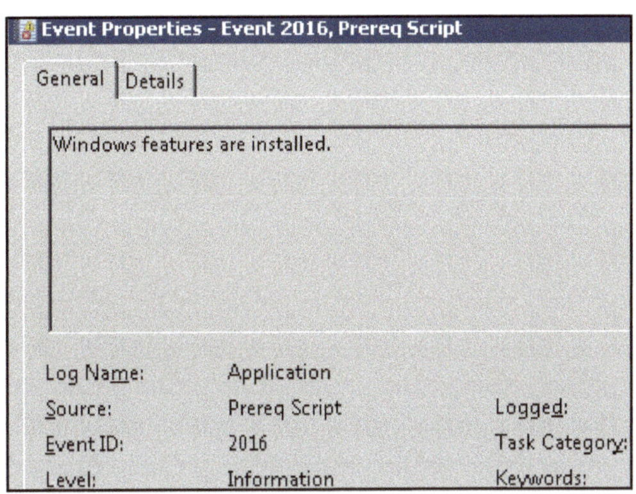


## Example 2

Same as the first example, the Write-EventLog cmdlet can be used for auditing purposes. In this example a PowerShell script is being used to correct UPNs on a set of users, updating them to the correct domain. Each time a UPN is changed, an event is recorded in the Application Log, the same is event will be logged for any UPN that is not changed. While this may not be efficient or orthodox, it provides a valid example of what could be done with the write-event log to assist in troubleshooting a script.

### Sample Code

```
$Users = Get-ADUser
$Domain = "Test.Com"

Foreach ($User in $Users) {
    $Alias = $User.Name
    $Upn = $Alias+"@"+$Domain
```

```
Try {
    Get-ADUser $User | Set-ADUser -UserPrincipalName $UPN -ErrorAction STOP
    Write-EventLog -LogName Application -EntryType Information -EventId 2016 -Source "UPN Script"
    -Message "UPN for $user is now set to $UPN."
} Catch {
    Write-EventLog -LogName Application -EntryType Warning -EventId 2016 -Source "UPN Script"
    -Message "The UPN for $user failed to change."
    }
}
```

A failed UPN change would be logged:    A successful event would be logged like this:

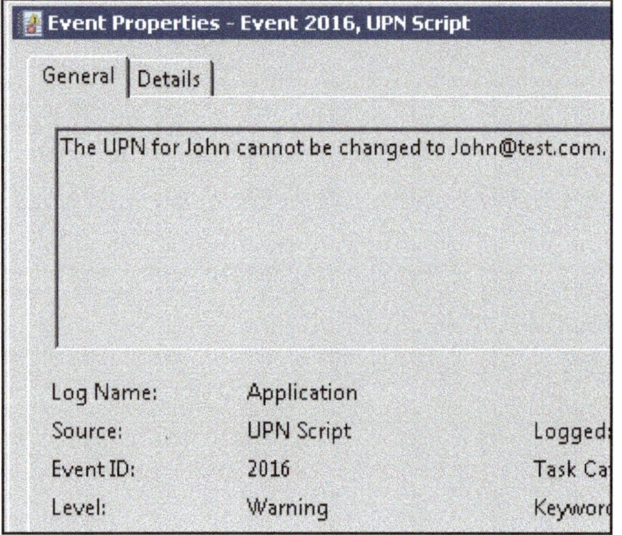

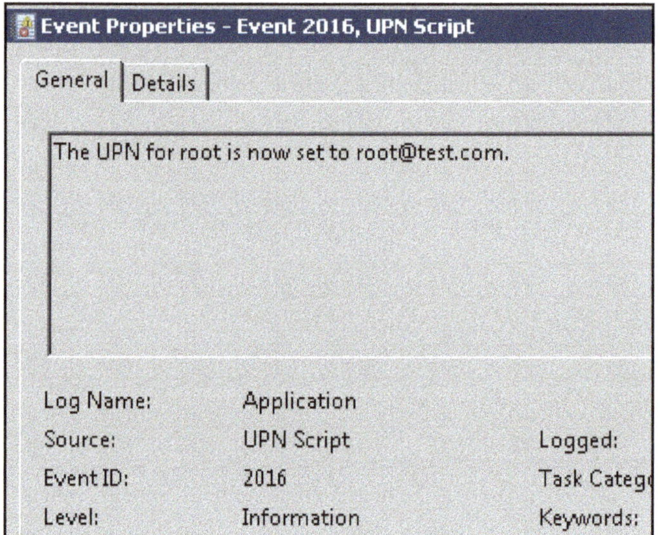

Notice the failed one is logged as a Warning and the successful change was logged as Information.  Before writing any events to the event log, the Source needs to be created beforehand:

```
New-EventLog –LogName Application –Source "UPN Script"
```

Without this, an error will be generated that the "source name" does not exist, and no event log entry would be generated.


# PowerShell ISE

While not the obvious choice for troubleshooting, one of the advantages of using the Windows PowerShell Integrated Scripting Environment (ISE) is that in a longer script ISE can visually assist in finding misconfigured parts of the script. For example, bad brackets have red squiggly lines under them.  What makes the ISE program even more powerful for troubleshooting PowerShell scripts, plugins can be installed that provide hints on misconfiguration, information on quotes that may be incorrect, and more.

When writing scripts and prior to executing them, make sure to load the script into PowerShell ISE along with a Plugin called ISE Steroids. Taken together, a script can be analyzed better, tweaks could be made or errors could be corrected before the script makes it into production.  Here are some examples of this:

## Example 1

If you were coding in notepad or similar ASCII editor, then PowerShell syntax issues would not be obvious:

```
Foreac ($Line in $Test) {
Write-Host 'This is a test.'
}
```

However, the same text, in PowerShell ISE with the ISE Steroids plugin loaded would look this:

```
2 foreac ($line in $test) {
3     write-host 'This is a test.'
4 }
```

Here is what the ISE is pointing out:

Foreach is misspelled which causes ISE to see think the brackets are wrong

```
2 foreac ($line in $test) {
3     write-host 'This is a test.'
4 }
```

## Example 2

Quotes.  As was discussed in Chapter 2  there are two types of quotes in PowerShell.  A single quote (') and a double quote (").  In PowerShell, what quote that is used can determine what can be placed in those quotes:

```
$alias = 'DScoles'

write-host 'The mailbox alias is $alias.'
write-host "The mailbox alias is $alias."
```

Using the ISE and ISE Steroids, we are able to see where the blocks of quotes start and end (the type of quotes does not matter, as long as they match.

```
write-host 'The mailbox alias is $alias.'    write-host 'The mailbox alias is $alias.'
write-host "The mailbox alias is $alias."    write-host "The mailbox alias is $alias."
```

A mistake in the quotes will be pretty obvious using the plugin and ISE:

```
write-host 'The mailbox alias is $alias."
write-host "The mailbox alias is $alias.'
```

However, if you were using Notepad the mistake may or may not be as obvious:

```
write-host 'The mailbox alias is $alias."
write-host "The mailbox alias is $alias.'
```

# Debugging

The ISE can also be used to set up various Breakpoints for in the script at certain lines, when variable values change, and when commands are run. Each of these have their value when it comes to PowerShell's debugging.

A Line Break allows for a pause at a certain point in the script. Could be good for running parts of the script at a time. Making troubleshooting easier by partitioning out the code looking for the weak points.

The Variable breakpoint allows for a script to pause whenever a variable's value has changed. This could be potentially good if a value should not be changing or if the script should be paused to examine what has happened already before the variable changes.

Command breakpoint is triggered when a certain command or function is about to run. Before that command or function is run, PowerShell will pause.

For each of these scenarios, the script is paused and while the script is paused, other commands can be run to examine the current state of the script. This includes checking variable values to running any command that provides output. In effect, this feature is even more useful than using Pause, Sleep or some of the other techniques listed in this chapter.

Breakpoints can also be enabled and disabled at will. This can be done via the menu. Below is an example of setting a Line breakpoint from the menu and what it looks like in the ISE window:

| Edit   View   Tools   Debug   Add-ons | |
| --- | --- |
| Step Over | F10 |
| Step Into | F11 |
| Step Out | Shift+F11 |
| Run/Continue | F5 |
| Stop Debugger | Shift+F5 |
| Toggle Breakpoint | F9 |
| Remove All Breakpoints | Ctrl+Shift+F9 |
| Enable All Breakpoints | |
| Disable All Breakpoints | |
| List Breakpoints | Ctrl+Shift+L |
| Display Call Stack | Ctrl+Shift+D |

```powershell
# variables
$Filepath = (Get-Item -Path ".\" -Verbose).FullName
$Server = $env:computername

foreach ($line in $bpa) {
    $Name = $Line.Replace("Microsoft/windows/","")
    $Model = $Line
    $CSV = "BPA-Results-$Name-$Server.csv"
    Invoke-BPAModel $Model -ErrorAction SilentlyContinue
    Get-BPAResult -BestPracticesModelId $Model -ErrorAction SilentlyContin
    $CSVFile = Import-CSV $CSV
    GenerateHTMLReport $Name $CSVFile $Filepath
}
```

# Try and Catch

Basic PowerShell scripting involves very little error correction or data validation. Using the Try and Catch coding pair is not exactly troubleshooting as it is more like error correction or error handling. Take for example a scenario where with some data or results, PowerShell works perfect. With other data, the same PowerShell cmdlet may fail or generate an error which causes the rest of the script to fail. In the below examples, the use of Try and Catch will be demonstrated as a key part of building an effective PowerShell script.

## Example 1 - WMI and CIM

WMI and CIM use different connection methodologies and because of this either CIM or WMI could fail depending on the server.   In the Exchange Server ecosystem, the Edge Transport role can be in a workgroup while all other Exchange servers are domain joined.  As such, CIM queries will fail against the Edge Transport Server role and because WMI will not work against servers that are not part of a domain, Try and Catch are perfect cmdlets to run queries against all Exchange 2016 servers without creating a separate set of code for non-domain servers.

In this scenario, there are two Edge Transport servers and four Mailbox Servers that need to be examined:

*RAM Query for all Exchange Servers*

 Base command for getting RAM on any server would look like this (CIM version):

```
(Get-CIMInstance -ComputerName $name -ClassName win32_PhysicalMemory -ErrorAction Stop | Measure-Object -Property Capacity -Sum).Sum/$GB
```

Same command (WMI version):

```
 (Get-WMIObject -Computer $Name -Class Win32_PhysicalMemory -ErrorAction Stop | Measure-Object -Property Capacity -Sum).Sum/$GB
```

Typically, in an organization's Exchange messaging environments there will be more mailbox role servers than transport servers or there won't be any edge transport servers at all, thus starting with CIM for a query method and using a WMI query as a fallback:

```
# Variables
$ExchangeServers = Get-ExchangeServer
$Fail = $False

Foreach ($Server in $ExchangeServers) {
   Try {
     $RAM = (Get-CimInstance -ComputerName $Server -ClassName W32_PhysicalMemory -ErrorAction
     STOP | Measure-Object -Property Capacity -Sum).Sum/1MB
   } Catch {
     $TryWmi = $True
   }
   If ($TryWmi) {
     ## WMI Depend\s on RPC.  CIM Depends on WinRM, but CIM failed, so we try WMI before we give
     up.
     Try {
       $RAM = (Get-WmiObject -Computer $Computer -Class Win32_PhysicalMemory -ErrorAction
       STOP | Measure-Object -Property Capacity -Sum).Sum/1MB
```

```
    } Catch {
        Write-Host "The server $Server cannot be queried." -ForegroundColor Red
        $Fail = $True
    }
}
If ($Fail -eq $False) {
    Write-Host "The server $Server has $RAM MB of RAM." -ForegroundColor Cyan
}

# Variable Reset
$Server = $Null
$RAM = $Null
$Fail = $False
}
```

In this scenario, Edge Transport servers would be queried by the WMI portion of the script (after CIM fails), while Mailbox role servers will be queried via CIM not having to fail back to WMI. However, the results will be the same and when all servers are up the results should look like the below example:

```
The server EDGE-EX01 has 16384 MB of RAM.
The server EDGE-EX02 has 16384 MB of RAM.
The server EX01 has 16384 MB of RAM.
The server EX02 has 16384 MB of RAM.
The server EX03 has 16384 MB of RAM.
The server EX04 has 16384 MB of RAM.
```

## EXAMPLE 2

While pairing CIM and WMI cmdlets is a good use of Try and Catch, this pair can also be used for error handling to enable the script to move forward or to not get hung on bad results or downed servers. Take for example a script checking for recommended settings on a list of Exchange servers or potential Exchange servers. One of these prerequisites would be disabling RC4 ciphers (https://support.microsoft.com/en-us/kb/2868725).

```
$RegistryPath1 = "HKLM:\SYSTEM\CurrentControlSet\Control\SecurityProviders\SCHANNEL\Ciphers\RC4 128/128\"
$Name = "Enabled"
$value = "0"

Try {
    New-ItemProperty -Path $RegistryPath1 -Name $Name -Value $Value -Force -ErrorAction STOP
} Catch {
    Write-Host "Cannot create the registry entry." -ForegroundColor Red
}
```

In the above code block, the purpose is to create a new registry entry (one of three) to disable the RC4 ciphers. The catch is meant to handle a failed registry entry creation. The script will report that the creation failed. With success, the block should display this:

```
Enabled       : 0
PSPath        : Microsoft.PowerShell.Core\Registry::HKEY_LOCAL_MACHINE\SYSTEM\CurrentControlSet\Control\SecurityProviders\SCHANNEL\Ciphers\RC4 128\128\
PSParentPath  : Microsoft.PowerShell.Core\Registry::HKEY_LOCAL_MACHINE\SYSTEM\CurrentControlSet\Control\SecurityProviders\SCHANNEL\Ciphers
PSChildName   : RC4 128/128
PSDrive       : HKLM
PSProvider    : Microsoft.PowerShell.Core\Registry
```

If the script fails, the script will produce this 'error':

```
Cannot create the registry entry.
```

The key is that '-ErrorAction STOP' forces the Try section to fail over and run the code from the Catch section, the failure happens when the registry entry fails either because the key exists or access denied occurs.


# ErrorAction

ErrorAction is useful in numerous scenarios. In the previous section of this chapter, ErrorAction was used within the Try and Catch framework in order to make it work properly. By using '-ErrorAction STOP' when a cmdlet fails in the 'TRY { }' section of the code errors or fails, the cmdlet is stopped and fails to the 'CATCH { }' section of PowerShell code. If no –ErrorAction were not specified, the Catch { } part of the code would never be executed.

ErrorAction can also be used to allow a command to continue silently without displaying an error message:

**Without**

```
[PS] C:\>Get-ExchangeServer EX02
The operation couldn't be performed because object 'EX02' couldn't be found on '16-TAP-DC01.16-TAP.Local'.
    + CategoryInfo          : NotSpecified: (:) [Get-ExchangeServer], ManagementObjectNotFoundException
    + FullyQualifiedErrorId : [Server=16-TAP-EX02,RequestId=196da8eb-1d51-4e29-ad1d-eb71a615bef4,TimeStamp=12/20/2016
    5:16:29 AM] [FailureCategory=Cmdlet-ManagementObjectNotFoundException] 8A8FB263,Microsoft.Exchange.Management.Syst
    emConfigurationTasks.GetExchangeServer
    + PSComputerName        : 16-tap-ex02.16-tap.local
```

**With**

```
[PS] C:\>Get-ExchangeServer EX02 -ErrorAction SilentlyContinue
[PS] C:\>_
```

Using the –ErrorAction SilentlyContinue may be what is needed for a script to keep moving or prevent the script from failing and causing further issues. However, in a troubleshooting scenario, removing these switches may be what is needed as its removal could generate error messages that could potentially point to the issue.

As an example, let's say a scheduled script takes an inventory of all Exchange mailbox servers and creates a chart that shows the server specs for each Exchange server. Now imagine that on a normal, weekly basis the script creates a report on ten Exchange 2016 servers. However, this week the report only has nine Exchange 2016 servers in the report with the RAM correct, the other one reports RAM as 0 GB. When reviewing the script code, most cmdlets appear to have an –ErrorAction switch configured.

To troubleshoot the issue, make a copy of the script and remove all –ErrorAction's in the script and save it as a different name. Now, if a server is not reporting back information on mailboxes running this copy of the script without the –ErrorAction switches should reveal any issues that the non-reporting server is experiencing.

```
$ExchangeServers = Get-ExchangeServer
Foreach ($Server in $ExchangeServers) {
    $RAM = (Get-CimInstance -ComputerName $Server -ClassName W32_PhysicalMemory -ErrorAction SilentlyContinue | Me
    Write-Host "The server $Server has $RAM GB of RAM." -ForegroundColor Cyan
}
```

First, run the script manually without the changes:

```
The server EX01 has 24 GB of RAM installed.
The server EX02 has 24 GB of RAM installed.
The server EX03 has 0 GB of RAM installed.
The server EX04 has 24 GB of RAM installed.
The server EX05 has 24 GB of RAM installed.
The server EX06 has 24 GB of RAM installed.
The server EX07 has 24 GB of RAM installed.
The server EX08 has 24 GB of RAM installed.
The server EX09 has 24 GB of RAM installed.
The server EX10 has 24 GB of RAM installed.
```

Then run the modified script with the –ErrorAction removed:

```
The server EX02 has 24 GB of RAM installed.
Get-CIMInstance : WinRM cannot complete the opera
service is enabled and allows access from this co
At C:\downloads\mailboxcheck.ps1:5 char:10
+     $RAM = (Get-CIMInstance -computername $serve
+
    + CategoryInfo          : ConnectionError: (r
    + FullyQualifiedErrorId : HRESULT 0x80338126,
    + PSComputerName        : EX03
The server EX04 has 24 GB of RAM installed.
The server EX05 has 24 GB of RAM installed.
The server EX06 has 24 GB of RAM installed.
The server EX07 has 24 GB of RAM installed.
The server EX08 has 24 GB of RAM installed.
The server EX09 has 24 GB of RAM installed.
```

From the error message, we see that WinRM was unable to connect to the server. With that error message, troubleshooting can now begin. Maybe the server failed, the firewall isn't working properly, or something else is preventing the remote PowerShell call from succeeding. The point is, the error message returned provides some clues as to the possible issues and it took a simple modification of an existing script to find. This is also a good example of where Try {} Catch {} could be used to handle the error better.


# Transcript

While not an active troubleshooting method, using the transcription feature in PowerShell provides value by recording what is entered into a PowerShell window and the resulting output from a script. Transcription will copy these entered cmdlets, their output and error messages to a txt file for an examination of what happened.

### Example

```
# Start Transcript Process
Start-Transcript -Path "C:\downyloads\report\ScriptLogging.txt" -NoClobber
# Starting the script part to be logged
Write-Host "This is the start of the script." -ForegroundColor White
# Getting Services
Write-Host "This is a list of services on my laptop." -ForegroundColor Green
Get-Service
# Getting Processes
Write-Host "This is a list of processes on my laptop." -ForegroundColor Red
Get-Process
# Ending the script
```

```
Write-Host "This is the end of the script." -ForegroundColor Cyan
# Ending the transcript process
Stop-Transcript
```

Transcript File Content

```
************************
Windows PowerShell transcript start
Start time: 20160730154709
Username: domain\user
RunAs User: domain\user
Machine: WorkLaptop (Microsoft Windows NT 6.3.9600.0)
Host Application: C:\Windows\System32\WindowsPowerShell\v1.0\powershell.exe
Process ID: 7756
************************
Transcript started, output file is C:\downloads\report\ScriptLogging.txt

Status    Name              DisplayName
------    ----              -----------
Running   AdobeActiveFile... Adobe Active File Monitor V14
Running   AdobeARMservice    Adobe Acrobat Update Service
Stopped   AeLookupSvc        Application Experience
Stopped   ALG                Application Layer Gateway Service
Running   AppHostSvc         Application Host Helper Service
Stopped   AppIDSvc           Application Identity
Running   Appinfo            Application Information
Running   Apple Mobile De... Apple Mobile Device Service
Stopped   AppMgmt            Application Management
Stopped   AppReadiness       App Readiness
Stopped   AppXSvc            AppX Deployment Service (AppXSVC)
```

```
Running   wuauserv          Windows Update
Running   wudfsvc           Windows Driver Foundation - User-mo...
Stopped   WwanSvc           WWAN AutoConfig
Running   ZeroConfigService Intel(R) PROSet/Wireless Zero Confi...
Stopped   ZuneNetworkSvc    Zune Network Sharing Service
Stopped   ZuneWlanCfgSvc    Zune Wireless Configuration Service


Id      : 6772
Handles : 504
CPU     : 4.140625
Name    : anuacui



Id      : 2448
Handles : 161
CPU     :
Name    : AppleMobileDeviceService
```

…….. continues listing processes ……

```
Id      : 3712
Handles : 257
CPU     :
Name    : ZeroConfigService



Id      : 6664
Handles : 88
CPU     : 0.03125
Name    : ZuneLauncher


************************
Windows PowerShell transcript end
End time: 20160730154715
************************
```

Notice that the PowerShell cmdlets that were contained in the script do not get recorded in the transcript file. The only items that are recorded is the output from each PowerShell cmdlet that was run. The exception is the header and the footer of the transcript file that are recorded. The header provides some information about the computer and user running the script, while the footer provides just the ending time.

Notice that the Start-Transcript cmdlet is using the '-NoClobber' switch. This switch simply prevents any other log files from being overwritten. If the script is being run multiple times and you want to overwrite the files, just remove the '-NoClobber' switch.

For troubleshooting, the Transcript is more useful on scripts that run unattended and only the output needs to be logged. Make sure to use date/timestamps for the file name. This will make troubleshooting much faster in case the file is copied or moved and the date / timestamp is not retained.

# Deciphering Error Messages

PowerShell error messages; yes, this is a bit of a nebulous concept. There are literally thousands of error messages that could occur in PowerShell. This section will not address them all. No book could truly address them all. This section of this chapter is simply here to help guide the troubleshooting process for these error messages. Let's start with the basics.

## Basic Steps

There are a lot of things that can go wrong in building and running a PowerShell script. As with any troubleshooting technique, start with the basics if the error message is not clear enough.

- Open the script in PowerShell IDE and look for syntax and formatting misuse clues
- Check the spellings of all cmdlets, variables, arrays, switches, etc.
- Check the value of each variable using write-host, a line with the variable name in it, or via a ISE breakpoint
- If the error message contains a line number, see if that line can be isolated or run by itself so that it can be picked apart
- Break out the section that is causing the error into a similar script or run the code one line at a time from the prompt
- Check permissions, does the script need to be run as an administrator?

## Sample Error Troubleshooting

Let's say you tried to start a service using the following cmdlet and got the error below:

```
Start-Service -Name "Remote Registry"
```

```
Start-Service : Service 'Remote Registry (RemoteRegistry)' cannot be started due to the following
error: Cannot start service RemoteRegistry on computer '.'.
At line:1 char:1
+ Start-Service -Name "Remote Registry"
+ ~~~~~~~~~~~~~~~~~~~~~~~~~~~~~~~~~~~~~~~
    + CategoryInfo          : OpenError: (System.ServiceProcess.ServiceController:ServiceControlle
   r) [Start-Service], ServiceCommandException
    + FullyQualifiedErrorId : CouldNotStartService,Microsoft.PowerShell.Commands.StartServiceComma
   nd
```

So, let's check the StartType of the Remote Registry service with this cmdlet:

Get-Service -Name "Remote Registry" | fl Name, StartType, Status

From the StartType returned, we can see the service is Disabled and therefore can't be started until the StartType is changed.

```
Name       : RemoteRegistry
StartType  : Disabled
Status     : Stopped
```

## Access Denied

Got an Access Denied error? The PowerShell windows or script may need to run as an Administrator. This can be done by right-clicking on the shortcut for Windows PowerShell and selecting "Run as Administrator".

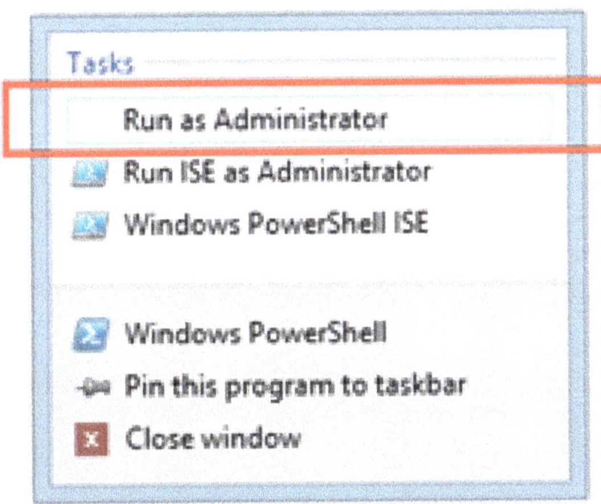


Opening PowerShell, using Run as Administrator allowed the Set-Service cmdlet to change the setting without error. It isn't uncommon to run into this issue as some PowerShell cmdlets require an elevated set of permissions in order to run. The use of 'Run as Administrator' should be limited to only when needed, versus doing it all the time. Elevated permissions should be restricted to an as needed basis. This will limit any possible exposure to malicious code running on a production server.

To fix the issue, a PowerShell cmdlet would be needed to change the startup mode from Disabled to something like Automatic. The cmdlet below will do this, but requires an elevated, administrator, PowerShell sessions:

Set-Service -Name "Remote Registry"-StartupType Automatic

Attempting to run this cmdlet, brings up an error "Access is denied" error, if not run as an Administrator:

```
Set-Service : Service 'Remote Registry (remoteregistry)' cannot be configured due to the following error: Access is
denied
At line:1 char:1
+ Set-Service -name remoteregistry -StartupType automatic
+
    + CategoryInfo          : PermissionDenied: (System.ServiceProcess.ServiceController:ServiceController) [Set-Servi
   ce], ServiceCommandException
    + FullyQualifiedErrorId : CouldNotSetService,Microsoft.PowerShell.Commands.SetServiceCommand
```

Back to the problem with starting the service, once the service Start Mode was set from Disabled to Automatic, the script now runs without error:

```
PS C:\> .\RemoteRegistryScript.ps1
PASSED - the Remote Registry Service is running.
PS C:\>
```

Because of this issue, a code block was put in place to check for the startup mode of the Remote Registry service:

**Added Code Block**

```
$StartUpMode = (Get-WmiObject Win32_Service | Where-Object {$_.Name -eq "RemoteRegistry"}).
StartMode
If ($StartUpMode -eq "Disabled") {
    Set-Service -Name RemoteRegistry -StartupType Automatic
    Start-Service -Name "Remote Registry"
    $StatusReg = (Get-Service -Name "Remote Registry").Status
}
```

# Variables

Variable content can be quite crucial in a PowerShell script. Script troubleshooting may include validating the content of variables. A variable used to store values may not be storing the value the way one might think it's storing. Let's examine one scenario where the content of a variable does not match the expected results:

```
Get-Mailbox "Damian" | fl PrimarySmtpAddress
```

This commend provides these results:

```
PrimarySmtpAddress
------------------
Damian@Domain.Com
```

Now, say we want to store this for later use? A temporary variable might be to appropriate approach. The problem becomes when the value that is stored turns out to be the wrong value because the property that is stored is not a single value property but actually a multi-valued property. Take the above command where the Primary SMTP Address for a mailbox is stored in a variable. At first glance it appears to be a single value property – a string that makes up an email address. However, let's see what it really is. First, store the SMTP address as a variable (below):

```
$PrimarySmtpAddress = (Get-Mailbox "Damian"). PrimarySmtpAddress
```

Now, using this primary SMTP address, let's attempt to query for the mailbox (yes, it is a circular reference, but it will make sense later):

```
Get-Mailbox $PrimarySmtpAddress
```

This provides some surprising results:

```
Cannot process argument transformation on parameter 'Identity'. Cannot convert the "Damian@domain.com" value of type
"Microsoft.Exchange.Data.SmtpAddress" to type "Microsoft.Exchange.Configuration.Tasks.MailboxIdParameter".
    + CategoryInfo          : InvalidData: (:) [Get-Mailbox], ParameterBindin...mationException
    + FullyQualifiedErrorId : ParameterArgumentTransformationError,Get-Mailbox
    + PSComputerName        : ex01.domain.com
```

Not exactly the results that were expected. What's happening here? The property in question, PrimarySMTPAddress, is actually a multi-value property. To see the values store, expand the contents of the variable with this command:

```
$PrimarySmtpAddress | fl
```

And these results:

```
Length          : 17
Local           : Damian
Domain          : domain.com
IsUTF8          : False
IsValidAddress  : True
```

Notice that the five values stored together, are all stored in the $PrimarySMTPAddress property. One solution to this problem is to store the address as a string instead, which will group these properties as we had originally expected:

```
[String]$PrimarySmtpAddress = (Get-Mailbox "Damian").PrimarySmtpAddress
Get-Mailbox $PrimarySmtpAddress
```

Then we get the desired results:

```
Name            Alias        ServerName    ProhibitSendQuota
----            -----        ----------    -----------------
Damian Scoles   Damian       ex01          Unlimited
```

Adding '| fl' after a variable name at the prompt, can be used to reveal if that variable is a multi-valued variable and therefore might need special handling to use it correctly.

Variables can also store empty values. Which may or may not be a desired result. The empty value could be because a PowerShell query (i.e. any mailbox on a certain server, where the name of the server is misspelled) did not work or an invalid value was provided for the query providing bad results (garbage in / garbage out). The $null value may not even provide any errors or cause the script to throw an error. The script may end up with invalid data as a results. Depending on the script, a check for the $null (or empty) variable may need to be put in place OR the cause of the empty (or null) variable may need to be investigate.

## Example

In this example, there are say 20 databases on four Exchange 2016 servers. A PowerShell script has been written to find all mailboxes on a certain database. At the tail end of the script is a nice section of code that handles the formatting to create an HTML report. The script is also run on a scheduled basis. Yet, for a database with 150 mailboxes on it, the HTML is completely empty.

### Sample Script Code

```
# HTML Formatting
$Css2='<Style>Table{Margin:Auto; Width:98%}
    Body{background-Color: Black; Color:White; Text-Align:Center;}
    th{Background-Color:Black; Color:White;}
    td{Background-Color:White; Color:Black; Text-Align:Center;}
</Style>'
# Gather mailbox information
```

```
$Database = "DB02"
Try {
   $Mailboxes = Get-Mailbox -Database $Database -ErrorAction STOP | Select-Object
   Name,Alias,ServerName,ProhibitSendQuota
} Catch {
   Write-Verbose "No mailboxes found in $Database"
}


[string]$FilePath = "C:\downloads\report\MailboxInforReport.html"
Write-Verbose "HTML report will be saved $FilePath"


# Format the HTML Report
$MailboxInfo = $Mailboxes |ConvertTo-Html -Fragment -As Table -PreContent "<h2>Current User
Attributes Before Import</h2>" | Out-String
$MailboxReport = ConvertTo-Html -Title "Mailbox Report"-Head "<h1>Exchange Mailbox Reporting</
H1><br>" -Body "$MailboxInfo $Css2"


# Generate Report
$MailboxReport | Out-File $Filepath
```

Troubleshooting the failed report generation will require multiple steps – check the variable values, check the code for the HTML report and check to see if any mailboxes exist in the database.  Because this book is a practical guide to PowerShell, let's examine the script to see where the problem lies.

As with any troubleshooting method starting with the absolute basics is key.  Starting with the source of the mailbox data used to generate the HTML report:

```
$Database = "DB02"
Try {
   $Mailboxes = Get-Mailbox -Database $Database -ErrorAction STOP | Select-Object Name, Alias,
   ServerName, ProhibitSendQuota
} Catch {
   Write-Verbose "No mailboxes found in $Database"
}
```

No error is generated with the above code block (save in 'TestCommand.ps1'):

```
[PS] C:\>.\TestCommand.ps1
[PS] C:\>_
```

So, the code block above still does not provide the answer.  The fact is, we know that there are mailboxes in every database on the server.  So, we did not get an error and the HTML report is blank.  Since the HTML report is generated from the $mailboxes variable its contents need to be validated. So, after the second attempt, with no error generated, we can do that by adding a line at the end of the script like this:

```
$Database = "DB02"
Try {
   $Mailboxes = Get-Mailbox -Database $Database -ErrorAction STOP | Select-Object
   Name,Alias,Servername,ProhibitSendQuota
```

```
} Catch {
    Write-Verbose "No mailboxes found in $Database"
}

$Mailboxes
```

The results are exactly the same:

```
[PS] C:\>.\TestCommand.ps1
[PS] C:\>_
```

This now proves that the $mailboxes variable is blank. However, no clues are provided by PowerShell. Let's isolate the code even further by just running the command without any extra switches or filters or variables. Just the base 'Get-Mailbox' to see if the data is good from the start:

```
$Database = "DB02"
Get-Mailbox -Database $Database
```

After this is run…. The problem becomes self-evident:

```
Couldn't find database "DB02". Make sure you have typed it correctly.
    + CategoryInfo          : NotSpecified: (:) [Get-Mailbox], ManagementObjectNotFoundException
    + FullyQualifiedErrorId : [Server=EX01,RequestId=38a89ba3-7ea3-49ee-a45f-cabd31ffe1b0,TimeSta
   =Cmdlet=ManagementObjectNotFoundException] D48A9886,Microsoft.Exchange.Management.RecipientTas
```

Thus, proving that Garbage In does indeed produce Garbage Out. Once the database name is corrected (in this case to DB01, the line displays mailbox correct. Then once the script is fixed (just changing the source database name), an HTML report is generated.

## Exchange Mailbox Reporting

### Current User Attributes Before Import

| Name | Alias | ServerName | ProhibitSendQuota |
|---|---|---|---|
| Administrator | Administrator | ex01 | Unlimited |
| Damian Scoles | Damian | ex01 | Unlimited |

The report generated is a bit awful looking, but it did work as planned. As you can see, checking data sources and the corresponding variables, can prove useful in determining the root of bad results.

# Arrays

Arrays can contain either a single line of values or an array of lines with data in them. To troubleshoot the contents of an array with PowerShell, there are two methods that could be used. If the data is stable, then the data only needs to validate it once. However, if the data source is more fluid or variable, it may need to be checked on a more constant basis.

**Method One**
```
$Array | ft
```

**Method Two**
```
Foreach ($Line in $Array) {
    $Array | ft
}
```

Each line that is stored in the array can now be evaluated and verified as good or bad data.  From there it can be determined if the data source is bad, or if the PowerShell command that gathered the data is bad, or that the script that is using the data in the array is not handling the datatypes correctly.


# Conclusion

Writing scripts isn't always a cut and dry process.  Details may need to be worked out, variable names vetted and uses need to be worked out.  Functions built, reporting code created and feedback to the user may need to be included.

This chapter covered several troubleshooting methods.  The methods are by no means exhaustive on troubleshooting PowerShell.  When troubleshooting script errors remember that there is no limit to the number of techniques described that can be used.  It isn't unusual to use more than three methods (Variables, Event Logs, commenting and write-host) on a single script to troubleshoot issues with it.

Before there is a real need for troubleshooting, practice with some of the above PowerShell cmdlets and syntax to get familiar with how these tools will work.  Make sure to also take advantage of the usual tools for PowerShell:

- ISE and ISE Steroids plugin
- Get-Help
- Search Engine

Putting all of it together will make building a successful script that much easier.

**18** # Miscellaneous

---

**In This Chapter**

- CIM and WMI
- Menus
- Aliases
- Foreach-Object (%)
- PowerShell Interface Customization

---

In this book, we've covered numerous topics from how to start out scripting, to server configuration, user configuration, to troubleshooting and more.  This chapter will cover a series of random topics in PowerShell.  The topics picked are, as with the rest of the book, based on practical experience and are ones that should prove useful in a production environment.

For this chapter, we'll cover CIM and WMI a bit more in-depth, menus, aliases, foreach-object filtering, and special permission cmdlets.  Each of these has its value when managing and working with Exchange 2016 servers.   CIM and WMI provides an interface into hardware / OS level settings that allow configuration of items like Pagefiles, Power Management settings and NIC Power Management to documenting RAM, CPUs and other hardware specific information about the Exchange server.

Aliases provide a way to customize PowerShell for easier coding.  These shortcuts simply make coding easier.  In addition to this, the shell can also be customized in terms of path, colors and window sizing.

An additional filtering option will also be covered in this chapter.  This cmdlet helps sort through or manipulate results of cmdlets and can be used to provide an 'in-flight' cleanup for results for readability.  Foreach-Object is indeed a useful cmdlet for your PowerShell scripts or one-liners.

# CIM and WMI

Chapter 2 discussed CIM and WMI briefly and what its function was for managing servers. This chapter will cover some real world examples and what you can do with the PowerShell cmdlets that surround this. Chapter 2 also covered some sample cmdlets on how to gather information on the Pagefile. The Pagefile settings require custom setting for Exchange servers because Microsoft's best practice to set this to RAM + 10 MB or 32,778 MB, with the latter being the maximum recommended for Exchange 2016 (Reference - https://technet.microsoft.com/en-us/library/aa996719(v=exchg.160).aspx). What if, however, there is a need to get quite a bit more information on the Exchange servers in the environment? Maybe the number of cores, RAM, current speed, power settings and more. How would this be accomplished? What other type of information can be seen that might be useful?

**Scenario**

You are the IT administrator for a large corporation with 42 Exchange servers world-wide. All servers are running Windows 2012 R2 and Exchange Server 2016 with the latest CU release. All servers are physical as per Microsoft's Preferred Architecture. As part of the formal documentation process for the company, IT management would like to get a report on the physical server's (1) CPU count, (2) RAM, (3) make and model as well as the (4) serial number of the server. For your own documentation, you want to check on the server settings for the (5) Pagefile, server (6) Server Power Management and (7) NIC Power Management.

For each Exchange Server, a total of seven individual bits of information need to be found. In order to properly store this, an Array or a PowerShell Object could be used to store this for each server. Ideally, storing the information would look like this:

Name, CPU, RAM, Make, Model, Serial #, Pagefile, Server Power Mgmt., NIC Power Mgmt.

First, what cmdlets are available for CIM:

Get-Command *Cim*

```
Cmdlet          Get-CimAssociatedInstance
Cmdlet          Get-CimClass
Cmdlet          Get-CimInstance
Cmdlet          Get-CimSession
Cmdlet          Invoke-CimMethod
Cmdlet          New-CimInstance
Cmdlet          New-CimSession
Cmdlet          New-CimSessionOption
Cmdlet          Register-CimIndicationEvent
Cmdlet          Remove-CimInstance
Cmdlet          Remove-CimSession
Cmdlet          Set-CimInstance
```

Get-CimInstance is the cmdlet that was used from Chapter 2 and to perform system level queries for servers. The hardest part of using the cmdlets to query CIM and WMI is knowing what classes to use to for your query. Using a search engine is a good way to find the right one.

To make queries for the Pagefile settings, the CIM classes are Win32_ComputerSystem, Win32_PagefileSettings and Win32_PagefileUsage.

With the first CIM class (Win32_ComputerSystem):

```
Get-CimInstance -ComputerName $Name -ClassName Win32_ComputerSystem | fl
```

```
Domain               : 16-TAP.Local
Manufacturer         : VMware, Inc.
Model                : VMware Virtual Platform
Name                 : 16-TAP-EX02
PrimaryOwnerName     : Windows User
TotalPhysicalMemory  : 10736947200
PSComputerName       : 16-tap-ex02
```

From just the results of this one cmdlet it's apparent that it provides the name of the server, the manufacture and model of the computer as well as the total Physical RAM installed. However, the CIM Class of Win32_ComputerSystem has far more values. The question is how to find these so a query can be run with PowerShell.

```
Get-CimClass Win32_ComputerSystem | fl
```

```
CimSuperClassName   : CIM_UnitaryComputerSystem
CimSuperClass       : ROOT/cimv2:CIM_UnitaryComputerSystem
CimClassProperties  : {Caption, Description, InstallDate, Name, Status, CreationClassName, NameFormat,
                      PrimaryOwnerContact, PrimaryOwnerName, Roles, InitialLoadInfo, LastLoadInfo,
                      PowerManagementCapabilities, PowerManagementSupported, PowerState, ResetCapability...}
CimClassQualifiers  : {Locale, UUID, dynamic, provider, SupportsUpdate}
CimClassMethods     : {SetPowerState, Rename, JoinDomainOrWorkgroup, UnjoinDomainOrWorkgroup}
CimSystemProperties : Microsoft.Management.Infrastructure.CimSystemProperties
CimClassName        : Win32_ComputerSystem
```

The CimClassProperties looks promising as there are more properties than can be displayed in the short amount of screen real estate – notice the '…' at the end of the properties list. Getting all the properties listed in that value (Screenshot is a small sample of values) looks like this:

```
(Get-CimClass Win32_ComputerSystem).CimClassProperties | ft Name,CimType,Qualifiers –Auto
```

## (1) CPU

Of the options in the 'Win32_ComputerSystem' class, NumberOfLogicalProcessors, fits one of the requirements in the list. From the above information, a CIM query of the Win32_ComputerSystem class can be performed and pull just the 'NumberOfLogicalProcessors' value:

```
$Name = "$Name" # Replace "
(Get-CimInstance -ComputerName $Name -ClassName Win32_ComputerSystem
).NumberOfLogicalProcessors
```

## (2) RAM

On the previous page, there is a 'TotalPhysicalMemory value from Get-CimInstance -Classname Win32_ComputerSystem'. The value is in Bytes and it needs to be converted to gigabytes. In order to do so, the RAM number needs to be divided by 1073741824. Then the value needs to be rounded to the nearest hundredth.

```
[Math]::Round($Value,2)
```

For the RAM size, a cmdlet needs to be queried via CIM:

```
(Get-CimInstance -ComputerName $Name -ClassName Win32_ComputerSystem ).TotalPhysicalMemory/1GB
```

The cmdlet above is then placed where the $value was from above:

```
[Math]::Round(((Get-CimInstance -ComputerName $Name -ClassName Win32_ComputerSystem
).TotalPhysicalMemory)/1GB,2)
```

## (3) Manufacturer and Model

From a previous section the 'Win32_ComputerSystem' class also contains the 'Manufacturer' and 'Model' of the server. Using this as a base:

```
Get-CimInstance -ComputerName $Name -ClassName Win32_ComputerSystem
```

Two cmdlets can be assembled to get these values:

```
(Get-CimInstance -ComputerName $Name -ClassName Win32_ComputerSystem).Manufacturer
(Get-CimInstance -ComputerName $Name -ClassName Win32_ComputerSystem).Model
```

## (4) Serial Number

For the Serial Number, this is usually stored in the BIOS for a server. Reviewing CIM classes for 'BIOS' a class called 'CIM_BIOSElement' is present.

```
(Get-CimInstance -ComputerName $Name -ClassName CIM_BIOSElement).SerialNumber
```

## (5) Pagefile

Automatic Pagefile value can be found in the Win32_ComputerSystem class:

```
Get-CimInstance -ComputerName $Name -ClassName Win32_ComputerSystem -Property *
```

```
ResetCapability                 : 1
AutomaticManagedPagefile        : True
AutomaticResetBootOption        : True
```

To get just the one value use this cmdlet:

```
(Get-CimInstance -ComputerName $Name -ClassName Win32_ComputerSystem).
AutomaticManagedPagefile
```

For the rest of the Pagefile values, a search of the various Win32 Classes reveals that there is a 'Win32_PagefileSetting' class. However, a query of this via Get-CimInstance reveals that there are no values and you get no errors:

```
Get-CimInstance -ComputerName $Name -ClassName Win32_PagefileSetting
```

The reason for an empty result is if the Pagefile is set to be managed. However, if the Pagefile is not managed, then values for the three settings will be found. To accommodate for this possibility an IF…ELSE check should be used for the 'AutomaticManagedPagefile' value. If it is true, then these three values need to be 'N/A' otherwise the three queries need to be run:

```
(Get-CimInstance -ComputerName $Name -ClassName Win32_PagefileSetting).InitialSize
(Get-CimInstance -ComputerName $Name -ClassName Win32_PagefileSetting).MaximumSize
(Get-CimInstance -ComputerName $Name -ClassName Win32_PagefileSetting).AllocatedBaseSize
```

## (6) Server Power Management

For Server Power Management, searching through the various classes for CIM with the keyword of Power, the WIN32_PowerPlan seems to point to the correct class for this query. However, a straight query, like the one below, does not work and will return a class does not exist error:

```
Get-CimInstance -ComputerName $Name -Class Win32_PowerPlan
```

Some 'Get-CimInstance' cmdlets require a NameSpace specified to get queries. The base of the NameSpace for this set of cmdlets is 'root/cimv2'. To checking for more NameSpaces, type in 'Get-CimInstance –Namespace root/cimv2' and hit tab to see if there are any more specific NameSpaces and there is:

```
Get-CimInstance –Namespace Root/Cimv2/Power <TAB>
```

If you keep hitting TAB you will see Win32_PowerPlan come up. With that name space, this cmdlet is possible (and functional):

```
Get-CimInstance -ComputerName $Name -Name Root\Cimv2\Power -Class Win32_PowerPlan
```

```
Caption          :
Description      : Automatically balances performance with energy consumption on capable hardware.
ElementName      : Balanced
InstanceID       : Microsoft:PowerPlan\{381b4222-f694-41f0-9685-ff5bb260df2e}
IsActive         : False
PSComputerName   :

Caption          :
Description      : Favors performance, but may use more energy.
ElementName      : High performance
InstanceID       : Microsoft:PowerPlan\{8c5e7fda-e8bf-4a96-9a85-a6e23a8c635c}
IsActive         : True
PSComputerName   :

Caption          :
Description      : Saves energy by reducing your computer's performance where possible.
ElementName      : Power saver
InstanceID       : Microsoft:PowerPlan\{a1841308-3541-4fab-bc81-f71556f20b4a}
IsActive         : False
PSComputerName   :
```

Now a query for the Power Policy with an 'IsActive' value of $true is needed. To do so, a filter of 'IsActive = $true" needs to be performed and the 'ElementName' value provides the Power Plan:

```
(Get-CimInstance -ComputerName $Name -Name Root\Cimv2\Power -Class Win32_PowerPlan -Filter "IsActive = 'True'").ElementName
```

Which should return "High performance" if set to the recommended, instead of the default "Balanced", plan:

```
High performance
```

## (7) NIC Power Management

Reviewing PowerShell cmdlets for Power Management cmdlets we find these:

```
Get-Command *Power*
```

```
CommandType     Name
-----------     ----
Function        Disable-NetAdapterPowerManagement
Function        Enable-NetAdapterPowerManagement
Function        Get-NetAdapterPowerManagement
```

Reviewing what the Get-NetAdapterPowerManagement cmdlet can provide:

Get-NetAdapterPowerManagement

```
InterfaceDescription     : vmxnet3 Ethernet Adapter
Name                     : Ethernet
ArpOffload               : Unsupported
NSOffload                : Unsupported
RsnRekeyOffload          : Unsupported
D0PacketCoalescing       : Unsupported
SelectiveSuspend         : Unsupported
DeviceSleepOnDisconnect  : Unsupported
WakeOnMagicPacket        : Enabled
WakeOnPattern            : Enabled
```

None of the values above provide what is needed.  Normally, at least from previous PowerShell experience, to expose extra properties:

Get-NetAdapterPowerManagement –Property * | fl

However, it does not work and it will return a parameter cannot be found error, the properties can be revealed by putting -property * after the Format-List:

Get-NetAdapterPowerManagement | fl –Property *

The 'AllowComputerToTurnOffDevice' value is the value that determines if the NIC can power itself off:

(Get-NetAdapterPowerManagement).AllowComputerToTurnOffDevice


**Script Assembly**

The first section is used to define variables for the script.  $ServerInfo array is defined to store all settings.  $ExchangeServers stores all Exchange Servers for the query.

```
# Variable Definition
$ServerInfo = @()
$ExchangeServers = Get-ExchangeServer
```

Each of the above queries need to be stored in variables:

```
$Name = $Server.Name
$CPU = (Get-CimInstance -ComputerName $Name -ClassName Win32_ComputerSystem).
NumberOfLogicalProcessors
$RAM = [Math]::Round(((Get-CimInstance -ComputerName $Name -ClassName Win32_
ComputerSystem).TotalPhysicalMemory)/1GB,2)
$Manufacturer = (Get-CimInstance -ComputerName $Name -ClassName Win32_ComputerSystem).
Manufacturer
$Model = (Get-CimInstance -ComputerName $Name -ClassName Win32_ComputerSystem).Model
$Serial = (Get-CimInstance -ComputerName $Name -ClassName Win32_ComputerSystem).
SerialNumber
$PagefileManaged = (Get-CimInstance -ComputerName $Name -ClassName Win32_ComputerSystem).
AutomaticManagedPagefile
$PFInit = (Get-CimInstance -ComputerName $Name -ClassName Win32_PagefileSettings).InitialSize
$PFMax = (Get-CimInstance -ComputerName $Name -ClassName Win32_PagefileSettings).
```

```
MaximumSize
$BaseSize = (Get-CimInstance -ComputerName $Name -ClassName Win32_PagefileSettings).
AllocatedBaseSize
$ServerPower = (Get-CimInstance -ComputerName $Name -Name Root\Cimv2\Power -ClassName
Win32_PowerPlan -Filter "IsActive = 'True'").ElementName
$Nic = (Get-NetAdapterPowerManagement).AllowComputerToTurnOffDevice
```

Then take all of the variables and put all the pieces together in a PowerShell object:

```
New-Object PSObject -Property @{
    Name = $Name
    CPU = $CPU
    RAM = $RAM
    Manufacturer = $Manufacturer
    Model = $Model
    SN = $SerialNumber
    PagefileManaged = $PagefileManaged
    PFInitialSize = $PFInit
    PFMaxSize = $PFMax
    PFBaseSize = $BaseSize
    ServerPowerMgmt = $ServerPower
    NICPowerMgmt = $NICPower
}
```

The PS Object will create a new line in the '$ServerInfo' variable that was configured in the beginning.

Complete Script Code

```
# Variable Definition
$ServerInfo = @()
$ExchangeServers = Get-ExchangeServer

$ServerInfo = Foreach ($Server in $ExchangeServers) {
    # Name
    $Name = $Server.Name

    # CPU
    $CPU = (Get-CimInstance -ComputerName $Name -ClassName Win32_ComputerSystem
    ).NumberOfLogicalProcessors

    # RAM
    $RAM = [math]::Round((((Get-CimInstance -ComputerName $Name -ClassName Win32_
    ComputerSystem ).TotalPhysicalMemory)/1GB,2)

    # Make/Model
    $Mfg = (Get-CimInstance -ComputerName $Name -ClassName Win32_ComputerSystem).
    Manufacturer
    $Model = (Get-CimInstance -ComputerName $Name -ClassName Win32_ComputerSystem).Model
```

```powershell
    # Serial Number
    $serialnumber = (Get-CimInstance -ComputerName $Name -ClassName CIM_BIOSElement).
    SerialNumber

    # Pagefile
    $PagefileManaged = (Get-CimInstance -ComputerName $Name -ClassName Win32_
    ComputerSystem).AutomaticManagedPagefile
    If ($PagefileManaged -ne $True) {
        $PFInit = (Get-CimInstance -ComputerName $Name -ClassName Win32_PagefileSetting).initialsize
        $PFMax = (Get-CimInstance -ComputerName $Name -ClassName Win32_PagefileSetting).
        MaximumSize
        $BaseSize = (Get-CimInstance -ComputerName $Name -ClassName Win32_PagefileSetting).
        AllocatedBaseSize
    } Else {
        $PFInit = "N/A"
        $PFMax = "N/A"
        $BaseSize = "N/A"
    }

    # Server Power Management
    $ServerPower = (Get-CimInstance -ComputerName $Name -Name root\cimv2\power -Class Win32_
    PowerPlan -Filter "IsActive = 'True'").ElementName

    # NIC Power Management
    $NICPower = (Get-NetAdapterPowerManagement).AllowComputerToTurnOffDevice

    # Put together data

    New-Object PSObject -Property @{
    Name = $Name
    CPU = $CPU
    RAM = $RAM
    Manufacturer = $Mfg
    Model = $Model
    SN = $SerialNumber
    PagefileManaged = $PagefileManaged
    PFInitialSize = $PFInit
    PFMaxSize = $PFMax
    PFBaseSize = $BaseSize
    ServerPowerMgmt = $ServerPower
    NICPowerMgmt = $NICPower
    }
}

$ServerInfo | fl
```

Script Results:

```
PageFileManaged PFInitialSize Manufacturer  PFBaseSize CPU      RAM    ServerPowerMgmt   Name          Model                   PFMaxSize
--------------- ------------- ------------   ---------- ---      ---    ---------------   ----          -----                   ---------
           True N/A           VMware, Inc.  N/A        2 CPUs  10 GB  High performance  16-TAP-EX01   VMware Virtual Platform N/A
          False 11238         VMware, Inc.             2 CPUs  10 GB  High performance  16-TAP-EX02   VMware Virtual Platform 11238
          False 11238         VMware, Inc.             2 CPUs  10 GB  High performance  16-TAP-EX03   VMware Virtual Platform 11238
           True 11238         VMware, Inc.  N/A        4 CPUs  24 GB  High performance  16-TAP-EX04   VMware Virtual Platform N/A
           True N/A           VMware, Inc.  N/A        4 CPUs  24 GB  High performance  16-TAP-EX05   VMware Virtual Platform N/A
           True N/A           VMware, Inc.  N/A        4 CPUs  24 GB  High performance  16-TAP-EX06   VMware Virtual Platform N/A
           True N/A           VMware, Inc.  N/A        4 CPUs  24 GB  High performance  16-TAP-EX07   VMware Virtual Platform N/A
          False 11238         VMware, Inc.             2 CPUs  10 GB  High performance  16-TAP-EX08   VMware Virtual Platform 11238
          False 11238         VMware, Inc.             2 CPUs  10 GB  High performance  16-TAP-EX09   VMware Virtual Platform 11238
          False 11238         VMware, Inc.             2 CPUs  10 GB  High performance  16-TAP-EX10   VMware Virtual Platform 11238
           True N/A           VMware, Inc.  N/A        4 CPUs  24 GB  High performance  16-TAP-EX11   VMware Virtual Platform N/A
           True N/A           VMware, Inc.  N/A        4 CPUs  24 GB  High performance  16-TAP-EX12   VMware Virtual Platform N/A
           True N/A           VMware, Inc.  N/A        4 CPUs  24 GB  High performance  16-TAP-EX13   VMware Virtual Platform N/A
```

# Menus

Building menus is not a task that is necessary for one off scripts. Menus should be used on scripts that will be run on multiple occasions, for example on multiple Exchange servers. Another reason to use it is for a reusable script, which is especially useful for consultants who run their scripts in dozens of environments a year. The menu simply makes running the script quicker and more flexible.

In a PowerShell script, the menu can consist of two parts. The first part is the text for the menu which is the visual part of the script. The menu can be simple and singular in color or very colorful like the example given in Chapter 2. The second part is the infrastructure or backend of the menu itself. This is where the executable code is stored and where coding needs to be performed in the form of functions that will complete the tasks the menu has called.

### Sample Menu Code

```
$menu = {
    Write-Host "*****************************************************************************"
    Write-Host "Exchange Server 2016 – Post Fixes"
    Write-Host "*****************************************************************************"
    Write-Host "1) Set Power Plan to High Performance"
    Write-Host "2) Disable Power Management for NICs"
    Write-Host "3) Disable SSL 3.0 Support"
    Write-Host "4) Disable RC4 Support"
    Write-Host ""
    Write-Host "98) Restart the Server"
    Write-Host "99) Exit"
    Write-Host ""
    Write-Host "Select an option.. [1-99]?"
}
```

The above menu has been snipped from a real script that is used to install prerequisites for Exchange Server 2016. The last section of the menu allows some Post Installation changes – server power plan, NIC power management, SSL 3.0 and RC4. By itself this menu is just a variable that holds a bunch of text that looks like a menu. Next, we need to build the backbone on the infrastructure part of the menu. This is where PowerShell will make calls to functions in the rest of the script to perform the functions you code for.

To start this section, construct a 'Do { } While' code block. The reason for this is that script will keep running options and displaying the menu until one of two exit codes are chosen. So the 'Do { } While' block would look something like this:

```
Do {
    Invoke-Command -ScriptBlock $Menu
    $Choice = Read-Host
} While ($Choice -ne 99)
```

Notice that with this code, the loop will keep displaying the menu after each option is chosen until the value of 99 is selected. At that point the script will stop and exit to a PowerShell prompt. The Read-Host will store the value type in $opt to be used for selecting which code block to run. Next, there needs to be a way to decide which option will run. What PowerShell cmdlet will allow for this?

```
Switch ($Choice)
```

However, a review of the help on 'Switch' does not reveal a lot of clue for its usefulness/functionality. However with a little bit of help from your favorite search engine, one can find this MSDN link for PowerShell functionality:

https://technet.microsoft.com/en-us/library/hh847750.aspx

We find that Switch will act like a condition tester, if a condition is fed to it will select that option within the Switch code section. For example:

```
$Choice = 3
    Switch ($Choice) {
    1 {Write-Host "1"}
    2 {Write-Host "2"}
    3 {Write-Host "3"}
}
```

The result of this will display the number 3:

Let's incorporate this into our menu infrastructure. Using the above as an example, we'll need to build code blocks for each function. To make this process simpler (in terms of the scope of the menu) functions have been precreated:

**HighPerformance**: Sets the servers Power Plan to High Performance
**PowerMgmt:** Turns off Power Management on all NICs
**DisableSSL3:** Disabled the use of SSL 3.0 due to vulnerabilities
**DisableRC4:** Disabled the use of the RC4 encryption on Exchange

With these functions created they can be referred to in each option code block:

**Option 1**

This option calls the HighPerformance function:

```
Function HighPerformance {
    Write-Host " "
    $HighPerf = Powercfg -l | %{if($_.Contains("High performance")) {$_.Split()[3]}}
    $CurrPlan = $(Powercfg -GetActiveScheme).Split()[3]
    if ($CurrPlan -ne $HighPerf) {
        PowerCfg -SetActive $HighPerf
```

```
        CheckPowerPlan
    } Else {
      If ($CurrPlan -eq $HighPerf) {
        Write-Host " "
        Write-Host "The power plan is already set to " -NoNewLine
        Write-Host "High Performance." -ForegroundColor Green
        Write-Host " "
      }
    }
  }
```

## Option 2

The option calls the PowerMgmt function:

```
Function PowerMgmt {
  Write-Host " "
  $NICs = Get-WmiObject -Class Win32_NetworkAdapter|Where-Object{$_.PNPDeviceID -NotLike
  "ROOT\*" -and $_.Manufacturer -ne "Microsoft" -and $_.ConfigManagerErrorCode -eq 0 -And
  $_.ConfigManagerErrorCode -ne 22}
  Foreach($NIC in $NICs) {
    $NICName = $NIC.Name
    $DeviceID = $NIC.DeviceID
    If([Int32]$DeviceID -lt 10) {
        $DeviceNumber = "000"+$DeviceID
    } Else {
        $DeviceNumber = "00"+$DeviceID
    }
    $KeyPath = "HKLM:\SYSTEM\CurrentControlSet\Control\Class\{4D36E972-E325-11CE-BFC1-
    08002bE10318}\$DeviceNumber"

    If(Test-Path -Path $KeyPath) {
        $PnPCapabilities = (Get-ItemProperty -Path $KeyPath).PnPCapabilities
        # Check to see if the value is 24 and if not, set it to 24
        If($PnPCapabilities -ne 24) {
            Set-ItemProperty -Path $KeyPath -Name "PnPCapabilities" -Value 24 | Out-Null
        }
        # Verify the value is now set to or was set to 24
        If($PnPCapabilities -eq 24) {
            Write-Host " "
            Write-Host "Power Management has already been " -NoNewline
            Write-Host "disabled" -ForegroundColor Green
            Write-Host " "
        }
      }
    }
  }
}
```

**Option 3**

The option calls the DisableSSL3 function:

```powershell
Function DisableSSL3 {
  Write-Host " "
  $TestPath1 = Get-Item -Path "HKLM:\System\CurrentControlSet\Control\SecurityProviders\
  SCHANNEL\Protocols\SSL 3.0" -ErrorAction SilentlyContinue
  $TestPath2 = Get-Item -Path "HKLM:\System\CurrentControlSet\Control\SecurityProviders\
  SCHANNEL\Protocols\SSL 3.0\Server" -ErrorAction SilentlyContinue
  $RegistryPath = "HKLM:\System\CurrentControlSet\Control\SecurityProviders\SCHANNEL\
  Protocols\SSL 3.0\Server"
  $Name = "Enabled"
  $Value = "0"
  $CheckVal1 = Get-ItemProperty -Path "$registrypath" -Name $Name -ErrorAction SilentlyContinue

  # Check for SSL 3.0 Reg Key
  If ($TestPath1 -eq $null) {
    $Key = (Get-Item  HKLM:\).OpenSubKey("System\CurrentControlSet\Control\SecurityProviders\
    SCHANNEL\Protocols", $true)
    $Key.CreateSubKey('SSL 3.0')
    $Key.Close()
  } else {
    Write-Host "The " -NoNewLine;Write-Host "SSL 3.0" -ForegroundColor Green -NoNewline
    Write-Host " Registry key already exists."
  }

  # Check for SSL 3.0\Server Reg Key
  If ($TestPath2 -eq $Null) {
    $Key = (get-item  HKLM:\).OpenSubKey("System\CurrentControlSet\Control\SecurityProviders\
    SCHANNEL\Protocols\SSL 3.0", $true)
    $Key.CreateSubKey('Server')
    $Key.Close()
  } Else {
    Write-Host "The " –NoNewLine
    Write-Host "SSL 3.0\Servers" -ForegroundColor Green –NoNewline
    Write-Host " Registry key already exists."
  }

  # Add the enabled value to disable SSL 3.0 Support
  If ($CheckVal1.Enabled -ne "0") {
    Try {
      New-ItemProperty -Path $registryPath -Name $Name -Value $Value –Force
      $Ssl++
    } Catch {
      $Ssl--
    }
```

```
    } Else {
        Write-Host "The registry value " -NoNewLine
        Write-Host "Enabled" -ForegroundColor Green -NoNewline
        Write-Host " exists under the SSL 3.0\Server Registry Key."
    }
} # End of Disable SSL 3.0 function
```

## Option 4

The option calls the DisableRC4 function:

```
# Disable RC4
Function DisableRC4 {
    Write-Host " "
    # Define Registry keys to look for
    $Base = Get-Item -Path "HKLM:\SYSTEM\CurrentControlSet\Control\SecurityProviders\SCHANNEL\
Ciphers\" -ErrorAction SilentlyContinue
    $Val1 = Get-Item -Path "HKLM:\SYSTEM\CurrentControlSet\Control\SecurityProviders\SCHANNEL\
Ciphers\RC4 128/128\" -ErrorAction SilentlyContinue
    $Val2 = Get-Item -Path "HKLM:\SYSTEM\CurrentControlSet\Control\SecurityProviders\SCHANNEL\
Ciphers\RC4 40/128\" -ErrorAction SilentlyContinue
    $Val3 = Get-Item -Path "HKLM:\SYSTEM\CurrentControlSet\Control\SecurityProviders\SCHANNEL\
Ciphers\RC4 56/128\" -ErrorAction SilentlyContinue

    # Define Values to add
    $RegistryBase = "Ciphers"
    $RegistryPath1 = "HKLM:\SYSTEM\CurrentControlSet\Control\SecurityProviders\SCHANNEL\Ciphers\
RC4 128/128\"
    $RegistryPath2 = "HKLM:\SYSTEM\CurrentControlSet\Control\SecurityProviders\SCHANNEL\Ciphers\
RC4 40/128\"
    $RegistryPath3 = "HKLM:\SYSTEM\CurrentControlSet\Control\SecurityProviders\SCHANNEL\
Ciphers\RC4 56/128\"
    $Name = "Enabled"
    $Value = "0"
    $Ssl = 0
    $Checkval1 = Get-ItemProperty -Path "$RegistryPath1" -Name $Name -ErrorAction SilentlyContinue
    $Checkval2 = Get-ItemProperty -Path "$RegistryPath2" -Name $Name -ErrorAction SilentlyContinue
    $Checkval3 = Get-ItemProperty -Path "$RegistryPath3" -Name $Name -ErrorAction SilentlyContinue
```

… And so on … See the current script here:

https://gallery.technet.microsoft.com/Install-Exchange-2016-48983e13

Notice that a comment is included in each option block for documentation purposes.  For the last two options the script provides a way to exit the script and reboot the server:

**Option 98**

```
98 {#       Exit and restart
   Restart-Computer -ComputerName LocalHost -Force
}
```

**Option 99**

```
99 {#       Exit
   Write-Host "Exiting..."
}
```

When option 99 is selected, the script exists because of the Do {} While code block.  Option 98 will also exit, but only because the server is rebooting at that moment.

Pulling all of the previous code together into one script:

```
$Menu = {
   Write-Host "******************************************************************"
   Write-Host " Exchange Server 2016 – Post Fixes"
   Write-Host "   ******************************************************************"
   Write-Host ""
   Write-Host "1) Set Power Plan to High Performance"
   Write-Host "2) Disable Power Management for NICs"
   Write-Host "3) Disable SSL 3.0 Support"
   Write-Host "4) Disable RC4 Support"
   Write-Host ""
   Write-Host "98) Restart the Server"
   Write-Host " 99) Exit"
   Write-Host ""
   Write-Host "Select an option.. [1-99]?"
}

Do {
   $Choice = Read-Host $Menu
   Switch ($Choice)   {

      1 { # Set power plan to High Performance as per Microsoft
         ormance
      }
      2 { # Disable Power Management for NICs.
        PowerMgmt
      }
      3 { # Disable SSL 3.0 Support
        DisableSSL3
      }
      4 { # Disable RC4 Support
        DisableRC4
      }
```

```
    98 {#         Exit and restart
        Restart-Computer -ComputerName LocalHost -Force
    }
    99 {#         Exit
        Write-Host "Exiting..."
    }
    Default {
        Write-Host "You haven't selected any of the available options. "
    }
  }
} while ($Choice -ne 99)
```

Running the script provides a menu as displayed below:

```
Last command:

        ****************************************************************
        Exchange Server 2016 - Post Fixes
        ****************************************************************

        1) Set Power Plan to High Performance
        2) Disable Power Management for NICs.
        3) Disable SSL 3.0 Support
        4) Disable RC4 Support

        98) Restart the Server
        99) Exit
Select an option.. [1-99]?: _
```

99 allows for the exit to exit:

```
Select an option.. [1-99]?: 99
Exiting...
```

If an option is typed in wrong, say 77:

```
        98) Restart the Server
        99) Exit

    Select an option.. [1-99]?: 77

You haven't selected any of the available options.
```

Any error message can be displayed here, this will help identify the issue of a wrong choice.  If Options 1 - 4 are chosen, and the script had the required functions, those functions would then be executed:

```
Select an option.. [1-99]?: 1

The power plan now is set to High Performance.
```

```
Select an option.. [1-99]?:  2

Power Management has already been disabled
```

```
Select an option.. [1-99]?: 3
The SSL 3.0 Registry key already exists.
The SSL 3.0\Servers Registry key already exists.
The registry value Enabled exists under the SSL 3.0\Server Registry Key.
```

```
Select an option.. [1-99]?: 4

The Ciphers Registry key already exists.

SubKeyCount : 0
View        : Default
Handle      : Microsoft.Win32.SafeHandles.SafeRegistryHandle
ValueCount  : 0
Name        : HKEY_LOCAL_MACHINE\SYSTEM\CurrentControlSet\Control\Securit


SubKeyCount : 0
View        : Default
Handle      : Microsoft.Win32.SafeHandles.SafeRegistryHandle
ValueCount  : 0
Name        : HKEY_LOCAL_MACHINE\SYSTEM\CurrentControlSet\Control\Securit
```

# Aliases

PowerShell aliases are shortened versions of PowerShell cmdlets.  Consider aliases to be a convenience in reducing the amount of text in a script.  Aliases are not necessary to writing a script but they do provide shortcuts to coding. Without aliases, each command in PowerShell just takes longer to type.  The downside of aliases is that normally PowerShell is a very readable scripting language using aliases can obscure the ability to read PowerShell in plain English.  Another downside is that there is no guarantee that the alias will exist in a different environment.  If the script is meant to be portable, it would be advisable to not use them or at least limit their usage.  If a script will be read by someone other than you, using aliases might make the script unreadable to others.

```
Get-Alias -Definition Foreach-Object

CommandType          Name
-----------          ----
Alias                % -> ForEach-Object
Alias                foreach -> ForEach-Object
```

However, what if you don't know the command that the alias is for?  The above can be reverse engineered to show all aliases.  To look up all aliases, simply type in 'Get-Alias':

```
CommandType          Name
-----------          ----
Alias                % -> ForEach-Object
Alias                ? -> Where-Object
Alias                ac -> Add-Content
Alias                asnp -> Add-PSSnapin
Alias                cat -> Get-Content
Alias                cd -> Set-Location
Alias                chdir -> Set-Location
Alias                clc -> Clear-Content
Alias                clear -> Clear-Host
Alias                clhy -> Clear-History
Alias                cli -> Clear-Item
Alias                clp -> Clear-ItemProperty
Alias                cls -> Clear-Host
Alias                clv -> Clear-Variable
Alias                cnsn -> Connect-PSSession
Alias                compare -> Compare-Object
Alias                copy -> Copy-Item
```

Without listing them all here, all told, there are 148 aliases defined.  What may be more interesting is that aliases can be created and modified.  This certainly provides for some flexibility or customization of PowerShell.

# New-Alias

If there is a desire to make custom aliases for PowerShell, this is the cmdlet to use.  Remember that this customization is a local customization and will not be useable on other servers, unless the alias is created on that server as well.

Get-Help New-Alias -Examples

```
----------------------------- EXAMPLE 1 -----------------------------

PS C:\>new-alias list get-childitem
This command creates an alias named "list" to represent the Get-ChildItem cmdlet.

----------------------------- EXAMPLE 2 -----------------------------

PS C:\>new-alias -name w -value get-wmiobject -description "quick wmi alias" -option ReadOnly
PS C:\>get-alias -name w | format-list *
This command creates an alias named "w" to represent the Get-WMIObject cmdlet. It creates a description, "quick wmi
pipes it to Format-List to display all of the information about it.
```

## Sample Usage

Take for example an environment that is migrating thousands of mailboxes to Office 365 and scripts are created to manage moving the users to Office 365 as well as manage the mailboxes once they are in Exchange Online.  In this scenario there are a few cmdlets that alias could be created using the New-RemoteMailbox, Enable-Remote-Mailbox, Set-RemoteMailbox and Remove-RemoteMailbox cmdlets.  A series of aliases could be created for these cmdlets which would assist both in the creation of a more efficient script or easier for the engineer to type in the cmdlet.  For simplicity sake, we'll use just the first letter of each word in the cmdlet for the alias.

To create these aliases, we'll use a series of New-Alias one-liners:

New-Alias erm Enable-RemoteMailbox –Description "For enabled Office 365 Mailboxes"
New-Alias nrm New-RemoteMailbox –Description "For creating new Office 365 Mailboxes"
New-Alias rrm Remove-RemoteMailbox –Description "For removing old Office 365 Mailboxes"
New-Alias srm Set-RemoteMailbox –Description "For managing Office 365 Mailboxes"

Example result of a new alias creation:

```
[PS] C:\>New-Alias nrm New-RemoteMailbox -Description "For creating new Office 365 Mailboxes"
[PS] C:\>Get-Alias nrm

CommandType        Name                                             ModuleName
-----------        ----                                             ----------
Alias              nrm -> New-RemoteMailbox
```

There are a few parameters that can be used to customize this new alias during creation.  One of the parameters is 'Option' which provides for a way to limit when the alias can be used – Global, Local, Script or Private.  An alias could be enabled for only when a script runs or only while in a local session.  The purpose of this option is to possibly isolate the usage of a cmdlet as to prevent unwarranted changes using the aliases.  A description should be added so that the purpose of the alias is known by others.

## Set-Alias

This cmdlet is used to modify any of the existing alias to the specifics that you may want to configure for a particular alias. One of the exceptions is if the alias is set to ReadOnly. To modify one of those aliases, a '-Force' switch must be used. Here are some sample uses of the cmdlet:

Get-Help New-Alias -Examples

```
------------------------  EXAMPLE 1  ------------------------

PS C:\>set-alias -name list -value get-childitem
This command creates the alias "list" for the Get-ChildItem cmdlet. After you create the alias, you can use "list"
in place of "Get-ChildItem" at the command line and in scripts.


------------------------  EXAMPLE 2  ------------------------

PS C:\>set-alias list get-location


This command associates the alias "list" with the Get-Location cmdlet. If "list" is an alias for another cmdlet,
this command changes its association so that it now is the alias only for Get-Location.
```

## Sample Usage

In practical terms, this cmdlet would likely only be used to modify existing aliases that you've created yourself. Taking some of the aliases created in the previous section, let's make sure that the aliases are locked down and cannot be changed:

```
Set-Alias erm Enable-RemoteMailbox  -Option ReadOnly
Set-Alias nrm New-RemoteMailbox   -Option ReadOnly
Set-Alias rrm Remove-RemoteMailbox  -Option ReadOnly
Set-Alias srm Set-RemoteMailbox  -Option ReadOnly
```

What's interesting is that this same cmdlet ('Set-Alias') can be used to create a new alias as well. For example, if a new alias were needed for creating a new mailbox on-premises. The Set-Alias could be used to create this alias as well:

```
[PS] C:\>set-alias nmop new-mailbox -Description "Create new mailbox on-premises"
[PS] C:\>
```

### Removing an Alias

Reviewing the PowerShell cmdlets with the word 'Alias' there are no cmdlet with the word 'remove' in it. How then can an alias be removed? If the solution cannot be found in PowerShell, then searching for a solution via your favorite search engine is the next step:

**Search string:**    remove powershell alias

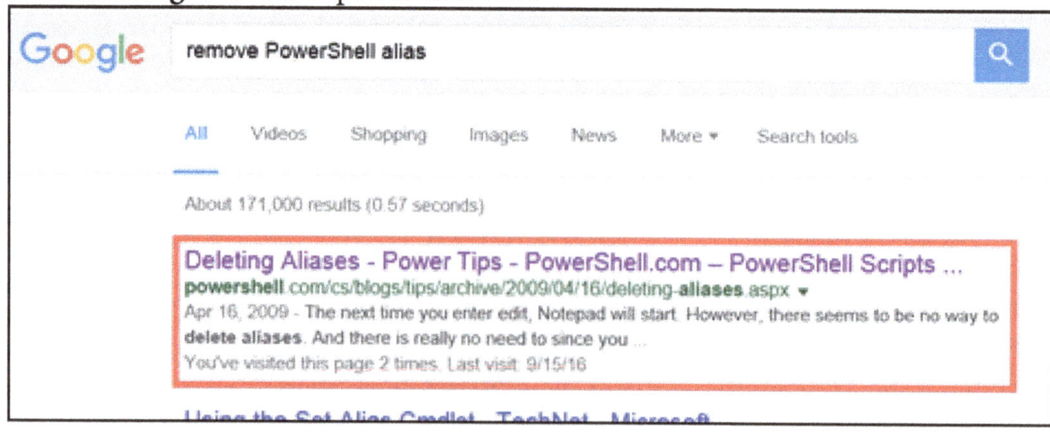

Reviewing the first link from the search, the solution to removing the alias is:

    Remove-Item Alias:<alias to remove>

To remove one of the previous aliases that were created use this cmdlet:

    Remove-Item Alias:nrm

However, there is an error:

```
[PS] C:\>remove-item alias:nrm
remove-item : Alias was not removed because alias nrm is constant or read-only.
At line:1 char:1
+ remove-item alias:nrm
+ ~~~~~~~~~~~~~~~~~~~~~~
    + CategoryInfo          : WriteError: (nrm:String) [Remove-Item], SessionStateUnauthorizedAccess
    + FullyQualifiedErrorId : AliasNotRemovable,Microsoft.PowerShell.Commands.RemoveItemCommand
```

That means the 'ReadOnly' setting that was applied worked as expected.  To remove the ReadOnly option, run this:

    Set-Alias nrm New-RemoteMailbox –Force –Option None
    Remove-Item Alias:nrm

```
[PS] C:\>set-alias nrm new-remotemailbox –force –option none
[PS] C:\>remove-item alias:nrm
[PS] C:\>_
```

Now if the alias is tried once more, PowerShell fails as the references has been removed:

```
[PS] C:\>nrm
nrm : The term 'nrm' is not recognized as the name of a cmdlet, function, script fi
spelling of the name, or if a path was included, verify that the path is correct an
At line:1 char:1
+ nrm
+ ~~~
    + CategoryInfo          : ObjectNotFound: (nrm:String) [], CommandNotFoundExcep
    + FullyQualifiedErrorId : CommandNotFoundException
```

In the end, creating your own aliases is not required, nor are they necessary, but creating custom aliases may be a more efficient way to write code in PowerShell.


# Foreach-Object (%)

While on the topic of PowerShell aliases, there are indeed some useful aliases that point to some rather useful cmdlets that we have not covered.  One useful alias is '%'.  What does the '%' symbol stand for or abbreviate in PowerShell.  We can still use the Get-Alias cmdlet, but we need some criteria for finding just the '%' character in the results.  If you recall from the Filtering section earlier in the book, the 'where' filter can help find the '%' symbol. From the screenshot, we also know that the field called 'Name' will contain the value:

    Get-Alias | Where {$_.Name -eq "%"}

```
CommandType     Name
-----------     ----
Alias           % -> ForEach-Object
```

By using that cmdlet we now know that the alias % refers to Foreach-Object. Some other examples of other aliases:

```
Get-Alias | Where {$_.Name -eq "ft"}
```

```
CommandType          Name
-----------          ----
Alias                ft -> Format-Table
```

```
Get-Alias | Where {$_.Name -eq "fl"}
```

```
CommandType          Name
-----------          ----
Alias                fl -> Format-List
```

Circling back to the '%' symbol or Foreach-Object. This particular alias provides for some interesting processing of data. Take for example a scenario where the Active Directory sites, costs and so on are not documented. IT Management wants this mapped out to help with troubleshooting AD replication issues that are having an impact on the Exchange system – mailbox moves, password changes and DNS changes.

In the end, a report that shows this criteria needs to be created and the PowerShell one-liner looks like this:

```
Get-ADReplicationSiteLink -Filter * | Select-Object Name, Objectclass, Cost, @{Expression={$_.
ReplicationFrequencyInMinutes};Label="Frequency"}, SitesIncluded | % { $Sites = $_.SitesIncluded;
$AllSites = @(); Foreach ($Line in $Sites) {$Site = $Line -Split ','; $SiteName = $Site[0].
Substring(3);$AllSites += $SiteName};$_.SitesIncluded = $AllSites;Return $_} | ft -Auto
```

```
Name                  Objectclass Cost Frequency Sitesincluded
----                  ----------- ---- --------- -------------
DEFAULTIPSITELINK     siteLink     100       180 {Corp,PBurg}
Corp to Chicago       sitelink     100       180 {Corp,Chi}
Corp to New York      sitelink     100       180 {Corp,NT}
Corp to LA            sitelink     100       180 {Corp,LA}
Corp to Mexico        sitelink     100       180 {Corp, Mex}
Corp to London        sitelink     100       180 {Corp,London}
```

OK. Maybe that was a bit too much at once. Think of the above as what IT Management is looking for. To learn how the Foreach-Object or '%' alias fit into this, start with the results of just the 'Get-ADReplicationSiteLink' that we need for the replication information.

```
Get-ADReplicationSiteLink -Filter *
```

```
Cost                            : 100
DistinguishedName               : CN=DEFAULTIPSITELINK,CN=IP,CN=Inter-Site Transports,CN=Sites,CN=Configuration,DC=domain,DC=com
Name                            : DEFAULTIPSITELINK
ObjectClass                     : siteLink
ObjectGUID                      : 5ae023d4-d407-4ae0-b650-8359c1344318
ReplicationFrequencyInMinutes   : 180
SitesIncluded                   : {CN=Corp,CN=Sites,CN=Configuration,DC=domain,DC=com, CN=Pburg,CN=Sites,CN=Configuration,DC=domain,DC=com}

Cost                            : 100
DistinguishedName               : CN=DEFAULTIPSITELINK,CN=IP,CN=Inter-Site Transports,CN=Sites,CN=Configuration,DC=domain,DC=com
Name                            : CorpToChicago
ObjectClass                     : siteLink
ObjectGUID                      : 5ae023d4-d407-4ae0-b650-8359c8976345
ReplicationFrequencyInMinutes   : 180
SitesIncluded                   : {CN=Corp,CN=Sites,CN=Configuration,DC=domain,DC=com, CN=Chicago,CN=Sites,CN=Configuration,DC=domain,DC=com}

Cost                            : 100
DistinguishedName               : CN=DEFAULTIPSITELINK,CN=IP,CN=Inter-Site Transports,CN=Sites,CN=Configuration,DC=domain,DC=com
Name                            : CorpToNewYork
ObjectClass                     : siteLink
```

Lots of good information there, it needs formatting and selecting five values – Name, ObjectClass, Cost, SitesIncluded and ReplicationFrequency – in table format:

```
Get-ADReplicationSiteLink -Filter * | ft Name,ObjectClass,Cost,ReplicationFrequency*,SitesIncluded
-Auto
```

```
Name                   ObjectClass Cost ReplicationFrequencyInMinutes SitesIncluded
----                   ----------- ---- ----------------------------- -------------
DEFAULTIPSITELINK      siteLink    100                            180 {CN=Corp,CN=Sites,CN=Configuration,DC=domain,DC=com, CN=Pbu
CorpToChicago          siteLink    100                            180 {CN=Corp,CN=Sites,CN=Configuration,DC=domain,DC=com, CN=Chi
CorpToNewYork          siteLink    100                            180 {CN=Corp,CN=Sites,CN=Configuration,DC=domain,DC=com, CN=Nev
CorpToLA               siteLink    100                            180 {CN=Corp,CN=Sites,CN=Configuration,DC=domain,DC=com, CN=LA,
CorpToMexico           siteLink    100                            180 {CN=Corp,CN=Sites,CN=Configuration,DC=domain,DC=com, CN=Mex
CorpToLondon           siteLink    100                            180 {CN=Corp,CN=Sites,CN=Configuration,DC=domain,DC=com, CN=Lon
```

The table looks alright, however the SitesIncluded field is a mess. Too much information, not specific enough to see the site names at first glance. The 'ReplicationFrequenecyInMinutes' column is also too wide. First, let's examine the field to see what data is in that field:

```
{CN=Corp, CN=Sites, CN=Configuration, DC=domain, DC=com, CN=Pburg, CN=Sites, CN=Configuration,
DC=domain, DC=com}
```

From the field data, we can determine that two sites are listed here – Corp and Pburg – the other information in this field is just 'noise' and not relevant. There are a couple ways to tackle splitting up this data. One method is to store just that field in a variable to manipulate the field and distill the results down to just the site names.

```
$SitesIncluded = (Get-ADReplicationSiteLink "DefaultIPSiteLink").SitesIncluded
$SitesIncluded
```

```
CN=Corp,CN=Sites,CN=Configuration,DC=domain,DC=com
CN=Pburg,CN=Sites,CN=Configuration,DC=domain,DC=com
```

As we saw from the Get-ADReplicationSiteLink cmdlet output earlier, each site is made up of multiple fields (think comma delimited CSV file) and that means that the values can be parsed out. Which means we can choose column one, as it contains the site name. How to do this?

In some ways, each site name (from above) is an array of values, with each field being separated by commas. This means that we can write some lines to isolate just the first column (where the site name is stored). First, we work with one site to store the SitesIncluded value in the $SitesIncluded variable:

```
$SitesIncluded = (Get-ADReplicationSiteLink "DefaultIPSiteLink").SitesIncluded
```

Then we need to define $AllSites as an array:

```
$AllSites = @()
```

Once that is established, a Foreach loop will be used to process each site in the $SitesIncluded variable.

```
Foreach ($Line in $SitesIncluded) {
```

Inside the loop we need to parse this out:

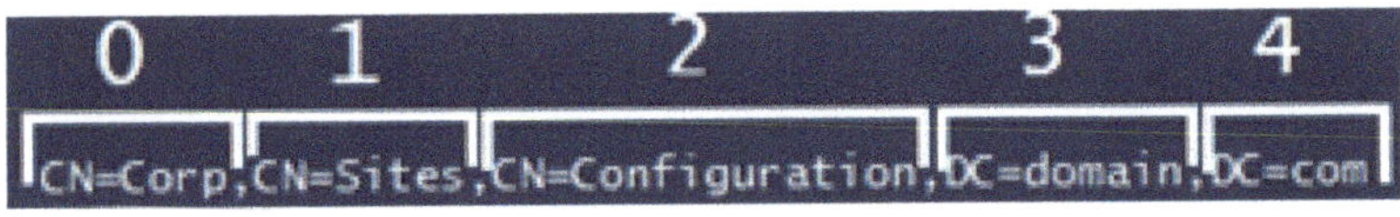


Each number above represents a positional value in the array variable. We only need the first of the five sections. We also don't want the "CN=". First we'll split the line using the ',' character as a delimiter:

```
$Site = $Line -Split ','
```

Then we select the first value in the array ($Site[0]) and only take the characters after the 3rd character and store it into the $SiteName variable:

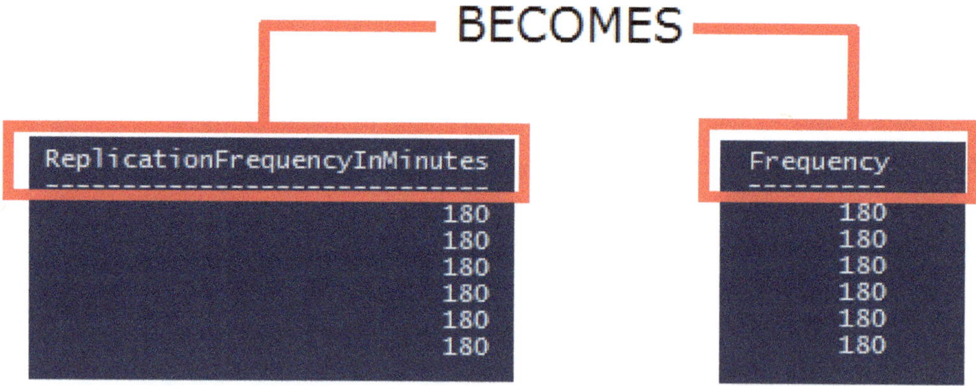


Then with each look the $SiteName is added to the $AllSites variable.

```
    $AllSites += $SiteName
}
```

Once completed, the site names stored in the variable for the DEFAULTSITELINK are Corp and PBurg:

```
Corp
Pburg
```

Now that we are able to get just the site names from that one value, the process needs to handle all the sites and in a single one-liner?  First, the base command once more:

```
Get-ADReplicationSiteLink -Filter * | Select-Object Name, ObjectClass, Cost,
ReplicationFrequencyInMinutes, SitesIncluded
```

This will choose the name, ObjectClass, ReplicationFrequency, Cost and SitesIncluded.  To make the Replication Interval column look better, change the formatting by specifying these changes:



```
@{expression={$_.ReplicationFrequencyInMinutes};label="Frequency"}
```

This will provide the replication frequency column with a much shorter header or label:



With the objects selected, the values are sent via a pipe to a code section started the alias for Foreach-Object followed by a starter bracket:

```
% {
```

This is then followed by two variable definitions. The first takes the object $_.SitesIncluded and stores it in a new variable called $Sites. This is done because in some of the cmdlets later, using $_.SitesIncluded will fail. The $All-Sites variable is also designated as an array for storing values and a ';' is used because all combined, to make it a one-liner:

```
$Sites = $_.SitesIncluded; $AllSites = @();
```

On to the filtering. In this section, a Foreach is used to go through each line stored in $Sites – which will have all the sites from each site link stored in it. Using the code for parsing the data on the last page, the code will split the values by the ',', then select the first section of the splitting and remove the 'CN=' part of the same value. All of this will then be stored in the $AllSites variable. Notice the ';' in the script. This means new line or next command. Without it, the one-liner would not work:

```
Foreach ($Line in $Sites) {$Site = $Line -split ','; $SiteName = $Site[0].Substring(3);$AllSites += $SiteName}
```

After the Foreach section is complete, the $AllSites variable has all the sites distilled to just the proper name. Then replace the old $_.SitesIncluded variable with the $AllSites data:

```
;$_.SitesIncluded = $AllSites
```

Then the new value is returned to the Select-Object from before the filter:

```
;Return $_}
```

Lastly, the data is displayed in a table formatted to fit with the '-Auto' switch:

```
| ft -Auto
```

With that completed, the one-liner from the start of this section is complete and ready to document Active Directory Sites. This same technique can be used with any PowerShell command that returns a field with multiple values that need to be cleaned up. The key is the Foreach-Object (%) cmdlet that allows the data manipulation before being displayed in the PowerShell window.

## Before

```
Name                 ObjectClass Cost ReplicationFrequencyInMinutes Sitesincluded
----                 ----------- ---- ---------------------------- -------------
DEFAULTIPSITELINK siteLink       100                           180 {CN=Corp,CN=Sites,CN=Configuration,DC=domain,DC=com, CN=Pbu
CorpToChicago     siteLink       100                           180 {CN=Corp,CN=Sites,CN=Configuration,DC=domain,DC=com, CN=Chi
CorpToNewYork     siteLink       100                           180 {CN=Corp,CN=Sites,CN=Configuration,DC=domain,DC=com, CN=New
CorpToLA          siteLink       100                           180 {CN=Corp,CN=Sites,CN=Configuration,DC=domain,DC=com, CN=LA,
CorpToMexico      siteLink       100                           180 {CN=Corp,CN=Sites,CN=Configuration,DC=domain,DC=com, CN=Mex
CorpToLondon      siteLink       100                           180 {CN=Corp,CN=Sites,CN=Configuration,DC=domain,DC=com, CN=Lor
```

## After

```
Name                 Objectclass Cost Frequency Sitesincluded
----                 ----------- ---- --------- -------------
DEFAULTIPSITELINK siteLink       100       180 {Corp,PBurg}
Corp to Chicago   sitelink       100       180 {Corp,Chi}
Corp to New York  sitelink       100       180 {Corp,NT}
Corp to LA        sitelink       100       180 {Corp,LA}
Corp to Mexico    sitelink       100       180 {Corp, Mex}
Corp to London    sitelink       100       180 {Corp,London}
```

# PowerShell Interface Customization

Working space is important in PowerShell and this means screen buffering.  Why is this important?   The default line buffer limit is 300 which can be too small depending on what script output of cmdlet output is being run.  For example, just running 'Get-Help New-ReceiveConnector' can overrun that buffer.  This makes it hard to use PowerShell to its fullest.  So, just changing the buffer size will make PowerShell that much easier to work with.

**Before** - 300 Character Buffer

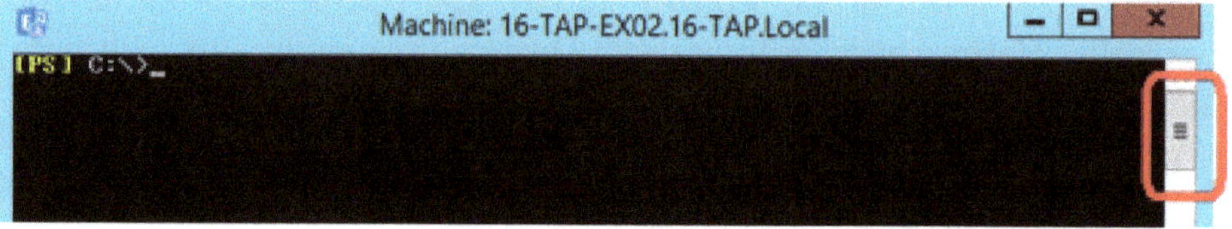


To make the change, click on the icon in the upper left and select Properties (see below):

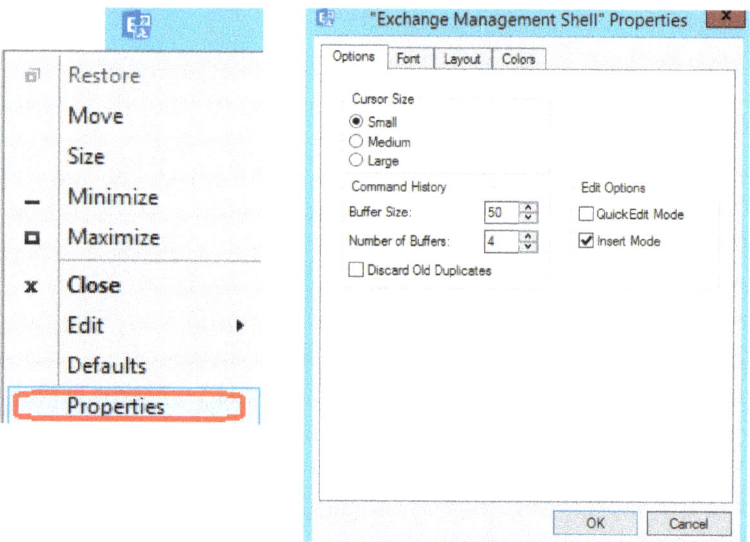


Adjust the 300 to 9999:

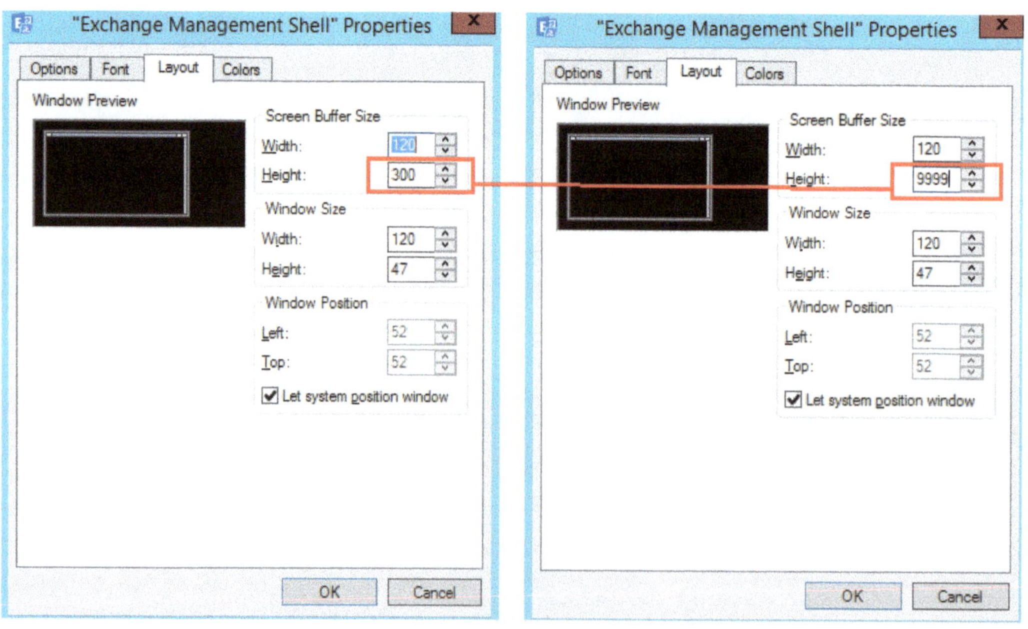

After - 9999 Character Buffer

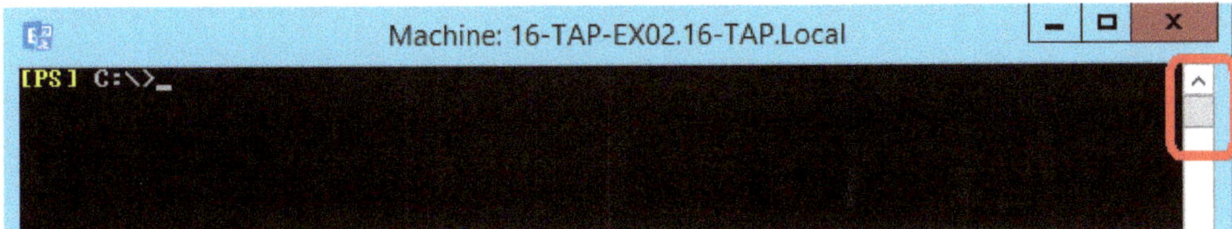

Notice the smaller size of the slider on the right.  Now output from most, if not all cmdlets, will not exceed the window buffer size.  If the output is in excess of 9999 lines, it may be better to export the results a TXT, CSV or some other sort of file.  Make sure to save these settings so as not to have to keep making this change.

In addition to the above, startup options can be created for the PowerShell window to customize it more.  There are several locations for customization files for PowerShell and they vary in their functionality.  The two we will work with for this chapter are:

**For all users - PowerShell**

> %windir%\system32\Windows¬PowerShell\v1.0\Microsoft.Powershell_profile.ps1

**Current user - PowerShell**

> %UserProfile%\Documents\WindowsPowerShell\Microsoft.Powershell_profile.ps1

Before creating a new one, verify that one has not yet been created.  Backup the old profile if needed for later.  First verify the current PowerShell profile:

$Profile

```
PS C:\> $Profile
C:\Users\administrator.16-TAP\Documents\WindowsPowerShell\Microsoft.PowerShell_profile.ps1
PS C:\>
```

To see if the file was already created and in use (if $True, then the file exists, otherwise it does not):

Test-Path $Profile

```
PS C:\> Test-Path $Profile
False
PS C:\>
```

In the above case, the profile has not been created and if we wish to add customizations we'll need to create our own file.

New-Item -Path $Profile –ItemType File –Force

```
PS C:\> New-Item -Path $Profile –ItemType File –Force


    Directory: C:\Users\administrator.16-TAP\Documents\WindowsPowerShell


Mode                LastWriteTime         Length Name
----                -------------         ------ ----
-a---         2/26/2017     6:49 PM              0 Microsoft.PowerShell_profile.ps1
```

Once the file has been created you can open this in your favorite editor.

**What Can Be Added to This File**

The following is a list of some of the customizations that can be performed with the profile file:

- Window sizing (height and width)
- Load custom scripts
- Windows colors

**Window Sizing and Coloring**

The size of the console is stored in this variable $Host which is a known variable in PowerShell.

```
$Host
```

```
PS C:\> $Host


Name              : ConsoleHost
Version           : 4.0
InstanceId        : 6d3a530c-8f0f-48cd-b4c1-0f5d73a3eb78
UI                : System.Management.Automation.Internal.Host.InternalHostUserInterface
CurrentCulture    : en-US
CurrentUICulture  : en-US
PrivateData       : Microsoft.PowerShell.ConsoleHost+ConsoleColorProxy
IsRunspacePushed  : False
Runspace          : System.Management.Automation.Runspaces.LocalRunspace
```

Notice the UI parameter is for the User Interface. To find out what is stored in it, run this:

```
$Host.UI
```

```
PS C:\> $Host.UI

RawUI
-----
System.Management.Automation.Internal.Host.InternalHostRawUserInterface
```

That was rather unhelpful, how do we see the values stored for the UI so that changes can be made?

```
$Host.UI.RawUI
```

```
PS C:\> $Host.UI.RawUI
ForegroundColor       : DarkYellow
BackgroundColor       : DarkMagenta
CursorPosition        : 0,43
WindowPosition        : 0,0
CursorSize            : 25
BufferSize            : 120,3000
WindowSize            : 120,50
MaxWindowSize         : 120,72
MaxPhysicalWindowSize : 242,72
KeyAvailable          : False
WindowTitle           : Administrator: Windows PowerShell
```

We now see the buffer size and Window Size as well as colors for the window. For this sample, the window will have a background of gray and a foreground of black. The buffer will be widened to 160 and shortened to 6000. Next the Window size will increase to 160 and then length to 85.

```
$Shell = $Host.UI.RawUI
$Shell.ForegroundColor = "Black"
$Shell.BackgroundColor = "Gray"
```

```
$Buffer = $Shell.BufferSize
$Buffer.Width = 160
$Buffer.Height = 6000
$Shell.BufferSize = $Buffer
$Window=$Shell.WindowSize
$Window.Width = 160
$Window.Height = 50
$Shell.WindowSize = $Window
```

The custom colors change the PowerShell window like this:

```
PS] C:\Windows\system32>cd \
PS] C:\>
PS] C:\>_
```

In the end, when the new customized PowerShell window is opened, there may be an error message displayed. The reason is that in order to load a script with the PowerShell window, the permissions for Script Execution need to be something above Restricted, which is the default permission. For example, the 'RemoteSigned' permission will allow the script to be loaded.

```
Set-ExecutionPolicy RemoteSigned
```

That will ensure the customizations will work. Loading scripts when opening a PowerShell window requires a couple of items. First changing the location of the PowerShell window to a directory where the scripts are stored:

```
Set-Location C:\Psscripts
```

As a final step of configuring the profile script, it could run another script stored the above folder:

```
.\ExchangeServices.PS1
```

The example script above, could simply list all of the Exchange services that are running on all Exchange Servers. Combing all of these steps together would results in this profile script:

```
# Load all shell parameters
$Shell = $host.UI.RawUI
$Shell.ForegroundColor = "Black"
$Shell.BackgroundColor = "Gray"
$Buffer = $Shell.BufferSize
$Buffer.Width = 160
$Buffer.Height = 6000
$Shell.BufferSize = $buffer
$Window=$Shell.WindowSize
$Window.Width = 160
$Window.Height = 50
$Shell.WindowSize = $Window
# Run Exchange Services check script
Set-Location C:\Psscripts
.\ExchangeServices.PS1
```

There are plenty of other options and additions that can be made to your PowerShell profile, but they will not all be listed here.

# B



# C

# G

## J

Join-path 53, 225, 227
Journal 206-208, 210-214, 217, 269
Journaled 194, 206, 207, 211, 217
Journalemailaddress 207, 214
Journaling xii, 146, 158, 161, 194, 206-214, 217
Journaling- 210
Journalingmailbox 207
Journalreportdecryptionenabled 216, 217
Junkemail 269

## K

Kerberos 69-72
Keypath 416
Keyword(s) 2, 22, 223, 277, 340, 410

## L

Lagged ix, 82, 84
Language 199, 253, 257, 258, 271, 272, 421
Languages 21
Largeitemlimit 323, 327
Larger 1, 179, 194, 234, 237, 281, 294, 327, 337
Lastfullbackup 144, 145
Lastname 246-248, 343-345
Lastoccurred 76, 77
Lastsuccesssync 318
Lastsyncattempttime 318
Latency 82, 85, 380, 381
Legacy 25, 32, 84, 109, 124, 304, 334, 335
Legacyarchivejournals 269
Legacyexchangedn 331
Legacyexchangedn-attribute-myth 331
Length(s) 11, 247, 308, 384, 431
Letter-spacing 171
Library 2, 38, 48, 49, 54, 56, 57, 61, 80, 120, 166, 177, 193, 322, 324, 325, 330, 335, 407, 415
License 208, 245, 310, 349-353, 355, 356
Licensed 194, 350, 351, 355
Licenseoptions 352, 356
Licensing xiv, 194, 216, 217, 336, 349, 352, 353, 355, 356
Licensinglocation 216
Limited 1, 55, 81, 146, 158, 164, 221, 246, 254, 311,

320, 322, 349, 375, 400
Limiteddetails 267
Limit-eventlog 96-98, 123
Limits 160, 267, 323, 327, 333
Line-height 171
Linked xii, 233, 236, 244, 245, 249, 258, 259, 261
Linkedcredential 249
Linkeddomaincontroller 249
Linkedmailuser 331
Linkedmasteraccount 249, 259
Listlog 76
Literalpath 368
Litigation 252, 342
Litigationholdenabled 342
Loadbalancer 108
Localcredentials 331
Localdc 331
Locale 199
Localized 202, 258, 272
Localizedefaultfoldername 258
Locallongfullpath 166
Location 13, 45, 50, 60, 89, 104, 106, 111-114, 117, 156, 190, 201, 206, 208, 224, 225, 227, 230, 231, 265, 267, 276, 283-285, 324-326, 351, 355-357, 369, 378, 380, 381, 432
Locations 85, 104, 144, 190, 248, 283, 381, 430
Locked 45, 309, 326, 330, 369, 423
Locking 68, 303
Logcheck 76
Logfilelocation 224, 227, 230, 231
Logfiles 320
Logfolderpath 111, 112, 114
Logged 69, 70, 75, 95, 145, 150, 165, 171, 213, 272, 293, 389-391, 397, 399
Logging x, xi, xii, xv, 68, 113, 124, 146, 147, 152-155, 158, 161, 164, 165, 188, 190, 208, 209, 219, 224, 359, 361, 380, 383, 389
Login-azurermaccount 351
Logintype 234, 237
466
Logname 77, 97, 98, 123, 389, 391
Logonformat 107, 108
Logparser 189
Longer 15, 21, 27, 28, 61, 66, 80, 82, 83, 85, 86, 88, 107, 109, 117, 162, 171, 175, 245, 252, 289, 297, 320, 326, 329, 387, 391, 421
Lookup 119, 186

# O

# P

## S

# T